Schriftenreihe wissenschaftlicher Abhandlungen
des Leo Baeck Instituts
47

Leo Baeck Institute New York

Catalog of the Archival Collections

edited by

FRED GRUBEL

in cooperation with

ALAN S. DIVACK
FRANK MECKLENBURG
MICHAEL A. RIFF
NUSI SZNAIDER

J.C.B. Mohr (Paul Siebeck) Tübingen

CIP-Titelaufnahme der Deutschen Bibliothek

Leo Baeck Institute:
Catalog of the archival collections / Leo Baeck Institute New York / ed. by Fred Grubel. In cooperation with Alan S. Divack ... – Tübingen : Mohr, 1990
  (Schriftenreihe wissenschaftlicher Abhandlungen des Leo-Baeck-Instituts ; 47)
  ISSN 0459-097X
  ISBN 3-16-145597-5
NE: Grubel, Fred [Hrsg.]; Catalog of the archival collections; Leo Baeck Institute: Schriftenreihe wissenschaftlicher Abhandlungen ...

© 1990 J.C.B. Mohr (Paul Siebeck) Tübingen and Leo Baeck Institute, Inc., New York, N.Y.

This book may not be reproduced, in whole or in part, in any form (beyond that permitted by copyright law) without the publisher's written permission. This applies particularly to reproductions, translations, microfilms and storage an processing in electronic systems.

Typeset by Typobauer, Scharnhausen and printed by Gulde-Druck GmbH in Tübingen; acid-free paper from Papierfabrik Gebr. Buhl in Ettlingen; bound by Heinrich Koch KG in Tübingen.

לזכר
שלמה בן שמואל לסינג
תרע״ה – תש״ן

The Leo Baeck Institute New York
dedicates its Archives to the memory
of
FRED W. LESSING
Chairman of the Board and Treasurer (1965–1990)
astute and prudent leader
most generous benefactor
and
beloved friend

CONTENTS

Preface   IX
    by Fritz Stern

Introduction   XI
    by Fred Grubel

Major Collections   1
    alphabetical listing with descriptions

Index   157
    to Major Collections

Small Collections   189
    alphabetical listing coded for contents

PREFACE

The history of German Jewry is inextricably linked to the history of modern Germany, that is to say, to the history of the world. German Jewry has come to be identified with its final fate, the dispersion and destruction of its members in the years of Hitler's rule. Before Hitler, German Jewry was a major presence in German life, especially in the century of emancipation. German Jews were disproportionately successful – but individual preeminence should not render oblivious the ordinary lives of Jews who often contributed much in quiet ways to German society. The many Jewish merchants, doctors and lawyers in small towns and large cities are but an example of what I have in mind.

History is reconstructed in many ways, but individuals as actors, as exemplars, even as victims, are indispensable to an understanding of the past. They exemplify life, which official documents or statistical evidence can merely state in abstract, anonymous form.

The record of German Jews is dispersed because of the final disaster. The Leo Baeck Institute has painstakingly collected the records of individuals, carefully compiled there for scholarly use; this Catalog should become a major help for historians of future generations. Here are the names, Jewish and Christian, that are world-famous; the obscure ones have their own representative function. Historians will always be grateful for this meticulously prepared aid to scholarship. The Catalog is also intrinsically a reminder of the past life, ordinary life, greatness, and tragedy. Given the role of New York in the lives of so many German Jews in the nineteenth and twentieth centuries, it is particularly fitting that a major depository should forever remain in this city.

New York, January 1990   FRITZ STERN

INTRODUCTION

Since earliest times communities have preserved their most treasured written records in buildings that were firmly rooted in their homeland. Indeed, the word *Archives* derives from *Archeion*, the town hall in which ancient Greeks housed their historic records.

The Jews were an exception. It is indicative of Jewish history that while others erected imposing structures for their treasures, Jews placed their Holy Commandments in a movable shrine, the Ark of the Covenant. This distinction prevailed for thousands of years, as Jews took their growing fount of written law and lore with them from country to country in the hope that a place of asylum might, finally, become a permanent home. In our own times, when the scourge of Nazism forced German Jewry to run for its life, refugees took their books, family papers and other documents with them, if little else.

One of the primary reasons for founding the Leo Baeck Institute was to create a place where these remnants of public and family archives could be collected and preserved for study and research. It was our hope that papers, books, documents and pictures – simple people's letters as well as scholars' manuscripts – would attest to centuries of Jewish life in German speaking lands.

That end has been achieved beyond all expectations. Today over 4,000 collections, 1,800 running feet of material, are housed in a beautiful East Side Manhattan townhouse that is home to the New York Leo Baeck Institute. The stories of how these collections found their way to the Institute are sometimes as fascinating as the material itself, their routes as complex as those of Jewish emigrants.

Jewish community records spanning 200 years are found in the collection of Jacob Jacobson, who spirited these documents out of Germany under the noses of the Nazis. The former director of the Archives of German Jews, Jacobson sent these "letters and packages" to London while doing forced labor in the Nazi genealogical office. After his death, his heirs donated them to the Leo Baeck Institute.

A portion of the literary estate of philosopher Franz Rosenzweig, including his correspondence with Martin Buber, was stranded on its way to Palestine, rediscovered in Tunisia after World War II and eventually entrusted to the Institute by Rosenzweig's family and friends.

Over 8000 pages of historical notes were painstakingly copied verbatim from important records of Baden and Hessen Jewry going back to the sixteenth century by teacher and historian Berthold Rosenthal, who feared that the originals might not survive Nazi savagery. He was right: in many cases the copy he brought with him out of Nazi Germany is the only extant text. Manuscripts of works by the Austrian writer Joseph Roth found their way to the Leo Baeck Institute from a hiding place – under the bed of a Parisian concierge – where they had eluded the grip of the Gestapo.

Collections in the Archives span the broadest range of subjects. Some focus on correspondence. A businessman living in Spain, originally a German, gave the LBI his copious correspondence about the refugees he had saved by helping them cross the

Spanish border. From an earlier time, there are hundreds of original letters written by the nineteenth century scholar Leopld Zunz, given to the LBI by an officer of the U.S. Army who, as a young man, had been a student at the Berlin Hochschule fuer die Wissenschaft des Judentums. When the student emigrated shortly before the War, Rabbi Leo Baeck entrusted these rare materials to him.

Other collections have prominent families as their focus. The literary estate of Julie Braun-Vogenstein is a particularly rich example as it contains the papers of four generations of distinguished families as well as the men and women drawn into their orbit. There are among others, her father, the prominent liberal Rabbi Heinemann Vogelstein; socialist leaders Heinrich and Lilly Braun and Victor Adler; and American industrialist and Jewish philanthropist Ludwig Vogelstein. Other material touches on lives ranging from courtiers of Napoleonic times to the antifascist resistsance martyr Adam von Trott zu Solz.

Yet another collection focuses on philosopher Moses Mendelssohn and his descendants. Max Kreutzberger, the first director of the New York Leo Baeck Institute had befriended members of the Mendelssohn family in post-war Germany. They, in turn, entrusted him with their entire archives – material dating back to the eighteenth century philosopher and his children. While most of this material was subsequently returned to the Mendelssohn family, photocopies and microfilms of the collection in its entirety are available in the Archives.

Twenty years ago the Institute published volume one of a catalog of its collections. Editor Max Kreutzberger, who was responsible for building up the library and launching the LBI Archives, selected three subject areas for that first volume: books and other material about Jewish communal history; Jewish serials, including newspapers, almanacs and periodicals; and the Institute's memoir collection.

This new catalog, written in English, is limited to the Institute's archival collections, which are presented in two sections. The first section includes 284 Major Collections, (each having more than one hundred items) and 3,825 Small Collections.

The Major Collections appear alphabetically and are numbered consecutively. The time span covered by the materials is listed immediately following the collection's name, which in most instances is the name of the donor. Each Major Collection is described at length and indexed.

Small Collections are only briefly described. The number of items in the collection is noted, as is whether photos (FO), genealogical material (GE), primary material (PM) and/or secondary material (SM) will be found. While Small Collections are neither numbered nor indexed, each entry will show one or more accession numbers (AR), as is the case with Major Collections.

When using the catalog, the reader should therefore first refer to the index as a guide to Major Collections, then scan the listing of Small Collections.

When requesting material, researchers should give the collection name, and preferably the AR and/or collection number as well. A description of the specific documentation desired will further facilitate locating material.

This new catalog includes all acquisitions received through 1988. Many years in preparation, it was condensed from an earlier, more voluminous draft. Consultants for that initial draft were the late Fritz Bamberger, vice-president of the Leo Baeck Institute in New York and professor emeritus at Hebrew Union College-Jewish Institute of Religion in New York; Francis X. Blouin, Jr., director, Bentley Historical Library, University of Michigan, Ann Arbor, Michigan; Fritz Stern, Columbia University, New York City; and Kurt Schwerin, librarian emeritus of the Law Library of Northwestern University in Chicago. The Institute thanks them for their cooperation and wise counsel.

The Institute is especially grateful for the painstaking, thorough work Steven Lowenstein, University of Judaism, Los Angeles, California and Sybil Milton, research curator, U.S. Holocaust Memorial Museum, Washington, D.C., devoted to the first draft while both were archivists of the LBI.

This present version represents the teamwork of members of the LBI's archival staff: Alan Divack, Frank Mecklenburg and Nusi Sznaider, with the assistance of Michael Riff, the LBI's former assistant director; the late Stephanie Stern, chief librarian until her death; and volunteer Steven Leopold, as well as the Archivist Diane Spielman.

Mr. Sznaider also transferred the entire manuscript to the in-house computer. Our deep appreciation and thanks are extended to each of them. Special thanks is also due to deputy director Robert A. Jacobs for his invaluable assistance. Each gave generously of their time and talents.

We wish to acknowledge the patience and practical advice of our publisher and friend, Georg Siebeck of Tübingen. And, finally, the LBI extends its deep gratitude to the Volkswagen-Stiftung in Hanover, particularly its Secretary General Rolf Möller, for their cooperation and very generous support, which made it possible to complete this project.

It is our sincere hope that this catalog – the first LBI book printed from computer disks – will become a valuable tool for studying and conducting research into the rich and tragic history of German speaking Jewry and that it will make the treasure trove of material at the Leo Baeck Institute accessible to an evergrowing community of scholars and interested laymen.

New York, NY., October 1989   FRED GRUBEL

MAJOR COLLECTIONS

1 ABRAHAM FAMILY
1755–1810   2.5 inches

Born in Poland, Jacob Abraham (1723–1800) worked in the mints of Dresden, Stettin, and Königsberg, and was appointed medallist at the Royal Mint at Berlin in 1751. Abraham Abramson, his son, (1754–1811) worked with him first, but later worked on his own. He was appointed a royal minter in 1781, and in 1792, became a member of the Preussische Akademie der Künste, Berlin.

Sixty-seven silver and copper medals struck by Abraham and Abramson from 1755 to 1810, of subjects including members of the Prussian court and royal family, Daniel Itzig, Immanuel Kant, and Moses Mendelssohn; this represents one of the largest collections of medals by these artists to survive the Nazi period.

Languages: German, French, Latin.
Donors: Mr. and Mrs. Fred Lessing, 1965.
Finding Aid: 2 catalogue cards.
Accession Number: AR 2638.

2 ADLER FAMILY
1863–1958   1 inch

The Adler family lived in Bavaria during the nineteenth century; some family members emigrated to the United States before 1900.

Family tree, family correspondence, telegrams, visiting cards, emigration documents, and notebooks.

Languages: German, Hebrew.
Donor: Selig Adler, 1958.
Finding Aid: 5 catalogue cards.
Accession Number: AR 228.

3 KARL ADLER
1787–1975   2 feet

Born in Buttenhausen, Württemberg on January 25, 1890, Karl Adler studied music at the Stuttgart Conservatory, of which he became director in 1922. He was a cofounder of the Verein zur Förderung der Volksbildung, an adult-education organization, and director of its music department. From 1926 he was a director of the Jüdisches Lehrhaus Stuttgart. After his dismissal from his other positions in 1933, he became director of the Stuttgarter Jüdische Kunstgemeinschaft, as well as leader of the music department of the Mittelstelle für jüdische Erwachsenenbildung, a division of the Reichsvertretung der deutschen Juden. From 1938 he directed the local emigration program until his own emigration to the United States in 1940. He taught music at various institutions, including Yeshiva University, and died in New York on July 10, 1973.

Correspondence of Karl Adler with individuals, including Theodor Bäuerle, Martin Buber, Alexander Dillmann, Theodor Heuss, Paul Hindemith, Otto Hirsch, Kurt Georg Kiesinger, Paul Rieger, and Hans Walz; correspondence with family members, including letters written as a soldier during World War I and the November Revolution.

Material on the career of Karl Adler as musician and music educator in Germany and the United States, including clippings, educational documents, programs, letters of congratulation and condolence, and obituaries.

Records of the Verein zur Förderung der Volksbildung, including programs, by-laws, memoranda, reports, commemorative publications, and correspondence; material on the Stuttgarter Konservatorium, a division of the Verein, of which Adler was director; material on Adler's dismissal in 1933, and on the operation of the Verein from then until its dissolution in 1936.

Records of the Stuttgarter Jüdische Kunstgemeinschaft and of the Jüdisches Lehrhaus, Stuttgart, including programs, correspondence, clippings, and statutes; material pertaining to Adler's work as director of the Mittelstelle Stuttgart, the local Jewish emigration agency, including reports to the Nazi administration and individual case histories.

Material on the Jewish community of Buttenhausen in the eighteenth and nineteenth centuries, including decrees, Schutzbriefe, wills, and other documents; clippings and other material on the fate of the community in the Nazi period, including the will of Naphtali Beringer, the town's last rabbi, and on memorials to them after the war.

Languages: German, English.
Donor: Grete Adler, 1986.
Finding Aid: 9-page inventory.
Accession Number: AR 7276.

4   SOLOMON ADLER-RUDEL
      1927–1948   2.5 inches

Born in Czernowitz, Austria-Hungary (now Chernovtsy, USSR), on June 23, 1894, Adler-Rudel was a social worker in Berlin and Vienna. From 1933 to 1936, he was executive secretary of the Reichsvertretung der deutschen Juden and a member of the executive committee of the Zionistische Vereinigung für Deutschland. In 1936, he emigrated to Great Britain, and in 1949 to Israel.

Adler-Rudel held important positions with the Association of Jewish Refugees, the World Zionist Organization, and the Leo Baeck Institute. He died in Jerusalem on November 14, 1975.

Speeches, essays, reports, statistics, and lecture notes by Adler-Rudel on Jews in Germany, problems of German-Jewish emigration, and the situation of refugees in Europe, the Americas, and Palestine.

Reports by others on conditions during World War II, including material on Arab fascists in Palestine, an account by a German diplomat on Lithuania under German occupation, and a report by Norbert Masur on a meeting with Heinrich Himmler in April 1945.

Languages: German, English, French, Yiddish.
Donor: LBI London, 1977.
Finding Aid: 7-page inventory.
Accession Number: AR 4473.

5   ERICH AHRENS
1913–1972   2 inches

Born in Breslau (now Wroclaw, Poland) on May 6, 1905, Ahrens grew up in Frankfurt am Main, where he worked as a shoe wholesaler and attended courses at the Freies Jüdisches Lehrhaus, Frankfurt. He emigrated to the United States in 1937 and died in New York City in 1977.

Papers related to Ahrens' career and to his and his wife's emigration to the United States.

Material on the Jüdisches Lehrhaus, including a manuscript "Franz Rosenzweig and the Men of the Frankfurt Lehrhaus," with reminiscences of Rosenzweig, Martin Buber, and Rabbi N. A. Nobel.

Languages: German, French, English.
Donor: Therese Ahrens, 1977.
Finding Aid: 2-page inventory.
Accession Number: AR 4384.

6   ALSACE AND LORRAINE: JEWISH COMMUNITIES
1809–c.1875   c. 2.5 feet

Records of the Consistoire Central des Israélites de France, as well as of the local consistories for the departments of Bas-Rhin and Haut-Rhin (Alsace) and Moselle and Meurthe-et-Moselle (Lorraine), in Strasbourg, Colmar, Metz and Nancy, including minutes, tax-lists, lists of rabbis, cantors, and notables, censuses of Jewish communities, and correspondence.

Records of 139 Jewish communities in Alsace and Lorraine, predominantly from the nineteenth century, including: correspondence of these communities, their rabbis, and consistories, with the state authorities and the departmental consistories; decrees and legislation of the state authorities; financial documents and records; material relating to the religious activities of the communities, including liturgy and kashrut; legal and financial documents of the communities; material on yeshivoth, seminaries, and other Jewish education, communal and general elections, synagogue construction, welfare institutions and activities, and other communal organizations.

Personal papers of Jews from these communities, including marriage and engagement contracts; wills and testaments; genealogies, family histories, and genealogical documents; educational documents and papers; legal and financial documents; business papers of the banker Jacob Moch of Hagenau.

Languages: French, German, Yiddish, Judeo-German.
Donor: Purchased, Z. Frydman, 1963, 1971.
Finding Aid: 16-page inventory.
Accession Number: AR 2863.

7 SIEGFRIED ALTMANN
1872–1961   2.5 inches

Born in Nikolsburg, Austria Hungary (now Mikulov, Czechoslovakia), on July 12, 1887, Altmann studied social work and became director of Israelitisches Blindeninstitut, Vienna. He emigrated to the United States in 1939 and served as business director of the Austrian Institute in New York from 1943 until 1958, when he became its director. He died in New York City on September 14, 1963.

Correspondence of Siegfried Altmann with individuals including Peter Altenberg, Richard Beer-Hofmann, Hermann Broch, Hirsch Perez Chajes, David Feuchtwang, Anna Freud, Max Hayek, Josef Kastein, Erich Kästner, Karl Kraus, Lotte Lehmann, Detlev von Liliencron, Arthur Schnabel, Rudolf Serkin, Friedrich Torberg, Siegfried Trebitsch, Bruno Walter, and Ignaz Ziegler. The correspondence deals with topics including Altmann's activities with the Blindeninstitut, and later with the Austrian Institute, among which is a benefit for the Vienna Opera in the late 1940s, with Zionism, and with literary and cultural matters.

Correspondence of the Austrian Jewish Representative Committee with the International Red Cross about concentration camps (1944–45).

Manuscripts by Richard Beer-Hofmann, including *Hochzeit des Todes Ariel Bension* (Vienna, 1920), and four handwritten drafts (62 pages) about Kabbalah, Spanish Jews, and Palestine.

Photo album of the Israelitisches Blindeninstitut (including poems by Ludwig August Frankl), and its guestbook from 1872 to 1939.

Ritual artifacts: Torah scroll and megillah owned by Chief Rabbi Hirsch Perez Chajes of Vienna, and his grandfather Zewi Hirsch ben Meir Chajes; and cedarwood Torah pointer owned by Ludwig August Frankl.

A memoir by Altmann is catalogued separately in the memoir collection.

Languages: German, English.
Donor: Siegfried Altmann, 1963.
Finding Aid: 10-page inventory.
Accession Number: AR 2899.

8 PAUL AMANN
1911–1958   5 feet

Born in Prague in 1884, Amann taught at a Gymnasium in Vienna and was also an author and translator, translating the works of Romain Rolland into German. He emigrated to France in 1939 and to the United States in 1941, where he taught at various colleges until his death in Fairfield, Connecticut, in 1958.

Correspondence with individuals and organizations, including American Committee for Refugee Scholars, Writers and Artists, Roland Bainton, Hugo Bergmann, Jean-Richard Bloch, Hermann Broch, Peter Demetz, Isaac Deutscher, Fischer Verlag, Hermann Hesse, Hajo Holborn, Christopher Isherwood, George Kennan, Hans Kohn, Thomas Mann, Romain Rolland, Adlai Stevenson, and Frederike Zweig.

Literary manuscripts and nonfiction works on history and politics, especially on the German Question, by Amann; diaries and reminiscences by Amann, concerning his experiences as a soldier in World War I, on life in Nazi Vienna, as an internee in the camp of Sables d'Olonne, Brittany, and as a refugee in the United States.

Case files of fifty-nine Jewish children evacuated from France to the United States in 1941; transcript of a security board hearing for Amann's daughter Eva in New Jersey, 1950.

Languages: German, English, French.
Donor: Dora Amann, 1967.
Finding Aids: 5-page inventory and name-index for correspondence.
Accession Number: AR 7157.

9 AMERICAN FEDERATION OF JEWS FROM CENTRAL EUROPE
1944–1946   1.25 feet

The American Federation of Jews from Central Europe was founded in New York in 1941 as the central representative agency of over thirty national and local organizations of victims of National Socialism from Central Europe. Its purpose was to safeguard the rights and further the interests of the refugees, as well as to sponsor social welfare programs.

Drafts and criticisms of a proposed restitution law for the American-occupied zone of Germany after World War II.

Questionnaire on former Jewish communal property in Germany, financial statements, supplementary correspondence for over 400 Jewish communities.

Languages: German, English.
Donor: American Federation of Jews from Central Europe, 1977.
Finding Aid: 10-page inventory organized by province and town.
Accession Number: AR 4420.

10   AMERICAN JEWISH JOINT DISTRIBUTION COMMITTEE
1933–1947   13.5 feet

The American Jewish Joint Distribution Committee (also known as the JDC) was founded on November 27, 1914, in order to facilitate and centralize the collection and distribution of funds by American Jews for Jews abroad. The JDC generally worked through Jewish organizations in the countries involved, rather than aiding individuals directly.

German case files of the JDC, 1933–1941, dealing with individuals' attempts to emigrate. Although the JDC was at first reluctant to aid individuals directly, this became necessary after the outbreak of World War II. Individuals whose case files may be found in this collection include: Ossip Flechtheim, Babette Gross, Kurt Grossmann, Albert Grzesinski, Erich Kästner, Alfred Kerr, Hermann Kesten, Siegfried Kracauer, Karl Meinhard, Franz Oppenheim, Wolfgang Panowsky, Joachim Prinz, Kurt Rosenfeld, Hans-Joachim Schoeps, Leopold Schwarzschild, Toni Sender, Kurt Singer, Heinrich Stahl, Friedrich Stampfer, and Bruno Weil.

The case files include papers and correspondence of organizations which collaborated with the JDC, including: American Jewish Committee, American Jewish Congress, Canadian Jewish Congress, Comité voor Joodsche Vluchtelingen, HIAS-HICEM, Hilfsverein der deutschen Juden, National Refugee Service, Reichsvertretung der deutschen Juden, Selfhelp for German Refugees, and United Jewish Appeal. Among individuals whose correspondence is contained in the case files are Cyrus Adler, Ernst Behrendt, Albert Einstein, Joseph Hyman, Bernhard Kahn, Herbert Katzki, J. B. Lightman, Robert Pilpel, Cecilia Razovsky, and Jeanette Robbins.

Italian case files of the JDC, 1945–1947, for displaced persons in Italy after the war, concerning attempts to contact friends and relatives, conditions in Italy, and attempts to emigrate.

Languages: English, German, French, Yiddish, Spanish, Italian, and others.
Donor: American Jewish Joint Distribution Committee, 1981.
Finding Aid: 10-page inventory.
Accession Number: AR 7196.

11   HANNAH ARENDT, EICHMANN IN JERUSALEM
1963–1966   2 inches

Born in Hanover on October 14, 1906, Hannah Arendt studied philosophy at the Universities of Marburg, Freiburg and Heidelberg. She emigrated to France in 1933 and to the United States in 1941, where she taught at several universities and achieved a reputation as a leading political philosopher. In *Eichmann in Jerusalem: A Report on the Banality of Evil* (New York, 1963), a reflection on the trial of Adolf Eichmann, she refuses to place the sole responsibility for the Holocaust on the Nazis, and assigns blame as well to the Allied nations and to the Jewish communal leaders who passively cooperated with the Nazis. She died in New York on December 4, 1975.

Notes, commentaries and press clippings concerning *Eichmann in Jerusalem* and the controversy which it caused, in particular regarding the question of collaboration by Jewish communal organizations, notably the Reichsvertretung der deutschen Juden, and the role of such leaders as Leo Baeck.

Languages: German, English.
Donors: Various, 1963–1966.
Finding Aid: 30 catalogue cards.
Accession Number: AR 255.

12   ARNHOLD FAMILY
1914–1933   1 inch

The Arnholds were a family of bankers.

Material on the history of the Arnholds and related families and their activities as bankers; press clippings and memorabilia about the family; in addition, a history of the Arnhold banking firm is available in the memoir collection.

Language: German.
Donor: American Joint Reconstruction Foundation, 1956.
Finding Aid: 6-page inventory.
Accession Number: AR 2920.

13   PAUL ARNSBERG
Undated   6 feet

Born in Frankfurt am Main on December 26, 1899, Arnsberg was a businessman, publisher, and civil servant, active in Jewish communal affairs and Zionism. In 1933 he emigrated to Palestine. He returned to Frankfurt in 1958, later becoming executive of the Jewish community, and died there on December 10, 1978.

This collection consists of approximately 1500 photographs, including over 500 portraits. Most pertain to the city of Frankfurt and its Jewish community, and deal with subjects dating from the twelfth century to the present. In addition to the individual portraits, it contains group portraits, particularly of Jewish communal organizations, and photos of the Rothschild family, synagogues and communal buildings, cemeteries, commercial establishments, institutions and municipal buildings, and street scenes. In addition, there are photographic reproductions of written material, such as business advertisements and calling cards, prayerbooks, and antisemitica.

Language: German.
Donor: Purchase, 1981.
Finding Aid: 69-page inventory.
Accession Number: AR 7206.

14 FELIX AUERBACH
1876–1926   10 inches

Born in Breslau (now Wroclaw, Poland) on November 12, 1856. Auerbach received a doctorate in physics at Heidelberg in 1875, and was named professor of physics at Jena in 1889, where he died on February 26, 1933.

Sixteen volumes of diaries, 1876–1891, written in Gabelsberger shorthand, dealing with personal, political, and scientific topics.

Correspondence and personal and family memorabilia.

Language: German (mostly written in Gabelsberger shorthand).
Donor: Mrs. Bruno Kisch, 1971.
Finding Aid: 2 catalogue cards.
Accession Number: AR 3958.

15 JULIUS BAB
c. 1895–1956   c. 5 feet

Born in Berlin on December 11, 1880, Bab was a theater critic and author, and cofounder of the Jüdischer Kulturbund in 1933. He emigrated to France in 1938, to the United States in 1940, and died in New York City on February 12, 1955.

Correspondence of Bab with individuals, including Hermann Bahr, Richard Beer-Hofmann, Eduard Bernstein, Lily Braun, Constantin Brunner, Pearl Buck, Richard Dehmel, Friedrich Gundolf, Maximilian Harden, Gerhart Hauptmann, Hermann Hesse, Hugo von Hofmannsthal, Arno Holz, Josef Kainz, Käthe Kollwitz, Selma Lagerloef, Gustav Landauer, Max Liebermann, Detlev von Liliencron, Thomas Mann, Fritzi Massary, Fritz Mauthner, Gustav Meyrink, Albert Mombert, Alexander Moissi, Franz Oppenheimer, Jacob Picard, Alfred Polgar, Walther Rathenau, Carl Schmitt, George Bernard Shaw, Georg Simmel, Carl Sternheim, Ernst Troeltsch, Fritz von

Unruh, Hans Vaihinger, Franz Werfel, Alma Mahler-Werfel, Carl Zuckmayer, and Stefan Zweig.

Diaries and appointment books 1895–1908 and 1935–1943; manuscripts of articles and lectures by Bab on literature, theater, and Jewish life; poetry; clippings and programs concerning Bab and his activities, 1905–1932.

The memoirs of Bab's wife, Elizabeth, are catalogued separately in the memoir collection.

Language: German.
Donor: Elisabeth Bab, 1958, 1961.
Finding Aid: 23-page inventory.
Accession Number: AR 196.

16   BERTHA BADT-STRAUSS
1941–1961   2.5 inches

Born in Breslau (now Wroclaw, Poland) on December 7, 1885, Bertha Badt-Strauss was an author who lived in Berlin until she emigrated to the United States in 1939. She died in Chapel Hill, North Carolina, on February 20, 1970.

Correspondence with individuals, including Elisabeth Bab, Julius Bab, Eli Elkana (pseudonym for Dr. Georg Michelsohn), and Jacob Picard.

Poetry by Eli Elkana and Julius Bab.

Language: German.
Donor: Albrecht Strauss, 1972, 1974, 1976.
Finding Aid: 5-page inventory.
Accession Number: AR 3945.

17   LEO BAECK
1864–1979   6 feet

Born in Lissa (now Leszno, Poland) on May 24, 1873, Baeck studied at the Universities of Breslau and Berlin and at the Jüdisch-theologisches Seminar, Breslau and the Hochschule für die Wissenschaft des Judentums in Berlin, receiving his doctorate in 1895 and rabbinical ordination in 1897. He served as a rabbi in Oppeln, Düsseldorf, and Berlin, as a lecturer at the Hochschule, and from 1933 to 1942 as president of the Reichsvertretung der deutschen Juden. Deported to Theresienstadt in 1943, he emigrated to Great Britain in 1945, and became chairman of the World Union for Progressive Judaism and first president of the Leo Baeck Institute. He died in London on November 1, 1956.

Correspondence of Leo Baeck with family members and other individuals, including Bertha Badt-Strauss, David Baumgardt, Ilse Blumenthal-Weiss, Martin Buber, Karl

D. Darmstaedter, Max Dienemann, Dora Edinger, Albert Einstein, Ismar Elbogen, Robert Raphael Geis, Nahum Glatzer, Max Gruenewald, Siegfried Guggenheim, Alfred Hirschberg, Graf Hermann Keyserling, Rudolf Loeb, Siegfried Moses, Dagobert Nellhaus, Max Plaut, Salman Schocken, Selma Stern-Taeubler, Baron Hans-Hasso von Veltheim, Chaim Weizmann, and Robert Weltsch.

Personal papers, including passport, educational documents, membership certificates, and congratulatory telegrams on Baeck's marriage to Natalie Hamburger; genealogy; obituaries of Leo Baeck.

Book-length and shorter manuscripts by Leo Baeck on history, philosophy, and theology, including *Die Rechtsstellung der Juden in Europa* and *Dieses Volk Israel*; sermons, speeches, prayers, lectures, and articles by Baeck.

Newspaper and journal articles and clippings by and about Baeck, about the Leo Baeck Prize, and about the controversies surrounding Hannah Arendt's *Eichmann in Jerusalem*; reviews of Leo Baeck's writings, unpublished Festschrift for Baeck's sixtieth birthday.

Tape of radio interview with Joachim Prinz about Baeck's activities in the 1930s.

Photos and sketches of Leo Baeck, including individual and group portraits, as well as some with other well known figures; photos of artworks and memorials; personal effects, including prayer shawl and phylacteries.

Languages: German, English, Hebrew, French.
Donors: Karl Guggenheim, 1957; Dagobert Nellhaus, 1964; Ruth Berlak, 1966–1971; LBI London, 1970–1979; and others, 1956–1980.
Finding Aids: 16-page inventory, 2-page inventory, 10-page inventory, and 282 catalogue cards.
Accession Numbers: AR 9001, AR 66, AR 363, AR 365, AR 2269, AR 2457, AR 3883, AR 3982, AR 7161.

18   LEO BAECK – LEONARD BAKER
1881–1977   10 inches

Born in Pittsburgh on January 24, 1931, Leonard Baker studied journalism at the University of Pittsburgh and Columbia University. He worked as a journalist and author, and wrote several books, including *Days of Sorrow and Pain: Leo Baeck and the Berlin Jews* (New York, 1978). He died on November 26, 1984.

Material, mostly photocopies, assembled by Baker for his biography of Leo Baeck, including personal documents; correspondence of Baeck with family members and others, including Martin Buber, Ernst Ludwig Ehrlich, Ismar Elbogen, Joseph Herman Hertz, Fritz Kaufmann, and Baron Hans-Hasso von Veltheim; manuscripts and clippings by and about Baeck; records of the Reichsvertretung der Juden in Deutschland; an anonymous report about Theresienstadt; and other documents from the Nazi period from the Institut für Zeitgeschichte and elsewhere.

Languages: German, English, French.
Donor: Leonard Baker, 1980.
Finding Aid: 23-page inventory.
Accession Number: AR 4851.

19 BAER-OPPENHEIMER FAMILY
1865–1945   10 inches

The Baers and the Oppenheimers lived in the town of Bruchsal, Baden, where they had a textile factory and a wholesale leather business. The family emigrated to the United States via Switzerland in 1939–1941.

Diaries, notebooks, personal documents, and correspondence of family members, including material on World War I, on the persecution of the Jews in Bruchsal, and on emigration to the United States.
Family and corporate histories.
Photos and drawings of the synagogue in Bruchsal.

Languages: German, English, Judeo-German.
Donor: Martin Baer, 1971.
Finding Aid: 3-page inventory.
Accession Number: AR 7044.

20 LEO BAERWALD
c. 1800–1963   2.5 inches

Born in Saaz, Austria-Hungary (now Zatec, Czechoslovakia) on October 20, 1883, Baerwald was ordained in 1911 after studying at the Jüdisch-theologisches Seminar, Breslau. He served as a rabbi in Munich, and emigrated to the United States in 1940, where he served as rabbi of Beth Hillel, a refugee congregation in Washington Heights, New York. He died in New York City on April 8, 1970.

Correspondence and personal documents of Baerwald, including letters from Julius Bab, Leo Baeck, and Michael Cardinal Faulhaber.
Clippings by and about Baerwald's life and activities.
Papers of Baerwald's ancestors Leiser Lazarus, Moritz Lazarus, and Arnold Lazarus, including manuscripts, autograph albums, correspondence, and photographs, 1820–1890.
Circulars and clippings about the Jewish communities of Hamburg and Munich; photos of synagogues in Bechhofen, Haigerloch, and Munich.

Languages: German, English, Hebrew.
Donor: Estate of Leo Baerwald, 1970.

LEO BAERWALD

Finding Aid: 8-page inventory.
Accession Number: AR 3677.

21   DAVID BAUMGARDT
1907–1971   24 feet

Born in Erfurt on April 20, 1890, Baumgardt studied philosophy at various universities, and was a lecturer and assistant professor at the University of Berlin, 1924–1935. He emigrated to Great Britain in 1935 and to the United States in 1939, where he taught at various colleges and was consultant in philosophy to the Library of Congress. He died in New York City on July 21, 1963.

Correspondence of Baumgardt including letters from the front to his family during World War I, and correspondence with Conrad Aiken, Hannah Arendt, Julius Bab, Bertha Badt-Strauss, Leo Baeck, Isaiah Berlin, Walter Benjamin, Hugo Bergmann, Kurt Blumenfeld, Ilse Blumenthal-Weiss, Martin Buber, John Dewey, Dora Edinger, Albert Einstein, Ismar Elbogen, Elisabeth Foerster-Nietzsche, Felix Frankfurter, Sigmund Freud, Georg Heym, Salomon Friedländer (Mynona), Max Gruenewald, Hermann Hesse (including photos, watercolors, autographed poems), Sidney Hook, Rudolf Kayser, Wolfgang Köhler, Hans Kohn, Georg Landauer, Heinrich Mann, Thomas Mann, Hans Margolius, Reinhold Niebuhr, Erwin Panofsky, Jacob Picard, Kurt Pinthus, Joachim Prinz, Hyman Rickover, Eleanor Roosevelt, Arthur Schlesinger, Hans Joachim Schoeps, Gershom Scholem, Toni Sender, Ernst Simon, Chaim Weizmann, Beatrice Webb, Robert Weltsch, and Arnold Zweig.

Manuscripts, articles, lectures, and offprints by and about Baumgardt on philosophy, ethics, religion, literature, politics, and other subjects; transcripts of conversations with Einstein and Freud.

Correspondence and reviews about publication of *Horizons of a Philosopher (the Festschrift for David Baumgardt)*.

Letters, notes, and manuscripts by Dorothy Canfield Fischer.

Photos of Baumgardt's family and friends.

Organizational records of the Zionist youth group Ha-Poel Ha-Zair, including minutes of the central council of the organization in Berlin and letters from Georg Landauer, Eugen Taeubler and Robert Weltsch, 1919–1921.

Languages: German, English, French, Spanish.
Donors: David Baumgardt, 1959; Rose Baumgardt, 1977.
Finding Aids: 8-page inventory, name-index to the correspondence.
Accession Number: AR 797.

22 RICHARD BEER-HOFMANN
1798–1945   1.7 feet

Born in Vienna on July 11, 1866, Richard Beer-Hofmann was the son of Hermann and Rosa Beer. On the death of his mother, he was adopted and raised by his uncle Alois Hofmann. He studied law, but worked as a poet, novelist, and dramatist, becoming a member of the "Young Vienna" literary circle. Many of his works deal with Jewish themes. He emigrated to the United States via Switzerland in 1939 and died in New York City on September 26, 1945.

Correspondence of Richard Beer-Hofmann and of other family members, including letters from Ludwig August Frankl, Fritz Mauthner, and Hedwig Mauthner.

Papers of the Beer and Hofmann families, including correspondence, vital records, wills and testaments, baptismal certificates of several family members, curricula vitae, military certificates, passports, school records and other educational documents, real estate and tax assessment papers, obituaries and diaries, samples of calligraphy and needlework. In addition, the Leo Baeck Institute's art collection has artwork and artifacts owned by the family.

Photographs of Richard Beer-Hofmann, family members, and friends, 1860–1945.

Languages: German, Hebrew, Czech, Croatian.
Donor: Miriam Beer-Hofmann Lens, 1960, 1981.
Finding Aid: 31-page inventory.
Accession Number: AR 910.

23 BEER-MEYERBEER FAMILY
1746–1969   4 inches

The Beers were a prominent Jewish family in Berlin in the eighteenth and nineteenth centuries. Jakob Herz Beer was a banker in Berlin and was married to Amalia Beer (1776–1854), a famous *salonière*. The three sons:

Jakob Meyer Beer, better known as Giacomo Meyerbeer (1791–1864), was a composer, remembered mainly for his grand operas. In 1842 he became the director of the Berlin Opera.

Michael Beer (1800–1833) was a poet and playwright. Beer's plays were performed at the Berlin Hoftheater and in Vienna.

Wilhelm Beer (1797–1850) was an astronomer, best known for his research on the surface of the moon; he joined and later succeeded his father in the family banking house.

Family trees, various documents, clippings, and photos of family members, including Giacomo Meyerbeer; material on related families.

Languages: German, English.
Donor: Lee Chudson, 1967–1971.
Finding Aid: 12-page inventory.
Accession Number: AR 3185.

24   MARTIN BERADT
1875–1949   2.5 inches

Born in Magdeburg on August 2, 1881, Martin Beradt studied law and practiced as an attorney in Berlin. He emigrated to the United States in 1940 and died in New York City on November 26, 1949.

Correspondence and personal documents of Beradt, including letters from Martin Buber, Max Brod, Constantin Brunner, Samuel Fischer, Hermann Hesse, and Walther Rathenau.

Essays by Beradt on legal questions and on Jewish folklore; reviews of his work.

Beradt's collection of autographs of Berthold Auerbach, Max Liebermann, and Lesser Ury.

Language: German.
Donor: Charlotte Beradt, 1964.
Finding Aid: 6-page inventory.
Accession Number: AR 2286.

25   BEREND & CO.
1769–1861   5 inches

The Berends were a family of merchants who founded a banking firm in Potsdam in the late eighteenth century. The firm moved to Berlin in 1812, and their interests expanded to include sugar refining in 1818. The firm was dissolved in 1880.

Letters of protection, residence, and citizenship for family members, eighteenth and early nineteenth centuries.

Notice of sale of two seats in the Potsdam synagogue, 1772.

Business correspondence of Berend & Co., including letters from Moritz August von Bethmann-Hollweg, S. Bleichröder, Jeremias Heinemann, August Neidhart Count von Gneisenau, Otto Lewald, Meyer Amschel Rothschild, and Salomon Mayer Rothschild.

Language: German, Hebrew.
Donor: Wallich, 1962.

Finding Aid: 7-page inventory.
Accession Number: AR 1571.

26   MARGARETE BERENT
1906–1965   2.5 inches

Born in Berlin on July 7, 1887, Margarete Berent became one of the first female lawyers in Germany. Besides her legal practice, she was active in feminist circles. She emigrated to the United States via Chile in 1939–1941 and died in New York City on June 23, 1965.

Correspondence, including letters from Leo Baeck, Hanna Karminski, Josephine Levy-Rathenau, Marie Elisabeth Lueders, and Alice Salomon.

Essays, petitions, speeches, clippings, and radio-speech transcripts on marital law and women's rights.

Clippings, professional certificates and diplomas, obituaries, and eulogies about Berent.

Languages: German, English.
Donor: Hildegard Brennan, 1965; Anna Hertz, 1966.
Finding Aid: 5-page inventory.
Accession Number: AR 2861.

27   BERLIN JEWISH COMMUNITY
1849–1979   8 inches

Records of the Jewish community of Berlin, including reports and correspondence; clippings, documents, pictorial material, and memorabilia of the community. The collection also contains minutes of the meetings of the executive committee, 1933–1935, 1938.

Languages: German, English.
Donors: Various, 1957–1979.
Finding Aid: 36 catalogue cards.
Accession Number: AR 88.

28 BERLIN THEATER
1913–1933   5 inches

Two scrapbooks containing Berlin theater programs, reviews and photos from newspapers and magazines of 450 performances in 30 Berlin theaters from 1913 to 1933.

Language: German.
Donor: Vera Rubin, 1966.
Finding Aid: 29-page inventory, with lists of performers.
Accession Number: AR 3048.

29 SELMA BERLINER
1833–1947   2.5 inches

Born in Danzig on October 6, 1860, Selma Berliner was a pianist and composer. She died in Berlin on July 12, 1925.

Photos, compositions by Selma Berliner; letters and cards from contemporary musicians.

Papers of the Berliner family, including photos of family members, family correspondence, vital, professional, and medical papers, awards, and obituaries, 1853–1947.

Language: German, Judeo-German.
Donor: Frida Berliner, 1961.
Finding Aid: 4-page inventory.
Accession Number: AR 1992.

30 JACOB BERNAYS
1853–1878   2.5 inches

Born in Hamburg on September 11, 1824, the son of Chacham Isaak Bernays (1792–1849), chief rabbi of Hamburg and an Orthodox leader, Bernays studied philology at the University of Bonn, receiving his doctorate in 1848. He taught at the University of Breslau and the Jüdisch-Theologisches Seminar Breslau and in 1866 was appointed assistant professor of philology and chief librarian at the University of Bonn, a post he retained until his death on May 27, 1881.

Letters from Bernays to Friedrich Wilhelm Ritschl, and from Christian Karl von Bunsen, Christian August Brandis, Heinrich Graetz, and Theodor Mommsen to Bernays.

Language: German.
Donor: Photocopied from originals at the New York Public Library, 1972.
Finding Aid: 7-page inventory.
Accession Number: AR 3974.

31 JACOB BERNAYS – HANS BACH
1820–1937   5 inches

Born in Stuttgart in 1902, Bach received a doctorate in German literature from the University of Berlin in 1928. He was an author and editor until his emigration to Great Britain in 1939, and continued his literary work there, including his biography of Bernays, *Jacob Bernays: Ein Beitrag zur Emanzipationsgeschichte der Juden und zur Geschichte des deutschen Geistes im neunzehnten Jahrhundert*. Bach died in London on December 5, 1977.

Autographs of Bernays and transcripts, made by Bach, of correspondence by Bernays, including correspondence with Georg von Bunsen, Christian Karl von Bunsen, Heinrich Graetz, Eduard Lasker, Theodor Mommsen, Max Mueller, Ernst Renan, and Franz von Roggenbach.

Material on Bernays's father, Rabbi Chacham Isaac Bernays, and about the controversies over education and religious practice among the Jews of Hamburg during the 1820s.

Correspondence of Hans Bach concerning his work on a projected edition of Jacob Bernays's collected writings, including correspondence with David Baumgardt, Werner Cahnmann, Max Gruenewald, and Hans Liebeschütz.

Languages: German, English.
Donor: Hans Bach, 1977.
Finding Aid: 3-page inventory.
Accession Number: AR 7168.

32 MICHAEL BEROLZHEIMER
17th cent. – 1942   1 foot

Born in Fürth on February 22, 1866, Michael Berolzheimer was a lawyer whose chief avocation was genealogy. He emigrated to the United States in 1939 and died in Mount Vernon, New York, on June 5, 1942.

Documents on the history of the Berolzheimer family.

Family trees of the Berolzheimers and related families.

Copies of censuses, vital records, and tax lists of the Jewish communities of Berolzheim, Fürth, Heidenheim, Mittelfranken, and Redwitz an der Rodach from the seventeenth through the nineteenth century, photos of cemeteries, ritual objects.

Languages: German, English, Hebrew.
Donor: Charles E. Berolzheimer, 1968–1973.
Finding Aid: 12-page inventory.
Accession Number: AR 4136.

33 CARL BEYTH
1835–1975   1.5 inches

Born in Bleicherode in 1903, Carl Beyth was a salesman until his emigration to Palestine, where he lived and worked in Kefar Shemaryahu.

Personal papers of family members and a history of the Jews of Bleicherode, 1835–1920.

Press clippings and fliers from World War I, the Revolution of 1918, the trial of Walther Rathenau's assassins, and about Jewish communities in the German Democratic Republic.

Language: German.
Donor: Carl Beyth, 1980.
Finding Aid: 3 catalogue cards.
Accession Number: AR 7175.

34 FRIEDRICH BILL
1914–1972   7.5 inches

Born in Prossnitz, Austria-Hungary (now Prosťejov, Czechoslovakia), in January 1894, Bill was a lawyer and journalist active in the Sozialdemokratische Partei Deutschlands (SPD) and vice-president of the Czechoslovak League for Human Rights. He emigrated to Ecuador in 1940, came to the United States in 1951, and died in New York City on October 26, 1976.

Memoirs of Bill's youth and his experiences during World War I in Prossnitz and Prague.

Articles, manuscripts, and clippings by and about Bill, including material about Social Democratic politics, the Nazis, life in emigration, and other cultural and political questions.

Material on Johannes Urzidil, including correspondence, poetry, and clippings.

Languages: German, Czech, Spanish, English.
Donor: Lucy Bill, 1979.
Finding Aid: 2-page inventory.
Accession Number: AR 7156.

35 FRANZ BLEI
1909–1915   2 inches

Born in Vienna in 1871, the author Franz Blei immigrated to the United States in 1941, and died in Westbury, New York, in 1942.

Correspondence of Franz Blei with the Georg Müller Verlag, 1909–1915.

Language: German.
Donors: Joachim Schöndorf, Albert Senzen, 1963.
Finding Aid: 6-page inventory.
Accession Number: AR 2933.

36 CHAIM BLOCH
1916–1969   7.5 feet

Born in Nagy Boscko, Austria-Hungary (now USSR) on June 27, 1881, Chaim Bloch was ordained as a rabbi and emigrated to Vienna in 1915. He served as a chaplain in the Austro-Hungarian army during World War I, and afterwards worked as an author in Vienna. He was the author of the Prager Golem. He emigrated to the United States via Great Britain in 1939. Bloch continued his literary work in the United States, and died in New York City on January 23, 1973.

Correspondence, including letters from Leo Baeck, Salo Baron, Julie Braun-Vogelstein, Martin Buber, Werner Cahnmann, Max Dienemann, Ismar Elbogen, Erich Fromm, Hermann Fürnberg, Nahum Glatzer, Nahum Goldmann, Max Gruenewald, Max Grunwald, Siegfried Guggenheim, Ernest Jones, Hermann Kesten, Guido Kisch, Adolf Kober, Franz Kobler, Joachim Prinz, Lessing Rosenwald, Ingrid Warburg, Alma Mahler-Werfel, and Franz Werfel.

Clippings and manuscripts on Judaism, Hasidism, Zionism, Nazi Germany, and on Bloch's life and work.

Languages: German, Yiddish, Hebrew, English.
Donor: Estate of Chaim Bloch, 1974.
Finding Aids: 1-page inventory, name-index to the correspondence.
Accession Number: AR 7155.

37 ARTHUR BLUHM
1809–1962   2.5 inches

Born in Polnisch-Cekzin (now Cekeyn, Poland) on October 23, 1899, Bluhm studied philosophy and theology at the Universities of Berlin and Würzburg and the Hochschule für die Wissenschaft des Judentums in Berlin, receiving his doctorate in 1924 and his rabbinical ordination in 1927. He served as a rabbi in Krefeld until his emigration to the United States in 1939, where he was the rabbi of the Jewish community of Amarillo, Texas, until his death on July 18, 1962.

Personal documents, clippings, photos, correspondence, manuscripts of speeches, and sermons, concerning the Jewish community of Krefeld, Bluhm's role in it, his imprisonment in Dachau in 1938, and the case of Jews from Burgenland imprisoned near Krefeld in 1938.

General correspondence including letters from Leo Baeck, Leo Baerwald, Ismar Elbogen, Julius Seligsohn, and the Reichsvertretung der deutschen Juden.

Papers of Abraham Sutro, chief rabbi of Westphalia, 1815–1869, including government circulars and decrees on Jewish life in the Napoleonic Kingdom of Westphalia and the Prussian province of Westphalia, among which is Jérôme Bonaparte's decree granting full civil rights to the Jews of Westphalia; records of the Konsistorium der Israeliten des Königreichs Westfalen; and Sutro's official correspondence concerning affairs of the Jewish communities of Beverungen, Münster, Oelde, Ossendorf, Paderborn, Soest, and Warburg.

Languages: German, Judeo-German, English.
Donor: Hannah Bluhm, 1962.
Finding Aid: 11-page inventory.
Accession Number: AR 1884.

38 B'NAI B'RITH
1890–1939   8 inches

B'nai B'rith (Sons of the Covenant) is a Jewish fraternal benevolent society founded in New York in 1843. The first lodge outside the United States was established in Germany in 1882 as the Grossloge für Deutschland, and by 1932, the German district had 103 lodges and nearly 15,000 members. In addition, districts were established in Austria, Czechoslovakia, Poland, Rumania, and Great Britain.

Correspondence, membership certificates, newsletters, notices concerning ritual and function, by-laws and minutes for B'nai B'rith lodges in Berlin, Budweis, Cologne, Düsseldorf, Frankfurt am Main, Konstanz, Mainz, Prague, Schneidemühl, and Stolp.

Languages: German, Czech.
Donor: Anonymous, 1974.

Finding Aid: 7 catalogue cards.
Accession Number: AR 4087.

39   B'NAI B'RITH – JEWISH PRESS AGENCIES
1933–1935   5 inches

Press bulletins, releases, and reports assembled by the headquarters of B'nai B'rith International from the Jewish Central Information Office, Jewish Telegraphic Agency, INPRESS (Independent Press Agency), and Comité voor bijzondere Joodsche Belangen. The material deals with the situation of Jews in Germany and elsewhere in Europe in the 1930s, including information on antisemitism, Nazi and antisemitic propaganda in Germany and elsewhere, economic conditions, emigration, Jewish professionals, the anti-Jewish boycott, the Nuremberg laws, and international reaction to the National Socialist regime.

Languages: German, English, Dutch, French.
Donor: B'nai B'rith International, Washington D.C., 1984.
Finding Aid: 10-page inventory.
Accession Number: AR 5316.

40   SALLY BODENHEIMER
15th cent.–20th cent.   4.5 cubic feet

Born in Rexingen on May 3, 1907, Bodenheimer emigrated to France in 1934 and Palestine in 1935. He returned to West Germany in 1962 and died in Frankfurt am Main in 1981. Bodenheimer was a collector of autographs, artworks, manuscripts, and rare printed materials.

Autographs of prominent individuals, including Berthold Auerbach, Leo Baeck, Alfred Ballin, Ludwig Bamberger, Michael Beer, Henri Bergson, Ludwig Börne, Max Born, Martin Buber, Benjamin Disraeli, Alfred Dreyfus, Paul Ehrlich, Albert Einstein, Ludwig Fulda, Léon Gambetta, Ludwig Geiger, Maximilian Harden, Henriette Herz, Hirsch Hildesheimer, Paul Landau, Else Lasker-Schüler, Moritz Lazarus, Fanny Lewald, Max Liebermann, Paul Lindau, Ludwig Meidner, Giacomo Meyerbeer, Moses Montefiore, Max Nordau, Bertha Pappenheim, Walter Rathenau, Lesser Ury, Chaim Weizmann, Leopold Zunz, Arnold Zweig, Frederike Zweig, and Stefan Zweig.

Clippings, letters, family trees, photos, and memorabilia about Paul Ehrlich and the Rothschild family.

Decrees, patents, authorizations, passports, letters of protection, residence permits, letters of municipal citizenship, notarial, business, and vital documents, and community and organizational stamps from Amsterdam, Austerlitz, Austria, Baden, Bavaria, Berlin, Breslau, Budapest, Cologne, Cottbus, Culmsee, East Frisia, Frankfurt am

Main, Gnesen, Hamburg, Hanover, Hessen, Holleschau, Landsberg an der Warthe, Leipzig, Moravia, Neustettin, Paderborn, the Palatinate, Posen, Prussia, Rhina, Schaumburg-Lippe, Schleswig, Thuringia, Vienna, and Württemberg.

Other miscellaneous items, including antisemitic caricatures and leaflets, Arabic documents, posters from World War I and the German Revolution of 1918, visiting cards, Stammbuch of Rebekka Bielefeld, 1821–1948.

Languages: German, Hebrew, Yiddish, French, English, Judeo-German, Arabic.
Donor: Purchase, 1977.
Finding Aid: 51-page inventory.
Accession Number: AR 7169.

41 JOSEPH BORNSTEIN
1941–1952   8 inches

Born in Cracow, Austria-Hungary (now Poland) on October 18, 1899, Bornstein moved to Berlin in 1905, emigrated to France in 1933, and to the United States in 1941. He was active as a literary agent, author and journalist. Bornstein died in New York City on June 23, 1952.

Correspondence of Bornstein, including letters from Hermann Kesten, Thomas Mann, Alfred Polgar, and Leopold Schwarzschild; also about the publication of American editions of the works of Hermann Hesse and Alberto Moravia.

Drafts, research notes, prospectuses, and reviews of books by Bornstein, including material on the murder of Carlo Tresca with letters by Elmer Davis and Norman Thomas.

Languages: German, English.
Donor: William Kallir, 1973.
Finding Aid: 8-page inventory.
Accession Number: AR 4082.

42 CARL BOSCHWITZ – HERMANN LEUBSDORF
1731–1959   5 inches

Carl Boschwitz (1877–1937) was a businessman who emigrated to the United States in 1914.

Hermann Leubsdorf was the great-great grandson of Brunella van Geldern, sister of Betty van Geldern, Heinrich Heine's mother.

Correspondence and other papers of Carl Boschwitz, mostly in connection with his work with the Prisoners of War Relief Committee (Kriegsgefangenen Fürsorge), later the Welfare Committee for Prisoners of War, and the Kolonialkriegerbank on behalf of German and Austrian POWs during and after World War I, 1914–1921, including correspondence with the German and Austrian embassies, the Deutsches Rotes Kreuz, and individual POWs; a letter from Reichskanzler Franz von Papen in 1932 discussing German domestic and foreign affairs, and the Nazi movement.

Papers of the Leubsdorf family and the van Geldern families, including wills, contracts, guild papers, and correspondence, including correspondence of Betty Heine (born Peira van Geldern), the mother of Heinrich Heine.

A manuscript prayerbook, *Seder u-tefilot Yom Kippur Katan*, containing prayers for the fast day preceding the New Moon as well as for other occasions, written in 1743–1744, and later owned by the van Geldern family.

Genealogies, and correspondence and other manuscripts dealing with the genealogies, of the Boschwitz, Leubsdorf, and van Geldern families, including correspondence of Hermann Leubsdorf with Wilhelm Levison.

Languages: German, English, Judeo-German, Hebrew, French.
Donor: Mrs. Karl Leubsdorf, 1983.
Finding Aid: 4-page inventory.
Accession Number: AR 7251.

43 JULIE BRAUN-VOGELSTEIN
1743–1971   40 feet

Born in Stettin (now Szczecin, Poland) on January 26, 1883, Julie Braun-Vogelstein became active in the Social Democratic movement, and was Heinrich Braun's secretary and his wife following the death of Lily Braun.
Active as an author, art historian, and journalist, she emigrated to the United States via France in 1935–1936. She was a member of the board of the Leo Baeck Institute, and she died in New York City on February 6, 1971. She assembled and preserved the papers of various members of her family, which are included in her collection.

1. Heinrich Braun and Lily Braun
Born in Budapest on November 23, 1854, Braun studied law and economics at the Universities of Vienna and Strasbourg. He joined the Sozialdemokratische Partei Deutschlands (SPD) and worked as an editor and journalist, becoming a leading representative of the party's revisionist wing. Braun died in Berlin on February 9, 1927.

Born Lily von Kretschman in Halberstadt on July 2, 1865, Lily Braun was a social worker and author, active in the German feminist movement and the SPD.
She died in Berlin-Zehlendorf on August 9, 1916.

Correspondence of Heinrich Braun with individuals, including Victor Adler, August Bebel, Eduard Bernstein, Lujo Brentano, Benedetto Croce, Kurt Eisner, Sigmund Freud, Wolfgang Heine, Benno Karpeles, Karl Kautsky, Isolde Kurz, Friedrich Meinecke, Paul Natorp, Heinrich de Man, Walther Rathenau, Werner Sombart, Ferdinand Tönnies, and Max Weber.

Correspondence of Lily Braun with individuals, including Mathilde von Colomb and Heinrich Braun.

Manuscripts, clippings, by and about Heinrich Braun and his political and journalistic activities, including minutes of the party court of the Frankfurt an der Oder-Lebus branch of the SPD concerning charges brought against him; related material from the SPD Congress in Dresden, 1903.

2. Otto Braun
Born in Berlin on June 27, 1897, the son of Heinrich and Lily Braun, Otto Braun died in combat in Marlecave, France, on April 29, 1918.

Juvenilia, memorabilia, and childhood and wartime correspondence of Otto Braun; material concerning Julie Braun-Vogelstein's biography of him, including correspondence and Lily Braun's diaries.

3. Ludwig Vogelstein
Born in Pilsen, Austria-Hungary (now Plzeň, Czechoslovakia), on February 3, 1871, Ludwig Vogelstein, the older brother of Julie Braun-Vogelstein, emigrated to the United States in 1896, becoming a successful entrepreneur and prominent American Jewish philanthropist. He died in New York City on September 23, 1934.

Family and business correspondence; speeches on metallurgy and Jewish affairs; and photos of New York City in the early twentieth century, and of his business.

4. Julie Braun-Vogelstein
Correspondence with family members and other individuals including Hasso von Seebach, Hannah Arendt, Ludwig Dehio, Henri de Man, Friedrich Meinecke, Eugen Rosenstock-Huessy, Toni Stolper, and Adam von Trott zu Solz.

Essays, research notes, manuscripts, and clippings on art history, politics, and philosophy, by Julie Braun-Vogelstein and others; proofs, drafts, and other material for her autobiography, and for biographies of Heinrich Braun, Otto Braun, and Ludwig Vogelstein.

Material on resistance to the Nazis, including a manuscript by Dietrich Bonhoeffer, and lists of individuals executed after July 20, 1944.

5. Heinemann Vogelstein
Born in Lage on February 13, 1841, Julie Braun-Vogelstein's father was a rabbi in Pilsen and Stettin, a leader of the liberal tendency in German Jewry, and a noted opponent of Zionism. He died in St. Moritz, Switzerland, on August 4, 1911.

Correspondence, including letters of Heinemann Vogelstein's wife, Rosa Vogelstein, as well as letters from other family members, colleagues, including Josef Heinemann, Siegmund Maybaum, Claude Montefiore, and N. A. Nobel, and organizations such as the Liberaler Rabbiner-Verband.

Sermons, pamphlets, and speeches concerning Zionism and other topics; autograph album; records of the Vereinigung für das liberale Judentum in Deutschland, and of the Liberaler Rabbiner-Verband. Religious documents, including shechita certificates, marriage contracts, rabbinical court decrees concerning divorce, and eighteenth-century manuscript commentaries on the Bible and the Kabbalah.

6. Hans von Kretschman and Jenny von Gustedt
Lily Braun's father, Hans von Kretschman, was a general in the Prussian army. He was born in Berlin on August 11, 1832, and died there on March 31, 1899.

Jenny von Gustedt, Lily Braun's grandmother, was born in Kassel on September 7, 1811, the illegitimate daughter of Jérôme Bonaparte, king of Westphalia. She died in 1890.

Correspondence, including letters of Hans von Kretschman to his wife and letters of Jenny von Gustedt to individuals, including the German Empress Augusta, Ottilie von Goethe, and Wolfgang von Goethe.

Autobiographies, wills, genealogies, and diaries of members of the Gustedt and Kretschman families; the autobiography of Lily Braun's sister Maria von Kretschman (alias Maria de Victorica), and photocopies of the files of her trial for espionage by the U.S. Department of Justice after World War I.

Languages: German, French, English, Italian, Hebrew, Judeo-German.
Donor: Julie Braun-Vogelstein, 1967.
Finding Aid: 33-page inventory.
Accession Number: AR 7163.

44 WALTER BRESLAUER
1928–1976   4 inches

Born in Berlin in 1890, Walter Breslauer studied law and from 1931 to 1936 was administrative director of the Jewish Community of Berlin. In 1936, he emigrated to Great Britain, where he was active in refugee affairs, becoming vice-president of the Council of Jews from Germany. He died in London on May 11, 1981.

Breslauer's correspondence, including letters from Leo Baeck.

Clippings by and about Breslauer, including articles on refugee life in Britain, restitution, and the work of the Council of Jews from Germany.

A memoir by Breslauer is catalogued separately, in the memoir collection.

Budget of the Jewish community of Berlin, 1936.

Languages: German, English.
Donor: Walter Breslauer, 1974, 1976.
Finding Aid: 9-page inventory.
Accession Number: AR 4129.

45 CONSTANTIN BRUNNER
1879–1952   7 feet

Born Leopold Wertheimer in Altona on September 19, 1862, Brunner was a writer and philosopher. He emigrated to the Netherlands and died in the Hague on August 17, 1937.

Correspondence of Brunner, both personal and in his capacity as editor of *Zuschauer*, including correspondence with Ernst Altkirch, Rose Ausländer, Ferdinand Avenarius, Martin Beradt, Aron Berman, Lothar Bickel, Martin Buber, Max Busyn, Theodor Fontane, Ludwig Fulda, Maximilian Harden, Gustav Landauer, Max Nordau, Wilhelm Raabe, Walther Rathenau, and Prince Emil von Schönaich-Carolath.

Manuscripts, clippings, and albums by and about Brunner.

Papers of members of the Brunner circle, including Selma van Leeuwen, Lotte Brunner-Stigter, and Magdalena Kasch, containing correspondence, diaries, reminiscences, and manuscripts primarily relating to Brunner, his ideas, and his followers; a memoir about Brunner by Ernst Altkirch, which is catalogued separately in the memoir collection.

Reports and circulars of the Internationaal Constantin Brunner Instituut.

Languages: German, Dutch.
Donor: Constantin Brunner Foundation, 1977.
Finding Aid: 50-page inventory.
Accession Number: AR 7159.

46 FREDERICK BRUNNER
1808–1971   1 foot

Born in Landau on December 11, 1895, Friedrich Brunner was a banker and collector of Rothschildiana and material for the history of banking. He emigrated to the United States in 1939, and served as vice-chairman of Arnhold, S. Bleichroeder, Inc., in New York, and as chairman of the board of the Leo Baeck Institute. He died in New Rochelle, New York, on July 19, 1974.

Correspondence with individuals from Landau, including Rabbi Caesar Seligmann, Rabbi Kurt Metzger, and Otto Brunner; manuscripts by Otto Brunner and Caesar Seligmann about Kristallnacht and the 1938 deportations from Landau, internment in Dachau, Gurs, and Les Milles, and emigration to the United States.

Clippings, manuscripts, correspondence, and documents relating to the Rothschild family and other prominent Jewish banking families; on the history of the Jews in Landau, Speyer, Neustadt, and other towns in the Palatinate, from the Middle Ages through the mid-twentieth century; and on other topics; fundraising circular, 1837, for the publication of a pamphlet advocating the emancipation of the Jews of Bavaria.

Fragments of organizational records of the American Federation of Jews from Central Europe, Verein der Pfälzer in Berlin, and Selfhelp for German Refugees, including reports of its efforts on behalf of the prisoners in Gurs.

Languages: German, English.
Donor: Edith Brunner, 1975, 1978.
Finding Aid: 22-page inventory.
Accession Number: AR 4237.

47   MARTIN BUBER
1921–1929   2.5 inches

Born in Vienna on February 2, 1878, Martin Buber studied philosophy and art history at various European universities, became active in the Zionist movement, and worked as an author, editor, and publisher. Moving to Berlin in 1906, and to Heppenheim near Frankfurt am Main in 1916, he published highly regarded philosophical and theological works. Buber emigrated to Palestine in 1938, where he taught at the Hebrew University in Jerusalem until his death on June 13, 1965.

Two-way exchange of letters between Martin Buber and Franz Rosenzweig concerning, among other matters, their translation of the Bible, the affairs of the Freies Jüdisches Lehrhaus, Frankfurt, and controversies surrounding the founding of the Hebrew University, Jerusalem.

Languages: German, Hebrew.
Donor: Nahum Glatzer, 1971.
Finding Aid: 13-page inventory.
Accession Number: AR 3866.

48   WILHELM BUCHHEIM
1902–1947   3 inches

Born in Rosenthal bei Marburg on December 28, 1887, Wilhelm Buchheim studied to become an elementary school teacher and, after army service during World War I, taught in the Jewish school in Essen. From 1933 to 1939, he was principal of the Jewish school in Dortmund. He emigrated to the United States via Great Britain in 1939–1940 and died in New York City on October 15, 1957.

Diaries of Buchheim, covering his experiences in World War I, life in Dortmund in the Nazi era, and his emigration; a family history by Buchheim which is catalogued separately in the memoir collection.

Manuscripts and newspaper clippings, many by Buchheim, on questions of pedagogy and antisemitism.

Photos of Buchheim and fellow pupils before World War I; as a soldier during the war; of Jewish teachers and pupils at the Israelitische Volksschule, Essen, and Städtische Israelitische Volksschule, Dortmund, 1919–1932; and of a 1934 seder in Herzebrock.

Languages: German, English.
Donor: Hannah Buchheim, 1960, 1979.
Finding Aid: 5-page inventory.
Accession Number: AR 2078.

49   MAX BUSYN
1919–1975   1.3 feet

Born in Lodz, Russia (now Poland) on November 16, 1899, Busyn lived in Berlin where he was an artist and follower of Constantin Brunner. Busyn emigrated to Palestine in 1934, returned to Germany in 1955, and died in Wiesbaden on August 12, 1976.

Clippings, correspondence, and manuscripts by Busyn and other members of the Brunner circle concerning Brunner and the Constantin Brunner Stichting.

Photos of Brunner and of Busyn's portraits of Brunner.

Languages: German, Hebrew, French, Dutch.
Donor: Jewish Community, Wiesbaden, 1977.
Finding Aid: 4-page inventory.
Accession Number: AR 7093.

50   CENTRALVEREIN DEUTSCHER STAATSBÜRGER JÜDISCHEN GLAUBENS – ALFRED HIRSCHBERG
1894–1961   8 inches

Born in Gnesen (now Gniezno, Poland) on September 27, 1901, Hirschberg was editor of the *C.V. Zeitung* from 1920 to 1938. He emigrated to Brazil in 1940 and died in Sao Paulo, Brazil, on September 20, 1971.

Circulars, pamphlets, clippings, reports concerning the Centralverein Deutscher Staatsbürger Jüdischen Glaubens, and Eugen Fuchs, its cofounder.
Minutes of Centralverein board meetings, 1894–1895, and of the 1927 general meeting.

Language: German.
Donor: Eva Hirschberg, estate of Alfred Hirschberg, 1972.
Finding Aid: 6-page inventory.
Accession Number: AR 3965.

51 MORITZ VON COHN
    1810–1902   7.5 inches

Born in Dessau on September 19, 1812, Cohn entered the family banking business and served as court banker and financial advisor to the kings of Prussia, later the German emperors, the Grand Duke of Baden, and other members of the German nobility. He died in Dessau on April 30, 1900.

Financial and personal correspondence of Cohn, along with supporting documents, including letters from S. Bleichröder, King Friedrich Wilhelm IV of Prussia, the German Emperors Friedrich III, Wilhelm II, and Wilhelm III, Grand Duke Friedrich II of Baden, Duke Friedrich I of Anhalt, Duke Ernst II of Sachsen-Coburg-Gotha, Prince Clodwig zu Hohenlohe-Schillingsfürst, and other German nobles and court officials.

Clippings, programs, and memorabilia from Cohn's life, including posters from the Revolution of 1848, and issues of *Kladderadatsch*, 1855–1856.

Papers of Moritz von Cohn's daughter, Julie von Oppenheim, and his father, Itzig Hirsch Cohn, including personal and business correspondence, in particular with the dukes of Anhalt-Cöthen-Dessau, photos, awards, and honors.

Language: German.
Donor: Gertrud Mazur, 1960.
Finding Aid: 26-page inventory.
Accession Number: AR 1120.

52 RUDOLF COHN
    1886–1971   2.5 inches

Born in Schneidemühl (now Pila, Poland) on April 23, 1862, Cohn studied medicine, receiving his doctorate at the University of Königsberg in 1886. He was a lecturer and assistant professor at Königsberg, specializing in pharmacology and physiological chemistry, and also continued in private medical practice. Cohn emigrated to Palestine in 1933 and died there in 1938.

Scientific manuscripts and articles by Cohn and others; clippings, honors, commendations, eulogies.

Language: German.
Donors: Mr. and Mrs. Jehuda Levin, 1973.
Finding Aid: 4-page inventory.
Accession Number: AR 4055.

53   ERNST HEINRICH COLLIN
1889–1955   1 inch

Born Ernst Heinrich Schoenfeld in Nordhausen on March 10, 1882, the poet Ernst Collin emigrated to Great Britain in the late 1930s and died in London on March 19, 1953.

Poems, photos, manuscripts, correspondence of Collin with Julius Bab, Max Brod, Erich von Kahler, and Else Lasker-Schüler.

Collin's diaries for the years 1900–1948 are catalogued separately in the memoir collection.

Language: German.
Donor: Margarete Collin, 1962.
Finding Aid: 3-page inventory.
Accession Number: AR 2916.

54   CONCENTRATION AND INTERNMENT CAMPS
1936–1965   1 foot

A miscellaneous group of small collections containing the following sets of material:

I. Files on various concentration and internment camps, as well as ghettos established by the Nazis, including Auschwitz, Buchenwald, Dauchau, Gurs, and Theresienstadt; smaller files on Gelsenberg, Isle of Man, Kulmhof, Lodz, Lublin, Maidanek, Mauthausen, Les Milles, Mittelbau, Sachsenhausen, St. Cyprien, Schatzlar, La Vernet, and Vichy. Material includes correspondence, manuscripts, clippings, photographs, work and other personal documents, ghetto scrip, records of relief agencies, and postwar Allied reports and documents on the camps.

II. Photocopies of Gestapo records concerning 26 political, criminal and racial prisoners, both Jews and non-Jews, held in various concentration camps, including material on arrest, transport, and the evaluation of behavior during incarceration.

III. Records of relief agencies, including American Friends Service Committee, American Jewish Joint Distribution Committee, Comité de coordination pour l'assistance dans les camps (also known as the Nimes Committee and the CCAC), OSE (Ouevre de Secours aux Enfants), Selfhelp for German Refugees, and Union internationale de secours aux enfants, which were concerned with internees in French camps, as well as with refugees who were interned in camps in Spain, 1939–1944; records of the Interallied Commission for Political Prisoners and Refugees in North Africa and the Joint Antifascist Refugee Committee dealing with internees, both Jewish and non-Jewish, in camps in Algeria and Morocco, 1942–1944.

Languages: German, French, English, Czech.
Donors: Various, 1959–1983.

Finding Aids: 221 catalogue cards, 3 inventories.
Accession Numbers: AR 402, AR 971, AR 2271, AR 2272, AR 2273, AR 2274, AR 2275, AR 2314, AR 2369, AR 2439, AR 3128, AR 3471, AR 3572, AR 3763, AR 3783, AR 3987, AR 4012, AR 5033, AR 5063, AR 5260, AR 5269, AR 5316, AR 7131, AR 7213, AR 9002.

55 CONE FAMILY
c. 1800–1965   5 inches

The Cones were a Bavarian Jewish family who emigrated to the United States in the nineteenth century.

Family history, along with supporting documents and photos.

Languages: English, German.
Donor: Sydney Cone Jr., 1972.
Finding Aid: 3-page inventory.
Accession Number: AR 7050.

56 CONFERENCE ON JEWISH MATERIAL CLAIMS AGAINST GERMANY
1958–1963   5 inches

The Conference on Jewish Material Claims against Germany was founded in 1951 by representatives of twenty-three Jewish organizations to obtain and administer funds for the rebuilding of destroyed Jewish communities and the compensation of victims of Nazi persecution.

Annual reports containing material on applications for funds and projects financed by the conference.

Language: English.
Donor: Frederick Elkan, 1971.
Finding Aid: 1 catalogue card.
Accession Number: AR 7136.

57 S. D. CRAMER
19th cent.–1938   2.5 inches

Photos of the Israelitische Religionsgesellschaft, the Orthodox separatist community of Frankfurt am Main including portraits of such prominent rabbis as: Samson Raphael Hirsch, Salmon Breuer, Joseph Breuer; photos of community schools, pupils, teachers, and members of burial society, choir and other community groups.

Photos of Frankfurt am Main including street scenes, private and public buildings, and the former Jewish ghetto.

Language: German.
Donor: S. D. Cramer, 1965.
Finding Aid: 5-page inventory.
Accession Number: AR 2991.

58   ARTHUR CZELLITZER
   1919–1958   2.5 inches

Born in Breslau (now Wroclaw, Poland) on April 5, 1871, Czellitzer was a physician who practiced in Berlin. His avocation was genealogy, and he was president of the Gesellschaft für jüdische Familienforschung. He was killed in Sobibor in 1943.

Personal papers of Czellitzer and his family, including clippings, manuscripts, and notebooks, primarily on Jewish genealogy.

By-laws, regulations, and membership lists of the Gesellschaft für jüdische Familienforschung.

Languages: German, English.
Donors: Margarete Czellitzer, 1961; Rosemary Stevens, 1972.
Finding Aid: 6 index cards.
Accession Number: AR 302.

59   KARL D. DARMSTAEDTER
   18th cent.–1972   5 inches

Born in Birkenau on September 25, 1892, Karl D.Darmstaedter emigrated to the United States via the Netherlands in 1939–1940. He settled in Washington, D.C., and was active as an author, poet, and professor of German. He died in 1984.

Correspondence and autographs, including letters from former residents of Mannheim, as well as Rabbi Joseph Carlebach, Rabbi Jacob Hoffman, Richard Beer-Hofmann, Jacob Rosenheim, Felix Theilhaber, Fritz von Unruh, and Karl Wolfskehl.

Clippings, notes, photos of synagogues and cemeteries, organizational records, and official and private documents about Jews in southwestern Germany, especially in Baden and the Palatinate including material from Alsberg an der Bergstrasse, Birkenau, Ettenheim, Grosbliederstroff, Karlsruhe, Königswart, Ladenburg, Memmingen, Mannheim, Neckarbischofsheim, Sugenheim, Weinheim, Worms, and Zwingenberg, as well as Amsterdam and Prague, from the eighteenth through the twentieth century.

Material on the Ephraim Deinard collection at the Smithsonian Institution in Washington, D.C.

Lists of refugees deported from Gurs and Rivesaltes internment camps; correspondence with former residents of Mannheim interned in Gurs and Récébédon, including Eugen Neter.

Languages: German, English, Hebrew.
Donor: Karl D. Darmstaedter, 1962, 1977.
Finding Aid: 12-page inventory.
Accession Numbers: AR 9003, AR 15, AR 2562, AR 3737, AR 3850, AR 3898, AR 3999.

60 DECREES
1614–1846   c. 10 inches

Various decrees issued by rulers before emancipation to the Jewish communities of the towns and provinces of Alsace, Augsburg, Austria, Baden, Bamberg, Berlin, Bohemia, Brandenburg, Braunschweig, Breslau, Cassel, Cologne, Dresden, Eisenach, Frankfurt am Main, Hanau, Hanover, Helmstädt, Hessen, Karlsruhe, Leipzig, Nassau, Nuremberg, Palatinate, Potsdam, Prussia, Rawicz, Rheinfels, Saxony, Schleswig, Schwerin, Vienna, Weinheim, Wolfenbüttel, and Würzburg. The decrees concern many aspects of life, including economic activity and taxation, settlement rights, and the regulation of the internal life of the Jewish communities.

Language: German.
Donors: Various donations and purchases, 1958–1978.
Finding Aid: 100 catalogue cards.
Accession Number: AR 379.

61 SALAMON DEMBITZER
1909–1964   c. 1.5 feet

Born in Cracow, Austria-Hungary (now Poland), on December 29, 1888, Dembitzer settled in Germany around the turn of the century, where he worked as an author and journalist. He emigrated to Holland in 1933, Belgium in 1935, and the United States in 1941. He moved to Australia in 1947, Switzerland in 1958, and died in Lugano, Switzerland, on October 11, 1964.

Correspondence with individuals including Julius Bab, Martin Buber, Manfred George, Nahum Goldmann, Kurt Kersten, Gustav Landauer, Primo Levi, Thomas Mann, Bertrand Russell, Philipp Scheidemann, August Vermeylen, and Hugo Zuckerman. Manuscripts of novels, poetry, short stories, and essays by Dembitzer; press clippings by and about him.

Photos and promotional material by publishers about his fiction.

Languages: German, Yiddish, transliterated Yiddish, English, Dutch.
Donors: Hertha Dembitzer, 1975; H. O. Willrich, 1977.
Finding Aid: 11-page inventory.
Accession Number: AR 4212.

62 MAX DIENEMANN
1898–1948   10 inches

Born in Krotoschin (now Krotoszyn, Poland) on September 30, 1875, Dienemann studied at the University of Breslau and the Jüdisch-theologisches Seminar, Breslau, receiving his doctorate and rabbinical ordination in 1898. He served as rabbi in Ratibor and Offenbach until his emigration to Palestine in 1938. He died in Tel Aviv on April 10, 1939.

Correspondence with individuals, including Chaim Bloch, Martin Buber, Ismar Elbogen, Siegfried Guggenheim, Richard Koch, Else Lasker-Schüler, Claude Montefiore, Franz Rosenzweig, and Eduard Strauss; letters written to Dienemann by inmates of Buchenwald concentration camp.

Dienemann's dissertation, articles and manuscripts by him on theology and Jewish history, and lecture notes for his Jewish history course during the 1930s at the Freies Jüdisches Lehrhaus, Frankfurt; sermons by Dienemann, and records kept by him of rabbinical duties performed in Offenbach.

Memoirs of Dienemann and his wife, Mally of their lives during World War I; additional memoirs of Mally are catalogued separately in the memoir collection.

Languages: German, Hebrew.
Donor: Mally Dienemann, 1957.
Finding Aid: 16-page inventory.
Accession Number: AR 3050.

63 SAMUEL ECHT-BERNHARD KAMNITZER
1929–1950   1 foot

Samuel Echt was born in Norgau, East Prussia (now USSR), on July 17, 1888. A teacher, historian, and Jewish communal leader in Danzig, he emigrated to Great Britain in 1939 and to the United States in 1948. He died in New York City on November 12, 1974.

Bernhard Kamnitzer was born in Dirschau (now Tczew, Poland) on October 25, 1890. He worked as a lawyer and served as a judge, legislator, and senator in the Free City of Danzig. He emigrated via Great Britain to the United States in 1938, where he was co-founder and president of the American Danzig Association. Kamnitzer died in New York City on July 15, 1959.

Correspondence and clippings by and about Kamnitzer and Echt, concerning the Free City of Danzig and its Jewish community, particularly during the 1930s; correspondence with former residents of Danzig in their countries of emigration, including those who were interned in Beau-Bassin, Mauritius.

Material on the life of Echt after his emigration to Great Britain and the United States.

Records of the Jewish community of Danzig, from the 1930s, concerning emigration. Manuscripts by Echt on the history of the Jews of Danzig, along with supporting material, including correspondence and photocopies of documents; additional manuscripts by Echt on the Jews of Danzig are catalogued separately in the manuscript collection.

Records of the founding meetings of the American Danzig Association.

Report on a trip to the USSR made by a Danzig trade delegation in 1929.

Memoirs by Gerald Meyer of childhood vacations in Carlsbad, and by Richard Simson of Elbing.

Languages: German, English.
Donors: Mrs. Frieda Echt, 1976; Eva Meyer, 1985.
Finding Aid: 1-page inventory.
Accession Number: AR 7016.

64 DORA EDINGER
1928–1977   3 inches

Born in Berlin in 1890, Dora Edinger studied social work at the University of Heidelberg and lived in Frankfurt am Main, where she taught at the Freies Jüdisches Lehrhaus and was active in the women's auxiliary of the B'nai B'rith and Jüdischer Frauenbund. She emigrated to the United States c. 1934, where she worked as a librarian and journalist and died in New York City on November 18, 1977.

Clippings by Edinger and others about social work, Jewish life, and Jewish education; issues of Jewish periodicals; interview with Edinger about Jewish feminism and women's organizations in Weimar and Nazi Germany; and letter of recommendation signed by Leo Baeck.

Edinger's manuscript entitled "Aus deutsch-jüdischen Kindheitserinnerungen," containing excerpts from the childhood memoirs of Meno Burg, Moritz Oppenheim, Therese Devrient, Fanny Lewald, Moritz Lazarus, Julius Bernstein, Eduard Bernstein, Franz Oppenheimer, Gustav Mayer, Theodor Lessing, Alice Salomon, Moritz Julius Bonn, Jakob Wassermann, Paul Rosenstein, Else Lasker-Schüler, Hermann Sinsheimer, Ernst Toller, Isolde Kurz, and Alla Nazimova.

Languages: German, English.
Donors: Dora Edinger, Marion Kaplan, 1975–1976.
Finding Aid: 9 catalogue cards.
Accession Number: AR 4182.

65 TILLY EDINGER
1832–1964   2.5 inches

Born in Berlin in 1897, Tilly Edinger was a zoologist and paleontologist who emigrated to the United States via Great Britain and died in Cambridge, Massachusetts in 1967.

Correspondence, clippings, offprints, manuscripts, vital documents, and genealogical material concerning Tilly Edinger and the Edinger family.

The memoirs of her father, the physician Ludwig Edinger, are catalogued separately in the memoir collection.

Languages: German, English.
Donors: Tilly Edinger, 1959; Gerhard M. Lidly, 1965, 1967.
Finding Aid: 6-page inventory.
Accession Number: AR 2718.

66 JULIE FISCHEL EHRENBERG
1844–1912   1.5 inches

Born in Prague on June 16, 1827, Julie Fischel married into the Ehrenbergs, a prominent family of Jewish educators. She died in Kassel on July 9, 1922.

Letters from Julie Fischel Ehrenberg to Adelheid Zunz and Leopold Zunz, some containing addenda by Julie Fischel Ehrenberg's husband, Philipp Ehrenberg, and some with addenda by other family members, including Samuel Meyer Ehrenberg. Material on the Samson Freischule, Wolfenbüttel, including annual reports, invitations to festivities, regulations, and the by-laws of the S. M. Ehrenberg school fund; and eulogies for Philipp Ehrenberg.

Language: German.
Donors: Nahum Glatzer, 1975; Martin Goldner, 1977.
Finding Aids: 2 catalogue cards, 8-page inventory.
Accession Numbers: AR 9004, AR 4245, AR 7069.

67 SAMUEL MEYER EHRENBERG
1763–1917   15 inches

Born in Braunschweig on October 16, 1773, Ehrenberg was a teacher and then principal of the Samson Freischule, Wolfenbüttel. He died in Wolfenbüttel on October 21, 1853.

Correspondence of Samuel Meyer Ehrenberg with Philipp Ehrenberg, Seligman M. Ehrenberg, Leopold Zunz, Adelheid Zunz, and Isaak Marcus Jost.

Marriage contract, will, financial papers, manuscripts, and autobiographies; eulogies of Samuel Meyer Ehrenberg and of other family members; letters from Frederick Ehrenberg, who emigrated to the United States in 1882; genealogies and family histories.

Languages: German, Hebrew, Judeo-German.
Donor: Nahum N. Glatzer, 1972–1977.
Finding Aid: 61-page inventory.
Accession Numbers: AR 9005, AR 4025, AR 4441.

68   EHRENBERG-ROSENZWEIG FAMILY
1742–1930   2.5 inches

Correspondence among members of the Ehrenberg and Rosenzweig families, including letters from Adam Rosenzweig and Richard Ehrenberg, as well as with other parties, including Leopold Zunz, Adelheid Zunz, Claire von Glümer, and Heinrich Heine.

Engagement contracts, marriage banns, school curricula and certificates, character references, eulogies, family histories, and other documents concerning family members.

Languages: German, Judeo-German, Hebrew.
Donor: Nahum Glatzer, 1978.
Finding Aids: 4-page inventory, index to Judeo-German and Hebrew words used in the correspondence.
Accession Number: AR 4584.

69   JULIE EHRENBERG-WICHELHAUSEN
1828–1846   1 inch

Born in 1813, Julie Ehrenberg-Wichelhausen died in 1847. She was the sister of the Jewish educator Samuel Meyer Ehrenberg.

Copies of letters by Julie Ehrenberg-Wichelhausen to Moritz Ehrenberg, Philipp Ehrenberg, Meyer Isler, and Felix Wichelhausen.

Copies of letters by Samuel Meyer Ehrenberg to Isaak Marcus Jost, Meyer Isler, and Leopold Zunz.

Photos and genealogical material.

Languages: German, Judeo-German.
Donor: Martin Goldner, 1977.
Finding Aid: 2 catalogue cards.
Accession Number: AR 7056.

70   RICHARD A. EHRLICH
1881–1969   5 inches

Born in Rogasen (now Rogozno, Poland) on February 22, 1888, Ehrlich was a printer and publisher. He moved to Berlin after World War I, and was deported to Theresienstadt in 1943. He emigrated to the United States in 1946, and lived in New York City.

Correspondence, including letters from Bertha Badt-Strauss and Albert Einstein. Reminiscences of life in Rogasen and Berlin; diary kept in Theresienstadt by Ehrlich's wife, Sophie Ehrlich; other material from Theresienstadt including ghetto scrip, postcards, documents, and photos from the Deggendorf displaced persons camp.

Transcripts, clippings, vital documents, pictures, memorabilia, unpublished manuscripts by Ehrlich, and genealogies of the Ehrlich, Kurtzig, and Alexander families; a history of the Ehrlich family is catalogued separately in the memoir collection.

Languages: German, English.
Donors: Hilde Berman, 1957; Richard A. Ehrlich, 1969.
Finding Aid: 13-page inventory.
Accession Number: AR 11.

71   ADOLF EICHMANN TRIAL
1961–1962   1 foot

Mimeographed copies and translations of minutes of the Adolf Eichmann trial, including proceedings of the Jerusalem district court and the Israeli Supreme Court.

Languages: German, French, English.
Donor: Anonymous, 1978.
Finding Aid: 1 catalogue card.
Accession Number: AR 7137.

72   ESTHER ELBIN FAMILY
1787–1976   1 inch

Esther Elbin, née Cohn, assembled genealogical material on the family of her mother, the Buchholz family, as well as the related Steinthal and Herz families.

Vital certificates, marriage and engagement contracts, letters of protection, residency certificates, Jewish oaths, military and business papers, diaries, correspondence, photos, obituaries, and genealogies of members of the Elbin (originally Elbogen), Buchholz, Steinthal, Herz, and Cohn families.

Typescript with related correspondence on life of Jewish Hungarian citizens in Germany during World War II.

Languages: German, English.
Donor: Esther Elbin, 1978.
Finding Aid: 6-page inventory.
Accession Number: AR 4651.

73   ISMAR ELBOGEN
1842–1974   6 feet

Born in Schildberg (now Ostrzeszow, Poland) on September 1, 1874, Elbogen studied at the University of Breslau and the Jüdisch-theologisches Seminar, Breslau, receiving his doctorate in 1898 and rabbinical ordination the following year. He taught at the Collegio Rabbinico Italiano, Florence, from 1899 to 1902 and at the Hochschule für die Wissenschaft des Judentums, Berlin from 1902 to 1938, when he emigrated to the United States. He died in New York City on August 1, 1943.

Correspondence of Ismar Elbogen with individuals, including Elias Auerbach, Julius Bab, Leo Baeck, Salo Baron, Markus Brann, Martin Buber, Umberto Cassuto, Ludwig Feuchtwanger, Ludwig Geiger, Robert Raphael Geis, Louis Ginzburg, Ignaz Goldziher, Max Gruenewald, Moritz Güdemann, Julius Guttmann, Bernhard Kahn, Mordechai Kaplan, Adolf Leschnitzer, Lily Montagu, Claude Montefiore, Adolph Oko, Paula Ollendorf, Bertha Pappenheim, Felix Perles, Koppel Pinson, Peter Reinhold, Julius Rosenwald, Cecil Roth, Caesar Seligmann, Selma Stern-Taeubler, Henrietta Szold, Hermann Vogelstein, and Stephen Wise.

Personal papers, diary of a trip to the United States in 1922–1923, photos of Elbogen and others, including the staff of the Hochschule, and clippings by and about him.

Lectures, research notes, and manuscripts, largely on Jewish history and liturgy; annotated copy of Elbogen's *Der jüdische Gottesdienst*, for a revised edition.

Papers of Regina Elbogen née Klemperer, including family papers, vital documents, and reminiscences of her youth; papers of the Elbogen's son, Herman Elbin; and genealogy of the Klemperer family.

Decree by King Friedrich I of Prussia in 1703 censoring a section of the *Aleinu* prayer.

Languages: German, English, Hebrew, Italian, Czech.
Donors: Herman Elbin, 1965–1979; Regina Elbogen, 1959; Robert Raphael Geis, 1963; University of Chicago Library, 1963; Aron Brand 1981; American Jewish Historical Society, 1981.
Finding Aids: 6 inventories; 10 catalogue cards.
Accession Numbers: AR 9006, AR 64, AR 695, AR 1179, AR 2050, AR 2374, AR 4961, AR 7032, AR 7209.

74 ELE TOLEDOT
1241–1824   32 volumes

Ele Toledot (These are the Generations) is a collection of transcriptions of genealogical records of the Jewish community of Frankfurt am Main, made by the lawyer and genealogist Shlomo Ettlinger from originals in the Stadtarchiv Frankfurt am Main. The material is divided into three parts, containing lists of the Jews of Frankfurt by date of death, along with biographical information; men by surname; women by first name; and supplementary lists of baptized Jews and miscellaneous data.

Languages: German, Hebrew.
Donor: Purchased from Stadtarchiv Frankfurt for the LBI by Hans Georg Hirsch, 1984.
Finding Aid: 1-volume index.
Accession Number: AR 5241.

75 WLADIMIR G. ELIASBERG
1926–1970   5 inches

Born in Wiesbaden on December 10, 1887, Eliasberg was a physician and psychiatrist. He emigrated to Austria in 1933, Czechoslovakia in 1937 and the United States in 1938. He died in New York City on June 22, 1969.

Correspondence of Eliasberg with individuals, including Manfred George, Thomas Mann, and Jacob Robinson.

Articles, clippings, and manuscripts on various questions, especially antisemitism.

Languages: German, English.
Donor: W. C. Eliasberg, 1968, 1972.
Finding Aid: 5-page inventory.
Accession Number: AR 3267.

76 ALFRED ELIASSOW
1883–1979   1 inch

Born in Königsberg (now Kaliningrad, USSR) on June 11, 1893, Eliassow was a physician who emigrated to the United States in 1937 and died in Genoa, Italy, on October 11, 1972.

Vital documents, military service papers, patent signed by German Emperor Wilhelm II, emigration papers, photos, family documents, and genealogy.

Languages: German.
Donor: Dora Eliassow, 1979.
Finding Aid: 3-page inventory.
Accession Number: AR 4745.

77 HANS ELTZBACHER
1781–1971   7.5 inches

Born in Cologne on November 30, 1893, to a family active in banking since the eighteenth century, the painter Hans Eltzbacher emigrated to Belgium in 1938 and died in the Netherlands on January 18, 1969.

Financial, business, and personal papers of the Eltzbacher family and related families, including correspondence, architectural plans, financial ledgers, wills and testaments, clippings, and eulogies; of particular interest is the business correspondence of Count Aloys zu Kaunitz-Rietberg with the banker Jacob Loeb Eltzbacher (1758–1825), who was based in Neuenkirchen, Westphalia, along with supporting documents and records; material on the career of the lawyer Carl Eltzbacher (1854–1936), including clippings on his candidacy to the Cologne city council in 1903 and correspondence, including a letter from Konrad Adenauer.

Reports, by-laws, and other material on the Jewish hospital in Cologne and the Israelitisches Asyl für Kranke und Altersschwache, Cologne, in the twentieth century.

Languages: German, Hebrew.
Donor: Mrs. Hans Schoemann, 1970.
Finding Aid: 12-page inventory.
Accession Numbers: AR 3623, AR 1134, AR 3781.

78 EMIGRATION
1864–1952   5 inches

A heterogeneous group of collections containing the following material: Material on efforts of Western European and North American Jews to assist Eastern European Jews in their emigration, including material on the persecution of Jews and Jewish refugees in Bielorussia, Czechoslovakia, Lithuania, Palestine, Poland, Rumania, and Russia; on the pogroms in Kishinev and Lvov; membership lists, programs, statutes, and reports on the activities of Jewish organizations, including Alliance Israélite Universelle, American Jewish Committee, American Roumanian Jewish Emancipation Committee, Bureau für soziale Arbeit in Warschau, Deutsches Zentralkomitee für die russischen Juden, HIAS-HICEM, Hilfsverein der deutschen Juden, Jewish World Relief Committee, Jüdisches Zentralkomitee für die Kriegsopfer, Verband jüdischer Studentenvereine, Centralverein deutscher Staatsbürger jüdischen Glaubens, and Zionistisches Centralbureau.

Material on the emigration of refugees from Nazi persecution, including clippings, and organizational records, particularly reports, memoranda, and minutes of meetings of ORT, Congrès Juif Mondial, Zentralvereinigung der österreichischen Emigranten Paris, the American Federation of Jews from Central Europe, and the Harmonie Club, New York; clippings and correspondence assembled by Mrs. James Lightfoot dealing with refugees in the 1930s, and with the possibility of settlement in Alaska.

Anonymous diary of 1832 dealing with emigration to Latin America.

Languages: German, French, English, Polish, Yiddish.
Donors: Various 1958–1983.
Finding Aid: 10-page inventory.
Accession Numbers: AR 9007, AR 1989, AR 2023, AR 4647, AR 4680, AR 5187.

79   OTTO FANTL
   1922–1938   3 inches

Three autograph albums collected by Fantl, containing autographs, epigrams, pictures, and newspaper clippings of famous artists, musicians, writers, and politicians, including Eduard Beneš, Max Brod, Karel Čapek, Fedor Chaliapin, Gabriel Fauré, Ludwig Fulda, Maxim Gorky, Magnus Hirschfeld, Alfred Kerr, Egon Kisch, Franz Lehar, Theodor Lessing, Erika Mann, Thomas Masaryk, André Maurois, Franz Molnar, Josef Wenzel Radetzky, Hermann Sudermann, and Rabindranath Tagore.

Languages: Czech, German, French, English, Russian.
Donor: Donald Guntz, 1964.
Finding Aid: 5-page inventory.
Accession Number: AR 2209.

80   ERNST FEDER
   1851–1972   11 feet

Born in Berlin on March 18, 1881, Ernst Feder was a journalist and editor of *Berliner Tageblatt* from 1919 to 1931. Feder emigrated to France in 1933 and to Brazil in 1941. He returned to Germany in 1957 and died in Berlin on March 29, 1964.

Correspondence of Feder and his wife, Erna Feder (née Zobel), with individuals and institutions, including Julius Bab, Moritz Julius Bonn, Erich Dombrowski, Manfred George, Kurt Grossmann, Ernst Hamburger, Gustav Heinemann, Theodor Heuss, Alfred Hirschberg, Bernhard Kahn, Kindler Verlag, Guido Kisch, Paul Löbe, Henry Morgenthau Jr., Ina Seidel, Ernst Simon, Fritz von Unruh, Bruno Weil, Robert Weltsch, Alfred Wiener, Theodor Wolff, Egmont Zechlin, Leon Zeitlin, Frederike Zweig, and Stefan Zweig.

Diaries by Feder recording his experiences from 1913 to 1962.

Manuscripts, photos of Feder and his wife, and clippings by and about Feder and his work.

Material on immigration to Brazil and on Nazi activities there; transcripts of the restitution case by *Norbert Wollheim against I.G. Farben*.

Languages: German, Portuguese, English, French.
Donor: Estate of Erna Feder, 1973.

Finding Aid: 5-page inventory.
Accession Number: AR 7040.

81 SIEGFRIED FEHL
1879–1955   2.5 inches

Siegfried Fehl was born in Nikolsburg, Austria-Hungary (now Mikulov, Czechoslovakia), on January 1, 1869. He studied dentistry at the University of Vienna, receiving his doctorate in 1895, and practiced in Vienna until his emigration to the United States in 1938. He died in Yonkers, New York, on July 26, 1955.

Educational, vital, and military service documents; honors and awards; photos of Fehl, of the synagogue and Jewish quarter of Nikolsburg, and of David Feuchtwang (1864–1932), a rabbi in Vienna; manuscript by Fehl about the history of Nikolsburg.

Correspondence, including a letter from Fehl's boyhood friend, Karl Renner.

Language: German.
Donor: Fred Fehl, 1970.
Finding Aid: 9 catalogue cards.
Accession Number: AR 3665.

82 LUDWIG FEUCHTWANGER
1908–1973   6 feet

Born in Munich on November 28, 1885, Ludwig Feuchtwanger was trained as a lawyer, but worked as an author, journalist, and publisher. He emigrated to Great Britain in 1939, where he was briefly interned on the Isle of Man. He died in Winchester, Great Britain, on July 14, 1947.

Correspondence with individuals, including Alexander Altmann, Werner Cahnmann, Guido Kisch, Raphael Straus, and Max Warburg; business correspondence with publishers and organizations; correspondence with family members, including his brother, the novelist Lion Feuchtwanger.

Manuscripts by Feuchtwanger on various topics, including the Jewish Question and history and sociology of the Jews; clippings by and about Feuchtwanger; and photos.

Curricula vitae, bibliographies, professional documents, and material relating to Feuchtwanger's search for employment in Great Britain, including letters of recommendation from Leo Baeck, Leo Baerwald, and Martin Buber.

Manuscripts by other individuals, including Bertha Badt-Strauss, Chaim Bloch, Werner Cahnmann, Dora Edinger, Georg Hermann, Hans Kohn, and Nelly Sachs.

Field letters from the Verein Mekor Chajim, an orthodox group affiliated with the Israelitische Religionsgesellschaft of Frankfurt am Main, to Jewish soldiers during World War I; sermons from the Nazi period by various rabbis, including: Alexander

Altmann, Joseph Carlebach, Max Eschelbacher, Moses Hoffmann, Jakob Horovitz, Alfred Jospe, Max Kapustin, Emil Levy, Siegmund Maybaum, Hermann Schreiber, Caesar Seligmann, and Hermann Vogelstein.

Languages: German, English, Hebrew.
Donors: Edgar and Martha Feuchtwanger, 1968.
Finding Aid: 21-page inventory.
Accession Number: AR 6001.

83   MARTA FRAENKEL
1870–1973   5 inches

Born in Cologne on December 19, 1896, Marta Fraenkel studied medicine, receiving her degree at the University of Frankfurt in 1923. She emigrated to Belgium c. 1934, and to the United States in 1938. She died in New York City on August 8, 1976.

Correspondence of Marta Fraenkel with friends and family members, school papers, diplomas, and certificates.

Papers of Marta Fraenkel's brother, the political scientist Ernst Fraenkel, including: education, employment, emigration and military service papers, correspondence with family members and other individuals, among them Hedwig Wachenheim and Ernst Lowenthal, and letters written during Fraenkel's service as legal advisor to the U.S. military government in South Korea after World War II.

Papers of the Fraenkel family, including genealogical materials, family histories, and photo albums.

Languages: German, English, French.
Donor: Gertrud Mainzer, 1976.
Finding Aid: 8-page inventory.
Accession Number: AR 4348.

84   ADOLF FRANK
1857–1958   4.6 feet

Born in Klötze on January 20, 1834, Frank was educated as an apothecary and went on to study chemistry, obtaining his doctorate at Göttingen in 1872. He worked in various industrial positions, specializing in agricultural chemistry, and died in Charlottenburg on May 30, 1916.

Business and scientific correspondence of Adolf Frank, concerning the fixation of atmospheric nitrogen, the affairs of the Städtischen Gasanstalt, Charlottenburg, and the scandals surrounding Professor Paul Wagner and the German chemical industry during World War I, including a letter from Fritz Haber.

Laboratory notebooks of Frank, his son Albert Frank, and their associates; research papers, lectures and professional opinions of Frank; clippings on the chemical industry, and material relating to patents.

Business records of chemical concerns, including the Cyanid Gesellschaft, the Vereinigte Chemische Werke, Brandenburg and the Bayerische Stickstoff Werke, containing its correspondence with I.G. Farben.

Obituaries, photo albums, and clippings about Frank and about German politics and culture.

A memoir by Frank is catalogued separately in the memoir collection.

Languages: German, English, French.
Donor: Robert Frank, 1968.
Finding Aid: 9-page inventory.
Accession Number: AR 7176.

85   HANS FRANKENBACH
1867–1969   4 inches

Born in Eisleben on November 13, 1894, Hans Frankenbach was a leather goods salesman and member of the Deutsche Liga für Menschenrechte and Deutsche Friedengesellschaft. He emigrated in 1933–1934 via Denmark to Sweden, where he was living in 1970.

Correspondence of Frankenbach, including letters from Lion Feuchtwanger, Helmut von Gerlach, Emil J. Gumbel, and a card from Hermann Hesse.

Personal documents, manuscripts, clippings, and photos of and about Frankenbach and his pacifist activities.

Family trees and various documents illustrating the history of the Frankenbach, Falkenburg, and Simon families.

Languages: German, English, Swedish, Danish, Judeo-German.
Donor: Hans Frankenbach, 1962, 1970.
Finding Aid: 4-page inventory.
Accession Number: AR 1583.

86 FRANKFURT AM MAIN, JEWISH COMMUNITY
1614–1978   5 inches

Clippings, correspondence, documents, circulars, posters, and pictorial material, including photos of prints from the fifteenth through the nineteenth century, of Jewish community of Frankfurt am Main and its cemeteries, synagogues, and other institutional buildings.

Fragments of records of Jewish communal organizations, including a protocol book of the Sustentations Verein für Lehrer und Commission from 1833–1875; a mohel book with entries from 1698–1836; clippings, photos, and other material on the Jewish school Philanthropin; membership lists of the burial society.

Document commemorating the laying of the cornerstone of the synagogue of the seccesionist Orthodox community in Frankfurt, the Israelitische Religionsgesellschaft, in 1852.

The art collection of the Leo Baeck Institute has prints dealing with the history of the Jews of Frankfurt from the seventeenth through the nineteenth century, depicting individual Jews, the Jewish quarter, synagogues, and the Fettmilch uprising of 1614.

Languages: German, Hebrew, Latin.
Donors: Various, 1958–1985.
Finding Aid: 34 catalogue cards.
Accession Number: AR 380.

87 JAKOB FREIMANN
1827–1937   1 inch

Born in Cracow, Austria-Hungary (now Poland), on October 1, 1866, Rabbi Jakob Freimann died in Berlin on December 24, 1937.

Correspondence of Freimann with rabbis, historians, philosophers, and orientalists, including Jacob Barth, Abraham Berliner, Markus Brann, A. Breitenbacher, Adolph Büchler, Max Grunwald, Moritz Güdemann, Harry Hirschfeld, David Hoffmann, Leopold Löwenstein, Joseph Perles, Sigmund Seligmann, Christoph Sigwart, and David Simonsen.

Autographs, including letters signed by Marcus Benedict, Martin Buber, Heinrich Graetz, and Paul Heyse.

Languages: German, Hebrew.
Donor: Kalman Schlesinger, 1969.
Finding Aid: 7-page inventory.
Accession Number: AR 3489.

88 JOHN H. E. FRIED
1946–1982   6.5 feet

Born in Vienna in 1905, John H. E. Fried is a lawyer and political scientist.
He emigrated to the United States in 1938, and received his doctorate at Columbia University in 1942. He served as a special consultant to the U.S. War Crimes Tribunal at Nuremberg from 1947 to 1949, and afterwards as a professor of political science at Lehmann College of the City University of New York and with the human rights and technical assistance divisions of the United Nations.
He lives in New York City.

Legal briefs prepared by Fried as legal consultant to the Nuremberg Tribunal; manuscripts, legal briefs, clippings, offprints, and memoranda by Fried and others, including Justice Robert Jackson and John J. McCloy, on war crimes, National Socialism, international law and human rights; proceedings of war crimes trials; proceedings of the Nuremberg tribunals.

Drafts and research notes by Fried for books on human rights and international justice.

Languages: English, German, French.
Donor: John H. E. Fried, 1984.
Finding Aid: 5-page preliminary inventory.
Accession Number: AR 7262.

89 KURT FRIEDLAENDER
1851–1956   3 inches

Born in Bromberg (now Bydgoszcz, Poland) on September 17, 1888, Kurt Friedlaender studied law at various universities and was a senior official in the provincial government of Pomerania. He emigrated to Great Britain in 1939 and died in London in 1968.

Papers about Kurt Friedlaender's education, professional career, honors awarded him, his dismissal from the civil service on "racial" grounds, his emigration, and restitution claims.

Vital, educational, professional, military service, financial papers, genealogies, will, honors and awards of other members of the Friedlaender family, including Dagobert Friedlaender (1826–1904), member of the Preussisches Herrenhaus (upper chamber of Prussian parliament).

Languages: German, English.
Donor: Bertha Friedlaender, 1968.
Finding Aids: 2-page inventory; 27 catalogue cards.
Accession Number: AR 6004.

90 FRIEDLÄNDER FAMILY, OPPELN
1811–1937   1.5 inches

The Friedländer family of Oppeln were brewers, industrialists, and local notables.

Real estate, tax, and financial documents concerning the affairs of the Friedländer family and the Schlossbrauerei M. Friedländer; family histories; photos of family members, the brewery, and the town.

Manuscript and correspondence of the author Robert Friedländer-Prechtl with Ernst Lissauer.

Language: German.
Donor: M. J. Friedländer, 1963.
Finding Aid: 4-page inventory.
Accession Number: AR 2133.

91 EFRAIM FRISCH
1894–1958   6 feet

Born in Stry, Austria-Hungary (now USSR) on March 1, 1874, Frisch studied at the Universities of Vienna, Berlin, and Kiel, and settled in Berlin around 1900. He was a writer, dramatist, and journalist, and was editor of *Der Neue Merkur* from 1914 to 1925. Frisch emigrated to Switzerland in 1933 and died in Ascona, Switzerland, on November 29, 1942.

Editorial and personal correspondence of Efraim Frisch and his wife, Fega Frisch, with individuals and institutions, including Richard Beer-Hofmann, Walter Benjamin, Gottfried Benn, Micha Berdyczewski (pseudonym Micha Bin-Gorion), Ernst Bloch, Martin Buber, Carl Burkhardt, Bruno Cassirer, Deutsche Verlagsanstalt, Edmond Fleg, *Frankfurter Zeitung*, Manfred George, Stefan Grossmann, Willy Haas, Konrad Hänisch, Ludo M. Hartmann, Wilhelm Hausenstein, Wolfgang Heine, Hermann Hesse, Georg Hirschfeld, Hugo von Hofmannsthal, Arthur Holitscher, Monty Jacobs, Siegfried Jacobsohn, Erich von Kahler, Hans Kauders, Rudolf Kayser, Friedrich Kayssler, Alfred Kerr, Hermann Kesten, Jacob Klatzkin, Siegfried Kracauer, Else Lasker-Schüler, Max Lehrs, Ferdinand Lion, Emil Ludwig, Heinrich Mann, Klaus Mann, Thomas Mann, Albrecht Mendelssohn-Bartholdy, Christian Morgenstern, Robert Musil, Carl von Ossietzky, Max Picard, Max Reinhardt, Eduard Rosenbaum, Lou Andreas-Salomé, Arno Schirokauer, Ignazio Silone, Hermann Struck, Eduard Stucken, Kurt Tucholsky, Alfred Vagts, Jakob Wassermann, Frank Wedekind, and Karl Wolfskehl.

Personal documents, manuscripts of Frisch's novels, short stories, essays, and book reviews; clippings by and about Ephraim and Fega Frisch and their work, including an essay by Alfred Vagts on *Der Neue Merkur*. Photos of Efraim and Fega Frisch and other literary personalities.

Languages: German, English, Yiddish.
Donor: Bella Schlesinger, 1965, 1966.
Finding Aids: 87-page inventory, 7 catalogue cards.
Accession Numbers: AR 9008, AR 1034, AR 2463, AR 2469, AR 2523, AR 2533, AR 2549, AR 3466, AR 3816, AR 4014.

92 FEGA FRISCH
1897–1958   2 inches

Born in Grodno, Russia, on November 8, 1878, Fega Lifschitz studied philosophy in Berlin and Zurich, and worked as a translator and author. She married Efraim Frisch in 1903, assisted him in his publishing enterprises, including the editing of *Der Neue Merkur*. She emigrated to Switzerland in 1933 and died in Ascona, Switzerland, on May 30, 1964.

Identification, curricula vitae, school and employment papers, and letters of recommendation, including one from Max Reinhardt.

Manuscript translations of a Russian essay of S. An-Ski on Yiddish folklore and of Yiddish works of Baruch Hager; reviews of translations by Fega Frisch.

Language: German.
Donor: Bella Schlesinger, 1965.
Finding Aid: 5-page inventory.
Accession Number: AR 2555.

93 HUGO FUCHS
1902–1934   2.5 inches

Born in Chemnitz (now Karl Marx Stadt) in 1878, Hugo Fuchs was rabbi of Chemnitz, and was active in the Vereinigung für das liberale Judentum in Deutschland. He emigrated to Argentina c. 1939 and died in Buenos Aires in 1949.

Correspondence of Fuchs concerning Keren Hayesod, including letters from Leo Baeck and Leo Baerwald, clippings of articles by Fuchs.

Photos and postcards of Jewish communities and synagogues in Czechoslovakia, Germany, Israel and other countries, and of paintings depicting Jewish life and well-known Jewish personalities.

Language: German.
Donor: Theodore Fuchs, 1960.
Finding Aid: 10-page inventory.
Accession Number: AR 1167.

94 ROBERT RAPHAEL GEIS
1928–1971   10 inches

Born in Frankfurt am Main on July 4, 1906, Robert Raphael Geis studied at the Jüdisch-theologisches Seminar, Breslau, the University of Cologne, and the Hochschule für die Wissenschaft des Judentums. He received his doctorate in 1929 and his rabbinical ordination in 1932. He served as a rabbi and religious teacher in Munich and Mannheim and as Landesrabbiner of Hessen, until he emigrated to Palestine in 1939. He returned to Europe in 1947, serving first as a rabbi in Zurich and Amsterdam before becoming Landesrabbiner of Baden from 1952 until 1956. From then until 1972 he was professor of Judaic studies at the University of Freiburg. He died in Baden-Baden on May 18, 1972.

Correspondence of Geis with family members, friends, and colleagues, including Leo Baerwald, Fritz Bamberger, Hugo Bergmann, Mally Dienemann, Regina Elbogen, Nahum Glatzer, Ludwig Goldschmidt, Max Gruenewald, Theodor Heuss, Jakob Horovitz, Hans Huber, Paul Josephthal, Jossef Kratzenstein, Miriam Beer-Hofmann Lens, Erich Lüth, Hermann Maas, Thomas Mann, Ignaz Maybaum, Martin Niemöller, Carlo Schmidt, Gershom Scholem, Caesar Seligmann, Ernst Simon, Margarete Susman, Harry Torczyner, Isak Unna, Robert Weltsch, Alfred Wiener, and Kurt Wilhelm; correspondence with the Zionistische Vereinigung für Deutschland and its local branches; and letters from students of Geis.

Topics of the correspondence include Geis' career as student, teacher, and rabbi; the activities of the Jewish communities in which he served; Jewish life in Germany under the Nazis; and Jewish life in Germany and elsewhere in Western Europe after World War II.

Educational documents from religious schools where Geis taught, including curricula, exams, and students' notebooks, papers, and assignments.

Languages: German, English, Hebrew.
Donor: Susanna Geis, 1986.
Finding Aid: 2 catalogue cards.
Accession Number: AR 7263.

95 HEDWIG GENG
1939–1963   1.5 inches

Born in Munich on April 23, 1891, Hedwig Geng was deported to Theresienstadt in 1943. She returned to Munich in 1945, emigrated to the United States in the late 1940s and was living in Albuquerque, New Mexico, in 1966.

Papers of Hedwig Geng from when she worked as a forced laborer in Munich, 1939–1942, her incarceration in Theresienstadt, and her residence in Munich after World War II, including correspondence with relatives abroad, decrees of the authorities, identification papers, photos, ghetto scrip, and poems and songs by concentration camp inmates.

Languages: German, English.
Donor: Hedwig Geng, 1962–1966.
Finding Aid: 8 catalogue cards.
Accession Number: AR 1587.

96 GERMAN ARMY PROCLAMATIONS
1915–1918   136 items

Multilingual German army proclamations issued during World War I, in Vilna, Warsaw, and German General Headquarters for the Eastern Front, containing regulations, announcements, warnings, war dispatches, and election list for Jewish elections in Leipaja.

Languages: German, Lithuanian, Polish, White Russian, Yiddish, Hebrew.
Donor: Anonymous, 1977.
Finding Aid: 2 catalogue cards.
Accession Number: AR 7076.

97 CARL GOLDMARK FAMILY
1836–1964   2.5 inches

Carl Goldmark, the son of Rubin Goldmark (1799–1860), was born in Kesztheley, Hungary, in 1830, and died in Vienna in 1915.
His brother Joseph was born in 1819. He emigrated to the United States in 1850 after taking part in the revolution of 1848 in Vienna. He died in New York c. 1882.

Family papers, including Hebrew dowry contract, prayer for pregnant women, and correspondence between family members who emigrated to the United States and those who remained in Budapest; correspondence with acquaintances in Goltsch-Jenikau, Austria-Hungary (now Golčuv-Jenikov, Czechoslovakia).

Languages: German, Judeo-German, Hebrew, English.
Donor: Mrs. Algernon Black, 1963.
Finding Aid: 6-page inventory.
Accession Number: AR 1909.

98   JULIUS GOLDSTEIN AND MARGARETE GOLDSTEIN
c. 1850–1943   4 feet

Born in Hamburg on October 29, 1873, Julius Goldstein studied philosophy in Jena, Berlin, and Darmstadt, completing his doctorate in 1899 and his habilitation in 1903. He was appointed Privat-Dozent at the Technische Hochschule, Darmstadt, in 1901. His appointment as professor in 1925 touched off a virulent antisemitic reaction. He was the founding editor of the journal *Der Morgen*, and also served as editor of *Darmstädter Zeitung*. He died in Darmstadt on June 25, 1929.

Born in Mainz in 1885, Margarete Neumann married Julius Goldstein in 1907. She was coeditor of *Der Morgen*, and continued to edit the journal until it ceased publication in 1938. She was active as a social worker and after her husband's death worked with the World Union for Progressive Judaism. In 1938, she married Leon Benevenisti and emigrated to Great Britain, where she died c. 1960.

Correspondence of Julius and Margarete Goldstein with each other, with relatives, and concerning the management of *Der Morgen*, including field letters from World War I and letters from Leo Baeck, Martin Buber, and Richard Koch. Diaries and appointment books of Julius and Margarete Goldstein, including Julius Goldstein's account of a meeting with Henri Bergson in 1911 and Margarete Goldstein's diaries of her lecture tour in America in 1923.

Press clippings concerning the activities of Margarete and Julius Goldstein; articles and manuscripts written by them.

Documents of the Goldstein family, education, citizenship and military papers of Julius Goldstein, and memoirs of his mother on her life in Hamburg during the second half of the nineteenth century.

Correspondence, reports, posters, and photos of Frauenhilfe im Krieg Darmstadt and related social work during World War I, and papers related to Margarete Goldstein's work in the 1930s and 1940s, including correspondence with Lily Montagu and a letter from Ramsey McDonald.

Languages: German, English, French, Danish, Dutch.
Donor: Via LBI London, 1979.
Finding Aid: 8-page inventory.
Accession Number: AR 7167.

99   LEO GOMPERTZ
1886–1967   4 inches

Born in Krefeld on January 15, 1887, Leo Gompertz lived in Gelsenkirchen, where he was a merchant, philanthropist, Jewish community leader, and director of Haus Bertha, a vacation camp and youth training and recreation center sponsored by the Reichsbund jüdischer Frontsoldaten. Gompertz emigrated to the United States via the Netherlands in 1939 and died in New York City on February 26, 1968.

Memoirs of Gompertz and others concerning Haus Bertha, correspondence with former members of Haus Bertha, clippings about, it and photos of its members and activities.

Languages: German, English.
Donors: Leo Gompertz, 1963, 1967; Mrs. J. Goldschmidt, 1969.
Finding Aid: 9 catalogue cards.
Accession Number: AR 1990.

100 WILLIAM GRAETZ
   1915–1974   7.5 inches

Born in Krojanke (now Krajenka, Poland) on October 18, 1879, Graetz was a banker who was chairman of German ORT and a member of the executive board of the Jewish community of Berlin. He emigrated to Switzerland in 1938, to Argentina via France in 1940, and to the United States in 1947, and died in Philadelphia on January 13, 1974.

Personal documents of William Graetz, including military papers, and membership and identity cards.

Records of ORT committees, minutes of executive committee meetings, correspondence and reports of the activities of ORT branches during the years 1926–1970 in Argentina, Bessarabia, Bolivia, Brazil, France, Germany, Hungary, Lithuania, Poland, South Africa, Switzerland, and the USSR, also including letters from Leo Baeck.

Records of the Jewish community of Berlin, in 1929 and 1930, including correspondence on juvenile care, financial reports, and meeting minutes.

Languages: German, English, Spanish.
Donors: Eva Herman, Frank Jacob, 1974.
Finding Aid: 13-page inventory.
Accession Number: AR 4121.

101 KURT GROSSMANN
   1933–1972   30 feet

Born in Berlin on May 21, 1897, Kurt Grossmann-Gilbert was a journalist and general secretary of the Deutsche Liga für Menschenrechte from 1926 to 1933. He emigrated to Czechoslovakia in 1933 and to France in 1938, where he was secretary of the Demokratische Flüchtlingsfürsorge. He emigrated to the United States in 1939 where he was an executive assistant to the World Jewish Congress, and died in St. Petersburg, Florida, on March 2, 1972.

Correspondence, both personal and concerning Deutsche Liga für Menschenrechte, Demokratische Flüchtlingsfürsorge, and other organizations, including letters from

Konrad Adenauer, Philipp Auerbach, Roger Baldwin, Eduard Beneš, Willy Brandt, Albert Einstein, Benjamin Ferencz, Manfred George, Nahum Goldmann, Emil J. Gumbel, Paul Hertz, Wieland Herzfelde, Theodor Heuss, Hermann Kesten, Joachim Lipschitz, Erich Lüth, Kurt Pinthus, Joachim Prinz, Hanns Reissner, Stephen Wise, and Norbert Wollheim.

Manuscripts of books and articles by Grossmann on numerous topics.

Transcripts of Nuremberg war-crimes trials and other postwar German trials of Nazi criminals.

Correspondence, clippings, memoranda, and reports on restitution and reparations, refugees and stateless persons after World War II, East Germany, the Jewish Question and the State of Israel, Neo-Nazism and antisemitism, and human rights; United Nations reports on migration and other matters.

Manuscripts, clippings and other research material on Carl von Ossietzky, for Grossmann's book about him, including correspondence with Rosalinda von Ossietzky.

Languages: German, English, Czech, French.
Donor: Purchased, Mr. and Mrs. Kurt Grossmann, 1967–1973.
Finding Aids: 7-page inventory, 114-page name-index to correspondence.
Accession Number: AR 7148.

102 MAX GRUENEWALD
1812–1984   4.5 feet

Born in Königshütte, Upper Silesia (now Chorzow, Poland), on December 4, 1899, Max Gruenewald studied at the Jüdisch-theologisches Seminar, Breslau, and at the university there. From 1925 until 1938 he served as a rabbi in Mannheim, and as president of the Jewish community from 1934 to 1938. He was a member of the executive committee of the Reichsvertretung der deutschen Juden. He emigrated to Palestine and then to the United States in 1939. In the United States, he worked for the Jewish Theological Seminary, New York, and for other Jewish foundations and organizations. He served as rabbi of Congregation B'nai Israel in Millburn, New Jersey, until his retirement in 1970. He was president of the New York branch of the Leo Baeck Institute from its foundation in 1955 until his retirement in 1985, and he remains president of its international board, an office which he assumed in 1974. He is also cofounder of the American Federation of Jews from Central Europe and the Philanthropic Fund. He lives in Millburn.

Correspondence of Gruenewald with institutions and individuals, including: American Zionist Emergency Council, Leo Baeck, Salo Baron, Arthur Biram, Julie Braun-Vogelstein, Rudolf Callmann, Karl D. Darmstaedter, Ida Dehmel, Saul Finkel, Jacob Hoffman, Guido Kisch, Hans Kohn, Bernhard Kolb, Liberal-jüdische Vereinigung, Judah Magnes, Ignaz Maybaum, Eva Reichmann, Reichsvertretung der deutschen Juden, Selfhelp for German Refugees, and Bernard Weinryb.

Correspondence, memoranda, reports, organizational records, and other material on emigration, internees in Gurs and St. Cyprien concentration camps, displaced persons, life in Germany in the 1930s, Zionism, the Jewish communities in Karlsruhe, Mannheim, and elsewhere in Baden before and after World War II, and on organizations, including the Fellowship for Reconciliation, Theodor Herzl Society, Yad Vashem, and Zionist Organization of America; material on a 100th anniversary album for the Jüdisch-theologisches Seminar, Breslau.

Manuscripts by Gruenewald on various Jewish topics; clippings by and about Gruenewald, and on areas of interest to him; manuscripts by others, including Jacob Picard and Karl Darmstaedter.

Genealogies of the Gruenewald family; material by and about Simon Gruenewald, Max's father, including memoirs.

Papers of Saul Horovitz (1859–1921), Max Gruenewald's father-in-law, a scholar of the history of the talmudic period, docent of religious philosophy and homiletics, and later Seminarrabbiner at the Jüdisch-theologisches Seminar, Breslau, on Jewish history, law, and philosophy, including manuscripts, sermons, and lecture notes.

Languages: German, English, Hebrew.
Donor: Max Gruenewald, 1981–1984.
Finding Aid: 8-page preliminary inventory.
Accession Number: AR 7204.

103 FALK VALENTIN GRUENFELD
1854–1961   5 inches

Originally from Silesia, the Gruenfelds were a family of textile manufacturers and retailers who established major retail firms in Berlin and Cologne.

Material concerning the family business, including excerpts from business correspondence, photos, advertisements, catalogues, bills, gift certificates, and price lists; reports, posters, clippings on the business in the Nazi era and its eventual "aryanization".

A memoir of Falk Valentin Gruenfeld by Heinrich Gruenfeld is catalogued separately in the memoir collection.

Languages: German, Judeo-German.
Donor: Stefi Jersch-Wenzel, 1968.
Finding Aid: 7-page inventory.
Accession Number: AR 2259.

104 FRANZ VIKTOR GRUENFELD
1911–1965   2 feet

Born in Berlin on November 24, 1895, Gruenfeld was active in the Gruenfeld family's textile business, and was also a student of graphology. He emigrated to the United States in 1937 and died in Zurich on November 21, 1965.

Notebook with sketches, documents, photos, letters and clippings on Gruenfeld and the family business.

Personal and business correspondence, including a letter from Fritz von Unruh and circular sent by Thomas Mann.

Clippings, manuscripts, offprints by Gruenfeld and others concerning graphology.

Languages: German, English.
Donors: Frank Victor, via Edith Tietz, 1965, 1966.
Finding Aid: 15-page inventory.
Accession Number: AR 3174.

105 LEOPOLD GRUENFELD
1908–1963   1.5 inches

Born in Vienna on June 26, 1894, Gruenfeld served in the Austrian army during World War I. He emigrated to France in 1938, where he was interned in the camps of Les Milles and Saint Nicholas. Upon his release in 1940, he lived in Nice, and emigrated to the United States via Morocco, Spain, and Portugal in 1942. He died in New York City on March 25, 1971.

Personal documents, letters from the field, military medals and photos of Gruenfeld and the Austrian army on the Eastern Front during World War I.

Documents concerning emigration from Austria and France, residence in Nice, and release from Les Milles and Saint Nicholas internment camps.

Languages: German, French, English, Bulgarian.
Donor: Paula Gruenfeld, 1973.
Finding Aid: 6 catalogue cards.
Accession Number: AR 4006.

106 MORITZ GÜDEMANN
1811–1918   1 foot

Born in Hildesheim on February 19, 1835, Moritz Güdemann studied at the Jüdisch-theologisches Seminar, Breslau, and became rabbi of Magdeburg in 1862. He became a maggid in Vienna in 1866, and was appointed chief rabbi in 1868. He wrote extensively on Jewish apologetics and education. His early ambivalent attitude to Zionism became strong opposition with his publication of *Nationaljudentum* in 1897. He died in Baden, near Vienna, on August 5, 1918.

Correspondence of Güdemann with family members, and other individuals, including Zacharias Fränkel, Heinrich Friedjung, Ludwig Max Goldberger, Heinrich Graetz, Max Grunwald, Julius Guttmann, Solomon Chaim Halberstam, Adolf Jellinek, David Kaufmann, Ignaz Kuranda, Moritz Königswarter, and Sigmund Maybaum.

Sermons (over six hundred), 1860–1918, organized chronologically and given by Güdemann on Sabbaths, holidays, and other occasions, including confirmations, weddings, funerals, and the Kaiser's birthday; manuscripts by Güdemann, including an obituary of Heinrich Graetz.

Personal, educational and family documents of Moritz Güdemann and other members of the family Güdemann; communications and awards from the governments of Austria and Vienna.

Communications and correspondence from various Jewish communities, including Vienna, Breslau, Hildesheim, Leipzig, and Magdeburg; synagogue regulations for Moravia from 1848, signed by Samson Raphael Hirsch.

Both originals and transcripts of Güdemann's memoirs are catalogued separately in the memoir collection; topics dealt with include the affairs of the Jewish community of Vienna, the beginnings of the Zionist movement, and the career of Theodor Herzl.

Languages: German, Hebrew, Judeo-German.
Donor: Syuta Güdemann, 1977.
Finding Aid: 4 catalogue cards.
Accession Number: AR 7067.

107 SIEGFRIED GUGGENHEIM
1791–1969   3 feet

Born in Worms on November 12, 1873, Siegfried Guggenheim was a lawyer, and chairman of the Jewish community of Offenbach from 1933 to 1938. He emigrated to the United States in 1939 and died in New York City on January 30, 1961.

Correspondence of Guggenheim and his wife with individuals, including Bertha Badt-Strauss, Leo Baeck, Leo Baerwald, Ismar Elbogen, Oskar Maria Graf, Max Gruenewald, Hermann Hesse, Otto Hirsch, Magdalena Kasch, Guido Kisch, Adolf

Kober, Thomas Mann, Jacob Picard, Nathan Stein, Selma Stern-Taeubler, Eugen Taeubler, Friedrich Torberg, Alfred Wiener, Karl Wolfskehl, and Stefan Zweig. Manuscripts, photos, and press clippings by Guggenheim and others on various topics, including: Jewish traditions, ritual art, Jews in Nazi Germany, and contemporary celebrities.

Records of the family Guggenheim, including family tree, family history, vital records, obituaries, papers of family members who emigrated to Chile, and other papers of family members.

Material concerning the Jewish communities of Offenbach and Worms from the eighteenth through the twentieth century, including correspondence, reports, circulars, regulations, programs, memorabilia, and press clippings.

Material concerning the Offenbacher Haggadah, edited by Guggenheim and acclaimed for its content and the quality of its printing, including correspondence, manuscripts, drafts, typography samples, printing blocks, and proofs.

Languages: German, Hebrew, English, Judeo-German, Spanish.
Donors: Siegfried and Eugenie Guggenheim, 1959, 1969; the New York Public Library, 1972.
Finding Aid: 45-page inventory.
Accession Number: AR 180.

108 EMIL J. GUMBEL
1914–1960   13.5 feet

Born in Munich on July 18, 1891, Emil J. Gumbel studied mathematics, economics, statistics, and physics at the universities of Munich, Berlin, and Heidelberg, where he completed his habilitation in statistics in 1923, and served as Privatdozent and professor. He joined the Unabhänhige Sozialdemokratische Partei Deutschlands (USPD) and later the Sozialdemokratische Partei Deutschlands (SPD), and was active in pacifist and left-wing causes. He was dismissed by the University of Heidelberg in 1932 because of his political activities, and emigrated to France, where he taught at Paris and Lyon, and was active in emigré politics. In 1940, he emigrated to the United States, where he taught at various institutions of higher learning. He died in Brooklyn on September 10, 1966.

Manuscripts, offprints, and clippings by Gumbel and others on statistics, in particular the theory of extreme values and mathematical limits; on the relation between his scientific and political interests; and on his professional career.

Manuscripts prepared by Gumbel for the OSS (Office of Strategic Services) on National Socialism in Germany and its political influence elsewhere in Europe.

Clippings, and scrapbooks of clippings, offprints, and other material assembled by Gumbel on his own career and political activities, including pacifist and socialist activity, his trips to the Soviet Union, and his expulsion from the faculty of the

University of Heidelberg; the history of the University of Heidelberg and right-wing political activity there; the growth of National Socialism and other right-wing political movements in Germany; right-wing terrorism and assassinations both before and after the Nazi seizure of power; concentration and internment camps and warcrimes trials; and World War II and the postwar plans of the allies.

Memos and publications of the Deutsche Liga für Menschenrechte; pamphlets of Jewish and underground organizations in Nazi Germany, and of various anti-Nazi groups abroad.

Languages: German, English, French, Dutch.
Donor: Estate of Emil J. Gumbel (1966–1985).
Finding Aid: 5-page preliminary inventory to the nonstatistical material.
Accession Number: AR 7267.

109 FRITZ HABER
1910–1964   2.5 inches

Born in Breslau (now Wroclaw, Poland) on December 9, 1868, Haber was a chemist, professor of chemistry at the Karlsruhe Technical Institute from 1903 to 1911, when he was appointed director of the Kaiser Wilhelm Institut für Physikalische Chemie. Haber received the Nobel Prize in 1919 for his work on the fixation of atmospheric nitrogen. He resigned his directorship in 1933 and died in Basel on January 19, 1934.

Photocopies of correspondence with Richard Willstätter and Chaim Weizmann.
Clippings, biographical material, family tree, and photos of Haber.

Language: German.
Donor: Karl Weigert, 1958–1962.
Finding Aid: 3-page inventory.
Accession Number: AR 182.

110 ERNST HAMBURGER
1913–1980   9.5 feet

Born in Berlin on December 30, 1890, Ernst Hamburger studied history, receiving his doctorate at the University of Berlin in 1918. After army service during World War I, he was an official in the Prussian Ministry of the Interior, and served as deputy from Breslau in the Prussian Landtag for the Sozialdemokratische Partei Deutschlands (SPD) from 1925 to 1933. In 1933 he emigrated to France, where he was a fellow of the Institut de droit comparé and the Institut de science de la presse in Paris. In 1940, he emigrated to the United States where he was on the faculty of the New School for Social Research and the faculty in exile of the École libre des hautes études. From 1948 to 1955 he was executive secretary of the Human Rights Division of the United

Nations. Hamburger was a member of the executive committee of the Leo Baeck Institute. He died in New York City on April 2, 1980.

Correspondence with individuals, including letters from Solomon Adler-Rudel, Immanuel Birnbaum, Julie Braun-Vogelstein, Arnold Brecht, Rudolf Breitscheid, John Caspari, Erna Feder, Ernst Feder, Ernst Fraenkel, Marta Fraenkel, Walter Friedlaender, Fred Grubel, Max Gruenewald, Albert Grzesinski, Helmut Hirsch, J. Edgar Hoover, Alvin Johnson, Rudolf Katz, Robert Kempner, Max Kreutzberger, E. G. Lowenthal, Cecile Lowenthal-Hensel, John J. McCloy, Alex Moeller, Siegfried Moses, Erich Ollenhauer, Arnold Paucker, Hanns Reissner, George Salomon, Richard Salomon, Toni Sender, Hans Simon, Hans Staudinger, Fritz Stern, Toni Stolper, Hugo Stransky, Hans Tramer, Hedwig Wachenheim, Herbert Weichmann, and Elsbeth Weichmann, and Robert Weltsch.

Personal papers, Hamburger's speeches in the Prussian Diet, notes for his lecture tours in the Federal Republic of Germany, and photos of Hamburger and others.

Lecture texts and notes for lectures given at the Academie de droit international, at the École libre des hautes études, in West Germany on behalf of the U.S. embassy.

Memoranda, speeches, correspondence, and related items from the period of Hamburger's work at the U.N., including a commentary on the Universal Declaration of Human Rights.

Manuscripts and research notes, including extensive biographical material for Hamburger's work on Jews in German public life during the Weimar Republic.

Clippings and offprints by Hamburger and others on Hamburger's life and publications, and on questions of history and politics.

Languages: German, English, French, Chinese.
Donors: Ernst Hamburger, 1978–1979; estate of Ernst Hamburger, 1980.
Finding Aids: 12-page inventory, name-index to the correspondence.
Accession Number: AR 7034.

111 HENNIGSON FAMILY
1832–1966   1 inch

The Hennigson family originated in Preussische Stargard and Tilsit, and is related to the Tiktin family by marriage.

Papers of the Hennigson and related families, including educational, medical, citizenship, and military service documents, wedding and funeral announcements, correspondence of family members, photos, and genealogies.

Languages: German, Hebrew
Donor: LBI London, 1972.
Finding Aid: 4-page inventory
Accession Number: AR 4114.

112 GEORG HERMANN
c. 1892–1977   10 feet

Born Georg Hermann Borchardt in Berlin on October 7, 1871, the novelist and writer Georg Hermann emigrated to the Netherlands in 1933. He is known best for such novels as *Jettchen Gebert* and *Henriette Jacoby*, which deal with problems of Jewish life in Germany. He was deported to Auschwitz and was killed there in 1943.

Correspondence with various individuals, including letters to Julius Bab, Bertha Badt-Strauss, Vicky Baum, Georg Bernhard, Max Brod, Martin Buber, Lyonel Feininger, Lion Feuchtwanger, Irene Forbes-Mosse, Sigmund Freud, Ludwig Fulda, Herbert Jonas, Käthe Kollwitz, Allert de Lange, Max Liebermann, Emil Ludwig, Thomas Mann, Arthur Schnitzler, Gustav Stresemann, Hermann Struck, Kurt Tucholsky, Heinrich Zille, Alfred Wiener, and Stefan Zweig.

Manuscripts of novels, short stories and poems, and of essays on various topics, including life in Berlin, German society and politics, Judaism, travel, art and literature; clippings by and about Hermann; and photos.

Dutch identification papers, food ration cards and stamps for Hermann, some under false names.

Autographs collected by Hermann, including letters by Theodor Fontane and Theodor Mommsen.

Languages: German, Dutch, English, French.
Donors: Hilde Villum Hansen, Eva Rothschild, 1964, 1974.
Finding Aid: 37-page inventory.
Accession Numbers: AR 9009, AR 2251, AR 3109, AR 7074.

113 HERTZ FAMILY
1835–1965   1 inch

The Hertz family originated in Rheinberg near Geldern, an old Jewish community. Emanuel Hertz of Rheinberg joined the Ulanen Regiment in Düsseldorf for three years voluntary service in 1835. His brother Kallmann Hertz died in uniform while fighting the insurrection in Baden in 1849.

Records of the Hertz family from the nineteenth century, including military papers, marriage contracts, business and personal correspondence, and clippings.

Obituaries, eulogies, speech manuscript, clippings, and list of publications of the Sozialdemokratische Partei Deutschlands (SPD) politician Paul Hertz (1888–1961). Hertz returned from exile in 1949 to become Senator for Economy and Credit in West Berlin.

Languages: German, English, Judeo-German.
Donors: Anna Hertz, Hannah Hertz, 1964.

Finding Aid: 3-page inventory.
Accession Number: AR 2452.

114 SALOMON HERZFELD
    1934–1968   1 inch

Born in Graz, Austria-Hungary, on February 14, 1875, Herzfeld settled in Essen, where he was a lawyer. In 1937, he became chairman of the Centralverein deutscher Staatsbürger jüdischen Glaubens. In 1939, he emigrated to Palestine. He died while visiting Argentina in 1948.

Photocopies of Gestapo records concerning Salomon Herzfeld, and notes by Alfred Hirschberg concerning Herzfeld's life.

Language: German.
Donor: Alfred Hirschberg, 1972.
Finding Aid: 3 catalogue cards.
Accession Number: AR 3976.

115 HIGH COMMISSION FOR REFUGEES FROM GERMANY
    1933–1936   1.6 feet

Founded in 1933, the League of Nations High Commission for Refugees from Germany was dissolved following the Evian Conference in 1938 and replaced by the Intergovernmental Committee on Political Refugees.

Copies of correspondence on the placement of German refugees from the office of High Commissioner James G. McDonald with numerous refugee-aid organizations and prominent individuals; copies of correspondence of Norman Bentwich, who served as McDonald's assistant.

Minutes of commission meetings, press releases, reports of commission subcommittees dealing with finances, passports, travel regulations and special problems of emigration by professionals.

Languages: English, French, German, Spanish.
Donor: Thomas Donnelly, 1979.
Finding Aid: 2 index cards.
Accession Number: AR 7162.

116 ESRIEL HILDESHEIMER
18th cent.–1895   1 inch

Born in Halberstadt in 1820, Esriel Hildesheimer studied at the yeshiva in Altona and at the universities of Berlin and Halle, receiving his doctorate in 1844. Along with Samson Raphael Hirsch, he was one of the founders and leaders of neo-Orthodoxy. He became rabbi in Eisenstadt, Austria-Hungary, in 1851, where he also founded a yeshiva, and at Congregation Adass Jisroel, Berlin, in 1869, founding the Rabbiner Seminar für das orthodoxe Judentum in 1873. His attempts to give secular learning a firm place in rabbinical studies brought him into conflict with more traditionally minded Orthodox Jews. He died in Berlin in 1899.

Letters to Esriel Hildesheimer from various individuals, mostly rabbis in Germany, Austria-Hungary, Palestine, Eastern Europe, and the United States, and institutions, including Akiba Lehren, David Neimann, Simcha Bunem Sofer, Yeshiva Etz-Hayyim, Jerusalem, and the Österreichisch- Ungarisch- Israelitische Gemeinde, Jerusalem; third-party correspondence of individuals and institutions, including Adolf Jellinek. Approximately one-half of the correspondence is transcribed.

Business records and other Hebrew documents of the Local-Comitee der israelitischen Armen- und Pilgerwohnungen auf Zion and other institutions in Jerusalem; a responsum from the eighteenth century.

Languages: Hebrew, German.
Donor: Purchased, Pampiere Wereld, Amsterdam, 1963.
Finding Aid: 3-page inventory.
Accession Number: AR 2373.

117 HELMUT HIRSCH
1935–1978   5.5 feet

Born in Wupperthal-Barmen on September 2, 1907, Hirsch emigrated to France in 1933, where he was active in refugee affairs. He emigrated to the United States in 1941, obtained a doctorate in history at the University of Chicago in 1945, and taught at various American colleges. In 1957, he returned to Germany, where he was active as a freelance writer and historian. Hirsch lives in Düsseldorf.

Correspondence concerning Hirsch's life in emigration and academic and political affairs, including correspondence with Fritz Epstein, Paul Froehlich, Rosi Froehlich, Louis Gottschalk, Georg Haupt, Hedda Korsch, Karl Korsch, Siegfried Marck, Maximilian Rubel, Hans-Joachim Schoeps, and Siegfried Thalheimer.

Manuscripts, radio scripts, and lecture notes by Hirsch and others.

Languages: German, English.
Donor: Helmut Hirsch, 1967–1978.

Finding Aid: 6-page inventory.
Accession Number: AR 3150.

118 ALFRED HIRSCHBERG
1935–1936   4 inches

Born in Gnesen (now Gniezno, Poland) on September 27, 1901, Hirschberg was a lawyer, from 1933 to 1938 director of the Berlin branch of the Centralverein deutscher Staatsbürger jüdischen Glaubens, and was also active in the leadership of the Reichsvertretung der deutschen Juden. He emigrated to France in 1939, and Brazil in 1940, where he was active in Jewish community affairs. He died in São Paulo, Brazil, on September 22, 1971.

Reports on the activities of the Reichsvertretung, especially in regard to emigration; minutes of its meetings, and budgets.

Language: German.
Donor: Eva Hirschberg, 1972.
Finding Aid: 5 catalogue cards.
Accession Number: AR 3975.

119 KURT HIRSCHFELD
1910–1965   6 feet

Born in Lehrte on March 10, 1902, Kurt Hirschfeld was a theatrical director and dramaturge in Darmstadt and, following his emigration to Switzerland in 1933, at the Neues Schauspielhaus, Zurich. He died in Zurich on November 8, 1964.

Correspondence of Hirschfeld with individuals and institutions including Theodor Adorno, Max Brod, Friedrich Dürrenmatt, Lion Feuchtwanger, Fega Frisch, Erich Kästner, Siegfried Kracauer, Ludwig Marcuse, Robert Musil, Martha Musil, Max Ophuls, Erwin Piscator, *Süddeutsche Zeitung*, Hans Sahl, Salman Schocken, Carlo Schmidt, Friedrich Torberg, Paul Tillich, Thornton Wilder, and Carl Zuckmayer.

Manuscripts, lecturers, clippings, photos, notebooks by Hirschfeld and others concerning the theater, plays, director's scripts, photos, and set designs.

Languages: German, Russian, French, English.
Donor: Tetta Hirschfeld, 1965.
Finding Aid: 9-page inventory.
Accession Number: AR 7066, AR 1563.

120 LILLY ISLER
1938–1946   2.5 inches

Born in Vienna c. 1910, Lilly Isler was a dressmaker who emigrated to the United States via Canada in 1939 and died in New York City in the 1960s.

Correspondence of Lilly Isler and her husband, Richard with her brother and mother concerning the events of Kristallnacht, of 1939–1941 in Vienna, of life in the United States, and of Isler's attempts to obtain a U.S. visa for her mother.

Language: German.
Donor: Gloria Isler, 1980.
Finding Aid: 1-page inventory.
Accession Number: AR 7173.

121 ISRAEL FAMILY
1714–1971   5 inches

The Israel family are descendants of Israel Jacob, who was permitted to reside in Berlin after 1741. Nathan Israel founded the Kaufhaus N. Israel in 1815, one of the most important concerns in Berlin. Its three branches were "aryanized" in 1939.

Documents, both originals and photocopies, relating to the history of the Israel family from the eighteenth through the twentieth century, including contracts, wills and testaments, letters of protection and vital documents; genealogies of the Israel and Adler families; photographs of family members and of their gravestones.

Material on the Kaufhaus N. Israel, including photos, publicity publications, the 1926 anniversary album, and the annual calendar albums for the years 1908, 1910, 1912, and 1914.

Correspondence of Wilfred Israel, in London, with Hanns Reissner and his family, who were living as refugees in Bombay, 1940–1943.

Languages: German, French, English.
Donor: Mrs. S. Behr, 1979.
Finding Aids: 5-page inventory, 4 catalogue cards.
Accession Numbers: AR 9010, AR 187, AR 783, AR 4790.

122 ITZIG FAMILY
1776–1969   5 inches

Daniel Itzig (1723–1799) was a banker and a minter; he served the Prussian state during the Seven Years' War. In 1764 he became the leader of the Berlin Jewish community. In 1796, he was appointed to the position of royal banker. He conceived of a school for poor Jewish children, where they would receive education in both religious and secular subjects. Such an institution was founded by his son, Isaak Daniel Itzig (1750–1806) as the Jüdische Freischule Berlin, in 1778.

Photocopies and transcripts of papers of Daniel Itzig and his son Isaak Daniel Itzig, including royal commissions, citizenship papers, testament, genealogies and family histories, and correspondence with Jüdische Freischule Berlin.

Autograph album of the Itzig family, 1784–1796.

Copies of papers of Arnold, August, and Nathan Mendelssohn from the early nineteenth century, including vital and military documents, copies of correspondence, and a travel log of a journey by Arnold to the Middle East.

List of 2,700 Jews in the Kurmark who were emancipated after March 11, 1812.

Languages: German, French.
Donor: Karoline Cauer, 1973.
Finding Aid: 4-page inventory.
Accession Numbers: AR 4191, AR 114.

123 JACOB JACOBSON
c. 1660–1958   18 feet

Born in Schrimm (now Srem, Poland) on November 27, 1888, Jacobson was an historian and archivist, as well as director of the Gesamtarchiv der deutschen Juden from 1920 to 1939. He was deported to Theresienstadt in 1943, emigrated to Great Britain in 1945, and died in Bad Neuenahr on May 31, 1968.

Records of the Jewish community of Berlin from the eighteenth and nineteenth centuries, including census lists, vital registers, cemetery lists and tombstone inscriptions, rabbinical court decisions, among them the divorce case of Simon Veit and his wife, the future Dorothea Schlegel; fliers, budgets, by-laws, and elections to the community executive committee.

Records of the Jewish communities of Hamburg, Altona, and Wandsbek from the eighteenth and nineteenth centuries, including the minute book of the burial society of the Sephardic Congregation Neve Salom, Altona, and record books (Pinkassim), vital registers, tax-lists, proclamations, letters of protection, financial reports, by-laws, ordinances, private documents, and correspondence of the German-Askenazic communities of Hamburg, Altona, and Wandsbek; photos of gravestones; minutes of the Loeb

Mindensche Brautstiftung, Altona-Hamburg, as well as records of other communal organizations.

Records of Jewish communities in Central Europe, including memorial books, correspondence, minutes, financial records, censuses, vital registers, mohel books, and cemetery lists from Allersheim, Altstrelitz, Arnswalde, Aurich, Bleicherode, Breslau, Danzig, Dresden, Düsseldorf, Dyhernfurth, Flatow, Frankfurt am Main, Frankfurt an der Oder, Fürth, Gnesen, Goch, the Hague, Haigerloch, Halberstadt, Halle an der Saale, Hanover, Harburg, Hechingen, Hörstein, Hürben, Jastrow, Karge, Königsberg, Koeslin, Krotoschin, Kurhessen, Kurmark, Landsberg an der Warthe, Lippe-Detmold, Lubacz, Märkisch-Friedland, Marburg, Meseritz, Mönchengladbach, Nackel, Neumark, Oberlangenstadt, Oberseemen, Pomerania, Posen Province, Potsdam, Prague, Prenzlau, Ravensburg, Reichensachsen, Rimpar, Sachsen-Meiningen, Sandersleben, Schermeisel, Schildberg-Bunzlau, Schleswig-Holstein, Schottland, Schwerin an der Warthe, Solm-Braunfels, Spangenberg, Tütz, Unruhstadt, Wallerstein, Westphalia, West Prussia, Wolfenbüttel, Züllichau, and Zwesten; transcriptions of documents, 1797–1806, dealing with the administration of territories annexed by Prussia in the partitioning of Poland, and particularly with the Jewish question.

Records of Jewish organizations, from the eighteenth through the twentieth century, including the minute book of the Gesellschaft der Freunde, Berlin; the correspondence of the Kassel branch of the Kartell jüdischer Verbindungen; by-laws, membership lists, or minutes of the tailors' mutual benefit society in Gnesen; the Gesellschaft jüdischer Handwerker, Berlin; the charitable society in Mattenbuden; and the burial societies in Rendsburg and Dyhernfurth.

Papers of Jacobson's grandfather Marcus Hirsch (1833–1907), chief rabbi in Prague and Hamburg, including correspondence with rabbis and Jewish communities in Altenhofen, Prague, Vienna, and towns in Hungary.

Papers of Jacobson's father, Moses Jacobson (1853–c.1930), rabbi in Schrimm, Gnesen, and Hamburg, including a eulogy for Eduard Lasker and a speech on the 125th anniversary of the Brüderverein Gnesen.

Jacobson's own memoirs of the years 1939–1945 are catalogued separately in the memoir collection.

Letters to Rabbi Leopold Löw, editor of Ben Chananja, and to Rabbi Löw Schwab from individuals, including Adolphe Crémieux, Samson Raphael Hirsch, Isaak Marcus Jost, and Ludwig Philippson.

Poetry, correspondence, notes, personal papers, clippings and other material from various individuals and communities, including memo by Max Bodenheimer about a meeting of Theodor Herzl with Kaiser Wilhelm II; papers of the bookdealer Julius Harrwitz; genealogical correspondence of Moritz Stern, librarian of the Jewish community of Berlin; eighteenth-century talmudic novellae written by members of the Fliess family; poetry of George Davidsohn, editor and parliamentary deputy for the Sozialdemokratische Partei Deutschlands (SPD); and a manuscript and notes by Selma Stern-Taeubler.

Languages: German, Hebrew, Yiddish, Judeo-German, Portuguese, French, Hungarian, Czech.
Donor: H. Jacobson, 1969.
Finding Aid: 39-page inventory.
Accession Number: AR 7002.

124 HANS JACOBY
1938–1980   5 inches

Born in Dresden on September 6, 1900, Hans Jacoby was educated as an artist.

He emigrated to the Netherlands in 1938, where he was interned in the Hoek van Holland refugee camp, to Shanghai in 1940, and to the United States in 1947. He died in Miami Beach, Florida.

Diaries, documents, correspondence, clippings, and photos concerning refugee life in the Netherlands and Shanghai; photos by Jacoby of the Seminole Indians of Florida, and of their art.

The art collection of the Leo Baeck Institute contains several artworks by Jacoby relating to his experiences.

Languages: German, English, Dutch, Chinese.
Donor: Hans Jacoby, 1979, 1980.
Finding Aid: 21-page inventory.
Accession Number: AR 4847.

125 JEWISH RESTITUTION SUCCESSOR ORGANIZATION (JRSO)
1947–1972   2.5 inches

The Jewish Restitution Successor Organization was founded by twelve Jewish organizations in 1947 to present claims against Germany and German individuals on behalf of deceased, heirless victims of Nazi persecution, as well as on behalf of disbanded organizations. The restitution funds obtained from these claims were distributed to the Council of Jews from Germany, the Jewish Agency, and the JDC.

Reports and memorandum on the organization's activities and its history; restitution claims for individuals and communities, including those of Altenstadt, Himbach, Mülheim/Ruhr, and Schotten.

Languages: German, English.
Donors: JRSO and others, 1960–1972.
Finding Aid: 3 index cards.
Accession Number: AR 1485.

126 JEWISH THEATER
1916–1950   c. 180 items

Posters, programs, and newspaper reviews for performances of Jewish theater in cities in Germany, Austria, and Lithuania, including theater produced by and about displaced persons in post-World War II Germany.

Languages: German, Hebrew, Yiddish, transliterated Yiddish.
Donor: Purchased, Z. Frydman, 1964.
Finding Aid: 4 catalogue cards.
Accession Number: AR 2371.

127 JEWISH VETERANS ASSOCIATION
1934–1973   1.5 feet

Successor organization to the Reichsbund Jüdischer Frontsoldaten, it was formed in New York City by refugees in 1938 as the Immigrants' Jewish Veterans Association, and dissolved in 1972–1973.

Correspondence, by-laws, minutes, financial records, photoalbums, and memorabilia of the association.

Languages: German, English.
Donor: Hugo Stransky, 1975.
Finding Aid: 3-page inventory.
Accession Number: AR 7012.

128 JEWS IN GERMANY, 1933–1945
1933–1974   5.5 inches

A miscellaneous collection combining correspondence, manuscripts, clippings, programs, and photo albums on Jewish life in Nazi Germany, antisemitism, resistance, youth groups, and victims of the Final Solution.

Languages: German, English, Yiddish, Hebrew, French, Russian, Czech, Polish, Dutch, Hungarian, Swedish.
Donors: Various sources, 1961; Association of Jewish Refugees, 1976.
Finding Aids: 5 catalogue cards, 13-page inventory.
Accession Number: AR 1441.

129 RUDOLF JOSEPH
1837–1963   5 inches

Born in Pforzheim on August 14, 1893, Joseph was an architect who emigrated to France in 1933 and to the United States in 1936. He died in New York City on January 17, 1963.

Manuscript and articles by Joseph on architecture, photos of his architectural works, and two 19th-century marriage contracts.

Languages: German, English, Hebrew, French.
Donor: Mrs. Rudolf Joseph, 1963.
Finding Aid: 3-page inventory.
Accession Number: AR 2180.

130 PAUL JOSEPHTHAL
1916–1963   10 inches

Born in Nuremberg on June 16, 1869, Josephthal was a toy manufacturer who served as a German army officer in Rumania during World War I. He emigrated to Palestine in 1939 and died in Tel Aviv on March 22, 1943.

Photo and clippings on Josephthal's military service; military orders, regulations, and notices issued by Josephthal and other German officers in Rumania; Josephthal's diaries from 1916–1918, when he was commander of a unit of German soldiers in Rumania.

Languages: German, Rumanian, English.
Donor: John Thal, 1963, 1975.
Finding Aid: 2 catalogue cards.
Accession Number: AR 4179.

131 ISAAK MARCUS JOST CORRESPONDENCE
1815–1860   2.5 inches

Born in Bernburg on February 22, 1793, Jost studied philosophy at Berlin and Göttingen, was a teacher at private Jewish schools, a journalist, historian, and advocate of religious reform. He died in Frankfurt am Main on November 20, 1860.

Correspondence of Jost with Samuel Meyer Ehrenberg and his son Philipp Ehrenberg, containing discussions about contemporary politics, Jewish education and scholarship, and the Jewish communities of Berlin and Frankfurt am Main.

Language: German.
Donor: Nahum N. Glatzer, 1976.

Finding Aid: 7-page inventory.
Accession Number: AR 4294.

132 HANS JUDA
1919–1972   5 inches

Born in Trier on September 25, 1904, Hans Juda was from 1927 a correspondent, and from 1928 an editor of the Handels-Zeitung of the Berliner Tageblatt. He emigrated to Great Britain in 1933, and died in London in 1975.

Personal documents, membership cards, correspondence, manuscripts, clippings on journalistic activities, including the 1932 Berlin world economic conference sponsored by the *Berliner Tageblatt*.

Languages: German, English, French.
Donor: LBI London, 1976.
Finding Aid: 2-page inventory.
Accession Number: AR 4352.

133 JÜDISCHER KULTURBUND
1933–1938   6 inches

The Jüdischer Kulturbund was established in April 1933 to provide employment for Jewish artists, musicians, and teachers who had been dismissed by the Nazis. They organized lecture series and theatrical and musical performances under the direct supervision and censorship of Staatskommissar Hans Hinkel, executive director of the Reichskulturkammer. The activities of the Kulturbund were severely curtailed after Kristallnacht and the organization ceased to exist in late 1941.

Transcript of the conference of the Jüdischer Kulturbund, Berlin, April 1935. Participants included Kurt Singer and Hans Hinkel.

Papers of local branches of the Kulturbund and their activities in Berlin, Düsseldorf, Hamburg, Kassel, and the Rhein-Ruhr, including cultural programs, invitations, bulletins, fliers, posters, and clippings.

Language: German.
Donors: Martin Goldschmidt, 1958, and others.
Finding Aids: 11-page inventory, 3-page inventory, 36 catalogue cards.
Accession Number: AR 2590.

134 FRANZ KAFKA
1913–1974   3 inches

Born in Prague on July 3, 1883, the author Franz Kafka died in Kerling near Vienna on June 3, 1924.

Photocopies, along with some originals, of Kafka's correspondence, as well as third-party correspondence of others, including letters from Felice Bauer, Grete Bloch concerning her son by Kafka, Max Brod, Martin Buber, Milena Jesenska, Gertrude Thieberger Urzidil, and Felix Weltsch.

Clippings, manuscripts, offprints, catalogues, albums, and pictorial material about Kafka and his work.

Languages: English, German, Czech, Hebrew, Italian.
Donors: Various, 1957–1980, including S. Fischer Verlag and Bildarchiv der Österreichischen Nationalbibliothek.
Finding Aid: 27 catalogue cards.
Accession Numbers: AR 1429, AR 3863.

135 ERICH VON KAHLER
1912–1979   c. 2 feet

Born in Prague on October 14, 1885, Kahler was a writer and essayist who taught literature at several German universities. He emigrated to Switzerland in 1933 and to the United States in 1938, where he continued his literary and scholarly activities. He died in Princeton, New Jersey, on June 28, 1970.

Originals and copies of correspondence of Kahler, his wife, Alice, and of his mother Antoinette von Kahler with individuals, including Leo Baeck, Richard Beer-Hofmann, Hermann Broch, Martin Buber, Albert Einstein, Efraim Frisch, Franz Kobler, Hans Kohn, Otto Loewi, Thomas Mann, Hans Rosenfeld, Franz Rosenzweig, Eduard Strauss, Margarete Susman, and Karl Wolfskehl.

Personal documents, clippings on Kahler, and reviews of his work; photos of Kahler, his relatives, the ancestral home in Brünn, and of Albert Einstein and other well known personalities.

Essays, speeches, articles, manuscripts by Kahler and others on the Jewish Question, Palestine, German-Jewish relations, Albert Einstein and Stefan George; a memoir by his mother, Antoinette.

Languages: German, English.
Donor: Alice von Kahler, 1962–1983.
Finding Aid: 23-page inventory.
Accession Numbers: AR 2141, AR 2242, AR 3890, AR 3905, AR 4816, AR 9022.

136 BERNHARD KAHN
1906–1963   7.5 inches

Born in Oscarsham, Sweden, on April 9, 1876, Bernhard Kahn was a lawyer, general secretary of the Hilfsverein der deutschen Juden, 1904–1921, European director of the American Jewish Joint Distribution Committee, 1921–1939, and director of the American Joint Reconstruction Foundation, 1924–1939. He emigrated to Great Britain in 1934, to the United States in 1937, and died in New York City on April 27, 1955.

Personal and professional correspondence of Bernhard Kahn, including correspondence with Paul Baerwald, Hilfsverein der deutschen Juden, Herbert H. Lehmann, and Felix Warburg.

Clippings, press releases, eulogies, photos of Kahn, identification, citizenship papers, and educational and professional certificates.

Kahn's memoirs are catalogued separately in the memoir collection.

Languages: German, French, English, Russian, Polish, Swedish, Hebrew, Yiddish.
Donor: Dora Kahn, 1958.
Finding Aid: 9-page inventory.
Accession Number: AR 416.

137 ERNST KANTOROWICZ
1908–1982   3 feet

Born in Posen (now Poznan, Poland) on May 5, 1895, Kantorowicz was a historian, who specialized in the Middle Ages. After serving in World War I, he fought with the Freikorps against the Poles in Posen, and against the Spartacist uprising in 1919. He received his doctorate at Heidelberg in 1921, and began teaching at Frankfurt am Main in 1930, receiving a chair in 1932. He was a member of the Stefan George Kreis, and is best known for his biography of Emperor Frederick II. He took a leave of absence to protest the antisemitic regulations instituted after the Nazis came to power, and was dismissed in 1934. He emigrated to Great Britain in 1938 and to the United States in 1939, where he taught at the University of California, Berkeley. He left as a result of the loyalty-oath controversy in 1951, and then served as professor at the Institute for Advanced Studies in Princeton until his death on September 9, 1963.

Correspondence on various topics, including emigration to the United States and Cuba; relocation in academic jobs; denazification and conditions in Germany after the war; and Kantorowicz's scholarship. In addition to family members, correspondents include Ernst Curtius, Ludwig Edelstein, Bernhard Flexner, Felix Frankfurter, Sidney Hook, Robert Maynard Hutchins, Ernst Kitzinger, Theodor Ernst Mommsen, John Ulric Nef, Kurt Riezler, Hans Rothfels, Fritz Saxl, Percy Ernst Schramm, Edward

Sproul, Gerd Tellenbach, Paul Tillich, Edward Tolman, Helen Waddell, Earl Warren, and Stanley Weigert.

Unpublished manuscripts, and offprints of articles and reviews by Kantorowicz, largely on medieval cultural history; a brief biography of him by Ralph Giesey.

Manuscripts, correspondence, legal briefs, clippings, and other material on the loyalty-oath controversy; material on Kantorowicz's tenure at the University of Frankfurt, and on his dismissal.

Manuscripts, correspondence, and other papers of family members; an art history essay by Gertrude Kantorowicz and a pamphlet of poetry from Theresienstadt; genealogies; and a manuscript on Simon Kaliphari of Posen.

Photos of Kantorowicz and of family members.

Papers of Richard Kandt (1867–1918), an African explorer and, from 1908–1914, administrator of Ruanda: poems, letters, maps, and obituaries.

Languages: German, English.
Donors: Ralph Giesey, 1982; Beate Salz, 1983.
Finding Aid: 11-page inventory.
Accession Number: AR 7216.

138 JOSEF KASTEIN AND SHULAMITH KASTEIN
1935–1982   4 inches

Born Julius Katzenstein in Bremen on October 6, 1890, Kastein studied law and economics and practiced law until his emigration to Ascora-Moscia, Switzerland, in 1927. He worked as a writer, concentrating on Jewish themes. His best-known work is *Eine Geschichte der Juden*. He emigrated to Palestine in 1935 and settled in Haifa, where he married Margarethe Vogl (who adopted the Hebrew name Shulamith) in 1936. While on a trip to Europe, she was separated from her husband by the outbreak of war in 1939, and eventually emigrated to the United States. Josef died in Haifa on June 13, 1946. Shulamith died in New York City in 1983.

Letters of Josef to Shulamith Kastein, including some poetry manuscripts; correspondence of Shulamith Kastein about her husband's work, with publishers and other individuals, including Alfred Dreyer, Friedrich Glaebe, and Nahum Glatzer.

Fiction and nonfiction manuscripts by Josef Kastein, including several catalogued separately in the Leo Baeck Institute's manuscript collection; his memoirs, entitled "Mosaiken," are catalogued in the memoir collection.

Clipping about Josef Kastein; material on Alfred Dreyer's work on him, including manuscripts, bibliographies, and a transcript of a radio interview.

Languages: German, English, Hebrew.
Donor: Estate of Shulamith Kastein, 1983.

Finding Aid: 3-page inventory.
Accession Number: AR 7227.

139 FELIX I. KAUFFMANN
1877–1946   2.5 inches

Born in Frankfurt am Main on February 7, 1878, Felix Kauffmann was a publisher and chairman of the Reichsbund Jüdischer Frontsoldaten for southwestern Germany. He emigrated to the United States via Portugal in 1941 and died in New York City on November 15, 1953.

Vital certificates, war medals, papers relating to employment, various Jewish organizations, and emigration; clippings about and correspondence with Leo Baeck.

Clippings on Kauffmann's business and on Jewish affairs.

Languages: German, English, French.
Donor: Philipp Feldheim, 1965.
Finding Aid: 6-page inventory.
Accession Number: AR 2633.

140 FRITZ KAUFMANN
1934–1958   2 inches

Born in Leipzig on July 3, 1891, Fritz Kaufmann studied philosophy at various universities, receiving his doctorate in 1924 at Freiburg, where he was a lecturer until 1933. In 1935 he emigrated via Great Britain to the United States, where he was a professor first at Northwestern University, and then at the University of Buffalo. He died in Zurich on August 9, 1958.

Correspondence with Oberrat der Israeliten Badens and Reichsvertretung der deutschen Juden concerning assistance for unemployed Jewish academics in Nazi Germany and Jewish adult education.

Short manuscripts by Kaufmann and others on philosophy.

Languages: German, English.
Donor: Luise Kaufmann, 1958.
Finding Aid: 13 catalogue cards.
Accession Number: AR 244.

141 KURT KERSTEN
1937–1961   2 feet

Born in Weldheiden bei Kassel on April 19, 1891, Kurt Kersten studied in Munich and Berlin and served in World War I. From 1919 to 1933 he worked as a freelance journalist in close association with left-wing expressionists. He made several trips to the USSR and contributed to the German Communist press.

He emigrated to Switzerland in 1934, Czechoslovakia the same year, France in 1937, and the United States via Morocco and Martinique, 1940–1945. He was active in exile affairs and continued to work as an author and publicist.

Kersten occasionally used the pseudonym Georg Forster. He died in New York City on May 18, 1962.

Correspondence with newspapers, journals, publishers, and individuals, including Jakob Altmaier, Julius Bab, C.F.W. Behl, Eduard Beneš, Joseph Bornstein, Elisabeth Castonier, Julius Deutsch, Alfred Döblin, John Dos Passos, Lion Feuchtwanger, Friedrich Wilhelm Foerster, Leonhard Frank, Claire Goll, Oscar Maria Graf, Babette L. Gross, Georg Grosz, Emil J. Gumbel, Willy Haas, Theodor Heuss, Kurt Hiller, Heinrich Eduard Jacob, Erich Kästner, Alfred Kerr, Hermann Kesten, Gustav Kiepenheuer, Emil Ludwig, Erika Mann, Monika Mann, Thomas Mann, Ludwig Marcuse, Walter Mehring, H. L. Mencken, Martin Niemöller, Franz Pfemfert, Jacob Picard, Kurt Pinthus, Erwin Piscator, Ernst Reuter, Ernst Rowohlt, Anna Seghers, Upton Sinclair, Dorothy Thompson, Fritz von Unruh, Veit Valentin, Bruno Weil, Thornton Wilder, and Duke Odo of Württemberg.

Manuscripts with notes and supplementary correspondence concerning the eighteenth-century naturalist and revolutionary Johann Georg Forster and on the last years of Rudolf Breitscheid and Rudolf Hilferding in Vichy France.

Published and unpublished manuscripts on cultural topics.

Language: German.
Donor: Alice David, 1967, 1968.
Finding Aid: 19-page inventory.
Accession Number: AR 4061.

142 ISIDOR KIEFER
1839–1961   10 inches

Born in Worms on May 25, 1871, Isidor Kiefer was a tin manufacturer, and chairman of the Jewish community of Worms. He emigrated to the United States via Belgium in 1934 and died in New York City on January 27, 1962.

Manuscript history, clippings, extensive photo collection, and sketches of the Jewish community synagogue and Jewish quarter of Worms; correspondence and community budget and census lists from the eighteenth and nineteenth centuries.

Languages: German, English.
Donor: Mrs. Rudolf Oppenheimer, 1962.
Finding Aid: 13-page inventory.
Accession Numbers: AR 1894, AR 3912.

143 ELIZABETH KITZINGER
1790–1965   5 inches

Born Elizabeth Merzbacher in Munich on April 21, 1881, Elizabeth Kitzinger was educated as a social worker and directed the Israelitische Jugendhilfe of Munich.

She emigrated to Palestine in 1939, to the United States in 1947, and died in Washington, D.C., on June 14, 1966.

Yearly reports of Israelitische Jugendhilfe and its predecessor organizations; professional correspondence of Elizabeth Kitzinger with other social workers including Alice Bendix and Henrietta Szold.

Family trees and documents concerning the Merzbacher and Strauss families.

Mohel books, including one of Rabbi Joseph Aub with entries from Munich and Fürth.

Fragment of governmental decree about Schutzjuden in Mergentheim and Heilbronn.
Photos of Elizabeth Kitzinger, Alice Bendix, and Henrietta Szold.

Languages: German, Hebrew, English.
Donor: Ernst Kitzinger, 1967.
Finding Aid: 6-page inventory.
Accession Number: AR 3086.

144 ADOLF KOBER
18th cent.–1956   8.5 feet

Born in Beuthen (now Bytom, Poland) on September 3, 1879, Adolf Kober received his doctorate at the University of Breslau in 1903 and his rabbinical ordination from the Jüdisch-theologisches Seminar, Breslau, in 1907. He was a rabbi in Wiesbaden from 1908 to 1918 and in Cologne from 1918 to 1939. In 1939 he emigrated to the United States and died in New York City on December 30, 1958.

Manuscripts and research notes on Jewish history, including the emancipation of the Jews, nineteenth century emigration of German Jews to the United States, Jewish education, and the Jewish communities of Heidelberg, Göttingen, Frankfurt am Main, Magdeburg, and especially Cologne and vicinity, including manuscripts of eighteenth-century chroniclers.

Organizational records of Congregation B'nai Jeshurun, New York, including minutes, budgets, lists of officers and clubs.

19th-century prayers, contracts, and prenuptial agreements.

Languages: German, English, Hebrew, Judeo-German, French.
Donor: Hanna Kober, 1956–1961.
Finding Aid: 5-page inventory.
Accession Number: AR 7188.

145 FRANZ KOBLER
1909–1965   c. 10 feet

Born in Vienna on December 18, 1882, Franz Kobler was a lawyer and author, active in pacifist circles. In 1938 he emigrated to the United States via Switzerland and Great Britain and died in Berkeley, California, on May 12, 1965.

Correspondence with individuals and organizations, including Else Lasker-Schüler, Ernst Lissauer, Margarete Susman, and the Leo Baeck Institute.

Manuscripts, notes, clippings, and supporting material for various essays, including one on Napoleon Bonaparte and the Jews.

Languages: German, English, Czech, French, Hebrew, Italian, Swedish.
Donor: Richard Kobler, 1968.
Finding Aid: 8-page inventory.
Accession Number: AR 7184.

146 BERNHARD KOLB
1756–1968   7.5 inches

Born in Sugenheim on September 22, 1881, Bernhard Kolb was business manager of the Jewish community of Nuremberg. He was deported to Theresienstadt in 1943, returned to Nuremberg in 1945, emigrated to the United States in 1947, and died in Vineland, New Jersey on October 16, 1971.

Material from the Jewish "self-administration" of Theresienstadt, including transport and deportation lists, lists of births, deaths, and organization memberships, proclamations, directives, and daily orders of the Council of Elders.

Records of the Nazi newspaper *Der Stürmer*, including denunciations and letters to the editor, Julius Streicher; reports on Streicher's activities promoting naturopathy and opposing vaccination.

Military propaganda photos of Jews before and during World War II in Western Poland, including destroyed synagogues and Jewish cemeteries in Kattowitz and Lublin.

Material on the post-World War II Jewish community of Nuremberg; a manuscript by Kolb on the history of the Jewish community of Nuremberg from its beginnings to 1945.

Letter of protection and by-laws of the Jewish community of Sugenheim.

Languages: German, French, English.
Donor: Bernhard Kolb, 1968.
Finding Aid: 7-page inventory.
Accession Number: AR 360.

147 MAX KOWALSKI
1916–1950   5 inches

Born in Kowal, Poland, on August 10, 1882, Max Kowalski grew up in Frankfurt am Main, received his law degree at the University of Marburg, and practiced law in Frankfurt. He was also active as a composer. He was an associate of Arnold Schoenberg and served as his lawyer. He was interned in Buchenwald in 1938 and emigrated to Great Britain the following year. He died in London on June 4, 1956.

Correspondence with individuals, including Richard Dehmel, Hermann Hesse, Arthur Holitscher, Paul Levi, Ernst Lissauer, Arno Nadel, Arthur Schnabel, Arnold Schoenberg, and Leo Sternberg.

Kowalski's law office files for the lawsuit of Arnold Schoenberg against the Frankfurt Opera House, 1930.

Clippings, albums, and theater programs written by Kowalski and others for concerts, including ones sponsored by Jüdischer Kulturbund and Jüdische Tonkünstler, Frankfurt; caricatures of musicians, and musical scores.

Photos of Kowalski and friends, autographed poetry and photos from Hesse.

Languages: German, Dutch, English.
Donor: Oscar Kowal, 1976.
Finding Aid: 2-page inventory.
Accession Number: AR 7049.

148 MAX KREUTZBERGER
1918–1972   9.5 feet

Born in Königshütte, Oberschlesien (now Chorzow, Poland), on January 31, 1900, Kreutzberger was a social worker and communal leader. He was director of the Zentralwohlfahrtsstelle der deutschen Juden until he emigrated to Palestine in 1935, where he led the Hitachduth Olej Germania, which dealt with the affairs of German immigrants. In 1948 he returned to Germany, where he was the special representative of the Jewish Agency and helped in the reclamation of property.
Emigrating to the United States in 1955, he became the first director of the Leo Baeck Institute. After his retirement in 1967, he moved to Locarno, Switzerland, and died there on November 22, 1978.

Photocopies of material assembled by Kreutzberger from various archives and libraries for a projected history of Germany Jewry during the Nazi period, focusing on such topics as the persecution of Jews, German-Jewish organizations, international aid, emigration and the Holocaust. Specific documents include records of the American Jewish Committee, HIAS-HICEM, Jewish Labor Committee, Preussischer Landesverband jüdischer Gemeinden, Reichsvertretung der deutschen Juden, Reichsvereinigung der Juden in Deutschland, and Zentralausschuss der deutschen Juden für Hilfe and Aufbau; memoirs by Bruno Blau, Fritz Fabian, Alexander Gutsfeld, Jacob Jacobson, Paula Littauer, Bruno Marcuse, Martha Mosse, Max Plaut, Georg Salzberger, and Bruno Weil; material by and about Cora Berliner, Georg Kareski, Arthur Prinz, Hanns Reissner, and Leo Wolff; a memorandum by Hans Reichmann on the arrest of Leo Baeck in 1935; material on the Evian Conference; and records of agencies of the German government during the Nazi period, including Gestapo files.

Unpublished author and subject indices to the Jüdische Rundschau, 1918–1919 and 1932–1936.

Languages: German, English, Hebrew, Yiddish.
Donor: Irmgard Foerg, 1981.
Finding Aid: 10-page inventory.
Accession Number: AR 7183.

149 HANS KRONHEIM
1856–1958   2.5 inches

Born in Crone an der Brahe on April 5, 1885, Hans Kronheim was the rabbi of the Jewish community of Bielefeld from 1917 to 1938. In 1938, he emigrated to the United States and died in Cleveland, Ohio, on October 1, 1958.

Material concerning the Jewish community of Bielefeld and Jewish organizations there, including membership lists, correspondence, circulars, programs, questionnaires, lists of deportees and survivors, photos, as well as synagogue statutes and photos from the neighboring communities of Borgholzhausen and Enger.

Manuscripts by Kronheim, including community history, other historical essays, and sermons.

Personal documents, certificates of Kronheim, reports and photos of soldiers killed in World War I.

Languages: German, English.
Donor: Kurt Rosenbaum, 1967.
Finding Aid: 4-page inventory.
Accession Number: AR 3156.

150 CARL LANDAUER
1934–1955   3 inches

Born in Munich on October 15, 1891, Carl Landauer received his doctorate in economics at the University of Heidelberg in 1915, and worked as a journalist and in various academic positions. He emigrated to the United States in 1934, where he became professor of economics at the University of California, Berkeley, and lived in Berkeley, California, after his retirement.

Photocopies of correspondence concerning assistance for refugee scholars, including correspondence with Academic Assistance Council, American Committee for Refugee Scholars, Writers and Artists, American Assistance Council, Hilfsverein der deutschen Juden, National Student Federation, Reichsvereinigung der Juden in Deutschland, and Selfhelp for German Refugees.

Languages: German, English.
Donor: Carl Landauer, 1977.
Finding Aid: 4 catalogue cards.
Accession Number: AR 7053.

151 GEORG LANDAUER
1656–1960   3 feet

Born in Cologne on November 17, 1895, Georg Landauer was a lawyer, journalist, and Zionist leader. He was a founder of the German branch of Ha-Poel Ha-Zair. After his emigration to Palestine in 1934, he was involved in politics in the Yishuv, especially as founder of Aliyah Hadasha, a party based in the German immigrant community, and in aliyah and absorption matters, particularly as financial director of Youth Aliyah. After statehood, he was involved in negotiating for reparations and restitution. He emigrated to the United States in 1953 and died in New York City on February 4, 1954.

Correspondence of Georg Landauer, along with related third-party correspondence, with individuals, including Leo Baeck, David Ben-Gurion, Norman Bentwich, Kurt Blumenfeld, Walter Breslauer, Hermann Broch, Martin Buber, Levi Eshkol, Benjamin Ferencz, Nahum Goldmann, Berl Katznelson, Hans Kohn, Max Kreutzberger, Judah Magnes, Siegfried Moses, Hans Reichmann, Felix Rosenblüth (later Pinchas Rosen), Hans Schäffer, Werner David Senator, Moshe Shertok, Ernst Simon, Moshe Smilansky, Henrietta Szold, Hans Tramer, Chaim Weizmann, and Alfred Wiener, on various topics, including Zionism, Jewish-Arab relations, immigration and Youth Aliyah, and restitution and reparations.

Essays, speeches, reports, and articles by Landauer and others on Zionism in Germany, the Yishuv and Israel (including material on Ha-Poel Ha-Zair, Brith Shalom, and Aliyah Hadasha), restitution, vocational retraining, and matters related to immigration and absorbtion.

Records, including memoranda, reports, publications, and correspondence of various organizations, including Zionistische Vereinigung für Deutschland; the German Department of the Jewish Agency, dealing with Zionist politics, restitution, reparations, and Israeli economic development; and Brith Shalom, dealing with Jewish-Arab relations.

Original documents concerning Jews in Central Europe, from the seventeenth through the twentieth century, including decrees, letters of protection, and citizenship papers largely from Frankfurt am Main and Hanover; manuscripts by Landauer, along with supporting material and research notes, on the legal status and economic activity of Jews in Central and Eastern Europe, from the Middle Ages to the twentieth century; minutes of meetings, posters, fliers, and clippings of the German soldiers' council in Poltava in the Ukraine, 1918–1919.

Papers of the Landauer family, including the doctoral dissertation of Georg Landauer's grandfather, Rabbi Gabriel Joshua Landauer, entitled "Der Judeneid." Photos, including an album of a Ludwig Tietz Handwerkerschule, in Yagur, Palestine, in the 1930s; administrative and military maps of Israel.

Languages: German, English, Hebrew, French.
Donor: Lou Landauer, 1970.
Finding Aid: 26-page inventory.
Accession Number: AR 6007.

152 GUSTAV LANDAUER
1888–1919   2.5 inches

Born in Karlsruhe in 1870, Landauer was a philosopher, literary critic, and anarchist-socialist writer and politician. In November 1918, he became a member of the central council of the revolutionary government of Kurt Eisner in Munich. After Eisner's assassination, he served briefly as commissar for public instruction in the Bavarian Soviet Republic. He was murdered on May 2, 1919, during the suppression of the revolutionary government.

Two notebooks by Landauer: one on a course of lectures in German literature given by Wilhelm Braune, 1888–1889; the other containing miscellaneous notes on politics and literature, written after 1895.

Manuscript pamphlet, 5 pages hand-bound, entitled "Weihnacht: Friede auf Erde," probably written December 1919, commemorating the last year of Landauer's life and containing drawings, poems, photos, vignettes, and quotations about Landauer and Eisner.

Photos, loose and in albums, of Landauer, his family, and the events of the Bavarian Revolution.

Language: German.
Donor: Marianne B. Luetke, 1983.

Finding Aid: 3-page inventory.
Accession Number: AR 7236.

153 FRANZ LANDSBERGER
1907–1964   1.5 inches

Born in Kattowitz (now Katowice, Poland) on June 14, 1883, Franz Landsberger was an art historian who emigrated to the United States in 1939 and died in Cincinnati, Ohio, on March 17, 1964.

Correspondence of Landsberger with individuals, including Leo Baeck, Theodor Heuss, Ernst Lissauer, Thomas Mann, Ludwig Meidner, Gilbert Murray, Erwin Panofsky, the painter Max Weber, and correspondence concerning the career and suicide of the painter Anita Rée.

Manuscripts, offprints, clippings by and about Landsberger, photos of him and others, and recommendations, including one by Max Friedländer.

Languages: German, English.
Donor: Mrs. Franz Landsberger, 1967–1970.
Finding Aid: 16 catalogue cards.
Accession Number: AR 2318.

154 EDUARD LASKER
1856–1971   5 inches

Born in Jarotschin (now Jarocin, Poland) on October 14, 1829, Eduard Lasker studied law in Breslau and participated in the revolution of 1848. He became an associate judge in Berlin in 1856, a member of the Prussian Landtag in 1865, and, in 1870, of the Reichstag. One of Germany's leading liberal politicians, his early support for Bismarck changed to increasingly vehement opposition. He remained active in Jewish affairs, and while in the Prussian Landtag, he was the sponsor of legislation allowing the ultra-Orthodox to secede from the Jewish community and form their own congregations. He died in New York City on January 5, 1884.

Will, obituaries, and membership cards of Lasker for various organizations as well as for the Reichstag of the North German Confederation and the German Empire, and for the Nationalverein; transcripts of some of his speeches; draft of a constitution of the North German Confederation with marginal comments by Lasker; and correspondence, including letters from Bernhard von Bülow, Otto von Bismarck, and liberal colleagues in Parliament.

Photos of Reichstag members, election pamphlets, visiting cards of fellow politicians, clippings about Lasker, and obituaries.

Languages: German, English.
Donors: Various, 1960–1966.

Finding Aid: 12-page inventory.
Accession Numbers: AR 1195, AR 2967.

155 HERTHA LEAB AND LEO LEAB
   1858–1981   6.5 feet

Hertha Marcus was born in Gilgenburg in 1901. She went to school in Stettin, and studied medicine in Berlin, before going to work in the Scherk perfume and cosmetics firm, where she became a leading executive. In 1929, she married Leo Liebeskind, a salesman with the firm who had been born in Berlin in 1897. They emigrated to the United States in 1938, and anglicized their names. Hertha set up a small cosmetics business. Leo died in New York in 1979, Hertha in 1981.

Correspondence of Hertha and Leo Leab, largely with friends and family members, concerning education, career choices, family matters, World War I and subsequent events, and emigration and refugee life.

Family documents, school papers, cookbooks, autograph albums, military service documents, and genealogies of Hertha and Leo Leab, the Liebeskind, Marcus, and Scherk families; extensive photo collection; documents and correspondence concerning emigration to the United States, and on the transfer of funds to Palestine; correspondence and legal and other documents relating to restitution.

Photos, clippings, advertisements, business and lab reports, and correspondence of the Scherk firm; correspondence and other papers of Hedda Marr cosmetics, a firm established by Hertha Leab in New York.

Languages: German, English.
Donor: Daniel Leab, 1981.
Finding Aid: 8-page inventory.
Accession Number: AR 7205.

156 LEITER FAMILY
   1911–1958   2.5 inches

Benno Leiter (1890–1958) was a manufacturer of women's garments. He lived through World War II as a laborer in Berlin.

Included in the collection are the papers of Benno Leiter's brother Siegfried Leiter, who married Minna Berliner (1891–1952), and died during World War I; she survived the Nazi years in Holland.

Citizenship papers, marriage certificates, genealogical materials, and photos of the Leiters and related families; police papers, postcards, and poetry from Theresienstadt.

Languages: German, English.
Donor: Dina Leiter, 1977.

Finding Aid: 5-page inventory.
Accession Number: AR 4448.

157 MEINHARDT LEMKE
1905–1962   5 inches

Born in Fordon (now Poland) on April 22, 1904, the author Meinhardt Lemke emigrated to the United States via Bolivia in 1939 and died in New York City on March 12, 1962.

Personal documents, diaries, literary manuscripts, and correspondence including letters from Thomas Mann and Ernst Wiechert concerning Lemke's work.

Musical scores, photos, albums, and clippings about the cantor Leopold Lemke.

Languages: German, Hebrew, English, Spanish.
Donor: Thea Rozenski, 1975.
Finding Aid: 3-page inventory.
Accession Number: AR 4235.

158 MIRIAM BEER-HOFMANN LENS
1867–1970   8 feet

Born in Vienna on September 4, 1897, Miriam Beer-Hofmann was the daughter of Richard and Paula Beer-Hofmann. She was the inspiration for her father's poem "Schlaflied für Miriam." She was employed as a social worker and married Ernst Czuckza, a social worker and businessman, in 1924. They emigrated to Amsterdam in 1934, Paris in 1936, Great Britain in 1938, and the United States in 1940.
They changed their surname to Lens when they were naturalized in 1947. Miriam Beer-Hofmann Lens died in New York in 1984.

Originals and transcriptions of correspondence between Richard and Paula Beer-Hofmann, 1896–1935, on a variety of topics, including family matters, current events, and Richard's professional activities as playwright and theatrical producer; correspondence of other members of the Beer-Hofmann family with each other and other individuals, including Kurt Blumenfeld, Walter Grossmann, Antoinette von Kahler, and Olga Schnitzler; correspondence of members of the Beer and Hofmann families in the nineteenth century.

Papers of members of the Beer-Hofmann family, including vital documents, business papers, passports and naturalization certificates, and educational documents, including Paula's notebooks from her conversion classes; obituaries of family members and letters of condolence; and reviews of works of Richard Beer-Hofmann.

Poetry, prose, and fiction manuscripts of Richard Beer-Hofmann, as well as notes and scripts for theatrical productions which he organized; poetry and fiction manuscripts of his son Gabriel Beer-Hofmann (a.k.a. Gabriel Marlowe) and Antoinette von Kahler.

Photos and photo albums from the mid-nineteenth through the twentieth century, of members of the Beer-Hofmann family and their activities, their house in Vienna, theatrical productions, and their friends and associates, including Martin Buber, Alexander Moissi, and members of the von Kahler family.

Languages: German, English.
Donor: Egon Radvany, executor of the estate of Miriam Beer-Hofmann Lens, 1984.
Finding Aid: 4-page preliminary inventory.
Accession Number: AR 7258.

159 LEO BAECK INSTITUTE
1955–1980   3 feet

Photo collection with pictures of the Leo Baeck Institute, New York, including buildings, staff, exhibitions, library and archival objects, pictures published in the *LBI Yearbook*, special events, and prominent visitors, including Theodor Heuss, Erich von Kahler, Annemarie Renger, Walter Scheel, and Axel Springer. Clippings concerning the Leo Baeck Institute, including transcripts of lectures held there, invitations to and descriptions of other events, reviews of exhibitions, publications, and news stories about accessions.

Languages: German, English, French.
Donor: LBI office files.
Finding Aid: c. 140 catalogue cards.
Accession Numbers: AR 9011, AR 230, AR 4349.

160 DANIEL LESSMANN
1813–1909   2.5 inches

Born in Soldin on January 18, 1794, Lessmann was an author who took part in the German national uprising against Napoleonic rule. He died in Wittenberg on September 1, 1831.

Letters from Lessmann to his family describing daily life, studies, travels, and his friend Heinrich Heine.
Manuscripts by Lessmann, including travel essays, poems, a Jewish history, and a play.
Clippings concerning Lessmann.

Languages: German, English, Judeo-German.
Donor: Purchased, 1979.
Finding Aid: 4-page inventory.
Accession Number: AR 4728.

161 LEOPOLD LEVI
1858–1966   10 inches

Born in Buttenhausen on May 6, 1870, Leopold Levi was a Stuttgart manufacturer and member of the Oberrat der Israeliten Württembergs from 1919 until its dissolution in 1939. He emigrated to the United States via Cuba, 1941–1943, and died in New York City on August 2, 1968.

Correspondence of Levi on various topics, including his emigration, his restitution claims, and the fate of friends and acquaintances in the Holocaust.

Excerpts from records of the Oberrat der Israeliten Württembergs, including decrees, reports, memoranda, minutes, and correspondence, with a letter from Ismar Elbogen.

Reports, clippings, and memorabilia, documenting the history of the Jews of Württemberg in the nineteenth and twentieth centuries, including reports on Jewish displaced persons in Württemberg in 1945, the postwar Jewish community there, and a nineteenth century prayerboard from the synagogue of Nordstetten.

Languages: German, English, Judeo-German, Hebrew.
Donors: Leopold Levi, 1963; Luise Blumenthal, 1976.
Finding Aids: 3-page inventory, 6-page inventory.
Accession Numbers: AR 9012, AR 1929, AR 2440, AR 7041.

162 WILHELM LEVISON
1823–1970   5 inches

Born in Düsseldorf on May 27, 1876, Levison received his doctorate in history at the University of Bonn in 1898, where he taught until his dismissal in 1935. A specialist in medieval history, he emigrated in 1939 to Great Britain and died in Durham, Great Britain, on January 17, 1947.

Correspondence, memoranda, and directives of the process of Gleichschaltung and aryanization at the University of Bonn; minutes of a meeting of the Verband deutscher Historiker in 1933.

Reports, records, protocols, and circulars of the Grossloge, the German branch of B'nai B'rith, collected by Josef Freundlich, Levison's father-in-law; notices of the Verband Nationaldeutscher Juden.

Family documents, family histories, and family trees of the Levison and Freundlich families.

Languages: German, English.
Donor: John Levison, 1972.
Finding Aid: 9-page inventory.
Accession Number: AR 3906.

163 CAROLA LEVY
1823–1975   2.5 inches

Born in Worms in 1893, Carola Levy (Mrs. Ferdinand Kaufmann) emigrated to Switzerland c. 1933 and later to the United States. She died in New Rochelle, New York, in 1975.

Papers of the Levy family from the nineteenth and twentieth centuries, including vital documents, certificates of honors and awards, autograph album, family memorabilia, clippings on the family, letters from and about Else Lasker-Schüler.

Manuscript histories of the Jews in Worms and Amorbach.

Languages: German, English, French, Judeo-German, Hebrew.
Donors: Mrs. Ferdinand Kaufmann, Henry M. Kaufmann, 1964–1978.
Finding Aid: 21 catalogue cards.
Accession Number: AR 257.

164 CLARA LEVYSOHN
1876–1908   6 inches

Clara Hermann was born on December 4, 1854 and married Ulrich Levysohn in 1876. Her date of death is unknown.

Letters of Ulrich Levysohn to his fiancée, Clara Hermann; correspondence of Clara Levysohn with Fritz Mauthner.

Miscellaneous items, including a photo of Mauthner.

Languages: German, Italian, Dutch, English.
Donor: Susanne Jacobs, 1971.
Finding Aid: 12-page inventory.
Accession Number: AR 3778.

165 MANFRED LEWANDOWSKI
1821–1971   5 inches

Born in Hamburg on September 1, 1895, Manfred Lewandowski was a composer and cantor in Berlin. He emigrated to France in 1938 and to the United States in 1939, and died in Philadelphia on September 8, 1970.

Correspondence, autographs, and photos of individuals, including Konrad Adenauer, Pablo Casals, Heinz Galinski, Nahum Goldmann, Teddy Kollek, Joachim Prinz, Josef (Yossele) Rosenblatt, Harry Truman, Richard Tucker, and Bruno Walter.

Personal documents, clippings, recordings, sheet music, photos of Manfred Lewandowski and other family members, including his great-uncle the cantor and composer Louis Lewandowski.

Photos, clippings, and manuscripts on German Jews in general and the Jewish community of Königsberg in particular.

Languages: German, English, French, Yiddish, Hebrew.
Donor: Nelly Lewandowski, 1976.
Finding Aid: 3-page inventory.
Accession Number: AR 7027.

166 MAX LIEBERMANN
1867–1978   3 inches

Born in Berlin on July 20, 1847, Max Liebermann was a painter influenced by impressionism. Although he was himself a rather conservative artist, he helped to found the Sezession, an organization of progressive artists in Berlin. In 1920, he was elected president of the Preussische Akademie der Künste, but was dismissed in 1933. He died in Berlin on August 2, 1935.

Correspondence of Liebermann, including letters to Bruno Cassirer, Paul Cassirer, and the art historian and museum director Max Lehrs, and letters on Liebermann's election as president of the Preussische Akademie der Künste.

Clippings by and about Liebermann, exhibition catalogues, and photos of him, his atelier, and his works.

The art collection of the Leo Baeck Institute contains numerous works by Liebermann.

Languages: German, English.
Donor: Purchased, 1959.
Finding Aids: 1-page inventory, 12 catalogue cards.
Accession Number: AR 847.

167 LILLI LIEGNER
1841–1974   2.5 inches

Born Lilli Buchheimer in Grossachsen on September 12, 1894, Lilli Liegner was a social worker and feminist who emigrated to the United States in 1936 and died in New York City in 1980.

Correspondence, including letters from Beate Guttmann, Paula Ollendorf, Ottilie Schoenewald, and Emmy Vogelstein.

Manuscripts, clippings, photoalbums and correspondence on women's education, job opportunities, and social work, on the Beate Guttmann Heim Breslau, and on the Jüdischer Frauenbund and its 1928 Congress; obituaries of Paula Ollendorf, Bertha Pappenheim, and Max Simonsohn. Genealogy of the Rawicz family, documents on the history of the Liegner family, and ritual artifacts.

Clippings from publications of the Schlesischer Hausfrauen-Bund in the 1930s.

Languages: German, English.
Donor: Lilli Liegner, 1962, 1972.
Finding Aid: 6-page inventory.
Accession Number: AR 1228.

168 LIEPMANN FAMILY
1871–1932   2 feet

Hugo Liepmann (1863–1925) was a psychiatrist and psychologist in Berlin. He taught at the university there and served as director of a mental health institute. He was the discoverer of Apraxia, a neurological disorder preventing coordination in certain activities.

Correspondence of Hugo Liepmann and his wife, Agatha née Bleichröder, with their parents, children, other relatives, and friends, including Agatha's letters from her trips to Egypt.

Language: German.
Donor: Charlotte Hamburger, 1976.
Finding Aid: 1 catalogue card.
Accession Number: AR 7021.

169 ERNST LISSAUER
1882–1937   5 feet

The author Ernst Lissauer was born in Berlin on December 16, 1882. He wrote poetry and drama, and is best known for "Hassgesang gegen England." He moved to Vienna in 1924 and died there on December 10, 1937.

Correspondence with publishing houses and theaters, and with individuals, including Julius Bab, Theodor Heuss, Heinrich Meyer-Benfey, Börries von Münchhausen, Kurt Schuschnigg, and Ina Seidel.

Unpublished diaries and notebooks for years 1905–1937, with the exception of the missing years 1918–1919 and 1932–1933.

Fiction and nonfiction manuscripts, poetry, essays, obituaries, and clippings, programs by and about Lissauer.

Language: German.
Donor: Mrs. Ernst Lissauer, 1961–1962.
Finding Aid: 10-page inventory.
Accession Number: AR 1735.

170 RUDOLF LOEB
  1865–1966   6 inches

Born in Elberfeld on November 21, 1877, Rudolf Loeb was a banker with Mendelssohn & Co. and consultant to the German and Russian governments. In the 1930s, he served as the Belgian general consul in Berlin. He emigrated to Argentina in 1939 and to the United States in 1948. He died in Boston on January 30, 1966.

Correspondence, including photocopies of letters from Otto von Bismarck, Bernhard von Bülow, the German Emperor Wilhelm II, and a letter from Hermann J. Abs describing the "aryanization" of the Mendelssohn banking firm in 1939.

Articles by Loeb and others on the Dawes Plan and other issues of politics and economics; theater and concert programs, mostly from Berlin, 1924–1925; honors from various governments, and a directory of the diplomatic corps in Berlin for 1937–1938; clippings on political, cultural, and financial topics; obituaries.

Photos of Loeb, his family, employees of the Mendelssohn banking firm.

Languages: German, English, Russian.
Donors: Eric and Walter Loeb, 1966–1970.
Finding Aid: 4-page inventory.
Accession Number: AR 4057.

171 ADOLF LOEBEL
  1900–1974   5 inches

Born in Baden c. 1900, Adolf Loebel survived World War II in hiding in Karlsruhe. He was president of the Jewish community of Heidelberg from 1945 to the early 1950s, when he emigrated to the United States. He was living in New York City in the mid 1970s.

Material on the Nazi persecution of the Jews including letters and circulars of the Reichsvereinigung der Juden in Deutschland, letters from a camp internee, a Gestapo list of Jews living in Baden, clippings on the survival of Loebel's daughter in hiding, and photos of deportations.

Material on Jews in post-World War II Germany, including the minutes of the 1949 Heidelberg conference on the future of Jews in Germany.

Clippings and photos on Jewish life in Baden in general and the towns of Bruchsal, Gailingen, Heidelberg, Karlsruhe, Mosbach, Rexingen, and Völkerheim.

Languages: German, English, Hebrew.
Donor: Adolf Loebel, 1975, 1976.
Finding Aid: 7-page inventory.
Accession Number: AR 4185.

172 JAKOB LOEWENBERG
1875–1971   9 inches

Born in Niederntudorf bei Paderborn on March 9, 1856, Loewenberg taught at the Jewish schools in Gesecke and Padberg, became director of a private Jewish girls' Realschule in Hamburg, and was active as a writer and poet. He died in Hamburg on February 2, 1929.

Correspondence with family members, educational and literary figures, including Ferdinand Avenarius, Richard Dehmel, and Detlev von Liliencron.

Manuscripts by Loewenberg on German literature, Jewish life, and his trips to the United States; manuscripts by others, including poems by Detlev von Liliencron and Gustav Falke.

Clippings about Loewenberg, his life and work; photos of him, family, and friends.

Teaching notebooks and other pedagogical materials, curricula vitae, recommendations, and diaries for the years 1881–1928; obituaries.

Languages: German, English, Hebrew.
Donor: Ernst Loewenberg, 1967–1972.
Finding Aid: 15-page inventory.
Accession Number: AR 1200.

173 RICHARD DETLEV LOEWENBERG
1911–1954   5 inches

Born in Hamburg on June 18, 1898, Richard Detlev Loewenberg was a psychiatrist who emigrated to Shanghai in 1933, to the United States in 1937, and died in Bakersfield, California, on April 29, 1954.

Manuscripts, clippings and offprints by Loewenberg on poetry, literature, and psychiatry; diaries, curricula vitae.

Languages: German, English, Japanese, Esperanto.
Donor: Ernst Loewenberg, 1969.
Finding Aid: 2-page inventory.
Accession Number: AR 6005.

174 PHILIPP LOEWENFELD
1909–1950   1 foot

Born in Munich on September 13, 1887, Philipp Loewenfeld was a journalist and lawyer with close ties to the Sozialdemokratische Partei Deutschlands (SPD), and an associate of Kurt Eisner. He emigrated to Switzerland in 1933, to the United States in 1938, and died in New York City on November 3, 1963.

Clippings, essays, and lectures on judicial, socio-political, and cultural-political topics.

Loewenfeld's extensive memoirs, dealing with the period before his emigration and in particular with politics in Bavaria from the Wilhelmine period until the Nazi takeover, are catalogued separately in the memoir collection.

Languages: German, English.
Donor: Mrs. Philipp Loewenfeld, 1965–1967.
Finding Aid: 10-page inventory.
Accession Number: AR 789.

175 ERNA MAGNUS
1912–1930s   2 feet

Born in Hamburg on February 26, 1896, Erna Magnus was a social worker who was engaged in an historical study of the Jewish community of Hamburg during the 1930s. She emigrated to the United States in 1939, held various social work and teaching positions, and lives in Cockeysville, Maryland.

Index cards containing biographical information on prominent Hamburg Jews from the eighteenth to the twentieth century.

Family tree of the Samson family covering the years 1733 to 1911.

Language: German.
Donor: Erna Magnus, 1980.
Finding Aid: 2-page inventory.
Accession Number: AR 7166.

176 ERNST MARCUS
1898–1976   2.5 inches

Born in Kamen on September 3, 1856, Ernst Marcus was a lawyer and philosopher. He died in Essen on October 29, 1928.

Correspondence of Marcus with family and with Salomon Friedländer (Mynona) concerning philosophical questions.

Clippings, offprints, and manuscripts by and about Marcus.

Marcus's memoirs are catalogued separately in the memoir collection.

Language: German.
Donor: Robert Marcus, 1976.
Finding Aid: 6-page inventory.
Accession Number: AR 4322.

177 MAX MARKREICH
1749–1961   4 feet

Born in Weener on October 11, 1881, Max Markreich (later Markrich) was a merchant and chairman of the Jewish community of Bremen from 1927 to 1938. He emigrated to the United States via Trinidad, 1939–1941, and died in San Francisco on November 27, 1962.

Correspondence of Markreich with family members concerning emigration, with material on the life of Markreich and others in Shanghai, South Africa, Marseilles, and Trinidad, on Jewish life in Germany after World War II, on restitution and on Markreich's historical writing, including correspondence with the Leo Baeck Institute, Yad Vashem, Bernhard Brilling, Adolf Kober, and Manfred Lewandowski.

Material on the history of the Jews of northwestern Germany, including manuscript histories of the Jews of Bremen and East Frisia along with clippings, offprints, photos, original documents and other supporting material documenting their social, economic and political history.

Correspondence, legal papers, clippings, and obituaries of members of the Markreich family, beginning in 1812, along with genealogical correspondence and family trees.

Organizational records of the Jewish community of Bremen, including minutes of the general meeting of the community, social work efforts, lists of inhabitants, speeches and correspondence of Markreich in his official capacity, and a list of Jews deported to Minsk. Records of organizations of German-Jewish refugees, including the papers of the Jewish Association of Trinidad, Congregation Shaare Zedek, Astoria, New York, and Hilfswerk für Juden in Bremen.

Languages: German, English, Hebrew.
Donor: Mary Schwarz, 1976.
Finding Aid: 6-page inventory.
Accession Number: AR 7048.

178 LUDWIG MARUM
1722–1984   8 inches

Born in Frankenthal, in the Palatinate, on November 5, 1885, Ludwig Marum studied law at Heidelberg and Munich and practiced in Karlsruhe. From 1914 to 1928, he was a member of the Sozialdemokratische Partei Deutschlands (SPD) of the Landtag of Baden, serving as Minister of Justice from 1918 to 1919. Marum was a member of the Reichstag from 1928 until 1933. On May 16, 1933 he was arrested and deported to Kislau concentration camp, where he was murdered on March 29, 1934.

Photocopies of the minutes of the council of ministers in Baden, November 1918; of clippings from the *Volksfreund*, a Social Democratic newspaper, relating to Marum's career, 1909–1918; of legal documents relating to the 1948 trial of those accused of Marum's murder; and of clippings about Marum from various sources, particularly on the fiftieth anniversary of his death.

Photos of Marum, family members, and associates, including one of the arrest of Marum and other Social Democrats.

Material on Marum's daughter, Elizabeth Lunau (born Elizabeth Marum) including documents concerning her incarceration in Gurs concentration camp, and her emigration to the United States.

Photocopies of family and vital documents of members of the Marum, Benedick, and Oppenheimer families, as well as of other families; and of documents of various Jewish communities, including a complaint of the Jewish community of Münzesheim against that of Michelfeld in 1751, and material concerning Jewish economic activity in Michelfeld in the early nineteenth century.

Languages: German, English, French.
Donor: Elizabeth Marum Lunau, 1982.
Finding Aid: 14 catalogue cards.
Accession Number: AR 4969.

179 FRITZ MAUTHNER
1765–1968   c. 9 feet

Born in Horitz, Austria Hungary (now Horice, Czechoslovakia), on November 22, 1849, Mauthner was an author, journalist, theatrical critic, and philosopher, known for his work on the philosophy of language. He moved to Berlin in 1876, to Freiburg im Breisgau in 1900, and died in Meersburg on June 29, 1923.

Correspondence with translators, newspapers, publishing houses, family members, and other individuals, including Berthold Auerbach, Ferdinand Avenarius, Julius Bab, Hermann Bahr, Ludwig Bamberger, Gerson von Bleichröder, Otto Braun, Martin Buber, Alfred Döblin, Johann Gustav Droysen, Kurt Eisner, Paul Ernst, Ernst Feder, Lion Feuchtwanger, Heinrich Friedjung, Walter Friedlaender, Ludwig Fulda, Edmond de Goncourt, Maximilian Harden, Hermann Hesse, Arno Holz, Siegfried Jacobsohn, Josef Kainz, Karl Kraus, Gustav Landauer, Helen Lange, Lilli Lehmann, Theodor Lessing, Detlev von Liliencron, Paul Lindau, Emil Ludwig, Ernst Mach, Helmut von Moltke, Theodor Mommsen, Rudolf Mosse, Erich Mühsam, Börries von Münchhausen, Engelbert Pernerstorfer, Josef Popper-Lynkeus, Walther Rathenau, Alexander Roda-Roda, Rene Schickele, Werner von Siemens, Georg Simmel, Helene Stöcker, Hermann Sudermann, Ferdinand Tönnies, Frank Wedekind, and Bruno Wille.

Clippings by and about Mauthner; manuscripts of essays, plays, poetry, proofs, offprints and articles by him; photos of Mauthner, friends, and family; diaries and notebooks of Mauthner, including a diary from the first years of World War I.

Personal and family documents from Horitz, Berlin and Prague; photos and photo albums of Mauthner's friends and of his family, particularly in Horitz.

Languages: German, French.
Donor: Wilhelm Restle, 1966–1971.
Finding Aid: 164-page inventory.
Accession Numbers: AR 9013, AR 3392, AR 3426, AR 3660, AR 3764.

180 MENDELSSOHN FAMILY
1761–1940   3 feet, 4 microfilm reels, one bound volume

Photocopies and microfilms of papers of members of the Mendelssohn family.
Several originals are in the possession of the Leo Baeck Institute, but most are in the possession of Robert von Mendelssohn, Berlin.

1. Moses Mendelssohn
The philosopher Moses Mendelssohn was born in Dessau on September 26, 1729, and died in Berlin on January 4, 1786.

Correspondence of Mendelssohn with individuals, including Christian Wilhelm Dohm, Meyer Hannover, August Hennings, F. H. Jacobi, Fromet Mendelssohn (née Fromet Guggenheim), Friedrich Nicolai, and Elise Reimarus; correspondence with other members of the Mendelssohn family; personal and business account books. Manuscript fragments by Moses Mendelssohn and by others concerning him.

2. Joseph Mendelssohn and Henriette Mendelssohn, née Meyer
Moses Mendelssohn's son, the banker Joseph Mendelssohn, was born in Berlin on August 11, 1770 and died there on November 24, 1848. He married Henriette Meyer, who was born in Alt-Strelitz in 1776 and died in Berlin in 1862.

Correspondence of Joseph and Henriette Mendelssohn with individuals including Professor Johann Buscher, Rahel Varnhagen von Ense, and Joseph's sister, Dorothea Schlegel; diaries of Henriette Mendelssohn, 1848–1854.

3. Benjamin Mendelssohn
Benjamin Mendelssohn, son of Joseph and Henriette Mendelssohn, was born in Berlin

on November 16, 1794, and took part in the uprising against Napoleon. He received his doctorate at the University of Kiel in 1827, taught geography at the University of Bonn, and died in Horchheim on August 24, 1874.

Correspondence with family and other individuals, including Moritz August von Bethmann-Hollweg, Christian August Brandis, Franz Mendelssohn, Joseph and Henriette Mendelssohn, Felix Mendelssohn-Bartholdy, Karl Immanuel Nitzsche, and Clemens Theodor Perthes; travel diaries, personal documents, and writings on the Napoleonic wars.

4. Alexander Mendelssohn
The banker Alexander Mendelssohn was born in Berlin on September 19, 1798, and died there on October 25, 1871.

Correspondence with Alexander von Humboldt.

5. Felix Mendelssohn-Bartholdy
The composer Felix Mendelssohn-Bartholdy was born in Hamburg on February 3, 1790 and died in Leipzig on November 4, 1847.

Correspondence with A. C. Schleinitz.

6. Franz von Mendelssohn and Enole Mendelssohn
The banker Franz Mendelssohn was born in Berlin on January 25, 1829, was ennobled in 1888, and died in Berlin on February 20, 1889. He was married to Enole Biarney, who had been born in Bordeaux on October 6, 1827, and died in Berlin on January 3, 1889.

Correspondence of Franz von Mendelssohn and Enole Mendelssohn with each other, with their son Franz von Mendelssohn, and with relatives and other individuals, including Clara Schumann.

School and military service papers of Franz von Mendelssohn; essays on economic, political, and historical questions, and eulogies of him, his wife, and his son.

7. Other Family Members
Fragments of correspondence, press clippings, and memorabilia concerning family members: Dorothea Schlegel, including correspondence with her former husband, Simon Veit, Paul Mendelssohn-Bartholdy, Abraham and Lea Mendelssohn-Bartholdy, Louise and Wilhelm Hensel, and Gustave Dirichlet.

8. Banking Firm Records
Records of the banking firm Mendelssohn & Co. as well as its predecessor firms: Joseph Mendelssohn & Co., Mendelssohn & Friedlaender, Gebrüder Mendelssohn & Co. Hamburg, Joseph & Abraham Mendelssohn Berlin, and Mendelssohn & Fränkel, including ledgers, account books, correspondence, contracts, and reports.

Languages: German, French, Hebrew, Judeo-German.
Donor: Robert von Mendelssohn.

Finding Aids: 7-page inventory; detailed table of contents of the family papers; 5-page inventory and 70 catalogue cards for the microfilm.
Accession Numbers: AR 9021, AR 7156.

181 JOHANNA MEYER
1846–1958   3 feet

Born Johanna Loevinson in Berlin on January 13, 1874, Johanna Meyer was a lecturer and author who gave speeches and readings in many of the Jewish communities in Germany. She was also an active member of the Jüdischer Frauenbund. She emigrated to the United States in 1938 and died in Philadelphia on April 24, 1958.

Correspondence with family members, friends and other individuals, including Julius Bab, Leo Baeck, Ilse Blumenthal-Weiss, Ludwig Hardt, Georg Hermann, and Max Pohl.

Clippings, manuscripts, lecture notes, programs, and albums on literature, Jewish topics, and cultural life in Germany in the 1920s and 1930s; Meyer's memoirs of her life before her marriage in 1901.

History and genealogy of the Loevinson family, along with supporting documents, including personal documents, photos and photoalbums, correspondence, wills, and obituaries; educational documents and doctoral dissertations of family members.

Material on Johanna Meyer's sister, Henriette May (1862–1928), a founder of the Jüdischer Frauenbund, including correspondence, documents, clippings, obituaries, and protocols of Frauenbund congresses in which she participated. Material on Meyer's brother, Ermanno (Hermann) Loevison (1863–1943), historian, archivist in Rome, and head of the Italian Archives in Bologna, including correspondence, photos, clippings, offprints and other publications, and material on his fate, and that of his family in the Holocaust. Loevison's diaries, 1886–1920, are catalogued separately in the memoir collection.

Languages: German, English, Italian, French.
Donors: Johanna Meyer, YIVO, and others, 1954–1978.
Finding Aid: Two 5-page inventories.
Accession Numbers: AR 299, AR 877, AR 3837, AR 7095, AR 9024.

182 OSCAR MEYER-RUDOLF HILFERDING
1902–1946   1 inch

Born in Berlin on December 18, 1876, Oscar Meyer was a lawyer and politician active in the Deutsche Demokratische Partei (DDP). He served in the Berlin City Council, the Prussian Landtag, and from 1924 to 1930, in the Reichstag. He emigrated to Switzerland in 1933, to Great Britain in 1939, and to the United States via Columbia in 1941. He was active in exile organizations, and died in Berkeley on January 1, 1965.

Born in Vienna on August 10, 1877, Hilferding studied medicine and became active in the socialist movement. In 1906, he moved to Berlin, wrote for and edited various socialist journals, and published *Das Finanzkapital* in 1910. After World War I, he was a leader of the Sozialdemokratische Partei Deutschlands (SPD) and a member of the Reichstag, serving as minister of finance in 1923 and again 1928–1929. He fled to France in 1933, and died in Paris, under mysterious circumstances, on February 12, 1941.

Much of the material in this collection consists of residual fragments of Hilferding's estate, which his widow probably gave to Meyer in the United States in the 1950s. Included are letters of August Bebel and Albert Einstein to Hilferding; letters of Rudolf and Rose Hilferding to Oscar and Margarethe Meyer; a postcard with photographs and signatures of Hilferding, Meyer, Heinrich Brüning, Paul Lejeune-Jung and Hans von Raumer, the members of the Reichstag delegation to the International Interparliamentary Conference in Rio de Janeiro, 1927; and a letter from Max Nordau.

Language: German.
Donor: Stephen Lehmann, 1984.
Finding Aid: 1-page inventory.
Accession Number: AR 7243.

183 WALTHER MEYER
1809–1940   2.5 inches

Born in Hanover on April 15, 1890, Walther Meyer was a lawyer and genealogist. He emigrated to Luxembourg in 1939, returned to Germany in 1946, and died in Bad Pyrmont on February 7, 1974.

Correspondence concerning genealogy with individuals and institutions, including Arthur Czellitzer, Ismar Elbogen, Gesamtarchiv der deutschen Juden, Gesellschaft zur Förderung der Wissenschaft des Judentums.

Family histories, including a history of the Eger family with supporting material, including excerpts from the Memorbuch of the Jewish community of Beverungen and the vital registers of the Jewish community of Rotenburg an der Fulda.

Correspondence of Nathan Adler (1803–1890), who became chief rabbi of Hanover in 1830, and of the British Empire in 1844, with Leffman Meyer, chairman of the Jewish community of Birdorf, with documents relating to Jewish law, fund-raising, and liturgy.

Languages: German, Judeo-German.
Donor: A. Meyer, 1977.
Finding Aid: 3-page inventory.
Accession Number: AR 7064.

184 HANNA DE MIESES
1833–1979   2.5 inches

Hanna de Mieses, née Koritzer, collected papers of the family of her husband as well as papers of the Koritzer family, and the related Pflaum and Gundolf families.

Papers of the de Mieses family and related families, including business and family correspondence and photos; included in this material is business correspondence of Adolph Koritzer, a fur trader of East European origins living in Leipzig, and engagement letters with his fiancée, Nanny Herzberg, 1856–1859; engagement letters of Marcus Pflaum and Emilie Hoeter, 1833; letters of the chess master Jacques Mieses (1865–1954); and correspondence and manuscripts of the literary historian Friedrich Gundolf (1880–1931); family trees and family histories.

Languages: German, French, English, Judeo-German.
Donor: Hanna de Mieses.
Finding Aid: 9-page inventory.
Accession Number: AR 4644.

185 MILCH FAMILY, BRESLAU
1813–1939   1 foot

Prominent members of the Milch family include Ludwig Milch (1867–1928), professor of mineralogy and geology at Greifswald and Breslau; and his son Werner Milch (1903–1950), a literary historian.
The Kauffmann and Silbergleit families were related to the Milch family by marriage. Wilhelm Silbergleit became a successful merchant in Myslowitz.

Papers of Milch and related families, including wills, membership cards, letters of Rabbi Wolf Aloys Meisel, baptismal certificates, clippings, photos, family history, and family tree.

Material on the literary historian Werner Milch (1903–1950), including articles on literary topics and autographs of Gerhart Hauptmann, Max Pinkus, and correspondence including letters from Karl Vietor.

Languages: German, Hebrew.
Donors: Various donors, 1963–1974.
Finding Aid: 14-page inventory.
Accession Number: AR 2281.

186 MILITARY TRIBUNALS NUREMBERG
1933–1949   2.5 feet

Originals and photocopies of Military Tribunal transcripts and final briefs of cases against Ernst von Weiszäcker and the following other defendants: Otto Dietrich Gottlob Berger, Ernst Wilhelm Bohle, Richard Walter Darre, Karl Ritter Otto von Erdmannsdorff, Friedrich Flick, Hans Kehrl, Wilhelm Keppler, Paul Körner, Lutz Schwerin von Krosigk, Hans Heinrich, M. Lammers, Otto Meissner, Paul Pleiger, Oswald Pohl, Emil Puhl, Karl Rasche, Hermann Röchling, Walter Schellenberg, Gustav Adolf Steengracht von Moyland, Wilhelm Stuckart, Edmund Veesenmayer, and Ernst Wörmann.

Supporting documents, including manual for trial of war crimes; reports from Greek and Polish war crimes offices; copies of orders concerning Nazi racial laws, and of orders and decrees from territories occupied by Germany; articles on German government and administration.

Languages: German, English, French, Danish.
Donor: German Consulate General, 1974.
Finding Aid: 4-page inventory.
Accession Number: AR 4334.

187 LUDWIG MISCH
1834–1967   5 inches

Born in Berlin on June 13, 1887, Ludwig Misch was educated as a lawyer but worked as a musical composer, music critic, and music teacher. Married to an "Aryan," he lived in Berlin through the Nazi era, and emigrated to the United States in 1947, where he continued his musical career. He died in New York City on April 22, 1967.

Correspondence with individuals including Wilhelm Furtwängler, Jakob Schoenberg, Max Unger, Bruno Walter; clippings, manuscripts of articles, reviews, and lectures on music and Jewish affairs.

Nazi era identification papers, Jewish star, and accounts by Misch and his wife of their experiences in Berlin during World War II.

Genealogies, photos, letters and identification papers; material on the Perl family, and the Löwenthal family of Schwerin; including photos, letters, papers, several architectural plans, and an autograph letter of Jacques Halévy.
Memoirs of Misch are also catalogued separately in the memoir collection.

Languages: German, English, French.
Donor: Ludwig Misch 1963–1967.
Finding Aid: 12-page inventory.
Accession Number: AR 2073.

188 MOSSE FAMILY
1767–1971   8.5 feet; 97 printed volumes

The Mosse family was prominent in publishing and advertising, and publishers of the *Berliner Tageblatt*, which was founded by Rudolf Mosse in 1867.

In addition to extensive personal and professional correspondence, papers of family members include: medical diplomas and Prussian citizenship papers of the physician Marcus Mosse (1807–1865); clippings and manuscripts concerning the publishers Rudolf Mosse (1843–1920) and Emil Mosse (1854–1911); correspondence and other papers of the attorney Albert Mosse (1854–1925), including correspondence with his daughter and son-in-law, Dora and Erwin Panofsky and material concerning his work drafting local government legislation for the government of Japan; clippings, correspondence, divorce papers, awards, and albums of Hans Lachmann-Mosse (1885–1944) and Felicia Lachmann-Mosse (1888–1944); affidavits and official documents from the Nazi era concerning Martha Mosse (1884–1980); papers of the psychiatrist Hilde Lachmann-Mosse (1912–1982), including material on black Americans, Reform Judaism, travel, and astrology; history and genealogy of the Mosse family.

Business records, publications, and clippings of the German and foreign branches of the Rudolf Mosse Verlag; papers of Alfred Schwabacher, director of the Swiss branches of the firm, including records of the Rudolf Mosse Verlag from Switzerland, Italy, and Yugoslavia, as well as those of affiliated companies, the Orbis A.G. Vaduz and the Treuga Holding Company, Switzerland; material on the restitution claims of the firm and family members.

Material on the Rudolf Mosse Stiftung, a nondenominational foundation which provided education for poor children.

Photos and photo albums of family members and their associates, activities, and properties.

Printed books, predominantly corporate histories and jubilee volumes, presented to Rudolf Mosse Verlag in 1917 on the occasion of its fiftieth anniversary by other firms, including Actien-Brauerei-Gesellschaft Friedrichshöhe, Julius Blüthner Pianofortefabrik, Berliner Börse, Berliner Börsen-Zeitung, Berliner Elektricitäts-Werke, Commerz- und Disconto Bank, Disconto Gesellschaft, Frankfurter Zeitung, Hamburg-Amerika Linie, Hannoverscher Courier, Königliche Porzellan-Manufaktur Berlin, Kölnische Zeitung, Krupp, Heinrich Lanz, Leipziger Buchdruckerei, Meissen, E. S. Mittler & Sohn Königliche Hofbuchhandlung, Nicolaische Buchhandlung, Norddeutscher Lloyd, Schichau-Werke, Schlesische Zeitung, Schultheiss' Brauerei, Schwäbischer Merkur, Siemens & Co. Hamburg, Teubner, Vossische Zeitung, F. G. Weidenmüller Antonsthal, Georg Westermann Braunschweig, and Wiener Zeitung.

Languages: English, German, French, Japanese, Turkish.
Donors: Walther Mosse, George Mosse et al., 1957–1985; Hans Panofsky, 1984; D. Broh, 1985.
Finding Aids: 11-page inventory, 5-page inventory, 3-page inventory.

Accession Number: AR 99.

189 MARGARET T. MUEHSAM
1913–1975   3.5 inches

Born Margarethe Meseritz in Berlin on September 18, 1891, Muehsam studied law and then worked as a journalist. She was married to John Edelheim from 1918 until his death in 1931, and was active in journalism, politics and Jewish affairs. She emigrated to the United States in 1938, where she continued her journalistic activities. She married Eduard Muehsam in 1946. She was a member of the board of directors of the Leo Baeck Institute, and died in New York City on May 26, 1975.

Clippings and manuscripts by Muehsam and others, on law, feminism, Jewish affairs and emigration possibilities, and the German press; curricula vitae, recommendations, and obituaries.

Memorabilia, including an 1885 prayerbook of the Berlin Reform community.

Languages: German, English.
Donor: Eduard Muehsam, 1958, 1975.
Finding Aid: 7-page inventory.
Accession Number: AR 720.

190 ERICH MÜHSAM
1896–1968   2.5 inches

Born in Berlin on April 6, 1878, Erich Mühsam was an author, poet, and anarchist. He was murdered in the Oranienburg concentration camp on July 10, 1934. After the death of her husband, Kreszentia Mühsam (Zenzl Mühsam) fled to Prague. In 1935, she moved to Moscow on the invitation of the Internationale Rote Hilfe. Imprisoned in 1938, she was eventually sent to Siberia and released in 1955, when she settled in East Berlin, where she died in 1962.

Correspondence of Erich Mühsam, and Kreszentia Mühsam including letters describing Erich's imprisonment in Oranienburg and Zenzl's incarceration in Siberia.

Manuscripts and published articles of Erich Mühsam.

Clippings, photos, and manuscripts, including transcripts of radio broadcasts on Erich and Kreszentia Mühsam.

Languages: German, English, French, Hebrew.
Donor: Hans Landau, 1976, 1977.
Finding Aid: 12-page inventory.
Accession Number: AR 1806.

191 SIEGFRIED SELIGMANN MÜHSAM
1801–1974   7.5 inches

Born in Landsberg an der Warthe (now Gorzow Wielkopolski, Poland) on September 2, 1838, Siegfried Seligman Mühsam studied pharmacy at the University of Königsberg, and after his apprenticeship and service in the Austro-Prussian War settled in Lübeck, where he had a pharmacy and was a member of the city council. He was the father of Erich Mühsam, the anarchist writer, and of Charlotte Landau-Mühsam, a member of the Lübeck City Council. He died in Lübeck on July 21, 1915.

Documents relating to Mühsam's education, army service, pharmaceutical practice; articles on his activities in Lübeck, including protocols of the Lübeck City Council for 1890 and 1901–1911; obituaries.

Papers of the Mühsam family, including genealogies, family histories, correspondence, memorabilia, religious education notebooks, and report on the educational activities of the Jewish community of Berlin, 1865.

The memoirs of Mühsam's daughter, Charlotte Landau-Mühsam, who was a member of the Lübeck City Council after him, are catalogued separately in the memoir collection.

Languages: German, Hebrew, Judeo-German.
Donors: Hans Landau, 1978; Gad Landau 1984.
Finding Aids: 7-page inventory, 4 catalogue cards.
Accession Number: AR 7112.

192 ARNO NADEL
1911–1973   2.5 inches

Born in Vilna on October 3, 1878, Arno Nadel emigrated to Germany in 1890 and settled in Berlin in 1895. In 1916, he became choir director of the Jewish community of Berlin. He is best known for his work as a musicologist, and for his transcriptions and adaptations of Jewish traditional and liturgical music. He also worked as a poet and an artist. He was killed in Auschwitz in 1943.

Manuscripts and clippings of poetry, and of music and literary criticism; photos of artwork by Nadel; a transcript of Nadel's diaries from 1941–1942; publications about Nadel; inventory of the papers of Nadel which are held by the Jewish National and University Library, Jerusalem; and various unrelated material.

The art collection of the Leo Baeck Institute contains many drawings and prints by Nadel.

Language: German.
Donor: Arsene Okon, 1965, 1976–1977.
Finding Aid: 3-page inventory.
Accession Number: AR 4314.

193 NATIONAL SOCIALISM
1920–1979   1 foot

A miscellaneous collection, containing reports, publications, including *Reichsgesetzblätter*, and artifacts of the Nazi party and regime, as well as numerous contemporaneous and postwar clippings on Nazi rule in Germany, antisemitism, and the Final Solution.

Languages: German, English, Hebrew, French.
Donor: Various, 1957–1979.
Finding Aid: c. 500 catalogue cards.
Accession Number: AR 119.

194 S. S. NAVEMAR – SAUL SPERLING
1941–1953   2 inches

The S.S. *Navemar*, of the Compania Española de Navegación Marítima, brought refugees from Seville to the United States in 1941 under wretched sanitary and safety conditions.

Papers of the plaintiffs' attorney, Saul Sperling, concerning the suit of the passengers of the S.S. *Navemar* against the owners of the ship; clippings from the legal and popular press.

Languages: English, German, Czech.
Donor: A. Sperling, 1969.
Finding Aid: 8 catalogue cards.
Accession Number: AR 3857.

195 EUGEN NETER
1880–1975   5 inches

Born in Gernsbach on October 29, 1876, Eugen Neter was a physician who settled in Mannheim in 1903. He was chairman of the Jewish community there, 1938–1940, was deported to Gurs concentration camp in 1940, emigrated to Palestine in 1946, and died in Deganiah, Israel, on October 10, 1966.

Articles, manuscripts and letters concerning the life of Eugen Neter and his family; memoirs, including a description of life at the front during World War I and one of conditions in the Gurs concentration camp, which is catalogued separately in the memoir collection.

Correspondence with and other material on Paul Eppstein, Hermann Mass, Pauline Maier, Julius Moses, and Nathan Stein.

Languages: German, Hebrew, English.
Donors: Mia Neter and others, 1962–1975.

Finding Aid: 8-page inventory.
Accession Number: AR 1619.

196 OSCAR H. NETTER FAMILY
1809–1972   4 inches

Born in Pforzheim on August 12, 1906, Oscar Netter emigrated to the United States c. 1939 and died in Miami Beach, Florida on February 22, 1974.

Detailed genealogies and histories of the Netter family with supporting papers, including clippings, scientific writings, and family and business documents. Photos, clippings, and pamphlet on the Jewish community of Bühl; clippings on Pforzheim.

Languages: German, English, Hebrew, Portuguese, Judeo-German, French.
Donor: Herbert Epstein, 1974.
Finding Aid: 5-page inventory.
Accession Number: AR 4097.

197 DER NEUE MERKUR
1918–1925   c. 4 feet

Der Neue Merkur was a literary and cultural magazine edited by Efraim Frisch. It appeared between 1914 and 1916, and 1919 and 1925.

Editorial correspondence of *Der Neue Merkur* with individuals and organizations, including Willy Andreas, Lou Andreas-Salomé, Gottfried Benn, Micha Berdyczewski (pseudonym Micha Bin-Gorion), Immanuel Birnbaum, Franz Blei, Ernst Bloch, Adolf Braun, Bertolt Brecht, Lujo Brentano, Max Brod, Martin Buber, Hans Carossa, Bruno Cassirer, R. N. Coudenhove-Kalergi, Ernst R. Curtius, Deutsche Verlagsanstalt, Alfred Döblin, Kasimir Edschmid, Wladimir Eliasberg, T. S. Eliot, Lion Feuchtwanger, Otto Flake, Friedrich Wilhelm Foerster, Bruno Frank, Manfred George, Helmut von Gerlach, André Gide, Ivan Goll, Oskar Maria Graf, Walter Gropius, Emil J. Gumbel, Willy Haas, Ludo M. Hartmann, Wilhelm Hausenstein, Willy Helpach, Alfred Henschke (Klabund), Hermann Hesse, Kurt Hiller, Hugo von Hofmannsthal, Arthur Holitscher, Ricarda Huch, Siegfried Jacobsohn, Erich von Kahler, Georg Kaiser, Rudolf Kayser, Hermann Kayserling, Kurt Kersten, Hans Kohn, Annette Kolb, Siegfried Kracauer, Albert Lamm, Ferdinand Lion, Ernst Lissauer, Philipp Loewenfeld, Emil Ludwig, Heinrich Mann, Leo Matthias, Albrecht Mendelssohn-Bartholdy, Julius Meyer-Gräfe, Robert Müller, Robert Musil, Alfred Neumann, Balder Olden, Franz Oppenheimer, José Ortega y Gasset, Max Osborn, Rudolf Pannwitz, Alfons Paquet, Max Picard, Erwin Piscator, Josef Ponten, Gustav Radbruch, Walther Rathenau, Theodor Reik, Alexander Roda-Roda, Joseph Alois Schumpeter, Leopold Schwarzschild, Kurt Singer, Friedrich Steinthal, Ernst Toller, Siegfried Trebitsch,

Ernst Troeltsch, Kurt Tucholsky, Alfred Vagts, Armin T. Wegner, Ernst Weiss, Felix Weltsch, Alfred Wolfenstein, Arnold Zweig.

Languages: German, French.
Donor: Fega Frisch, 1958.
Finding Aid: 85-page name-index to the correspondence.
Accession Number: AR 7141.

198   ARTHUR NEUSTADT AND HERTA NEUSTADT
1888–1974   5 inches

Born in Borek (now Borek Wielkopolski, Poland) on April 8, 1888, Arthur Neustadt was a furniture dealer in Danzig who emigrated to the United States in 1939, helping to transport the Judaica collection of the community of Danzig. He died in New York City in 1958.

Born in Annen on March 28, 1896, Herta Segall married Arthur Neustadt in 1920, emigrated to the United States in 1939, and was living in New York City in the 1970s.

Birth certificates, passports, wedding announcements, autograph and photo albums, including a series of photos of Arthur Neustadt as soldier in World War I.

Correspondence concerning family and business affairs, restitution, emigration, and the Free City of Danzig.

Languages: German, English, Italian, Spanish, Hebrew.
Donors: Mr. and Mrs. Kurt Gelles, 1978.
Finding Aid: 1-page inventory.
Accession Number: AR 4593.

199   W. G. NIEDERLAND
1950–1981   10 inches

Born in Schippenbeil on August 19, 1904, William G. Niederland is a psychiatrist who emigrated to the United States via Italy and the Philippines in 1935 and lives in Englewood, New Jersey.

Psychiatric case-files by Niederland and others of concentration camp survivors and of Jews who lived in hiding, compiled in connection with restitution claims; material on gypsies and on the children of survivors, including the Winterstein affair, in which children of survivors were prosecuted for actions against former SS members; and articles, manuscripts, and a transcript of a radio interview with Niederland on the survivors syndrome and on the psychological roots of creativity. (Privacy restrictions apply to the use of psychiatric case files.)

Languages: German, English.
Donor: William G. Niederland, 1979, 1981.

Finding Aid: 3-page inventory.
Accession Number: AR 7165.

200 ELSA OESTREICHER
1878–1961   3 inches

Born Elsa Herz in Berlin on November 6, 1878, Elsa Oestreicher worked as a cook and cooking teacher. She was deported to Theresienstadt in 1942, and emigrated via Sweden to the United States in 1946. She died in New York City in 1963.

Material from Elsa Oestreicher's incarceration in Theresienstadt, including censored mail, birthday and New Year's cards, ghetto scrip, poems, and memoirs.
Cookbook manuscripts, instructional material, diplomas, and correspondence relating to culinary arts.

Personal documents, references, correspondence, photos, and genealogical material.

Photos of Jewish communities of Beerfelden and Frankfurt am Main.

Languages: German, English.
Donor: Jenny Lissner, 1957.
Finding Aid: 3-page inventory.
Accession Number: AR 328.

201 ERICH OFFENBACHER
1835–1939   2 inches

Born in Frankfurt am Main on June 11, 1909, Erich Offenbacher was a physician who emigrated to Holland in 1933, and to the United States in 1939, and lives in New York City.

Material on the Oppenheimer family, including a family tree, photos of family members, educational, army service, residency, and vital documents; memorial volume for Erich Offenbacher's great-grandfather, the antiques dealer Selig Goldschmidt.

Languages: German, Judeo-German, Dutch, French.
Donor: Erich Oppenheimer, 1979.
Finding Aid: 8 catalogue cards.
Accession Number: AR 4687.

202 KLAUS OLIVEN
1807–1909   1.5 inches

The Oliven family originated in Lissa in Posen. The collection contains material on Heimann Oliven (died in 1873); his son Julius Oliven, who was in the clothing business, and his grandson Fritz Oliven, a lawyer.

Family histories of the Oliven, Schottlaender (of Lissa), and Meyer (of Hanover) merchant families, including some business papers and testaments.

Languages: German, Judeo-German.
Donor: Klaus Oliven.
Finding Aid: 3 catalogue cards.
Accession Number: AR 3172.

203 ORGANIZATIONS
1792–1980   3 feet

An artificial collection which contains fragmentary organizational records, including brochures, pamphlets, minutes, membership lists, newsletters, correspondence, clippings, and photos from Agudath Israel, Akademie für die Wissenschaft des Judentums, Akademischer Verein für jüdische Geschichte und Literatur, Allgemeiner Rabbinerverband in Deutschland, American Federation of Jews from Central Europe, American Jewish Joint Distribution Committee, Arbeitsgemeinschaft jüdisch-liberaler Jugendvereine Deutschlands, Bar Kochba, Prague, Bildungsverein deutscher Juden, Blau-Weiss, B'nai B'rith-Grossloge für Deutschland-Berlin and Cologne lodges, Bund Deutsch-Jüdischer Jugend, Center for Holocaust Studies, Centralverein Deutscher Staatsbürger jüdischen Glaubens, The Circle (Organization for Refugee Architects), Congregation Habonim, New York, Council of Jews from Germany, Deutsch-Israelitischer Gemeindebund, Deutsch-Jüdische Jugend Gemeinschaft, Freie Vereinigung für die Interessen des orthodoxen Judentums, Genealogical Society of Utah, Gesellschaft der Freunde Berlin, Gesellschaft der Freunde der Hebräischen Universität Jerusalem, Gesellschaft für jüdische Familienforschung, Gesellschaft für jüdische Volkskunde, Gesellschaft zur Förderung der Wissenschaft des Judentums, Gesellschaft zur Förderung wirtschaftlicher Interessen von in Deutschland wohnhaften oder wohnhaft gewesenen Juden, Hechaluz, Hilfsverein der Juden in Deutschland, Hilfsverein für die jüdischen Taubstummen in Deutschland, Hilfswerk für jüdische Künstler und Geistesarbeiter Berlin, Irgun Oleh Merkas Europa, Israelitischer Literatur-Verein, Jewish Agency, Jewish Philanthropic Fund of 1933, Jewish Restitution Successor Organization, Jüdische Buchgemeinde, Jüdische Welthilfskonferenz, Jüdische Winterhilfe, Jüdischer Frauenbund, Jüdischer Kulturbund (includes material from Berlin, Düsseldorf, Hamburg, Kassel, Rhein-Ruhr), Jüdischer Lehrerverein, Jugend-Aliyah (Youth Aliyah), Jung-Jüdischer Club Leipzig, Kameraden: deutschjüdischer Wanderbund, Kartell jüdischer Verbindungen (KJV), Kartell-Convent deutscher Studenten jüdischen Glaubens, Keren Hayessod, Keren Kayemeth, Kreditverein für Handel und Gewerbe, Licaria, Liederkranz, Makkabi, Mekize Nirdamim, National Foundation for Jewish Culture, Nationaljüdische Jugend Deutschlands, ORT, Preussischer Landesverband jüdischer Gemeinden, Rabbinerverband in Deutschland, Rashi Association for the Preservation of Jewish Cultural Monuments in Europe, Reichsbund jüdischer Frontsoldaten, Reichsverband des jüdischen Mittelstandes, Resource von 1794: Vereinigung der Kaufleute jüdischen Glaubens in Berlin, Selfhelp for German Refugees, Tarbuth Foundation, United Restitution Organization, Verband der deutschen Juden, Verband der jüdischen Jugendvereine Deutschlands, Verband jüdischer Heimatvereine, Verband nationaldeutscher Juden, Verein Freunde der Taubstummen Jedide Ilmin, Verein Israelitischer Lehrer, Verein zur Abwehr des Antisemitismus, Verein zur Förderung der Kunst, Vereinigung der liberalen Rabbiner Deutschlands, Versicherungsverein "Die Hilfe", Weltverband für religiös-liberales Judentum, Wissenschaftlich-gesellige Verbindung- Wirceburgia, World Congress of Jewish Studies, World Jewish Congress, World Union for Progressive Judaism, Zentralausschuss der deutschen Juden für Hilfe und Aufbau, Zentralwohlfahrtsstelle der deutschen Juden, Zionistische Vereinigung für Deutschland.

Languages: German, English, Hebrew, Yiddish.
Donors: Various, 1957–1978.
Finding Aid: c. 400 catalogue cards.
Accession Numbers: Numerous.

204 LEOPOLD PERL FAMILY
1845–1962   1 inch

Born in Berlin on January 17, 1845, the physician Leopold Perl died there on August 25, 1909. His descendants emigrated from Nazi Germany to Great Britain.

Educational, professional, vital, and military service papers of Leopold Perl; honors and awards.

Papers of Perl's descendants, especially his daughter Katherine Perl (1884–?), concerning her education, work as a trade school teacher, dismissal from the civil service in 1933 and emigration to Great Britain, and her application for restitution.

Languages: German, English, French.
Donor: Dr. Suschitzky, 1967–1972.
Finding Aid: 12 catalogue cards.
Accession Number: AR 3143.

205 JOSEPH PERLES FAMILY
1808–1924   1 foot

Born in Baja, Hungary, on November 26, 1835, Joseph Perles received his rabbinical ordination at the Jüdisch-theologisches Seminar, Breslau, in 1862. He was a rabbi in Posen until 1871, and then in Munich until his death in 1894. His son, Felix Perles, born in 1874, was a rabbi in Königsberg from 1899 until his death in 1933. Hedwig Perles, the wife of Felix, was a social worker in Königsberg. She emigrated to Palestine, where she died in 1954.

Correspondence with institutions and individuals, including Wilhelm Bacher, Jacob Bernays, Joseph Bloch, Philip Bloch, Salomon Buber, Albert Cohen, Hermann Cohen, Ignaz von Döllinger, Zacharias Fränkel, Ludwig Geiger, Heinrich Graetz, Max Grünbaum, Moritz Güdemann, Solomon Chaim Halberstam, Esriel Hildesheimer, Adolf Jellinek, Moritz Jutrozinski, Zadoc Kahn, Gustav Karpeles, Emanuel Kirschner, Moritz Lazarus, Rochus Liliencron, Leopold Lipschitz, Isidore Löb, Theodor Löwenfeld, Samuel David Luzzatto, Claude Goldsmith Montefiore, Moses Montefiore, Marco Mortara, Salomon Neumann, Solomon Schechter, David Simonsen, Nahum Sokolow, and Leopold Zunz.

Manuscripts, clippings, and offprints of sermons by Joseph Perles and other rabbis; by-laws, 1854, and a report, 1875, of the Jüdisch-theologisches Seminar, Breslau; correspondence of Perles on the selection of a director for the seminary.

Correspondence of Joseph Perles as rabbi of Munich, as well as supporting documents assembled by him dealing with the affairs of the community, including questions of religious reform, liturgy, education, kashrut, participation in public ceremonies, and relations with the secular authorities; official correspondence with the communities of Augsburg, Kitzingen, and Rotterdam.

Clippings and correspondence of Felix Perles about the work of Adolf von Harnack, and about Liberal Judaism.

Papers and correspondence of Hedwig Perles, largely about Russian Jewish refugees in Königsberg, 1904–1905.

Languages: German, Hebrew, French, Italian, English.
Donors: Purchase from Kalman Schlesinger, 1961; donation by Hans Perles, 1980.
Finding Aids: 29-page inventory, 5-page inventory, 4-page inventory, 9 catalogue cards.
Accession Numbers: AR 9014, AR 1351, AR 2945, AR 4884, AR 4911, AR 4993.

206 PERLMANN FAMILY
1852–1977   4 inches

The Perlmanns were a family of merchants and businessmen in Königsberg. This collection was assembled by Herbert Perlmann, who was born in Königsberg in 1886, and emigrated to Great Britain in 1939, to the United States in 1941, and lived in Louisiana and Chicago.

Personal documents, photos, curricula vitae, correspondence, articles, and emigration and business papers, by and about members of the Perlmann and related families, including the Jolowicz, Spiero, and Lewald families; genealogies and family histories.

Clippings, photos, and correspondence by and about Heinrich Spiero, a literary critic, convert to Christianity, and founder of the Paulus Bund, and organization of "non-aryan" Christians; essays by his daughter, the art historian Sabine Gova.

Clippings and photos concerning the Jewish community of Königsberg.

Languages: English, German, French.
Donor: Herbert Perlmann, 1959–1976.
Finding Aid: 8-page inventory.
Accession Number: AR 886.

207 ALFRED PHILIPPSON
1872–1953   4 inches

Born in Bonn on January 1, 1864, Alfred Philippson received his doctorate in geography at Leipzig in 1886, his habilitation in Bonn in 1891 and taught at the Universities of Halle, Bern, and Bonn. He was deported to Theresienstadt in 1942, returned to Bonn in 1945, and died there on March 28, 1956.

Correspondence with individuals, including Leo Baeck, Sven Hedin, Wilhelm Levison, and Ferdinand von Richthofen.

Identification and military service papers, clippings, diaries, memoirs, academic papers, curricula vitae, honorary medals and awards.

Material of Philippson and his wife, Dora Philippson, from their imprisonment in Theresienstadt, including correspondence, identity cards, ghetto scrip, and lectures.

Languages: German, French, English.
Donor: Dora Philippson, 1967.
Finding Aid: 12-page inventory.
Accession Number: AR 3245.

208 LUDWIG PHILIPPSON FAMILY
1810–1961   10 inches

Born in Dessau on December 27, 1811, Ludwig Philippson received his doctorate at the University of Berlin, was rabbi in Magdeburg from 1833 to 1861, and was also active as a publicist and journalist. He was the founder of the *Allgemeine Zeitung des Judentums*. He moved to Bonn in 1862 and died there on December 29, 1889.

Birth and marriage certificates and wills; transcripts of Ludwig Philippson's letters; short manuscripts by him; articles, clippings and lectures concerning him.

Papers of other family members, including correspondence dating back to 1810, photos, memoirs, biographies, diaries, and educational and vital documents of Philippson's son, the geographer Alfred Philippson (1864–1953), his brother, the physician Phoebus Philippson (1807–1870), his nephew, the physician Moritz Philippson (1833–1877), and others; genealogies and family history of the Philippson and Gottschalk families.

Languages: German, Judeo-German, French, Dutch, Hebrew, English.
Donors: Purchase from Pampiere Wereld, 1965; donation by Barbara Jacobson and Stephen Lustig, 1983.
Finding Aid: 6-page inventory.
Accession Numbers: AR 9015, AR 2679, AR 2846.

209 JACOB PICARD
1882–1964   12 feet

Born in Wangen on November 1, 1883, Jacob Picard was a lawyer who practiced in Cologne and was also active as an author and journalist. He emigrated to the United States in 1940, returned to Germany in 1958, and died in Konstanz on January 10, 1967.

Correspondence with family members, including letters from the front in World War I, letters concerning a memorial to Gertrud Colmar and other correspondence with individuals and institutions, among them: Karl Adler, Paul Amann, American Committee for Refugee Scholars, Writers and Artists, American Jewish Congress, Aufbau, Julius Bab, Bertha Badt-Strauss, Bernhard Brilling, Werner Cahnmann, Conference on Jewish Material Claims against Germany, Ludwig Feuchtwanger, Oskar Maria Graf, Max Gruenewald, Ludwig Hardt, Hermann Hesse, Theodor Heuss, Otto Hirsch, Jewish Publication Society, Jüdischer Kulturbund, Kurt Kersten, Hans Kohn, Leo Baeck Institute, Paul Mayer, Caroline Norment, Kurt Pinthus, Joachim Prinz, Reichsvereinigung der Juden in Deutschland, Franz Rosenzweig, Nelly Sachs, Selfhelp for German Refugees, Isaac Bashevis Singer, Nathan Stein, *Stuttgarter Zeitung*, Selma Stern-Taeubler, Karl Vietor, Alfred Wiener, and Stefan Zweig.

Court papers in Picard's divorce case and his suit against Schweizerische Volksbank.

Manuscripts by Picard, including a biography of Franz Sigel, an 1848 revolutionary and Union general during the American Civil War; clippings of articles by and about him; and diaries for the years 1906–1950.

Genealogy of the Picard family, and papers, including vital documents and correspondence, of Picard's parents.

Photos of Jakob Picard, family members, and others; photographs from World War I.

Picard's memoirs are catalogued separately in the memoir collection.

Languages: German, English, French.
Donor: R. van Dijk Picard, 1969.
Finding Aid: 38-page inventory.
Accession Number: AR 6016.

210 PINKUS FAMILY
1696–1976   15 feet

The Pinkuses were a family of textile manufacturers whose factory in Neustadt, Upper Silesia (now Prudnik, Poland), was one of the largest producers of fine linens in the world. Joseph Pinkus became a partner in the firm S. Fränkel when he married Auguste Fränkel, the daughter of the owner. Their son Max Pinkus (1857–1934) was director until 1926. His son Hans Pinkus managed the company until it was "aryanized" after Kristallnacht. He emigrated to Great Britain with his family in 1939, and died there in 1977, after an unsuccessful attempt to rebuild the firm in Bavaria.

Correspondence of family members with each other and with others including Johannes Avenarius, Anton Belda, Paul Ehrlich, Max Oberländer, Kurt Schwerin and Hermann Stehr; material dealing with the political activities of family members; their involvement with Jewish and other philanthropies in Breslau, Neustadt, and elsewhere; Max Pinkus's role on the home front during the World War I, and in the disputes over the territorial changes in Silesia after the war; Hans Pinkus's education, fraternity membership, and duels; his experiences as a POW in France and Switzerland, including his matriculation at Bern; and his activities in the Konstanz soldiers' council and as a founding member of the Reichsvereinigung ehemaliger Kriegsgefangener.

Records of businesses owned by the Pinkus family from the mid-nineteenth century through the period after World War II, including correspondence, manuscripts, business reports, tax and financial records, legal papers, advertising material, newspaper clippings, and sample books from the firms of S. Fränkel Neustadt, Spinnerei Vorwärts Brackwede, Schlesische Flachs-Werke Kaundorf, Süddeutsche Leinenweberei Augsburg, Schlesische Feinweberei, S. Fränkel Augsburg, and Hronover Baumwollspinnerei.

Manuscripts and clippings about the family and its activities, Nazism and antisemitism, and Paul Ehrlich and the Paul Ehrlich Stiftung.

Papers of family members, including vital documents, membership cards, awards, medals, diaries, travel journals, legal papers, tax records, wills and testaments; genealogies and family histories, along with supporting documents, of the Pinkus family and related families, including the Deutsch and Fränkel families.

Photos of family members, their friends and associates, and of their business, travel, and other activities.

Material on the literary activities of Max Pinkus, including material on his activity as a book collector, particularly his renowned collection of Silesian literature; transcriptions of his correspondence with Gerhart Hauptmann; clippings, programs, and other material on plays of Hauptmann, especially *Vor Sonnenuntergang* and *Die Finsternisse*, whose protagonists were inspired by Max Pinkus; bibliographies of Hauptmann's work compiled by Pinkus; and offprints, clippings, correspondence, and manuscripts of Hauptmann scholars C.F.W. Behl and Walter Reichart.

Material on the Jews of Silesia, including reports of meetings of the chairmen of the Jewish communities of Upper Silesia during the 1930s, letter of privilege for the Jews of Zülz issued in 1699, and decrees on the Jews of Silesia signed by the German Emperor, Karl VI and King Friedrich II of Prussia.

Languages: German, English, French.
Donors: Hans Pinkus, 1957–1976; Jon Peters, 1985.
Finding Aid: 26-page inventory.
Accession Number: AR 7030.

211 KOPPEL S. PINSON
1931–1964   2.5 inches

Born in Postawy, Lithuania on February 11, 1904, Koppel Pinson came to the United States with his parents in 1907. He received his doctorate in history at Columbia University in 1934 and taught from 1934 to 1961 at various branches of the City University of New York. Pinson's academic specialty was German history, and he was active in assisting refugee scholars during the 1930s. He died in New York City in 1961.

Correspondence of Pinson with Hans Kohn, Emil Lederer, Thomas Mann, and Robert Weltsch.

Book reviews and curricula vitae.

Languages: German, English, Hebrew, Yiddish.
Donor: Hilde Pinson, 1976.
Finding Aid: 11-page inventory.
Accession Number: AR 4310.

212 MAX PLAUT
1944–1950   4 inches

Born in Sorau (now Zary, Poland) on October 17, 1901, Max Plaut was a lawyer and Jewish communal official, head of the Jewish community of Hamburg, 1938–1943, and head of the Bezirkstelle Nordwestdeutschland of the Reichsvereinigung der Juden in Deutschland, 1939–1943. In 1944 he emigrated to Palestine, as part of an exchange program with Germans interned there. He returned to Germany in 1950, and lived in Bremen and Hamburg. He died in Hamburg on March 8, 1974.

Correspondence of Plaut, 1944–1950, dealing primarily with the fate of the Jews of Hamburg during the Holocaust, and with related problems of restitution, along with supporting material; material on the fate of functionaries of the Reichsvereinigung, including lists of those interned in Theresienstadt, Lodz, Auschwitz, Vittel, and elsewhere.

Inventory of papers of Max Plaut, and of the Plaut family, on deposit at the Staatsarchiv Bremen.

Languages: German, English, Hebrew.
Donors: Ruth Plaut, 1977, via E. G. Lowenthal, 1978.
Finding Aid: 2 catalogue cards.
Accession Number: AR 7094.

213 VICTOR POLZER
1899–1966   4 inches

Born in Vienna on September 5, 1892, the editor, author, and journalist Victor Polzer emigrated to the United States in 1938 and died in New York City on February 16, 1965.

Correspondence, including letters from Hermann Broch and Thomas Mann.

Vital documents and educational and military papers.

Articles, interviews, lectures, stories by Polzer.

Languages: German, English.
Donor: Annie Polzer, 1966.
Finding Aid: 10-page inventory.
Accession Number: AR 3683.

214 ARTHUR PRINZ
1891–1980   5 feet

Born in Guatemala City on December 3, 1898, Arthur Prinz moved to Berlin with his family in 1904. He studied economics, history, and philosophy at the University of Berlin, receiving his doctorate in 1923. He taught at Humboldt Hochschule, Berlin, from 1926 until his dismissal in 1933. From 1935 until 1939, he worked for the Hilfsverein der Juden in Deutschland, and edited its journal *Jüdische Auswanderung*. He emigrated to Palestine in 1939, and to the United States in 1948, where he became professor of economics at Fairleigh Dickenson University. He died in San Diego on August 27, 1981.

Correspondence with individuals and institutions, including American Jewish Joint Distribution Committee, Kurt Blumenfeld, Council of Jews from Germany, Julius Curtius, Freie jüdische Volkshochschule, Berlin, Hans Bernd von Haeften, HIAS-HICEM, Joachim Prinz, Reichsbund jüdischer Frontsoldaten, Alexander Rüstow, Anita Warburg, Max Warburg, Robert Weltsch, Alfred Wiener, and Zionistische Vereinigung für Deutschland.

Family documents; diaries of Prinz for 1908–1919, and 1940; his memoirs of the Nazi period; and material on Prinz's dismissal from his teaching position at Humboldt Hochschule.

Manuscripts and research notes on economics, emigration, and exile life, Jewish history and affairs, Karl Marx, and Marxism, Zionism, and other topics; an extensive collection of clippings and offprints by Prinz and others on these subjects.

Material on the Hilfsverein and Prinz's work there, including correspondence, manuscripts, publications, and a satirical play.

Languages: German, English, Spanish.
Donor: Fanny Prinz, 1982.
Finding Aid: 11-page inventory.
Accession Number: AR 5103.

215 REICHSVERTRETUNG DER DEUTSCHEN JUDEN
1933–1963   9 inches

The Reichsvertretung der deutschen Juden was founded in 1933 as a federation of Jewish organizations and regional and local Jewish communities to represent German Jewry in dealing with the Nazi authorities. In 1934, the Nazi government renamed it the Reichsvertretung der Juden in Deutschland. It was dissolved in 1938 and was replaced in 1939 by the Reichsvereinigung der Juden in Deutschland, a compulsory organization of all Jews living in Nazi Germany, as defined by the Nuremberg laws.

Correspondence of Georg Hirschland on the founding of the Reichsvertretung, including letters from Leo Baeck, Otto Hirsch, and Max Warburg.

Minutes of Reichsvertretung meetings; budgets; reports on their own activities, conditions of Jewish life in Germany, and Jewish emigration.

Clippings from various periodicals, relating to the Reichsvertretung and emigration, including pictorial material.

Language: German.
Donor: John Herold, Aufbau, 1957, 1965.
Finding Aid: 3-page inventory.
Accession Number: AR 221.

216 HANNS REISSNER
1953–1976   2.5 feet

Born in Berlin on November 29, 1902, the historian Hanns Reissner emigrated to India in 1939, the United States in 1948, and died in Philadelphia on August 6, 1977.

Correspondence with individuals and institutions, including Bernhard Brilling, Lion Feuchtwanger, the Central Zionist Archives, and the Leo Baeck Institute. Clippings, research notes, photographs, and manuscripts by Reissner and others on topics in Jewish history, including the Mendelssohn family and the anti-Nazi boycott; genealogical researches; and material on Jewish communities in the Caribbean.

Languages: German, English.
Donors: Mrs. Hanns Reissner via Herbert Strauss, 1977.
Finding Aid: 3-page inventory.
Accession Number: AR 7105.

217 PAUL RIEGER
18th c.–1939   2 feet

Born in Dresden on July 4, 1870, Paul Rieger was a rabbi and historian. He studied at the Jüdisch-theologisches Seminar, Breslau, and at the University of Breslau, receiving his doctorate in 1894, and pursued further studies at the Lehranstalt für die Wissenschaft des Judentums and the University of Berlin. He served as rabbi in Potsdam, preacher at the Israelitischer Tempelverband Hamburg, and afterwards as Landesrabbiner in Braunschweig and Stuttgart. He died in Stuttgart on July 10, 1939.

Correspondence of Rieger with individuals, including Berthold Auerbach, George Alexander Kohut, Martin Philippson, and Hermann Vogelstein.

Manuscripts, lectures, offprints and clippings by Rieger on Jewish history, Judaism and Christianity, antisemitism and Jewish civil rights, and philosophy; Rieger's research notes for his dissertation on material culture in the Talmud and research notebooks on the Jews of Spain and on Jewish communities in Württemberg; reviews of his work, particularly on the history of the Jews of Rome, which he co-authored with Hermann Vogelstein.

Photos of Rieger, his associates, and their rabbinical activities.

Minute book and register of the Kuratorium des Vereins Arbeitstätte in Hamburg, 1906–1909, an organization to provide work for unemployed young Jews, particularly recent immigrants.

Records of the Jewish community of Freudental in Württemberg from the eighteenth century.

Languages: German, Hebrew, Judeo-German, English.
Donor: Martin Rieger, 1986.
Finding Aid: 5-page preliminary inventory.
Accession Number: AR 7275.

218 EDOUARD RODITI
c. 1931–1980   3.5 feet

Born in Paris on June 6, 1910, the author and art critic Edouard Roditi lives there today.

Short biographies of Jewish artists, particularly of the school of Paris, photos of their works, and exhibition catalogues; clippings relating to Jewish art; exhibition catalogues of Jewish ritual art.

Miscellaneous clippings, reviews, and translations, by Roditi and others, on various topics, including Sephardic culture; a memoir by Otto Freundlich of his experiences as a German artist in Paris during World War I.

Languages: French, English, Portuguese, German, Dutch, Spanish, Hebrew.
Donor: Edouard Roditi, 1971–1980.
Finding Aid: 37-page inventory.
Accession Number: AR 7058.

219 ROSENFELD FAMILY
1746–1945   5 inches

The Rosenfeld family was a family of physicians and cantors from southern Germany. Callmann Isaac Rosenfeld (1756–1851) served as a cantor in Berlichingen. His son Leopold Rosenfeld (1813–1880) studied medicine in Heidelberg in the 1830s and worked as a physician in Adelsheim. His son Gustav Rosenfeld (1844–1904) also studied medicine in Heidelberg and later served in the Franco-Prussian War. His son Fritz Rosenfeld (1877–?) studied medicine in Würzburg.

Papers of the Rosenfeld, Rosenthal, and Lublinski families, including vital, academic, and professional documents, some bearing on medical education and service, business contracts, and correspondence.

A copy of a 1945 deposition by Manfred Rommel, on the circumstances of the death of his father, Field Marshal Erwin Rommel.

Languages: German, Judeo-German.
Donor: S. Brill, 1962.
Finding Aid: 6-page inventory.
Accession Number: AR 1544.

220 BERTHOLD ROSENTHAL
1650–1957   6 feet

Born in Liedolsheim on January 17, 1875, Berthold Rosenthal was a schoolteacher and genealogist. He emigrated to the United States in 1939 and died in Omaha, Nebraska, on December 16, 1957.

Manuscripts, clippings, correspondence on the history of the Jews in Baden and on the genealogy of Jewish families there. Copies of tax, census, and cemetery lists, mohel books, Memorbücher of the Jewish communities of Altdorf, Bad-Durkheim, Baden, Baden-Baden, Durlach, Beisheim, Bergen, Bieskastel, Bödigheim, Buchen, Epstein, Grünstadt, Hanau-Lichtenberg, Hembsbach, Hessen, Hochberg, Krautheim, Kuppenheim, Landau, Leiningen, Leutershausen, Limpertheim, Lorsch, Mannheim, Markelfingen, Meckesheim, Neckarbischofsheim, Obergrombach, Palatinate, Speyer, Wertheim, and Worms from the seventeenth through the nineteenth century.

Organizational records of the Naphtali-Epstein Verein, Karlsruhe, Jewish schoolteachers' association, including minutebooks, by-laws, budgets, correspondence, and membership lists.

Rosenthal's memoirs dealing with his emigration are catalogued separately in the memoir collection.

Languages: German, English, Hebrew.
Donor: Johanna Rosenthal, 1959.
Finding Aid: 23-page inventory.
Accession Number: AR 638.

221 ROSENZWEIG FAMILY
1777–1938   6 inches

Papers of the ancestors of Franz Rosenzweig.

Vital certificates, marriage and engagement contracts, school papers, military papers, letters, poems, photos, and clippings concerning members of the Rosenzweig, Ehrenberg, and Eisenberg families; correspondence of Adam Rosenzweig, including letters from Samuel Meyer Ehrenberg and Leopold Zunz.

Languages: German, Hebrew, Judeo-German.
Donor: Louis Rosenzweig, 1958.
Finding Aid: 9-page inventory.
Accession Numbers: AR 9016, AR 410, AR 421.

222 FRANZ ROSENZWEIG
1837–1960   3 feet

Born in Kassel on December 25, 1886, Franz Rosenzweig studied philosophy and history at the Universities of Berlin and Freiburg, receiving his doctorate in 1917. Although he for a time contemplated conversion to Christianity, he rejected this course and returned to Judaism with increasing commitment. After army service in World War I, he founded the Freies Jüdisches Lehrhaus, Frankfurt. He was the author of several philosophical works, most prominently *Der Stern der Erlösung*, and collaborated with Martin Buber on a translation of the Hebrew Bible. He died in Frankfurt after a long and debilitating illness on December 10, 1929.

Correspondence of Rosenzweig and his wife, Edith Rosenzweig, with individuals, including Leo Baeck, Isaac Breuer, Martin Buber, Joseph Carlebach, Karl D. Darmstaedter, Max Dienemann, Richard Ehrenberg, Victor Ehrenberg, Nahum Glatzer, Margarete Goldstein, Oscar Loerke, Eugen Mayer, Friedrich Meinecke, Alfred Mombert, Hermann Oncken, Eugen Rosenstock-Huessy, Fritz Schwarzschild, Caesar Seligmann, Ernst Simon, Rudolf Stahl, Bruno Strauss, Eduard Strauss, Margaret Susman, Gershom Scholem, Karl Wolfskehl, and Arnold Zweig.

Manuscripts on various topics including diaries for 1905–1914 and 1922, and drafts and annotated galleys of part of *Der Stern der Erlösung*; clippings about Rosenzweig and his work; photos of Rosenzweig.

Course announcements and descriptions for the Freies Jüdisches Lehrhaus, Frankfurt, and Rosenzweig's lecture notes for courses at the Lehrhaus.

Album presented to Rosenzweig on his fortieth birthday including testimonials from S. Y. Agnon, Hermann Badt, Bertha Badt-Strauss, Fritz Goitein, and Jacob Rosenheim, in addition to several of the above-mentioned correspondents.

Genealogies and histories of Rosenzweig and Ehrenberg families; obituaries, poems, letters, photos of family members; diaries and memoirs of family members, including Adele Rosenzweig's memoirs of Franz's childhood.

Languages: German, English, Hebrew, Latin.
Donor: Edith Scheinmann-Rosenzweig, 1959–1960, 1980.
Finding Aid: 55-page inventory.
Accession Numbers: AR 3001, AR 5043.

223 FRANZ ROSENZWEIG-MARTIN BUBER
1913–1929   1.5 feet

Franz Rosenzweig collaborated with Martin Buber on several projects, the most important of which was a translation of the Hebrew Bible.

Typescripts and handwritten manuscripts by Buber and Rosenzweig on various topics, including political theory, philosophy, and literature; seminar papers from Rosenzweig's university years; twenty-two notebooks containing parts of the Rosenzweig-Buber Bible translation, and correspondence between the two about the translation.

Languages: German, English, Hebrew, Greek.
Donor: Nahum N. Glatzer, 1974, 1975.
Finding Aid: 14-page inventory.
Accession Number: AR 4193.

224 JOSEPH ROTH
1906–1970   2 feet

Born in Brody, Austria-Hungary (now USSR) on September 26, 1894, Joseph Roth lived in Berlin after World War I, where he worked as a journalist and author. He emigrated to France in 1933, was active in exile politics, and died in Paris on May 27, 1939.

Correspondence of Joseph Roth, including letters from family members, letters to Blanche Gidon, and correspondence with publishers, including Gustav Kiepenheuer Verlag, Allert de Lange Verlag, Querido Verlag, and Viking Press. Manuscripts by Roth, including the novels *Hundert Tage* and *Trotzki*, excerpts from *Radetzkymarsch*, chapters of other novels, novellas, poems, and essays; clippings and offprints.

Manuscripts, clippings, and reviews about Roth and his work; photos of Roth, friends, and relatives.

Correspondence, papers, photos, clippings, and other material relating to the Leo Baeck Institute's Joseph Roth Symposium, 1970.

Languages: German, English, French, Polish, Russian, Hebrew.
Donor: Purchase 1962; Mrs. C. Birmann, 1963, 1970.
Finding Aid: 29-page inventory.
Accession Number: AR 1836.

225 JOSEPH ROTH – JOSEPH BORNSTEIN
1926–1939   7.5 inches

Born in Cracow, Austria-Hungary (now Poland) on October 18, 1899, Bornstein moved to Berlin in 1905, emigrated to France in 1933 and to the United States in 1941. He was active as a literary agent, author, and journalist. Bornstein died in New York City on June 23, 1952. Part of Roth's papers were found in Bornstein's literary estate.

Correspondence of Roth with individuals, including Lion Feuchtwanger, Victor Gollancz, Egon Kisch, Rudolf Leonhard, Prinz Hubertus Löwenstein, Emil Ludwig, Heinrich Mann, Thomas Mann, Walter Mehring, Alfred Neumann, Carl von Ossietzky, Max Picard, Alfred Polgar, Max Reinhardt, Albert Sarraut, Rene Schickele, Leopold Schwarzschild, Dorothy Thompson, Ernst Toller, and Stefan Zweig.

Poetry manuscripts and miscellaneous notes by Roth, membership and press cards, hotel bills, and other memorabilia.

Language: German.
Donor: William Kallir, 1973.
Finding Aid: 12-page inventory.
Accession Number: AR 4152.

226 HANS J. SACHS
1844–1971   5 inches

Born in Breslau (now Wroclaw, Poland), on August 11, 1881, Hans J. Sachs studied and practiced dentistry. He emigrated to the United States in 1938 and was living in New York City in 1971.

School papers, doctoral diploma, patents, essays on dentistry, and letters of recommendation, including one written by Albert Einstein.

Papers of Sachs's father, the dentist Wilhelm Sachs, who emigrated to the United States in 1868, where he received his dental education before returning to Breslau, and of his grandfather Joseph Wilhelm Sachs, including photos, memorabilia, essays and articles on dentistry, and awards and honors.

Languages: German, English, French.
Donor: Hans J. Sachs, 1958, 1970, 1971.
Finding Aid: 9-page inventory.
Accession Number: AR 2564.

227 JULIUS SACHS
1944–1968   1 foot

Born in Vienna on June 12, 1882, the journalist and translator Julius Sachs emigrated to the United States via Great Britain in 1940 and died in New York City in the early 1970s.

Draft of a German-English thesaurus along with correspondence and recommendations concerning the thesaurus project.

Languages: German, English.
Donor: Margaret Bush, 1976.
Finding Aid: 6 catalogue cards.
Accession Number: AR 7042.

228 NELLY SACHS
1891–1971   1 foot

Born in Berlin on December 10, 1891, the poet and dramatist Nelly Sachs emigrated to Sweden in 1940. She won the Nobel Prize for literature in 1966 and died in Stockholm on May 12, 1970.

Photocopies of correspondence of Nelly Sachs, including a letter to Paul Celan. Clippings, exhibition catalogues and programs, theater programs, radio transcripts, tape recordings, and photos concerning Nelly Sachs's life and work, largely assembled in connection with the Leo Baeck Institute's exhibition on Sachs in 1967; tapes and photos of performances of the opera *Eli*, whose libretto was written by Sachs.

Manuscripts of letters and poems, sent to Hannah Labus.

Languages: German, English, Swedish, French, Dutch, Hebrew.
Donors: Various sources, 1958–1971.
Finding Aids: Index cards and 17-page inventory.
Accession Numbers: AR 3991, AR 3239.

229 SIEGMUND SALFELD
1862–1978   5 inches

Born in Stadthagen on March 24, 1843, Siegmund Salfeld studied philosophy and theology in Berlin and Tübingen, receiving his doctorate in 1870. From 1870 to 1880 he was rabbi in Dessau, and from 1880 until his retirement in 1918 in Mainz. He died in Mainz on May 1, 1926.

Correspondence with individuals, including Leo Baeck, Markus Brann, Martin Buber, Gotthard Deutsch, Ismar Elbogen, Gustav Karpeles, Moritz Lazarus, and Martin Philippson.

Educational documents, awards and honors, historical manuscripts, lecture notes, sermons, and a bibliography of Salfeld's historical writings.

Clippings, programs concerning Salfeld and his career and on the dedication of the new synagogue in Mainz, 1912.

Photographs of Salfeld and family members; genealogy of the Salfeld family.

Languages: German, Hebrew, Judeo-German.
Donor: Ruth Salfeld, 1976.
Finding Aid: 4 catalogue cards.
Accession Number: AR 7017.

230 ALBERT SALOMON
1926–1959   10 inches

Born in Berlin on December 8, 1891, Albert Salomon received his doctorate in sociology at Heidelberg in 1921 and taught at various German institutions, including the Hochschule für Politik. In 1935 he emigrated to the United States, where he taught at the New School for Social Research. Salomon died in New York City in December 1966.

Correspondence of Albert Salomon with individuals, including Charles Beard, Walter Benjamin, Arnold Brecht, Felix Frankfurter, Felix Gilbert, Waldemar Gurian, Theodor Heuss, Robert Maynard Hutchins, Herbert Lehmann, Robert Lynd, Erwin Panofsky, Talcott Parsons, Alice Salomon, Hans Schäffer, Arthur Schlesinger Jr., Edward Shils, Adlai Stevenson, Leo Strauss, Marianne Weber, and Kurt Wolff.

Manuscripts and course outlines by Salomon and others.

Salomon's memoirs are catalogued separately in the memoir collection.

Photos of Israel shortly after statehood.

Languages: German, English, French.
Donor: Albert Salomon, 1962, 1964.
Finding Aid: 8-page inventory.
Accession Number: AR 4091.

231 ALICE SALOMON
1877–1961   2 inches

Born in Berlin on April 19, 1872, Alice Salomon was a social worker, educator and feminist who emigrated to the United States in 1937 and died in New York City on August 30, 1948.

Professional and vital certificates, diplomas, honors, awards, and essays on feminism and social work; notes on her interrogation by the Gestapo.

Manuscript of Salomon's autobiography, entitled "Character Is Destiny," written after her emigration to the United States.

Genealogy of the Salomon family with supporting materials.

Languages: German, English.
Donor: Hannah S. Janovsky, 1971.
Finding Aid: 4-page inventory.
Accession Number: AR 3875.

232 RICHARD G. SALOMON
1884–1979   7 inches

Born in Berlin on April 22, 1884, Richard Salomon converted to Lutheranism in 1902 and studied history, receiving his doctorate at the University of Berlin in 1907. He was professor of history at the University of Hamburg from 1919 to 1934, when he was dismissed on racial grounds. After emigrating to the United States in 1937, he taught at Kenyon College in Gambier, Ohio. He died in Mount Vernon, Ohio on February 3, 1966.

Correspondence pertaining to Salomon's career and his emigration; clippings, off-prints, and essays by and about Salomon; material relating to his employment by the OSS (Office of Strategic Services), including a letter from Herbert Marcuse; vital, educational, and military papers.

Material, largely satirical, on the Nichtarische Bach-Cantaten Gesellschaft. Genealogy of the Salomon family.

Memoirs of Salomon's father, Georg Anton Salomon (1849–1916), are catalogued separately in the memoir collection, as is a diary of his son of a trip to Germany after World War II.

Languages: German, English, Latin.
Donor: George Salomon, 1966–1974.
Finding Aids: 6-page inventory, 11 catalogue cards.
Accession Number: AR 3862.

233 SALOMONSOHN FAMILY
1806–1848   2.5 inches

Members of the Salomonsohn family lived in Copenhagen and in the Posen Province in the first half of the nineteenth century.

Letters of Gedalja Salomonsohn, his wife, Ernestine Salomonsohn, and his parents, Rabbi Schachne Salomonsohn and Rachel Salomonsohn.

Essays and letters by Schachne Salomonsohn and others on religious law, as well as religious documents.

Languages: Hebrew, Judeo-German, German.
Donor: Ms. Rischowski, 1974.
Finding Aids: 2 catalogue cards, 50-page introduction to the collection with elaborations and translations of several items into English.
Accession Number: AR 4137.

234 HANS SCHÄFFER
1933–1968   11 feet

Born in Breslau (now Wroclaw, Poland) on April 11, 1886, Hans Schäffer was a lawyer, financial expert, and civil servant. After World War I, he worked in the German Ministry of Commerce, and was concerned in particular with the problems of inflation and reparations. He was senior official in the German Ministry of Finance, 1929–1932, when he became director of the Ullstein Verlag, where he served until his dismissal by the Nazis in 1933. Beginning in 1933, he oversaw the liquidation and reorganization of the Swedish Match Company (STAB), along with Allen Dulles and Jean Monnet, following the death of its owner, Ivar Kreuger. He emigrated to Sweden with his family in 1936, where he worked as an investment advisor and was active in Jewish affairs. After 1957 he served as the president of the Council of Jews from Germany. He died in Jönköping, Sweden, on March 20, 1967.

Correspondence of Hans Schäffer, discussing, among other topics, the fall of the Weimar Republic, the conditions of Jews in and Jewish refugees from Nazi Germany, politics and resistance in Nazi Germany, the economic policies of Hjalmar Schacht, conditions in Europe during World War II, the Holocaust, post-World War II Germany, restitution and reparations, the founding of the State of Israel, and conditions in India shortly after its independence. Among Schäffer's correspondents are Hermann J. Abs, Konrad Adenauer, Solomon Adler-Rudel, Johannes Avenarius, Bertha Badt-Strauss, Leo Baeck, Cora Berliner, Count Folke Bernadotte, Julie Braun-Vogelstein, Heinrich Brüning, Carl J. Burckhardt, Allen Dulles, Manfred George, Dag Hammarskjold, Paul Hertz, Theodor Heuss, Rudolf Hilferding, Rose Hilferding, Otto Hirsch, Wilfred Israel, Hans Jacoby, Hannah Karminski, Georg Landauer, Emil Lederer, Adolf Leschnitzer, Hans Luther, John J. McCloy, Lise Meitner, Carl Melchior, Robert von Mendelssohn, Mendelssohn & Co. Amsterdam, Jean Monnet, Fritz Naphtali, Notgemeinschaft deutscher Wissenschaftler im Ausland, Ludwig Quidde, Reichsvertretung der deutschen Juden, Hanns Reissner, Alexander Rustow, Hans-Joachim Schoeps, Werner David Senator, Georg Solti, Hans Staudinger, Else Staudinger, Stockholms Enskilda Bank, Svenska Handelsbank, Fritz Tarnow, Gottfried Reinhard Treviranus, Hermann Ullstein, Veit Valentin, Jacob Wallenberg, Erich Warburg, Fritz Warburg, Max Warburg, Siegmund Warburg, Robert Weltsch, and Alfred Wiener.

Memorandum on conditions of Jews in Germany, 1933; memorandum on career and bankruptcy of Ivar Kreuger, the Swedish "match king" and financier.

A memoir by Schäffer is catalogued separately in the memoir collection.

Languages: German (some in Stolze-Schrei shorthand), English, Swedish, French.
Donors: Hans Schäffer, 1964; Eva Schäffer, 1968.
Finding Aids: 6-page inventory, 105-page name index to the correspondence.
Accession Number: AR 7177.

235 HANS SCHÄFFER-ECKHARD WANDEL
1918–1971   2.5 inches

Eckhard Wandel (born 1942) worked as a historian at the economic seminar at the University of Tübingen.

Material collected by Wandel for his biography of Hans Schäffer, including recollections of Schäffer by contemporaries and associates; clippings, reviews concerning Schäffer and his work; photocopies of excerpts from Schäffer's diaries and of reports and memoranda he wrote.

Languages: German, French, Swedish, English, Hebrew.
Donor: Eckhard Wandel, 1976.
Finding Aid: 2-page inventory.
Accession Number: AR 7023.

236 BRUNO SCHINDLER
1867–1967   3 inches

Born in Leschnitz (now Lesnica, Poland) on October 16, 1882, the educator and sinologist Bruno Schindler emigrated to Great Britain in 1933 and died in London on July 29, 1964.

Curricula vitae, school papers, and obituaries of Bruno Schindler.

Papers of the journalist James Heckscher (1834–1909), reporter for Reuters, including correspondence between Heckscher and Austen Chamberlain, Edward Grey, Paul Landau, Moses Montefiore, Ivan Turgenev, members of the House of Lords, and the British Foreign Office.

Notes and clippings, obituaries and photos of Heckscher.

Languages: German, English, French.
Donor: Georg Schindler, 1961, 1965.
Finding Aid: 8-page inventory.
Accession Numbers: AR 9018, AR 1369, AR 2520.

237 ALFRED SCHIROKAUER
1889–1932   3.5 feet

Born in Breslau (now Wroclaw, Poland) on July 13, 1880, the author Alfred Schirokauer lived in Berlin, emigrated to Austria in 1933, and died in Vienna on October 27, 1934.

Correspondence with publishers, manuscripts of novels and shorter works, and newspaper serializations of Schirokauer's writing.

Language: German.
Donor: Mrs. Hartman, 1978.
Finding Aid: 3-page inventory.
Accession Number: AR 7107.

238 FRANZ SCHOENBERNER
1927–1969   10 inches

Born in Berlin on December 18, 1892, Franz Schoenberner was a writer and editor of *Simplicissimus*, 1929–1933. He emigrated to France in 1933, to the United States in 1941, and died in New Jersey in April 1970.

Photocopies of Schoenberner's literary estate, the originals of which are in possession of the Hoover Institution on War, Revolution and Peace, Stanford University.

Correspondence with publishers and with individuals, including Albert Einstein, D. H. Lawrence, Heinrich Mann, Klaus Mann, Reinhold Niebuhr, Upton Sinclair, and Stefan Zweig.

Manuscripts of Schoenberner and his wife, Eleonora Schoenberner, also known as Ellen Caren, and clippings by and about Schoenberner.

Languages: German, English, French.
Donors: Stefan Congrot-Butlar via Joy Chute of PEN, 1979.
Finding Aid: 7-page inventory.
Accession Number: AR 7164.

239 OTTILIE SCHOENEWALD
1905–1961   5 inches

Born in Bochum on December 21, 1883, Ottilie Schoenewald was a social worker and feminist, and last president of the Jüdischer Frauenbund, 1934–1939. She was also a member of the Preussicher Landesverband der jüdischen Gemeinden. She emigrated to the United States via the Netherlands and Great Britain in 1939 and died in New York City on May 18, 1961.

Correspondence of Schoenewald with institutions and individuals, including Leo Baeck, Klara Caro, Dora Edinger, Alfred Hirschberg, Selma Jolowicz, Hannah Karminski, Ernst Lowenthal, and Lilli Marx.

Manuscripts, clippings, and offprints of articles, lectures, and speeches, by Schoenewald and others, on feminism, social work, the Jüdischer Frauenbund, post-World War II Germany, U.S. immigration laws, and denazification. Material on Bertha Pappenheim, including reminiscences of her, clippings, letters of condolonce and obituaries; essays and speeches on Pappenheim by Schoenewald.

Records of the Jüdischer Frauenbund, mostly from the 1930s, including minutes of local and district organizations, reports, circulars, material on the homes and other institutions run by the organization and its branches, photos of the home at Neu-Isenburg, and material on the dissolution of the organization in 1939 and on attempts to rebuild the organization after World War II.

Records of the International Council of Jewish Women, including minutes of the central and national committees and official correspondence.

Schoenewald's memoirs are catalogued separately in the memoir collection.

Languages: German, English.
Donor: Ms. Berch, 1962.
Finding Aid: 8-page inventory.
Accession Number: AR 3896.

240 LEOPOLD SCHWARZSCHILD
1940–1955   4.5 feet

Born in Frankfurt am Main on December 8, 1891, Leopold Schwarzschild was a journalist, economist, and editor of *Das Tagebuch*, 1923–1933. He emigrated to France in 1933, where he played an active role in emigré politics, editing *Das Neue Tagebuch*, 1933–1939. Schwarzschild emigrated to the United States in 1940 and died in Santa Margherita, Italy, on October 2, 1950.

Correspondence with individuals and organizations, including Clifford Case, Max Eastman, the Emergency Rescue Committee, Bruno Frank, Manfred George, Hermann Kesten, H.R. Knickerbocker, Alfred Knopf, Emil Ludwig, Erika Mann, Klaus Mann, James G. McDonald, Maxwell Perkins, Victor Polzer, Curt Riess, Ernst Rowohlt, Friedrich Sternthal, Max Warburg, Franz Werfel, and Carl Zuckmayer.

Manuscripts of articles, speeches, and radio broadcasts by Schwarzschild; manuscripts and reviews of his books, including *World in Trance* and *The Red Prussian*.

Languages: German, English.
Donor: Valerie Schwarzschild, 1956, 1962.
Finding Aid: 3-page inventory.
Accession Number: AR 7043.

241 HERBERT SEELIGER
1936–1959   4.5 inches

Born in Neumark, West Prussia (now Poland), on March 15, 1903, Herbert Seeliger was a lawyer, administrator, and general secretary of the Jewish Community of Berlin, 1936–1940. He emigrated to the United States via Shanghai in 1940, and died in New York City on July 4, 1964.

Personal papers, including manuscripts and clippings on the communal affairs and history of the Jewish community of Berlin; reports about the activities of the community, including the conduct of religious services, 1937–1941, and on the situation of Jews in Berlin, October 1945.

Photos of synagogues and other communal buildings in Berlin, and of leaders of the Jewish community.

Languages: German, English.
Donor: Mrs. Herbert Seeliger, 1965.
Finding Aid: 5-page inventory.
Accession Number: AR 3957.

242 RUDOLPH SEIDEN
1845–1958   10 inches

Born in Langenwang, Austria, on August 13, 1900, Rudolph Seiden was a chemist and Zionist activist. He emigrated to the United States in 1935 and died in Kansas City, Missouri, on June 12, 1965.

Personal and editorial correspondence by contributors to Seiden's three pamphlets: *Von und über Juden*, *Pro Zion*, and *Nichtjuden über den Kulturwert des Judentums*, including letters from Paul Amann, Friedrich Austerlitz, Otto Bauer, Siegfried Bernfeld, Franz Blei, Max Brod, Martin Buber, Eduard David, Hans Delbrück, Heinrich Friedjung, Moritz Heimann, Kurt Hiller, Karl Kautsky, Hans Kohn, Arthur Landsberger, E. M. Lilien, Erich Mühsam, Arno Nadel, Alfred Nossig, Franz Oppenheimer, Oswald Redlich, Hugo Salus, Philipp Scheidemann, Arthur Schnitzler, Hermann Stehr, Werner Sombart, Ferdinand Tönnies, Bruno Walter, Otto Warburg, and Max Weber.

Letters and postcards between third parties from Rudolf Seiden's autograph collection: Berthold Auerbach, Maximilian Harden, Eduard Hanslick, Arthur Holitscher, Gustav Karpeles, Moritz Lazarus, Ludwig Wihl, and Carl Zuckmayer. Unpublished manuscripts and accompanying correspondence on anti- and philosemitism by contributors including Max Brod, Lujo Brentano, Asis Domet, Karl Henckell, Kurt Hiller, Walter von Molo, Arno Nadel, Hugo Salus, and Ferdinand Tönnies.

Seiden's correspondence, manuscripts, and newspaper stories about Jewish resettlement in Alaska in the 1930s; clippings of his articles about Palestine and the Jewish Question; and his writings on chemistry.

Minutes and circulars of the sports group Hakoah, Vienna, and Austrian Zionist organizations, 1930s.

Manuscripts collected by Seiden's clearinghouse, Foreign Authors Syndicate, Kansas City, Missouri, 1938–1940.

Languages: German, Italian, English.
Donor: Rudolph Seiden, 1958.
Finding Aids: 25-page inventory, 9 catalogue cards.
Accession Number: AR 406.

243 RUDOLF JAKOB SIMONIS
1749–1965   12 feet

Born in Berlin on September 13, 1893, the genealogist Rudolf Simonis emigrated to Sweden in 1937 and died in Stockholm on December 17, 1965.

Material on the Simonis family, including an album containing vital documents, military service and citizenship papers, prayerbooks, and commemorative publications; photos of family members; family history and correspondence on genealogy and other topics.

Correspondence includes letters from Leo Baeck, Alfred Ballin, Hugo Bergmann, Berliner Zionistische Vereinigung, Arthur Czellitzer, Heinrich von Friedberg, Jacob Javits (about Heinrich Eduard Jacob), Reichsbund jüdischer Frontsoldaten, Berlin, and Emperor Wilhelm II.

Genealogical notes for four hundred Jewish families from Sweden, Berlin, and northern Germany, covering the period from the sixteenth through the twentieth century.

Manuscripts and clippings; special issues of newspapers, including memorial numbers for personalities and anniversary issues for German-Jewish organizations; research notes on famous Jewish individuals, Zionism, the Jewish Question, and Jewish communities in Germany and elsewhere, including copies of pre-emancipation lists of tolerated Jews.

Languages: German, Swedish, Judeo-German.
Donor: Brigit Simonis, 1976.
Finding Aid: 9-page inventory.
Accession Number: AR 7019.

244 KURT SINGER
1855–1953   3.5 inches

Born in Berent (now Koscierzyna, Poland) on October 11, 1885, Kurt Singer was a physician, conductor and musicologist, as well as music critic for the socialist newspaper *Vorwärts*. From 1935 to 1938, he served as director of the Jüdischer Kulturbund. He emigrated to Holland in 1939, and was deported to Theresienstadt in 1942. He died there in 1944.

Correspondence, including letters from Max Friedländer, Wilhelm Furtwängler, and Siegfried Ochs, some of it dealing with Singer's book on the choral music of Anton Bruckner.

Manuscripts of articles and speeches by and about Singer and his activities in the Jüdischer Kulturbund; reviews of Singer's writings.

Papers of Singer's father, the Hungarian-born Moritz Singer, who served as rabbi in Koblenz, including letters from Helmuth von Moltke and Duke Friedrich I of Baden; educational documents from his studies at the Universities of Berlin and Jena, including a dissertation, as well as academic reports signed by Moritz Lazarus, Heymann Steinthal, and Theodor Mommsen; personal documents; and material on the community of Koblenz.

Languages: German, Hebrew, Hungarian, Latin.
Donors: M. Nitke, 1964; B. Gellen, 1964.
Finding Aid: 7-page inventory.
Accession Number: AR 3100.

245 HEINRICH STAHL
1926–1941   c. 2 feet

Born in Berlin on April 13, 1868, Heinrich Stahl was an insurance executive active in Jewish communal affairs, and chairman of the Jewish community of Berlin, 1933–1942. In 1942, he was deported to Theresienstadt, where he died on November 11 of that year.

Business correspondence and correspondence of Stahl in his official capacity as chairman of the Jewish community of Berlin, 1939–1940, including a report on a trip to London, Belgium, and Paris in 1939 to survey the condition of Jewish refugees, and a report on emigration, 1940.

Photo albums of Jewish orphanages, old-age homes, and vocational retraining schools in Berlin, Weissensee, and Landsberg an der Warthe, the sports groups of the Reichsbund jüdischer Frontsoldaten, and the activities of Jüdische Winterhilfe, Berlin.

Language: German.
Donors: Sophie Stahl, Ted Heubner, and Gaby Lessing via James Fotes, 1980.

Finding Aid: 3-page inventory.
Accession Number: AR 7171.

246 LEOPOLD STEIN
   1802–1910   2.5 inches

Born in Burgpreppach on November 5, 1810, Leopold Stein was a teacher, publicist, and rabbi who was also known as a poet and dramatist. He served in Burgkundstadt and became rabbi of Frankfurt am Main in 1844. A prominent advocate of Reform Judaism, he resigned his position due to a conflict with the leadership of the community in 1862. He died in Frankfurt on December 2, 1882.

Correspondence with individuals, including Albert Cohn, Isaac Adolphe Crémieux, David Einhorn, Abraham Geiger, James de Rothschild, and Salomon Ludwig Steinheim.

Essays, poetry, and a diary from 1830 by Stein; pictures and photos of him; articles about Stein and his work.

Correspondence of Stein's teacher, Aron Wolfssohn (1754–1835), including a letter appointing him principal of the Jewish school in Breslau, and letters from Emmanuel Osmund and from Amalia, Jakob Herz, and Michael Beer, the parents and brother of Giacomo Meyerbeer, and dealing in part with his education.

Languages: German, Hebrew, Judeo-German.
Donor: Bettina Machol-Stein, 1968.
Finding Aid: 8-page inventory.
Accession Number: AR 3263.

247 NATHAN STEIN
   1865–1959   3 inches

Born in Neckarsulm on November 11, 1857, Nathan Stein was a jurist, and president of the Mannheim District Court, 1914–1922, the first Jew in Germany to be appointed to such a position. He died in Mannheim on May 8, 1927.

Correspondence of Stein, including a letter from Hjalmar Schacht congratulating him on his retirement.

Documents about Stein's education, career awards, and honors; clippings and obituaries about Stein.

Language: German.
Donor: Nathan Stein, 1959.
Finding Aid: 8 catalogue cards.
Accession Number: AR 529.

248 S. THEODOR STEIN
1865–1965   2.5 inches

Born in Burgkundstadt on April 2, 1840, S. Theodor Stein studied physics and medicine at various European universities, receiving doctorates in 1862 and 1864. Besides his medical practice, he engaged in extensive research on the application of physics to medicine. He died in Frankfurt am Main on September 27, 1891.

Certificates of honor, titles, clippings, and offprints by and about Stein; letters from prominent individuals, including the German Emperor Wilhelm I, the German Crown Prince Friedrich Wilhelm, and Helmuth von Moltke.

Languages: German, English, French, Spanish, Hungarian.
Donor: Bettina Machol-Stein, 1968.
Finding Aid: 5-page inventory.
Accession Number: AR 3262.

249 STEINER FAMILY, LAUPHEIM
1828–1935   2 feet

Simon H. Steiner, born c. 1826, was the founder of the hops trading firm of the same name in Laupheim near Ulm. The wife of Simon H. Steiner was Emilie, née Einstein. They had four sons, two of whom, Louis and Samuel, went into the business of their father. Samuel continued the business in New York. Louis married Hedwig Reinemann, who had been born in Chicago in 1868. Engagement contracts, vital, educational, and business documents, and military service and citizenship papers of members of the Steiner family; papers of members of the Reinemann family who had settled in Chicago in the nineteenth century; photos of family members.

Letters written to Hedwig and Louis Steiner by their sons Heinrich and Julius from the front during World War I.

Languages: German, Hebrew, Judeo-German, English, French.
Donor: H. Simon, for the estate of Julius Steiner, 1979.
Finding Aid: 7-page inventory.
Accession Number: AR 4713.

250 HUGO STEINER-PRAG
1900–1955   10 inches

Born in Prague on December 12, 1880, Hugo Steiner-Prag was one of the leading graphic artists of his time. He moved to Germany in 1901 and served as professor at the Academy of Graphic Arts and the Printing Trade in Leipzig from 1907 until his dismissal in 1933, when he emigrated to Czechoslovakia. He emigrated to Sweden in 1938, and to the United States via the USSR and Japan in 1941, and died in New York City on September 10, 1945.

Notes and outlines for courses and lectures; unfinished memoirs, manuscripts on literary topics, and clippings of articles written by Steiner-Prag; and diaries of a trip to Spain, 1925, and of emigration, 1941, and a memoir of his youth in Prague.

Clippings about Steiner-Prag's work, programs, exhibition catalogues, honors and awards.

Photos about Steiner-Prag, of Prague, its Jewish quarter and cemetery, and of Hasidic rabbis; photo negatives of Steiner-Prag's work.

The art collection of the Leo Baeck Institute contains numerous works by Steiner-Prag, including the printing blocks for a decorated Machzor.

Languages: German, English, Czech, Swedish
Donor: Eleanor Steiner-Prag, 1962.
Finding Aid: 10-page inventory.
Accession Number: AR 1723.

251 HUGO STEINTHAL
1922–1967   7 inches

Born in Saarbrücken on July 27, 1893, Hugo Steinthal received his doctorate at the University of Breslau in 1921. He was rabbi in Saarbrücken until his emigration to France in 1935. After the World War II, he returned to Germany and died in Saarbrükken in 1961.

Manuscripts and research notes for a history of the Saarland and Lorraine and their Jewish communities from the earliest times until 1935; Steinthal's doctoral dissertation on the status of Jews in the Merovingian and Carolingian empires.

Languages: German, French.
Donor: Pierre Steinthal, 1967.
Finding Aid: 3 catalogue cards.
Accession Number: AR 4056.

252 LUIS STERN
1940–1970   2 inches

Born Ludwig Stern in Mannheim c. 1890, Luis Stern emigrated to Spain in the early 1930s and was living in Barcelona in 1975.

Correspondence, clippings, manuscripts concerning Stern's efforts to assist Jewish refugees interned in France and in the Miranda de Ebro internment camp in Spain, including letters from camp inmates.

Languages: German, French, Spanish, English.
Donor: Luis Stern, 1969, 1970.

Finding Aid: 8 catalogue cards.
Accession Number: AR 3728.

253 SELMA STERN-TAEUBLER
1713–1960   2.5 feet

Born in Kippenheim bei Lahr on July 24, 1890, Selma Stern studied history, receiving her doctorate at the University of Munich. She married the historian Eugen Taeubler, and published historical works including a study of the Jews and the Prussian state in the eighteenth century. In 1941 she emigrated to the United States, where she was the archivist at the American Jewish Archives in Cincinnati Ohio. In 1960 she retired to Switzerland, and died in Basel, Switzerland on August 17, 1981.

Manuscripts and research notes on Jews in eighteenth century Prussia, including material on Schutzjuden, government deliberations, and decrees and transcripts of other original documents; statistical tables concerning the Jews of Berlin, Halberstadt, Halle an der Saale, Kleve-Mark, Magdeburg, Mark Brandenburg, Minden, Moers, Pomerania, Potsdam, Ravensburg, Lower Silesia, and Tecklenburg.

Diaries of Selma Stern-Taeubler, from c. 1900–1946; memoir and poetry manuscripts.

Language: German.
Donor: Selma Stern-Taeubler.
Finding Aid: 2-page inventory, 1979.
Accession Number: AR 7160.

254 HANS STERNHEIM
1870–1977   2 feet

Born in Heidelberg on November 22, 1900, the author Hans Sternheim emigrated to the United States in 1939 and lived in Sommerville, New Jersey, and died in Racine, Wisconsin, c. 1985.

Correspondence and other material by Sternheim and others relating to Jewish life under the Nazis, and to Sternheim's emigration and life as a refugee.

Manuscripts, photos, and correspondence about the Jewish communities of Viernheim and Bensheim, including material about the deportation of the men of the Bensheim community after Kristallnacht.

Genealogy of the Sternheim family, with supporting documents.

Memoirs by Sternheim dealing with lives of his parents Rudolf and Helene, are catalogued separately as part of the memoir collection.

Languages: German, English.
Donor: Hans Sternheim, 1965.

Finding Aid: 80-page inventory.
Accession Number: AR 2988.

255 TONI STOLPER AND GUSTAV STOLPER
1875–1982   8 feet

Born Antonie Kassowitz in Vienna on November 22, 1890, Toni Stolper was an economist and journalist. She married Gustav Stolper in 1921, and moved with him to Germany in 1925. After their emigration to the United States in 1933, she was a founder of Selfhelp for German Refugees, and was active in the American Council for Emigrés from the Professions. She moved to Canada in 1975, and returned to the United States in 1983. She died October 18, 1988.

Born in Vienna on July 25, 1888, Gustav Stolper was an economist, politician, journalist and editor. After his emigration to Germany, he became editor of *Der Deutsche Volkswirt* and was a leader of the Deutsche Demokratische Partei (DDP). After his emigration to the United States, he worked as an economic consultant for business and government. Shortly before his death, he served as a member of the Hoover Commission on Germany. He died in New York City on December 27, 1947.

Correspondence of Toni and Gustav Stolper with family members and other individuals, including Willy Brandt, Julius Braunthal, Julie Braun-Vogelstein, Heinrich Brüning, Gerd Bucerius, Margaret Chapman (Storm Jameson), Fritz Demuth, Allen Dulles, Ernst Hamburger, Hildegard Hamm-Brücher, Paul Hertz, Theodor Heuss and members of the Heuss family, Herbert Hoover, Carl Landauer, Lilo Linke, Oscar Meyer, Robert Moses, Martin Niemöller, Ilona Polanyi, Hans Schäffer, Else Staudinger, Hans Staudinger, Adlai Stevenson, Dorothy Thompson, Paul Tillich, Ernst Toch, and Gottfried Reinhard Treviranus.

Manuscripts and clippings by Toni Stolper on economics, contemporary Germany, and international affairs, and journalistic manuscripts with related correspondence; diaries of Toni and Gustav Stolper, and of other family members.

Clippings about the Stolpers and reviews of their works; pamphlets and clippings by and about Theodor Heuss.

Genealogy of the Kassowitz family.

Photos of the Stolpers, family members, friends and associates, including Heuss, his paintings, and his family.

Languages: German, English.
Donor: Toni Stolper, 1983.
Finding Aids: 6-page inventory; 16-page name-index to correspondence.
Accession Number: AR 7212.

256 HUGO STRANSKY
1855–1970   3 inches

Born in Prague on May 4, 1905, Hugo Stransky was a rabbi in Nachod and Zilina, Czechoslovakia, until his emigration to Great Britain in 1939. He moved to Australia in 1945, to New Zealand in 1952, and to the United States in 1955. He was an active member of Mizrachi, and he served as rabbi of Beth Hillel, a refugee congregation in New York City's Washington Heights. He emigrated to Israel in 1976, and died in Kefar Saba on March 31, 1983.

Letters from Bernhard Kolb concerning religious life in Theresienstadt.

Clippings and manuscripts on Jews in Germany and the Netherlands, Nazism, war crimes, antisemitism, and sermons by Stransky and others; copies of material from the Maurice Frankenhuis collection.

Reports, statutes, minutes of Jewish Veterans Association, and about Jewish military chaplains.

Prayerbooks from the nineteenth century, including one for emigrants to America, printed in Fürth, 1855.

Languages: German, Dutch, Hebrew.
Donor: Hugo Stransky, 1976.
Finding Aid: 4 catalogue cards.
Accession Number: AR 7039.

257 RAPHAEL STRAUS
1915–1946   2.5 feet

Born in Karlsruhe on February 25, 1887, the historian Raphael Straus emigrated to Palestine in 1933, and to the United States in 1945, and died in New York City on May 3, 1947.

Correspondence, manuscripts, and research notes on Jewish history, including histories of the Jews of Augsburg, Munich, Pappenheim, and Regensburg, Zionism, and Jews in Palestine and North Africa; biographies of Moses Montefiore and the Baal Shem of Michelstadt.

Languages: German, English, Hebrew.
Donor: Erna Strauss, 1958.
Finding Aid: 3-page inventory.
Accession Number: AR 628.

258 EDUARD STRAUSS
1896–1952   4 feet

Born in Kreuznach on February 18, 1876, Eduard Strauss was a chemist and philosopher. After receiving his doctorate in chemistry at the University of Berlin in 1899, he worked as a nutritional chemist in various clinics in Frankfurt am Main. He taught at the Freies Jüdisches Lehrhaus from 1920 to 1933. He emigrated to the United States via Italy and Cuba in 1938 and died in New York City on August 23, 1952.

Correspondence of Strauss with individuals, including Martin Buber, Nahum Glatzer, Richard Koch, and Franz Rosenzweig.

Offprints, clippings, manuscripts, essays, and book reviews by Strauss on Judaism, Christianity, history, philosophy, politics, the philosopher Franz Rosenzweig, and B'nai B'rith; lectures from and essays about the Freies Jüdisches Lehrhaus, Frankfurt; and a diary for the years 1937–1939.

A drawing of Martin Buber by Gertrud Metzger and a poem by Jacob Picard.

Languages: German, English.
Donor: C. Trier, 1971.
Finding Aid: 18-page inventory.
Accession Number: AR 7192.

259 WILLIAM STRAUSS
1856–1971   1 foot

Born in Hanover on January 10, 1904, William Strauss was a banker and economist who emigrated to the United States in 1939 and died in Palo Alto, California, on August 2, 1971.

Correspondence with individuals, including Hans Pinkus and Hanns Reissner.

Manuscripts, research notes, and clippings on banking and on the economic history of German Jews.

History of the Strauss family and related families with supporting documents.

Artifacts collected by Strauss, including kabbalistic amulets.

Languages: German, English, Hebrew.
Donor: Anna Strauss, 1972.
Finding Aid: 20-page inventory.
Accession Number: AR 7178.

260 MARGARETE SUSMAN
1903–1972   4 inches

Born in Hamburg on October 14, 1872, the author and philosopher Margarete Susman emigrated to Switzerland in 1933 and died on January 16, 1966. Her married name was Margarete von Bendemann.

Correspondence with individuals, including Gertrude Kantorowicz, Ignaz Jastrow, Franz Rosenzweig, Georg Simmel, and Karl Wolfskehl.

Memoirs, photos, and clippings by and about Susman.

Languages: German, English.
Donors: Various donors, 1959–1972.
Finding Aid: 15 catalogue cards.
Accession Numbers: AR 9019, AR 1166, AR 1398, AR 2066, AR 3022.

261 ARNOLD TÄNZER
1845–1971   5 inches

Born in Pressburg, Austria-Hungary (now Bratislava, Czechoslovakia) on January 30, 1871, Arnold (also known as Aron) Tänzer received his doctorate at the University of Berlin. He served as rabbi in Hohenems and Meran, Austria, and in Göppingen, where he died on March 19, 1937.

Manuscripts and clippings by Tänzer and David Baumgardt, obituary, and photos of him as a field chaplain during World War I with members of Jüdische Volksküche, Biala.

Typescripts of correspondence of Moritz Lazarus with individuals, including: Berthold Auerbach, Georg Brandes, and Heymann Steinthal.

A genealogy of the Einstein family prepared by Tänzer.

A memoir by Tänzer, dealing largely with experiences during World War I, is catalogued separately in the memoir collection.

Languages: German, Hebrew.
Donor: Fritz Taenzer, 1958, 1963.
Finding Aid: 12 catalogue cards.
Accession Numbers: AR 485, AR 3682.

262 HEINRICH TOCZEK
1825–1973   2.5 inches

Born in Frankfurt an der Oder on March 9, 1898, Heinrich Toczek received his doctorate at the University of Berlin in 1923, and practiced as a physician until his emigration to the United States in 1938. He lived in New York City and died on April 26, 1977.

Vital documents, photos, and educational, military, and professional papers of Heinrich Toczek and family members; correspondence with friends and family members; correspondence and other documents concerning Toczek's dismissal from his position on racial grounds in 1933, and his reinstatement because he was a veteran of World War I.

Genealogy of the Toczek family.

Languages: German, English.
Donor: Peter Toczek, 1979.
Finding Aid: 9-page inventory.
Accession Number: AR 4763.

263 NORBERT TROLLER
1900–1982   7 feet

Born in Brünn, Austria-Hungary (now Brno, Czechoslovakia) in 1900, Norbert Troller served as a soldier in World War I, spending time as a prisoner-of-war in Italy. After the war he studied architecture in Brno and Vienna and worked as an architect in Brno until the German occupation of Czechoslovakia. He was deported to Theresienstadt in 1942, where he worked as an architect for the Jewish self-adminstration of the camp, and produced works of art as well. In 1944 he was imprisoned by the Gestapo, and was sent to Auschwitz later that year. After liberation, he lived briefly in Cracow, and then reopened his architectural business in Prague and Brno. He emigrated to the United States in 1948 and worked for the National Jewish Welfare Board in New York designing Jewish community centers, before opening his own practice. He died in 1984.

Extensive autobiographical manuscript by Troller, with illustrations and other supporting material, discussing his family and community, his early life, and his experiences during and after the Holocaust.

Material relating to Troller's career as an architect, including educational documents, professional papers, clippings, and blueprints.

Extensive photograph collection documenting Troller's life and work in Czechoslovakia and the United States, including photos of buildings designed by him in both countries; photocopies of artwork by Troller, many from his time at Theresienstadt, including items from the Leo Baeck Institute's art collection.

Material relating to an exhibit of Troller's work at the Yeshiva University Museum in 1982.

The art collection of the LBI also has an extensive collection of artwork of Troller's from his time in Theresienstadt.

Languages: German, English, Czech.
Donor: Doris Rauch, 1985.
Finding Aid: 6-page preliminary inventory.
Accession Number: AR 7268.

264 VIKTOR ULLMANN
1943–1977   1 inch

Born in 1898, Viktor Ullmann studied music with Arnold Schoenberg in Vienna in the 1920s and following that taught and conducted in Prague. He composed operas and other musical works before World War II, and continued to compose after his deportation to Theresienstadt. He composed the music for *Der Kaiser von Atlantis* in 1944, and in the same year he was deported to Auschwitz, where he was murdered.

Photocopies of fragments of the score of *Der Kaiser von Atlantis*, and of a score for piano adapted by Kerry Woodard; the complete libretto, which was written by the poet Peter Kien (1919–1944).

Correspondence, programs, clippings, and reviews of performances of the opera from the 1970s, including one sponsored by the Leo Baeck Institute at the Brooklyn Academy of Music.

Languages: German, English, Dutch.
Donors: Various, assembled by LBI New York and LBI London, 1977.
Finding Aid: 6 catalogue cards.
Accession Number: AR 4403.

265 JOHANNES URZIDIL AND GERTRUDE THIEBERGER URZIDIL
1753–1977   17 feet

Born in Prague on February 3, 1896, the writer and poet Johannes Urzidil emigrated to the United States in 1939 and died in Rome on November 2, 1970. Born Gertrude Thieberger in Goltsch-Jenikau, Austria-Hungary (now Golčuv Jenikov, Czechoslovakia), on July 20, 1898, the writer and poet Gertrude Urzidil emigrated with her husband to the United States in 1939 and died in New York City on June 12, 1977.

Correspondence of Johannes and Gertrude Urzidil with individuals, including Julius Bab, Eduard Beneš, Hugo Bergmann, Petr Bezruč, Ilse Blumenthal-Weiss, Heinrich

Böll, Hermann Broch, Max Brod, S. D. Cramer, Kasimir Edschmid, Margot Einstein, Willy Haas, Ludwig Hardt, Hermann Hesse, Erich von Kahler, Mascha Kaleko, Hermann Kesten, Noa Kiepenheuer, Otto Klemperer, Walter Koch, Hans Kohn, Max Kreutzberger, Thomas Mann, Walter Mehring, Jacob Picard, Kurt Pinthus, Anna Seghers, William Shirer, Peter Stadelmayer, Georg Szell, Friedrich Thieberger, Dorothy Thompson, Fritz von Unruh, Felix Weltsch, Robert Weltsch, Alma Werfel, Franz Werfel, and Carl Zuckmayer.

Manuscripts, clippings, transcripts, offprints of fiction and nonfiction works of the Urzidils; diaries, honors and awards, and obituaries.

Clippings about Johannes Urzidil, Franz Kafka, and other literary topics.

Photo albums with pictures of the Urzidils' and of family and friends, including Max Brod, Albert Einstein, Hermann Hesse, Franz Kafka, Dorothy Thompson, and Franz Werfel.

Papers of the Urzidil and Thieberger families, including vital, educational, and professional documents, beginning in the eighteenth century, and including the document releasing one of Urzidil's ancestors from serfdom.

A memoir by Gertrude Urzidil is catalogued separately in the memoir collection.

Languages: German, Czech, English, Latin.
Donors: Estate of Johannes Urzidil and Gertrude Thieberger Urzidil, 1977.
Finding Aid: 14-page inventory.
Accession Number: AR 7110.

266 VALENTIN FAMILY
    1677–1970   1.5 feet

The Valentins were a Berlin family whose ancestors settled there in the seventeenth century.

Vital documents, letters of protection and municipal citizenship, autograph albums, wills and testaments, marriage contracts, memoirs, obituaries, and clippings concerning members of the Valentin family, the family business, the freight-movers Jacob & Valentin, and related families, including the Abraham, Behrend, Löwen, and Mannheimer families; noteworthy documents include memoirs of the banker Samuel Liepmann Löwen, 1824, and records of the Prussian minter and medalist Jacob Abraham, 1753, as well as photocopies of records of his son, the minter Abraham Abramson.

Family histories, family trees, and correspondence with individuals about genealogy, including Bernhard Brilling and Jacob Jacobson.

Photos of family members, their home, and their business.

Languages: German, Hebrew.
Donor: Martha Valentin, 1970.

Finding Aid: 17-page inventory.
Accession Number: AR 3818.

267 GERTRUDE VAN TIJN
1934–1973   3 inches

Born in Braunschweig on July 4, 1891, Gertrude van Tijn was a social worker who lived in the Netherlands after 1915. She was a member of the Joodsche Raad, Amsterdam, during World War II, but in 1943 she was deported to Westerbork concentration camp, and then to Bergen-Belsen. In 1944 she was sent to Palestine as part of an exchange for German civil internees, and following the war she served as a social worker for the JDC in Shanghai. In 1948 she came to the United States and lives in Portland, Oregon.

Vital and professional documents, and clippings about van Tijn's career; correspondence with organizations, and with individuals, including Norman Bentwich.

Material on the Werkdorp Wieringen, an agricultural training camp for German-Jewish refugees in Holland, including correspondence, photos, circulars, and reports.

Reports by van Tijn on the occupied Netherlands, on concentration camps, and on the situation of Jewish refugees in Shanghai.

Van Tijn's memoirs are catalogued separately in the memoir collection.

Languages: Dutch, English, German, Hebrew.
Donor: Gertrude van Tijn.
Finding Aid: 16 catalogue cards.
Accession Number: AR 3477.

268 RAHEL VARNHAGEN VON ENSE
1793–1974   2.5 inches

Born in Berlin on May 26, 1771, Rahel Levin was an author and salon hostess. She married Karl August Varnhagen von Ense in 1814 and died in Berlin on March 7, 1833.

Transcripts of excerpts of Varnhagen's correspondence with: Wilhelm Bokelmann, Gustav Brinkmann, Rebecca Friedländer, Frederike Robert, and Ludwig Robert.

Copy of *Rahel: Ein Buch des Andenkens für ihre Freunde*, edited by Karl August Varnhagen von Ense, 1834, with handwritten annotations by Hannah Arendt.

Articles on Varnhagen.

Languages: German, English.
Donor: F. H. Eisner, 1965.
Finding Aid: 15 catalogue cards.
Accession Number: AR 2923.

269 VEIT-SIMON FAMILY
   1784–1913   2.5 inches

The Veits and the Simons were families of prominent Jewish businessmen and booksellers in eighteenth- and nineteenth- century Berlin.

Papers of the Veit and Simon families, including: passports, letters of protection, contracts, testaments, and a real-estate deed signed by Moses Mendelssohn, father-in-law of Simon Veit.

Personal and business correspondence of family members with individuals and institutions, including Moses Mendelssohn, Meyer Amschel Rothschild, Karl von Savigny, Dorothea Schlegel, Moritz Veit, Philipp Veit, and the Jewish community of Berlin.

Languages: German, Hebrew.
Donor: Etta Japha, 1973.
Finding Aid: 10-page inventory.
Accession Numbers: AR 9020, AR 2543, AR 4015.

270 VIERFELDER FAMILY
   1694–1956   2.5 feet

The Vierfelders were a family of merchants, and rabbis in Buchau, Württemberg.

Illustrated history and genealogy of the Vierfelder family of Buchau, Württemberg, along with articles and manuscripts about the town, its Jewish community, and its synagogues; material on former residents of Buchau who served in the allied armies during World War II, including reports on conditions there after the war; photos of family members and of the synagogues and other buildings of the communities of Buchau and Kappel; Jewish ritual objects and books containing handwritten notes.

Languages: German, Hebrew.
Donor: Morris Vierfelder, 1959.
Finding Aid: 5-page inventory.
Accession Number: AR 890.

271 WASSERMANN FAMILY
   1860–1948   5 inches

Members of the Wassermann family were bankers in Bamberg before emigrating to the United States.

Family history and genealogies, vital certificates, obituaries, military service papers, photos and photo albums of family members, their house, and their bank; a family history by David Wassermann is catalogued separately in the memoir collection.

Program for the twenty-fifth anniversary of the dedication of the Bamberg synagogue.

Languages: German, English.
Donor: M. Wassermann, 1958, 1969.
Finding Aid: 7 catalogue cards.
Accession Number: AR 269.

272 BRUNO WEIL
   1854–1965   8.5 feet

Born in Saarlouis on April 4, 1883, Bruno Weil received his doctorate in law at the University of Würzburg in 1906, and was a lawyer in Strasbourg, 1910–1914, and Berlin, 1920–1935. He was executive secretary of the Centralverein deutscher Staatsbürger jüdischen Glaubens and active in the Deutsche Demokratische Partei (DDP). In 1935 he emigrated to Argentina, and he lived in France, 1939–1940, before emigrating to the United States. In America, he was a founder of the Axis Victims League and the American Association of Former European Jurists. Weil died in New York City on November 11, 1961.

Correspondence on various topics, including Weil's libel suit against Henry Torres in 1942, his restitution case, and the organization of victims of Nazi persecution. Correspondents include Konrad Adenauer, Frederick Aron, Philipp Auerbach, Manfred George, Alfred Hirschberg, Joseph Klibansky, Alexandre Millerand, Henry Morgenthau, Fritz Moses, Joseph Panholzer, Kurt Rosenfeld, Paul Tager, and Julius Weigert.

Diaries (with photos) of World War I experiences, internment in La Vernet camp, 1940, and a trip to Germany in 1948.

Clippings of articles by and about Weil, and on politics in Alsace and Lorraine before and after the World War I, Jews in Weimar and Nazi Germany and in emigration, antisemitism, and restitution.

Manuscripts of books by Weil, and of articles, essays, and speeches about the Dreyfus Affair, Jews in Germany, and other topics.

Material on the Kartell-Convent deutscher Studenten jüdischen Glaubens, including meeting minutes, correspondence, circulars, and clippings.

History and genealogy of the Weil family.

Languages: German, French, English, Spanish.
Donor: Gerda Flaum, 1968.
Finding Aid: 10-page inventory.
Accession Number: AR 7108.

273 ROBERT WELTSCH
1883–1981   13 feet

Born in Prague on June 20, 1891, Robert Weltsch was active as a student in Zionist youth groups. After World War I he moved to Berlin, where he edited the German Zionist newspaper *Jüdische Rundschau* from 1919 to 1938. In 1939 he emigrated to Palestine where he edited the *Jüdische Welt-Rundschau*, 1939–1940. In 1945, Weltsch moved to London, where he was correspondent of the daily *Ha-aretz*, one of the founders of the Leo Baeck Institute, and editor of its Yearbook, 1956–1971. He returned to Israel in 1978 and died in Jerusalem on December 22, 1982.

Correspondence with family members, including letters from the front in World War I and from later years, and with other individuals, including: Solomon Adler-Rudel, Alexander Altmann, Hannah Arendt, Chaim Arlosoroff, Leo Baeck, David Baumgardt, Hugo Bergmann, Isaiah Berlin, Siegfried Bernfeld, Kurt Blumenfeld, Ilse Blumenthal-Weiss, Julie Braun-Vogelstein, Hermann Broch, Max Brod, Martin Buber, Albert Einstein, Amos Elon, Joseph Cardinal Frings, Manfred George, Nahum Glatzer, Nahum Goldmann, Georg Halpern, Ernst Hamburger, Hugo Hermann, Erich von Kahler, Siegmund Kaznelson, Hans Kohn, Max Kreutzberger, Gustav Krojanker, Georg Landauer, Gustav Landauer, Miriam Beer-Hofmann Lens, Hans Liebeschütz, Gerda Luft, Judah Magnes, Heinrich Margulies, Siegried Moses, Koppel Pinson, Joachim Prinz, Eva Reichmann, Felix Rosenblüth (later Pinchas Rosen), Gustav Schocken, Salman Schocken, Gershom Scholem, Werner David Senator, Ernst Simon, Christoph Stölzl, Hans Tramer, Johannes Urzidil, Max Warburg, Chaim Weizmann, Felix Weltsch, and Arnold Zweig.

Correspondence of Weltsch as editor of *Jüdische Rundschau* and *Jüdische Welt-Rundschau*; correspondence on Zionist affairs, in particular on the 1929 Arab uprising in Palestine and its repercussions.

Personal papers of Robert Weltsch and other family members, including his diaries and notebooks from various periods, and of his father, Theodor Weltsch, from the 1870s; manuscripts and other material on Jewish life in Prague.

Speeches, reports, essays, and journalistic dispatches by Weltsch on Zionism, Jewish-Arab and Jewish-German relations, displaced persons in post-World War II Europe, the Nuremberg war crimes trials, and the founding of the State of Israel; clippings of articles by Weltsch.

Clippings and manuscripts by others on Zionism and Jewish affairs, including a report by Hans Kohn on Zionist activities among former POWs in Siberia in 1919, and a 1915 speech by Moshe Smilansky.

Records of the Komitee für den Osten concerning the situation of East European Jewry at the end of World War I, including memoranda by Max Bodenheimer and Franz Oppenheimer; records of the Verband Jüdischer Studentenvereine in Deutschland from the 1920s and of the Jewish student fraternity Bar Kochba, Prague, including reports, minutes, membership lists and correspondence of its Israeli alumni association;

correspondence and minutes of Brith Shalom, an organization which favored Arab-Jewish cooperation and a bi-national state, and Ha-Poel Ha-Zair, a Zionist labor party; correspondence of the Zionistische Vereinigung für Deutschland and of Aliyah Hadasha, a German-Jewish party in the Yishuv.

Papers of Solomon Adler-Rudel, including records of the Arbeiterfürsorgeamt der jüdischen Organisationen Deutschlands and of Poalei Zion, relating to East European Jewish workers in Germany, their working and living conditions and political activities; correspondence and other material on the Evian Conference and on emigration from Nazi Germany in the 1930s and from German-occupied Europe during World War II, including reports of the Movement for the Care of Children from Germany; research notes and manuscripts by Adler Rudel for his biography of Baron Maurice de Hirsch.

Languages: German (including many items in Gabelsberger shorthand), Hebrew, Czech, English, Yiddish.
Donor: Robert Weltsch, 1965–1982.
Finding Aids: 8-page inventory, 8-page name-index to the post–1945 correspondence.
Accession Number: AR 7185.

274 ALFRED WERNER
c. 1938–1979   7.5 feet

Born in Vienna on March 30, 1911, the art critic and journalist Alfred Werner emigrated to the United States in 1940 and died in New York City in 1979.

Clippings and offprints of articles by Werner on various topics, including refugees, American responses to the Holocaust, Judaism, German Jews, Jewish artists and art; manuscript essays on artists; correspondence with publishers.

Photos of artworks, and of Jewish life in Austria, Czechoslovakia, France, Israel, and Italy.

Languages: German, English, Spanish.
Donors: Dr. and Mrs. Alfred Werner, 1979.
Finding Aid: 100-page inventory, with indices.
Accession Number: AR 7158.

275 WILLY WERTHEIMER
1900–1974   6 inches

Born in Hardheim on March 26, 1897, Willy Wertheimer emigrated to the United States c. 1939 and lives in New York City.

Personal correspondence, including a letter from Albert Schweitzer; several memoirs by Wertheimer which are catalogued separately in the memoir collection.

Manuscripts, photos, press clippings, and memorabilia on Jewish soldiers in the World War I, Nazi Germany, genealogy, and Israel.

Languages: German, English.
Donor: Willy Wertheimer, 1957–1980.
Finding Aid: 66 catalogue cards.
Accession Number: AR 798.

276 WIENER LIBRARY ARCHIVES
1880–1967   260 microfilm reels

The Wiener Library was founded in Amsterdam in 1934 by David Cohen and Alfred Wiener as the Jewish Central Information Office, to assemble and transmit information on National Socialism to Jewish leaders and organizations. In 1939, the seat of the institute was transferred to London, where it continued its efforts during World War II, providing, in particular, valuable documentation of war crimes. After the death of Alfred Wiener in 1964, Walter Laqueur became director of the Wiener Library.

The Press Archives of the Wiener Library, consisting of clippings from newspapers, pamphlets, posters, fliers, and other public documents, primarily from Germany and Great Britain but also from countries in Europe, the Arab World, Africa and Asia, and North and South America, concerning Nazi Germany and its society, politics, ideology, economy and foreign policy, opposition to its government, official antisemitism, and the condition and treatment of Jews; on Fascism and antisemitism throughout the world in the 1930s; on World War II: the course of the war, conditions in the belligerent countries, the Final Solution, and war crimes trials; and on Jews and antisemitism in the postwar world.

In addition to the Press Archives, this collection contains records of organizations, mostly from the 1930s and 1940s, including: Brussels Relief Committee; Comité voor Bijzondere Joodsche Belangen; Comité voor Joodsche Vluchtelingen; Council for German Jewry, London; Deutsche Arbeitsfront; Far Eastern Jewish Central Information Bureau; Hilfsverein für jüdische Studierende, Berlin (1890–1910); Intergovernmental Committee on Refugees; Jewish Cultural Reconstruction; Jewish Refugee Committee, Leeds; Jüdischer Kulturbund; Das Lanterndl (the Lantern, a theater group of Austrian emigrés); Reichsbund jüdischer Frontsoldaten; Reichsvereinigung der Juden in Deutschland; and Reichsvertretung der deutschen Juden.

Documents presented to the Nuremberg Trials of Major German War Criminals, 1945–1946, dealing with the Nazi persecution of the Jews.

Other archival holdings of the Wiener Library, including material on the German occupation of Austria, Bukovina, Czechoslovakia, Luxembourg, Poland, and Yugoslavia during World War II; Gestapo records on Jewish organizations in Erfurt; documentation of the deportation of Jews from Mährisch Ostrau (Moravska Ostrava) to Nisko, October 1939; transcripts of the postwar trial of Ilse Koch; correspondence of the Jewish community of Danzig with the Senate of the Free City, 1933–1939; material on Nazi activity in Spain captured by the Republicans during the Spanish Civil War; papers of Cecil Roth on Italian Jewry in the facist period; papers of Wilfred Israel on politics in Weimar and Nazi Germany; documents from concentration and internment camps, including Buchenwald, Dachau, Hadjerat Mguil (Algeria), Lodz, and Theresienstadt; the diaries of Eva Noack-Mosse from Theresienstadt, 1945; documents on gypsies under Nazi rule; circulars and publications of the Reichsministerium für Justiz, 1942–1944; and material for a biography of Heinrich Himmler.

Languages: German, English, French, Spanish, Dutch, Swedish, Danish, Norwegian, Polish, Ukrainian, Arabic, Hebrew, Yiddish, Italian, and Others.
Donor: Wiener Library with the assistance of the National Endowment for the Humanities, 1980.
Finding Aid: 85-page reel guide.
Accession Number: AR 7187.

277 ERNST WOLF
1724–1960   4 inches

Born in Dresden on May 21, 1874, Ernst Wolf emigrated to the United States in 1892 and died in New York City on January 15, 1960.

Papers of the Wolf family, including letters of protection, patents, diaries, passports, vital documents, school certificates, business records, family correspondence, and genealogies.

Languages: German, Hebrew, Judeo-German.
Donor: Mrs. Ernst Wolf, 1960.
Finding Aid: 5-page inventory.
Accession Number: AR 1113.

278 ROBERT WOLFERS
1811–1968   3 inches

Born in Berlin on September 19, 1884, Robert Wolfers was an asphalt manufacturer and street-paving contractor who emigrated to the United States in 1940 and died in Miami, Florida, in 1968.

Correspondence, clippings, photos, memorabilia, vital documents, and education, business, and military service papers of Robert Wolfers, his family, and the astronomer Jakob Wolfers; genealogies of the Wolfers family.

Letters and speech draft by Gustav Stresemann.

Languages: German, English, French.
Donor: Robert Wolfers, 1961–1962.
Finding Aid: 29 catalogue cards.
Accession Number: AR 1312.

279 FRIEDA WUNDERLICH
1919–1969   3.5 feet

Born in Berlin on November 8, 1884, Frieda Wunderlich received a doctorate in economics at the University of Freiburg in 1919, held academic and state positions, and was a member of the Berlin City Council and Prussian Landtag for the Deutsche Demokratische Partei (DDP). She emigrated to the United States in 1933, where she taught at the New School for Social Research, and died in East Orange, New Jersey, on December 29, 1965.

Correspondence, including letters from Alvin Johnson and Thomas Mann.

Manuscripts of lectures, speeches, articles on labor relations, trade union policies, labor and economy in Nazi Germany, social insurance, women and politics; course outlines and notes; diary of 1936–1937; clippings and offprints by and about Wunderlich.

Photos of Wunderlich and of the faculty of the New School.

Languages: German, English.
Donor: Eva Wunderlich, 1967.
Finding Aid: 3-page inventory.
Accession Number: AR 3230.

280 LEON ZEITLIN
1927–1966   6 inches

Born in Memel (now USSR) on February 23, 1876, Leon Zeitlin received a doctorate in economics at the University of Leipzig in 1902 and was employed as a journalist and business association representative. He was active in the Deutsche Demokratische Partei (DDP) and a member of the Prussian Landtag. In 1933 he emigrated to Great Britain, where he continued his journalistic activities. He died in London on June 21, 1967.

Correspondence of Zeitlin with individuals and institutions, including Conference on Jewish Material Claims against Germany, Nahum Goldmann, Max Horkheimer, Walter von Molo, Harold Reinhart, Karl Heinrich Rengstorf, W. W. Simpson, Joachim Tiburtius, UNESCO, and Alfred Wiener.

Manuscripts, offprints and clippings by and about Zeitlin, and on Otto von Bismarck, Christian-Jewish relations, human rights, and economics; an essay by Hans-Jochen Vogel about a trip to Israel, 1964.

Languages: German, English.
Donor: LBI London, 1974.
Finding Aid: 9-page inventory.
Accession Number: AR 4128.

281 ADELHEID ZUNZ
1844–1873   3 inches

Born in Pyrmont on April 2, 1802, Adelheid Bermann married Leopold Zunz in 1822 and died in Berlin on August 18, 1874.

Letters by Adelheid Zunz with postscripts by her husband, Leopold Zunz, written to Julie Ehrenberg née Fischel.

Language: German.
Donor: N. Glatzer, 1976.
Finding Aid: 6-page inventory.
Accession Number: AR 4293.

282 LEOPOLD ZUNZ
1815–1939   4 feet

Born in Detmold on August 10, 1794, Leopold Zunz was educated at the Samson Freischule, Wolfenbüttel, and the Universities of Berlin and Halle, receiving his doctorate at the latter institution in 1821. He was a schoolteacher, journalist, and historian, an advocate of religious reform and one of the founders of the Wissenschaft des Judentums. Zunz died in Berlin on March 17, 1886.

Correspondence of Zunz and his wife, Adelheid Zunz, née Berman with friends and relatives, including Philipp Ehrenberg, Samuel Meyer Ehrenberg, Salomon von Hönigsberg, and Meyer Isler.

List of the Zunz collection at the Hochschule für die Wissenschaft des Judentums in Berlin, drawn up by Franz Biermann in 1939; an autograph list by Zunz of his library.

Calling cards of Zunz's visitors.

Photocopies of Zunz's papers deposited at the Jewish National and University Library, Jerusalem, including lectures, sermons, essays, and correspondence; minutes of meetings of the Verein für Kultur und Wissenschaft des Judentums, and reports by its members.

Languages: German, French, English, Hebrew, Italian.
Donor: Franz Biermann, 1970.
Finding Aids: 20-page inventory, 18-page name-index to the visiting cards.
Accession Number: AR 3648.

283 STEFAN ZWEIG-SIEGMUND WARBURG
1917–1943   1 inch

Born in Vienna on November 28, 1881, Stefan Zweig was one of the leading German-language authors of his generation, writing in many genres-prose, poetry, drama, and fiction. He emigrated to Great Britain in 1934, to the United States in 1940 and to Brazil in 1941. He committed suicide in Petropolis, near Rio de Janeiro on February 23, 1942. Born in Tübingen on September 30, 1902, Siegmund Warburg worked as a banker in Hamburg. He emigrated to Great Britain in 1934 and continued his work as a banker, as well as activities on behalf of Jewish causes. He was knighted in 1964, and died in London on October 18, 1982.

Correspondence of Zweig and Warburg from 1923–1941, but mostly following 1934, dealing with, amongst other topics, National Socialism, Zweig's travels, life in exile and the political and literary activities of the emigrés, the death of Sigmund Freud, and World War II; correspondence of Zweig and Warburg with others, including Hermann Hesse and Felix Warburg; a brief obituary of Zweig by Warburg.

Languages: English, German.
Donors: Anna Biegun and George Warburg, via Joshua Sherman, 1986.

Finding Aid: 17-page inventory.
Accession Number: AR 7277.

284 INDIVIDUAL AUTOGRAPHS
c. 1750–1968   c. 3 feet

This is an artificial collection of autograph material of varied provenance assembled by the Leo Baeck Institute through gifts and purchases. This material contains the most important of the archives' small collections. In the early years of the institute, many autograph items were separated from their collections of origin and organized as individual small collections. In most cases, information about their provenance has been lost. Because of the importance and interest of this material, it has been presented in this volume as an appendix, and described as if it were a large artificial collection.

The material consists of autograph and holograph correspondence, poetry, prose and dramatic manuscripts, musical scores, and autographed photographs and published works.

The collection contains autograph material of individuals including: Peter Altenberg, Berthold Auerbach, Julius Bab, Hugo Ball, Albert Ballin, Ludwig Bamberger, Ludwig Barnay, Karl Beck, Michael Beer, Walter Benjamin, Eduard Bernstein, Otto von Bismarck, Leo Blech, S. Bleichröder, Ernest Bloch, Max Born, Ludwig Börne, George Brandes, Markus Brann, Max Brod, Max Bruch, Martin Buber, Hans von Bülow, Enrico Caruso, Bruno Cassirer, Paul Celan, Daniel Chwolson, Ferdinand Cohn, Leopold Damrosch, Eduard Devrient, Benjamin Disraeli, Alfred Döblin, Albert Ehrenstein, Paul Ehrlich, Albert Einstein, Kurt Eisner, Lyonel Feininger, Lion Feuchtwanger, Theodor Fontane, Ludwig August Frankl, Sigmund Freud, David Friedländer, Salomon Friedländer (Mynona), Friedrich II, King of Prussia, Efraim Frisch, Ludwig Fulda, Abraham Geiger, Johann Wolfgang von Goethe, Ottilie von Goethe, Henriette Goldschmidt, Lazarus Goldschmidt, Ignaz Goldziher, Heinrich Graetz, Friedrich Gundolf, Fritz Haber, Jacques Halevy, Maximilian Harden, Heinrich Heine, Alfred Henschke (Klabund), Henriette Herz, Marcus Herz, Theodor Herzl, Magnus Hirschfeld, Hugo von Hofmannsthal, Edmund Husserl, Heinrich Eduard Jacob, Siegfried Jacobsohn, Johann Jacoby, Ignaz Jastrow, Joseph Joachim, Isaak Marcus Jost, James Joyce, Franz Kafka, Ernst Kantorowicz, Hannah Karminski, Meyer Kayserling, Alfred Kerr, Otto Klemperer, Erich Korngold, Julius Korngold, Karl Kraus, Gustav Landauer, Else Lasker-Schüler, Ferdinand Lassalle, Moritz Lazarus, Daniel Lessmann, Fanny Lewald, Ernst Lissauer, Ernst Lubitsch, Emil Ludwig, Gustav Mahler, Ludwig Marcuse, Fritz Mauthner, Ludwig Meidner, Moses Mendelssohn, Felix Mendelssohn-Bartholdy, Giacomo Meyerbeer, Walter von Molo, Theodor Mommsen, Moses Montefiore, Erich Mühsam, Alfred Neumann, Max Nordau, Jacques Offenbach, Franz Oppenheimer, Emil Orlik, Max Pallenberg, Alfred Polgar, Walther Rathenau, Max Reinhardt, Gabriel Riesser, Alexander Roda-Roda, Meyer Amschel Rothschild, Anton Rubenstein, Arthur Ruppin, Nelly Sachs, Felix Salten, Dorothea Schlegel, Arthur Schnitzler, Arnold Schoenberg, Albert Schweitzer, George

INDIVIDUAL AUTOGRAPHS 156

Bernard Shaw, Werner Sombart, Leopold Sonnenfeld, Richard Strauss, Hermann Struck, Abraham Sutro, Richard Tauber, Ernst Toller, Kurt Tucholsky, Karl August Varnhagen von Ense, Rahel Varnhagen von Ense, Johannes Veit, Philipp Veit, Bruno Walter, Jakob Wassermann, Hile Wechsler, Alma Werfel, Franz Werfel, Chaim Weizmann, Richard Willstätter, David Wolfssohn, Karl Wolfskehl, Adelheid Zunz, Leopold Zunz, Arnold Zweig, and Stefan Zweig.

Languages: German, English, Hebrew, Judeo-German, French.
Donors: Numerous donations and purchases, 1956–1986.
Finding Aids: Catalogue cards.
Accession Numbers: Numerous.

INDEX

TO MAJOR COLLECTIONS

Abraham, Jacob, 1, 266
Abraham family, 1, 266
Abramson, Abraham, 1, 266
Abs, Hermann J., 170, 234
Academic Assistance Council, 150
Academie de droit international, 110
Actien-Brauerei-Gesellschaft Friedrichshöhe, 188
Adass Jisroel (Berlin), 116
Adenauer, Konrad, 77, 101, 165, 234, 272
Adler, Cyrus, 10
Adler, Karl, 3, 209
Adler, Nathan, 183
Adler, Victor, 43
Adler family, 2, 121
Adler-Rudel, Solomon, 4, 110, 234, 273
Adorno, Theodor, 119
Agnon, S. Y., 222
Agudath Israel, 203
Ahrens, Erich, 5
Aiken, Conrad, 21
Akademie für die Wissenschaft des Judentums, 203
Akademischer Verein für jüdische Geschichte und Literatur, 203
Alaska, 78, 242
Alexander family, 70
Algeria, 54
Aliyah Hadasha, 151, 273
Allersheim, 123
Allert de Lange Verlag, 224
Allgemeine Zeitung des Judentums, 208
Allgemeiner Rabbinerverband in Deutschland, 203
Alliance Israélite Universelle, 78, 246
Alsace, 6, 60, 272
Alsberg an der Bergstrasse, 59
Altdorf, 220
Altenberg, Peter, 7, 284
Altenhofen, 123
Altenstadt, 125
Altkirch, Ernst, 45
Altmaier, Jakob, 141
Altmann, Alexander, 82, 273
Altmann, Siegfried, 7
Altona, 123
Altstrelitz, 123
Amann, Paul, 8, 209, 242
American Assistance Council, 150
American Association of Former European Jurists, 272
American Committee for Refugee Scholars, Writers and Artists, 8, 150, 209

American Council for Emigrés from the Professions, 255
American Danzig Association, 63
American Federation of Jews from Central Europe, 9, 46, 78, 203
American Friends Service Committee, 54
American Jewish Committee, 10, 78, 148
American Jewish Congress, 10, 209
American Jewish Joint Distribution Committee, 10, 54, 125, 136, 203, 214, 267
American Joint Reconstruction Foundation, 136
American Roumanian Jewish Emancipation Committee, 78
American Zionist Emergency Council, 102
Amorbach, 163
Amsterdam, 40, 59, 94, 116, 188, 267
An-Ski, S., 92
Anarchism, 152, 190
Andreas, Willy, 197
Andreas-Salomé, Lou, 91, 197
Anti-Nazi movements
 in Germany, 17, 43, 108, 234, 276
 outside Germany, 43, 108, 182, 211, 234, 240, 272, 276, 283
Anti-Zionism, 43, 106
Antisemitism, 13, 39, 40, 48, 50, 75, 78, 86, 98, 101, 109, 117, 128, 135, 136, 146, 193, 217, 242, 256, 272, 276, 280. See also Nazi Germany and persecution of Jews
Arbeiterfürsorgeamt der jüdischen Organisationen Deutschlands, 273
Arbeitsgemeinschaft jüdisch-liberaler Jugendvereine Deutschlands, 203
Architecture
 commercial, 13, 263, 266, 271,
 residential, 13, 263, 271
 See also Synagogue architecture
Arendt, Hannah, 11, 17, 21, 43, 268, 273
Argentina, 100
Arlosoroff, Chaim, 273
Arlosoroff, Gerda, 273
Arnhold family, 12
Arnhold, S. Bleichroeder Inc. (New York), 46
Arnsberg, Paul, 13
Arnswalde, 123
Aron, Frederick, 272
Assimilation, 6, 22, 66, 67, 68, 69, 86, 90, 109, 122, 123, 131, 169, 180, 188, 191, 206, 210, 221, 231, 246, 266, 268, 269, 270, 281, 282. See also Domestic life; Salons
Aub, Joseph, 143

INDEX

Auerbach, Berthold, 24, 40, 179, 217, 242, 261, 284
Auerbach, Elias, 73
Auerbach, Felix, 14
Auerbach, Philipp, 101, 272
Aufbau, 209
Augsburg, 60, 205, 257
Augusta (German Empress), 43
Aurich, 123
Auschwitz (concentration camp), 54, 212, 263
Auslaender, Rose, 45
Austerlitz, 40
Austerlitz, Friedrich, 242
Austria; allied occupation, 7
Austrian Institute (New York), 7
Austrian Jewish Representative Committee, 7
Austrian Jewry, 7, 8, 22, 36, 40, 60, 81, 105, 106, 116, 120, 123, 158, 224, 225, 242, 276. See also Czechoslovak Jewry; East European Jewry; Hungarian Jewry
Austro-Prussian War, 180, 222, 248
Autograph albums, 43, 79, 122, 155, 163, 266
Avenarius, Ferdinand, 45, 172, 179
Avenarius, Johannes, 210, 234
Axis-Victims-League, 272

Baal Shem of Michelstadt, 257
Bab, Elisabeth, 16
Bab, Julius, 15, 16, 20, 21, 53, 61, 73, 80, 112, 141, 169, 179, 181, 209, 265, 284
Bach, Hans, 31
Bacher, Wilhelm, 205
Bad-Durkheim, 220
Baden, 40, 59, 60, 94, 102, 171, 178, 220
Baden-Baden, 220
Badt, Hermann, 222
Badt-Strauss, Bertha, 16, 17, 21, 70, 82, 107, 112, 209, 222, 234
Baeck, Leo, 11, **17, 18**, 20, 21, 26, 36, 37, 40, 44, 64, 73, 82, 93, 98, 100, 102, 107, 135, 139, 148, 151, 153, 207, 215, 222, 229, 234, 239, 243, 273
Baer family, 19
Baerwald, Leo, 20, 37, 82, 93, 94, 107
Baerwald, Paul, 136
Bahr, Hermann, 15, 179
Bainton, Roland, 8
Baker, Leonard, 18
Baldwin, Roger, 101
Ball, Hugo, 284
Ballin, Albert, 284
Ballin, Alfred, 40, 243
Bamberg, 60, 271
Bamberger, Fritz, 94

Bamberger, Ludwig, 40, 179, 284
Banks and banking, 6, 12, 25, 40, 46, 51, 77, 170, 180, 234, 259, 266, 271, 283
Bar Kochba (Prague), 203, 273
Barnay, Ludwig, 284
Baron, Salo, 36, 73, 102
Barth, Jacob, 87
Bas-Rhin, 6
Basel, 188
Bauer, Felice, 134
Bauer, Otto, 242
Bäuerle, Theodor, 3
Baum, Vicky, 112
Baumgardt, David, 17, **21**, 31, 261, 273
Bavaria, 32, 40, 46, 123, 174, 205
Bayerische Stickstoff Werke, 84
Beard, Charles, 230
Beate Guttmann Heim Breslau, 167
Bebel, August, 43, 182
Bechhofen, 20
Beck, Karl, 284
Beer, Agnes, 158
Beer, Amalia, 23, 246
Beer, Jakob Herz, 23, 246
Beer, Jakob Meyer. See Meyerbeer, Giacomo
Beer, Michael, 23, 40, 246, 284
Beer, Sigmund, 158
Beer, Wilhelm, 23
Beer family, 22, 23
Beerfelden, 200
Beer-Hofmann, Gabriel, 158
Beer-Hofmann Lens, Miriam. See Lens, Miriam Beer-Hofmann
Beer-Hofmann, Naemah, 158
Beer-Hofmann, Paula, 158
Beer-Hofmann, Richard, 7, 15, **22**, 59, 91, 135, 158
Behl, C.F.W., 141, 210
Behrend family, 266
Behrendt, Ernst, 10
Beisheim, 220
Bekennende Kirche, 231
Belda, Anton, 210
Belgium, 245
Ben Chananja, 123
Bendemann, Margarete von. See Susman, Margarete
Bendix, Alice, 143
Benedick family, 178
Benedict, Marcus, 87
Beneš, Eduard, 79, 101, 141, 265
Ben-Gurion, David, 151
Benjamin, Walter, 21, 91, 230, 284
Benn, Gottfried, 91, 197

Bensheim, 254
Bentwich, Norman, 115, 267
Beradt, Martin, 24, 45
Berdyczewski, Micha, 91, 197
Berend and Co. (bank), **25**
Berent, Margarete, 26
Bergen, 220
Bergen-Belsen (concentration camp), 267
Berger, Otto Dietrich Gottlob, 186
Bergmann, Hugo, 8, 21, 94, 243, 265, 273
Bergson, Henri, 40, 98
Beringer, Naphtali, 3
Berlin, 1, 23, 25, **27**, 38, 40, 44, 60, 70, 100, 112, 116, 121, 122, 123, 131, 132, 133, 166, 168, 170, 179, 181, 187, 188, 189, 191, 192, 203, 214, 241, 243, 245, 253, 266, 268, 269, 276, 278
    University of, 108, 168, 244
    West; Jewish life after 1950, 27, 80, 113
Berlin, Isaiah, 21, 2
Berlin Theater, 28
Berliner, Abraham, 87
Berliner Börse, 188
Berliner Börsen-Zeitung, 188
Berliner, Cora, 148, 243
Berliner Elektricitäts-Werke, 188
Berliner, Selma, 29
Berliner Tageblatt, 80, 132, 188
Berliner Zionistische Vereinigung, 243
Berman, Aron, 45
Bermann, Adelheid. See Zunz, Adelheid
Bern, 188
Bernadotte, Count Folke, 234
Bernays, Isaac, 31
Bernays, Jacob, 30, 31, 205
Bernfeld, Siegfried, 242, 273
Bernhard, Georg, 112
Bernstein, Eduard, 15, 43, 64, 284
Bernstein, Julius, 64
Berolzheim, 32
Berolzheimer, Michael, 32
Berolzheimer family, 32
Bessarabia, 100
Bethmann-Hollweg, Moritz August von, 25, 180
Beverungen, 37, 183
Beyth, Carl, 33
Bezruč, Petěr, 265
Biala, 261
Biarney, Enole, 180
Bickel, Lothar, 45
Bielefeld, 149
Bielefeld, Rebekka, 40
Bielorussia, 78

Biermann, Franz, 282
Bieskastel, 220
Bildungsverein deutscher Juden, 203
Bill, Friedrich, 34
Bin-Gorion, Micha. See Berdyczewski, Micha
Biram, Arthur, 102
Birdorf, 183
Birkenau, 59
Birnbaum, Immanuel, 110, 197
Bismarck, Otto von, 154, 170, 280, 284
Blau, Bruno, 148
Blau-Weiss, 203
Blech, Leo, 284
Blei, Franz, 35, 197, 242
Bleicherode, 33, 123
Bleichröder, Agatha, 168
Bleichröder, Gerson von, 179
Bleichröder, S., 25, 51, 284
Bloch, Chaim, 36, 62, 82
Bloch, Ernest, 284
Bloch, Ernst, 91, 197
Bloch, Grete, 134
Bloch, Jean-Richard, 8
Bloch, Joseph, 205
Bloch, Philipp, 205
Bluhm, Arthur, 37
Blumenfeld, Kurt, 21, 151, 158, 214, 273
Blumenthal-Weiss, Ilse, 17, 21, 181, 265, 273
Blüthner, Julius, Hofpianofabrik, 188
B'nai B'rith, 38, 39, 64, 162, 203, 258
Bodenheimer, Max, 123, 273
Bodenheimer, Sally, 40
Bödigheim, 220
Bohemia, 60
Bohle, Ernst Wilhelm, 186
Bokelmann, Wilhelm, 268
Bolivia, 100
Böll, Heinrich, 265
Bonaparte, Jerome, 37
Bonhoeffer, Dietrich, 43
Bonn, Moritz Julius, 64, 80
Bonn, University of, 162, 207
Borchardt, Georg Hermann. See Hermann, Georg
Borgholzhausen, 149
Born, Max, 40, 284
Börne, Ludwig, 40, 284
Bornstein, Joseph, 41, 141, **225**
Boschwitz, Carl, 42
Boschwitz family, 42
Brandenburg, 60
Brandes, Georg, 261, 284
Brandis, Christian August, 30, 180

INDEX

Brandt, Willy, 101, 255
Brann, Markus, 73, 87, 229, 284
Braun, Adolf, 197
Braun, Heinrich, 43
Braun, Lily, 15, 43
Braun, Otto, 43, 179
Braun-Vogelstein, Julie, 36, **43**, 102, 110, 234, 255, 273
Braune, Wilhelm, 152
Braunschweig, 60
Braunthal, Julius, 255
Brazil, 80, 100, 283
Brecht, Arnold, 110, 230
Brecht, Bertolt, 197
Breitenbacher, A., 87
Breitscheid, Rudolf, 110, 141
Bremen, 177
Brentano, Lujo, 43, 197, 242
Breslau (now Wroclaw, Poland), 40, 60, 106, 123, 185, 210, 46
 University of, 73
Breslauer, Walter, 44, 151
Breuer, Isaac, 222
Breuer, Joseph, 57
Breuer, Salmon, 57
Brewing industry, 90, 249
Brilling, Bernhard, 177, 209, 216, 266
Brinkmann, Gustav, 268
Brith Shalom, 151, 273
Broch, Hermann, 7, 8, 135, 151, 213, 265, 273
Brod, Max, 24, 53, 79, 112, 119, 134, 197, 242, 265, 273, 284
Bruch, Max, 284
Bruchsal, 19, 171
Bruckner, Anton, 244
Brüderverein (Gnesen), 123
Brüning, Heinrich, 182, 234, 255
Brünn, 135, 263
Brunner, Constantin, 15, 24, **45**, 49
Brunner, Frederick, 46
Brunner, Otto, 46
Brunner-Stigter, Lotte, 45
Brussels Relief Committee, 276
Buber, Martin, 3, 5, 17, 18, 21, 24, 36, 40, 45, **47**, 61, 62, 73, 82, 91, 98, 112, 134, 135, 151, 158, 179, 197, 222, **223**, 229, 242, 258, 273, 284
Buber, Salomon, 205
Bucerius, Gerd, 255
Buchau, 270
Buchen, 220
Buchenwald (concentration camp), 54, 62, 107, 254, 276
Buchheim, Wilhelm, 48

Buchheimer, Lilli, 167
Büchler, Adolph, 87
Buck, Pearl, 15
Budapest, 40, 97
Budweis, 38
Bühl, 196
Bukovina, 276
Bülow, Bernhard von, 154, 170
Bülow, Hans von, 284
Bund Deutsch-Jüdischer Jugend, 203
Bunsen, Christian Karl von, 30, 31
Bunsen, Georg von, 31
Burckhardt, Carl J., 234
Bureau für soziale Arbeit in Warschau, 78
Burg, Meno, 64
Burgenland, 37
Burgkundstadt, 246
Burial societies, 6, 37, 57, 59, 86, 123, 127, 161, 203
Burkhardt, Carl, 91
Buscher, Johann, 180
Business and economic history, 4, 6, 12, 13, 19, 22, 25, 39, 40, 43, 46, 51, 60, 77, 84, 88, 90, 103, 104, 115, 116, 122, 130, 132, 139, 142, 149, 150, 151, 155, 158, 170, 177, 178, 180, 184, 188, 195, 198, 202, 210, 214, 229, 234, 235, 245, 255, 259, 266, 269, 271, 277, 279, 280
Busyn, Max, 45, **49**
Buttenhausen, 3

Cahnmann, Werner, 31, 36, 82, 209
Callmann, Rudolf,102
Canadian Jewish Congress, 10
Capek, Karel, 79
Caren, Ellen. See Schoenberner, Eleonora
Caribbean Jewish communities, 177, 216
Carlebach, Joseph, 59, 82, 222
Carlsbad, 63
Caro, Klara, 239
Carossa, Hans, 197
Caruso, Enrico, 284
Casals, Pablo, 165
Case, Clifford, 240
Caspari, John, 110
Cassel, 60
Cassirer, Bruno, 91, 166, 197, 284
Cassirer, Paul, 166
Cassuto, Umberto, 73
Castonier, Elisabeth, 141
CCAC (Comité de coordination pour l'assistance dans les camps), 54
Celan, Paul, 228, 284

Center for Holocaust Studies, 203
Central Zionist Archives, 216
Centralverein Deutscher Staatsbürger Jüdischen Glaubens, 50, 78, 114, 188, 203, 272
Chajes, Hirsch Perez, 7
Chajes, Zewi Hirsch ben Meir, 7
Chaliapin, Fedor, 79
Chamberlain, Austen, 236
Chapman, Margaret, 255
Charlottenburg, 84
Chemical industry, 84
Chemnitz, 93
Christianity, Jewish attitudes towards, 17, 45, 62, 205, 217, 224, 258, 280
Chwolson, Daniel, 284
Circle, The (Organization for Refugee Architects), 203
Clodwig, Prince zu Hohenlohe-Schillingsfürst, 51
Cohen, Albert, 205
Cohen, David, 276
Cohen, Hermann, 205
Cohn, Albert, 246
Cohn, Emil. See Ludwig, Emil
Cohn, Esther, 72
Cohn, Ferdinand, 284
Cohn, Itzig Hirsch, 51
Cohn, Moritz von, 51
Cohn, Rudolf, 52
Cohn family, 72
Collegio Rabbinico Italiano (Florence), 73
Collin, Ernst Heinrich, 53
Colmar, 6
Colmar, Gertrud, 209
Cologne, 38, 40, 60, 77, 144, 188, 203
Colomb, Mathilde von, 43
Comité de coordination pour l'assistance dans les camps, 54
Comité voor bijzondere Joodsche Belangen, 39, 276
Comité voor Joodsche Vluchtelingen, 10, 276
Commerz- und Disconto-Bank, 188
Communism, 108, 110, 117, 141, 190, 240
Compania Espanola de Navigacion Maritima, 194
Concentration and internment camps, 7, 8, 17, 18, 37, 43, 46, **54**, 59, 70, 82, 88, 95, 102, 105, 107, 108, 120, 124, 146, 149, 156, 171, 178, 188, 190, 195, 199, 200, 207, 212, 234, 252, 254, 256, 263, 264, 267, 272, 276
Cone family, 55
Conference On Jewish Material Claims Against Germany, 56, 209, 280

Congregation B'nai Jeshurun (New York), 144
Congregation Habonim (New York), 203
Congregation Neve Salom (Altona), 123
Congregation Shaare Zedek (Astoria, N.Y.), 177
Congrès Juif Mondial, 78
Conservatism (political), 180
Consistoire Central des Israélites de France, 6
Constantin Brunner Stichting, 49
Conversion
    from Judaism, 22, 60, 74, 109, 123, 160, 180, 185, 206, 231, 232, 268
    to Judaism, 22, 158
Cookbooks, 155, 200, 205
Copenhagen, 233
Cosmetic industry, 155
Cottbus, 40
Coudenhove-Kalergi, R. N., 197
Council for German Jewry (London), 276
Council of Jews from Germany, 44, 125, 203, 214
Courtship, 98, 155, 164, 180, 184. See also Marriage
Cramer, S. D., 57, 265
Crémieux, Adolphe Isaac, 123, 246
Croce, Benedetto, 43
Culmsee, 40
Curtius, Ernst R., 137, 97
Curtius, Julius, 214
Cyanid Gesellschaft, 84
Czech League for Human Rights, 34
Czechoslovak Jewry, 22, 34, 38, 54, 81, 93, 97, 106, 123, 134, 135, 145, 179, 203, 250, 256, 263, 265, 273, 274, 276
Czechoslovakia, 78, 101, 265
Czellitzer, Arthur, 58, 183, 243

Dachau (concentration camp), 37, 46, 54, 120, 254, 276
Damrosch, Leopold, 284
Danzig, 63, 123, 198, 276
Darmstadt, 98
Darmstädter Zeitung, 98
Darmstaedter, Karl D., 17, **59**, 102, 222
Darre, Richard Walter, 186
David, Eduard, 242
Davidsohn, George, 123
Davis, Elmer, 41
DDP. See Deutsche Demokratische Partei
Decrees, 6, 40, **60**, 121, 123, 143, 151, 210, 253
Deggendorf (displaced persons camp), 70
Dehio, Ludwig, 43

Dehmel, Ida, 102
Dehmel, Richard, 15, 147, 172
Deinard, Ephraim, 59
Delbrück, Hans, 242
Dembitzer, Salamon, 61
Demetz, Peter, 8
Demokratische Flüchtlingsfürsorge, 101
Demuth, Fritz, 255
Deportations, 46, 54, 59, 70, 72, 95, 146, 149, 171, 177, 186, 188, 193, 195, 212, 234, 252, 254, 267, 276. See also concentration and interment camps; Holocaust; Nazi Germany
Dessau, 229
Deutsch, Gotthard, 229
Deutsch, Julius, 141
Deutsch family, 210
Deutsch-Israelitischer Gemeindebund, 203
Deutsch-Jüdische Jugend Gemeinschaft, 203
Deutsche Demokratische Partei (DDP), 182, 255, 272, 280
Deutsche Friedengesellschaft, 85
Deutsche Liga für Menschenrechte, 85, 101, 108
Deutsche Verlagsanstalt, 91, 197
Deutscher, Isaac, 8
Deutsches Rotes Kreuz, 42
Deutsches Zentralkomitee für die russischen Juden, 78
Devrient, Eduard, 284
Devrient, Therese, 64
Dewey, John, 21
Diaries, 8, 14, 15, 19, 22, 43, 45, 48, 53, 70, 72, 73, 78, 80, 98, 124, 130, 157, 169, 172, 173, 180, 181, 192, 207, 208, 209, 210, 214, 222, 232, 235, 246, 250, 253, 255, 258, 265, 272, 273, 276, 279. See also Memoirs
Dienemann, Mally, 62, 94
Dienemann, Max, 17, 36, **62**, 222
Dillmann, Alexander, 3
Dirichlet, Gustave, 180
Disconto Gesellschaft, 188
Discrimination. See Antisemitism; Nazi Germany – Persecution of Jews
Displaced persons, 10, 70, 95, 126, 161, 171, 273, 276
Disraeli, Benjamin, 40, 284
Divorce, 43, 123, 188, 209, 255
Döblin, Alfred, 141, 179, 197, 284
Dohm, Christian Wilhelm, 180
Döllinger, Ignaz von, 205
Dombrowski, Erich, 80
Domestic life
  18th cent., 42, 123, 180, 268
  19th cent., 2, 22, 42, 43, 64, 66, 68, 97, 98, 123, 131, 158, 168, 177, 179, 180, 181, 184, 185, 188, 201, 208, 210, 221, 222, 231, 232, 233, 243, 249, 266, 268, 269, 281, 282
  20th cent., 43, 83, 98, 120, 155, 158, 168, 177, 188, 198, 209, 210, 222, 232, 249, 255, 266
  See also Marriage
Domet, Asis, 242
Dortmund, 48
Doubs, 6
Dresden, 60, 123, 277
Dreyer, Alfred, 138
Dreyfus, Alfred, 40
Droysen, Johann Gustav, 179
Dulles, Allen, 234, 255
Durlach, 220
Dürrenmatt, Friedrich, 119
Düsseldorf, 38, 123, 133, 203
Dyhernfurth, 123

East European Jewry, 36, 60, 78, 96, 100, 116, 123, 126, 130, 136, 146, 224, 261, 273, 276. See also Austrian Jewry; Czechoslovak Jewry; Hungarian Jewry
East European Jews in Germany, 60, 61, 62, 78, 91, 92, 123, 126, 184, 192, 205, 217, 224, 273. See also Hungarian Jews in Germany
East Frisia, 40, 177
Eastman, Max, 240
Echt, Samuel, 63
École libre des hautes études, 110
Edelheim, Margarethe, 189
Edelstein, Ludwig, 137
Edinger, Dora, 17, 21, **64**, 82, 239
Edinger, Ludwig, 65
Edinger, Tilly, 65
Edinger family, 65
Edschmid, Kasimir, 197, 265
Education
  higher, 207
    before 1871, 22, 160, 208, 219
    1871–1918, 73, 98, 168, 181, 210, 219, 244, 250, 276
    1918–1933, 73, 98, 108, 123, 137, 214, 232, 250 279
    after 1933, 108, 162
  Jewish, 5, 17, 37, 73, 86, 205, 246, 258
  of adults, 5, 47, 62, 64, 82, 98, 140, 222, 258
  primary and secondary, 144, 220
    1871–1918, 66, 172, 181
    1918–1933, 48, 143, 167, 172

after 1933, 48, 143
religious, 6, 86, 94, 131, 144, 191
See also Vocational retraining; Students' societies
Eger family, 183
Egypt, 168
Ehrenberg, Frederick, 67
Ehrenberg, Julie, 281
Ehrenberg, Julie Fischel, 66
Ehrenberg, Moritz, 69
Ehrenberg, Philipp, 66, 67, 69, 131, 282
Ehrenberg, Richard, 68, 222
Ehrenberg, Samuel Meyer, 66, **67**, 69, 131, 221, 282
Ehrenberg, Seligman M., 67
Ehrenberg, Victor, 222
Ehrenberg family, 68, 221, 222
Ehrenberg-Wichelhausen, Julie, 69
Ehrenstein, Albert, 284
Ehrlich, Ernst Ludwig, 18
Ehrlich, Paul, 40, 210, 284
Ehrlich, Richard A., 70
Ehrlich, Sophie, 70
Ehrlich family, 70
Eichmann, Adolf, 11
Eichmann, Adolf; Trial, 71
Einhorn, David, 246
Einstein, Albert, 10, 17, 21, 40, 70, 101, 135, 182, 226, 238, 265, 273, 284
Einstein, Margot, 265
Einstein family, 61
Eisenach, 60
Eisenberg family, 221
Eisenstadt, 116
Eisner, Kurt, 43, 152, 174, 179, 284
Elbin, Esther, 72
Elbin, Herman, 73
Elbing, 63
Elbogen, Ismar, 17, 18, 21, 36, 37, 62, **73**, 107, 183, 229
Elbogen, Regina, 94
Elbogen family, 72
Ele Toledot, 74
Eliasberg, Wladimir, 75, 197
Eliassow, Alfred, 76
Eliot, T. S., 197
Elkana, Eli, 16
Elon, Amos, 273
Eltzbacher, Carl, 77
Eltzbacher, Hans, 77
Eltzbacher, Jacob Loeb, 77
Eltzbacher family, 77
Emancipation, 40
  Alsace, 6

Baden, 220
Bavaria, 46
Bremen, 177
France, 6, 145
Lorraine, 6, 251
Prussia, 122, 123, 253, 269
Rhineland, 144
Saarland, 251
Westphalia, 37
See also Jewish communities – pre-Emancipation
Emergency Rescue Committee, 240
Emigration and immigration
  before 1933, 2, 42, 43, 55, 67, **78**, 97, 100, 136, 144, 205, 226, 249, 256, 262
  1933–1945, 3, 10, 17, 39, 54, **78**, 100, 115, 118, 136, 148, 189, 214, 215, 245, 274, 276
  Argentina, 272
  Australia, 267
  Belgium, 61
  Bolivia, 157
  Brazil, 80, 283
  Canada, 120
  Chile, 107
  Cuba, 137
  Czechoslovakia, 101, 250
  Ecuador, 34
  France, 8, 15, 54, 78, 80, 101, 105, 108, 110, 117, 141, 165, 177, 182, 188, 224, 225, 238, 252, 272
  Great Britain, 4, 21, 44, 48, 63, 82, 89, 98, 121, 137, 147, 162, 188, 204, 206, 210, 280, 283
  India, 121
  Martinique, 141
  Netherlands, 45, 61, 112, 124, 224, 225, 267
  North Africa, 54
  Palestine, 4, 49, 52, 62, 94, 102, 138, 151, 155, 212, 214, 257, 267, 273
  Shanghai, 124, 267
  Spain, 54, 194, 252
  Sweden, 85, 228, 234, 235, 243, 250
  Switzerland, 19, 91, 119, 163, 188, 260
  Trinidad, 177
  United States, 3, 5, 7, 8, 15, 16, 19, 20, 21, 34, 36, 37, 41, 43, 46, 48, 61, 63, 64, 65, 73, 75, 76, 78, 83, 101, 102, 105, 107, 108, 110, 117, 120, 127, 129, 135, 137, 139, 140, 141, 142, 143, 144, 145, 146, 149, 150, 153, 155, 157, 158, 159, 161, 165, 170, 173, 174, 177, 178, 188, 194, 198, 206, 209, 211, 213, 216,

220, 226, 227, 230, 231, 232, 238, 239, 240, 241, 242, 250, 253, 254, 255, 256, 257, 258, 259, 262, 265, 271, 272, 275, 278, 279, 283
   USSR, 190
   after 1945; 10
      Australia, 61
      Great Britain, 17
      Israel, 195
      Switzerland, 61
      United States, 63, 70, 95, 150, 187, 200, 214, 263
   See also East European Jews in Germany; Holocaust; Hungarian Jews in Germany; Nazi Germany
Enger, 149
Enlightenment, 6, 67, 68, 123, 131, 180, 268, 269, 281, 282
Eppstein, Paul, 195
Epstein, 220
Epstein, Fritz, 117
Erdmannsdorff, Karl Ritter Otto von, 186
Erfurt, 276
Ernst, Paul, 179
Ernst II (Duke of Sachsen-Coburg-Gotha), 51
Eschelbacher, Max, 82
Eshkol, Levi, 151
Essen, 48
Ettenheim, 59
Ettlinger, Shlomo, 74
Evian Conference (1938), 78, 100, 148, 234, 273, 276. See also Emigration and immigration – 1933–1945
Exile literature, 8, 16, 22, 59, 61, 91, 112, 119, 135, 141, 158, 224, 225, 228, 234, 238, 242, 265, 283
Expressionism, 134, 141, 166, 197

Fabian, Fritz, 148
Falke, Gustav, 172
Falkenburg family, 85
Fantl, Otto, 79
Far Eastern Jewish Central Information Bureau, 276
Faulhaber, Michael Cardinal, 20
Faure, Gabriel, 79
Feder, Erna, 80, 110
Feder, Ernst, 80, 110, 179
Fehl, Siegfried, 81
Feininger, Lyonel, 112, 284
Fellowship for Reconciliation, 102
Feminism, 26, 43, 64, 167, 189, 231, 239. See also Women
Ferencz, Benjamin, 101, 151

Fettmilch Uprising, 86
Feuchtwang, David, 7, 81
Feuchtwanger, Lion, 82, 85, 112, 119, 141, 179, 197, 216, 225, 284
Feuchtwanger, Ludwig, 73, **82**, 209
Finkel, Saul, 102
Fischel, Julie, 281
Fischer, Dorothy Canfield, 21
Fischer, Samuel, 24
Fischer Verlag, 8, 134
Flake, Otto, 197
Flatow, 123
Flechtheim, Ossip, 10
Fleg, Edmond, 91
Flexner, Bernhard, 137
Flick, Friedrich, 186
Fliess family, 123
Foerster, Friedrich Wilhelm, 141, 197
Foerster-Nietzsche, Elisabeth, 21
Folklore, 24, 123, 177, 221, 270
Fontane, Theodor, 45, 112, 284
Forbes-Mosse, Irene, 112
Foreign Authors Syndicate, 242
Forster, Johann Georg, 141
Fraenkel, Ernst, 83, 110
Fraenkel, Marta, 83, 110
France, 80, 101, 218
   Vichy period, 54, 105, 141, 182, 272
   See also French Jewry
Franco-Prussian War, 6, 180, 204, 219
Frank, Adolf, 84
Frank, Albert, 84
Frank, Bruno, 197, 240
Frank, Leonhard, 141
Fränkel, Auguste, 210
Fränkel, Zacharias, 106, 205
Fränkel family, 210
Frankenbach, Hans, 85
Frankenbach family, 85
Frankenhuis, Maurice, 256
Frankfurt am Main, 13, 38, 40, 57, 60, 74, 82, **86**, 123, 131, 144, 151, 200, 201, 246
   Opernhaus, 147
   University of, 137
Frankfurt an der Oder, 43, 123
Frankfurter, Felix, 21, 137, 230
Frankfurter Zeitung, 91, 188
Frankl, Ludwig August, 7, 22, 284
Fraternal organizations, 38, 123, 162, 203, 258
Frauenhilfe im Krieg, 98
Freiburg, University of, 94
Freie jüdische Volkshochschule (Berlin), 214
Freie Vereinigung für die Interessen des orthodoxen Judentums, 203

Freies Jüdisches Lehrhaus (Frankfurt), 5, 47, 62, 64, 222, 258
Freimann, Jakob, 87
French Jewry, 6, 100, 218, 246, 274. See also France
Freud, Anna, 7
Freud, Sigmund, 21, 112, 283, 284
Freudental (Württemberg), 217
Freundlich, Josef, 162
Freundlich, Otto, 218
Freundlich family, 162
Fried, John H. E., 88
Friedberg, Heinrich von, 243
Friedjung, Heinrich, 106, 179, 242
Friedlaender, Dagobert, 89
Friedlaender, Kurt, 89
Friedlaender, Walter, 110, 179
Friedlaender family, 89
Friedländer, David, 284
Friedländer, Max, 153, 244
Friedländer, Rebecca, 268
Friedländer, Salomon (Mynona), 21, 176, 284
Friedländer family, 90
Friedländer-Prechtl, Robert, 90
Friedrich I (Duke of Anhalt), 51
Friedrich I (Grand Duke of Baden), 244
Friedrich I (King of Prussia), 73
Friedrich II (Grand Duke of Baden), 51
Friedrich II (King of Prussia), 210, 284
Friedrich III (German Emperor), 51
Friedrich Wilhelm (German Crown Prince), 248
Friedrich Wilhelm IV (King of Prussia), 51
Frings, Joseph Cardinal, 273
Frisch, Efraim, 91, 92, 135, 197, 284
Frisch, Fega, 91, **92**, 119
Froehlich, Paul, 117
Froehlich, Rosi, 117
Fromm, Erich, 36
Fuchs, Eugen, 50
Fuchs, Hugo, 93
Fulda, Ludwig, 40,, 45, 79, 112, 179, 284
Fürnberg, Hermann, 36
Fürth, 32, 123, 143
Furtwängler, Wilhelm, 187, 244

Gailingen, 171
Galinski, Heinz, 165
Gambetta, Leon, 40
Geiger, Abraham, 246, 284
Geiger, Ludwig, 40, 73, 205
Geis, Robert Raphael, 17, 73, **94**
Gelsenberg (concentration camp), 54
Gelsenkirchen, 99
Genealogical Society of Utah, 203
Genealogy, 2, 6, 12, 17, 19, 23, 25, 32, 33, 40, 42, 46, 48, 55, 58, 59, 65, 67, 68, 69, 70, 72, 73, 74, 76, 77, 82, 83, 85, 90, 97, 102, 103, 107, 111, 113, 121, 122, 123, 137, 139, 143, 144, 146, 149, 162, 163, 166, 167, 175, 177, 178, 179, 181, 183, 184, 185, 187, 188, 191, 196, 200, 201, 202, 206, 208, 209, 210, 216, 219, 220, 221, 222, 229, 231, 232, 243, 249, 254, 255, 259, 261, 262, 265, 266, 269, 270, 271, 272, 275, 277, 278
Geng, Hedwig, 95
Georg Müller Verlag, 35
George, Manfred, 61, 75, 80, 91, 101, 197, 234, 240, 272, 273
George, Stefan, 135
Gerlach, Helmut von, 85, 197
German Army Proclamations, 96
German Democratic Republic, 190
  Jewish communities of, 33
Germany
  politics and government; before 1871, 51, 154, 180
    national unification, 6, 154, 180
  politics and government
    1871–1918, 43, 50, 51, 65, 77, 84, 89, 137, 154, 170, 174, 178, 180, 188, 191,
    1918–1933, 26, 33, 42, 43, 50, 80, 91, 98, 108, 110, 112, 132, 170, 174, 178, 182, 188, 189, 190, 191, 193, 197, 210, 234, 235, 238, 255, 272, 273, 276, 279, 280
    1933–1945. See Nazi Germany
    allied occupation; 1945–1949, 9, 43, 83, 95, 101, 110, 126, 137, 141,150, 174, 177, 186, 187, 209, 210, 234, 239, 241, 255, 270, 272, 273, 276
  Federal Republic of, 17, 101, 110, 113, 141, 209, 210, 232, 234, 239, 255, 272, 273
    Jewish communities of, 17, 86, 94, 101, 102, 110, 117, 142, 146, 149, 161, 171, 177, 199, 207, 210, 239, 256, 272, 276
Gesamtarchiv der deutschen Juden, 123, 183
Gesecke, 172
Gesellschaft der Freunde (Berlin), 123, 203
Gesellschaft der Freunde der Hebräischen Universität Jerusalem, 203
Gesellschaft für jüdische Familienforschung, 58, 203
Gesellschaft für jüdische Volkskunde, 203
Gesellschaft jüdischer Handwerker (Berlin), 123
Gesellschaft zur Förderung der Wissenschaft des Judentums, 183, 203

INDEX
168

Gesellschaft zur Förderung wirtschaftlicher Interessen von in Deutschland wohnhaften oder wohnhaft gewesenen Juden, 203
Gestapo records, 114, 148, 171, 231, 276
Gide, André, 197
Gidon, Blanche, 224
Giesey, Ralph, 137
Gilbert, Felix, 230
Ginzburg, Louis, 73
Glaebe, Friedrich, 138
Glatzer, Nahum, 17, 36, 94, 138, 222, 258, 273
Glümer, Claire von, 68
Gneisenau, August Neidhart Count von, 25
Gnesen, 40, 123
Goch, 23
Goethe, Johann Wolfgang von, 284
Goethe, Ottilie von, 43, 284
Goethe, Wolfgang von, 43
Goitein, Fritz (later Shlomo Dov), 222
Golčuv-Jenikov, 97
Goldberger, Ludwig Max, 106
Goldmann, Nahum, 36, 61, 101, 151, 165, 273, 280
Goldmark, Carl family, 97
Goldschmidt, Henriette, 284
Goldschmidt, Lazarus, 284
Goldschmidt, Ludwig, 94
Goldschmidt, Selig, 201
Goldstein, Julius, 98
Goldstein, Margarete, 98, 222
Goldstein family, 98
Goldziher, Ignaz, 73, 284
Goll, Claire, 141
Goll, Ivan, 197
Gollancz, Victor, 225
Goltsch-Jenikau, 97
Gompertz, Leo, 99
Goncourt, Edmond de, 179
Gorky, Maxim, 79
Göttingen, 144
Gottschalk, Louis, 117
Gottschalk family, 208
Graetz, Heinrich, 30, 31, 87, 106, 205, 284
Graetz, William, 100
Graf, Oskar Maria, 107, 141, 197, 209
Great Britain; politics and government, 236
Greece, German occupation, 186
Grey, Edward, 236
Gropius, Walter, 197
Grosbliederstroff, 59
Gross, Babette L., 10, 141
Grossloge für Deutschland. See B'nai B'rith
Grossmann, Kurt, 10, 80, **101**

Grossmann, Walter, 158
Grossmann, Stefan, 91
Grosz, Georg, 141
Grubel, Fred, 110
Gruenewald, Max, 17, 21, 31, 36, 73, 94, 102, 107, 110, 209
Gruenewald, Simon, 102
Gruenewald family, 102
Gruenfeld, Falk Valentin, 103
Gruenfeld, Franz Viktor, 104
Gruenfeld, Heinrich, 103
Gruenfeld, Leopold, 105
Gruenfeld family, 104
Grünbaum, Max, 205
Grünstadt, 220
Grunwald, Max, 36, 87, 106
Grzesinski, Albert, 10, 110
Güdemann, Moritz, 73, 87, **106**, 205
Guggenheim, Fromet. See Mendelssohn, Fromet
Guggenheim, Siegfried, 17, 36, 62, **107**
Guggenheim family, 107
Gumbel, Emil J., 85, 101, **108**, 141, 197
Gundolf, Friedrich, 15, 184, 284
Gundolf family, 184
Gurian, Waldemar, 230
Gurs (concentration camp), 46, 54, 59, 102, 178, 195, 252
Gustedt, Jenny von, 43
Gutsfeld, Alexander, 148
Guttmann, Beate, 167
Guttmann, Julius, 73, 106
Gypsies. See Nazi Germany; persecution of Gypsies

Ha-aretz, 273
Ha-Poel Ha-Zair, 21, 151, 273
Haas, Willy, 91, 141, 197, 265
Haber, Fritz, 84, **109**, 284
Hadjerat Mguil (concentration camp), 276
Haeften, Hans Bernd von, 214
Hagenau, 6
Hager, Baruch, 92
Hague, 123
Haigerloch, 20, 123
Hakoah (Vienna), 242
Halacha. See Jewish law
Halberstadt, 123, 253
Halberstam, Solomon Chaim, 106, 205
Halévy, Jacques, 187, 284
Halle an der Saale, 123, 253
Halpern, Georg, 273
Hamburg, 20, 31, 40, 98, 123, 133, 172, 175, 203, 212, 217

University of, 232
Hamburg-Amerika Linie, 188
Hamburger, Ernst, 80, **110**, 255, 273
Hamburger, Natalie, 17
Hamm-Brücher, Hildegard, 255
Hammarskjold, Dag, 234
Hanau, 60
Hanau-Lichtenberg, 220
Hänisch, Konrad, 91
Hannover, Meyer, 180
Hannoverscher Courier, 188
Hanover, 40, 60, 123, 151, 183, 202, 242
Hanslick, Eduard, 242
Harburg, 123
Harden, Maximilian, 15, 40, 45, 179, 242, 284
Hardt, Ludwig, 181, 209, 265
Harmonie Club (New York), 78
Harnack, Adolf von, 205
Harrwitz, Julius, 123
Hartmann, Ludo M., 91, 197
Hasidism, 36, 250
Haupt, Georg, 117
Hauptmann, Gerhart, 15, 185, 210
Haus Bertha, 99
Hausenstein, Wilhelm, 91, 197
Haut-Rhin, 6
Hayek, Max, 7
Hebrew University (Jerusalem), 47
Hechaluz, 203
Hechingen, 123
Heckscher, James, 236
Hedda Marr Cosmetics, 155
Hedin, Sven, 207
Heidelberg, 144, 171
    University of, 14, 108
Heidenheim, 32
Heilbronn, 143
Heimann, Moritz, 242
Heine, Betty, 42
Heine, Heinrich, 42, 68, 160, 284
Heine, Wolfgang, 43, 91
Heinemann, Gustav, 80
Heinemann, Jeremias, 25
Heinemann, Josef, 43
Helmstädt, 60
Helpach, Willy, 197
Hembsbach, 220
Henckell, Karl, 242
Hennigson family, 111
Hennings, August, 180
Henschke, Alfred, 197, 284
Hensel, Louise, 180
Hensel, Wilhelm, 180
Hermann, Clara. See Levysohn, Clara

Hermann, Georg, 82, **112**, 181
Hermann, Hugo, 273
Hertz, Emanuel, 113
Hertz, Joseph Herman, 18
Hertz, Kallmann, 113
Hertz, Paul, 101, 113, 234, 255
Hertz family, 113
Herz, Henriette, 40, 248
Herz, Marcus, 284
Herz family, 72
Herzberg, Nanny, 184
Herzebrock, 48
Herzfeld, Salomon, 114
Herzfelde, Wieland, 101
Herzl, Theodor, 106, 123, 284
Hesse, Hermann, 8, 15, 21, 24, 41, 85, 91, 107, 147, 179, 197, 209, 265, 283
Hessen, 40, 60, 94, 123, 220
Heuss, Theodor, 80, 94, 101, 141, 153, 159, 169, 209, 230, 234, 255
Heuss family, 255
Heym, Georg, 21
Heyse, Paul, 87
HIAS-HICEM, 10, 78, 148, 214
High Commission for Refugees from Germany, 115
Hildesheim, 106
Hildesheimer, Esriel, 116, 205
Hildesheimer, Hirsch, 40
Hilferding, Rose, 182, 234
Hilferding, Rudolf, 141, **182**, 234
Hilfsverein der deutschen Juden, 10, 78, 136, 150, 203, 214
Hilfsverein für die jüdischen Taubstummen in Deutschland, 203
Hilfsverein für jüdische Studierende (Berlin), 276
Hilfswerk für Juden in Bremen, 177
Hilfswerk für jüdische Künstler und Geistesarbeiter (Berlin), 203
Hiller, Kurt, 141, 197, 242
Himbach, 125
Himmler, Heinrich, 4, 276
Hindemith, Paul, 3
Hinkel, Hans, 133
Hirsch, Helmut, 110, **117**
Hirsch, Marcus, 123
Hirsch, Maurice de, 273
Hirsch, Otto, 3, 107, 209, 215, 234
Hirsch, Samson Raphael, 57, 86, 106, 123
Hirschberg, Alfred, 17, **50**, **80**, 114, 118, 239, 272
Hirschfeld, Georg, 91
Hirschfeld, Harry, 87

Hirschfeld, Kurt, 119
Hirschfeld, Magnus, 79, 284
Hirschland, Georg, 215
Hitachduth Olej Germania, 148
Hochberg, 220
Hochschule für die Wissenschaft des Judentums (Berlin), 17, 37, 73, 94, 282. See also Wissenschaft des Judentums
Hochschule für Politik, 230
Hoek van Holland (internment camp), 124
Hoeter, Emilie, 184
Hoffman, Jacob, 59, 102
Hoffmann, David, 87
Hoffmann, Moses, 82
Hofmann, Alois, 158
Hofmann, Bertha, 158
Hofmann family, 22
Hofmannsthal, Hugo von, 15, 91, 197, 284
Holborn, Hajo, 8
Holidays and festivals, Jewish, 48, 59, 107, 270
Holitscher, Arthur, 91, 147, 197, 242
Holleschau, 40
Holocaust, 4, 7, 10, 11, 54, 59, 70, 71, 72, 88, 95, 108, 128, 146, 148, 149, 171, 177, 181, 186, 192, 193, 195, 199, 200, 207, 212, 234, 256, 263, 264, 267, 273, 274, 276,
  life in hiding, 171, 187, 199
  survivors, 10, 126, 149, 161, 171, 177, 199, 234, 263, 273
  See also Nazi Germany; World War II
Holz, Arno, 15, 179
Hönigsberg, Salomon von, 282
Hook, Sidney, 21, 137
Hoover Commission on Germany, 255
Hoover, Herbert, 255
Hoover Institution on War, Revolution and Peace (Stanford, Calif.), 238
Hoover, J. Edgar, 110
Horice, 179
Horitz, 179
Horkheimer, Max, 280
Horovitz, Jakob, 82, 94
Horovitz, Saul, 102
Hörstein, 123
Hronover Baumwollspinnerei, 210
Huber, Hans, 94
Huch, Ricarda, 197
Humboldt, Alexander von, 180
Humboldt Hochschule (Berlin), 214
Hungarian Jewry, 97, 100, 116, 123, 205. See also Austrian Jewry; East European Jewry
Hungarian Jews in Germany, 72, 205, 244. See also East European Jews in Germany

Hürben, 123
Husserl, Edmund, 284
Hutchins, Robert Maynard, 137, 238
Hyman, Joseph, 10

I.G. Farben, 80, 84
Immigrants' Jewish Veterans Association, 127
India, 121, 234
INPRESS (Independent Press Agency), 39
Institut de droit comparé, 110
Institut de science de la presse, 110
Institut für Zeitgeschichte, 18
Institute for Advanced Studies (Princeton), 137
Interallied Commission for camps in Spain, 54
Interallied Commission for Political Prisoners and Refugees in North Africa, 54
Intergovernmental Committee on Refugees, 276
Internationaal Constantin Brunner Instituut, 45
International Council of Jewish Women, 239
International Red Cross, 7
Internationale Rote Hilfe, 190
Internment of aliens, 8, 43, 63, 82, 177, 252, 272
Irgun Oleh Merkas Europa, 203
Isherwood, Christopher, 8
Isle of Man (internment camp), 82
Isler, Lilly, 120
Isler, Meyer, 69, 282
Israel, Nathan, 121
Israel, Wilfred, 121, 234, 276
Israel family, 121
Israel, State of, 93, 101, 151, 230, 234, 273, 274, 275, 280
  Supreme Court, 71
  See also Emigration and Immigration; Palestine
Israelitische Jugendhilfe Munich, 143
Israelitische Religionsgesellschaft (Frankfurt am Main), 57, 82, 86
Israelitische Volksschule Essen, 48
Israelitischer Literatur-Verein, 203
Israelitischer Tempelverband (Hamburg), 217
Israelitisches Asyl für Kranke und Altersschwache (Cologne), 77
Israelitisches Blindeninstitut (Vienna), 7
Italian Jewry, 73, 181, 274
  fascist period, 276
Italy, 10, 181, 188

Itzig, Daniel, 122
Itzig, Isaak Daniel, 122
Itzig family, 122

Jackson, Robert, 88
Jacob, Heinrich Eduard, 141, 243, 284
Jacob, Israel, 121
Jacob & Valentin, 266
Jacobi, F. H., 180
Jacobs, Monty, 91
Jacobsohn, Siegfried, 91, 179, 197, 284
Jacobson, Jacob, 123, 148, 266
Jacobson, Moses, 123
Jacoby, Hans, 124, 234
Jacoby, Johann, 284
Jameson, Storm. See Chapman, Margaret
Japan, 188
Jastrow, 123
Jastrow, Ignaz, 260, 284
Javits, Jacob, 243
J.D.C. See American Jewish Joint Distribution Committee
Jellinek, Adolf, 106, 116, 205
Jena, University of, 14, 244
Jerusalem, 116
Jesenska, Milena, 134
Jewish Agency, 148, 151, 203
Jewish Association of Trinidad, 177
Jewish Central Information Office, 39, 276
Jewish communities
  leadership, 3, 6, 17, 18, 27, 37, 40, 44, 86, 93, 102, 106, 107, 121, 123, 136, 142, 143, 146, 148, 151, 161, 163, 171, 177, 183, 195, 203, 212, 214, 215, 229, 241, 244, 245, 267, 270, 272
  pre-Emancipation, 1, 3, 25, 32, 40, 59, 60, 73, 74, 86, 122, 123, 142, 143, 144, 145, 146, 151, 163, 177, 178, 217, 220, 243, 251, 253, 257, 266, 269
Jewish Cultural Reconstruction, 276
Jewish Labor Committee, 148
Jewish law, 6, 31, 43, 59, 87, 102, 106, 116, 123, 183, 205, 233
Jewish National and University Library (Jerusalem), 192, 282
Jewish Philanthropic Fund of 1933, 203
Jewish press, 39, 82, 148, 189, 208
Jewish Publication Society, 209
Jewish Refugee Committee (Leeds), 276
Jewish Restitution Successor Organization (JRSO), 125, 203
Jewish Telegraphic Agency, 39
Jewish Theater, 126

Jewish thought, 5, 17, 18, 20, 30, 31, 43, 47, 62, 73, 82, 87, 91, 102, 106, 112, 131, 138, 205, 217, 222, 223, 246, 258, 260, 261, 282
Jewish Veterans Association, 127, 256
Jewish World Relief Committee, 78
Jews in Germany, 1933–1945, 128
Joachim, Joseph, 284
Johnson, Alvin, 110, 279
Joint. See American Jewish Joint Distribution Committee
Joint Antifascist Refugee Committee, 54
Jolowicz, Selma, 239
Jolowicz family, 206
Jonas, Herbert, 112
Jones, Ernest, 36
Joodsche Raad (Amsterdam), 267
Joseph, Rudolf, 129
Josephthal, Paul, 94, **130**
Jospe, Alfred, 82
Jost, Isaak Marcus, 67, 69, 123, **131**, 284
Joyce, James, 284
Juda, Hans, 132
Judaism. See also Holidays and festivals; Jewish law; Jewish thought; Liturgy and ritual; Professions and occupations – rabbis
Judaism (movements), 6, 82, 203
  liberal and reform, 17, 43, 93, 98, 102, 131, 188, 189, 205, 208, 217, 246, 282
  orthodox, 31, 57, 59, 86, 116
Jüdische Auswanderung, 214
Jüdische Buchgemeinde, 203
Jüdische Freischule (Berlin), 122
Jüdische Rundschau, 148, 273
Jüdische Tonkünstler (Frankfurt), 147
Jüdische Volksküche (Biala), 261
Jüdische Welt-Rundschau, 273
Jüdische Welthilfskonferenz, 203
Jüdische Winterhilfe, 203, 245
Jüdischer Frauenbund, 64, 167, 181, 203, 239
Jüdischer Kulturbund, 3, 15, **133**, 147, 203, 209, 244, 276
Jüdischer Lehrerverein, 203
Jüdisches Zentralkomitee für die Kriegsopfer, 78
Jüdisch-theologisches Seminar (Breslau), 17, 30, 73, 106, 144, 205
Jugend-Aliyah. See Youth Aliyah
Jung-Jüdischer Club, 203
Jutrozinski, Moritz, 205

Kafka, Franz, 134, 265, 284
Kahler, Alice von, 135
Kahler, Antoinette von, 135

INDEX

Kahler, Erich von, 53, 91, **135**, 159, 197, 265, 273
Kahler family, 158
Kahn, Bernhard, 10, 73, 80, **136**
Kahn, Zadoc, 205
Kainz, Josef, 15, 179
Kaiser, Georg, 197
Kaiser Wilhelm Institut für Physikalische Chemie, 109
Kaleko, Mascha, 265
Kaliphari, Simon, 137
Kameraden: deutsch-jüdischer Wanderbund, 203
Kamnitzer, Bernhard, 63
Kandt, Richard, 137
Kantorowicz, Ernst, 137, 284
Kantorowicz, Gertrude, 137, 260
Kaplan, Mordechai, 73
Kappel, 270
Kapustin, Max, 82
Kareski, Georg, 148
Karge, 123
Karl VI (German Emperor), 210
Karlsruhe, 59, 60, 102, 171, 178, 220
Karminski, Hannah, 26, 234, 239, 284
Karpeles, Benno, 43
Karpeles, Gustav, 205, 229, 242
Kartell-Convent deutscher Studenten jüdischen Glaubens, 203, 272
Kartell jüdischer Verbindungen, 123, 203
Kasch, Magdalena, 45, 107
Kassel, 94, 123, 133, 203
Kassowitz, Antonie. See Stolper, Toni
Kassowitz family, 255
Kastein, Josef, 7, **138**
Kastein, Shulamith, 138
Kästner, Erich, 7, 10, 119, 141
Kattowitz, 146
Katz, Rudolf, 110
Katzenstein, Julius, 138
Katzki, Herbert, 10
Katznelson, Berl, 151
Kauders, Hans, 91
Kauffmann family, 185
Kauffmann, Felix I., 139
Kaufhaus N. Israel, 121
Kaufmann, David, 106
Kaufmann, Fritz, 18, **140**
Kaunitz-Rietberg, Count Aloys zu, 77, 43, 242
Kayser, Rudolf, 21, 91, 197
Kayserling, Hermann, 197
Kayserling, Meyer, 284
Kayssler, Friedrich, 91

Kaznelson, Siegmund, 273
Kehrl, Hans, 186
Kempner, Robert, 110
Kennan, George, 8
Keppler, Wilhelm, 186
Keren Hayessod, 93, 203
Keren Kayemeth, 203
Kerr, Alfred, 10, 79, 91, 141, 284
Kersten, Kurt, 61, **141**, 197, 209
Kesten, Hermann, 10, 36, 41, 91, 101, 141, 240, 265
Keyserling, Graf Hermann, 17
Kiefer, Isidor, 142
Kien, Peter, 264
Kiepenheuer, Gustav, 141
Kiepenheuer, Noa, 265
Kiepenheuer Verlag, 224
Kiesinger, Kurt Georg, 3
Kindler Verlag, 80
Kirschner, Emanuel, 205
Kisch, Egon, 79, 225
Kisch, Guido, 36, 80, 82, 102, 107
Kishinev, 78
Kitzingen, 205
Kitzinger, Elizabeth, 143
Kitzinger, Ernst, 137
Klabund. See Henschke, Alfred
Kladderadatsch, 51
Klatzkin, Jacob, 91
Klemperer, Otto, 265, 284
Klemperer family, 73
Kleve-Mark, 253
Klibansky, Joseph, 272
Knickerbocker, H. R., 240
Knopf, Alfred, 240
Kober, Adolf, 36, 107, **144**, 177
Koblenz, 244
Kobler, Franz, 36, 135, **145**
Koch, Ilse, 276
Koch, Richard, 98, 258
Koch, Walter, 265
Koeslin, 123
Köhler, Wolfgang, 21
Kohn, Hans, 8, 21, 82, 102, 135, 151, 197, 209, 211, 242, 265, 273
Kohut, George Alexander, 217
Kolb, Annette, 197
Kolb, Bernhard, 102, **146**, 256
Kollek, Teddy, 165
Kollwitz, Käthe, 15, 112
Kölnische Zeitung, 188
Kolonialkriegerdank, 42
Komitee für den Osten, 273
Königliche Porzellan-Manufaktur Berlin, 188

Königsberg, 123, 165, 205, 206
Königswart, 59
Königswarter, Moritz, 106
Konsistorium der Israeliten des Königreichs Westfalen, 37
Konstanz, 38, 209, 210
Koritzer, Adolph, 184
Koritzer family, 184
Körner, Paul, 186
Korngold, Erich, 284
Korngold, Julius, 284
Korsch, Hedda, 117
Korsch, Karl, 117
Kowalski, Max, 147
Kracauer, Siegfried, 10, 91, 119, 197
Kratzenstein, Jossef, 94
Kraus, Karl, 7, 179, 284
Krautheim, 220
Kreditverein für Handel und Gewerbe, 203
Krefeld, 37
Kretschman, Hans von, 43
Kretschman, Lily von. See Lily Braun
Kretschman, Maria von, 43
Kreuger, Ivar, 234, 235
Kreutzberger, Max, 110, **148**, 151, 265, 273
Kriegsgefangenen Fürsorge, 42
Kristallnacht. See Pogrom (November 1938)
Krojanker, Gustav, 273
Kronheim, Hans, 149
Krosigk, Lutz Schwerin von, 186
Krotoschin, 123
Krupp, 188
Kulmhof (concentration camp), 54
Kuppenheim, 220
Kuranda, Ignaz, 106
Kurhessen, 123
Kurmark, 122, 123
Kurtzig family, 70
Kurz, Isolde, 43, 64

Labus, Hannah, 228
Lachmann-Mosse, Felicia, 188
Lachmann-Mosse, Hans, 188
Lachmann-Mosse, Hilde, 188
Ladenburg, 59
Lagerloef, Selma, 15
Lamm, Albert, 197
Lammers, Hans Heinrich M., 186
Landau, 46, 220
Landau, Paul, 40, 236
Landau-Mühsam, Charlotte, 191
Landauer, Carl, 150, 255
Landauer, Gabriel Joshua, 151
Landauer, Georg, 21, **151**, 234, 273, 284

Landauer, Gustav, 15, 45, 61, **152**, 179, 273
Landauer family, 151
Landsberg an der Warthe, 40, 123, 245
Landsberger, Arthur, 242
Landsberger, Franz, 153
de Lange, Allert, 112. See also Allert de Lange Verlag
Lange, Helene, 179
Lanterndl ("The Lantern"), 276
Lanz, Heinrich (agricultural equipment firm), 188
Lasker, Eduard, 31, 123, **154**
Lasker-Schüler, Else, 40, 53, 62, 64, 91, 145, 163, 284
Lassalle, Ferdinand, 284
Laupheim, Steiner family, 249
Lawrence, D. H., 238
Lazarus, Arnold, 20
Lazarus, Leiser, 20
Lazarus, Moritz, 20, 40, 64, 205, 229, 242, 244, 261, 284
Leab, Hertha, 155
Leab, Leo, 155
Lederer, Emil, 211, 234
Leeuwen, Selma van, 45
Lehar, Franz, 79
Lehmann, Herbert H., 136, 230
Lehmann, Lilli, 179
Lehmann, Lotte, 7
Lehranstalt für die Wissenschaft des Judentums. See Hochschule für die Wissenschaft des Judentums.
Lehren, Akiba, 116
Lehrs, Max, 91, 166
Leiningen, 220
Leipaja, 96
Leipnik, 106
Leipzig, 40, 60, 184, 203, 250
Leipziger Buchdruckerei, 188
Leiter, Benno, 156
Leiter family, 156
Leiter, Siegfried, 156
Lejeune-Jung, Paul, 182
Lemke, Leopold, 157
Lemke, Meinhardt, 157
Lens, Miriam Beer-Hofmann, 94, **158**, 273
Leo Baeck Institute, 17, 102, 110, 148, 145, **159**, 177, 189, 209, 216, 224, 228, 264, 273
Leonhard, Rudolf, 225
Leschnitzer, Adolf, 73, 234
Lessing, Theodor, 64, 79, 179
Lessmann, Daniel, 160, 284
Leubsdorf family, 42

INDEX

Leubsdorf, Hermann, 42
Leutershausen, 220
Levi, Leopold, 161
Levi, Paul, 147
Levi, Primo, 61
Levin, Rahel. See Varnhagen von Ense, Rahel
Levison, Wilhelm, 42, **162**, 207
Levison family, 162
Levy, Carola, 163
Levy, Emil, 82
Levy family, 163
Levy-Rathenau, Josephine, 26
Levysohn, Clara, 164
Levysohn, Ulrich, 164
Lewald, Fanny, 40, 64, 284
Lewald, Otto, 25
Lewald family, 206
Lewandowski, Louis, 165
Lewandowski, Manfred, 165, 177
Liberal-jüdische Vereinigung, 102
Liberaler Rabbiner-Verband, 43
Liberalism (political), 77, 80, 98, 110, 154, 182, 188, 231, 235, 240, 255, 272, 280
Liberal Judaism. See Judaism (movements) – liberal and reform
Licaria, 203
Liebermann, Max, 15, 24, 40, 112, **166**
Liebeschütz, Hans, 31, 273
Liebeskind family, 155
Liederkranz, 203
Liegner, Lilli, 167
Liegner family, 167
Liepmann, Hugo, 168
Liepmann family, 168
Lifschitz, Fega. See Frisch, Fega
Lightman, J. B., 10
Lilien, E. M., 242
Liliencron, Detlev von, 7, 15, 172, 179
Liliencron, Rochus, 205
Limpertheim, 220
Lindau, Paul, 40, 179
Linke, Lilo, 255
Lion, Ferdinand, 91, 197
Lippe-Detmold, 123
Lipschitz, Joachim, 101
Lipschitz, Leopold, 205
Lissa, 202
Lissauer, Ernst, 90, 145, 147, 153, **169**, 197, 284
Lithuania, 4, 78, 100
Littauer, Paula, 148
Liturgy and ritual, Jewish, 37, 40, 59, 73, 107, 123, 142, 144, 183, 189, 192, 205, 256, 70

Löb, Isidore, 205
Löbe, Paul, 80
Local-Comitee der israelitischen Armen- und Pilgerwohnungen auf Zion, 116
Lodz (ghetto), 212, 276
Loeb Mindensche Brautstiftung (Altona-Hamburg), 123
Loeb, Rudolf, 17, **170**
Loebel, Adolf, 171
Loerke, Oscar, 222
Loevinson, Johanna, 181
Loevison, Ermanno (Hermann), 181
Loevinson family, 181
Loewenberg, Jakob, 172
Loewenberg, Richard Detlev, 173
Loewenfeld, Philipp, 174, 197
Loewi, Otto, 135
London, 245
Lorraine, 6, 251, 272
Lorsch, 20
Löw, Leopold, 123
Löw, Schwab, 123
Löwen, Samuel Liepmann, 266
Löwen family, 266
Löwenfeld, Theodor, 205
Löwenstein, Leopold, 87
Löwenstein, Prinz Hubertus, 225
Lowenthal, Ernst G., 83, 110, 239
Löwenthal family, 187
Lowenthal-Hensel, Cecile, 110
Lubacz, 123
Lübeck, 191
Lubitsch, Ernst, 284
Lublin, 146
Lublinski family, 219
Ludwig, Emil, 91, 112, 141, 179, 197, 225, 240, 284
Ludwig Tietz Handwerkerschule, 151
Lueders, Marie Elisabeth, 26
Luft, Gerda, 273
Lunau, Elizabeth, 178
Lüth, Erich, 94, 101
Luther, Hans, 234
Luxembourg, 94
  German occupation of, 276
Luzzato, Samuel David, 205
Lvov, 78
Lynd, Robert, 230

Maas, Hermann, 94, 195
McCloy, John J., 88, 110, 234
McDonald, James G., 115, 240
McDonald, Ramsey, 98

Mach, Ernst, 179
Magdeburg, 106, 144, 253
Magnes, Judah, 102, 151, 273
Magnus, Erna, 175
Mahler, Gustav, 284
Mahler-Werfel, Alma, 15, 36
Mährisch Ostrau (Moravska-Ostrava), 276
Maidanek (concentration camp), 54
Maier, Pauline, 195
Mainz, 38, 229
Makkabi, 203
Man, Heinrich de, 43
Man, Henri de, 43
Mann, Erika, 79, 141, 240
Mann, Heinrich, 21, 91, 197, 225, 238
Mann, Klaus, 91, 238, 240
Mann, Monika, 141
Mann, Thomas, 8, 15, 21, 41, 61, 75, 91, 94, 104, 107, 112, 135, 141, 153, 157, 211, 213, 225, 265, 279
Mannheim, 59, 94, 102, 195, 220
Mannheimer family, 266
Marburg, 123
Marck, Siegfried, 117
Marcus, Ernst, 176
Marcus, Hertha, 155
Marcus family, 155
Marcuse, Bruno, 148
Marcuse, Herbert, 232
Marcuse, Ludwig, 119, 141, 284
Margolius, Hans, 21
Margulies, Heinrich, 273
Mark Brandenburg, 253
Markelfingen, 220
Märkisch-Friedland, 123
Markreich, Max, 177
Markreich family, 177
Marlowe, Gabriel, 158
Marriage, 6, 40, 59, 72, 97, 123, 129, 144, 177, 181, 221, 266. See also Courtship; Domestic life
Marseilles, 177
Marum, Elizabeth, 178
Marum, Ludwig, 178
Marum family, 178
Marx, Karl, 214
Marx, Lilli, 239
Masaryk, Thomas, 79
Massary, Fritzi, 15
Masur, Norbert, 4
Mattenbuden, 123
Matthias, Leo, 197
Mauritius, 63
Maurois, André, 79

Mauthausen (concentration camp), 256, 267
Mauthner, Fritz, 15, 22, 164, **179**, 284
Mauthner, Hedwig, 22
May, Henriette, 181
Maybaum, Ignaz, 94, 102
Maybaum, Siegmund, 43, 82, 106
Mayer, Eugen, 222
Mayer, Gustav, 64
Mayer, Paul, 209
Meckesheim, 220
Mehring, Walter, 141, 225, 265
Meidner, Ludwig, 40, 153, 284
Meinecke, Friedrich, 43, 222
Meinhard, Karl, 10
Meisel, Wolf Aloys, 185
Meissen, 188
Meissner, Otto, 186
Meitner, Lise, 234
Mekize Nirdamim, 203
Mekor Chajim, Verein, 82
Melchior, Carl, 234
Memmingen, 59
Memoirs, 7, 8, 12, 15, 34, 44, 45, 48, 53, 62, 63, 64, 65, 67, 70, 84, 98, 99, 102, 103, 106, 123, 135, 136, 138, 148, 174, 176, 181, 187, 191, 195, 200, 207, 208, 209, 214, 218, 220, 222, 230, 231, 232, 234, 239, 250, 253, 254, 260, 261, 263, 265, 266, 267, 271, 275. See also Diaries
Memorbücher, 59, 123, 183, 220
Mencken, H. L., 141
Mendelssohn, Alexander, 180
Mendelssohn, Arnold, 122
Mendelssohn, August, 122
Mendelssohn, Benjamin, 180
Mendelssohn, Enole, 180
Mendelssohn, Franz, 180
Mendelssohn, Franz von, 180
Mendelssohn, Franz von, Jr., 180
Mendelssohn, Fromet, 180
Mendelssohn, Henriette, 180
Mendelssohn, Joseph, 180
Mendelssohn, Moses, 180, 269, 284
Mendelssohn, Nathan, 122
Mendelssohn, Robert von, 234
Mendelssohn & Co., 170, 180
Mendelssohn & Co. (Amsterdam), 234
Mendelssohn & Fränkel, 180
Mendelssohn-Bartholdy, Abraham, 180
Mendelssohn-Bartholdy, Albrecht, 91, 197
Mendelssohn-Bartholdy, Felix, 180, 284
Mendelssohn-Bartholdy, Lea, 180
Mendelssohn-Bartholdy, Paul, 180

INDEX

Mendelssohn family, 122, **180**, 216
Mergentheim, 143
Merzbacher, Elizabeth, 143
Merzbacher family, 143
Meseritz, 123
Meseritz, Margaret, 189
Metz, 6
Metzger, Gertrud, 258
Metzger, Kurt, 46
Meurthe-et-Moselle, 6
Meyer, Gerald, 63
Meyer, Henriette, 180
Meyer, Johanna, 181
Meyer, Leffman, 183
Meyer, Margarethe, 182
Meyer, Oscar, 182, 255
Meyer, Walther, 183
Meyer-Benfey, Heinrich, 169
Meyer-Gräfe, Julius, 197
Meyer family, 202
Meyerbeer, Giacomo, 23, 40, 246, 284
Meyerbeer family, 23
Meyrink, Gustav, 15
Michelfeld, 178
Michelsohn, Georg, 16
Michelstadt, 257
Mieses, Hanna de, 184
Mieses, Jacques, 184
Mieses family, 184
Migration. See Emigration and immigration
Milch, Werner, 185
Milch family, 185
Military service
    19th cent., 113, 204
    World War I, 8, 21, 43, 48, 98, 105, 127, 130, 149, 151, 188, 195, 198, 209, 210, 213, 222, 224, 249, 261, 263, 273, 272, 275, 278. See also Reichsbund jüdischer Frontsoldaten
Military Tribunals Nuremberg, 186. See also Nuremburg Trial of Major German War Criminals, 1945–1946; War Crime Trials
Miller, Alexandre, 272
Millerand, Alexandre, 272
Les Milles (concentration camp), 46, 105
Minden, 253
Minsk (ghetto), 212
Miranda de Ebro (internment camp), 54, 252
Misch, Ludwig, 187
Mittelbau (concentration camp), 54
Mittelfranken, 32
Mittelstelle für Jüdische Erwachsenenbildung, 3

Mittelstelle Stuttgart, 3
Mittler, E. S., & Sohn, Königliche Hofbuchhandlung, 188
Moch, Jacob, 6
Moeller, Alex, 110
Moers, 253
Mohel books, 6, 86, 123, 143, 177, 220
Moissi, Alexander, 15, 158
Molnar, Franz, 79
Molo, Walter von, 242, 280, 284
Moltke, Helmuth von, 179, 244, 248
Mombert, Albert, 15
Mombert, Alfred, 222
Mommsen, Theodor, 30, 31, 112, 179, 244, 284
Mommsen, Theodor Ernst, 137
Mönchengladbach, 123
Monnet, Jean, 234
Montagu, Lily, 73, 98
Montefiore, Claude, 43, 73, 205
Montefiore, Moses, 40, 205, 236, 257, 284
Moravia, 40, 106
Moravia, Alberto, 41
Moravska Ostrava (Mährisch Ostrau), 276
Der Morgen, 98
Morgenstern, Christian, 91
Morgenthau, Henry, 272
Morgenthau, Henry Jr., 80
Morocco, 54
Mortara, Marco, 205
Mosbach, 171
Moselle, 6
Moses, Fritz, 272
Moses, Julius, 195
Moses, Robert, 255
Moses, Siegfried, 17, 110, 151, 273
Mosse, Albert, 188
Mosse, Emil, 188
Mosse, Eva, 276
Mosse, Marcus, 188
Mosse, Martha, 148, 188
Mosse, Rudolf, 179, 188
Mosse family, 188
Movement for the Care of Children From Germany, 273
Muehsam, Margaret T., 189
Mueller, Max, 31
Mühsam, Erich, 179, **190**, 191, 242, 284
Mühsam, Kreszentia, 190
Mühsam, Siegfried Selegmann, 191
Mühsam family, 191
Mülheim/Ruhr, 125
Müller, Robert, 197
Münchhausen, Börries von, 169, 179

Munich, 20, 82, 94, 95, 143, 152, 174, 188, 205, 257
Münster, 37
Münzesheim, 178
Murray, Gilbert, 153
Music, 3, 7, 23, 29, 133, 147, 157, 165, 228, 264
Musil, Martha, 119
Musil, Robert, 91, 119, 197
Mynona. See Friedländer, Salomon

Nackel, 123
Nadel, Arno, 147, **192**, 242
Nancy, 6
Naphtali-Epstein Verein (Karlsruhe), 220
Naphtali, Fritz, 234
Napoleon, 145
Napoleonic Wars, 6, 37, 123, 160, 180, 221
Nassau, 60
National Foundation for Jewish Culture, 203
National Refugee Service, 10
National Socialism (movement), 42, 108, **193**, 276
  outside Germany, 39, 80, 276
National Student Federation, 150
Nationaljüdische Jugend Deutschlands, 203
Nationalverein, 154
Natorp, Paul, 43
Navemar (S.S.), **194**
Nazi Germany, 36, 80, 108, 128, 182, 193, 234, 235, 255, 276, 279, 283
  Jewish communal and cultural life, 3, 4, 15, 17, 18, 27, 31, 44, 48, 50, 57, 64, 73, 82, 94, 99, 102, 107, 118, 133, 136, 140, 143, 147, 148, 161, 181, 214, 215, 232, 239, 241, 244, 245, 275
  persecution of Gypsies, 199, 276
  persecution of Jews; 1933–1941, 3, 4, 8, 9, 10, 11, 17, 18, 19, 21, 26, 27, 37, 39, 46, 48, 50, 54, 59, 62, 65, 70, 78, 82, 88, 89, 95, 98, 99, 100, 102, 103, 109, 110, 112, 114, 115, 118, 120, 133, 136, 137, 139, 140, 142, 146, 147, 148, 150, 151, 155, 156, 161, 162, 166, 170, 171, 186, 187, 188, 192, 195, 199, 204, 207, 210, 211, 212, 214, 215, 232, 239, 245, 254, 256, 258, 262, 267, 272, 273, 278
  persecution of Jews; 1942–1945. See Holocaust
  political repression, 34, 43, 110, 178, 186, 188, 189, 190, 231, 240, 272
  See also Anti-Nazi movements; Antisemitism; Concentration and internment camps; Emigration and immigration – 1935–1945; National Socialism; World War II
Nazimova, Alla, 64
Neckarbischofsheim, 59, 220
Nef, John Ulric, 137
Neimann, David, 116
Nellhaus, Dagobert, 17
Neter, Eugen, 59, **195**
Netherlands, 124, 256, 267
  German occupation of, 267
Netter, Oscar H., family, **196**
Der neue Merkur, 91, 92, **197**
Neuenkirchen, 77
Neues Schauspielhaus (Zurich), 119
Neumann, Alfred, 197, 225, 284
Neumann, Margarete, 98
Neumann, Salomon, 205
Neumark, 123
Neustadt, 46
Neustadt, Arthur, **198**
Neustadt, Herta, **198**
Neustadt, Upper Silesia, 210
Neustettin, 40
New School for Social Research (New York), 110, 230, 279
New York City, 43
Nichtarische Bach-Cantaten Gesellschaft, 232
Nicolai, Friedrich, 180
Nicolaische Buchhandlung, 188
Niebuhr, Reinhold, 21, 238
Niederland, W.G., **199**
Niemöller, Martin, 94, 141, 255
Nikolsburg, 81
Nimes Committee (Comité de coordination pour l'assistance dans les camps), 54
Nisko, 276
Nitzsche, Karl Immanuel, 180
Noack-Mosse, Eva, 276
Nobel, N. A., 5, 43
Nordau, Max, 40, 45, 182, 284
Nordeutscher Lloyd, 188
Nordstetten, 161
Norment, Caroline, 209
North Africa, 257
Nossig, Alfred, 242
Notgemeinschaft deutscher Wissenschaftler im Ausland, 234
Nuremberg, 60, 146
Nuremberg Trial of Major German War Criminals, 1945–1946, 9, 88, 101, 146, 186, 273, 276. See also War Crime Trials

Obergrombach, 220
Oberländer, Max, 210

INDEX

Oberlangenstadt, 123
Oberrat der Israeliten Badens, 140
Oberrat der Israeliten Württembergs, 161
Oberseemen, 123
Ochs, Siegfried, 244
Occupations. See Professions and occupations
Odo (Duke of Württemberg), 141
Oelde, 37
Oestreicher, Elsa, 200
Offenbach, 62, 107
Offenbach, Jacques, 284
Offenbacher, Erich, 201
Oko, Adolph, 73
Old age homes, 203, 245. See also Welfare institutions and organizations
Olden, Balder, 197
Oliven, Klaus, 202
Oliven family, 202
Ollendorf, Paula, 73, 167
Ollenhauer, Erich, 110
Oncken, Hermann, 222
Ophuls, Max, 119
Oppeln, 90
Oppenheim, Franz, 10
Oppenheim, Julie von, 51
Oppenheim, Moritz, 64
Oppenheimer, Franz, 15, 64, 197, 242, 273, 284
Oppenheimer family, 19, 178, 201
Oranienburg (concentration camp), 190
Orbis A.G. (Vaduz), 188
Orlik, Emil, 284
ORT (Organization for Rehabilitation Through Training), 78, 100, 203
Ortega y Gasset, José, 197
Orthodox Judaism. See Judaism (movements)- orthodox
Osborn, Max, 197
OSE (Oevre de Secours aux Enfants/Organization for Protection of Health and Child Care), 54
Osmund, Emmanuel, 246
OSS (Office for Strategic Services), 108, 232
Ossendorf, 37
Ossietzky, Carl von, 91, 101, 225
Ossietzky, Rosalinda von, 101
Österreichisch-Ungarisch-Israelitische Gemeinde (Jerusalem), 116

Pacifism, 85, 101, 108, 145, 190
Padberg, 172
Paderborn, 37, 40
Paetel, Karl, 108

Palatinate, 40, 46, 59, 60, 142, 220
Palestine
  19th cent., 116, 122, 246
  20th cent., 4, 78, 135, 138, 151, 257, 273
  See also Emigration and immigration; Israel, State of; Zionism
Pallenberg, Max, 284
Panholzer, Joseph, 272
Pannwitz, Rudolf, 197
Panofsky, Dora, 188
Panofsky, Erwin, 21, 153, 188, 230
Panowsky, Wolfgang, 10
Papen, Franz von, 42
Pappenheim, 257
Pappenheim, Bertha, 40, 73, 167, 239
Paquet, Alfons, 197
Paris, 6, 218, 245
Parsons, Talcott, 230
Passos, John Dos, 141
Paucker, Arnold, 110
Paul Ehrlich Stiftung, 210
Paulus Bund, 206
Perkins, Maxwell, 240
Perl, Katherine, 204
Perl, Leopold, 204
Perl family, 187, 204
Perles, Felix, 73, 205
Perles, Hedwig, 205
Perles, Joseph, 87, **205**
Perlmann family, 206
Pernerstorfer, Englebert, 179
Perthes, Clemens Theodor, 180
Pfemfert, Franz, 141
Pflaum, Marcus, 184
Pflaum family, 184
Pforzheim, 196
Philanthropy. See Welfare Institutions and organizations
Philippson, Alfred, 207, 208
Philippson, Dora, 207
Philippson, Ludwig, 123, **208**
Philippson, Martin, 217, 229
Philippson, Moritz, 208
Philippson, Phoebus, 208
Philippson family, 208
Philosophy, Jewish. See Jewish thought
Picard, Jacob, 15, 16, 21, 102. 107, 141, **209**, 258, 265
Picard, Max, 91, 197, 225
Picard family, 209
Pilpel, Robert, 10
Pinkus, Hans, 210, 259
Pinkus, Joseph, 210

Pinkus, Max, 185, 210
Pinkus family, 210
Pinson, Koppel, 73, **211**, 273
Pinthus, Kurt, 21, 101, 141, 209, 265
Piscator, Erwin, 119, 141, 197
Plaut, Max, 17, 148, **212**
Pleiger, Paul, 186
Poalei Zion, 273
Pogrom (November 1938), 9, 19, 27, 37, 46, 48, 62, 114, 120, 128, 133, 148, 186, 214, 254
Pogroms in Eastern Europe, 78, 205
Pohl, Max, 181
Pohl, Oswald, 186
Poland, 78, 100, 276
Poland, partition of, 123
Polanyi, Ilona, 255
Polgar, Alfred, 15, 41, 225, 284
Poltava, 151
Polzer, Victor, 213, 240
Pomerania, 123, 253
Ponten, Josef, 197
Popper-Lynkeus, Josef, 179
Posen (city), 40, 137, 205
Posen (province), 123, 233
Potsdam, 25, 60, 123, 253
Prague, 34, 38, 59, 123, 179, 188, 250, 265, 273
Prenzlau, 123
Pressburg, 116
Preussische Akademie der Künste, 166
Preussische Stargard, 111
Preussischer Landesverband jüdischer Gemeinden, 148, 203
Prinz, Arthur, 148, **214**
Prinz, Joachim, 10, 17, 21, 36, 101, 165, 209, 214, 273
Prisoners of War. See World War I – prisoners of war
Prisoners of War Relief Committee, 42
Professions and occupations
  architects, 129, 263
  archivists, 53, 123, 181
  art critics, 112, 218, 274
  art historians, 43, 153, 206
  artists, 24, 49, 77, 124, 153, 166, 192, 218, 250, 263, 274
  astronomers, 23, 278
  authors, 8, 15, 16, 22, 34, 35, 36, 41, 43, 45, 53, 61, 90, 91, 107, 112, 119, 134, 141, 145, 152, 157, 158, 164, 169, 172, 179, 181, 190, 197, 209, 213, 218, 224, 225, 228, 237, 238, 242, 250, 254, 260, 265, 268, 272, 283,
  bankers, 6, 12, 23, 25, 40, 46, 51, 77, 100, 122, 170, 180, 184, 234, 259, 266, 271, 283
  biochemists, 40, 52, 210
  biologists, 248
  booksellers, 123, 269
  cantors, 6, 57, 157, 165, 219
  chemists, 84, 109, 242, 258
  chess players, 184
  civil servants, 89, 110, 234, 235, 247
  composers, 23, 97, 147, 165, 180, 264
  conductors, 244
  cooks, 200
  dentists, 81, 226
  dramatists, 23, 119, 158
  dressmakers, 120
  economists, 132, 150, 182, 214, 234, 235, 240, 255, 259, 279, 280
  editors, 45, 91, 92, 188, 197, 213, 273
  educators, 3, 206, 231
  engineers, 129
  explorers, 137
  genealogists, 183, 243
  geographers, 180, 207, 208
  geologists, 185
  graphic artists, 250
  graphologists, 104
  historians, 17, 18, 82, 87, 110, 117, 123, 131, 137, 144, 162, 181, 211, 214, 216, 217, 229, 232, 251, 253, 257, 279
  home economists, 200
  industrial workers, 217, 273
  industrialists, 19, 43, 84, 90, 103, 104, 155, 210, 278
  journalists, 34, 41, 43, 80, 82, 91, 98, 101, 110, 132, 141, 151, 179, 188, 189, 190, 197, 209, 213, 224, 225, 227, 236, 238, 240, 254, 255, 265, 272, 273, 274
  judges, 247
  lawyers, 24, 26, 44, 77, 88, 89, 110, 145, 147, 151, 154, 174, 178, 183, 187, 188, 194, 202, 209, 234, 235, 247, 272
  lecturers, 181
  lexicographers, 227
  literary critics, 15, 91, 112, 119, 152, 179, 184, 185, 197, 206, 213, 218, 265
  mathematicians, 108
  medallists, 1, 266
  merchants, 19, 22, 99, 103, 121, 123, 155, 184, 185, 198, 201, 202, 206, 210, 266, 269, 270
  mineralogists, 185
  minters, 1, 122
  mohelim, 6

music critics, 187, 244
musicians, 3, 7, 29, 97, 133, 187, 192, 244, 264
musicologists, 192
orientalists, 82, 87
paleontologists, 65
pharmacists, 191
pharmacologists, 52
philanthropists, 99
philologists, 30, 31, 59, 135
philosophers, 21, 45, 47, 49, 87, 91, 98, 135, 140, 152, 164, 176, 179, 180, 222, 223, 258, 260
physicians, 22, 52, 65, 75, 76, 83, 122, 188, 195, 204, 208, 210, 219, 244, 248, 262
physicists, 14
poets, 23, 53, 59, 138, 172, 192, 224, 228, 264, 265
political scientists, 83, 88, 110
politicians, 43, 110, 113, 152, 154, 178, 182, 191, 255, 272, 279, 280
printers, 221
psychiatrists, 75, 173, 188, 199
psychologists, 168
publishers, 82, 139, 188
rabbis, 5, 6, 17, 18, 20, 31, 36, 37, 43, 57, 62, 73, 93, 102, 106, 116, 123, 144, 149, 151, 183, 185, 205, 208, 217, 229, 233, 244, 246, 251, 256, 261, 270
sales personnel, 5, 85, 103, 155
sinologists, 236
social workers, 4, 7, 64, 65, 98, 136, 143, 167, 181, 188, 195, 205, 231, 239, 267, 279
sociologists, 230, 279
soldiers. See Military service
statisticians, 108
tailors, 123
teachers, 48, 67, 131, 172, 204, 220, 246
theater critics, 15, 179
theologians, 17, 18, 20, 45, 47, 62, 73, 87, 205, 222, 223
translators, 8, 92, 213, 223, 227, 265
university teachers, 8, 14, 21, 22, 30, 31, 52, 59, 73, 83, 98, 108, 109, 110, 117, 135, 137, 140, 150, 153, 162, 168, 180, 207, 208, 211, 214, 230, 232, 236, 250, 279
zoologists, 65
Prossnitz, 34
Protected Jews. See Schutzjuden
Prussia, 1, 40, 60, 123
Prussian Landtag, 110, 154, 280
Public health administration, 83
Publishing industry, 82, 132, 139, 188
Puhl, Emil, 186

Querido Verlag, 224
Quidde, Ludwig, 234

Raabe, Wilhelm, 45
Rabbiner Seminar für das orthodoxe Judentum, 116
Rabbinerverband in Deutschland, 203
Radbruch, Gustav, 197
Radetzky, Wenzel, 79
Rasche, Karl, 186
Rashi Association for the Preservation of Jewish Cultural Monuments in Europe, 203
Rathenau, Walther, 15, 24, 33, 40, 43, 45, 179, 197, 284
Ratibor, 62
Raumer, Hans von, 182
Ravensburg, 123, 253
Rawicz, 60
Rawicz family, 167
Razovsky, Cecilia, 10
Récébédon (concentration camp), 59
Redlich, Oswald, 242
Redwitz an der Rodach, 32
Rée, Anita, 153
Reform Judaism. See Judaism (movements) – liberal and reform
Refugee-aid organizations, 9, 10, 46, 54, 56, 78, 102, 136, 148, 150, 203, 255, 272, 273, 276. See also Emigration and immigration
Refugee organizations, 9, 78, 127, 144, 203, 272, 276. See also Emigration and immigration – 1933–1945
Refugee scholars, relocation of, 8, 21, 52, 73, 83, 108, 110, 115, 117, 135, 137, 140, 150, 153, 162, 211, 214, 230, 232, 250, 255, 279. See also Emigration and immigration – 1933–1945
Regensburg, 257
Reichart, Walter, 210
Reichensachsen, 123
Reichmann, Eva, 102, 273
Reichmann, Hans, 148, 151
Reichsbund jüdischer Frontsoldaten, 99, 127, 139, 203, 214, 243, 245, 276. See also Military service (World War I); Veterans' organizations
Reichstag, 154

Reichsverband des jüdischen Mittelstandes, 203
Reichsvereinigung der Juden in Deutschland. See Reichsvertretung der deutschen Juden
Reichsvereinigung ehemaliger Kriegsgefangener, 210
Reichsvertretung der deutschen Juden, 3, 4, 10, 11, 17, 18, 37, 102, 118, 140, 148, 150, 171, 209, 212, 215, 234, 239, 276
Reichsvertretung der Juden in Deutschland. See Reichsvertretung der deutschen Juden
Reik, Theodor, 197
Reimarus, Elise, 180
Reinemann family, 249
Reinhardt, Max, 91, 92, 225, 284
Reinhart, Harold, 280
Reinhold, Peter, 73
Reissner, Hanns, 101, 110, 121, 148, **216**, 234, 259
Renan, Ernst, 31
Rendsburg, 123
Renger, Annemarie, 159
Rengstorf, Karl Heinrich, 280
Renner, Karl, 81
Reparations, 9, 56, 101, 141, 151, 234, 272, 273, 280. See also Restitution
Resource von 1794: Vereinigung der Kaufleute jüdischen Glaubens in Berlin, 203
Restitution, 9, 21, 43, 44, 56, 80, 86, 101, 110, 119, 125, 146, 151, 155, 161, 177, 188, 198, 199, 204, 210, 212, 234, 235, 239, 272, 273. See also Reparations
Reuter, Ernst, 141
Reuters, 236
Revolution of 1848–1849, 6, 51, 97, 113, 122, 131, 180, 209, 269
Revolution of 1918–1919, 33, 40, 151, 152, 155, 174, 178, 190, 210
Rexingen, 171
Rhein-Ruhr, 133, 203
Rheinfels, 60
Rhina, 40
Richthofen, Ferdinand von, 207
Rickover, Hyman, 21
Rieger, Paul, 3, **217**
Riess, Curt, 240
Riesser, Gabriel, 284
Riezler, Kurt, 137
Riga (ghetto), 212
Rimpar, 123
Ritschl, Friedrich Wilhelm, 30
Robbins, Jeanette, 10
Robert, Frederike, 268
Robert, Ludwig, 268

Robinson, Jacob, 75
Röchling, Hermann, 186
Roda-Roda, Alexander, 179, 197, 284
Roditi, Edouard, 218
Rogasen, 70
Roggenbach, Franz von, 31
Rolland, Romain, 8
Romanticism, 180
Rome, 181
Rommel, Erwin, 219
Rommel, Manfred, 219
Roosevelt, Eleanor, 21
Rosen, Pinchas. See Rosenblüth, Felix
Rosenbaum, Eduard, 91
Rosenblatt, Josef (Yossele), 165
Rosenblüth, Felix, 151, 273
Rosenfeld, Callmann Isaac, 219
Rosenfeld, Fritz, 219
Rosenfeld, Gustav, 219
Rosenfeld, Hans, 135
Rosenfeld, Kurt, 10, 272
Rosenfeld, Leopold, 219
Rosenfeld family, 219
Rosenheim, Jacob, 59, 222
Rosenstein, Paul, 64
Rosenstock-Huessy, Eugen, 43, 222
Rosenthal, Berthold, 220
Rosenthal family, 219
Rosenwald, Julius, 73
Rosenwald, Lessing, 36
Rosenzweig, Adam, 68, 221
Rosenzweig, Adele, 222
Rosenzweig, Edith, 222
Rosenzweig, Franz, 5, 47, 62, 135, 209, 221, **222**, 223, 258, 260
Rosenzweig family, 68, 221, 222
Rotenburg an der Fulda, 183
Roth, Cecil, 73, 276
Roth, Joseph, 224, 225
Rothfels, Hans, 137
Rothschild, James de, 246
Rothschild, Meyer Amschel, 25, 269, 284
Rothschild, Salomon Mayer, 25
Rothschild family, 13, 40, 46
Rotterdam, 205
Rowohlt, Ernst, 141, 240
Ruanda, 137
Rubel, Maximilian, 117
Rubenstein, Anton, 284
Rudolf Mosse Stiftung, 188
Rudolf Mosse Verlag, 188
Rumania, 78, 130
Ruppin, Arthur, 284
Russell, Bertrand, 61

INDEX

Russia, 78
Russian Literature, 92
Rüstow, Alexander, 214, 234

S. Fränkel (Neustadt), 210
Saarland, 251
Sachs, Hans J., 226
Sachs, Joseph Wilhelm, 226
Sachs, Julius, 227
Sachs, Nelly, 82, 209, **228**, 284
Sachs, Wilhelm, 226
Sachsen-Meiningen, 123
Sachsenhausen (concentration camp), 54
Sahl, Hans, 119
Saint Cyprien (concentration camp), 54
Saint Nicholas (concentration camp), 105
Salfeld, Siegmund, 229
Salomon, Albert, 230
Salomon, Alice, 26, 64, 230, **231**
Salomon, George, 110, 232
Salomon, George Anton, 232
Salomon, Richard, 110, **232**
Salomon family, 231, 232
Salomonsohn, Ernestine, 233
Salomonsohn, Gedalja, 233
Salomonsohn, Rachel, 233
Salomonsohn, Schachse, 233
Salomonsohn family, 233
Salons, 23, 66, 180, 265, 268. See also Assimilation
Salten, Felix, 284
Salus, Hugo, 242
Salzberger, Georg, 148
Samson family, 175
Samson Freischule (Wolfenbüttel), 66, 67, 282
Sandersleben, 123
Sarraut, Albert, 225
Savigny, Karl von, 269
Saxl, Fritz, 137
Saxony, 60
Schacht, Hjalmar, 234, 247
Schäffer, Hans, 151, 230, **234, 235**, 255
Schatzlar (concentration camp), 54
Schaumburg-Lippe, 40
Schechter, Solomon, 205
Scheel, Walter, 159
Scheidemann, Philipp, 61, 242
Schellenberg, Walter, 186
Scherk (cosmetics company), 155
Scherk family, 155
Schermeisel, 123
Schichau-Werke, 188
Schickele, Rene, 179, 225
Schildberg-Bunzlau, 123

Schindler, Bruno, 236
Schirokauer, Alfred, 237
Schirokauer, Arno, 91
Schlegel, Dorothea, 123, 180, 269, 284
Schleinitz, A. C., 180
Schlesinger, Arthur, 21
Schlesinger, Arthur Jr., 230
Schlesische Feinweberei, 210
Schlesische Flachs-Werke (Kaundorf), 210
Schlesische Zeitung, 188
Schlesischer Hausfrauen-Bund, 167
Schleswig-Holstein, 40, 60, 123
Schlossbrauerei M. Friedländer, 90
Schmidt, Carlo, 94, 119
Schmitt, Carl, 15
Schnabel, Arthur, 7, 147
Schneidemühl, 38
Schnitzler, Arthur, 112, 242, 284
Schnitzler, Olga, 158
Schocken, Gustav, 273
Schocken, Salman, 17, 119, 273
Schoenaich-Carolath, Prince Emil von, 45
Schoenberg, Arnold, 147, 284
Schoenberg, Jakob, 187
Schoenberner, Eleonora, 238
Schoenberner, Franz, 238
Schoenewald, Ottilie, 167, **239**
Schoenfeld, Ernst Heinrich, 53
Schoeps, Hans-Joachim, 10, 21, 117, 234
Scholem, Gershom, 21, 94, 222, 273
Schotten, 125
Schottlaender family, 202
Schottland, 123
Schramm, Percy Ernst, 137
Schreiber, Hermann, 82
Schrimm, 123
Schultheiss' Brauerei, 188
Schumann, Clara, 180
Schumpeter, Joseph Alois, 197
Schuschnigg, Kurt, 169
Schutzjuden, 25, 40, 60, 72, 74, 77, 121, 122, 123, 143, 146, 151, 210, 253, 266, 269, 277
Schwabacher, Alfred, 188
Schwäbischer Merkur, 188
Schwarzschild, Fritz, 222
Schwarzschild, Leopold, 10, 41, 197, 225, **240**
Schweitzer, Albert, 275, 284
Schweizerische Volksbank, 209
Schwerin an der Warthe, 60, 123
Schwerin, Kurt, 210
Seebach, Hasso von, 43
Seeliger, Herbert, 241
Segall, Herta, 198

Seghers, Anna, 141, 265
Seidel, Ina, 80, 169
Seiden, Rudolph, 242
Selfhelp for German Refugees, 10, 46, 54, 102, 150, 203, 209, 255
Seligmann, Caesar, 46, 73, 82, 94, 222
Seligmann, Sigmund, 87
Seligsohn, Julius, 37
Senator, Werner David, 151, 234, 273
Sender, Toni, 10, 21, 110
Sephardim in Germany, 60, 123
Serkin, Rudolf, 7
Sermons, 17, 37, 43, 62, 82, 102, 106, 123, 149, 205, 229, 256, 282
Shanghai, 124, 177, 267
Shaw, George Bernard, 15, 284
Shertok, Moshe, 151
Shils, Edward, 230
Shirer, William, 265
Siberia, 273
Siemens & Co. Hamburg, 188
Siemens, Hermann Werner von, 179
Sigel, Franz, 209
Sigwart, Christoph, 87
Silbergleit family, 185
Silesia:
  Lower, 253
  Upper, 210
Silone, Ignazio, 91
Simmel, Georg, 15, 179, 260
Simon, Ernst, 21, 80, 94, 151, 222, 273
Simon, Hans, 110
Simon family, 85, **269**
Simonis, Rudolf Jakob, 243
Simonis family, 243
Simonsen, David, 87, 205
Simonsohn, Max, 167
Simplicissimus, 238
Simpson, W. W., 280
Simson, Richard, 63
Sinclair, Upton, 141, 238
Singer, Isaac Bashevis, 209
Singer, Kurt, 10, 133, 197, **244**
Singer, Moritz, 244
Sinsheimer, Hermann, 64
Smilansky, Moshe, 151, 273
Socialism, 34, 41, 43, 108, 110, 113, 117, 122, 141, 152, 174, 178, 182, 214, 231. See also Anarchism; Communism; Sozialdemokratische Partei Deutschlands
Soest, 37
Sofer, Simcha Bunem, 116
Sokolow, Nahum, 205
Soladentenrat, Poltava, 151

Solm-Braunfels, 123
Solti, Georg, 234
Sombart, Werner, 43, 242, 284
Sonnenfeld, Leopold, 284
South Africa, 100, 177
South Korea, 83
Sozialdemokratische Partei Deutschlands (SPD), 34, 43, 108, 110, 113, 123, 174, 178, 182. See also Socialism
Spain, 250, 276
Spangenberg, 123
Spanish Civil War, 276
SPD. See Sozialdemokratische Partei Deutschlands
Sperling, Saul, 194
Speyer, 46, 220
Spiero, Heinrich, 206
Spiero family, 206
Spinnerei Vorwärts (Brackwede), 210
Springer, Axel, 159
Sproul, Edward, 137
St. Cyprien (concentration camp), 102
Staatsarchiv Bremen, 212
STAB (Swedish Match Company), 234
Stadelmayer, Peter, 265
Stadtarchiv Frankfurt am Main, 74
Städtische Israelitische Volksschule Dortmund, 48
Städtischen Gasanstalt (Charlottenburg), 84
Stahl, Heinrich, 10, **245**
Stahl, Rudolf, 222
Stampfer, Friedrich, 10
Staudinger, Else, 234, 255
Staudinger, Hans, 110, 234, 255
Steengracht von Moyland, Gustav Adolf, 186
Stehr, Hermann, 210, 242
Stein, Leopold, 246
Stein, Nathan, 107, 195, 209, **247**
Stein, Theodor S., 248
Steiner, Hedwig, 249
Steiner, Louis, 249
Steiner family, 249
Steiner-Prag, Hugo, 250
Steinheim, Salomon Ludwig, 246
Steinthal, Friedrich, 197
Steinthal, Heymann, 244, 261
Steinthal, Hugo, 251
Steinthal family, 72
Stern, Fritz, 110
Stern, Ludwig, 252
Stern, Luis, 252
Stern, Moritz, 123
Stern-Taeubler, Selma, 17, 73, 107, 123, 209, **253**

Sternberg, Leo, 147
Sternheim, Carl, 15
Sternheim, Hans, 254
Sternheim family, 254
Sternthal, Friedrich, 240
Stettin, 155
Stevenson, Adlai, 8, 230, 255
Stöcker, Helene, 179
Stockholms Enskilda Bank, 234
Stolp, 38
Stolper, Gustav, 255
Stolper, Toni, 43, 110, **255**
Stölzl, Christoph, 273
Stransky, Hugo, 110, **256**
Strasbourg, 6
Straus, Raphael, 82, **257**
Strauss, Bruno, 222
Strauss, Eduard, 62, 135, 222, **258**
Strauss, Leo, 230
Strauss, Richard, 284
Strauss, William, 259
Strauss family, 143, 259
Streicher, Julius, 146
Stresemann, Gustav, 112, 278
Struck, Hermann, 91, 112, 284
Stuckart, Wilhelm, 186
Stucken, Eduard, 91
Students' societies, 203, 210, 272, 273. See also Education, higher
Der Stürmer, 146
Stuttgart, 3
Stuttgarter Jüdische Kunstgemeinschaft, 3
Stuttgarter Konservatorium, 3
Stuttgarter Zeitung, 209
Süddeutsche Leinenweberei (Augsburg), 210
Süddeutsche Zeitung, 119
Sudermann, Hermann, 79, 179
Sugenheim, 59, 146
Susman, Margarete, 94, 135, 145, 222, **260**
Sutro, Abraham, 37, 284
Svenska Handelsbank, 234
Sweden, 234, 235, 243
Swedish Match Company (STAB), 234
Switzerland, 100
Synagogue architecture, 6, 13, 19, 20, 27, 37, 57, 59, 81, 86, 93, 107, 129, 142, 206, 241, 263, 270, 271, 274
Szell, Georg, 265
Szold, Henrietta, 73, 143, 151

Taeubler, Eugen, 21, 107
Taeubler, Selma Stern. See Stern-Taeubler, Selma
Tager, Paul, 272

Tagore, Rabindranath, 79
Tänzer, Arnold, 261
Tarbuth Foundation, 203
Tarnow, Fritz, 234
Tauber, Richard, 284
Technische Hochschule Darmstadt, 98
Tecklenburg, 253
Tellenbach, Gerd, 137
Teubner, 188
Textile and clothing industry, 19, 103, 104, 121, 202, 210
Thalheimer, Siegfried, 117
Theater, 15, 28, 119, 126, 133, 145, 158, 179, 181, 197, 210, 276
Theater, Berlin, 28
Theilhaber, Felix, 59
Theodor Herzl Society, 102
Theresienstadt (concentration camp), 17, 18, 43, 54, 70, 95, 123, 137, 146, 149, 156, 188, 200, 207, 212, 256, 263, 264, 276
Thieberger, Friedrich, 265
Thieberger, Gertrude. See Urzidil, Gertrude Thieberger
Thieberger family, 265
Thomas, Norman, 41
Thompson, Dorothy, 141, 225, 255, 265
Thuringia, 40
Tiburtius, Joachim, 280
Tillich, Paul, 119, 137, 255
Tilsit, 111
Titkin family, 111
Toch, Ernst, 255
Toczek, Heinrich, 262
Toczek family, 262
Toller, Ernst, 64, 197, 225, 284
Tolman, Edward, 137
Tönnies, Ferdinand, 43, 179, 242
Torberg, Friedrich, 7, 107, 119
Torczyner, Harry, 94
Torres, Henry, 272
Tramer, Hans, 110, 151, 273
Travel (professional and recreational), 73, 112, 122, 160, 168, 172, 180, 188, 210, 250
Trebitsch, Siegfried, 7, 197
Tresca, Carlo, 41
Treuga Holding A.G. (Switzerland), 188
Treviranus, Gottfried Reinhard, 234, 255
Trinidad, 177
Troeltsch, Ernst, 15, 197
Troller, Norbert, 263
Trott zu Solz, Adam von, 43
Truman, Harry, 165
Tucholsky, Kurt, 91, 112, 197, 284
Tucker, Richard, 165

Turgenev, Ivan, 236
Tütz, 123

Ullmann, Viktor, 264
Ullstein, Hermann, 234
Unabhängige Sozialdemokratische Partei Deutschlands (USPD), 108
UNESCO, 280
Unger, Max, 187
Union internationale de secours aux enfants, 54
United Jewish Appeal, 10
United Nations, 88, 101, 110
United Restitution Organization, 203
United States:
  Civil War, 209
  politics and government, 137, 230
University of California, Berkeley, 137, 150
Unna, Isak, 94
Unruh, Fritz von, 15, 59, 80, 104, 141, 265
Unruhstadt, 123
Ury, Lesser, 24, 40
Urzidil, Gertrude Thieberger, 134, **265**
Urzidil, Johannes, 34, 273, **265**
Urzidil family, 265
USPD (Unabhängige Sozialdemokratische Partei Deutschlands), 108
USSR, 63, 100

Vagts, Alfred, 91 197
Vaihinger, Hans, 15
Valentin, Veit, 141, 234
Valentin family, 266
Van Geldern, Peira, 42
Van Geldern family, 42
Van Tijn, Gertrude, 267
Varnhagen von Ense, Karl August, 268, 284
Varnhagen von Ense, Rahel, 180, **268**, 284
Veesenmayer, Edmund, 186
Veit, Johannes, 284
Veit, Moritz, 269
Veit, Philipp, 269, 284
Veit, Simon, 123, 180, 269
Veit family, 269
Veltheim, Hans-Hasso Baron von, 17, 18
Verband der deutschen Juden, 203
Verband der jüdischen Jugendvereine Deutschlands, 203
Verband deutscher Historiker, 162
Verband jüdischer Heimatvereine, 203
Verband jüdischer Studentenvereine, 78, 273
Verband Nationaldeutscher Juden, 162, 203
Verein Arbeitstätte in Hamburg, 217

Verein der Freunde der Taubstummen Jedide Ilmin, 203
Verein der Pfälzer in Berlin, 46
Verein für Kultur und Wissenschaft des Judentums, 282
Verein Israelitischer Lehrer, 203
Verein Mekor Chajim (Frankfurt am Main), 82
Verein zur Abwehr des Antisemitismus, 203
Verein zur Förderung der Kunst, 203
Verein zur Förderung der Volksbildung, 3
Vereinigte Chemische Werke (Brandenburg), 84
Vereinigung der liberalen Rabbiner Deutschlands, 203
Vereinigung für das liberale Judentum in Deutschland, 43, 93
Vermeylen, August, 61
La Vernet (concentration camp), 54, 272
Versicherungsverein "Die Hilfe", 203
Veterans' organizations, 99, 127, 139, 149, 203, 210, 245, 256. See also Reichsbund jüdischer Frontsoldaten
Victorica, Maria de, 43
Vienna, 7, 8, 22, 40, 60, 81, 106, 120, 123, 158, 242, 283
  Opera, 7
Vierfelder family, 270
Viernheim, 254
Vietor, Karl, 185, 209
Viking Press, 224
Vilna, 96
Vittel (concentration camp), 212
Vocational retraining, 78, 99, 100, 128, 151, 245, 267. See also Education; Emigration and immigration
Vogel, Hans-Jochen, 280
Vogelstein, Emmy, 167
Vogelstein, Heinemann, 43
Vogelstein, Hermann, 73, 82, 217
Vogelstein, Ludwig, 43
Vogelstein, Rosa, 43
Vogl, Margarethe, 138
Volksfreund, 178
Völkerheim, 171
Vossische Zeitung, 188

Wachenheim, Hedwig, 83, 110
Waddell, Helen, 137
Wagner, Paul, 84
Wallenberg, Jacob, 234
Wallerstein, 123
Walter, Bruno, 7, 165, 187, 242, 284
Walz, Hans, 3

Wandel, Eckhard, 235
Wandsbek, 123
Wangen, 209
War Crime Trials, 9, 71, 88, 101, 146, 178, 186, 273, 276
Warburg, 37
Warburg, Anita, 214
Warburg, Erich, 234
Warburg, Felix, 136, 283
Warburg, Fritz, 234
Warburg, Ingrid, 36
Warburg, Max, 82, 214, 215, 234, 240, 273
Warburg, Otto, 242
Warburg, Siegmund, 234, **283**
Warren, Earl, 137
Warsaw, 96
Washington Heights (New York City), 127, 256
Wassermann, Jakob, 64, 91, 284
Wassermann family, 271
Webb, Beatrice, 21
Weber, Marianne, 230
Weber, Max, 43, 153, 242
Wechsler, Hile, 284
Wedekind, Frank, 91, 179
Wegner, Armin T., 197
Weichmann, Elsbeth, 110
Weichmann, Herbert, 110
Weidenmüller, F.G. (Antonsthal), 188
Weigert, Julius, 272
Weigert, Stanley, 137
Weil, Bruno, 10, 80, 141, 148, **272**
Weil family, 272
Weimar Republic. See Germany – politics and government – 1918–1933
Weinheim, 59, 60
Weinryb, Bernard, 102
Weiss, Ernst, 197
Weissensee, 245
Weiszäcker, Ernst von, 186
Weizmann, Chaim, 17, 21, 40, 109, 151, 273, 284
Welfare Committee for Prisoners of War, 42
Welfare institutions and organizations, 6, 7, 10, 40, 54, 56, 66, 67, 77, 78, 86, 100, 106, 116, 123, 136, 143, 144, 146, 148, 149, 150, 167, 177, 181, 188, 191, 203, 205, 210, 214, 215, 217, 231, 239, 245, 267, 273
Weltsch, Felix, 134, 197, 265, 273
Weltsch, Robert, 17, 21, 80, 94, 110, 211, 214, 234, 265, **273**
Weltsch, Theodor, 273
Weltverband für religiös-liberales Judentum, 203
Werfel, Alma, 265, 284
Werfel, Franz, 15, 36, 240, 265, 284
Werkdorp Wieringen, 267
Werner, Alfred, 274
Wertheim, 220
Wertheimer, Leopold. See Brunner, Constantin
Wertheimer, Willy, 275
West Prussia, 123
Westerbork (concentration camp), 267
Westermann, Georg (Braunschweig), 188
Westphalia, 37, 77, 123
Wichelhausen, Felix, 69
Wiechert, Ernst, 157
Wiener, Alfred, 80, 94, 107, 112, 151, 209, 214, 234, 276, 280
Wiener Library, 276
Wiener Zeitung, 188
Wihl, Ludwig, 242
Wilder, Thornton, 119, 141
Wilhelm I (German Emperor), 248
Wilhelm II (German Emperor), 51, 76, 123, 170, 243
Wilhelm III (German Emperor), 51
Wilhelm, Kurt, 94
Wille, Bruno, 179
Wills and testaments, 3, 6, 22, 42, 43, 67, 77, 89, 121, 122, 123, 154, 181, 185, 202, 208, 210, 266, 269
Willstätter, Richard, 109, 284
Winterstein affair, 199
Wise, Stephen, 73, 101
Wissenschaft des Judentums, 17, 18, 30, 62, 66, 67, 68, 69, 73, 82, 102, 106, 123, 131, 140, 203, 205, 217, 221, 229, 246, 281, 282
Wissenschaftlich-gesellige Verbindung, Wirceburgia, 203
Wolf, Ernst, 277
Wolf family, 277
Wolfenbüttel, 60, 67, 123, 282
Wolfenstein, Alfred, 197
Wolfers, Jakob, 278
Wolfers, Robert, 278
Wolfers family, 278
Wolff, Kurt, 230
Wolff, Leo, 148
Wolff, Theodor, 80
Wolfskehl, Karl, 59, 91, 107, 135, 222, 260, 284
Wolfssohn, Aron, 246
Wolfssohn, David, 284
Wollheim, Norbert, 80, 101
Women
  in politics, 26, 43, 191, 239, 279

education of, 66, 83, 167, 172, 181, 231, 239, 255
employment of, 26, 29, 83, 98, 120, 143, 155, 167, 181, 200, 204, 208, 231, 239, 255, 279
Women's organizations, 38, 64, 167, 181, 203, 239. See also Feminism
Woodward, Kerry, 264
World Congress of Jewish Studies, 203
World Jewish Congress, 101, 203
World Union for Progressive Judaism, 17, 98, 203
World War I, 6, 8, 19, 21, 33, 34, 40, 42, 43, 48, 62, 82, 84, 91, 96, 98, 105, 114, 127, 130, 136, 139, 149, 151, 155, 158, 163, 169, 174, 179, 188, 195, 198, 209, 210, 213, 218, 222, 224, 231, 249, 261, 263, 272, 273, 275, 278
  espionage, 43
  prisoners of war, 42, 210, 263, 273
World War II, 4, 10, 54, 88, 108, 123, 186, 187, 219, 234, 240, 270, 273, 276, 283
  resistance, 43, 108, 234
Wörmann, Ernst, 186
Worms, 59, 107, 142, 163, 220
Wunderlich, Frieda, 279
Württemberg, 40, 94, 161, 217, 270
Würzburg, 60

Yad Vashem, 102, 177
Yeshiva Etz-Hayyim (Jerusalem), 116
Yeshiva University, 263
Yiddish literature, 36, 61, 92, 107, 126
Youth Aliyah, 121, 151, 203
Youth movement, 99, 128, 203, 242, 245, 273
Yugoslavia, 188, 276

Zechlin, Egmont, 80
Zeitlin, Leon, 80, **280**
Zentralausschuss der deutschen Juden für Hilfe und Aufbau, 148, 203
Zentralvereinigung der österreichischen Emigranten (Paris), 78
Zentralwohlfahrtsstelle der deutschen Juden, 148, 203
Ziegler, Ignaz, 7
Zille, Heinrich, 112
Zionism, 4, 7, 17, 21, 36, 40, 47, 82, 85, 93, 94, 106, 109, 110, 123, 135, 138, 145, 148, 151, 211, 214, 234, 242, 243, 257, 267, 273. See also Anti-Zionism; Emigration and immigration – Israel and Palestine; Israel, State of; Palestine
Zionist Organization of America, 102
Zionistische Vereinigung für Deutschland, 94, 151, 203, 214, 273
Zionistisches Centralbureau, 78
Zuckerman, Hugo, 61
Zuckmayer, Carl, 15, 119, 240, 242, 265
Züllichau, 123
Zülz, 210
Zunz, Adelheid, 66, 67, 68, **281**, 282, 284
Zunz, Leopold, 40, 66, 67, 68, 69, 205, 221, 281, **282**, 284
Zurich, 94, 119, 188
Zuschauer (Halbmonatsschrift für Kunst, Literatur und Öffentliches Leben) , 45
Zweig, Arnold, 21, 40, 197, 222, 273, 284
Zweig, Frederike, 8, 40, 80
Zweig, Stefan, 15, 40, 80, 107, 112, 209, 225, 236, 238, **283**, 284
Zwesten, 123
Zwingenberg, 59

SMALL COLLECTIONS

ALPHABETICAL LISTING CODED FOR CONTENTS

FO SM **AACHEN; JEWISH COMMUNITY**
Gallery with children's art exhibition;
transparencies depicting synagogue
2 items
AR 5183, AR 7063

FO **ABRAHAM AARON**
Court medailleur, Schwerin,
1735–1825
Photos
8 items
AR 3010

PM **LUDWIG ABRAHAM**
1871–ca. 1944
Identification cards
3 items
AR 3337

FO PM **DON ISAAK ABRAVANEL**
1437–1508
Medal issued by Jewish Community,
Berlin (1937) with photo
2 items
AR 2498

PM **SIMON ACKERMANN**
Report on pogrom of November
1938 in Baden
2 items
AR 2537

SM **ALFRED ADLER**
Physician, psychologist, 1870–1937
Newspaper article (1971)
1 item
AR 4674

GE **FRANK J. ADLER**
born 1923 Frankfurt a. M.
Prints on Adler and Schwarzadler
families, curriculum vitae
3 items
AR 4791

FO **FRIEDRICH ADLER**
Austrian politician, 1879–1960
Photos
3 items
AR 2758

PM **FRIEDRICH ADLER**
Writer, 1857–1938
Etching by R. Meyerhofer
1 item
AR 4678

FO SM **FRIEDRICH ADLER (HAMBURG)**
Architect, 1878–1942
Photo of stained glass window, article
about Adler
1 item
AR 1217

PM **GEORG ADLER**
1863–1908
Autographs
2 items
AR 2461

SM **HANS GUENTHER ADLER**
Author, 1910–
Festschrift for his 65th birthday
1 item
AR 4239

SM **HUGO CHAIM ADLER**
Composer of synagogue music,
1894–1955
Eulogy
1 item
AR 217

GE **KARL ADLER**
Letters about Lerchethal family
2 items
AR 3734

SM **KURT ADLER**
Conductor, 1905–1977
Obituaries
2 items
AR 4466

PM **LEO ADLER**
Cantor, rabbi, 20th cent.
Correspondence with libraries, E.
Kirschner and others about
synagogue music (1907–1932)
22 items
AR 723

FO **MAX ADLER**
Sociologist, 1873–1937
Photo of portrait
1 item
AR 2685

PM **SAMUEL ADLER**
Letter to Adler in Philadelphia from
his father and others in Wuerzburg, in
Latin and Hebrew script (1848)
1 item
AR 7051

FO = Photos · GE = Genealogical Material · PM = Primary Material · SM = Secondary Material

FO SM **VIKTOR ADLER**
Austrian politician, socialist,
1852–1918
Photo of portrait, article about Adler
4 items
AR 2759

SM **HELENE ADOLF**
Poem "Belvedere in Wien"
1 item
AR 3479

FO SM **THEODOR WIESENGRUND ADORNO**
Sociologist, 1903–1969
Clippings, photos
8 items
AR 2279

FO SM **SAMUEL JOSEF AGNON**
Hebrew author, 1966 Nobel Prize for Literature, 1888–1970
Photo of medal, special issue of *Haaretz* in his honor (1966), article about Agnon's work
6 items
AR 3034

PM **EDITH AHLFELD**
born 1893, Barmen
Various personal documents and notices
19 items
AR 5024

GE PM **JOSEF AHLFELD**
Photocopies of documents: notes and memos starting 1844, mostly dealing with family history since 1781
1 item
AR 4733

PM **AKTIONSAUSSCHUSS JÜDISCHER DEUTSCHER**
1933 circular letter
1 item
AR 5145

PM **ALBERSWEILER; JEWISH COMMUNITY**
Register of Jewish name changes (1808)
1 item
AR 4916

GE **CURT ALBU**
Family tree with correspondence of relatives
2 items
AR 1

PM **HARRY ALDERMAN**
Legal brief of City of Frankfurt a.M. concerning openings of stores outside Ghetto by Jews (1671); decrees about Jews by governments of Nuremberg (1770), Prussia (1770), Austria (1750/1810); leaflets announcing antisemitic meeting to be addressed by Adolf Stoecker (1891)
7 items
AR 7052

SM **SCHOLEM ALEICHEM**
Writer, 1859–1916
Commemorative stamps; clipping; typescript on Scholem Aleichem
4 items
AR 1645

FO SM **KURT ALEXANDER**
Administrator, 1893–1962, head of United Restitution Organization
Photo; obituary
2 items
AR 1640

PM SM **ROBERT ALEXANDER**
Composer, organist, 1883–1966
List of compositions; life story of Robert Alexander, curriculum vitae
5 items
AR 3030

SM **SALOMON MICHAEL ALEXANDER**
Anglican bishop, 1799–1845
Biographies; articles
2 items
AR 3492

FO PM SM **WALTER ALEXANDER**
Berlin Jewish Community official, 1878–1949
Clippings; letter; photo
5 items
AR 2

SM **H. J. ALLEN**
Clippings
2 items
AR 5258

FO = Photos · GE = Genealogical Material · PM = Primary Material · SM = Secondary Material

PM **ALLENSTEIN; JEWISH COMMUNITY**
Cornerstone document of synagogue (1876)
1 item
AR 2866

FO **ALLERSHEIM, BAVARIA; JEWISH COMMUNITY**
Photo of cemetery
1 item
AR 4232

FO **ALSBACH A.D. BERGSTRASSE; JEWISH COMMUNITY**
Photos of cemetery
7 items
AR 3568

FO **ALTDORF, BADEN; JEWISH COMMUNITY**
Photo of synagogue
1 item
AR 2486

GE **ALTEN FAMILY**
Family documents (1846–1964)
3 items
AR 7171

FO PM **PETER ALTENBERG (BORN**
SM **RICHARD ENGLAENDER)**
Author, 1859–1919
Clippings; unpublished poem; lecture on Altenberg; photos of portraits; autographs
40 items
AR 397, AR 844

SM **JACOB ALTMAIER**
Obituary, 1963
1 item
AR 2298

SM **ADOLF ALTMANN**
Rabbi, 1879–1944
Article (1979)
1 item
AR 4836

FO PM **ALEXANDER ALTMANN**
SM Rabbi, professor of philosophy, 1906–1987
Letters; photos; report; photocopies
6 items
AR 796

GE **ALTSCHUELER FAMILY**
Family tree, related documents
5 items
AR 3801

SM **ALZEY; JEWISH COMMUNITY**
Article, 1927
1 item
AR 137

PM **PAUL AMANN**
Professor of French, translator, 1884–1958
Letters from Thomas Mann
9 items
AR 3305

FO PM **KENNETH AMBROSE**
1919–
Resumé, photo
2 items
AR 1678

PM **AMERICAN FEDERATION OF JEWS FROM AUSTRIA**
Circulars, invitations (1946–1948)
4 items
AR 4013

SM **AMERICAN GATHERING**
Congressional Record (April 7, 1983)
1 item
AR 5128

SM **AMERICAN JEWISH COMMITTEE**
Brochure (1976)
1 item
AR 4301

PM **ANDERNACH; JEWISH COMMUNITY**
Questionnaire about community (1958)
1 item
AR 819

FO SM **GUENTHER ANDERS (BORN STERN)**
Author, born 1902
Clipping; photo
2 items
AR 3984

FO GE **LEOPOLD VON ANDRIAN**
Poet, 1875–1951
Family tree and sketch
2 items
AR 3918

FO = Photos · GE = Genealogical Material · PM = Primary Material · SM = Secondary Material

FO **ANGELTUERN; JEWISH COMMUNITY**
Photos of former synagogue
3 items
AR 3877

GE **HERBERT ANGERTHAL**
Family tree and sketch
1 item
AR 1380

PM **ANHALT; JEWISH COMMUNITY**
List of communities; letter about Jewish figures in Anhalt
2 items
AR 3446

GE **ANHAUCH FAMILY**
Austrian noble family, Czernowitz
Family tree
2 items
AR 1767

PM **SIMON ANKER**
born 1845
Letters; certificates; antisemitic paper about Anker (1937)
9 items
AR 1218

PM **ANNABERG; JEWISH COMMUNITY**
Estimated value of former communal property
1 item
AR 3447

FO SM **ANSBACH; JEWISH COMMUNITY**
Article (1962); transparencies depicting synagogue
2 items
AR 2936, AR 7228

FO GE **ANSCHEL FAMILY; WESTPHALIA**
Family history; copies of photos
1 item
AR 5282

GE **HERZ ANSCHELL**
1779–1847
"Genealogy of a Jewish Family: The descendants of Herz Anschell" by W. Rosenstock
1 item
AR 4474

PM **RUTH ANSELM**
Dancer-Soloist with Deutsches Opernhaus, Berlin
Portfolio of Ruth Anselm dedicated to Heinrich Stahl (1939)
1 item
AR 7171

PM **JULES ANSPACH**
Mayor of Brussels, 1825–1879
Medal
1 item
AR 4848

SM **RAHEL APFEL**
Eulogies
1 item
AR 736

SM **JENNY APOLANT**
Social worker, 1874–1925
Manuscripts; clipping
3 items
AR 4853

GE PM **RUDY APPEL FAMILY**
Family tree of Appel-Hofmann family, including related Loewenstein, Willstaetter, and Stein families; translation of diary of Benjamin Willstaetter (1813–1818); Yiddish notes on noteworthy events, Krefeld (1805–1811)
3 items
AR 3614

PM **ADOLF APT**
Commercial employee, 1814– ?
Personal papers
15 items
AR 3784

GE PM **RUDOLF APT**
1897–1979
Memoir; correspondence; family papers
3 items
AR 7180

SM **OTTO ARENDT**
Statesman, economist, 1854–1936
Typescript about him by Ernst Hamburger
1 item
AR 2650

FO = Photos · GE = Genealogical Material · PM = Primary Material · SM = Secondary Material

PM **RANDOLPH ARENSBERG**
Receipt books for R. Arensberg; city of Drausfeld (1847–1889 and 1894–1932)
2 items
AR 4586

PM **CHAIM ARLOSOROFF**
Invitation
1 item
AR 2534

SM **FRANK ARNAU**
Journalist
Miscellaneous articles in German newspapers: photocopies and clippings (1933–1964)
17 items
AR 2107

SM **ARNHOLD AND S. BLEICHROEDER, NEW YORK**
Story about banking family and firm; photo copies and clippings
7 items
AR 4843

GE **ARNOLD FAMILY, IBENHAUSEN**
Family tree since 1769
1 item
AR 4732

PM **HELINE ARNOLD**
Nurse, 1845–1905
Decoration (medal), 1870/71
2 items
AR 2625

FO GE **ARNSTEIN FAMILY**
Austrian noble family
Family tree; photos; copies of portraits
7 items
AR 1768

SM **EMIL ARON**
Physician
List of medical publications, (1881–1931)
1 item
AR 3782

SM **HERMANN ARON**
Electrical engineer, physicist, 1845–1918
Clipping; prints on Hermann Aron
3 items
AR 2127

SM **WILLIAM ARON**
Bibliography of his publications (1958)
1 item
AR 210

PM **GEBRUEDER ARONS BANKHAUS**
Letter
1 item
AR 2079

PM **DAVID ARONSFELD**
1873–1967
Memoirs about Jewish life
2 items
AR 7182

SM **LOUIS ARONSOHN**
Banker, member of Prussian Landtag, 1850–1928
Typescript on Aronsohn by Ernst Hamburger
1 item
AR 2651

GE **ARONSTEIN FAMILY**
Aronstein and Bueren family trees (18th cent.)
2 items
AR 273

SM **ART HISTORY**
Judaica and other works of art; Sotheby Park Bernét catalogue (1929)
1 item
AR 2354

GE **HANS ARZT FAMILY**
Family histories; genealogy
32 items
AR 4608

FO **BRUNO ASCH**
1890–1940
Photo
1 item
AR 1170

PM **M. ASCH**
Confirmation booklet (1859)
1 item
AR 3810

SM **SCHALOM ASCH**
Playbill
1 item
AR 3856

FO = Photos · GE = Genealogical Material · PM = Primary Material · SM = Secondary Material

SM **SIGISMUND ASCH**
Physician
Photocopy of newspaper clipping;
Curt Colden, "Der Alte Asch"
1 item
AR 539

PM **ASCHBACH, OBERFRANKEN; JEWISH COMMUNITY**
Excerpts of chronicle (1870–1970)
1 item
AR 4795

PM SM **LEO ASCHER FAMILY**
Composer
List of contents of Leo Ascher collection, poem by Franzi Ascher
17 items
AR 3741

FO PM **SELMAR ASCHHEIM**
Physician, 1878–1965
Photo; address for his 75th birthday
4 items
AR 3592

FO SM **A. ASHER & CO.; BOOKDEALER**
Berlin bookstore
Photos; clippings
15 items
AR 2213

FO PM **BERTHOLD AUERBACH (BORN**
SM **MOSHE BARUCH AUERBACH)**
Author, 1812–1882
Clippings; photo of his tombstone; autographs (1844–1873)
22 items
AR 1095, AR 1146

PM SM **ELIAS AUERBACH**
Physician, author 1882–1971
Restitution Court decision (1964); obituary
2 items
AR 2608

PM SM **HENRY (HEINZ) AUERBACH**
Lawyer, owner of film companies, 1890–
Documents; correspondence; clippings
8 items
AR 7098

PM **KURT AUERBACH**
Letter from Prussian Minister of Interior concerning possibility of admission to pharmacology examination (1935)
1 item
AR 3735

PM **LEOPOLD AUERBACH**
Physician, 1828–1897
Invitation
2 items
AR 3768

GE **MOSES AUERBACH FAMILY**
Family tree (ca. 1475), Regensburg; also Wolff and Friedlaender families
1 item
AR 3531

SM **SIEGFRIED M. AUERBACH**
Industrialist 1886– ?
Biographical notes; clippings
3 items
AR 3687

FO PM **RAOUL AUERNHEIMER**
Author 1876–1947
Photos; autographs
4 items
AR 2686, AR 553

SM **AUFBAU**
New York Times article (Nov. 16, 1984) "A Sense of Duty Sustains a Newspaper for Exiles"
1 item
AR 5314

SM **AUFHAUSEN, AALEN; JEWISH COMMUNITY**
Article
2 items
AR 2449

FO SM **AUGSBURG; JEWISH COMMUNITY**
Photo; forty negatives of synagogue interior and exterior; paper about industry in Augsburg (18th cent.)
6 items
AR 990

SM **AURICH; JEWISH COMMUNITY**
Exhibit catalogue about the community
1 item
AR 4638

FO = Photos · GE = Genealogical Material · PM = Primary Material · SM = Secondary Material

FO PM **AUSCHWITZ (CONCENTRATION**
SM **CAMP)**
Clippings; photos; manuscripts
32 items
AR 2271

SM **ROSE AUSLAENDER**
Poet, ca. 1907–1988
Articles about her phonograph records of poetry readings
13 items
AR 4353

GE **AUSPITZ FAMILY**
Family tree
1 item
AR 1769

FO **AUSTRIA; JEWISH COMMUNITY**
Photos of synagogues in Bohorodczany, Chlodorow, Zloczow, Zmigrod
3 items
AR 2877

FO **BAAL-SCHEM VON MICHELSTADT (BORN ISAAC LOEW WORMSER)**
Rabbi, died 1848
Photo of tombstone
1 item
AR 769

GE **BACH FAMILY, WUERTTEMBERG**
Family history, family tree from Mueringen and Dettensee
3 items
AR 3802

FO SM **GERSON BACH**
Office manager, *Syndicus* of Verband Deutscher Waren- und Kaufhäuser, 1865–1943
Biography; photos
3 items
AR 1684

FO SM **HANS I. BACH**
Historian, 1902–1977
Newspaper article; photos; obituary
6 items
AR 4461

GE **BACH-MEHLER FAMILY**
Family tree from 1540, biography of Rabbi Judah Mehler, (1660–1751)
2 items
AR 4

PM **FRANCES BACHARACH**
Woven challah cover; megillah (handwritten)
2 items
AR 4463

FO PM **SALOMON BACHENHEIMER**
Jewish religious teacher, 1863–1936
Letters; photos; documents relating to Jewish communities in northern Germany (1878–1933)
52 items
AR 3674

FO SM **WILHELM BACHER**
Hungarian scholar, 1850–1913
Photo; cross-references
2 items
AR 3195

PM **BACHRACH-STEG; JEWISH COMMUNITY**
14 tables; sketches of former synagogue
2 items
AR 5182

FO **BAD DUERKHEIM; JEWISH COMMUNITY**
Photo
1 item
AR 3727

FO PM **BAD HOMBURG V.D. HOEHE;**
SM **JEWISH COMMUNITY**
Clipping; manuscript; negatives and photocopies of synagogue photos
6 items
AR 190

SM **BAD KOENIG; JEWISH COMMUNITY**
Newspaper article (1983)
1 item
AR 5181

FO **BAD NAUHEIM; JEWISH COMMUNITY**
Photos of synagogue
2 items
AR 7211

FO PM **BADEN-BADEN; JEWISH COMMUNITY**
Photo of pogrom (1938); letters
7 items
AR 2560

FO = Photos · GE = Genealogical Material · PM = Primary Material · SM = Secondary Material

FO PM **BADEN; JEWISH COMMUNITY**
Government decrees, histories, photos
15 items
AR 138

PM **FREDERICK BADEN-WALDAUER**
Engineer, author, 1884–
Letters to Baden-Waldauer, including acknowledgement by Harry Truman
3 items
AR 3972

SM **BENNO BADT**
High school teacher, Breslau
Advertisement for textbook on biblical history
3 items
AR 2852

PM SM **SAMUEL BAECK**
Rabbi, father of Leo Baeck, 1834–1912
Letters; article on 25th anniversary of his death
4 items
AR 2382

PM **HEINRICH BAEHR**
1897–1981
Poems and various documents on Theresienstadt
30 items
AR 4700

PM **HUGO BAEHR**
Circular concerning curfew and release of Jews from concentration camps (Ulm, November 1938)
1 item
AR 1219

PM **ABRAHAM BAER**
Cantor, 1834–1894
Page of music by Baer (Hashkivenu)
1 item
AR 3303

GE PM **CARL BAER FAMILY, FRANKFURT A.M**
Documents (1789–1845); military safe-conduct pass (Berlin 1806); documents of Freudenberg family (Sinsheim, 1840–1850)
16 items
AR 2390

GE PM **HIRSCH BAER FAMILY**
Schutzbrief Hirsch Baer (1806); family documents
3 items
AR 5150

GE PM **JOSEPH BAER**
SM Bookdealer, Joseph Baer & Co.
Bibliography, family tree of descendants, excerpts about history of firm
5 items
AR 157

GE **JULIUS BAER**
Family letters 1817–1825, Hebrew marriage contract (New York, 1876), record of marriage
6 items
AR 2095

GE **LEO BAER FAMILY, NUERENBRECHT**
Family tree
1 item
AR 2488

PM SM **RICHARD BAER**
Physician, 1897–1965
Report; by-laws of Kameradschaftshilfe of Preles camp, Switzerland (1943); obituary
2 items
AR 486

FO SM **SELIGMANN BAER**
Jewish scholar, 1825–1898
Articles; photos of memorial plaque
2 items
AR 1052

FO **ALEXANDER BAERWALD**
Architect, 1877–1937
Photo
1 item
AR 1172

SM **BAERWALD FAMILY**
Catalogue cards of books by family members
1 item
AR 3529

PM **HERMANN BAERWALD**
Translation of correspondence with Eduard Lasker
1 item
AR 744

SM **MORITZ BAERWALD**
Politician, 1860–1919
Typescript by Ernst Hamburger
1 item
AR 2653

SM **PAUL BAERWALD**
Banker, philanthropist, son of
Hermann Baerwald, 1871–1961
Manuscript (5 pp.), "The Papers of
Paul Baerwald" (with Herbert
H. Lehmann Papers at Columbia
University)
1 item
AR 4735

FO **ADOLF VON BAEYER**
Nobel Prize 1905, chemist,
1836–1917
Photo
1 item
AR 2760

SM **BAIRSDORF B. BAMBERG;
JEWISH COMMUNITY**
Article
1 item
AR 3015

FO PM **BAISINGEN; JEWISH
COMMUNITY**
Comment on chronicle of anti-Jewish
riot during 1848; photos of megillah
3 items
AR 7089

PM **BALDENBURG; JEWISH
COMMUNITY**
Answer to questionnaire about Jewish
community
1 item
AR 815

PM **ERNST BALL**
Poem
1 item
AR 1534

PM **HUGO BALL**
Writer; leader of Dadaist movement,
1886–1927
Ball-Schohl correspondence; sheet
music
15 items
AR 7129

PM **K. J. BALL-KADURI**
Historian, 1891–1976
Letter
1 item
AR 4776

PM **ALBERT BALLIN**
Director General of Hamburg-
America Line 1857–1918
Postage stamps, telegram from Kaiser
Wilhelm II; autographs
7 items
AR 26, AR 833

GE **BALLIN FAMILY, HEBENHAUSEN**
Photocopies of handwritten
genealogy
1 item
AR 4919

PM SM **BAMBERG; JEWISH COMMUNITY**
Articles about Bamberg; antisemitic
article; community meeting minutes
(1832–39, 1928, 1936–65)
8 items
AR 2399

FO PM **MAX BAMBERGER-BEYFUS**
Organizer of fairs and exhibits,
1881–1944
Photos; letter of recommendation
5 items
AR 1782

FO **FRANZ BAMBERGER**
Banker, politician, 1856–1926
Photo
1 item
AR 3425

PM SM **FRITZ BAMBERGER**
Jewish scholar, editor, vice-president
of Leo Baeck Institute, 1902–1984
Articles; course catalogues; clippings;
letters; typescript about Berliner
Bibliophiles (1934–1977)
36 items
AR 349, AR 349a

GE **HIRSCH MICHAEL BAMBERGER
FAMILY**
Family tree from 1506
1 item
AR 905

FO = Photos · GE = Genealogical Material · PM = Primary Material · SM = Secondary Material

PM **LUDWIG BAMBERGER**
Politician, 1823–1899
Autographs
38 items
AR 2773, AR 345

PM **MAX BAMBERGER**
Translator, 1846–1929
Biographical sketch
1 item
AR 3515

FO PM **RUDOLF BAMBERGER**
Banker, 1824–1910
Correspondence about Rudolf and Ludwig Bamberger; photo
5 items
AR 3424

SM **SIMON BAMBERGER**
Governor of Utah, 1845–1926
List of biography about Bamberger, article about him
3 items
AR 1313

PM SM **EUGEN BANDEL**
Article; letter
2 items
AR 6

FO PM SM **EUGEN BANDMANN**
Social Democratic politician, president of City Council of Breslau and Silesian Landtag, 1874–1948
Obituaries; photos; letters about Bandmann
4 items
AR 7

FO **EDWARD BANETH**
Rabbi, 1855–1930
Photo
1 item
AR 3196

FO **ROBERT BARANY**
Physician, 1876–1936, Nobel Prize, 1915
Photo
1 item
AR 3058

PM **KLAUS BARBIE**
Nazi criminal
U.S. Government exhibits to report of U.S. Attorney General (1983)
1 item
AR 5198

SM **BARBY A.D. ELBE; JEWISH COMMUNITY**
Excerpt from book on Jewish community
1 item
AR 4183

FO SM **ISSAY BARMAS**
Violin teacher at Stern Conservatory, Berlin, 1872–1946
Photo; article
2 items
AR 2413

PM **LUDWIG BARNAY**
1842–1924
Letters; documents; autographs
5 items
AR 372

SM **HANS BARON**
Literary historian, 1900–
Article on Baron (Aufbau, 1980)
1 item
AR 4891

PM SM **SALLY BARON**
Rabbi, 1874–
Notes; articles; sermons by Baron
21 items
AR 825

FO SM **SALO WITTMEYER BARON**
Jewish historian, 1895–1990
Photo; newspaper articles
3 items
AR 2777

PM SM **JACOB BAROSIN**
Artist
Biography; autobiography; clippings
3 items
AR 5309

PM **ADOLF BARTELS**
Anti-Semitic author, 1862–1945
Autograph
1 item
AR 1865

FO = Photos · GE = Genealogical Material · PM = Primary Material · SM = Secondary Material

PM **JACOB BARTH**
Orientalist, 1851–1914
Autograph
1 item
AR 4995

SM **BARUCH FAMILY, ASCHEN**
Article about a family of engravers
from Aschen (19th cent.)
1 item
AR 533

PM **BASCH FAMILY, WOLLSTEIN**
Excerpt from list of naturalized Jews
in Grand Duchy of Posen, certificate
of naturalization (1836–1847)
2 items
AR 3421

SM **FRANZ BASS**
Physician, 20th cent.
Articles about Theresienstadt
3 items
AR 1423

FO SM **ROBERT BASS**
Physician, 20th cent.
Photo; typescript about Bass
3 items
AR 1422

SM **ELSE BASSERMANN**
Artist
Obituary; newspaper clipping
2 items
AR 1214

GE PM **JACOB BASSEVI VON TREUENBERG**
ca. 1570–1634
Typescript about Bassevi; family tree
2 items
AR 3480

GE **BATTENFELD, HESSEN; JEWISH COMMUNITY**
23 photos of cemetery; records
2 items
AR 5199

FO SM **LUDWIG BATZNER**
Businessman, 1901–
Photo; letter; business catalogue
3 items
AR 516

PM SM **BAUER FAMILY, BUTTENWIESEN**
Documents and history of town and
Bauer family
33 items
AR 4029

FO **LUDWIG BAUERNFREUND**
Industrialist, 1889–1959
Photos of cannery factory
20 items
AR 3033

PM **FRITZ BAUM**
Speech about antisemitism
1 item
AR 906

PM **H. A. BAUM FAMILY**
Letters by H. A. Baum to his wife
Augusta, letters between Ernst
Horowitz and H. F. Sachs (19th
century)
12 items
AR 4282

FO PM **PAULA BAUM**
SM Photos of former synagogue of
Elmshorn including officials; articles;
programs
19 items
AR 1314

SM **VICKY BAUM**
Author, 1888–1960
Newspaper clippings; correspondence
with Carl Ostertag
7 items
AR 1344, AR 5130

GE **FANNY BAUMANN FAMILY**
Parchment marriage contracts, one
with Portuguese signatures
(Hamburg, 1871, 1876, 1891)
3 items
AR 2425

PM **KURT BAUMANN**
Artist
Manuscript (20 pp.), plan for the
establishment of Deutsch-Jüdischer
Kulturbund (Berlin 1907; US 1939)
1 item
AR 5299

FO = Photos · GE = Genealogical Material · PM = Primary Material · SM = Secondary Material

PM **BAUTZEN; JEWISH COMMUNITY**
Estimated value of former community property
1 item
AR 3448

PM **BAVARIA; JEWISH COMMUNITY**
List of Jewish communities, article, list of Jews in Franconian towns (1709–1736); instructions for Jewish teachers (1828); copy of petition to Bavarian government against Augsburg Reform Jewish synod (1871); government instructions during Nazi period; handwritten history (ca. 1912)
9 items
AR 991

GE PM **BAYERTHAL FAMILY**
SM Family tree, certificates; letters of congratulation; eulogy for Hedwig Bayerthal
8 items
AR 165

PM **BAYREUTH; JEWISH COMMUNITY**
Community papers concerning requests by Schendel Hirsch and her family for charity (1805–1819)
2 items
AR 2606

FO **DAVID BECHER**
Lithograph
1 item
AR 3584

GE **BECHER FAMILY, BERLIN**
Biography of family members
3 items
AR 4023

FO SM **BECHHOFEN; JEWISH COMMUNITY**
Photos; articles about synagogue
7 items
AR 448

PM **ERNST BECHHOFF**
Document giving exemption from wearing of Jewish Star; wife's certificate proving Aryan descent
2 items
AR 4649

PM **KARL BECK**
Poet, 1817–1879
Poem (handwritten); autograph
2 items
AR 1505

FO **BENNO BECKER**
Painter, born Momel 1860
Photo
1 item
AR 2761

PM **BECKER FAMILY**
Identity papers of tenor Jacob Hirsch Neuburger (1831–1881); poetry album of Koehler family, eastern Germany (1833)
3 items
AR 876

GE **BECKER-HOCKENHEIMER FAMILY**
Family trees and history of three branches of family
3 items
AR 5091

SM **JOERG BECKER**
Article: "Racism in Children's Books" (Germany, 1978, 20 pp.)
1 item
AR 4668

SM **JUREK BECKER**
Writer, born Lodz 1938
Newspaper clipping (Germany 1938)
1 item
AR 4620

SM **BECKUM; JEWISH COMMUNITY**
Article
1 item
AR 134

FO **BEELITZ; INSTITUTE FOR MENTALLY RETARDED CHILDREN**
Photo
1 item
AR 1947

FO PM **RICHARD BEER-HOFMANN**
SM Poet, 1866–1945
Poetry, letters by Beer-Hofmann, articles, aphorisms, photo of his wife and daughter; autographs (also Large Collection AR 914)

FO = Photos · GE = Genealogical Material · PM = Primary Material · SM = Secondary Material

59 items
AR 745, AR 854, AR 3081

FO PM **MICHAEL BEER**
SM Brother of Giacomo Meyerbeer, 1880–1952
Article; photo; handwritten manuscript of Clytemnestra tragedy
3 items
AR 2182, AR 1096

FO **C. F. W. BEHL**
Lawyer 1889–1968
Photo
1 item
AR 1171

SM **THERESE BEHR-SCHNABEL**
Obituary: Aufbau (February 6, 1959)
1 item
AR 746

PM **HERMAN BEHREND**
Certificate of war decoration
1 item
AR 389

GE **ITZIG BEHREND**
Merchant, 1773–1845
Family tree of descendants
1 item
AR 4443

SM **ALEX BEIN**
Historian, born 1904
Newspaper article on Bein
1 item
AR 4565

PM **ALFRED BEIT**
Banker, 1853–1906
Letter
1 item
AR 2810

PM **ABRAHAM BELAIS**
Rabbi of Algiers, 1773–1853
Collection book (ca. 1836)
1 item
AR 2961

SM **EHUD BEN-EZER**
Book review of *Unease in Zion* by R. Furstenberg (July 22, 1975)
1 item
AR 4587

SM **PAUL BEN-HAIM**
Composer, born 1897, Munich
Newspaper article on Ben-Haim
1 item
AR 4479

PM **ELIEZER BEN-YEHUDAH**
1858–1922
Israeli postage stamp in his honor
1 item
AR 1643

GE **BENARIO FAMILY, OBERNBREIT**
Family tree (18th–20th cent.)
1 item
AR 3397

FO **GUSTAV BENARIO**
1868–1948
Photo
1 item
AR 1173

SM **HUGO BENARIO**
Art collector
Clippings about his art collection
3 items
AR 2504

GE **BENNY BENDA**
Bookdealer, Lausanne
Notes on descendants
1 item
AR 3742

PM **LAZARUS BENDAVID**
Philosopher, 1762–1832
Autograph
1 item
AR 2615

FO **EDUARD BENDEMANN**
Painter, 1811–1889
Photos
2 items
AR 2688

PM **EMIL BENDHEIM**
Army certificate, program
2 items
AR 1220

PM SM **BENDHEIM FAMILY, AUERBACH**
Hessian passport (1857); articles
5 items
AR 4421

FO = Photos · GE = Genealogical Material · PM = Primary Material · SM = Secondary Material

PM **LEO BENDIT**
Government document about loan by Kauffmann Benedick (Fuerth, 1790)
1 item
AR 3301

FO PM **JOSEF BENDIX**
Engineer, officer; died 1904 in combat in German Southwest Africa
Photos; letters
25 items
AR 4736

SM **LUDWIG BENDIX**
Lawyer, 1877–1954
Articles
2 items
AR 3380

PM **MARCUS BENDIX FAMILY, FREIENWALDE**
Government documents concerning taxes and business of members of Bendix and Doebrin families; family correspondence (1786–1855)
19 items
AR 3973

FO SM **BENEDICK FAMILY**
Obituaries; photo
4 items
AR 950

FO **MORITZ BENEDIKT**
Physician, 1835–1920
Photo
1 item
AR 2689

FO PM **WALTER BENJAMIN**
SM Literary critic, 1892–1940
Articles; photos; program of exhibit; autographs
6 items
AR 420, AR 1322

PM **EPHRAIM LOEB BENTHEIM**
Will, decision by Ephraim Loeb Bentheim Foundation, Darmstadt (1842–1892)
2 items
AR 1557

FO **LUDWIG BERNHARD BEREND**
Chemist, (born 1847, Koblenz)
Photo
1 item
AR 3577

PM SM **WALTER A. BERENDSOHN**
Professor, literary critic, 1884–197?
Articles; reviews; autograph
13 items
AR 310, AR 1827

FO **ALBAN BERG**
Composer, 1885–1935
Photos
2 items
AR 2691

PM **GUSTAVO BERG**
Memorial tablet
1 item
AR 1221

FO SM **BERGEN B. FRANKFURT A.M; JEWISH COMMUNITY**
Article; photo of burning synagogue (1938)
2 items
AR 2383

SM **BERGEN-ENKHEIM; JEWISH COMMUNITY**
Article
1 item
AR 2052

PM **JULIUS BERGER**
Letter; report by Rudolf Rochocz
2 items
AR 1566

PM **KURT BERGER FAMILY, BERLIN**
Documents; letters
12 items
AR 4669

FO SM **LUDWIG BERGER**
Theater director, 1892–1969
Article; photo
2 items
AR 2762

PM **ERNST BERGMANN**
Physician, 1896–
Autobiography
1 item
AR 4280

FO SM **HUGO BERGMANN**
Philosopher, 1883–1975
Photos; obituary
13 items
AR 2345

FO = Photos · GE = Genealogical Material · PM = Primary Material · SM = Secondary Material

PM **JOHN H. BERGMANN**
Re: Jews in Swabia; "The Bergmanns of Laupheim" (manuscript)
21 items
AR 4861, AR 4861a

FO **ELISABETH BERGNER**
Actress, 1897–
Photos
2 items
AR 2406

SM **HERMANN L. BERLAK**
Trustee *Syndikus* of the Reichsverband des Kreditgebenden Einzelhandels
Articles
47 items
AR 3517

GE **BERLIN FAMILY, FUERTH**
Family tree
1 item
AR 206

PM **BERLIN; JEWISH EDUCATIONAL INSTITUTIONS**
Lectures (1931–34)
3 items
AR 3564

FO PM **BERLIN; JEWISH YOUTH HOME &**
SM **APPRENTICE HOME**
Articles; photos; caricature of director
4 items
AR 4982

PM **BERLIN; JÜDISCHES LEHRHAUS**
Plans
3 items
AR 2602

FO SM **BERLIN; LEHRANSTALT FÜR DIE WISSENSCHAFT DES JUDENTUMS**
Articles; photos
6 items
AR 730

PM **LOEB MAYER BERLIN**
Chief Rabbi, Kingdom of Westphalia, 1738–1814
Handwritten sermon; notes about Berlin family
2 items
AR 7132

FO **BERLIN; TEACHERS' SEMINARY**
Photos
11 items
AR 3107

SM **WALTER BERLIN**
Obituary (London Nov. 1963)
1 item
AR 2080

FO **ABRAHAM BERLINER**
Professor, historian, 1883–1915
Photos
2 items
AR 2949

PM **CORA BERLINER**
Social worker, 1890–1942
Autographs
38 items
AR 1578, AR 1315

PM **BERLINER FAMILY; FLATOW**
Business papers (1789–1898)
4 items
AR 2575

FO PM **BERLINER FAMILY, HANNOVER**
SM Photos; wedding certificate; clippings; government documents; baby costume for circumcision
33 items
AR 1906

PM **FANNI BERLINER**
born 1812, Harburg
Poetry journal (40 p.)
1 item
AR 4389

PM SM **GERTRUD BERLINER**
Author, 1909–
Letters; typescript of stories and drawings by Berliner; clippings; photos of family members; gravestone
62 items
AR 1227

PM **HERBERT LEE BERLINER**
Documents about Benjamin Berliner, teacher (1811–1838)
5 items
AR 4454

FO = Photos · GE = Genealogical Material · PM = Primary Material · SM = Secondary Material

GE PM **KURT BERLINER FAMILY**
Family history; copy of poetry book
with drawings (1820); correspondence
7 items
AR 1579

FO PM **SARAH BERLINER**
Flyer of American Association of
University Women; photo
2 items
AR 1316

PM **SIEGFRIED BERLINER**
Economist, born 1884
Carbon-copy items dealing with
career of Berliner
25 items
AR 5280

PM **NAPTHALI BERLINGER**
Teacher
Documents from 1913–1933
6 items
AR 4688

PM **RABBI BERLINGER**
Rabbi born Berlichingen
Letter
1 item
AR 7077

PM SM **WALTER BERNARD**
Professor
Correspondence and clippings;
correspondence with Constantine
Brunner
2 inches
AR 7221

PM **BERNAYS FAMILY**
Seal
1 item
AR 4234

PM **KARL BERNAYS**
Journalist, 1815–1879
Curriculum vitae
1 item
AR 4737

PM **MICHAEL BERNAYS**
Autograph
1 item
AR 1508

SM **PAUL BERNAYS**
Mathematician, 1888–1977
Obituary (Sept. 27, 1977): *Neue
Züricher Zeitung*
1 item
AR 4591

PM **BENNO BERNEIS**
Painter, pilot World War I,
1883–1916
Letters relating to his death (1916)
5 items
AR 4738

FO PM **ARNOLD BERNEY**
Historian, 1897–1943
Biographical sketch; photos
3 items
AR 2843

FO SM **GEORG BERNHARD**
Editor of *Vossische Zeitung, Pariser
Tageblatt,* and *Pariser Tageszeitung*,
1875–1944
Photo; clipping; press release
3 items
AR 2690

PM **BERNHARDT FAMILY**
Family letters and documents (19th
cent.)
14 items
AR 978

PM **BARUCH BERNHEIM**
Jewish communal leader, Karlsruhe
19th cent.
Government letters about medal and
audience with Grand Duke
2 items
AR 4267

PM **SAMUEL BERNHEIM**
1903–
Documents of Nazi period
3 items
AR 4693

PM SM **OTTO BERNHEIMER**
1877–1960
Letter; newspaper articles
7 items
AR 1654

FO = Photos · GE = Genealogical Material · PM = Primary Material · SM = Secondary Material

SM **SAMUEL BERNHEIMER**
1812–1888
Newspaper clipping
1 item
AR 4701

PM **AARON BERNSTEIN (PSEUD. OF A. RUBENSTEIN)**
Writer, editor, 1812–1844
Autographs
2 items
AR 3755

PM **ALEX BERNSTEIN**
1862–1941
Histories of Jews in Westphalia
16 items
AR 4187

SM **ARNOLD BERNSTEIN**
Shipping line operator, 1888–1971
Newspaper article; obituary
2 items
AR 4592

FO PM **EDUARD BERNSTEIN**
Socialist politician, 1850–1932
Etching; photo; autographs
4 items
AR 3125, AR 832

FO GE **BERNSTEIN FAMILY, CHEMNITZ**
PM Family history; certificates; biography of Julius Bernstein; eulogies; annual reports and by-laws of Marschel Frank Sachs Corporation; photos of synagogue of Chemnitz; correspondence
41 items
AR 386, AR 747

FO PM **FELIX BERNSTEIN**
SM Mathematician, statistician, 1878–1956
Obituary; photos; correspondence
25 items
AR 1679

SM **HUGO BERNSTEIN**
Publisher
Newspaper clipping, "150 years Duemmler" (1958)
1 item
AR 555

FO **ULRICH BERNSTEIN**
1914–1949
Photo
1 item
AR 1907

GE **BERNSTEIN-ZEDEK FAMILY**
Genealogy
1 item
AR 4690

PM **PAULINE BERNZWEIG**
Yahrzeit scroll (1931)
1 item
AR 5119

SM **HEINRICH BEROLZHEIMER**
Newspaper clipping
1 item
AR 92

PM **JULIUS BERSTL**
1893–
Autograph
1 item
AR 1751

PM **BERTON FAMILY**
Photocopy of document (1707)
1 item
AR 4892

PM **BERWANGEN; JEWISH COMMUNITY**
Death register (1851–1869)
1 item
AR 4304

FO PM **CAROLINE BETTELHEIM**
Etching, 1862; autograph
2 items
AR 2058–2059

SM **ERNEST H. BETTMANN**
Physician, 1900–1988, Berlin
Magazine article
1 item
AR 4566

PM SM **DR. OTTO BETTMANN**
Newspaper clipping (1981)
1 item
AR 5099

PM **BEUERN; JEWISH COMMUNITY**
Community record book, 1822–1915
5 items
AR 1575

FO = Photos · GE = Genealogical Material · PM = Primary Material · SM = Secondary Material

FO PM **BEUTHEN (NOW BYTOM,**
SM **POLAND); JEWISH COMMUNITY**
Photo of synagogue; correspondence; documents about Kulturbund deutscher Juden (1934–1938); articles; report about Beuthen in the 1880's; Jewish community budget (1936)
11 items
AR 543

GE PM **BEUTHNER FAMILY**
Certificate of citizenship (1796); notes for family tree
2 items
AR 3551

SM **NAFTALI BEZEM**
Painter, born 1924, Essen
Catalogue exhibition
1 item
AR 4529

FO SM **CHAIM NACHMAN BIALIK**
Hebrew poet, 1873–1934
Clippings; photo; postage stamp in his honor
5 items
AR 1174

PM SM **BIBLIOPHILEN**
Article about Berliner Bibliophilen-Freunde, photo report
3 items
AR 3559

PM **JACK BIBO**
Report about Theresienstadt
1 item
AR 209

GE **BICKART FAMILY**
Genealogy of Bickart family (1925)
1 item
AR 5039

GE PM **LOTHAR BICKEL**
Physician, member of Constantin Brunner circle, 1902–1950
Material about Bickel and his relationship to Freud
3 items
AR 3494

SM **HUGO BIEBER**
Obituary (Sept.30, 1950)
1 item
AR 1016

SM **JOHANNES ROGALLA VON BIEBERSTEIN**
Newspaper clipping
8 items
AR 4508

GE PM **BIELEFELD FAMILY COLLECTION**
Documents; family tree
7 items
AR 3831

FO **BIELEFELD FAMILY, KARLSRUHE**
Photos of family portrait (19th cent.)
10 items
AR 4269

PM **BIELEFELD; JEWISH COMMUNITY**
Last list of Jewish residents and of deportation
1 item
AR 7248

PM SM **DR. LUDWIG BIELSCHOWSKY**
Bookcover collections; articles
2 items
AR 2214

SM **F. R. BIENENFELD**
Obituary (May 26, 1961)
1 item
AR 1222

PM **MORITZ BIESENTHAL**
Report on Battle of Sedan (1870); photocopies of birth and marriage certificates
2 items
AR 5200

FO PM **BILLIGHEIM; JEWISH COMMUNITY**
Photos of synagogue; reports
4 items
AR 2472

PM **BILLIGHEIMER FAMILY**
Family documents; *Schutzbrief*; family corrrespondence about Gurs
12 items
AR 3542

FO PM **SAMUEL BILLIGHEIMER**
SM Historian of Jewish philosophy 1889–
Articles; correspondence including letters from Martin Buber; photos
42 items
AR 3413

FO = Photos · GE = Genealogical Material · PM = Primary Material · SM = Secondary Material

FO PM **FRIEDRICH BILSKI**
Physician, 1894–1976
Memoirs as a doctor and a Jew (152 pp.)
1 item
Mem 28

FO **BINAU/BADEN; JEWISH COMMUNITY**
Photo of synagogue, cemetery
5 items
AR 4071

SM **RUDOLF G. BINDING**
Newspaper clipping on "Binding Letters", *Der Spiegel*, 1957
1 item
AR 84

PM **EPHRAIM BING**
Schutzbrief; military discharge, Hessen (1832, 1835)
2 items
AR 4476

FO PM **ERNEST BING FAMILY**
Letters; photos
18 items
AR 1789

PM **BING FAMILY**
Letters
2 items
AR 201

GE **BING FAMILY, FRANKFURT**
Family history and accompanying letters
2 items
AR 4086

SM **ROBERT BING**
1878–1956
Obituary; bibliography
2 items
AR 33

PM SM **BINGEN; JEWISH COMMUNITY**
Article; histories
2 items
AR 3240

FO **BINSWANGEN; JEWISH COMMUNITY**
Photo of synagogue
1 item
AR 369

PM **CLARA G. BINSWANGER**
Correspondence; memoir
17 items
AR 5231

FO PM **BIRKENAU, ODENWALD; JEWISH**
SM **COMMUNITY**
Article; photo of synagogue; list of Jews; photostats of *Kennkarte* of Jews in Birkenau (1930)
13 items
AR 2268

FO PM **EDUARD BIRNBAUM**
Cantor, 1852–1920
Photo; sheet music
2 items
AR 3302

SM **BISCHWILLER, ALSACE; JEWISH COMMUNITY**
Articles
2 items
AR 993

SM **BITBURG; JEWISH COMMUNITY**
Article
1 item
AR 3691

PM **JAMES H. BLACK**
Letters
2 items
AR 3213

FO **JULIUS BLAU**
Photo
1 item
AR 1676

FO PM **LEO BLAU**
Report card; photos from Jüdische Reformrealgymnasium Cologne
8 items
AR 1638

FO PM **LEO BLECH**
SM Composer and conductor, 1871–1958
Photo; concert program; autographs
15 items
AR 2085, AR 1727

PM **CARL BLEIBTREU**
Literary historian, 1859–1928
Autographs
16 items
AR 4181

FO = Photos · GE = Genealogical Material · PM = Primary Material · SM = Secondary Material

BLEICHROEDER ARCHIVES

SM BLEICHROEDER ARCHIVES
Lists of Bleichroeder Archives; items on Bleichroeder, Rothschild, Oppenheimer/Köln, Schwabach families
6 items
AR 4739

PM GERSON VON BLEICHROEDER
Banker, 1822–1893
Correspondence
7 items
AR 2955

PM JULIUS BLEICHROEDER
Banker (Younger brother of Gerson von Bleichroeder)
Letter dealing with banking firm of Bleichroeder (1978)
1 item
AR 4653

PM S. BLEICHROEDER
Letter, June 6, 1883 handwritten autograph
1 item
AR 1317

PM FRITZ BLEY
Editor, writer, 1853–1931
Autographs
12 items
AR 4180

SM JEKUTHIEL BEN ISAAK BLITZ
First translator of Hebrew Bible into Judeo-German
Newspaper clipping
1 item
AR 5247

SM DAVID LUDWIG BLOCH
born 1910, Huss, Bavaria, Artist
Biography; essays; clippings about his shows
3 items
AR 7199

PM ERNEST BLOCH
Composer, 1880–1959
Autographs
3 items
AR 4985

FO SM ERNST BLOCH
Philosopher, writer, 1885–1977
Clippings; photos; obituaries
11 items
AR 219

PM BLOCH FAMILY, HAMBURG, BERLIN
Family documents
9 items
AR 1018

GE BLOCH FAMILY, LANGENDORF
Family tree (18th–20th cent.)
1 item
AR 3358

SM HELENE BLOCH
Dentist
Newspaper clipping (1957)
1 item
AR 47

PM IWAN BLOCH
1872–1922
Autograph
1 item
AR 2618

PM JOSEPH BLOCH
Editor of *Sozialistische Monatshefte*, 1871–1916
Typescript about Bloch by Ernst Hamburger
1 item
AR 2654

FO JOSEPH SAMUEL BLOCH
Rabbi, 1850–1923
Photo
1 item
AR 3197

FO PM KONRAD BLOCH
SM Nobel Prize-winning biochemist, 1912–
Clippings; photos; autographs
5 items
AR 2364, AR 2455

PM LIPPMAN BLOCH
Pamphlet
1 item
AR 4177

FO = Photos · GE = Genealogical Material · PM = Primary Material · SM = Secondary Material

FO SM **MARTIN BLOCH**
Painter, 1883–1954
Photos of exhibition catalogue;
clippings; prints
7 items
AR 907

FO PM **W. H. BLOCH FAMILY**
Papers of Naumann Simonsohn;
letters signed by King Friedrich
Wilhelm III of Prussia; copy of
portrait; personal documents;
materials for Bloch family tree;
photos
13 items
AR 1577

FO SM **ALEXANDER BLOCK**
Russian author, 1818–1895
Photo
1 item
AR 2765

SM **ERNEST BLUM**
Social worker, 1901–
Newspaper clippings
4 items
AR 2853

PM **WILLI BLUM**
Letter from Joachim von Ribbentrop
to Blum (1929)
1 item
AR 1913

PM **EDUARD BLUMBERG**
Physician
Letters, documents (1933–1979)
29 items
AR 4818

SM **GINA BLUMENFELD**
Poster for film (1978, 1979)
1 item
AR 4948

SM **KURT BLUMENFELD**
Politician, Zionist leader, 1884–1963
Clippings
5 items
AR 1019

SM **MOSES BLUMENFELD**
Religion teacher, 1821–1902
Newspaper clipping, 1967
1 item
AR 3347

PM SM **WALTER BLUMENFELD**
Psychologist, 1882–1967
Manuscripts; correspondence;
obituary
4 items
AR 489

PM SM **FRITZ BLUMENTHAL**
Physician, artist, born 1913, Mainz
Miscellaneous articles; letters
8 items
AR 4882

PM **JACQUES BLUMENTHAL**
Composer, artist, 1829–1908
Autograph
1 item
AR 1428

PM **OSCAR BLUMENTHAL**
Writer, 1852–1917
Autographs
6 items
AR 545

PM **ROY BLUMENTHAL**
Eulogy address; telegram
1 item
AR 4774

PM SM **ILSE BLUMENTHAL-WEISS**
Writer
Correspondence; newspaper clippings
76 items and tape
AR 1020

PM **KARL THEODOR BLUTH**
1892–
Autograph
1 item
AR 1752

FO PM **ISMAR BOAS**
SM Physician, 1851–1938
Certificates; honors; poems;
obituaries; photos
18 items
AR 1374

SM **BOCHOLT, WESTPHALIA; JEWISH COMMUNITY**
Clippings with articles on one-time
Jewish residents
1 item
AR 5311

FO = Photos · GE = Genealogical Material · PM = Primary Material · SM = Secondary Material

PM SM **BOCHUM; JEWISH COMMUNITY**
Print of synagogue interior; article on cemetery
2 items
AR 344

PM **ALFRED BOCK**
Writer, 1859–1932
Newspaper clipping
1 item
AR 1318

SM **WERNER BOCK**
Writer
Obituary (1962)
1 item
AR 1580

SM **LOEB BODENHEIMER**
Rabbi of Krefeld, 1807–1868
Obituary
1 item
AR 3509

PM **MARTHA BODENHEIMER**
Tallit bag (red velvet)
1 item
AR 2879

SM **BODENTEICH; CEMETERY**
Article on school project relating to cemetery
1 item
AR 5228

FO PM **BOEDIGHEIM; JEWISH**
SM **COMMUNITY**
Photos; article; reports; correspondence
26 items
AR 418

FO SM **ERICH BOEHM**
Photo of Leo Baeck; correspondence
18 items
AR 2229

SM **FRANZ BOEHM**
Lawyer, 1895–1977
"Against antisemitism" (clipping)
2 items
AR 4477

PM **HANS BOEHM**
List of letters written to Boehm
1 item
AR 1860

PM **MAX BOEHM**
Industrialist, collector, 1874–1944
Material on Theresienstadt
34 items
AR 4154

FO PM **HILDEGARD BOEHME**
Social worker, teacher, 1884–1943
Correspondence concerning her work with Red Cross, her fate at Auschwitz; photo; list of property of Hannah Karminski
37 items
AR 235

FO PM **LUDWIG BOERNE (BORN LOEB BARUCH)**
Author, 1786–1837
Photos; autographs
4 items
AR 2797, AR 1097

SM **G. H. E. BOGENG**
Bibliophile, 1881–1962
Newspaper clipping (1962)
1 item
AR 2215

SM **NIELS BOHR**
Physicist, 1885–1962
Newspaper clippings
2 items
AR 2199

SM **CURT BOIS**
Musician, Actor
Newspaper clippings
3 items
AR 2200

SM **ALFRED J. BOLLET**
Physician, 1809–1885
Magazine article about Jacob Henle, physician (1978)
1 item
AR 4567

PM **HEINRICH BOLLWEG**
History of *Grafschaft* of Rietberg, 1768–1807
1 item
AR 5053

PM SM **CURT BONDY**
Psychologist, 1894–1972
Correspondence; articles
35 items
AR 4714

FO = Photos · GE = Genealogical Material · PM = Primary Material · SM = Secondary Material

SM **BONN; JEWISH COMMUNITY**
Review
2 items
AR 3428

SM **MORITZ JULIUS BONN**
Economist
Newspaper clipping
1 item
AR 2201

SM **RICHARD BORCHARD**
Ship owner
Newspaper clipping (1964)
1 item
AR 2588

GE **BORCHARDT FAMILY**
Family tree
3 items
AR 50

PM **FANNY BORCHARDT**
1817–1855
Poetry album
2 items
AR 2984

PM **HIRSCH ISAAC BORCHARDT**
Will
1 item
AR 4509

PM SM **RUDOLPH BORCHARDT**
Author and poet, 1877–1945
Typescript; clippings; letters to Dencke; autograph
6 items
AR 263, AR 1371

PM **E. L. BORCHERT**
Cookbook (handwritten)
1 item
AR 4617

PM **BORCHHEIM FAMILY**
Letter; Prussian decree
6 items
AR 1680

FO PM **MAX BORN**
SM Nuclear physicist, Nobel Prize winner, 1882–1970
Biography; clippings; photos; correspondence; autographs
15 items
AR 1225, AR 1984

PM **HERMINE BOSETTI**
Artist
Autograph
1 item
AR 1529

FO **BOSKOWITZ, MORAVIA; JEWISH COMMUNITY**
Photos
13 items
AR 3432

FO PM **RUDOLF BRACH**
Merchant in Texas, 1829–1907
Photo; memoir
2 items
AR 4359

PM **BRAFMANN FAMILY**
Will (Kissingen, 1798; copy, 1838)
1 item
AR 374

FO PM **OTTO BRAHM**
Writer, director
Photo; autographs
3 items
AR 1958, AR 2676

FO **MAX BRAHN**
Labor arbitrator, 1873–1944
Photo
1 item
AR 3115

SM **LOUIS DEMBITZ BRANDEIS**
Associate Justice of U.S. Supreme Court, 1856–1941
Index of microfilm collection at the University of Louisville
1 item
AR 5270

SM **BRANDENBURG; JEWISH COMMUNITY**
Articles
2 items
AR 4618

FO PM **GEORG BRANDES**
Danish author, literary historian, 1842–1927
Photo of painting by Liebermann; autograph

FO = Photos · GE = Genealogical Material · PM = Primary Material · SM = Secondary Material

2 items
AR 2693, AR 447

FO SM **GUENTHER BRANDT**
Minister; helped save Jews during Nazi period
Photo; article
2 items
AR 5172

PM SM **HENRY WALTER BRANN**
Philosopher, 1903–1973
Photocopy of article on Brann; correspondence with Leo Baeck Institute
2 items
AR 4788

PM SM **MARKUS BRANN**
Historian, 1848–1920
Correspondence; clippings; autographs
2 items
AR 3198, AR 3789

PM **RABBI BRANN**
Rabbi, father of Marcus Brann
Letter
1 item
AR 8

PM **JACOB BRAUDE**
Jewish community leader, 1902–1977
Typescript of biography by Alexander Carlebach
1 item
AR 7127

PM **ADOLF BRAUN**
German socialist, 1862–1929
Biography by Ernst Hamburger
1 item
AR 2655

PM **FELIX BRAUN**
Writer, 1885–
Autograph
1 item
AR 1719

PM SM **LILY BRAUN**
Writer, 1865–1916
Autograph; newspaper clipping
2 items
AR 2684, AR 1869

SM **OTTO BRAUN**
Politician, 1872–1955
Newspaper clippings
5 items
AR 4530

PM **OTTO BRAUN**
Writer, 1897–1919
Copy of handwritten prayer for Julie Vogelstein
1 item
AR 3266

PM **LUDWIG BRAUNFELS**
1810–1885
Letters to friends (1836–1849)
3 items
AR 1793

SM **BRAUNSBACH; JEWISH COMMUNITY**
Article
1 item
AR 2506

PM **BRAUNSCHWEIG; 'EZ CHAJIM'**
Society for the poor
By-laws (1834)
1 item
AR 4205

SM **BRAUNSCHWEIG; JEWISH COMMUNITY**
Articles
8 items
AR 3692

FO **ABRAHAM BRAVMANN**
Photo
1 item
AR 1176

SM **ARNOLD BRECHT**
Lawyer, 1884–1977
Obituary, 1977
1 item
AR 4467

SM **BERTOLT BRECHT**
Playwright, poet, 1898–1956
Theater program; clipping
2 items
AR 1556

FO = Photos · GE = Genealogical Material · PM = Primary Material · SM = Secondary Material

PM SM **GEORG BREDIG**
Chemist and educator, 1868–1944
Articles
3 items
AR 2386

SM **MARCUS BREGER**
Rabbi
Newspaper clippings (1964)
2 items
AR 2262

FO **BREISACH; JEWISH COMMUNITY**
Photos
4 items
AR 2473

FO PM **BREITNER FAMILY, VIENNA**
Letters to Hugo Breitner; photo
8 items
AR 3319

SM **ARNO BREKER**
Sculptor
Newspaper clipping, 1981
1 item
AR 5002

FO PM **BREMEN; JEWISH COMMUNITY**
SM Issue of *Bremer Woechentliche Nachrichten* (1743); copies of decree on Jews, (1815, 1820); list of Jewish businesses in Bremen compiled by the Nazis; photo of synagogue; list of deportations (1942)
10 items
AR 146

GE **BREMER FAMILY**
Family tree including index cards
2 items
AR 2395

SM **BREMKE; JEWISH COMMUNITY**
Article (1938)
1 item
AR 3988

PM **LUJO BRENTANO**
Historian
Excerpt from autobiography concerning Jewish Oath
1 item
AR 12

PM SM **LOUISE CATHERINE BRESLAU**
Painter, 1856–1927
Correspondence; clippings
4 items
AR 4510

FO PM **BRESLAU (NOW WROCLAW,**
SM **POLAND); JEWISH COMMUNITY**
Poem in honor of King Friedrich Wilhelm II. (1786); article; photos; catalogue of Jewish community library
30 items
AR 2355

PM **BRESLAU (THEOLOGICAL SEMINARY)**
List of lecture-catalogue (1938); list of biblical manuscripts; biography of Dr. Israel Rabin
12 items
AR 2044

PM SM **WALTER BRESLAUER FAMILY, POSEN**
Materials on election in Posen; court case; list of publications
7 items
AR 2365

GE **ERNST VON BRESSENDORF**
Genealogy of Breslau, Dessauer, von Bressendorf families
6 items
AR 3229

FO PM **BRETTEN, JEWISH COMMUNITY**
SM Photos of synagogue and cemetery; articles; *Memorbook* (1725)
9 items
AR 2799

PM **MAX BRETZFELDER**
Letter from Thomas Mann about Ludwig Thomas
2 items
AR 1224

SM **JOSEPH BREUER**
Rabbi, 1882–1980
Obituary, 1980
1 item
AR 4862

FO = Photos · GE = Genealogical Material · PM = Primary Material · SM = Secondary Material

FO SM **FRITZ BRILL**
Exhibition catalogue (1982),
Berlinische Gallerie (photos); article
2 items
AR 5144

SM **BERNHARD BRILLING**
Rabbi, historian, died 1987
Clippings; reprints
10 items
AR 139

PM **BRILON; JEWISH COMMUNITY**
Program for synagogue service on
birthday of King Friedrich Wilhelm
IV (1840)
1 item
AR 3317

FO PM **HERMANN BROCH**
SM Author, 1886–1951
Articles; photos; correspondence;
letters to Broch about rescuing Franz
Blei; Broch's report on activities in
rescuing German writers
35 items
AR 1022

FO PM **BROCK FAMILY**
SM Marriage contract; photo; article
5 items
AR 951

PM **FELIX BROCK**
1865–1941
Curriculum vitae; recommendation
3 items
AR 2375

SM **LEO BROD**
Writer
Newspaper clipping (1977)
1 item
AR 4568

FO PM **MAX BROD**
SM Writer, critic, 1884–1968
Articles; photo; letters; autographs
19 items
AR 1023, AR 856

PM **ERNST BRODER FAMILY**
Letters (1942–1963)
2 items
AR 2030

SM **HENRYK M. BRODER**
Writer, born 1946 in Katowice
Photocopy of newspaper clipping
(1981)
1 item
AR 5047

FO **FRIEDRICH S. BRODNITZ**
Physician, member of Board of
Directors, Leo Baeck Institute
Photo
1 item
AR 4428

FO **JULIUS BRODNITZ**
Lawyer, 1866–1936; president of
Central-Verein Deutscher
Staatsbürger jüdischen Glaubens
Photo with wife
1 item
AR 1175

SM **DANIEL BRODY**
Newspaper article for his 80th
birthday
1 item
AR 2113

FO **HEINRICH BRODY**
1868–1942, Chief Rabbi of Prague
Photo
1 item
AR 3199

PM SM **DAVID BRONSEN**
Professor of German, Washington
University, St. Louis, Missouri
Letter; articles
3 items
AR 3300

FO PM **BRUCH-KASSEL COLLECTION**
Karl Georg Fritz Kassel, leather
manufacturer, 1897–1982
Family documents: letters; photos,
miscellaneous clippings
1 foot
AR 7229

PM **MAX BRUCH**
Composer, 1838–1920
Autographs
5 items
AR 215

FO = Photos · GE = Genealogical Material · PM = Primary Material · SM = Secondary Material

FO **BRUCHSAL; JEWISH COMMUNITY**
Photos of synagogue
2 items
AR 2474

GE **BRUCK FAMILY**
Family history by Alfred Julius Bruck (1946, 1951)
6 items
AR 3940

PM **FERDINAND BRUCKNER (BORN THEODOR TAGGER)**
Writer, 1891–1958
Autographs
3 items
AR 1111, AR 2489

FO **ADOLF BRUELL**
Teacher of religion, 1846–1908
Photo (reproduction)
1 item
AR 3200

PM **BRUELL FAMILY**
1809 testament; letter concerning antisemitism
3 items
AR 4119

FO PM **IGNAZ BRUELL**
Composer, 1846–1907
Photo; autographs
3 items
AR 2809, AR 1104

FO **BRUENN, MORAVIA (NOW BRNO, CZECHOSLOVAKIA); JEWISH COMMUNITY**
Photo of memorial and of Jewish Real-Gymnasium
1 item
AR 2792

SM **SIEGFRIED BRUENN**
Obituary by Ismar Elbogen in monthly report of Freemason Lodge for Germany (1916)
1 item
AR 1811

PM SM **CONSTANTIN BRUNNER (BORN LEO WERTHEIMER)**
Philosopher, 1862–1937
Typescript; reprints; clippings; articles; circular; correspondence; autograph

25 items
AR 1024, AR 1509

SM **ILSE BRY**
Librarian, 1905–1974
Photocopy of magazine article (1976)
1 item
AR 4740

SM **MARGARETE BUBER-NEUMANN**
Writer
Newspaper clipping (1977)
1 item
AR 4480

FO PM **BUCHAU; JEWISH COMMUNITY**
Histories; family register (1809–1853); Einstein family tree; synagogue photos
14 items
AR 449

FO PM **BUCHEN; JEWISH COMMUNITY**
Photo of synagogue; reports
12 items
AR 2475

FO SM **WALTER G. BUCHHOLZ**
Judge, 1892–1980
Photo (1968); obituary (1980)
2 items
AR 3461

PM **JULIUS BUCHWALD**
Composer, 1909–1970
Musical compositions; fictional manuscripts (1938)
13 items
AR 4312

FO PM **GUSTAV BUCKY**
SM Physician, pioneer in X-ray technology
Miscellaneous magazine and newspaper articles; obituary (1963)
5 items
AR 1319

SM **BUDAPEST; JEWISH COMMUNITY**
Article on medieval synagogue
1 item
AR 2891

FO = Photos · GE = Genealogical Material · PM = Primary Material · SM = Secondary Material

FO **BUDWEIS (NOW CESKE BUDEJOVICE, CZECHOSLOVAKIA); JEWISH COMMUNITY**
Photograph of remnant of ancient building
1 item
AR 7035

PM **ARTHUR BUECHLER**
Certificates
3 items
AR 4230

SM **BUEDINGEN; JEWISH COMMUNITY**
Articles
2 items
AR 4849

FO SM **BUEHL; JEWISH COMMUNITY**
Article; photo of synagogue
3 items
AR 2154

PM **ALFRED BUEHLER**
Born 1927, Vienna
School report cards; passport; diary of trip to Shanghai (1940)
28 items
AR 4817

PM **HANS VON BUELOW**
Letter to Franz Brendel, Leipzig (1858)
1 item
AR 1721

PM **BUER; JEWISH COMMUNITY**
Stamp
1 item
AR 3618

PM **HERBERT BUKY**
Journalist, 1901–
Personal papers; restitution material
1 foot
AR 5143

PM **BULLERJAHN**
Circular of Committee for Bullerjahn
1 item
AR 2500

PM **BUND DEUTSCHER REVOLUTIONÄRER SOZIALISTEN**
Program, BDRS London, 1941/1942
1 item
AR 4921

GE PM **JOSEF HANS BUNZEL**
Sociologist, 1907–1975
Inventory of Bunzel Collection; family histories
5 items
AR 7071

PM **JULIUS BUNZL**
List of errors and inaccuracies of *Our Crowd* by Steven Birmingham
3 items
AR 3516

SM **BURCHARDT & SÖHNE**
Issues of *Vossische Zeitung*, advertising (1849)
2 items
AR 2505

PM **JAKOB BURCKHARDT**
Letter about Burckhardt's book, *Meine Danziger Mission* (1960)
1 item
AR 1002

FO **EUGEN BURG**
Actor, died 1944
Photos (1908, 1925)
2 items
AR 2407

SM **JOSEF BURG**
Politician, born 1909, Dresden
Newspaper article (1979)
1 item
AR 4712

PM **BURGHEIM FAMILY**
Marriage contract; family letters (19th cent.)
11 items
AR 2902

SM **BURGKUNSTADT; JEWISH COMMUNITY**
Article
1 item
AR 4655

FO = Photos · GE = Genealogical Material · PM = Primary Material · SM = Secondary Material

PM **BURGPREPPACH; JEWISH COMMUNITY**
Report of donation (1918)
1 item
AR 1690

SM **WILHELM BUSCH**
Newspaper clipping (1960), "Busch & die Juden"
1 item
AR 1794

FO **BUSENBERG; JEWISH COMMUNITY**
Photo
1 item
AR 3726

PM SM **BUTTENHAUSEN; JEWISH COMMUNITY**
Schutzbrief; regulation, 1787; articles
34 items
AR 2057

PM **BUTTENWIESEN; JEWISH COMMUNITY**
Short history; deportation lists
2 items
AR 5170

PM **BUTZBACH; JEWISH COMMUNITY**
History
1 item
AR 5115

PM **HENRY BUXBAUM**
Physician, family practitioner
Memoir (260 pp.)
1 item
Mem 12

PM **ALICE CAHN FAMILY**
Heimatschein (1830)
1 item
AR 437

FO **ARTHUR CAHN FAMILY**
Photos of synagogue and street in Muelheim, Wuertemberg (19th and 20th cent.)
10 items
AR 1681

FO **MARX CAHN**
Veteran of Napoleonic Wars
Photos of tombstone
2 items
AR 4111

SM **MAX L. CAHN**
Lawyer, 1889–1967
Eulogies
1 item
AR 3333

PM **SALOMON CAHN**
Marriage contract (1842); documents
3 items
AR 4654

PM **WILHELM CAHN**
1839–1920
Manuscripts
3 items
AR 347

PM SM **WERNER J. CAHNMANN**
Sociologist, 1902–1980
Reprints; correspondence; transcript of interview; articles on Nazism and various Jewish topics
57 items
AR 556

PM **CALENDARS**
Hebrew calendars (18th–19th cent.)
1 item
AR 2574

FO PM **RUDOLF CALLMANN**
SM Lawyer, 1892–1976
Obituaries; photos; biographical information; program
5 items
AR 2231

SM **S. CALVARY & CO. BOOKS**
Obituary for Otto Mayer, part-owner of the firm (1964)
1 item
AR 2546

FO SM **ELIAS CANETTI**
Novelist, 1905–
Clipping; photo
2 items
AR 2299

FO = Photos · GE = Genealogical Material · PM = Primary Material · SM = Secondary Material

FO **CANNSTATT; JEWISH COMMUNITY**
Photo of synagogue
1 item
AR 2656

PM **GEORG CANTOR**
Mathematician, 1845–1918
Letter
1 item
AR 562

PM **CARICATURES**
Caricatures of Jews (19th cent.)
26 items
AR 2826

FO SM **JOSEPH CARLEBACH**
Chief Rabbi of Altona, 1883–1942
Photos of him and his synagogue; obituary
10 items
AR 1025

GE **CARO FAMILY**
Family tree dating from the Middle Ages
1 item
AR 4412

PM SM **KLARA CARO (BORN BEERMANN)**
Wife of Rabbi Isidor Caro of Cologne, 1886–1979
Obituary; manuscript
2 items
AR 4808

PM **ENRICO CARUSO**
Tenor, 1873–1921
Drawn self-portrait
1 item
AR 3313

FO PM SM **SUZANNE CARVALLO-SCHUELEIN**
Painter, 1883–1972
Catalogue to 1911 Exhibition; clippings; photographs of works including Jakob Wassermann
3 items
AR 5079

SM **JOHN CASPARI**
Social worker, politician, 1888–
Newspaper clippings (1972, 1978)
2 items
AR 4522

PM **EVA CASPARY**
1905–
Emigration papers Shanghai and Australia; autobiography
11 items
AR 1910

PM **LEOPOLD CASPER**
1859–1959
Speech at confirmation (1873)
1 item
AR 3481

PM **A. CASSEL**
Rabbi
Sermon (1866)
2 items
AR 749

SM **SIR ERNEST CASSEL**
Excerpt of article about Cassel by Arthur de Breycha-Vauthier (1960)
1 item
AR 2387

FO PM **OSKAR CASSEL**
Lawyer, politician, 1849–1923
Photo; portrait; letters
4 items
AR 2430

PM **RENE CASSIN**
French politician, 1887–
Autograph
1 item
AR 3930

FO PM SM **BRUNO CASSIRER**
Publisher, 1872–1941
Article; photo; autograph
3 items
AR 1321, AR 2645

FO SM **ERNST CASSIRER**
Philosopher, 1874–1945
Article; photo
2 items
AR 542

GE SM **CASSIRER FAMILY, BERLIN**
Article; family tree
1 item
AR 4122

SM **H. W. CASSIRER**
Philosopher, son of Ernest Cassirer, 1904–1979
Obituary, *AJR Information* (April 1979)
1 item
AR 4747

PM **HUGO CASSIRER**
Publisher
Autograph
1 item
AR 2646

PM **MAX CASSIRER**
Industrialist
Speech at inauguration of the Max Cassirer Haus (1969)
1 item
AR 3702

FO PM **PAUL CASSIRER**
SM Art dealer, publisher, 1871–1926
Photos; catalogue; article
5 items
AR 1320

SM **DE CASTRO FAMILY**
Article about family by H. J. Schoeps
1 item
AR 3334

FO SM **PAUL CELAN**
Writer, 1920–1970
Photo; articles
5 items
AR 2766

FO PM **CELLE; JEWISH COMMUNITY**
Photos of synagogue; letter
10 items
AR 3855

SM **CEMETERIES, JEWISH**
Article on cemeteries in northern Germany
1 item
AR 5243

PM **CEREMONIAL RELIGIOUS OBJECTS**
Megillot Esther (Esther scrolls)
3 items
AR 4827

PM **CEREMONIES AND RITUALS**
Religious objects; photos; folders of lithographs
18 items
AR 75

PM **MARC CHAGALL**
Painter, 1887–1985
Clipping; postcard; reproduction
3 items
AR 3689

FO SM **SIR ERNST BORIS CHAIN**
Biochemist (Nobel Prize winner, 1945), 1906–
Article; photo
2 items
AR 3119

FO SM **HIRSCH PERETZ CHAJES**
Chief Rabbi of Vienna, 1876–1927
Photo; article
4 items
AR 2462

PM **SERGE CHARCHOUNE**
Painter, born 1888, Russia
Essays on Charchoune; letter; drawing
5 items
AR 4748

GE **CHASKEL-BURSCH FAMILY, BERLIN**
Family tree
1 item
AR 1381

FO PM **CHEMNITZ (NOW KARL MARX STADT, EAST GERMANY); JEWISH COMMUNITY**
Letter on communal history (Enrique Hamburger); photo of synagogue ruins; inventory of former community property
10 items
AR 813

GE PM **CHODZIESNER FAMILY**
Passport; articles, including obituary poem signed by G. Chodziesner
7 items
AR 1749

FO = Photos · GE = Genealogical Material · PM = Primary Material · SM = Secondary Material

PM **ISIDOR CHOYKE**
Lawyer, 1856–1920
School papers; correspondence; patent signed by Kaiser Wilhelm II
26 items
AR 1341

PM **ERNST CHRISTFELS**
Poetry book
1 item
AR 1953

SM **CHRISTIAN CHURCHES AND JEWS, 1933–1945**
Clippings; articles
11 items
AR 2351, AR 4707

SM **CHRISTIAN-JEWISH DIALOGUE**
Radio dialogue, clipping regarding program
2 items
AR 5097

PM **DANIEL CHWOLSON**
1819–1911
Autograph
1 item
AR 2619

FO **FELIX COBLENZ**
Rabbi, 1863–1923
Photo
1 item
AR 1177

SM **CARL COHEN**
Clippings
3 items
AR 3338

GE PM **EDUARD COHEN FAMILY**
Bismarck's doctor, 1820–1884
Notes on conversations with Bismarck, condolence letter from Bismarck; family tree; family correspondence
15 items
AR 3785

SM **ELIOT COHEN**
American journalist, 20th cent.
Article
1 item
AR 59

SM **FRIEDRICH COHEN**
Clipping, "Hedwig Bouvier zum Gedächtnis" (1960)
1 item
AR 2216

FO PM **GERSON COHEN**
SM Former chancellor of Jewish Theological Seminary of America
Photos; articles; program
7 items
AR 2819

FO PM **HERMANN COHEN**
SM Philosopher, 1842–1918
Correspondence with Friedrich Alfred Lange; articles on Cohen and the Marburg School; photos
70 items
AR 1026

SM **ISRAEL COHEN**
Magazine clipping, "Herzl's Debut in London" (1956)
1 item
AR 78

SM **MARTIN COHEN**
Publisher, 1905–1962
Newspaper clipping
1 item
AR 1795

PM **ABRAHAM COHN**
Letter
1 item
AR 1477

SM **ALBERT COHN**
Dealer; antique books
Newspaper clipping (1960)
1 item
AR 1027

PM SM **ALFRED COHN**
Physician, 1881–1965
Eulogies; obituaries; documents
21 items
AR 4085

PM **BERNHARD M. COHN**
Rabbi of Congregation Habonim
Speech
1 item
AR 5012

FO = Photos · GE = Genealogical Material · PM = Primary Material · SM = Secondary Material

PM **COHN BROTHERS**
Article
1 item
AR 1478

FO PM **EMIL BERNHARD COHN**
SM Rabbi, 1881–1948
Photo; articles; sermon; letters from
Leo Baeck, Martin Buber, Theodor
Heuss, Max Nordau, Stefan Zweig
19 items
AR 793

SM **ERNEST COHN**
Newspaper clipping (1932)
1 item
AR 1872

PM SM **FERDINAND COHN**
Botanist, 1828–1898
Newspaper clipping; autograph
2 items
AR 4781, AR 1510

PM **GEORG LUDWIG COHN**
Lawyer, 1845–1918
Religious class notebook
1 item
AR 979

PM **HUGO COHN**
Excerpt from letter
1 item
AR 80

PM **JOSEPH COHN FAMILY, RAWITSCH**
Prussian government documents
issued to family members, 1828–77
6 items
AR 2297

PM **JULIUS COHN**
Rabbi
Farewell sermon (Ulm, 1939)
1 item
AR 1233

PM **LOUIS MARCUS COHN**
Saddler, 1813–1898
Diaries; excerpts from German
writers
4 items
AR 4619

PM **LUDWIG ADOLF COHN**
Historian, 1834–1871
University papers; memberships in
historical associations; personal papers
41 items
AR 3891

FO PM **OSKAR COHN**
1869–1936, Social Democrat,
member of German Reichstag
Notes; photos
2 items
AR 4213

PM **BRUNO COHNBERG**
Lawyer, 1872–1934
Certificates; recommendations;
biographical sketch
3 items
AR 4167

PM **FRITZ COHNSTAEDT**
Speech
1 item
AR 1614

PM SM **COLLEGIUM MUSICUM JUDAICUM; AMSTERDAM**
Programs; newspaper clippings
15 items
AR 4987

PM **PAUL COLLIN**
Manuscript
1 item
AR 2114

FO PM **COLOGNE; JEWISH COMMUNITY**
Photos of synagogue; charity form;
clippings; government documents
about Jews in Cologne, 1816–1851
16 items
AR 998

PM **ISAAC SAMSON COMA**
Schutzbrief (Mainz, 1757)
1 item
AR 2398

PM **CONCERT PROGRAMS**
Assorted programs (1885–1932)
77 items
AR 2094

FO = Photos · GE = Genealogical Material · PM = Primary Material · SM = Secondary Material

SM **CLARIBEL CONE**
Art collector, 1864–1929
Articles concerning Cone sisters and
Gertrud Stein
2 items
AR 4478

PM **CONFERENCE ON JEWISH
MATERIAL CLAIMS AGAINST
GERMANY**
Circulars, memorandum, reports
(1959–1961)
6 items
AR 65

SM **CONFERENCE USA-SAN JOSE,
CALIF.**
Article on first Western Religious
Conference on Holocaust (1977)
1 item
AR 4380

PM **CONFERENCE USA-ST. LOUIS,
MO.**
Circular; programs; lectures; seminar
25 items
AR 4281

PM **CONFIRMATION**
Confirmation notebook
1 item
AR 3868

GE PM **CONITZER KONZERN**
Firm history; family genealogy
4 items
AR 14

FO PM **LEWIS CONN**
SM 1872–
Articles; manuscripts; photos;
correspondence with Albert
Schweitzer
14 items
AR 436

SM **COOKBOOKS**
Cookbooks, 1842–1932
4 items
AR 3527

PM **GUSTAV COPPEL**
Industrialist, 1830–1914
Brochure
1 item
AR 4494

PM **COSEL; JEWISH COMMUNITY**
Manuscript
1 item
AR 3713

PM **COUNCIL OF JEWISH CULTURAL
AGENCIES**
Program
1 item
AR 4702

PM **COUNCIL OF JEWISH
FEDERATION AND WELFARE
FUNDS, INC.**
Reports
1 item
AR 4080

PM **CLEMENTINE CRAMER**
Watercolors
9 items
AR 2018

SM **ERNST J. CRAMER**
Member of Board of Leo Baeck
Institute, manager of Springer Verlag,
editor *Die Welt*, 1913–
Articles
3 items
AR 4218

PM **JOHN D. CRAMER**
Letters about John D. Cramer from
his father S. D. Cramer to Leo Baeck
Institute
2 items
AR 2836

PM **CONSTANTIN CRAMER VON
LAUE**
Letters including correspondence
with Leo Baeck (1942, 1946)
3 items
AR 4134

SM **CUXHAVEN; JEWISH
COMMUNITY**
Article on Jews in district of
Ritzebuettel and Cuxhaven
1 item
AR 5242

FO SM **CZERNOWITZ (NOW CERNAUTI,
USSR); JEWISH COMMUNITY**
Rabbi's sermon (1928)
1 item
AR 5180

FO SM **CZIESCHOWA, UPPER SILESIA; JEWISH COMMUNITY**
Photo: synagogue and church; article
2 items
AR 4949

SM **DACHAU; JEWISH COMMUNITY**
Article on Jewish community of Dachau
1 item
AR 7241

GE PM **DAHL-SAMSON FAMILY**
Documents; genealogy
15 items
AR 4741

PM **MORITZ DAHLERBRUCH**
1887–
Miltary papers; certificates from Nazi welfare organizations; photos; miscellaneous papers about Jewish community activities
19 items
AR 2384

PM **LEOPOLD DAMROSCH**
Music manuscript
1 item
AR 1981

PM **MAX DANIEL FAMILY**
Pharmacist
Religious objects early 19th cent.; prayer for King Friedrich Wilhelm III; 19th cent. documents; family documents; recommendation by Leo Baeck
63 items
AR 1644

GE PM **ALBERT DANN FAMILY**
Businessman, 1868–1960
Family reminiscences; manuscripts; correspondence
36 items
AR 98

GE **DANNENBAUM SISTERS**
Family tree
1 item
AR 1382

PM SM **ALBERT DANZIG**
Author, 1882–1908
Biography, typescripts of plays by Danzig (1900); foreword to Danzig's play *Matthias Wolfram*
3 items
AR 3274

FO PM **DANZIG; JEWISH COMMUNITY**
Photos of synagogue; letter about emigration (1939); printed statement (1806)
16 items
AR 1722

FO PM **DANZIG; ROSENBAUM SCHOOL**
Photo of Rosenbaum School (1937); list of students
2 items
AR 5288

PM SM **DARMSTADT; JEWISH COMMUNITY**
Clippings; copy of Darmstadt Haggadah
8 items
AR 243

PM **MORITZ DAVID**
Rabbi in Bochum
Letters to Siegfried Guggenheim
4 items
AR 176

SM **LUCY DAVIDOWICZ**
Historian
Articles; reviews
5 items
AR 4306

SM **DAVIDSOHN FAMILY**
Eulogy
1 item
AR 1785

PM **SIMON DAVIDSON**
Admission to lodge, San Francisco (1858)
1 item
AR 3279

PM **THOMAS DEHLER**
Letter
1 item
AR 1877

FO PM **MAX DEHN**
1878–1952
Photos; biographical data
3 items
AR 3226

FO = Photos · GE = Genealogical Material · PM = Primary Material · SM = Secondary Material

FO **DELMENHORST, OLDENBURG; JEWISH COMMUNITY**
Photo of synagogue
1 item
AR 4419

FO GE **DEMBINSKY FAMILY, BRESLAU**
PM Two petitions (1805); military papers (1872); photos; notes about family tree
7 items
AR 1323

SM **DEPORTATION-JEWS OF BERLIN**
Indictment vs. Otto Bovensiegen (1970); documentation about the deportation of Jews from Berlin by Nazis
1 item
AR 7257

PM **BERNHARD DERNBURG**
Finance Minister of Germany, 1865–1937
Speech to Reichstag about revision of the Treaty of Versailles (1920)
1 item
AR 3865

PM **DERNBURG FAMILY**
Letters about family history
3 items
AR 1480

FO **DERTINGEN; JEWISH COMMUNITY**
Photos of synagogue
4 items
AR 2927

PM **DESSAU; JEWISH COMMUNITY**
Answers to questionnaire
1 item
AR 821

FO PM **PAUL DESSAU**
SM Composer, 1894–1979
Photos; postcard; obituary
3 items
AR 4970

GE **DESSAUER FAMILY, VIENNA**
Articles about family
2 items
AR 2935

FO PM **MAX DESSOIR**
Philosopher, 1867–1947
Photo of oil painting; autograph
2 items
AR 2172, AR 1828

FO **DETMOLD; JEWISH COMMUNITY**
Photos of synagogue
2 items
AR 400

FO PM **ERNST DEUTSCH**
SM Actor, 1890–1969
Articles; photos; autographs
6 items
AR 1655, AR 3345

PM **HENNY DEUTSCH**
1831–1918
Autographs
4 items
AR 2642

GE PM **HERMANN DEUTSCH FAMILY**
Family documents; testament; recommendations; membership certificates; papers concerning Hugo Deutsch on Hermann Boehm's execution by the French (1871)
18 items
AR 1889

FO PM **RICHARD DEUTSCHMANN**
Opthamologist, 1852–1935
Medals; photo
2 items
AR 2471

PM **EDUARD DEVRIENT**
Artist, 1801–1877
Autograph
1 item
AR 835

GE **DEVRIENT FAMILY**
Family tree
4 items
AR 213

GE **DEVRIES FAMILY**
Family tree
1 item
AR 2837

FO = Photos · GE = Genealogical Material · PM = Primary Material · SM = Secondary Material

PM **LEO-JEHUDA DIAMENT**
Died at Auschwitz, 1944
Typescript
1 item
AR 988

SM **DICKER FAMILY**
Jewish family from Czechoslovakia
Book: *A Jewish Family Trail; The Dickers and Their Mates* (New York 1977, privately printed)
1 item
AR 7123

FO **BERNHARD DIEBOLD**
1886–1945
Photo with dedication (1928)
1 item
AR 1829

FO PM **DIEDENHOFEN (NOW THIONVILLE, FRANCE); JEWISH COMMUNITY**
Manuscript; photos of synagogue
3 items
AR 4009

PM SM **MAX DIENEMANN**
Rabbi, 1875–1939
Clippings; letters
6 items
AR 60, AR 3050

FO PM **ZEVI H. WOLF DIESENDRUCK**
Philosopher, 1890–1940
Biographical notes; photo
2 items
AR 4049

PM **DIEZ A.D. LAHN; CHILDREN'S HOME**
Jewish home for children
Circulars 1887, 1880, 1920
5 items
AR 3546

PM SM **DIEZ/A.D. LAHN; JEWISH COMMUNITY**
Articles; copies of official records
7 items
AR 4943

PM **ERNST DINGFELDER**
1902–
Certificates
5 items
AR 4088

GE **DINKELSPIEL FAMILY**
History of Dinkelspiel family, Mannheim; family tree
2 items
AR 4942

PM **BENJAMIN DISRAELI**
Autograph
1 item
AR 532

PM **DITTIGHEIM; JEWISH COMMUNITY**
Letter
1 item
AR 4283

PM **DOBRIN FAMILY**
Personal documents; business and personal correspondence mostly in Hebrew; honorary citizenship; papers relating to deportation (1770–1940)
93 items
AR 4034

SM **DOBRUSKA FAMILY, BRUENN**
Article
1 item
AR 4252

PM **DOBRZYCA; JEWISH COMMUNITY**
Circular
1 item
AR 3550

GE PM **DOCTOR FAMILY; MEININGEN**
Documents; genealogical notes
11 items
AR 4908

FO PM **ALFRED DOEBLIN**
Author, 1878–1957
Photos; autographs
12 items
AR 86, AR 837

PM **DOERNBERG-DINKELSBUEHLER**
Various family documents (1818–1955)
1 item
AR 5276

FO = Photos · GE = Genealogical Material · PM = Primary Material · SM = Secondary Material

PM SM **B. F. DOLBIN**
Artist, 1883–1971
Articles; exhibit catalogue
6 items
AR 2300

PM **ERICH DOMBROWSKI**
Journalist
Autographs
2 items
AR 1830

PM **DORTMUND; JEWISH COMMUNITY**
Material about Theodor-Herzl Club, Dortmund Zionistische Vereinigung, Verein Jung-Juda; correspondence 1911–1914
14 items
AR 3178

FO PM **ELISE DOSENHEIMER**
1868–
Photo; list of books
2 items
AR 1481

PM **DR. BLOCH-PROF. ZUCKER**
Jewish members of Austrian Parliament
Printed certificate honoring their speeches against antisemitism, 1890
1 item
AR 1017

PM **H. L. DRAKER**
Microfilms: copies of Jewish Vital Statistics Registers east of Oder-Neisse
2 items
AR 7143

FO PM **DRESDEN; JEWISH COMMUNITY**
SM Budget (1938); photos of synagogue; articles; information about property; typescript; clippings
22 items
AR 140

GE PM **DRESDNER FAMILY**
Family documents
5 items
AR 4207

GE PM **KURT M. DRESEL**
SM Professor, physician, 1892–1951
Publications by Dresel; Bach family tree; citizenship document (1814)
66 items
AR 1178

FO SM **L. DREY**
Physician
Photo; offprints
5 items
AR 2263

GE **DREYDEL FAMILY**
Genealogical dates from 1785
1 item
AR 4855

GE PM **DREYER FAMILY**
Family tree of Dreyer-Loewenstein-Marx-Hardt families; marriage certificate (1877)
2 items
AR 989

FO PM **ALFRED DREYFUS**
SM 1859–1935
Paintings; prints; photos; texts
7 items
AR 2165

FO GE **DREYFUS-HEIMERDINGER-GUGGENHEIMER FAMILIES**
Family tree; photos of Baden communities of Schmieheim, Altdorf, Ettenheim, Friesenheim, Kippenheim
19 items
AR 4734

FO GE **DREYFUSS FAMILY, MANNHEIM**
PM Family tree; photos of documents, including citizenship, receipts, certificates concerning medal; letter and answer from Dachau (1766, 1860–1938)
16 items
AR 3937

PM **ISIDOR DREYFUSS**
Physician
Certificates
6 items
AR 4107

FO = Photos · GE = Genealogical Material · PM = Primary Material · SM = Secondary Material

FO PM **FELIX DREYSCHOCK**
Musician, 1860–1906
Biographical sketch; photo
2 items
AR 2414

SM **DROVE; JEWISH COMMUNITY**
History; newspaper clipping (1984)
1 item
AR 5294

PM **ERICH DRUCKER**
Businessman, 1905–
Business correspondence;
manuscripts; memoir; poems
13 items
AR 3176

FO PM **SALLY DRUCKER**
SM German soldier, World War I, died 1917
Photos; medal; letters; clippings
17 items
AR 3031

PM **SIMON DUBNOW**
Historian, 1860–1941
Autograph
1 item
AR 4148

GE **DUENKELSBUEHLER FAMILY**
Family trees of Duenkelsbuehler and Ochs families, Fuerth
2 items
AR 750

SM **LAZAR DUENNER**
Rabbi, 1876–
Article
1 item
AR 2524

PM **DUENSBACH; JEWISH COMMUNITY**
Drawing of synagogue
1 item
AR 4336

FO PM **DUESSELDORF; JEWISH COMMUNITY**
Photos of synagogue; print of Recke's asylum, 1826 (missionary institution)
5 items
AR 3570

PM **DUISBURG; JEWISH COMMUNITY**
History of Jews in Duisburg (1933–1945); name lists
1 item
AR 7239

PM SM **HELEN DUKAS**
Correspondence; photocopies of Einstein items; ID card with Einstein's signature; newspaper clippings
8 items
AR 5152

FO PM **ABRAHAM G. DUKER**
Historian, 1907–
Biographical sketch; photo
2 items
AR 3907

GE **ERNST DULKEN FAMILY**
Genealogy
1 item
AR 3573

PM **HENRY DUNANT**
Swiss philanthropist, 1826–1910
Proposal for International Society for the Renewal of the Orient (1866)
2 items
AR 4455

PM **HANS DUSCH**
Organist of Jewish community of Aachen
Music for Kaddish sheet music
3 items
AR 3139

PM **ALBERT DZIALOSZYNSKI**
Document: appointment as: *Kommerzienrat* by Wilhelm II
1 item
AR 5138

PM SM **EAST PRUSSIA; JEWISH COMMUNITY**
Jewish religion curriculum (1901–1903); article
6 items
AR 2939

PM **EBERBACH; JEWISH COMMUNITY**
Program of the dedication of new synagogue (1913); speech by Benjamin Levy; typescript on history of community in Eberbach

FO = Photos · GE = Genealogical Material · PM = Primary Material · SM = Secondary Material

3 items
AR 1412

PM **SIEGFRIED EBERHARDT**
Letter expelling him from Reichsschriftumskammer (1937)
1 item
AR 2838

PM **GEORG EBERS**
1837–1898
Autographs
9 items
AR 443

SM **EBERSWALDE; JEWISH COMMUNITY**
Clipping
1 item
AR 1413

PM **KARL EBERT**
Actor, 1917–
Autograph
1 item
AR 1831

PM **EBSTEIN FAMILY, BRESLAU, WOHLAU**
Family documents (1855–1882) especially concerning testament; purchase of estate (*Rittergut*)
9 items
AR 1879

FO SM **JOHANNES ECK**
Theologian, 1486–1543
Portrait etching
1 item
AR 3482

PM **JOSEPH JOHN EDELHEIM**
Certificate of Hamburg citizenship
1 item
AR 61

PM **IGNATIUS F. EDENBURG**
Doctor of Medicine diploma of University of Budapest (1914)
1 item
AR 5069

SM **EDENKOBEN; JEWISH COMMUNITY**
Article
1 item
AR 7081

FO GE **AKIBA EGER**
Rabbi in Posen, 1761–1837
Family trees; photos
5 items
AR 367

GE **EGER FAMILY**
Family history, genealogies
5 items
AR 21

FO PM **EVA EHRENBERG**
Voluntary war worker during First World War
Photos; poem; letter
7 items
AR 3664

FO PM **PHILIPP AND JULIE EHRENBERG**
Photos; letter
6 items
AR 2811

GE PM **RICHARD EHRENBERG**
Economist, 1857–1921
Typescript history of Ehrenberg and Fischel families, (1918); autograph
2 items
AR 7088, AR 2597

PM **V. L. EHRENBERG**
Professor
Letters from Leo Baeck; drawing by Adam Rosenzweig
4 items
AR 1232

PM **BONWIT EHRENFELD**
Hebrew marriage contract *Ketuba*, 1843
1 item
AR 768

GE **EHRENSTAMM FAMILY**
Family history
1 item
AR 541

PM SM **ALBERT EHRENSTEIN**
Author, 1886–1950
Poem and drawing by Kokoschka for Ehrenstein, review of book by Ehrenstein; autograph
3 items
AR 2719, AR 1720

FO = Photos · GE = Genealogical Material · PM = Primary Material · SM = Secondary Material

GE **EHRLICH-AUERBACH FAMILY**
Family tree of related Cohn, Hagelberg, Rother, Hirschfeld, Goldschmidt, Silberstein, Ehrenstamm, and Steinschneider families from Breslau, Chonitz, and Posen
12 items
AR 17

SM **ERNST LUDWIG EHRLICH**
Newspaper clipping, "Judaica Lectures at Zurich University" (1962)
1 item
AR 1967

PM SM **EUGEN EHRLICH**
Historian, professor of law, 1862–1922
Letters; testament; notes; clippings
12 items
AR 3908

PM **HEINRICH EHRLICH**
Author, 1822–1899
Autograph
1 item
AR 2501

SM **MAX EHRLICH**
Performer, died 1943, Auschwitz
Newspaper ad of first engagement (1920)
1 item
AR 2490

PM SM **PAUL EHRLICH**
Biologist, Nobel Prize winner, 1854–1915
Clippings; autograph; letters and cards
37 items
AR 339, AR 1728

PM **TONI EHRLICH FAMILY**
Engagement contract, 1800
1 item
AR 392

PM **BARUCH EHRMANN**
Document concerning secret emigration of Baruch Ehrmann (Hoechst im Odenwald, 1854)
3 items
AR 6008

GE PM **HERZ EHRMANN**
Marriage contract (1825); family trees (1767–1903); 1767 manuscript
5 items
AR 4153

PM **RUDOLF R. EHRMANN**
Letters about the family
2 items
AR 2245

FO **JONATHAN E. EIBENSCHUETZ**
Chief Rabbi of Altona, Hamburg, and Wandsbeck, 1690–1764
Photo
1 item
AR 3580

PM **EICH BEZIRK WORMS; JEWISH COMMUNITY**
Inventory of community property
1 item
AR 3449

FO GE **GUSTAV EICHELGRUEN FAMILY,**
PM **WESTPHALIA AND MAGDEBURG**
History of Stresemann and Eichelgruen families; family documents; photo; autograph by Gustav Stresemann
6 items
AR 3398

PM **EICHHOLHZEIM; JEWISH COMMUNITY**
Information
1 item
AR 2856

FO SM **JULIE EICHHOLZ**
1849–1918
Photo; memorial article
2 items
AR 1941

PM SM **MAX EICHHOLZ**
Lawyer, local political leader, 1881–1943
Articles; biographical sketch
4 items
AR 2598

FO **EICHSTETTEN; JEWISH COMMUNITY**
Photos
10 items
AR 2476

FO = Photos · GE = Genealogical Material · PM = Primary Material · SM = Secondary Material

GE PM **EICHTHAL FAMILY**
Ennobled Bavarian banking family
Family tree; history; report
concerning a bank by Freiherr von
Eichthal (1843)
4 items
AR 1770

SM **EGON EICHWALD**
Chemist, 1883–1943
Memorial article
1 item
AR 62

PM SM **NATHAN EIDINGER FAMILY**
Rumanian industrialist, 1879–1945
Clippings; family papers; letter to
Eidinger from Count Czernin (1918);
materials on Bukovina
88 items
AR 7033

SM **ALBERT EINSTEIN – BETTY NEWMAN COLLECTION**
Newspaper clippings; Einstein stamps; posters
37 items
AR 4988

FO PM **ALBERT EINSTEIN**
SM Physicist, Nobel Prize winner, 1879–1955
Clippings; letters and notes by Einstein; photos; items commemorating Einstein; Einstein family tree; autographs
181 items
AR 136, AR 1147

FO SM **ALBERT EINSTEIN CENTENNIAL EXHIBIT**
Leo Baeck Institute, 1979 – contents of catalogue, research materials for exhibition, mathematical drafts, correspondence, photos
2 items
AR 4858

FO PM **ALFRED EINSTEIN**
Physician
Photo; letter by his widow
2 items
AR 2232

FO PM **FRED EINSTEIN**
SM Letters by Albert Einstein; photo; correspondence concerning Max Einstein U.S. Civil War; clipping
15 items
AR 3171

SM **RUTH EIS**
Painter
Exhibit catalogue
1 item
AR 4217

FO PM **EISENACH; JEWISH COMMUNITY**
Manuscript; Festchrift; photos of synagogue, including burning synagogue
7 items
AR 3404

FO PM **EISENSTADT, BURGENLAND; JEWISH COMMUNITY**
Photos of Jewish quarters; synagogue; Jewish ritual objects and arts
65 items
AR 2388

FO PM **H. LUDWIG EISENSTADT**
SM Physician, 1872–1918
Articles; photos; notes
16 items
AR 122

FO PM **JULIUS EISENSTADT**
1895–1942
Letter; photos
8 items
AR 123

FO PM **BRUNO EISNER**
Pianist
Photo; business card; letters (1956, 1959)
4 items
AR 538

PM **HEINRICH EISNER**
Head of Berlin Jewish community, 1850–1918
Typed copies; business memorial
6 items
AR 2028

FO PM **KURT EISNER**
Revolutionary socialist, 1867–1919; Prime Minister of Bavaria
Police files; photos; circular from soldiers' council; autographs

FO = Photos · GE = Genealogical Material · PM = Primary Material · SM = Secondary Material

7 items
AR 1812, AR 2616

PM **CHAIM EITINGON**
Correspondence with Goerdeler
(1932)
1 item
AR 5057

PM SM **JULIUS ELBAU**
1881–1965, Publisher and chief editor
Vossische Zeitung
Personal items; correspondence;
articles
25 items
AR 4596

PM **ELBERFELD; JEWISH COMMUNITY**
Letter
1 item
AR 3468

PM **SIEGFRIED ELIAS**
1904–
Curriculum vitae
1 item
AR 2128

FO PM **BENNO ELKAN**
SM Sculptor, 1877–1960
Photos of works; letters; articles
18 items
AR 2016

FO GE **ELKAN FAMILY**
PM Memorabilia; documents; photos;
family tree; correspondence;
genealogy, including Parchim and
Bruel families, Mecklenburg
44 items
AR 1960

FO **FREDERICK W. ELKAN**
Photo album of ceremonial religious
objects; photo album of synagogues
80 items
AR 4039, AR 4040

PM SM **JULIUS ELKAN, BANKING HOUSE**
Notes about the family;
correspondence with Goethe; articles
29 items
AR 2238

PM **KURT ELKAN**
Certificates
2 items
AR 1584

PM **SALLY ELKAN**
1816–1893
Silver medal; letter
2 items
AR 2497

SM **WOLF ELKAN**
Physician, 20th cent.
Medical articles
4 items
AR 1459

GE **ELLERN FAMILY, FUERTH**
Family tree from 1600; Gruenbaum
family tree from 1490
2 items
AR 3510

PM **HERMAN ELLERN**
1892–
Album
2 items
AR 4360

FO **ELMSHORN; JEWISH COMMUNITY**
Photos
2 items
AR 3360

FO **ARTHUR ELOESSER**
Literary historian, 1870–1938
Photo
1 item
AR 2695

PM SM **ERICH ELOW**
Writer, cabaret performer 20th cent.
Correspondence; clippings; programs
including letter from Martin Buber
34 items
AR 1280

PM **HEDWIG ELSAESSER**
Music and text of children's Hebrew
songs
1 item
AR 7120

FO = Photos · GE = Genealogical Material · PM = Primary Material · SM = Secondary Material

GE PM **ELSBACH FAMILY**
History of family and business, Marsden
1 item
AR 4531

GE PM **BAER ELTZBACHER FAMILY**
Family documents (1797–1828)
7 items
AR 4350

PM **EMDEN; JEWISH COMMUNITY**
Typescript
1 item
AR 4220

PM **MEYER JACOB EMDEN**
19th cent. diary (1832); testament of M.J. Emden (1865); testament of Betty Emden (1876)
2 items
AR 3838

FO **EMMENDINGEN; JEWISH COMMUNITY**
Photos of synagogue
4 items
AR 2477

PM **EMS; JEWISH COMMUNITY**
Inventory
2 items
AR 3469

PM **EMS; JEWISH ORPHANAGE**
Jewish home for orphans and girls
Circulars
1 item
AR 3547

PM SM **MEYER EMS FAMILY**
Documents; correspondence; articles
75 items
AR 3177

PM SM **ENCYCLOPAEDIA JUDAICA**
Articles; circulars
5 items
AR 1296

SM **ENDINGEN; JEWISH COMMUNITY**
Clippings (1967–1970)
4 items
AR 3241

PM **EDUARD ENGEL**
1851–1941
Autograph
1 item
AR 1790

PM **FRITZ ENGEL**
1867–1934
Autograph
1 item
AR 2491

PM **ITZIG ENGELMANN**
Policeman, 1811–
Professional certificate
1 item
AR 3650

PM **ENZYKLOPAEDIE DES JUDENTUMS**
Circular
1 item
AR 4677

GE **EPHRAIM FAMILY, HAMBURG**
Family tree (1665–1938)
1 item
AR 1129

FO **VEITEL HEINE EPHRAIM**
Photos
2 items
AR 2627

GE **EPHRUSSI FAMILY**
Family tree, explanation
2 items
AR 1771

PM **EPPELSHEIM; JEWISH COMMUNITY**
Inventory
1 item
AR 3450

PM **LION EPPENSTEIN OF LUBLINITZ**
Documents; letters from 1798
11 items
AR 4913

SM **PAUL EPPSTEIN**
Social worker, 1902–1944
Articles on Eppstein and on his death at Theresienstadt
11 items
AR 804

FO = Photos · GE = Genealogical Material · PM = Primary Material · SM = Secondary Material

PM **ERNST H. EPSTEIN**
Businessman, 1870–1922
Cash books
4 items
AR 4165

GE **EPSTEIN FAMILY, FRANKFURT A.M.**
Family tree from 1627
1 item
AR 3508

PM **FELIX EPSTEIN**
Banker
Material concerning Salomon Heine; will; material about 125th anniversary of the Hamburg Jewish Hospital; Hamburg Bank (1872, 1873)
4 items
AR 3904

PM **JULIUS EPSTEIN**
Author
Autograph
1 item
AR 2492

PM **JULIUS PAUL EPSTEIN**
Letters; Jewish calendar for Wuerttemberg
3 items
AR 2609

FO **LUCY EPSTEIN**
Artist
Photo
1 item
AR 1180

FO **THEOBALD EPSTEIN**
Educator, 1836–1928
Photo
1 item
AR 1181

FO **TILLY EPSTEIN**
Educator, 1881–
Photo
1 item
AR 1182

FO PM **ERFURT; JEWISH COMMUNITY**
Articles; photo of city; interior of new synagogue
4 items
AR 2880

GE **ERLANGER FAMILY, FRANKFURT A.M.**
Family tree with explanations
1 item
AR 1772

FO PM **PHILIPP ERLANGER**
Sculptor, painter, 1870–1934
Biographical articles; letter; photos
58 items
AR 636

PM **IRMA C. ERMAN**
Poet, 20th cent.
Collection of poems, including Sandburg translations by E. Blumenberg
4 items
AR 4106

GE PM **ERNST FAMILY, WESERITZ, BOHEMIA**
Family trees; letters
2 items
AR 4077

PM **ERNESTINE ESCHELBACHER**
1858–
Prussian government documents concerning Ernestine Eschelbacher Stiftung and its dissolution in late 1930's
2 items
AR 4124

PM **MAX ESCHELBACHER**
Rabbi, 1880–1964
Obituary
1 item
AR 2437

PM **ESCHKOL-VERLAG**
Documents concerning Eschkol-Verlag (Dr. Nachum Goldmann), and its debt to Berlin Jewish community (1931–1939)
5 items
AR 3232

FO **ESCHWEGE; JEWISH COMMUNITY**
Photos of synagogue (interior and exterior)
2 items
AR 5140

PM **SHAUL ESH**
Paper on origins of
Reichsvereinigung der Juden in
Deutschland
1 item
AR 3283

FO **BERNHARD FREIHERR VON ESKELES**
1753–1839
Photo of lithograph
1 item
AR 2767

GE **ESKELES FAMILY, VIENNA**
Family tree and explanation
2 items
AR 1773

FO PM **ESSEN; JEWISH COMMUNITY**
SM Clippings; photos of synagogue; article about 1938 pogrom
33 items
AR 1588

PM **ESSENHEIM; JEWISH COMMUNITY**
Estimated value of community property
1 item
AR 3451

FO **ESSINGEN, NEAR LANDAU; JEWISH COMMUNITY**
Photos of synagogue
6 items
AR 4682

FO PM **ESSLINGEN; JEWISH**
SM **COMMUNITY**
Clippings; circular; letter; photos of Jewish orphanage
11 items
AR 2583

PM **ESSLINGEN; JEWISH ORPHANAGE**
Jewish institution for orphans and educational institution
Commemorative coin
1 item
AR 4502

FO GE **ESSLINGER FAMILY**
PM Otto Leib family tree; photocopies of documents; photos
5 items
AR 4991

GE **ETTLINGER FAMILY**
Family tree
1 item
AR 3606

FO **JACOB ETTLINGER**
Rabbi, 1798–1871
Photo
1 item
AR 2291

SM **L. J. ETTLINGER**
Newspaper clipping (1957 article on 125 years hardware wholesaler)
1 item
AR 1950

PM **EUBIGHEIM; JEWISH COMMUNITY**
Manuscript
1 item
AR 3827

PM **HERBERT EULENBERG**
Author
Clipping, 1951
1 item
AR 2217

PM **FRANZ EULENBURG**
Economist, 1867–1943
5 page typescript
1 item
AR 3423

SM **EWIGER JUDE**
Bibliography of works on the subject
1 item
AR 2024

SM **ERICH EYCK**
Historian, 1893–1964
Newspaper clippings
2 items
AR 2138

FO PM **FRITZ FABIAN**
1877–
Curriculum vitae; photos; documents from Nazi period, including Theresienstadt (1942–1962)
6 items
AR 2657

FO = Photos · GE = Genealogical Material · PM = Primary Material · SM = Secondary Material

PM **HANS ERICH FABIAN**
Jewish communal leader, Berlin
Reports on activities of Lehranstalt
für die Wissenschaft des Judentums
Berlin; memorandum on collection of
material concerning history of Jews in
Germany 1933–45
3 items
AR 4324

PM **LILLY FABIAN**
Widow of Fritz Fabian, 1892–1981
Documents from Theresienstadt
19 items
AR 7234

PM SM **EMIL L. FACKENHEIM**
Philosopher, 1916–
Program; article
2 items
AR 3429

FO GE **MANFRED FACKENHEIM FAMILY**
Family tree and family documents
(1827–1975); material on the related
Meyer and Heimann families; photo
13 items
AR 1281

PM **GEORG JOSEPH FAJANS**
Industrialist, 1911–
Curriculum vitae
1 item
AR 4837

SM **DR. FALCKSON**
Issue of *Der Teutsche* (1846)
1 item
AR 2031

SM **BERNHARD FALK**
Lawyer, 1867–1944
Clippings; articles
2 items
AR 3567

GE PM **HUGO AND MARGARETHE FALKENHEIM**
Letters
2 items
AR 4168

PM **KARL FARKAS**
Autograph
1 item
AR 1832

FO PM **FELIX FECHENBACH**
1894–1933
Letters; photos; articles; poems
(1914–1940)
52 items
AR 1709

PM SM **PAUL FECHTER**
Writer, 1880–1958
Letters; articles
80 items
AR 2111

FO PM **ERNST FEDER**
SM Journalist, 1881–1964
Typescripts; articles; photos
27 items
AR 1003

PM **PAUL FEDERN**
Student of Freud
Document of honorary membership
in Psychoanalytical Society
1 item
AR 2405

PM **FEHMARN; JEWISH COMMUNITY**
Reports
2 items
AR 3285

PM **ISAAK FEIBELMANN**
Marriage certificate (1824)
1 item
AR 3443

GE PM **FEIGENBAUM FAMILY**
Family tree, family documents (19th cent.)
13 items
AR 1911a

PM **FRANZ AND ANNA FEIGL**
Papers of Franz Feigl, 1899–1963;
papers of wife Anna from
Theresienstadt (1942–1945)
4 items
AR 5269

GE **FEILCHENFELD FAMILY**
Family chronicle with photos (1950)
1 item
AR 4295

FO = Photos · GE = Genealogical Material · PM = Primary Material · SM = Secondary Material

PM SM **HUGO FEILCHENFELD**
Ophthalmologist
Articles by and about Feilchenfeld;
letter to Thomas Mann; program in
memory of Kristallnacht
10 items
AR 3739

PM **WERNER FEILCHENFELD**
Businessman, economic advisor,
1895–
Manuscripts; memoranda on Israel
and Middle East; restitution claims
and transfers of funds from Nazi
Germany
20 items
AR 4081

PM **MARIA FEIN**
Actress
Photo-postcard 1917
1 item
AR 2408

FO PM **LYONEL FEININGER**
Painter, 1871–1956
Photo; autograph
2 items
AR 2696, AR 1672

FO PM **SIGMUND FEIST**
Educator, 1865–1943
Personal papers; correspondence;
photos of Reichenheim Orphanage
10 items
AR 3059, AR 5142

PM **ROLF FELDKRAN**
1915–
Correspondence and documents
regarding his stay in Switzerland
(1934, 1935)
10 items
AR 4430

PM **BERTHA FELDMANN FAMILY**
Birth, marriage certificate
2 items
AR 2237

PM **FANNY FELDMANN**
Letter
1 item
AR 469

FO PM **FRITZ FELDSTEIN FAMILY**
Correspondence; photos concerning
attempted immigration to America
(1938–1941)
25 items
AR 3250

SM **FELLHEIM; JEWISH COMMUNITY**
Clipping
1 item
AR 2149

PM **BERNHARD FELSENTHAL**
Rabbi
Notes on Felsenthal's immigration,
travel (1854–1857)
1 item
AR 103

SM **FEUCHTWANGER FAMILY,
FUERTH**
Article, "A Family of Bankers," 1968
1 item
AR 3399

PM **FRITZ FEUCHTWANGER**
Report on a trip in Germany
(November 1978)
1 item
AR 4857

PM SM **LION FEUCHTWANGER**
Author, 1884–1958
Copies of articles by and about
Feuchtwanger and his estate; photos;
programs; memorials; East German
stamp in his honor; material on
family tree; autographs
15 items
AR 1234, AR 838

SM **SIGBERT FEUCHTWANGER**
Lawyer; vice-president of Munich
Jewish community, died 1956
Clipping of 10th anniversary of death
(1966)
1 item
AR 4330

PM **ISAAC FEUERRING**
Zionist leader, 1889–1937
Brochure in his memory
1 item
AR 3314

FO **JOHN HOWARD FIELDS**
President H. J. Fields & Co; member of Board of Directors, Leo Baeck Institute
Photo
1 item
AR 4066

PM **KURT FILBERT**
Challah cover, tefillin
2 items
AR 4835

PM **FILEHNE; JEWISH COMMUNITY**
Cicumcision registers (1812–1864), with explanatory letter
3 items
AR 2470

PM **JACOB FINDER FAMILY**
Citizenship papers of family members; other documents, 1820–1855
4 items
AR 3056

PM **GEORG FINK**
Author, 1879–1944
Autographs
9 items
AR 4208

SM **FIORINO FAMILY**
Articles
2 items
AR 468

PM **FIRMS: BANKS**
Lists of participants at meeting of expanded executive committee of the Centralverband der Deutschen Bank und Bankiergewerbes
1 item
AR 4276

PM **FISCHBACH; JEWISH COMMUNITY**
Persecution of Jews in Fischbach, 1935–1944 (42 pp.)
1 item
AR 7172a

FO GE **OSKAR FISCHEL**
PM Art historian, 1870–1939
Autographs
2 items
AR 1753

SM **ALFRED JOACHIM FISCHER**
Clipping, "Juden in Island," 1957
1 item
AR 32

FO PM **JOHANNA FISCHER FAMILY**
Family documents (1882–1939); photos
21 items
AR 4289

PM **ILSE FISCHER-REITBOECK**
Poet, writer
Prints
3 items
AR 4703

SM **SAMUEL FISCHER**
Publisher
Clippings; articles
8 items
AR 1004

FO **ADOLF FISCHHOF**
Austrian statesman
Photo
1 item
AR 2697

FO **EMIL FLANTER**
Jewish educator and teacher, 1860–1921
Biographical data and photo
1 item
AR 510

GE **GEORG FLATOW FAMILY**
Genealogies of Flatow, Wiener, and Toeplitz families
7 items
AR 4901

FO **ALFRED FLECHTHEIM**
Art dealer, 1878–1937
Photo
1 item
AR 2698

SM **EDMOND FLEG**
French writer, 1874–1964
Articles on his death
2 items
AR 4594

FO = Photos · GE = Genealogical Material · PM = Primary Material · SM = Secondary Material

SM **FLEHINGEN; JEWISH COMMUNITY**
Clipping
1 item
AR 2478

GE PM **FLEISCHER FAMILY**
Curricula vitae; personal papers; family tree; history of family business; Nazi evaluation of W. Fleischer fortune according to 1938 law
23 items
AR 3641

PM **MOSES FLEISCHHACKER FAMILY**
Information on family, school diploma, Kassel (1824)
2 items
AR 3284

SM **FLEISCHMANN-ZADIKOW**
Karel Fleischmann, M.D., 1899–1944
"Der Bildhauer Zadikow ist gestorben" (German translation)
1 item
AR 5305

PM SM **PHILLIP FLESCH**
Poet
86 poems and essays; indexes to volumes of poetry; articles
14 items
AR 2981

FO PM **JOSEPH FLOCH**
Artist, 1895–1977
Memoirs; articles; art catalogues; photos; family material
3 items
AR 7218

PM **FLOERSCHEIM FAMILY, BATTENBERG**
Letter of municipal citizenship (1865)
1 item
AR 1236

SM **DAVID FLUSSER**
Newspaper clipping, "Is There a Jewish Art?"
1 item
AR 1912

SM **HERBERT FOERDER**
Banker, 1901–1970
Obituary (1970)
1 item
AR 3690

PM **THEODOR FONTANE**
Author, 1819–1898
Autograph
1 item
AR 1530

FO PM **ERNEST O. FONTHEIM**
SM Photos; notes; articles on emigration; deportation; various clippings on Nazi period
7 items
AR 4941

PM **FORT ONTARIO REFUGEE CENTER**
Preliminary list of refugees in center (1944–1945)
1 item
AR 5313

GE **FOULD FAMILY**
Family tree and explanation
2 items
AR 1774

FO **DAVID AND JONAS FRAENCKEL**
Negatives of 19th cent. photos
1 item
AR 3844

GE **ISAAC FRAENCKEL**
Rabbi
Family tree
1 item
AR 1237

GE SM **LIEPMANN FRAENCKEL**
Painter, 1772–1857
Photos of family trees; copies of articles
8 items
AR 3011

FO **ALBERT FRAENKEL**
Physician, 1848–1918
Photo
1 item
AR 2699

PM **BERMAN FRAENKEL**
Rabbi, 1650–1708
Testament (1707)
1 item
AR 3069

FO = Photos · GE = Genealogical Material · PM = Primary Material · SM = Secondary Material

PM **BERNHARD FRAENKEL**
Physician, 1836–1911
Photo
1 item
AR 2700

PM **DANIEL FRAENKEL, UPPER SILESIA**
1822–1890
Biography
1 item
AR 5253

PM SM **ERNST FRAENKEL**
Economist, 1898–1975
Lecture; obituary
2 items
AR 1558

SM **EUGEN FRAENKEL**
Physician
Clipping (1960)
1 item
AR 1656

FO GE **FRAENKEL FAMILY**
PM Genealogical tables; family history; photos
36 items
AR 3751

PM **FRAENKEL FAMILY, BERLIN**
Schutzbrief; letters from Friedrich II of Prussia
6 items
AR 7145

PM **JACOB FRAENKEL**
Marriage contract (1853)
1 item
AR 1343

FO PM **JONAS FRAENKEL**
SM Literary critic, 1879–1965
Review and articles; photos; autobiographical sketch; correspondence
22 items
AR 1536

PM **JOSEPH FRAENKEL FAMILY**
Poems; songs; housekeeping record book 1867; notebook 1811
22 items
AR 3097–3099

GE SM **KOPPEL FRAENKEL FAMILY**
Magazine article; genealogy
1 item
AR 2264

SM **MEIER FRAENKEL**
Article
1 item
AR 1796

GE PM **JAMES FRANCK**
Physicist, born 1882 (Nobel Prize 1925)
Letters; genealogy
5 items
AR 2977, AR 1985

GE **FRANCKEN FAMILY, GELDERN**
32–page family history (1791–1901)
1 item
AR 5126

FO PM **JOHN A. FRANCKEN**
Aachen Synagogue photos; letter
2 items
AR 5054

SM **FRANCONIA; JEWISH COMMUNITY**
Article on Christian-Jewish relations in Main-Franconia during Middle Ages
1 item
AR 4799

FO SM **ABRAHAM FRANK**
Rabbi, 1840–1918
Photo; articles
3 items
AR 3583

FO PM **ANNE FRANK**
1929–1945
Letter from Otto Frank; plaque; photos (including one of her hiding place)
11 items
AR 1394

SM **BENNO FRANK**
Actor
Newspaper articles
2 items
AR 809

FO = Photos · GE = Genealogical Material · PM = Primary Material · SM = Secondary Material

FO PM **BRUNO FRANK**
Author
Photo; autograph
7 items
AR 866, AR 2586

PM **FRANK & CO., DEPARTMENT STORE**
Business ads (1894, 1898)
2 items
AR 5003

GE PM **EDGAR FRANK FAMILY**
SM Family tree, genealogical notes; articles; postcards
10 items
AR 1029

PM **FRANK FAMILY, ERFURT**
Cable book
1 item
AR 3538

PM **FRANK FAMILY, TAUBERBISCHOFSHEIM**
Marriage contract and dowry receipt; testament; ornament (1674–1860)
4 items
AR 2996

PM **HELEN FRANK FAMILY, RAUSCHENBERG**
Family and community documents
7 items
AR 4974

GE **ISAAC MEYER FRANK**
Family tree Herford/Westfalen; family notes
1 item
AR 1616

SM **(JEHUDA) LEOPOLD FRANK**
Jewish community leader, 1887–1962
Eulogy
1 item
AR 3315

GE PM **LOEB FRANK**
Engagement contract
2 items
AR 3921

FO SM **LUDWIG FRANK**
Socialist politician, 1874–1914
Photo of portrait; obituaries; article
4 items
AR 2717

SM **PAUL FRANK**
Physician, 1867–1936
Article; obituary
2 items
AR 4966

FO **PAUL GEORG FRANK**
Physician, 1873–1954
Photo
2 items
AR 1231

SM **PHILIPP FRANK**
Physicist, 1884–1966
Obituary
1 item
AR 4793

SM **RUDOLF FRANK**
Author
Newspaper clipping (1961)
1 item
AR 1585

PM **LEO S. FRANKEL FAMILY**
Marriage contracts; Torah mantle
2 items
AR 4719

FO PM **ZACHARIAS FRANKEL**
Rabbi, president of the Jewish Theological Seminary, Breslau, 1801–1875
Manuscript; article; photo
4 items
AR 2903

PM **M. FRANKENHUIS**
Note concerning Theresienstadt (May 1945)
1 item
AR 1030

SM **ALFRED FRANKENSTEIN**
Clippings, The Last Days of German Jewry; report on "Jüdisches Nachrichtenblatt"
2 items
AR 1005

SM **FRANKENSTEIN, SANITÄTSRAT**
Physician
Article (1932)
1 item
AR 1352

FO = Photos · GE = Genealogical Material · PM = Primary Material · SM = Secondary Material

PM **FRANKFURT/ODER; JEWISH COMMUNITY**
Program; items concerning orphanage; sale of chometz
3 items
AR 3286

GE **FRANKFURT-TRAGER FAMILY**
Family history
1 item
AR 5162

PM **DAVID FRANKFURTER**
Assassin of Gustloff, head of Swiss Nazi party, born 1909
Restitution application and accompanying letter; autograph
3 items
AR 1482, AR 3316

PM **FRANKFURTER FAMILY**
Birth and marriage certificates (1853/1882)
2 items
AR 4399

FO PM **NAPTHALI FRANKFURTER**
Rabbi of Hamburg, 1810–1866
Letters; sermon manuscript; photo autographed by Berthold Auerbach (1829–34, 1862)
10 items
AR 4224

FO **RICHARD FRANKFURTER**
Politician
Photo
1 item
AR 1183

PM **SALOMON FRANKFURTER**
Philologist, librarian, 1856–1941
Letter of congratulations on 80th birthday
1 item
AR 3532

SM **FRANKFURTER ZEITUNG**
Articles on the paper (1924, 1943)
2 items
AR 368

SM **FRANKISTS**
Articles about Frankist sect, letter from Eva Frank (1801)
3 items
AR 175

FO PM **LUDWIG AUGUST FRANKL**
Poet, president of Jewish community of Vienna, 1810–1894
Photos; lithographs; autographs
5 items
AR 2701, AR 1511

SM **VIKTOR E. FRANKL**
Psychiatrist
Aufbau article (1977)
1 item
AR 4413

SM **WALTER FRANKL**
Teacher
Newspaper article
1 item
AR 5004

FO PM **KARL EMIL FRANZOS**
Writer, 1848–1904
Photo; autograph
2 items
AR 2702, AR 1493

PM **FREDERICK II OF PRUSSIA**
Autograph (1769)
1 item
AR 1494

SM **HERBERT FREEDEN**
Article about German Jews in Israel
1 item
AR 22

SM **FREDDY FREEDMAN**
Obituary
1 item
AR 4749

GE **FREEMAN FAMILY**
Family tree since 1740
2 items
AR 540

SM **FREEMASONS**
Article about "Juden and Freimaurer" and covering letter
2 items
AR 3671

FO **FREIBURG I. BR.; JEWISH COMMUNITY**
Photos of synagogue and community buildings
3 items
AR 141

FO = Photos · GE = Genealogical Material · PM = Primary Material · SM = Secondary Material

FO PM **ARON FREIMANN**
  Bibliographer, professor, 1871–1948
  Obituary; photos; prospectus of a
  book by Freimann
  6 items
  AR 1184

SM **ANNA FREUD**
  Psychologist
  Clippings
  2 items
  AR 2337

FO PM **SIGMUND FREUD**
SM Psychiatrist, 1856–1939
  Articles about Freud; photos;
  correspondence; autographs
  34 items
  AR 1031, AR 827

FO **FREUDENBERG A.M; JEWISH COMMUNITY**
  Photo of synagogue
  2 items
  AR 4082

PM SM **FREUDENBERG (DRESS SHOP, ELBERFELD)**
  Article and letter about dress shop
  and Freudenberg
  2 items
  AR 3043

PM **MARGOT S. FREUDENBERG**
  Audiocassete about life in Hanover
  1 item
  AR 7146

PM **FREUDENREICH FAMILY, URSPRINGEN**
  Items on families in Urspringen
  2 items
  AR 4722

PM **GEORG GERSON FREUDENSTEIN**
  Report on Palestine trip (1913)
  1 item
  AR 5048

FO PM **FREUDENTHAL; JEWISH COMMUNITY**
  Cemetery register (1884–1946);
  clipping with picture of synagogue
  2 items
  AR 2553, AR 4893

PM **FREUND FAMILY, BEUTHEN**
  School and marriage certificates;
  passports from period of Upper
  Silesian Plebiscite; photos; notes by
  Leo Baeck
  11 items
  AR 2658

PM **ISMAR FREUND**
  Historian and Berlin Community
  Leader, 1876–1956
  Photostats; letters; petitions by the
  Preussischer Landesverband Jüdischer
  Gemeinden (1925)
  7 items
  AR 4169

PM **ROBERT FREUND FAMILY**
  Documents, Ph.D certificate of
  Robert Freund
  4 items
  AR 1349

PM **RUDOLF FREUND**
  Typescript about Jews in agriculture
  in Silesia
  1 item
  AR 1032

FO PM **WILHELM FREUND**
  Lawyer, 1831–1915
  Personal papers; photo; letters and
  patents dealing with Freund's career;
  appointments
  72 items
  AR 73

FO PM **BERTHOLD FREUNDLICH**
  Papers concerning life in hiding in
  Berlin during Second World War;
  typescript letters; clippings; photos
  9 items
  AR 3774

FO PM **LEO FREUNDLICH**
  Member of Austrian parliament, died
  1953
  Letters; photos
  5 items
  AR 3339

PM **ALEXANDER MORITZ FREY**
  1881–1957
  Autographs
  7 items
  AR 1979

FO = Photos · GE = Genealogical Material · PM = Primary Material · SM = Secondary Material

FO SM **ERICH FREY**
Lawyer, 1883–1964
Photo; obituary
2 items
AR 2301

FO GE **FRIDBERG FAMILY**
PM Family tree; copy of death certificate; photos (ca. 1860's)
7 items
AR 1689

FO PM **ALFRED FRIED**
Journalist, pacifist, Nobel Prize 1911, 1864–1921
Photo; autograph
2 items
AR 2976, AR 1372

FO PM **FRIED & ALSBERG**
Photo and letter concerning firm
1 item
AR 3044

FO **ERICH FRIED**
Author, 1921–
Photos
2 items
AR 3062

FO SM **FRIEDBERG, HESSIA; JEWISH COMMUNITY**
Photo; article
4 items
AR 4796

PM **LEOPOLD FRIEDBERG FAMILY**
Correspondence about family history; family coat of arms
8 items
AR 2032

PM SM **EGON FRIEDELL**
Historian, actor, 1878–1938
Newspaper clipping (1949); autograph
2 items
AR 2855, AR 1033

GE PM **MAX FRIEDEMANN FAMILY**
Family history and document (1813)
2 items
AR 2025

PM SM **RICHARD FRIEDENTHAL**
Author, chairman of P.E.N., 1896–1979
Obituary; clippings
3 items
AR 2316

SM **RUDOLPH FRIEDENTHAL**
Sections of book about North German Emancipation Law, 1867–1868
1 item
AR 2012

GE **FRIEDENWALD FAMILY**
Report on family
1 item
AR 1486

FO **HEINRICH FRIEDJUNG**
Historian, 1851–1920
Photo
1 item
AR 2703

SM **ALBERT H. FRIEDLAENDER**
Rabbi, 1927–
Newspaper clippings
3 items
AR 3359

PM **DAGOBERT FRIEDLAENDER**
Banker, 1826– ?
Biographical information; copy of appointment to the Prussian House of Lords
2 items
AR 1350

FO PM **DAVID FRIEDLAENDER**
Manufacturer, religious reformer, 1750–1834
Photo of portrait, ex libris; autograph
2 items
AR 3151, AR 1512

SM **FRIEDLAENDER FAMILY, BEUTHEN**
Article about Friedlaender mining firm
1 item
AR 3811

GE **FRIEDLAENDER FAMILY, BRESLAU**
Genealogical material (1925–1940)
51 items
AR 763

FO = Photos · GE = Genealogical Material · PM = Primary Material · SM = Secondary Material

GE PM **FRIEDLAENDER-HAGADORN FAMILY**
Giershagen / Westphalia
Genealogy; correspondence
2 items
AR 5105

PM **FRITZ FRIEDLAENDER**
Letters to Friedlaender from Leo Baeck, Ismar Elbogen, Max Wiener (1935–1972)
9 items
AR 3938

PM SM **FRITZ FRIEDLAENDER**
Historian, 1901–1980
Personal material; memoirs; clippings; manuscripts
2.5 feet
AR 7201

GE **JOACHIM MOSES FRIEDLAENDER FAMILY**
Family tree
1 item
AR 97

FO PM SM **MAX FRIEDLAENDER**
Art historian, museum director, 1867–1958
Photos; university papers; letters of appointment; letter from Wilhelm von Bode; clippings; autographs
33 items
AR 487, AR 2420

PM **MAX J. FRIEDLAENDER**
1867–1958
Autograph
1 item
AR 1754

SM **RAPHAEL FRIEDLAENDER**
Dealer in antique books
Newspaper article (1959)
1 item
AR 784

PM **S. FRIEDLAENDER**
Pseudonym Mynona, 1871–1946
Autographs (1921–1929)
11 items
AR 859

PM **WALTER FRIEDLAENDER**
Professor of social welfare, born 1891
Curriculum vitae
1 item
AR 1345

SM **WALTER FRIEDLAENDER**
Art historian, 1873–1966
Clipping
1 item
AR 3393

PM **FRIEDA FRIEDLANDER**
Concerning orphaned Jewish child in France (1945/46); other items about France, Canada; correspondence
39 items
AR 4994

PM **DAVID FRIEDMAN**
Artist, 1893–
Curriculum vitae
1 item
AR 4545

PM **FRIEDMAN – S.S. *ST. LOUIS***
Concerning family's emigration from Germany via S.S. *St. Louis*
1 item
AR 7223

PM **ABRAHAM FRIEDMANN**
Menu with signatures of guests, including King Ferdinand of Bulgaria
2 items
AR 2270

PM **BASCHA FRIEDMANN**
Program and ticket for Friedmann's recitation of German translation of Yiddish poetry (Berlin, 1922)
1 item
AR 3777

FO PM **THEODOR FRIEDRICHS**
Physician, 1894–
Photos; notes
5 items
AR 4863

PM SM **BERTY FRIESLAENDER-BLOCH**
Clippings; correspondence with Konrad Adenauer, Nikita Kruschev, Pope John XXIII, and others
31 items
AR 7121

FO = Photos · GE = Genealogical Material · PM = Primary Material · SM = Secondary Material

PM **LILI FROEHLICH**
Bound volume of Froehlich's parents' bridal correspondence while she was engaged
1 item
AR 7026

FO **ERICH FROMM**
Photo
1 item
AR 5177

PM **EDUARD FUCHS**
Historian
Autograph (1922)
1 item
AR 839

PM **ERNST FUCHS**
Lawyer, 1859–1929
Biographical sketches; curriculum vitae
2 items
AR 1586

PM SM **EUGEN FUCHS**
Lawyer, 1856–1923, chairman of Central-Verein deutscher Staatsbürger jüdischen Glaubens
Articles by Fuchs; letters to his son; obituaries
17 items
AR 1813

PM **FUCHS FAMILY**
18th cent. advertisements; certificates of marriage; personal documents; Hebrew and German prayers (1749–1874)
22 items
AR 242

SM **FRANZ EUGEN L. FUCHS**
Lawyer, died 1942
Obituary
1 item
AR 1540

FO **HUGO FUCHS**
Rabbi in Chemnitz, 1878–1949
Photo with Hebrew inscription
1 item
AR 790

PM **LEOPOLD FUCHS**
Family birth, marriage, and citizenship certificates, 1826–1859
6 items
AR 3268

PM **HERMANN FUERNBERG**
Correspondence and family papers (1939–1945)
1.5 feet
AR 7194

SM **JULIUS FUERST**
Rabbi
Article (1958)
1 item
AR 1035

PM **JULIUS FUERST**
Author, 1896–1919
Manuscripts; poems including "Jude und Jude," ca. 1914
14 items
AR 3895

PM **MORITZ FUERST**
Physician
M.D. diploma (Jena 1889)
1 item
AR 127

GE PM **MORITZ FUERST FAMILY, HAMBURG**
Family history; family tree; citizens oaths; military papers; membership paper in the Hamburg Jewish community (1848)
15 items
AR 104

SM **HANS FUERSTENBERG**
Book collector
Newspaper article (1960)
1 item
AR 2218

FO PM **FUERTH; JEWISH COMMUNITY**
Community documents; photos (1814–1945)
8 items
AR 994

FO PM **FULDA FAMILY**
Reminiscences of Ferdinand Fulda (1836–1916) and other family members; photos
2 items
AR 5295

FO = Photos · GE = Genealogical Material · PM = Primary Material · SM = Secondary Material

FO SM **FULDA; JEWISH COMMUNITY**
Photo of synagogue; articles
10 items
AR 2450

FO PM **LUDWIG FULDA**
Author, 1862–1939
Autographs (1902, 1927); photos
14 items
AR 530, AR 2250

PM **FUTTER FAMILY**
Letters of appointment for Nathan
Gottschalk, *Hoflieferant* (1887);
professional documents
6 items
AR 1238

PM **SIEGMUND GABRIEL FAMILY**
Family documents, including
certificates of birth, marriage,
citizenship, military, apprenticeship,
and university papers
22 items
AR 4248

PM **GAERTNER FAMILY**
Mainz wine merchants
Will; inventory of property;
advertising circular; correspondence
from the 1930's
29 items
AR 2443

PM **JONAS GAERTNER**
Marriage certificate (Geroda, 1841)
1 item
AR 467

FO PM **GAILINGEN; JEWISH**
SM **COMMUNITY**
Photos of synagogue and deportation
of October 1940; clippings;
typescripts
17 items
AR 2431

PM **ARTHUR GALLINER**
Artist, 1878–1961
Exhibit catalogue
1 item
AR 3717

SM **HELMUT GALLINER**
1910–1969, Librarian, Leo Baeck
Institute
Obituaries
2 items
AR 4711

SM **JULIUS GALLINER**
Rabbi, 1872–1949
Articles by Galliner (1922)
4 items
AR 3070

SM **SIEGFRIED GALLINER**
Rabbi
Obituary, *Aufbau* (1960)
1 item
AR 1036

FO **JOSEPH GALLINGER**
Lawyer
Photo
1 item
AR 1185

SM **MAHATMA GANDHI**
Excerpts from book about Gandhi's
reaction to German pogroms, 1938
1 item
AR 156

PM SM **EDUARD GANS**
Philosopher, 1797–1839
Lectures; writings; doctoral degree;
articles
23 items
AR 24

PM **EDWARD GANS, BERKELEY**
Numismatist
Catalogue of coins from his
collection; marriage contract;
correspondence concerning
foundation of a Jewish publishing
firm, (1936–1937)
3 items
AR 1037

GE PM **GANZ FAMILY**
Genealogies; family trees;
correspondence
13 items
AR 743

FO = Photos · GE = Genealogical Material · PM = Primary Material · SM = Secondary Material

PM SM **FEDOR GANZ**
Writer, painter, 1910–
Correspondence; clippings; personal papers; published works
8 items
AR 7238

PM **THERESE GANZ**
Bonnet for circumcision, Siegburg
1 item
AR 1919

PM **GANZMANN; BAMBERG**
Chalitza (levirate marriage) certificate (1875)
1 item
AR 5083

PM **MOSES GASTER**
Rabbi, historian, 1856–1939
Inventory of Gaster papers in London
1 item
AR 4433

PM **LAZARUS GATZERT**
Copy of defense statement at his treason trial in Darmstadt (1850)
1 item
AR 3859

FO SM **PETER GAY**
Historian born Peter Froehlich, 1923
Photo and article by Gay
2 items
AR 3920

SM **HERMANN P. GEBHARDT**
Newspaper article, "Eichmann Prozess" (Uruguay 1961)
1 item
AR 1814

FO **GEBWEILER/ALSACE; JEWISH COMMUNITY**
Photo of synagogue
1 item
AR 4397

FO GE **ABRAHAM GEIGER**
PM Rabbi, 1810–1874
Photos; family trees; personal letters; autographs
17 items
AR 29, AR 1098

FO SM **ROSY GEIGER-KULLMANN**
Composer, 1886–1964
Obituary; photo
4 items
AR 2349

FO **LAZARUS GEIGER**
Philosopher, 1829–1870
Photo (1852)
1 item
AR 3201

PM SM **LUDWIG GEIGER**
Historian, 1848–1919
Letters by Geiger to Gotthard Deutsch (1900–1915); obituary; autograph
13 items
AR 71, AR 860

PM **RUDOLF GEIGER**
Lawyer, Jewish community leader, 1873–1956
Notes about his biography, including obituary
4 items
AR 2389

FO SM **GELSENKIRCHEN; JEWISH COMMUNITY**
Clippings; photo of synagogue
13 items
AR 2424

FO SM **GEMUENDEN A.D. WOHRA; JEWISH COMMUNITY**
Clipping; photo
2 items
AR 2784

PM **GEMUENDEN, LOWER FRANCONIA; JEWISH COMMUNITY**
Printout of church sermon on history of Jews in Germany since 1695
1 item
AR 4846

PM **GENEALOGICAL SOCIETY OF UTAH**
Material on Genealogical Society of Utah
2 items
AR 4468

FO = Photos · GE = Genealogical Material · PM = Primary Material · SM = Secondary Material

FO PM **MANFRED GEORGE**
Journalist, 1893–1965
Curriculum vitae; photo
2 items
AR 2233

PM SM **STEFAN GEORGE**
Poet, 1868–1933
Clippings and typescripts; letter about Stefan George and his circle
5 items
AR 1038

PM **ARTHUR GERBER**
Author, born 1882
Autograph
1 item
AR 1729

PM **LEOPOLD GERBER**
1854–
Birth and marriage certificates (19th cent.)
4 items
AR 4599

PM **GERMAN-AMERICAN TRI-CENTENNIAL**
Programs for 1983 visit of Karl Carstens, President of Federal Republic of Germany
1 item
AR 5236

PM SM **GERMANIA JUDAICA LIBRARY, COLOGNE**
Clippings, articles, circulars concerning Germania Judaica Library in Cologne Library, Cologne (1959–1980)
33 items
AR 1285

SM **FRIEDRICH GERNSHEIM**
Composer, 1839–1916
Articles
7 items
AR 2190

SM **GERRESHEIM B. DUESSELDORF; JEWISH COMMUNITY**
Article
1 item
AR 4290

GE **ARON GERSON FAMILY**
Family tree
2 items
AR 4631

GE **GERSON-GRUETERS-COHN-DANIELS FAMILY**
Genealogies since 1785 (196 pp.)
1 item
AR 5078

PM **HERMANN GERSON**
Textile entrepreneur
Offprint
1 item
AR 3363

PM **MAX GERSON**
Letters by Mrs. John Foster Dulles and Albert Schweitzer (1959)
3 items
AR 770

FO **E. A. GERSTENBERG**
Educator
Photo
1 item
AR 1039

GE **GERSTLE FAMILY**
Excerpts from statistical records about family members (1794–1930)
6 items
AR 4036

PM **FRIEDRICH HEINRICH WILHELM GESENIUS**
Protestant theologian, Hebraist, 1786–1842
Manuscript of lecture
1 item
AR 4138

SM **SZYJA GEWUERZ-FREUND**
Book collector
Article (Zurich, 1961)
1 item
AR 1606

SM **TIM GIDAL**
Photographer, reporter (born Ignaz Nachum Gidalowitch, 1909, Munich)
Newspaper articles
5 items
AR 4338

FO = Photos · GE = Genealogical Material · PM = Primary Material · SM = Secondary Material

PM **GIESSEN; JEWISH COMMUNITY**
Circulars about Jewish communal affairs (1830, 1836, 1843); text of German songs for Yom Kippur
8 items
AR 2931

GE **GILBERT FAMILY**
Notes on family tree, originally Ginsberg
1 item
AR 1028

FO **FELIX GILBERT**
Historian, 1905–
Photo of Moses Mendelssohn miniature with covering letter
2 items
AR 4518

FO PM **JULIUS GIMNICHER FAMILY**
Family papers, including citizen's oath; photos of Hamburg temple; Shanghai material
9 items
AR 1242

FO PM **HERBERT GINSBERG**
Binder (138 p.) including photos and manuscript on the story of the "Herbert Ginsberg Collection"
1 item
AR 5274

FO PM **GISSIGHEIM; JEWISH COMMUNITY**
Report; photos of synagogue
5 items
AR 3024

PM **ARTUR GLAESER**
Author, 1895–1951
Curriculum vitae
1 item
AR 3368

SM **RUDOLF GLANZ**
Writer
Book review of his *Geschichte des niederen jüdischen Volkes in Deutschland*
1 item
AR 3636

SM **SELMA GLANZ**
Article by Adolf Gaspary (1936)
1 item
AR 1325

PM SM **CURT GLASER**
Art historian, 1879–1943
Correspondence with Max J. Friedlaender, Heinrich Woelfflin, Wilhelm von Bode; manuscripts obituaries
18 items
AR 1240

PM **MYRO GLASS**
Cantor in Indianapolis
Exchange of letters concerning persecution of Jewish musicians (1933)
1 item
AR 4354

FO **SALOMON GLASS**
Protestant theologian, 1593–1656
Photo of woodcut
1 item
AR 3483

PM SM **NAHUM N. GLATZER**
Historian, 1903–
Clippings; manuscript for Leo Baeck Memorial Lecture No.10 (1966)
14 items
AR 148

PM SM **GLEIWITZ (NOW GLIWICE, POLAND); JEWISH COMMUNITY**
Excerpts from books, typescripts, circulars, 1751–1967; deportation list
12 items
AR 151, AR 5089

PM **DAVID GLICK**
Died 1964
Letters from Gestapo, U.S. consulate, and certificate for David Glick; article about Glick's mission to Berlin (1937, 1938)
5 items
AR 1239

PM **GLOGAU FAMILY, BERLIN, HAMBURG**
Family letters (1910–1923)
4 items
AR 3860

PM **HENRIK M. GLOGAU**
Friendship album (1843–1850)
2 items
AR 4256

FO = Photos · GE = Genealogical Material · PM = Primary Material · SM = Secondary Material

FO **GLOGAU; JEWISH COMMUNITY**
Photos of synagogue
3 items
AR 4247

PM **GNESEN (NOW GNIEZNO, POLAND); JEWISH COMMUNITY**
Programs; circular
4 items
AR 995

FO SM **LEOPOLD GODOWSKY**
Pianist, 1870–1938
Article about Godowsky; photo
3 items
AR 2415

SM **GOEPPINGEN; JEWISH COMMUNITY**
Newspaper article about old synagogue (1979)
1 item
AR 4894

PM **SIGMUND GOERITZ**
History of Goeritz knitting firm
1 item
AR 199

FO PM SM **GOERLITZ; JEWISH COMMUNITY**
Photo of synagogue; clippings; typescript
9 items
AR 4588

PM **GOETHE GYMNASIUM**
Retrospect on occasion of 50th anniversary (Easter 1982) of graduating class of 1932, reunion and photographs
1 item
AR 5094

PM **JOHANN WOLFGANG VON GOETHE**
Writer, poet, statesman, 1749–1832
Autographs; documents by Goethe concerning legal cases involving Jews (1782–1785)
3 items
AR 1490, AR 152

PM **OTTILIE VON GOETHE**
1796–1872
Autographs (1859–1866)
3 items
AR 1987

PM **GOETTINGEN; JEWISH COMMUNITY**
Questionnaire (1958)
1 item
AR 817

PM **ISRAEL GOLDBAUM**
Hebrew poem by Goldbaum (1843)
1 item
AR 7103

PM **GOLDBERG FAMILY**
Report about the family and its activities in the theater
1 item
AR 81

PM **JULIUS GOLDBERG**
Songsheet for Zionist seminar (Lehnitz, 1935), compiled by Goldberg
1 item
AR 897

FO SM **FELIX GOLDMANN**
Rabbi, 1882–1934
Photos; obituaries
5 items
AR 2677

SM **GEORG GOLDMANN**
Eulogy (1936)
1 item
AR 1353

PM **JAKOB GOLDMANN**
Honorary degree of "Morenu" for Jakob Goldmann, Hindenburg (now Zabrze, Poland), 1923
1 item
AR 2932

SM **NACHUM GOLDMANN**
Articles
3 items
AR 1615

PM SM **PHILIPP GOLDMANN**
Rabbi of Eschwege, 1808–1894
Biographical data; trial sermon (1829); manuscript; printed sermon on his 50th anniversary
3 items
AR 7122

PM **CARL GOLDMARK**
1830–1915
Autographs
3 items
AR 1668

FO **JOSEF GOLDMARK**
Physician, politican, 1818–1881
Photo
1 item
AR 2768

FO PM **MARTIN G. GOLDNER**
Physician, died 1987
Photo; report by Goldner
2 items
AR 3136

SM **GERHARD GOLDSCHLAG**
Composer
Musical works
1 item
AR 3096

SM **ADOLF GOLDSCHMIDT**
Art historian
Articles
2 items
AR 2303

FO **ALFRED GOLDSCHMIDT**
Physician, 1865–1934
Photo
1 item
AR 1697

GE **AMSEL ISAAK GOLDSCHMIDT**
Genealogical information and covering letter
2 items
AR 4355

SM **E. P. GOLDSCHMIDT**
Book collector
Articles
2 items
AR 898

FO PM **ERNST DANIEL GOLDSCHMIDT**
Theologian, librarian, 1895–1972
Photos; clippings; correspondence with Max Gruenewald
65 items
AR 3919

PM **GOLDSCHMIDT FAMILY, FUERTH**
Original government documents including citizenship paper; business licenses; marriage papers (1817–1871)
6 items
AR 3704

GE **GOLDSCHMIDT FAMILY, VIENNA**
Family tree and explanations
2 items
AR 1775

GE PM **GOLDSCHMIDT FAMILY, WITZENHAUSEN**
Family tree; documents dealing with family including title of court bankers to the Duke of Sachsen-Coburg and Gotha
3 items
AR 164

PM **HEINRICH GOLDSCHMIDT FAMILY, VIENNA**
Identification papers; school papers of Heinrich and Melitta Goldschmidt; passenger list (1939); interview and program concerning rescued Torah scroll (1939)
19 items
AR 4519

FO PM **HENRIETTE GOLDSCHMIDT**
SM Social worker, 1825–1920
Articles about Goldschmidt; photos; clippings; postcard about her obituary; autographs
11 items
AR 501, AR 2905

SM **HERMANN LEWIN GOLDSCHMIDT**
Article about Jewish relationship to Germany (1959)
1 item
AR 1040

PM **JAKOB GOLDSCHMIDT**
Banker, 1881–1955
Documents on Dresdner Bank and Darmstaedter & National Bank. Legal brief against Dresdner Bank by executor of Goldschmidt estate
3 items
AR 4361

FO = Photos · GE = Genealogical Material · PM = Primary Material · SM = Secondary Material

FO PM **LAZARUS GOLDSCHMIDT**
Orientalist, talmudist, 1871–1950
Photo; autographs
15 items
AR 3202, AR 4001

PM **LEON GOLDSCHMIDT**
Humorous poem for his 50th birthday (1912)
1 item
AR 3812

SM **LEVIN GOLDSCHMIDT**
Politician, 1829–1879
Sections of his book *Zur Reichstagswahl* (1887)
1 item
AR 2825

PM **LISEL GOLDSCHMIDT**
Wall hanging for Passover
1 item
AR 7141

GE PM **MARTIN E. GOLDSCHMIDT**
Gold scale; Goethe medallion; genealogy; synagogue order, Hamburg (1858/1859)
8 items
AR 2260

GE **GOLDSCHMIDT-OLDENBURG FAMILY, ALTONA**
Family tree
1 item
AR 318

GE PM **SALOMON BENEDIKT GOLDSCHMIDT FAMILY**
Business papers; documents; accounting records; genealogical material; personal papers; diary (1832–1969)
26 items
AR 100

FO **THEODOR V. GOLDSCHMIDT**
Photos
2 items
AR 2769

SM **VICTOR GOLDSCHMIDT**
Article, "Die Familie Cassirer" (1926)
1 item
AR 30

GE **WOLF GOLDSCHMIDT**
Wolf Wilhelm Goldschmidt, Ehrenbreitstein family tree
1 item
AR 1383

FO **HENRY GOLDSCHMIEDT**
Photo of Dr. Goldschmiedt's family
1 item
AR 4812

PM **M. W. GOLDSMITH**
Judeo-German letter with translation (1799)
1 item
AR 5204

GE **ALFRED H. GOLDSTEIN**
born 1916 in Guesten near Juelich
Family tree since 1717
1 item
AR 4798

PM **FRITZ GOLDSTEIN (later Frederick Mitchell)**
Pharmacist, 1874–1959
Papers depicting education as pharmacist in Germany
35 items
AR 2839

SM **ISAAK GOLDSTEIN**
Clipping, Gerhard Ziegler: "Mit einem Trauerrand" (1962)
1 item
AR 2304

PM SM **KURT GOLDSTEIN**
Physician, 1879–1965
Bibliography (1903–1958); letter
2 items
AR 481

FO SM **MORITZ GOLDSTEIN**
Editor, critic, 1880–1977
Photos; clippings; obituary
7 items
AR 2277

PM SM **IGNAZ GOLDZIHER**
Historian, 1850–1921
Articles; autographs
4 items
AR 1859, AR 150

FO = Photos · GE = Genealogical Material · PM = Primary Material · SM = Secondary Material

SM **CLAIRE GOLL**
Writer, 1891–1977
Obituaries
2 items
AR 4506

PM **IVAN GOLL**
Writer, 1891–1950
Autograph
1 item
AR 1861

SM **VICTOR GOLLANCZ**
Publisher
Newspaper clipping (1960)
1 item
AR 1590

PM **JULIUS GOMPERTZ**
Poem by Gompertz
1 item
AR 2013

FO SM **THEODOR GOMPERZ**
Philosopher, 1832–1912
Photo of Gomperz, his grave; clipping
4 items
AR 2084

FO **HEINRICH GOMPERZ**
Philosopher, son of Theodor Gomperz, 1873–1942
Photo
1 item
AR 2704

PM SM **EMERY I. GONDOR**
Psychiatrist, 20th cent.
Copy of Gondor's drawings of Ernst Toller and Klabund; reprints of his articles on child psychology
4 items
AR 4016

PM SM **HAROLD H. GORDON**
Rabbi
Curriculum vitae; obituary (1977)
2 items
AR 4438

PM **MAX GORDON FAMILY**
Military papers of Jacob Israel Gordon; copies of birth records and plebiscite voting pass from Upper Silesia (1921)
6 items
AR 2062

PM **GOSLAR FAMILY**
Personal papers; correspondence; business papers; concessions, certificates (1779–1974)
21 items
AR 4094

SM **GOSLAR; JEWISH COMMUNITY**
Articles
2 items
AR 4544

PM **CONRAD L. GOSSELS FAMILY**
Naturalization certificate (1862); name change certificate from Schulenklopper to Gossels; other personal documents
13 items
AR 4906

FO **GOSSMANNSDORF/MAIN; JEWISH COMMUNITY**
Photo of synagogue
1 item
AR 2155

SM **EBERHARD GOTHEIN**
Economist, 1853–1923
Gothein's lecture "Soziologie der Panik"
1 item
AR 899

PM **GOTTHEINER FAMILY**
Marriage papers; birth certificate; letter of municipal citizenship
4 items
AR 1041

GE PM **GOTTHELFT FAMILY**
Owners of *Kasseler Tageblatt*
Family trees and history; clippings about family business and family members (1953–1969)
9 items
AR 35

SM **ERNEST GOTTLIEB**
Publisher, 1903–1961
Newspaper obituary (1961)
1 item
AR 1607

FO = Photos · GE = Genealogical Material · PM = Primary Material · SM = Secondary Material

PM **GOTTSCHALK FAMILY**
Letter from Baron von Cohn and his daughter Julie Oppenheim to family members (1895)
2 items
AR 901

PM **GOTTSCHALK FAMILY, MAINZ**
Letter from Saxon government answering petition concerning freedom of commerce for Gustav Gottschalk (1843), marriage record, commission as first lieutenant (1843–1889)
3 items
AR 1291

GE PM **SIEGMUND GOTTSCHALK**
Family tree; baptismal certificate; letter of protection; certificates of citizenship and school; marriage papers; genealogical notes (1808–1919)
15 items
AR 4469

PM **SCHMUEL MOSES GOTTSTADT**
Citizenship document (Rastenberg, 1820)
1 item
AR 5005

SM **ROLF GRABOWER**
Financial official in Bavaria, 1883–1963
List of publications and catalogue exhibit in his memory
2 items
AR 4704

FO **ADOLF GRABOWSKY**
Author, 1880–
Photo
1 item
AR 2705

GE **GRADENWITZ FAMILY**
Family tree
2 items
AR 2396

GE PM **GRAEFENBERG FAMILY**
Military papers; family trees (1870–1933)
4 items
AR 231

FO PM **HEINRICH GRAETZ**
Historian, 1817–1891
Photos; clippings; correspondence; autographs
63 items
AR 154, AR 862

PM **LEO GRAETZ**
Poem
1 item
AR 466

FO PM **PAUL GRAETZ**
Actor, 1890–1938
Photos; poems; obituaries; autographs
22 items
AR 2706, AR 858

GE **GEORGE GRAETZER**
1907–
Letter with genealogical dates since 1843
1 item
AR 4481

PM SM **HEINRICH GRAF**
Correspondence concerning antisemitism; articles (1946–1960)
4 items
AR 4866

SM **OSKAR MARIA GRAF**
Author, 1894–1967
Catalogue of exhibit at University of Hampshire Library (1974)
1 item
AR 4296

PM **FELIX GRAFE**
Executed by Nazi government
Farewell letters to family; bill for execution costs
3 items
AR 1421

PM **ALEXANDER GRANACH**
Actor, 1890–1945
Poster of exhibit at Akademie der Künste (Berlin, 1971)
2 items
AR 3830

SM **LOUIS A. GRATZ**
Major in Union Army during American Civil War
Article about Gratz
1 item
AR 1908

FO = Photos · GE = Genealogical Material · PM = Primary Material · SM = Secondary Material

PM **MICHAEL GRATZ**
1740–1811
Letterbook (1769–1772)
1 item
AR 1042

PM **NICOLAI GRAUDAN**
Autograph (1935)
1 item
AR 3020

PM **GRAUSSMANN FAMILY**
1878–1939
Birth certificates; report cards; passports
12 items
AR 4979

PM **LEO GREINER**
Writer
Autograph (1906)
1 item
AR 2948

FO GE **SIMON GRELLING**
PM 1853–1928
Family tree; photos of family portraits; memorandum about family history
4 items
AR 205

PM **SAMUEL GRIESBACH**
1849–
Military service document (1870–1875)
1 item
AR 3795

FO PM **GRIESHEIM B. DARMSTADT; JEWISH COMMUNITY**
Photos; list of Jews
7 items
AR 7012, AR 1295

FO PM **MAX GRIESHEIM**
Photos of Griesheim and World War I memorial with his name, clippings concerning material
5 items
AR 1573

SM **BROTHERS GRIMM**
Newspaper article, "Bookdealers' letters about Grimm Brothers" (1957)
1 item
AR 96

PM **ADOLF GRIMME**
1889–1963, Prussian Minister of Education and Religious Affairs
Letters to Sigmund Freud, Edmund Husserl, Else Lasker-Schueler, Max Liebermann, Max Scheler (1917–34); original letter to Wilhelm Gaede (1947)
39 items
AR 3723

GE **EPHRAIM GROEDEL-LOEB CASSEL (CASSELLA) FAMILY**
Family tree
1 item
AR 3925

PM SM **ROBERT GROETSCH**
Journalist, 1878–1946, editor of *Dresdner Volkszeitung*
Articles and manuscripts in his memory
3 items
AR 4209

PM **LAZARUS GROS**
Military papers (1847–1871)
2 items
AR 3839

PM **GROSS-BREESEN (SCHOOL FOR EMIGRATION)**
Correspondence (1938–1956)
20 items
AR 3686

SM **FELIX GROSS**
Writer
Obituary (*Aufbau*, 1960)
1 item
AR 1336

PM **GROSS-GERAU; JEWISH COMMUNITY**
Brochure
1 item
AR 4501

PM SM **F. S. GROSSHUT**
Manuscript; clippings (1927–1959)
22 items
AR 1559

FO = Photos · GE = Genealogical Material · PM = Primary Material · SM = Secondary Material

PM SM **KURT R. GROSSMAN**
Author, 1897–1972
Speech by Grossman about
antisemitism; clippings; obituaries
8 items
AR 1591

PM **SAMUEL GROSSMAN**
Certificate of honorary citizenship,
Muensterberg (1873)
1 item
AR 153

PM **STEFAN GROSSMANN**
Autograph (1928)
1 item
AR 1427

SM **MARTIN GROTJAHN**
Physician
Articles on Freud
4 items
AR 3346

FO SM **FRED GRUBEL**
Lawyer, secretary of Leo Baeck
Institute, born 1908
Articles; photos
2 items
AR 3695

PM **HEINRICH GRUEBER**
Lecture at Leo Baeck Institute (1964)
3 items
AR 4753

PM **WALTER GRUENBAUM FAMILY**
History of family business;
application for restitution
2 items
AR 4683

PM SM **A. GRUENBERG**
Review by Max Brod; court decision
2 items
AR 1248

SM **ARTHUR GRUENEBAUM**
Newspaper clipping, "Establish
Arturo Gruenebaum Mining Metall.
Chair." (January, 1958)
1 item
AR 237

GE **GRUENEWALD FAMILY**
Family tree
2 items
AR 7117

PM SM **MAX GRUENEWALD**
Rabbi, president of Leo Baeck
Institute, 1899–
Letters of protection; petitions;
business and personal papers;
clippings
23 items
AR 155

FO **SIMON GRUENEWALD**
Teacher, Jewish Community of
Siegen
Photo
1 item
AR 5246

FO **ALFRED GRUENFELD**
Pianist, 1852–1924
Photos
6 items
AR 2763

FO PM **HEINRICH GRUENFELD**
Cellist, 1855–1931
Programs of his concerts; clippings;
photos; autographs
30 items
AR 2086, AR 1288

PM **GRUENSFELD; JEWISH
COMMUNITY**
Report
1 item
AR 3025

PM **LOLA GRUENTHAL**
Correspondence with Bertolt Brecht,
Sigmund Freud, Hugo von
Hofmannsthal, Arthur Schnitzler;
copies of autographs by Felix
Mendelsohn-Bartholdy and Giacomo
Meyerbeer
11 items
AR 4600

SM **DAVID GRUENWALD**
Article
1 item
AR 465

FO PM **GEBRUEDER GRUMACH A. G.**
Letters about the company; photo
3 items
AR 1565

FO = Photos · GE = Genealogical Material · PM = Primary Material · SM = Secondary Material.

FO **KURT H. GRUNEBAUM**
President N.Y. Hanseatic Corp.
Photo
1 item
AR 4067

PM **ERNEST G. GRUNSFELD**
Diaries (1908–1927); correspondence;
notebooks; correspondence with
Julius Rosenwald
5 items
AR 7146

GE PM **GRUNSFELD FAMILY**
Family trees; articles about family
members; poems
4 items
AR 956

PM **CLARA GRUNWALD**
Autographs (1941–1944)
5 items
AR 7014

FO **MAX GRUNWALD**
Rabbi, 1871–1953
Photo
1 item
AR 2774

PM **HERSCHL GRYNSZPAN**
Letters concerning history of
Sachsenhausen concentration camp
(1942)
2 items
AR 3645

SM **GSELLIUS FAMILY**
Antique book dealers
Article (1959)
1 item
AR 1043

PM SM **JULIUS GUCKENHEIMER**
Articles about St. Cyprien
concentration camp; photo of
prisoners; handwritten Yom Kippur
prayers from the camp;
correspondence about the camp
(1963); poem
6 items
AR 2278

PM **ROSALIE GUDEMANN**
Prussian decree denying her residency
rights; summons in case involving
illegal lottery (1850–1851)
2 items
AR 4253

PM SM **ERIKA GUETERMANN**
Poet, translator
Clippings; correspondence; typescript
of Else Lasker-Schueler translations
17 items
AR 1893

SM **HEINRICH GUETERMANN**
Publisher
Obituary (1963)
1 item
AR 2305

SM **GUETERSLOH; JEWISH COMMUNITY**
Newspaper article (1978)
1 item
AR 4694

SM **EDWIN GUGGENHEIM**
Lawyer
Review of Festschrift (1965)
1 item
AR 4331

PM **JULIUS AND PAULINE GUGGENHEIM**
Curricula vitae, letters, reminiscences
by Julius on his arrest by Nazis; letter
from Jewish community in
Goeppingen (1937–1940)
17 items
AR 4561

PM SM **KARL GUGGENHEIM**
Reprints; typescripts; articles; book
*Refugiados Immigrados Nuevos
Chilenos*, including letter to president
of Jewish communities of Chile
12 items
AR 179

PM **LEOPOLD GUGGENHEIM**
Mayor of Gailingen
Letter certifying that Guggenheim
was mayor of Gailingen (1870–1884)
2 items
AR 1940

FO = Photos · GE = Genealogical Material · PM = Primary Material · SM = Secondary Material

FO SM **EMIL J. GUMBEL**
Mathematician, journalist, 1891–1966
Articles on statistics; photo
20 items
AR 1502

FO **SIEGFRIED GUMBEL**
President of Jewish Community of
Wuerttemberg from 1935
Photo
1 item
AR 2548

SM **GUMBINNEN; JEWISH
COMMUNITY**
Clipping
1 item
AR 5495

GE **GUMPERTZ FAMILY**
Family tree of Gumpertz-May-
Frankfurter families
1 item
AR 160

GE **GUNDERMANN FAMILY**
Family tree, 18th–20th cent.
1 item
AR 359

SM **GUNDERSHEIM; JEWISH
COMMUNITY**
Clipping
1 item
AR 2599

PM SM **FRIEDRICH GUNDOLF**
Writer, literary historian, 1880–1931
Clippings; autographs
3 items
AR 1862, AR 803

PM SM **LUBA GURDUS**
Author born 1914 in Bialystok,
Poland
Curriculum vitae; reviews;
correspondence
5 items
AR 4754

FO PM **GURS (CONCENTRATION CAMP)**
Clippings; photos; letters; reports
concerning Gurs
52 items
AR 2273

PM **MARCUS GUSDORFF**
Marriage contract (1838)
1 item
AR 4755

FO GE **GUTENBERG FAMILY**
PM SM Birth, death, and marriage certificates
(1854–1926); family letter, deed for
real estate; clipping; photo
20 items
AR 782

PM **FERDINAND GUTHEIM**
Gymnasium teacher, 1865–1934
Letters from Hans F. K. Guenther
about his racial theories (1920–1933)
4 items
AR 3140

GE **GUTHMANN FAMILY, GROSS-
GERAU**
Family tree, 18th–20th cent.
1 item
AR 4622

PM **ERICH GUTKIND**
Letter to Martin Buber (1915)
1 item
AR 3651

FO **DAVID VON GUTMANN**
1834–1912
Photos
3 items
AR 2770

FO GE **GUTMANN FAMILY, HAMBURG**
18th–20th cent.
Family tree; photos of family
members
11 items
AR 561

GE **GUTMANN FAMILY,
PHILLIPSBURG**
Family tree, 18th–20th cent.
6 items
AR 4199

PM **HERMANN GUTMANN**
Leaflet from Kapp Putsch; letter from
Stuttgart City Council (1919, 1920)
2 items
AR 1044

FO = Photos · GE = Genealogical Material · PM = Primary Material · SM = Secondary Material

SM **JOSEPH GUTMANN**
Art historian
Articles
2 items
AR 2240, AR 5114

FO PM **META GUTMANN**
SM Clippings; family letters; material on fate of family members during World War II; family photos
24 items
AR 1627

GE **MOSES GUTMANN**
Family tree
4 items
AR 1402

PM **NATHAN GUTMANN**
1807–1889
Wanderbuch (1825–1832)
1 item
AR 113

PM **RUDOLPH GUTMANN**
Announcement of founding of Gebrueder Gutman Textiles, Berlin, 1868
1 item
AR 2589

PM **GUTTMANN FAMILY, KATTOWITZ**
Documents dealing with the Guttmann family during the Nazi period
5 items
AR 1046

PM **GUTTMANN FAMILY, VIENNA**
Family documents
5 items
AR 1047

FO **JACOB GUTTMANN**
Rabbi
Photo
1 item
AR 3203

FO SM **JULIUS GUTTMANN**
Philosopher, 1880–1950
Newspaper articles; photo
6 items
AR 1045

PM SM **LUDWIG GUTTMANN**
Physician, 1899–
Curriculum vitae; clippings
3 items
AR 4307

PM **ALEX HAAS**
Letters on survival of Jews living underground in Holland during World War II
2 items
AR 2558

PM SM **ELISE HAAS**
Poet
Poems; correspondence; clippings (1937–1965)
25 items
AR 2669

GE **HAAS FAMILY, BADEN**
Family tree, 18th–20th cent.
1 item
AR 4601

GE **HAAS FAMILY, FUCHSSTADT**
Genealogy of Haas and related families (1800–1900)
10 items
AR 7224

SM **LUDWIG HAAS**
Politician, 1875–1930
Obituaries
3 items
AR 1091

SM **OTTO HAAS**
Book dealer, 1874–1955
Obituaries
6 items
AR 440

PM **RUBEN HAAS**
Marriage contract (1828)
1 item
AR 3524

PM SM **WILLY HAAS**
Writer, 1891–
Newspaper clippings by and about Haas; autographs
16 items
AR 1403, AR 1833

FO = Photos · GE = Genealogical Material · PM = Primary Material · SM = Secondary Material

PM **F. HAASE LEATHER FACTORY**
History of the leather factory
(1766–1916)
1 item
AR 3903

PM **FRIEDRICH HAASE**
1826–1911
Autograph
1 item
AR 2173

FO PM **HUGO HAASE**
Socialist, 1863–1919
Photos and photocopies; letters to
Haase
6 items
AR 2707

PM **JOSEPH HAASE**
Certificate of the award of the Iron
Cross 2nd class (1873)
1 item
AR 4231

PM **TERRY HAASS**
Graphic artist, 1923–
Exhibition catalogue; circulars; letters
8 items
AR 4376

PM SM **HANS HABE**
Writer, 1911–1977
Obituary; autograph
2 items
AR 4482, AR 1870

GE **HABER FAMILY**
Family tree, 18th–19th cent.
2 items
AR 1776

PM **GUSTAV HABER**
Verdict of commission of inquiry of
dental association of Frankfurt a.d.
Oder in regard to charges brought
against Haber (1920)
1 item
AR 4405

PM **HABIMA**
Program of performance of Habima
troupe (Berlin, 1930)
1 item
AR 1048

FO **MAX HACHENBURG**
Lawyer, 1860–1951
Photo
1 item
AR 3571

GE **HACHENBURGER FAMILY**
Family tree (18th–20th cent.)
3 items
AR 715

SM **ERNST MAX HACKE**
Antiquarian
Article (1963)
1 item
AR 2317

PM **FRIEDRICH HACKER**
Poem on Holocaust
1 item
AR 2392

PM **EDMUND HADRA**
Document awarding Hadra the
Knight's Cross (1918)
2 items
AR 1249

PM **HAENDLER FAMILY**
Vital registration documents
concerning family history
11 items
AR 3435

SM **RUDOLPH HAGELSTANGE**
Article about metamorphosis of
antisemitism
1 item
AR 183

PM SM **ERICH G. HAGEN**
Clippings; sketches
6 items
AR 2401

SM **ARNOLD HAHN**
Author, 1882–1963
Obituary
1 item
AR 2115

GE **ERICH HAHN FAMILY**
Family tree (19th–20th cent.)
1 item
AR 3123

FO = Photos · GE = Genealogical Material · PM = Primary Material · SM = Secondary Material

SM **FRED HAHN**
Historian, 20th cent.
Reviews of Hahn's book *Lieber Stürmer*
15 items
AR 4573

FO SM **HUGO HAHN**
Rabbi, 1893–1967
Photo; obituaries
6 items
AR 2184, AR 4831

SM **KURT HAHN**
Educator
Articles; newspaper clippings
7 items
AR 1561

GE PM **MARCUS HAHN FAMILY**
Family tree since 1781; baptismal certificate (1933)
3 items
AR 4829

FO **HAIGERLOCH; JEWISH COMMUNITY**
Photos of synagogue, explanatory note
5 items
AR 3280

FO SM **OTTO HAINEBACH**
Photo; obituaries
2 items
AR 1574

PM **ALEXANDER HAINDORF**
Letter
1 item
AR 1049

FO PM **HAINSTADT; JEWISH COMMUNITY**
Reports; photos
13 items
AR 3026

GE PM **FRED HALBERS (BORN FRITZ**
SM **HALBERSTAEDTER)**
Actor, artist, born 1894, Berlin
Family trees; newspaper clippings; photocopies of paintings; correspondence

109 items
AR 2867

FO PM **HALBERSTADT; JEWISH**
SM **COMMUNITY**
Photo of synagogue; programs; excerpt of *Memorbuch*; article; summary of community history; articles
8 items
AR 2289

FO **HEINRICH HALBERSTAM**
Photos
2 items
AR 2661

PM **JACQUES FROMENTAL HALEVY**
1799–1868
Autograph
1 item
AR 846

FO GE **EDWIN HALLE**
PM SM 1895–
Photos; album and text concerning Jewish sport association in 1934; genealogy; personal papers; clippings
57 items
AR 1250

PM **HALLE; JEWISH COMMUNITY**
Exhibition catalogue on Jewish Community in Halle (1982)
1 item
AR 5213

GE **VON HALLE FAMILY**
Family tree (17th–20th cent.)
16 items
AR 2372

PM **HALLENSTEIN FAMILY**
Family documents (1796–1914)
6 items
AR 4574

PM **CHARLES HALLGARTEN**
Philantropist, 1838–1908
Letter from Lujo Brentano (1908); letter from Alfred Vagts (1981)
2 items
AR 5013

FO **S. HALLO AND SON**
Photos
9 items
AR 401

FO = Photos · GE = Genealogical Material · PM = Primary Material · SM = Secondary Material

PM **EPHRAIM HAMBURG**
Actor, 1824–1913
Brief biography
1 item
AR 4146

PM **HAMBURG (HOUSEKEEPING SCHOOL FOR GIRLS)**
Plans; letters
7 items
AR 4717

FO PM **HAMBURG; JEWISH COMMUNITY**
Clippings; circulars; decrees; photos; 19th cent. marriage contracts
74 items
AR 193

PM **BIANCA HAMBURGER**
Social worker
Certificates
Verdienstkreuz (1917–1939)
3 items
AR 4978

PM **HAMBURGER FAMILY, HANAU**
Family history and related documents
3 items
AR 2532

PM **GUSTAV HAMBURGER**
Program for wedding of Gustav Hamburger and Emilie Milch (1843)
2 items
AR 1532

GE PM **SIEGFRIED HAMBURGER**
Torah mantle and family tree of Hamburger families (17th–20th cent.)
2 items
AR 1252

GE **JENTE HAMELN**
Family tree
2 items
AR 2063

PM **HAMELN; JEWISH COMMUNITY**
Jewish cult objects (exhibition, 1981); extract by Thomas High from the Jewish community records
2 items
AR 5058

SM **HAMM; JEWISH COMMUNITY**
Clipping
1 item
AR 996

GE **HANAU FAMILY**
Family tree (1700–1900)
3 items
AR 3324

PM **HANAU; JEWISH COMMUNITY**
Microfilm "Juden in Hanau, Bergen and Bornheimer Berg;" photostat of handwritten copies of decrees concerning Jews (1556–1609)
8 items
AR 2363

FO **OSCAR HANDLIN**
Historian, 1915–
Photo
1 item
AR 2708

FO GE **HANOVER; JEWISH COMMUNITY**
PM SM Photos of synagogues and cemeteries; articles on Jewish community and institutions; genealogies; correspondence
40 items
AR 1685

PM **HANOVER, KINGDOM; JEWISH COMMUNITY**
German and Hebrew letters on synagogue, 1828–1864; rules; complaints of small Jewish communities
7 items
AR 5131

PM **IRENE HARAND**
Material on Harand Bewegung, Viennese Jewish pacifist group, including stamps of famous Jews
6 items
AR 3325

FO PM **HARBURG; JEWISH COMMUNITY**
Photos of synagogue and of town; letter about the synagogue
4 items
AR 3500

PM SM **MAXIMILIAN HARDEN (BORN FELIX WITKOWSKI)**
Journalist, 1861–1927
Clippings; autographs
7 items
AR 2191, AR 335

FO = Photos · GE = Genealogical Material · PM = Primary Material · SM = Secondary Material

FO PM **HARDHEIM; JEWISH**
SM **COMMUNITY**
Typescripts; photos of ritual bath, cemetery, synagogue, and views of town; articles
39 items
AR 2551

PM **ERNST HARDT**
1876–1947
Autographs
3 items
AR 840

PM **LUDWIG HARDT**
1886–
Autograph
1 item
AR 1634

SM **VEIT HARLAN**
Newspaper clipping, "Veit Harlan's Rolle im Dritten Reich" (1962)
1 item
AR 1592

SM **WILHELM HARMELIN**
Lawyer, 1900–1967
Eulogy
1 item
AR 4051

FO GE **WALTER HAROLD FAMILY**
PM Photo album; papers of Isaac family; genealogies
70 items
AR 4156

PM **HARRIS-BRANDES FAMILY**
Family letters (1892–1903)
9 items
AR 781

PM **FRANK A. HARRIS**
Circulars containing information on former residents of Nuremberg and Fuerth, including Henry Kissinger (1977–1979)
3 items
AR 7080

PM **EARL G. HARRISON**
Commissioner of immigration and naturalization
Lecture; report (1943)
2 items
AR 184

GE **HARTIG FAMILY**
Family history (1726–1963)
1 item
AR 3326

FO **LUDO M. HARTMANN**
Historian, politician, 1865–1924
Portrait
2 items
AR 3585

FO **MORITZ HARTMANN**
Writer, 1821–1872
Portrait
1 item
AR 2709

FO PM **WALTER HASENCLEVER**
SM Writer, 1890–1940
Portraits; clipping; autographs
4 items
AR 223, AR 1506

PM **KIBBUTZ HASOREA**
Chronology; report on emigration from Germany (1939)
3 items
AR 7101

PM **SIMON HATSCHEK**
Artisan's passbook (*Wanderbuch*), 1816–1826
2 items
AR 4189

SM **HAUDE & SPENER**
Publishers
Newspaper article, "350 years Haude & Spener" (written 1964)
1 item
AR 2255

FO PM **MARTIN HAUSER**
Zionist, 1913–
Diaries; photos
23 items
AR 4465

FO **HAUSMANN-STIFTUNG**
Photo of building which housed Hausmann-Stiftung
16 items
AR 4520

FO = Photos · GE = Genealogical Material · PM = Primary Material · SM = Secondary Material

PM **HERMANN HAYMANN**
Physician, 1879–1955
Short autobiographical sketch by
Haymann, accounts to his children of
life in Nazi-occupied Europe in 1940's
4 items
AR 3216

FO **SIMON HAYUM**
Attorney, president of Jewish
Assembly for Wurttemberg and
Lemberg until 1939, 1867–1948
Photo
1 item
AR 3327

PM **FRIEDRICH HEBBEL**
1813–1863
Autograph (1862)
1 item
AR 2011

PM **HEBRAICA**
Parchment document on laws of
conversion to Judaism, Hebrew (9th
or 10th cent.); *ketubah* (Fuerth, 1883);
businessman's account book
(1840–1844); other papers
4 items
AR 7142

PM **HEBREW PUBLISHING COMPANY**
Jewish New Year greeting cards
41 items
AR 7099

PM **JOSEPH HEBRONI**
Sculptor, 1888–1963
Exhibition catalogue
1 item
AR 4756

FO PM **HECHINGEN; JEWISH COMMUNITY**
SM
Photos of synagogue before and after
destruction; minutes; clippings
10 items
AR 2376

PM **EMMA HECHT**
1874–1977
Letters to Emma Hecht from her
sisters Marie Odenheimer and Klara
Eberstadt on their experiences in Gurs
concentration camp and in Germany
after World War II
61 items
AR 4470

PM **PAUL HECHT**
Cantor, 20th cent.
Correspondence with Yad Vashem on
memoirs and activities as director of
Kultusabteilung in Berlin
10 items
AR 3475

FO PM **RENA HECHT**
SM Photos; letters; clippings on Jewish
community in Michelstadt
9 items
AR 1050

SM **JAKOB HEGNER**
Publisher, 1882–1962
Obituaries
3 items
AR 1798

PM **HEIDELBERG; JEWISH COMMUNITY**
Documents; reports from 1737;
orders to Jewish community
8 items
AR 4896

PM SM **MARTHA HEIDEN**
Violinist, 1878–1963
Festschrift for Heiden (1938); notes
about her
2 items
AR 3520

PM SM **GERTRUD HEIDENFELD**
Letters; clippings
3 items
AR 1051

FO **HEIDENHEIM; JEWISH COMMUNITY**
Negatives of synagogue
1 item
AR 7062

FO SM **WOLF HEIDENHEIM**
1757–1832
Clippings; photos
5 items
AR 1053

FO = Photos · GE = Genealogical Material · PM = Primary Material · SM = Secondary Material

PM SM **HEINRICH HEIDENHEIMER**
Clippings; letters
2 items
AR 500

FO **LUDWIG HEIDENHEIMER**
President of Jewish Community in Mainz (1880)
Photo
1 item
AR 823

SM **HEIDINGSFELD/LOWER FRANCONIA; JEWISH COMMUNITY**
Article on Jewish community with photo of synagogue (1978)
1 item
AR 4838

PM **JASCHA HEIFETZ**
Musician, 1901–
Concert programs (1912, 1915)
2 items
AR 2087

PM **KARL HEIGEL**
Historian, 1842–1915
Autograph (1889)
1 item
AR 3055

FO PM **ADOLF HEILBERG**
SM Lawyer, 1858–1936
Photo; clippings; letters, including one of proceedings excluding Heilberg from practicing law (1933)
19 items
AR 1054

PM **AUGUST HEILBORN**
Letter to Heilborn (1865)
1 item
AR 1358

PM SM **HEILBRONN, DISTRICT; JEWISH COMMUNITY**
Photocopies of documentation: "Jews in the Lowland"; newspaper article on different Jewish communities in area (1982)
36 items
AR 5109

PM **HEILBRONN FAMILY**
Documents concerning real estate ownership; concessions for manufacturing; correspondence concerning building of a railroad (1704–1893)
58 items
AR 4157

SM **HEILBRONN; JEWISH COMMUNITY**
Articles
4 items
AR 1483

GE **HEILBRUNN FAMILY**
Family tree (17th–20th cent.)
2 items
AR 4143

PM **SIEGFRIED FRITZ HEILBRUNN**
Reminiscences
3 items
AR 3438

FO **OTTO HEILBUT**
Photos
7 items
AR 1639

FO PM **EDUARD HEILFRON**
Lawyer, 1860–1938
Biography; photo
3 items
AR 513

FO PM **ERNST HEILMANN**
SM Socialist politician, journalist, 1881–1940
Photo; curriculum vitae; list of publications
3 items
AR 1914

SM **SIGMUND A. HEILNER**
Published diary concerning immigrant life in American West (1859–1861)
6 items
AR 4471

GE **HEIMAN FAMILY, OBERDORF, WURTTEMBERG**
Family tree
1 item
AR 4897

FO = Photos · GE = Genealogical Material · PM = Primary Material · SM = Secondary Material

FO SM **HUGO HEIMANN**
Socialist politician, 1859–1951
Clippings; eulogy; photo
7 items
AR 208

PM **JACOB HEIMANN FAMILY**
Documents concerning family
property (1807–1868)
7 items
AR 3462

FO PM **MORITZ HEIMANN**
SM Author, 1868–1925
Autographs (1923); portrait; eulogy
5 items
AR 3297, AR 2207

GE **HEIMERDINGER FAMILY, ALSACE**
Family tree, since 1550
1 item
AR 5022

FO PM **CLARA HEINE FAMILY**
Personal documents; photos
(1862–1962)
18 items
AR 1915

PM **ELIAS HEINE**
Photocopy of diary and annotated
English translation (1836–1837)
2 items
AR 4850

FO **HEINE FAMILY**
Photos
3 items
AR 7029

FO PM **HEINRICH HEINE**
SM Author, 1799–1856
Articles; commemorative stamps and
plaquette; photos; letters; autographs
80 items
AR 38, AR 855

GE **MARGARETHE HEINE**
Family tree (12th–20th cent.)
1 item
AR 1384

PM **SALOMON HEINE**
Banker, 1767–1844
Memorial medals; letters by Heine
7 items
AR 181

PM **THOMAS THEODOR HEINE**
Artist, 1867–1948
Clippings; drawings; autographs
21 items
AR 1671, AR 841

PM **DAVID HEINEMAN**
Lawyer, politician, born 1865 Detroit,
Mich.
Biography
1 item
AR 5214

PM **ELKAN HEINEMANN**
Banker, 1859–1941
Biography
1 item
AR 3381

PM **HEINEMANN FAMILY, LUENEBURG**
Documents; family papers since 1811
38 items
AR 2973

PM **FRIEDEL HEINEMANN FAMILY**
Vaccination and death certificates of
family members (mid 19th cent.)
3 items
AR 1916

SM **FRITZ HEINEMANN**
Philosopher, 1889–1970
Clippings on Heinemann exhibition
in Lueneburg
12 items
AR 4095

SM **ISAAC HEINEMANN**
List of publications
1 item
AR 218

FO PM **WALTER HEINEMANN**
SM Physician
Correspondence, including letter
from Albert Einstein; photos from
liberated concentration camps
published by Americans; documents
concerning emigration; clippings
91 items
AR 865

SM **HEINSHEIM; JEWISH COMMUNITY**
Clipping
1 item
AR 2479

FO = Photos · GE = Genealogical Material · PM = Primary Material · SM = Secondary Material

GE PM **HEINSINS FAMILY**
Documents; curriculum vitae;
genealogy also of Meyer family;
corresponence
14 items
AR 5006

PM **BERTHOLD HELD**
1868–1931
Autograph (1927)
1 item
AR 1968

PM SM **ROBERT O. HELD**
Lawyer, 1889–
Clippings; two speeches
3 items
AR 2116

FO **ERNST D. HELLINGER**
Mathematician, 1883–1950
Photo
1 item
AR 3227

PM **HELLINGER FAMILY**
Naturalization patent, Posen (1834);
postcard (Poland, 1941); traveling
directions to Lisbon (1941)
3 items
AR 5077

GE **HELLMANN-BACH FAMILY**
Family tree (17th–20th cent.)
1 item
AR 2584

SM **BERTHA HELLMANN**
1861–1917
Eulogy
1 item
AR 53

FO PM **HEMSBACH; JEWISH COMMUNITY**
By-laws of burial society; reports;
photos; documentation on Jews of
Hemsbach
8 items
AR 142

PM **ELIAS HENSCHEL**
Physician, 1755–1839
Poems; writers notebook including
sketching and embroideries
2 items
AR 3357

PM **FANNY HENSEL**
1805–1847
Catalogue of exhibition on 125th
anniversary of her death (Berlin,
1972)
1 item
AR 3941

SM **SEBASTIAN HENSEL**
Newspaper article (1936)
1 item
AR 1055

FO **WILHELM HENSEL**
Photos of portraits, including Beer
family, Mendelssohn family, Rahel
Varnhagen; list of portraits in Hensel's
collection (1794–1861)
99 items
AR 314

PM **FELIX HEPNER**
Estate owner, Silesia
Estate account books; other records
15 items
AR 7210

PM SM **GEORG HERLITZ**
Historian, 1885–1968
Articles; obituaries
2 items
AR 2547

PM **HERMANN SAMUEL HERMANN**
Family document
1 item
AR 3638

PM **HERRLINGEN; JEWISH EDUCATIONAL INSTITUTION**
Correspondence (1928–32)
11 items
AR 4686

PM **FERDINAND L. HERRMANN**
Material concerning Bavarian
Commission for Restitution; statistics
81 items
AR 4188

SM **HELENE HERRMANN (BORN SCHLESINGER)**
Literary historian, 1877–1944
Article (1982)
1 item
AR 5088

FO = Photos · GE = Genealogical Material · PM = Primary Material · SM = Secondary Material

PM SM **HUGO HERRMANN**
Editor, 1887–1940
Obituary (1940); tape: "My Trip to Galicia"
2 items
AR 3504, AR 5132

PM **KLAUS J. HERRMANN**
Family documents (18th–19th cent.)
8 items
AR 1278

PM **MAX HERRMANN**
1865–1942
Autograph (1935)
1 item
AR 1731

PM **HERBERT HERRMANNS**
Autographs
6 items
AR 753

PM **HERRNSTADT FAMILY**
Mortgage (1838)
1 item
AR 1265

FO PM **HERSCH FAMILY**
Photos; manuscripts including plays by Heinrich Hersch and translations of Moliere; personal papers of Eugen Hersch, painter (1905–1957)
34 items
AR 3543, AR 3544

FO GE **MAX HERSCHEL**
PM Manufacturer, Jewish community leader, 1840–1921
Poems; photos; sermon on his 70th birthday; family tree (1745–1930)
12 items
AR 4333

FO SM **GUSTAV HERTZ**
Physicist, 1887–1975
Obituary; photo
3 items
AR 2202

PM **HEINRICH HERTZ**
Physicist, 1857–1894
Commemorative stamp of Deutsche Bundespost
1 item
AR 37

SM **HENRIETTE HERTZ**
Newspaper article, "Fünfzig Jahre Bibliotheka Hertziana" (1963)
1 item
AR 2129

PM **WILHELM HERTZ**
Publisher, 1822–1901
Notes on his family
1 item
AR 3964

SM **MENNO HERTZBERGER**
Antique book dealer, 1897–
Newspaper article (1977)
1 item
AR 4511

PM SM **SALOMON HERXHEIMER**
Rabbi, 1801–1884
Personal documents; sermons; prayers by Herxheimer; articles
21 items
AR 4832

PM **ARTHUR & FLORA HERZ**
Letters from Camp les Milles (Xerox copies)
15 items
AR 4909

PM SM **EMIL HERZ**
Editor, 1877–
Clippings; letters
3 items
AR 2538

PM **EMIL HERZ**
Correspondence with Jacob Gruenewald (1861–1877); family letters
73 items
AR 2171

SM **HAENLE HERZ**
Musician, 1780–1851
Obituary notice
1 item
AR 3234

FO PM **HENRIETTE HERZ**
SM Photo; clipping; autographs
10 items
AR 2350, AR 732

FO = Photos · GE = Genealogical Material · PM = Primary Material · SM = Secondary Material

PM **JACOB HERZ FAMILY**
Family documents (19th cent.)
3 items
AR 1241

GE PM **LOUIS HERZ FAMILY**
Family documents, family trees
(1833–1939)
14 items
AR 2561

PM **MARCUS HERZ**
1747–1803
Autographs
2 items
AR 1991

FO **MEYER NAFTALI HERZ**
Rabbi
Photo; 17th cent. portraits
2 items
AR 2993

GE PM **HERZBERG FAMILY**
Family history; family tree
(1730–1930)
9 items
AR 4575

GE PM **HERZBERG FAMILY, BERLIN**
Family trees, records of four
generations; citizenship papers
68 items
AR 3675

FO SM **GERHARD HERZBERG**
Physicist, 1904–
Clippings; photos
4 items
AR 3909

GE **HERMANN HERZBERG**
1826–1926
Booklet (1903) on genealogy of
Herzberg, Eltzbacher, Westfeld,
Frankenstein families
1 item
AR 5219

PM **ARNOLD HERZFELD FAMILY**
Family papers from the first half of
19th cent.
6 items
AR 2907

PM **JOSEPH HERZFELD**
Communist politician, 1853–1939
Biographical notices
1 item
AR 3942

SM **LEVI HERZFELD**
Rabbi
Newspaper article, *Braunschweiger
Zeitung* (1961)
1 item
AR 1562

SM **ISAAK HERZFELDER**
Lawyer, 1836–1904
Clipping
1 item
AR 4533

FO GE **THEODOR HERZL**
PM SM Zionist, 1860–1904
Letters; reprints; clippings about
Herzl and early Zionist congresses;
family tree; photos; autographs
43 items
AR 185, AR 1982

PM SM **ERNST HERZOG**
Memoirs; personal documents,
clippings, collection of theater
programs concerning Jewish exile
community in Shanghai (1940's)
23 items
AR 3935

GE **HERZOG FAMILY, HESSLOCH**
Herzog and Lambert genealogy
3 items
AR 3806

PM **WILHELM HERZOG**
Writer, 1884–1960
Biography
1 item
AR 1781

FO PM **CHARLES (KARL) HESS**
1902–
Memoirs (1940–1946); photos of
Westerbork camp, Holland; Bergen-
Belsen trial 1945; letters of
recommendation (1945)
5 items
AR 4938

FO = Photos · GE = Genealogical Material · PM = Primary Material · SM = Secondary Material

GE **HESS FAMILY**
Family tree (18th–20th cent.)
1 item
AR 1331

FO PM **WILLY HESS**
Musician, 1859–
Photo; biographical notes
2 items
AR 2416

FO **WOLF HESS**
Photos (ca. 1840) of oil paintings
2 items
AR 1186

PM SM **HERMANN HESSE**
Writer
Newspaper articles; autographs
12 items
AR 167, AR 180

PM **HERMANN HESSELBERGER**
Hop merchant, 1882–1922
Certificate that Hesselberger was awarded Iron Cross 1st class (1918); military medals
3 items
AR 4249

FO PM **HESSEN; JEWISH COMMUNITY**
SM Clippings; list of communities; decree on Jews 1809; microfilm concerning court case 1538; photos; articles
16 items
AR 997

PM **HEUMANN FAMILY**
Family papers (mid–19th cent.)
5 items
AR 118

FO **GEORG VON HEVESY**
Chemist, Nobel Prize 1943, 1885–1966
Photo under glass
1 item
AR 2974

PM **GEORG HEYM**
Poet, 1888–1912
Newspaper articles (1962, 1965)
2 items
AR 2192

FO PM **CURT L. HEYMANN**
SM Journalist, 1894–1969
Clippings; photos; World War I diary (1916–1917)
13 items
AR 4259

PM **EMILIE HEYMANN**
Letter concerning Heymann's life underground in Germany during World War II
1 item
AR 2097

GE PM **HEYMANN FAMILY**
Family tree (19th–20th cent.); correspondence
8 items
AR 1385

FO GE **FRITZ HEYMANN**
PM SM Journalist, editor, 1898–
Clippings; photos; article on Heine's genealogy; curriculum vitae; autographs
15 items
AR 764, AR 3312

SM **HARTWIG HEYMANN**
Dissertation in philosophy about Hitler, written in Trinidad, 1939
1 item
AR 5232

GE PM **HEINRICH HEYMANN**
Documents (1806, 1889); memoir; family tree
4 items
AR 5127

PM **OTTO HEYMANN**
License to deal in cloth (1811); passport (1813); material concerning Gurs concentration camp
11 items
AR 1918

SM **WERNER RICHARD HEYMANN**
Artist
Obituary (1961)
1 item
AR 1216

PM **LEVI HEYNE**
Letter of protection (1768)
1 item
AR 189

FO = Photos · GE = Genealogical Material · PM = Primary Material · SM = Secondary Material

PM **PAUL HEYSE**
Author, 1830–1914
Autographs
3 items
AR 946

PM **HICEM**
Protocol of meeting of the executives of Harmony Club, New York, June 1935
1 item
AR 4089

PM **HICEM, KREUTZBERGER**
Reports of various organizations for refugees
32 items
AR 4729

SM **WOLFGANG HIDESHEIMER**
Writer
Newspaper article (1964)
1 item
AR 2306

SM **RAOUL HILBERG**
Historian, 20th cent.
Commentary on Hilberg's book, *The Destruction of the European Jews*
2 items
AR 3696

SM **HILDESHEIM; JEWISH COMMUNITY**
Clipping
1 item
AR 3318

SM **HIRSCH HILDESHEIMER**
Historian, 1855–1910
Miscellaneous articles and print: "Der echte Talmud"
3 items
AR 1487

FO **RUDOLF HILFERDING**
German Finance Minister, 1877–1941
Photo
1 item
AR 2710

PM **FERDINAND HILLER**
Composer, 1811–1885
Autographs
5 items
AR 2117

PM **MAKSYMILIAN HILPPERTS**
Identity cards; work cards and other registration certificates while underground in Izdebno, Poland (1942–1944)
6 items
AR 3308

FO PM **HINDENBURG (NOW ZABRZE, POLAND); JEWISH COMMUNITY**
Photo of synagogue; festive programs
3 items
AR 2915

GE **HINRICHSEN FAMILY**
Genealogies of Hinrichsen, Roth, Guestrow families
3 items
AR 5007

FO PM **ALBERT F. HIRSCH**
Professor of literature, 1888–
Personal documents; photo (1914–1939)
19 items
AR 1187

PM **HIRSCH AUF GEREUTH FAMILY**
Business papers; patent of nobility from Bavarian State Archives, Munich, (1811–1964); Vienna Archives 1863–1890; YIVO Institute Films, misc. items, history
37 items
AR 2110, AR 1777, AR 3946, AR 3947, AR 7002

FO PM **BETTY HIRSCH**
SM Teacher of the blind, 1877–1961
Clippings; letters; photo
31 items
AR 1551

PM **EDITH J. HIRSCH**
Economist, 20th cent.
Curriculum vitae
1 item
AR 3756

SM **EMIL HIRSCH**
Dealer in antique books
Newspaper clippings (1954, 1959)
2 items
AR 785

FO = Photos · GE = Genealogical Material · PM = Primary Material · SM = Secondary Material

GE PM **HIRSCH FAMILY, HALBERSTADT**
Family history; vital documents
(18th–20th cent.)
18 items
AR 3064, AR 1136–1141

PM **HIRSCH FAMILY, MERGENTHEIM**
Business contracts; personal
documents; correspondence
(1832–1895)
96 items
AR 1159

PM **HIRSCH FAMILY, SCHWETZ**
Certificates; orders; medals
(1899–1916)
7 items
AR 2515

PM **HIRSCH FAMILY, THORN**
Family papers (mid–19th cent.); letter
of municipal citizenship (1848)
3 items
AR 3328

SM **FELIX E. HIRSCH**
Article, "First Hundred Days of
Hitler's Nightmare" (1958)
1 item
AR 324

GE PM **FRANZ EDUARD HIRSCH**
Physician
Family tree; family history
(1934–1936)
2 items
AR 1386

FO PM **GUSTAV HIRSCH**
SM Industrialist, 1822–1898
Correspondence; photos; clippings
relating to the Hirsch family and
family ironworks (1847–1946)
17 items
AR 2008

FO PM **JULIUS HIRSCH**
SM Economist, 1883–1961
Obituaries; clippings; curriculum
vitae; bibliographical notices; photo
39 items
AR 1254

SM **KARL JAKOB HIRSCH**
Writer, painter, 1892–1952
Exhibition (1967) described in article
1 item
AR 3697

PM **MEIER HIRSCH**
Mathematician, 1770–1851
Biographical data
2 items
AR 4955

FO SM **OTTO HIRSCH**
Lawyer, civil servant, 1885–1941
Articles; clippings; photos
28 items
AR 234

FO PM **PAUL HIRSCH**
SM 1868–1940, Politician, Prussian
Minister President
Photos; clippings concerning Hirsch's
political career; correspondence
including a letter from Gustav Noske
35 items
AR 3382

FO SM **RAHEL HIRSCH**
Physician, biologist, 1870–1943
Photos; clippings relating to Hirsch
14 items
AR 2610

PM **ROSETTA HIRSCH FAMILY**
Testaments; correspondence; book of
poetry (1813–1961)
19 items
AR 1330

FO PM **RUDOLF HIRSCH**
SM Physician, 1904–
Poems; clippings; photos; documents
of Hirsch's parents
6 items
AR 3032

FO PM **SAMSON RAPHAEL HIRSCH FAMILY**
Rabbi, 1808–1888
Photo; notes on family
11 items
AR 902

PM **THEODOR HIRSCH**
Business executive, 1888–
Notes on his life in Nazi Germany;
documents concerning his
emigration; letter from Leo Baeck
(1941)
3 items
AR 3275

FO = Photos · GE = Genealogical Material · PM = Primary Material · SM = Secondary Material

FO PM **ALFRED HIRSCHBERG**
SM Jewish community leader, 1901–1971
Photo; obituaries; short biographies
5 items
AR 3698

FO **JOHANNA HIRSCHBERG**
1803–1871
Photo
1 item
AR 1188

PM **MAX HIRSCHBERG**
Speech on his 80th birthday
1 item
AR 3418

PM **WALTHER HIRSCHBERG**
Musician, 1889–1960
Biographical notices; concert programs
2 items
AR 3840

PM **HIRSCHEL FAMILY, BRESLAU**
Marriage license; family letters (early 19th cent.)
4 items
AR 3646

FO **HIRSCHFELD FAMILY, FRANKFURT A.M**
Family portraits (19th cent.)
3 items
AR 4452

SM **GEORG HIRSCHFELD**
Author, 1873–1942
Newspaper clippings
2 items
AR 3487

PM **JACOB HIRSCHFELD**
Passport (1863)
1 item
AR 3969

SM **L. HIRSCHFELD**
Rabbi
Photocopy of newspaper article: induction of Dr. L. Hirschfeld as rabbi in Giessen
1 item
AR 4957

PM **MAGNUS HIRSCHFELD**
Physician, 1868–1935
Letter to Hirschfeld (1897); autograph
2 items
AR 1700, AR 765

FO **KURT M. HIRSCHLAND**
Photo
1 item
AR 1189

FO GE **SIMON HIRSCHLAND FAMILY**
SM Photos; family tree; clippings
7 items
AR 766

PM **J. HIRSCHMANN**
Business card (mid–19th cent.)
1 item
AR 2508

PM **SELMA HIRSCHMANN**
Two Torah-binders
2 items
AR 2577

SM **HIRSCHWALD'SCHE BUCHHANDLUNG**
Newspaper article, "150 yrs. Hirschwald'sche Buchhandlung"
1 item
AR 2966

GE **ALLEN T. HIRSH JR COLLECTION**
Genealogies
1 item
AR 5284

FO **JULIUS EDUARD HITZIG**
Criminologist, 1780–1849
Photo of lithograph
1 item
AR 2956

FO **HOCHBERG; JEWISH COMMUNITY**
Photo of synagogue
12 items
AR 759

FO PM **JULIUS HOCHFELD**
Engineer, 1880–1959
Photo; curriculum vitae; professional certificates
8 items
AR 2456

FO = Photos · GE = Genealogical Material · PM = Primary Material · SM = Secondary Material

FO **HOCHHAUSEN; JEWISH COMMUNITY**
Photos of former synagogue and site
5 items
AR 3878

SM **ROLF HOCHHUTH**
Playwright
Newspaper clippings about play *The Deputy*
33 items
AR 2000

GE **HOCHSTAEDTER FAMILY**
Family tree (19th–20th cent.)
1 item
AR 4757

FO **JACOB VAN HODDIS**
Photo, dedication (early 19th cent.)
2 items
AR 4495

FO **HOECHBERG; JEWISH COMMUNITY**
Photos of synagogue; notes; photos of students
4 items
AR 4108

FO SM **HOECHST; JEWISH COMMUNITY**
Clipping; photo of synagogue
1 item
AR 4109

PM **ARNOLD HOELLRIEGEL**
Author, 1883–1939
Correspondence concerning new edition of Hoellriegel's novel *Das Urwald Schiff* (early 1960's)
13 items
AR 4390

GE PM **HOENIG FAMILY**
Genealogy; material from some Jewish communities in Germany
24 items
AR 5076

PM SM **HOEXTER FAMILY**
Clippings and reports on the family and their work in education of deaf (1915–1963)
7 items
AR 2068

PM **FRIEDRICH HOEXTER FAMILY**
Memorial family history books; material on careers and emigration (1920's and 1930's)
22 items
AR 3082

PM **FRIEDRICH WILHELM HOEXTER**
German passport and U.S. immigration material
6 items
AR 2445

FO PM **HANS JOHN HOEXTER**
SM Painter, writer, 1884–1938
Photo; clippings; autobiographical notices; letters by Hoexter
15 items
AR 3826

SM **HUGO HOFFMAN**
Lawyer
Newspaper article (1960)
1 item
AR 1256

FO SM **JACOB HOFFMAN**
Rabbi in Frankfurt a. M., 1881–1956
Photo; newspaper articles
13 items
AR 2017

FO PM **LEO HOFFMANN FAMILY**
Letters to Hoffmann; photo of Hoffmann and his grandfather Rabbi David Hoffman
5 items
AR 4705

PM **BANESH HOFFMANN**
Mathematician
Curriculum vitae
1 item
AR 4062

FO **DAVID HOFFMANN**
Rabbi, 1843–1921
Photo
1 item
AR 2793

SM **MOSES HOFFMANN**
Rabbi
Obituary in *Aufbau*
1 item
AR 494

FO = Photos · GE = Genealogical Material · PM = Primary Material · SM = Secondary Material

PM **RUTH HOFFMANN**
Author, 1893–
Speech in honor of Ruth Hoffmann
3 items
AR 3276

PM **SIEGFRIED HOFFMANN**
Lawyer, 1878–1950
Biographical notice
1 item
AR 2465

SM **E. VON HOFMANNSTHAL**
Newspaper article (1955)
1 item
AR 1488

GE PM **HOFMANNSTHAL FAMILY**
Family tree (18th–20th cent.); family coat of arms
4 items
AR 107

FO SM **HUGO VON HOFMANNSTHAL**
Poet, playwright, 1874–1929
Photo; clippings
15 items
AR 1657

SM **PETER R. HOFSTAETTER**
Newspaper clippings
2 items
AR 2307

PM **STELLA BERGER-HOHENFELS**
1859–1920
Autograph
1 item
AR 1834

PM **ADOLF HOHENSTEIN**
Biography, including account of experiences in East Africa during First World War
1 item
AR 1489

PM **ARTHUR HOLITSCHER**
1869–1939
Autographs
2 items
AR 1373

PM **FELIX HOLLAENDER**
Letters
5 items
AR 2648

FO PM **GUSTAV HOLLAENDER**
Musician, 1855–1915
Photo; concert programs; biographical notice
15 items
AR 2088

PM SM **LUDWIG HOLLAENDER**
Lawyer, 1877–1936
Clippings by Hollaender; obituaries; memorials
9 items
AR 186

PM **HOLLANDER STIFTUNG, ALTONA**
Dowry endowments from 1795
1 item
AR 5240

SM **HOLOCAUST**
Clippings on scholarly, artistic, and media portrayals of Holocaust (1972)
49 items
AR 4546

PM **HOLOCAUST; EXHIBITION**
Five exhibit-size posters on the Holocaust
1 item
AR 5960

PM **HOLOCAUST-SURVIVORS**
Studies on survivors and children of survivors
2 items
AR 5099

PM **ISAAK HOLZER**
Rabbi
Certificate of ordination from Breslau Rabbinical Seminary (1901)
3 items
AR 3464

PM **JULIUS HOMBERGER**
Physician, 1839–1872
Biography
1 item
AR 4758

GE **HOMBURGER FAMILY**
Family tree (18th–20th cent.)
2 items
AR 266

FO = Photos · GE = Genealogical Material · PM = Primary Material · SM = Secondary Material

SM **FRITZ HOMEYER**
Antique book dealer, 1881–
Newspaper clippings
2 items
AR 1799

SM **FRITZ HOMMEL**
Anthropologist
Newspaper clipping, "Arier & Semiten"
1 item
AR 1874

SM **OSCAR HOMOLKA**
Actor, 1901–1978
Obituary
1 item
AR 4534

PM **EMANUEL LOEW HOPF**
1794–1866
Identification card; business license
3 items
AR 4284

FO **HORB; JEWISH COMMUNITY**
Photos
2 items
AR 3035

PM **ABRAHAM HORN**
Death certificate; will (1944)
2 items
AR 4684

SM **ABRAHAM HORODISCH**
Publisher
Newspaper clipping (1963)
1 item
AR 2308

SM **BELA HOROVITZ**
Publisher
Newspaper clipping (1959)
1 item
AR 767

FO **ABRAHAM HOROWITZ**
Photo
1 item
AR 1191

FO PM **JACOB HOROWITZ**
Rabbi
Photo; eulogy pronounced by Rabbi Horowitz (1885)
2 items
AR 1190

PM **JITZCHAK HOROWITZ**
Letter from Horowitz to Dr. M. N. Nathan, executive secretary of Jewish community in Hamburg (ca. 1840)
1 item
AR 4657

PM **JOSEF HOROWITZ**
Rabbi
Festive program in honor of Rabbi Horowitz, Frankfurt a. M
1 item
AR 2001

PM **MARCUS HOROWITZ**
Rabbi, 1844–1910
Biographical notices; festive program; bronze plaque on occasion of 25th anniversary of Horovitz's functioning as rabbi in Frankfurt a. M
4 items
AR 320

PM **ERNST HORWITZ**
Banker; manager of Banking House Mendelssohn, 1848–1925
Speeches; correspondence
8 items
AR 4930

FO **KURT HORWITZ**
Actor, director, 1897–
Photo (1960)
1 item
AR 2764

PM **LUDWIG HORWITZ**
Autograph (1921)
1 item
AR 2002

PM **HOTTENBACH B. BERNKASTEL; JEWISH COMMUNITY**
By-laws of Israelitische Religionsgesellschaft (1908)
1 item
AR 4112

SM **MARTIN HOXTER**
Newspaper clippings
2 items
AR 1600

FO = Photos · GE = Genealogical Material · PM = Primary Material · SM = Secondary Material

FO PM **BRONISLAW HUBERMANN**
SM Musician, 1882–1947
Photo; concert programs; clippings; autographs
8 items
AR 1593, AR 2569

PM **HUETTENHEIM; JEWISH COMMUNITY**
Birth, marriage, death registers of communities in the 19th cent.; papers of burial society, lists of Jews for 1726, 1835, 1912
9 items
AR 4381

PM **BOLAND HUGHES**
Physician
Speech, "A Constructive Answer to Auschwitz and Judenfeindschaft" (1965) and program
2 items
AR 2526

FO PM **RICHARD HULDSCHINER FAMILY**
Bibliographical list; portrait
2 items
AR 3743

FO **ALEXANDER VON HUMBOLDT**
Portrait
2 items
AR 2778

FO PM **HUNDHEIM; JEWISH COMMUNITY**
Letter; photos
6 items
AR 3027

PM SM **SELMA HURWITZ**
Obituaries; concert program (1855)
3 items
AR 1257

FO PM **EDMUND HUSSERL**
Philosopher, 1859–1938
Photos; autograph
4 items
AR 2446, AR 873

GE **HUTZLER FAMILY**
Genealogy and family trees
3 items
AR 5055

PM **ICHENHAUSEN; JEWISH COMMUNITY**
Letter
1 item
AR 4068

GE **IKELHEIMER FAMILY**
Vital documents (1869–1924)
6 items
AR 2868

PM **ILLEREICHEN; JEWISH COMMUNITY**
Letter
1 item
AR 2824

SM **ILLINGEN; JEWISH COMMUNITY**
Article, "History of Illingen Jews" (1981)
1 item
AR 4971

FO **IMPFINGEN; JEWISH COMMUNITY**
Photo of synagogue
2 items
AR 3879

SM **INSTITUTE FOR RESEARCH OF GERMAN EXILE LITERATURE, UNIVERSITY OF STOCKHOLM**
Papers from symposia (1971–1975)
13 items
AR 4611

SM **INSTITUTE FOR THE STUDY OF MODERN JEWISH LIFE; NEW YORK**
Papers from 1976 conference on Jewish fertility
9 items
AR 4262

SM **INSTITUTE FOR YIDDISH LEXICOLOGY, NEW YORK**
Photoprint of *Great Dictionary of the Yiddish Language*
1 item
AR 4263

PM **INTERNATIONAL COMMITTEE OF THE HISTORY OF THE SECOND WORLD WAR**
Conference reports (1974–1975)
13 items
AR 4236

FO = Photos · GE = Genealogical Material · PM = Primary Material · SM = Secondary Material

SM **INTERNATIONAL TEACHERS' CONFERENCE TEL-AVIV**
Publication on antisemitism issued at Tel-Aviv (1980)
1 item
AR 5245

SM **EDUARD ISAAC**
Chemist, 1882–
Clipping (1977)
1 item
AR 4486

FO **JOSEPH ISAACSOHN**
Photo (1861)
1 item
AR 1192

PM **J.J. ISAACSON**
Painter, 1859–1943
Clippings; exhibition catalogue; biography
12 items
AR 2098

PM **PINCUS ISACOWITZ**
License
1 item
AR 4642

FO SM **KURT HARALD ISENSTEIN**
Sculptor, 1898–1980
Articles; photo
8 items
AR 4698

PM **ISERLOHN; JEWISH COMMUNITY**
Notes
2 items
AR 3242

FO SM **ISRAEL**
Clippings; transcripts; copies of printed reports; photos of Palestine and Israel (1938)
27 items
AR 188

SM **ARTHUR ISRAEL**
Physician
Newspaper clippings
2 items
AR 2022

GE **KURT ISRAEL FAMILY, HANOVER**
Genealogy
1 item
AR 4910

PM **SAMUEL ISRAEL**
Decision of rabbinical court, Altona (1820)
1 item
AR 3798

PM **ISRAEL SONS BERLIN**
Family papers; photo dept. store
13 items
AR 783

FO PM **WILFRED ISRAEL**
1899–1943
Letters to India (1940–1943); family photos
6 items
AR 187

PM **JOSEFS ISRAELS**
Painter, 1824–1911
Autograph
1 item
AR 1099

PM **EDGAR ISTEL**
Composer, 1880–
Autograph
1 item
AR 2820

FO **BRUNO ITALIENER**
Rabbi
Photo
1 item
AR 1193

GE **ITZIG VON BERG**
Family tree (1730–1858)
1 item
AR 1497

PM SM **BENNO JACOB**
Rabbi, theologian, 1862–1945
Correspondence; reviews; essay
38 items
AR 2118

FO PM **HEINRICH EDUARD JACOB**
SM Writer, 1889–1967
Obituary; clippings; photos; copy of correspondence; autographs
6 items
AR 1498, AR 5188, AR 552

PM **LEIB JACOB**
18th cent. life in Hesse-Kassel
1 item
AR 5304

FO = Photos · GE = Genealogical Material · PM = Primary Material · SM = Secondary Material

SM **P. WALTER JACOB**
Writer
Book announcement, Buenos Aires (1945)
1 item
AR 1608

SM **ERWIN JACOBI FAMILY**
Musicologist
Family articles: Strassburg, Frankfurt, Hamburg
7 items
AR 3210

GE **JACOBI FAMILY**
Family tree (18th–20th cent.)
5 items
AR 116

GE **JACOBI FAMILY**
Family tree (1905)
1 item
AR 1387

PM **LOTTE JACOBI**
Photographer
Catalogue (1979)
1 item
AR 4759

PM **PAUL JACOBI**
Physician, 1890–
Family papers from 1836
12 items
AR 117

PM SM **LUDWIG JACOBOWSKI**
Author, 1868–1900
Newspaper clippings; autographs
6 items
AR 3353, AR 373

FO PM **MONTY JACOBS**
Writer, 1875–1945
Reminiscences of Isaak Babel; photo; autograph
3 items
AR 2711, AR 1755

PM **MORITZ JACOBSOHN**
Military service documents (1870's)
11 items
AR 1258

PM **MOSES JACOBSOHN**
Rabbi, 1853–1907
Autograph
1 item
AR 2559

FO PM **SIEGFRIED JACOBSOHN**
Author, 1881–1927
Photo; autographs
13 items
AR 2381, AR 1650

PM **ALBERT JACOBSON FAMILY**
Personal documents (1847–1971)
42 items
AR 3794

FO PM **ISRAEL JACOBSON**
Educator, 1768–1828
Photo; letters; poem
5 items
AR 1297

PM **M. JACOBSON**
Family business documents (1820's)
7 items
AR 6014

FO PM **MAX JACOBSON FAMILY**
Photos; family documents; material related to Theresienstadt
41 items
AR 3793

PM **MANASSE ITZIG JACOBOWITZ**
Petition (1817)
1 item
AR 874

PM **ALFRED JACOBY**
Song presented at a Bar Mitzvah (1916)
1 item
AR 5279

SM **GERHARD JACOBY**
Lawyer
Obituary (1960)
1 item
AR 1298

PM **GUSTAV JACOBY**
Letter (1873)
1 item
AR 2943

FO = Photos · GE = Genealogical Material · PM = Primary Material · SM = Secondary Material

FO PM **JOHANN JACOBY**
Politician, 1805–1877
Photo; autograph
2 items
AR 2712, AR 734

PM **MARGARETE JACOBY**
Letters; lectures; short history of
Olga-Sternhaus
6 items
AR 1262

SM **MAX JACOBY**
Physician, 1845–1912
Article, Berlin 1979
1 item
AR 4924

PM **NORBERT JACQUES**
Author, 1880–1954
Autograph
1 item
AR 1378

SM **JACQUIER & SECURIUS**
Bankers
Newspaper clippings (1938, 1957)
3 items
AR 245

FO **ERNST JAECKH**
1875–1959
Photos
6 items
AR 3374

GE **HANNS JAEGER-SUNSTENAU**
List of family trees of ennobled Jewish
families
1 item
AR 1787

PM **DR. BENNO JAFFE**
Industrialist, 1840–1923
Biographical notices
1 item
AR 18

GE PM **JAFFE FAMILY, POSEN**
Family trees; family documents;
correspondence
25 items
AR 4037

PM **LUDWIG JAFFE**
Doctor
Official papers, mid–19th cent.
4 items
AR 1243

GE **MORDECHAI JAFFE**
Family tree (17th–20th cent.)
1 item
AR 4515

FO **PHILLIPP JAFFE**
Photo
1 item
AR 1263

FO SM **ADOLF JANDORF**
Merchant, warehouse owner,
1870–1932
Obituaries; photos
11 items
AR 3144

GE **JAPHA FAMILY, FRAUSTADT**
Genealogy
3 items
AR 5050

FO **JAROCZYNO; JEWISH
COMMUNITY**
Photo
1 item
AR 132

FO PM **IGNAZ JASTROW**
Economist, 1856–1937
Photo; autographs
41 items
AR 2713, AR 1112

FO **ADOLF JELLINEK**
Rabbi, 1820–1893
Photo
1 item
AR 2987

FO **HERMANN JELLINEK**
Author executed in Vienna,
1822–1848
Photo
1 item
AR 2714

SM **JENA; JEWISH COMMUNITY**
Deportation story: newspaper
clipping (1975)
1 item
AR 5259

FO = Photos · GE = Genealogical Material · PM = Primary Material · SM = Secondary Material

PM **ANNA JERUSALEM FAMILY**
Educational, military papers
(mid–19th cent.)
5 items
AR 1130

FO **ELSE JERUSALEM**
Writer, 1877–
Photo (1920)
1 item
AR 2957

FO **JERUSALEM; JEWISH COMMUNITY**
Photos of Shaare Zedek Hospital
2 items
AR 7035

FO SM **LEOPOLD JESSNER**
Theater director, 1878–1945
Photo; newspaper article
2 items
AR 2715

PM **JESSURUN FAMILY COLLECTION**
Copies of statutes of Portuguese community, Hamburg (1660); other items of Hamburg Jewish community from 1772
12 items
AR 1213

FO **EUGEN JETTEL**
Painter, 1845–1901
Photo
1 item
AR 2716

PM **JEWISH COLONIZATION ASSOCIATION**
Reports (late 19th cent.); notes on archives
9 items
AR 2596

FO PM **JEWISH COMMUNITIES;**
SM **GENERAL**
Vital statistics; records from German Jewish communities; issue of *Familienschutz*; list of synagogues; photos (1898–1918)
6 items
AR 322, AR 7035, AR 5167

SM **JEWISH EDUCATIONAL INSTITUTIONS; GENERAL**
Articles on education of Jewish teachers (1957)
5 items
AR 224, AR 4225

SM **JEWISH THEOLOGICAL SEMINARY, NEW YORK**
Report (1977)
1 item
AR 4537

PM **JEWS IN AFRICA**
Memorial album (1954)
1 item
AR 490

PM **JEWS IN ALASKA**
Letter to Secretary of State suggesting creation of a refugee haven in Alaska
3 items
AR 4760

SM **JEWS IN AUSTRALIA**
Clippings (1967–1979)
2 items
AR 3354

PM SM **JEWS IN AUSTRIA**
Decree of Emperor Franz I (1759); clippings; pamphlets (1848)
28 items
AR 379, AR 403

PM SM **JEWS IN BELGIUM**
Articles on trials of Nazis (1981, 1982); Nazi orders relating to Jews (1942)
7 items
AR 5093

SM **JEWS IN BOHEMIA**
Clipping on ennobled Jewish families in Bohemia (1966)
1 item
AR 4196

SM **JEWS IN CUBA**
Clippings (1939)
2 items
AR 1801

FO = Photos · GE = Genealogical Material · PM = Primary Material · SM = Secondary Material

FO PM **JEWS IN CZECHOSLOVAKIA**
SM 1800 decree; birth certificate (1822); revolutionary appeal (1848); photos; clippings; manuscript
18 items
AR 495

SM **JEWS IN DENMARK**
Clippings (1967–1970)
3 items
AR 3296

SM **JEWS IN THE DOMINICAN REPUBLIC**
Clippings
2 items
AR 3917

PM SM **JEWS IN ENGLAND**
Clippings; papers relating to refugee industries; articles
6 items
AR 3761

SM **JEWS IN EUROPE**
List of sources, volume of *European Judaism*
2 items
AR 4170

PM SM **JEWS IN FRANCE**
Reports from Jewish committees in France; clippings
26 items
AR 4078

PM SM **JEWS IN GERMANY; MIDDLE AGES**
Reproduction of prints; clipping
4 items
AR 3130

PM **JEWS IN GERMANY; 16TH AND 17TH CENT.**
Lists of trials involving Jews
1 item
AR 2539

PM SM **JEWS IN GERMANY; 18TH CENT.**
Clippings; reproductions; 18th cent. decrees
113 items
AR 4444, AR 379

PM SM **JEWS IN GERMANY; 19TH CENT.**
19th cent. laws, petitions, program of Reform Jews, post 1848 trials involving Jews; articles; records of Prussian Parliament; poem
29 items
AR 2377, AR 1223

FO PM **JEWS IN GERMANY; 1900–1933**
SM Clippings; photos; correspondence; inflation scrip
27 items
AR 557, AR 1309, AR 515

FO PM **JEWS IN GERMANY; 1946–1978**
SM Miscellaneous collection combining correspondence, manuscripts, clippings, programs, and photo albums on Jewish life in Germany after 1945 (including report concerning mental condition of former concentration camp prisoners)
152 items
AR 4197, AR 491–0493, AR 124, AR 1445–1447, AR 1560, AR 1921, AR 2426, AR 2540, AR 2908, AR 3539, AR 4643, AR 4604, AR 4451, AR 4928, AR 4340, AR 4656

FO PM **JEWS IN HUNGARY**
SM Photos; clipping; proclamation (1868)
5 items
AR 3378

SM **JEWS IN ITALY**
Clippings, Fascist Union circular on racial questions; booklet on Deportion Resistance
7 items
AR 1594

SM **JEWS IN JAPAN**
Clipping, story of Jews in World War II in Japan
3 items
AR 4299, AR 5291

PM **JEWS IN LICHTENSTEIN**
Stamps
1 item
AR 3329

PM SM **JEWS IN LITHUANIA**
Clipping; manuscript translations
5 items
AR 4761

FO = Photos · GE = Genealogical Material · PM = Primary Material · SM = Secondary Material

FO PM **JEWS IN THE NETHERLANDS**
SM Photos; articles; decrees of Jewish Council in Amsterdam
22 items
AR 1677

FO PM **JEWS IN POLAND**
SM World War I circulars from German government in Warsaw; clippings; photos of Warsaw Ghetto (1943); articles
53 items
AR 1555

SM **JEWS IN PORTUGAL**
Clippings
4 items
AR 394

SM **JEWS IN ROUMANIA**
Clipping
1 item
AR 4553

PM SM **JEWS IN RUSSIA**
Clipping; personal item
2 items
AR 4432

PM SM **JEWS IN SHANGHAI**
Clippings; registration pass; experiences
11 items
AR 2509

SM **JEWS IN SOUTH AMERICA**
Clippings; reports; circulars; articles
9 items
AR 1440

FO **JEWS IN SPAIN**
Photo
1 item
AR 3749

PM SM **JEWS IN SWITZERLAND**
Transcript of Bern *Protocols of the Elders of Zion* trial (1934); pamphlets; clippings on Jews in Switzerland; Swiss policies towards Jewish refugees during the 1930's; list of Jews sent from Theresienstadt (1945)
52 items
AR 34, AR 7213

FO PM **JEWS IN THE UNITED STATES**
SM Photos of portraits; clippings; petition to President Franklin D. Roosevelt; refugee material; material on USA committees
48 items
AR 177

PM SM **JOSEPH JOACHIM**
Violinist, 1831–1907
Concert programs; autographs
93 items
AR 2089, AR 445

PM **JOACHIMSSOHN FAMILY**
Passport; marriage contract; membership certificate (1830's)
3 items
AR 872

FO PM **GEORG JOACHIMSTHAL**
Physician, professor of medicine
Photo; biographical notes
2 items
AR 2042

FO SM **JOEHLINGEN; JEWISH COMMUNITY**
Clipping with photo
1 item
AR 2801

SM **KARL JOEL**
1864–1934
Articles; obituaries
14 items
AR 1800

SM **ANNA MARIA JOKL**
Clipping, "2nd World Congress for Jewish Studies" (1957)
1 item
AR 27

SM **ERNST JOKL**
Book review (1958)
1 item
AR 1299

PM **JOLOWICZ FAMILY**
Family documents (mid–19th cent.)
3 items
AR 1686

FO = Photos · GE = Genealogical Material · PM = Primary Material · SM = Secondary Material

PM SM **HEYMANN JOLOWICZ**
Rabbi, 1816–1875
Essays; speeches; doctoral diploma;
curriculum vitae; portrait
16 items
AR 3163

SM **LEO JOLOWICZ**
Newspaper article (1961)
1 item
AR 2219

PM **JONAS FAMILY**
Family history (19th cent.)
1 item
AR 1131

SM **KLAUS W. JONAS**
Literary historian, 1920–
Clipping; article
2 items
AR 3540

SM **REGINA JONAS**
Rabbi, 1902–1944
Article
1 item
AR 4886

PM **RUDOLF JONAS**
History of a Ruhr Basin coal mine;
reminiscences of emigration to
United States (1930's)
5 items
AR 4171

SM **CHARLES JORDAN**
Article, "Reds and Arabs in Prague
Death" (1967)
1 item
AR 3403

FO **ALBERT JOSEF**
Kommerzienrat; president of
Landesverband Palatinat
Photo
1 item
AR 2812

PM **DANIEL JOSEPH**
Passport (1815); marriage permit
(1819)
2 items
AR 1335

PM **ERNST JOSEPH**
Postcards (1890's)
2 items
AR 1337

PM **JACQUES JOSEPH**
Biographical notice (1926)
1 item
AR 3705

FO PM **RAPHAEL JOSEPHSOHN**
1861–1934
Portrait; appointment as notary;
eulogy
3 items
AR 4625

GE **JOSEPHTHAL FAMILY**
Family trees (1932–1975)
3 items
AR 319

FO GE **FRANZ JOURDAN FAMILY**
PM Portrait; family tree; correspondence;
letters from Maximilian Harden
13 items
AR 2528

PM **JAMES JOYCE**
Author, 1882–1941
Autograph
1 item
AR 3076

GE **JOSEPH JUDA**
Family tree (18th–20th cent.)
1 item
AR 1628

PM **SALOMON JUDASSOHN**
1831–1902
Autograph
1 item
AR 2821

SM **JÜDISCHER VERLAG; BERLIN**
Literary Index (1920)
1 item
AR 4422

SM **ELISABETH JUNGMANN-
BEERBOHM**
Obituaries (1959)
3 items
AR 963

FO = Photos · GE = Genealogical Material · PM = Primary Material · SM = Secondary Material

SM **JUTROSINSKI FOUNDATION**
Charter for Reichenheimsches
orphanage, Berlin (1980's)
1 item
AR 89

FO GE **JUTROSINSKY FAMILY**
PM SM Clippings; manuscripts; family trees
and genealogy; photos
13 items
AR 7019

SM **STELLA KADMON**
Theatrical director, 1902–
Biography; clippings; articles
6 items
AR 4391

PM SM **FRANZ KAFKA EXHIBITIONS**
Obituaries; correspondence; publicity
concerning exhibitions
58 items
AR 4623

FO **ANTOINETTE KAHLER**
Author, 1862–1951
Photo
1 item
AR 3095

PM **JOSEFINE KAHLER-HOFMANN**
1868–1945
Autographs
2 items
AR 1404

PM **ANSELM KAHN**
Letters
2 items
AR 25

PM SM **ARNO KAHN**
Photocopies of correspondence;
photos; articles relating to history of
Jews in Westphalia, Rhineland and
Westerbork camp, Netherlands
4 items
AR 7253

FO **ARTHUR KAHN**
Physician, author, 1850–1928
Photo
1 item
AR 2878

PM **ARTHUR KAHN AND FRITZ (SON)**
1851–1928
Papers of Arthur Kahn; family papers;
correspondence; programs; memoirs
of travels including trips to United
States (1889); clippings and writings;
papers of Fritz Kahn, physician and
naturalist
3.5 feet
AR 7144

SM **ERNST KAHN**
Obituary (1963)
1 item
AR 2185

PM **KAHN FAMILY, LICHTENAU/BADEN**
Purchase contracts real estate (1807, 1837); other documents
11 items
AR 4963

PM SM **FRITZ KAHN**
Physician, writer, 1888–1968
Albums with clippings; Jewish
population statistics (1921);
manuscript outline
5 items
AR 3534

PM **HERBERT KAHN**
Manuscript
1 item
AR 250

FO SM **JULIUS KAHN**
Photo of German army, First World
War; clipping
2 items
AR 4805, AR 2208

SM **JULIUS KAHN**
1861–1924
Clipping
1 item
AR 4805

SM **LISA KAHN**
Writer, 1927–
Clipping
1 item
AR 4362

FO = Photos · GE = Genealogical Material · PM = Primary Material · SM = Secondary Material

SM **LOTHAR KAHN**
Literary historian
Articles on Nazis in German fiction
and Lion Feuchtwanger
5 items
AR 1264

PM **MANFRED KAHN**
Letter; poems
3 items
AR 1266

PM SM **ROBERT L. KAHN**
Literary historian
List of publications; accounts of
advanced studies and research, Rice
University, Texas (1965);
correspondence
3 items
AR 3038

FO PM **SALOMON KAHN FAMILY**
Photos; army documents (1840–1933)
6 items
AR 1292

PM **FRITZ KAISER-BLUETH FAMILY**
Wanderbuch (1820's); letter signed
Konrad Adenauer (1933)
2 items
AR 2544

SM **GEORG KAISER**
Author
Clipping, "The Last Days of
Gruenheid" (1957)
1 item
AR 58

SM **KAISER WILHELM GESELLSCHAFT**
Press releases; history; articles about
Adolf von Harnack
6 items
AR 2353

FO SM **KAISERSLAUTERN; JEWISH COMMUNITY**
Clipping; photos of synagogues; list
of Judaica; 1968 article on new Jewish
community
8 items
AR 343

GE **KALAHORA FAMILY**
Family tree (15th to 20th cent.)
1 item
AR 317

PM SM **MASCHA KALEKO**
Writer, 1907–
Clippings; letters
3 items
AR 4483

PM **SALOMON KALIPHARI**
Autobiography (18th cent.)
1 item
AR 4762

GE **KALISCH FAMILY**
Family tree (18th to 20th cent.)
1 item
AR 4782

PM **ARNOLD KALISCHER**
Lawyer
Lectures; silver Kiddush cup
3 items
AR 3637

FO GE **KALISCHER FAMILY**
SM Photos; clippings; family genealogies
23 items
AR 1748

SM **HIRSCH KALISCHER**
Rabbi and Zionist, 1795–1874
19th cent. biographical notices
5 items
AR 1868

GE **KALISKI FAMILY**
Family tree (16th to 20th cent.)
2 items
AR 4400

GE PM **KALLIR FAMILY**
SM Family documents; correspondence;
various honors awarded to family
members; clippings; family trees
85 items
AR 1520, AR 1522, AR 1524

SM **OTTO KALLIR**
Art dealer, 1894–1978
Obituary (1978)
1 item
AR 4666

PM **HILDE KALLMANN**
Physicist, 1908–1968
Dissertation abstract; life history;
notes on Mossner family;
correspondence with Julie Braun
Vogelstein

FO = Photos · GE = Genealogical Material · PM = Primary Material · SM = Secondary Material

58 items
AR 4692, AR 4658

PM **MARTIN KALLMANN**
1867–1911
Dissertation on development of music through electricity
1 item
AR 5210

SM **RICHARD KALLMANN**
Newspaper
5 items
AR 3813

GE **ISAAC KALLMES**
Family tree (16th–19th cent.)
1 item
AR 251

FO PM **EMMERICH KALMAN**
SM Composer, 1882–1953
Photos; obituary; autograph
5 items
AR 964, AR 4706

SM **RICHARD KANDT**
Physician, 1867–1918
Clipping on Kandt
1 item
AR 2840

PM **A. J. KANN**
Royal license (Bavaria 1821)
1 item
AR 1267

FO **ROBERT A. KANN**
Historian
Photo
1 item
AR 2252

PM **GISELA KANOPKA**
Educator
Description of life under Nazis and subsequent emigration
1 item
AR 5156

PM SM **ALFRED KANTOROWICZ**
Author, 1899–1979
Articles; correspondence
7 items
AR 404

FO GE **KANTOROWICZ FAMILY**
PM Family trees; photos; funeral address (1835)
10 items
AR 439

SM **HERMANN KANTOROWICZ**
Lawyer, 1877–1940
Clipping
1 item
AR 4627

FO **MAX KANTOROWITZ**
Photo
1 item
AR 1194

SM **HERMANN KAPAUNER**
Biographical notice; clippings
Landsberg/Warthe
3 items
AR 254

SM **MARION A. KAPLAN**
Book review, "The Jewish Feminist Movement in Germany 1904–1938"
Israelitisches Wochenblatt for Switzerland (1981)
1 item
AR 4944

SM **VICTOR KAPLAN**
Inventor
Article on Kaplan's turbine invention
1 item
AR 5290

PM **KAPP FAMILY**
Estate settlement (1905)
1 item
AR 1905

PM **KAPRALIK FAMILY**
Statutes of Society to Support the Poor in Czernowitz (1871)
1 item
AR 5300

GE **KARFUNKEL FAMILY**
Family tree (17th–19th cent.)
2 items
AR 1687

PM **ALFRED KARGER**
Speech
1 item
AR 1268

FO = Photos · GE = Genealogical Material · PM = Primary Material · SM = Secondary Material

SM **HEINZ KARGER**
Publisher, 1895–1959
Obituary (1959)
1 item
AR 965

SM **S. KARGER**
Clipping about S. Karger Publishers (1961)
1 item
AR 1816

FO PM **KARLSRUHE; JEWISH**
SM **COMMUNITY**
Photos of synagogues; clippings; prayers on marriage of Carl Ludwig Friedrich to Stephanie Napoleon (1806)
6 items
AR 2036

FO SM **MARTHA KARLWEIS**
Photo; bibliography
3 items
AR 1595

FO PM **HANNAH KARMINSKI**
SM Feminist, 1897–1942
Correspondence; photos; clippings; autograph
24 items
AR 330, AR 3769, AR 3902

PM **GUSTAV KARPELES**
Literary historian, 1848–1909
Autographs
2 items
AR 828

PM **HERMANN KASACK**
Author, 1896–1966
Autograph
1 item
AR 4867

PM **MAGDALENA KASCH**
Essay
1 item
AR 3269

PM **MARIE LUISE VON KASCHNITZ**
Writer, 1901–
Autographs
2 items
AR 3439

FO **F. KASKELINE**
Photo postcard
1 item
AR 4554

PM SM **KASSEL; JEWISH COMMUNITY**
Clippings; drawing of synagogue; tax bill (1827)
5 items
AR 454

PM **KASTOR FAMILY**
Photocopies of statistical documents of Kastor family (1786–1903); family documents concerning cutlery business in Solingen and United States (1870–1982)
2 items
AR 5237

PM **SIMON KATSER**
Physician, 1810–1893
Personal documents
18 items
AR 3776

FO SM **MAX KATTEN**
Rabbi, died 1957
Photo; clippings
9 items
AR 3071

FO PM **SIR BERNARD KATZ**
Biophysicist, Nobel Prize winner, 1911–
Photo; autograph
2 items
AR 3853, AR 4250

PM **GEORG KATZ**
Physician (20th cent.)
Essays
5 items
AR 3402

PM SM **HANNAH L. KATZ**
Program; biographies of Max Herrmann literary historian (1865–1942); poetry of Jüdischer Frauenbund
15 items
AR 3367

GE **LOUIS KATZ, BRUCHSAL**
Genealogy (since 1759)
1 item
AR 4914

FO = Photos · GE = Genealogical Material · PM = Primary Material · SM = Secondary Material

SIMON KAUFMANN FAMILY

SM **RICHARD KATZ**
Newspaper clipping (article on 75th birthday, 1963)
1 item
AR 2310

SM **RUDOLF KATZ**
Lawyer
Clipping on occasion of 65th birthday (1960)
1 item
AR 1658

FO GE **WALTER E. KATZ**
PM 1893–1972
Military papers; photos; family trees; genealogical material
27 items
AR 3986

PM **RABBI MEIR KATZENELLENBOGEN**
Rabbi
Short biography (1846)
1 item
AR 105

FO PM **A. KATZENSTEIN**
Photos of family members and family business; family artwork
8 items
AR 4227

PM **FRITZ R. KATZENSTEIN FAMILY**
Letters of protection; citizen letters; certificates; appointments (1777–1876)
23 items
AR 3635

SM **FRITZ KAUFFMANN**
Chemist
Newspaper clippings (1964)
2 items
AR 2311

FO GE **MEYER KAUFFMANN**
Family tree (18th–19th cent.); portraits of Kauffmann, his wife, their textile factory (ca. 1850)
3 items
AR 79

SM **THEKLA KAUFFMANN**
Social worker, 1883–1980
Newspaper clipping (1973); funeral oration (1980)
2 items
AR 4976

GE PM **CAROLA KAUFMANN**
1893–1975
Genealogical papers and correspondence; family documents; matters pertaining to Worms, Mainz, other towns
113 items
AR 257

FO SM **DAVID KAUFMANN**
Rabbi, 1852–1899
Photo; clippings
3 items
AR 1875

GE **KAUFMANN FAMILY**
Family tree (19th–20th cent.)
1 item
AR 2003

PM **KAUFMANN FAMILY, DÜRKHEIM**
Business and official papers; photocopies of family documents
25 items
AR 4931

SM **HANS KAUFMANN**
Newspaper article, "To the 50th anniversary of the Jews in Chile" (1956)
1 item
AR 252

SM **HENRY KAUFMANN; VIERNHEIM, HESSEN**
1860–1955
Obituaries (1955, Pittsburgh)
2 items
AR 3287

SM **RICHARD V. KAUFMANN**
Art collector
Clippings
4 items
AR 4770

PM **SIMON KAUFMANN FAMILY**
Family letters (mid 19th cent.); residence permit (1819)
5 items
AR 4484

FO = Photos · GE = Genealogical Material · PM = Primary Material · SM = Secondary Material

SM **WALTER KAUFMANN**
Philosopher, 1921–1980
Obituaries (1980)
2 items
AR 4905

FO PM **KAULA FAMILY**
Photo postcard Nanette Heine, born Kaula; painting (1829)
1 item
AR 2034

FO GE **KAULLA FAMILY**
PM Family trees and documents (1759–1842); histories; photos
30 items
AR 496

SM **RUDOLF KAYSER**
Literary historian
Obituary (1964)
1 item
AR 2312

PM **MEYER KAYSERLING**
Rabbi, 1829–1905
Centenary medallion; autographs
3 items
AR 3874, AR 2004

PM **KEIBEL FAMILY**
Family papers (19th cent.)
4 items
AR 967

GE PM **KEILER FAMILY**
Family tree (17th–20th cent.); passport; ration cards (ca. 1940)
4 items
AR 1253

PM **JULIUS KELLER**
Letters, documents relating to Jewish youth groups in Mannheim (1930's), including a letter from Martin Buber
13 items
AR 3122

FO PM **BENZION KELLERMANN**
Rabbi, 1869–1923
Photos; writings; correspondence
11 items
AR 1197

FO GE **KEMPNER FAMILY**
Photo album (19th cent.); family tree (18th–20th cent.)
2 items
AR 3212

FO **ROBERT M. W. KEMPNER**
Lawyer, historian, 1899–
Group photo
1 item
AR 3977

FO PM **ALFRED KERR**
SM Author, 1867–1947
Photos; clippings; short manuscripts; autographs
14 items
AR 2203, AR 733

FO SM **HERMANN KESTEN**
Author, 1900–
Clippings; photo
14 items
AR 968

PM **HERMANN KEYSERLING**
1880–1946
Autograph
1 item
AR 1411

PM SM **KIEL; JEWISH COMMUNITY**
Report on Jewish school (1891–1892); articles
5 items
AR 6002

PM **ANTON KIPPENBERG**
Director of Insel Verlag, 1874–1950
Correspondence, early history of Insel Verlag
37 items
AR 3145

PM SM **KIPPENHEIM; JEWISH COMMUNITY**
Program; clippings
5 items
AR 2904

PM **KIRCHEN; JEWISH COMMUNITY**
Article
1 item
AR 3233

FO = Photos · GE = Genealogical Material · PM = Primary Material · SM = Secondary Material

FO **KIRCHHAIN; JEWISH COMMUNITY**
Photo of synagogue
1 item
AR 4115

SM **WALTHER KIRCHNER**
Article, "Siemens & AEG and the Electrification of Russia"
1 item
AR 5220

PM **KIRN A.D. NAHE; JEWISH COMMUNITY**
Letter
1 item
AR 3470

SM **KIRRWEILER; JEWISH COMMUNITY**
Article
1 item
AR 4864

SM **BRUNO KIRSCHNER**
Economist
Newspaper clippings
2 items
AR 2313

PM SM **BRUNO KISCH**
Professor of medicine, 1890–1966
Letter; clipping
3 items
AR 3414

FO SM **GUIDO KISCH**
Professor of law, 1889–
Clippings; photo
10 items
AR 787

SM **KISHINEV PROGROM**
Newspaper clippings (1903)
3 items
AR 4940

PM **KISSINGEN; CHILDREN'S HOME**
Jewish children's home
Report on history of children's hospitals; circular on Israelitische Kur Hospiz (1919)
2 items
AR 3222

PM SM **KISSINGEN; JEWISH COMMUNITY**
Article on history of Kissingen Jews; correspondence
4 items
AR 3118

FO SM **HENRY A. KISSINGER**
Political scientist, diplomat, 1923–
Clippings; photo
7 items
AR 4041

PM **MARCUS KITCZALES**
Certificate of mental competency (1826)
1 item
AR 290

FO **ALFRED KLAAR**
Editor, 1848–1927
Photo
2 items
AR 2694

PM **KLABUND (PSEUD. OF ALFRED HENSCHKE)**
1891–1928
Autographs
3 items
AR 446

SM **JAKOB KLATZKIN**
Philosopher, Zionist, 1882–1948
Clipping
1 item
AR 4555

FO PM SM **IRMA KLAUSNER-CRONHEIM**
Physician, 1874–1959
Eulogy; diplomas; portrait of her and her family members
10 items
AR 751

FO PM **EGON KLEBE**
Physician, musician, 1887–1957
Photo; biography; compositions
4 items
AR 3916

PM **ALFRED KLEE**
Poster
2 items
AR 2535

PM **MAX KLEE**
Painter, 1866–1928
Poem of appreciation of Klee (1934), with translation
2 items
AR 4958

FO PM **WILHELM KLEEMANN**
Banker, Jewish community leader, 1869–
Photos; diplomas
8 items
AR 799

FO **HENRY L. KLEIN**
Served in cavalry in U.S. Civil War
Photo
1 item
AR 4547

SM **JULIUS KLEIN**
General, journalist
Clippings (1950's–1970's)
16 items
AR 754

SM **MELANIE KLEIN**
Physician
Article in *London Times*, obituary: "Exploring the Child's Mind" (1960)
1 item
AR 1659

FO **KLEIN SCHUETTUEBER BOHEMIA; JEWISH COMMUNITY**
Photo of synagogue
1 item
AR 7035

PM **KLEINBARDORF; JEWISH COMMUNITY**
Typescripts
3 items
AR 129

FO **KLEINEICHHOLZHEIM; JEWISH COMMUNITY**
Photos of former synagogue
3 items
AR 3880

PM SM **KLEINHEUBACH/BAVARIA; JEWISH COMMUNITY**
Articles; list of names (1942)
11 items
AR 4865

FO PM **OTTO KLEMPERER**
SM Composer, conductor, 1885–1973
Photos; clippings; compositions; autographs
23 items
AR 260, AR 2140, AR 7097

FO **VIKTOR KLEMPERER**
Literary historian, 1881–
Portrait
1 item
AR 2772

FO **FRED KLESTADT**
Industrialist
Portrait
2 items
AR 3146

PM **EDUARD KLEY**
Rabbi, school teacher, 1818–1840
Biography
1 item
AR 4424

FO PM **EDITH KLOPFER**
Family photo, correspondence (early 20th cent.); photo of nursery and daycare center for children of employees of the Weiss woolens factory in Silesia
12 items
AR 969

PM SM **WALTER KNOCHE**
Meteorologist, 1881–1941
Article; obituary; correspondence
6 items
AR 1271

PM SM **HUGO KNOEPFMACHER**
Lawyer, librarian, research analyst; 1890–1980
Personal and family papers; correspondence; restitution papers; essays; clippings
55 items
AR 7172

PM **KOBERN A.D. MOSEL; JEWISH COMMUNITY**
Fragment of prayer shawl
2 items
AR 1286

FO = Photos · GE = Genealogical Material · PM = Primary Material · SM = Secondary Material

PM **KOBLENZ; JEWISH COMMUNITY**
Deportation lists of Gestapo (1942)
1 item
AR 7085

PM **DORA KOBLER**
Pamphlet on Leo Pinsker and Emma Lazarus
1 item
AR 4582

PM **ALFRED KOCH**
Awards and medallions given to soldier A. Koch during World War I
1 item
AR 5153

PM **ILSE KOCH**
1906–1951
Manuscript by Alan Steinweis, "The Case of Ilse Koch"
1 item
AR 4768

PM SM **RICHARD KOCH**
Physician, 1882–1949
Bibliography; biography
2 items
AR 3744

FO **RICHARD KOEBNER**
Historian, 1885–1958
Photo
1 item
AR 2779

FO PM **KOENIGHEIM; JEWISH COMMUNITY**
Photos of synagogue; information on Jews in community
5 items
AR 2480

FO PM SM **KOENIGSBERG; JEWISH COMMUNITY**
Clippings; list of Jews deported from Koenigsberg; photos; articles
36 items
AR 1815

FO PM **CARL KOENIGSBERGER FAMILY**
Businessman, 1894–1960
Photo; family papers (early 19th cent.)
7 items
AR 1244

PM **KOENIGSHUETTE; JEWISH COMMUNITY**
Report on school year (1914–1915)
1 item
AR 224

FO **KOENIGSWART, BOHEMIA; JEWISH COMMUNITY**
Photos of synagogue
4 items
AR 2156

GE PM **KOENIGSWARTER FAMILY**
Family trees (18th–20th cent.); correspondence
13 items
AR 960

FO **KOEPENICK; JEWISH COMMUNITY**
Photo
1 item
AR 6011

SM **ARTHUR KOESTLER**
Author
Clipping (1962)
1 item
AR 1802

PM **KOETHEN; JEWISH COMMUNITY**
List of Jewish family names
1 item
AR 4175

FO **RABBI MOSES SAMUEL KOHEN**
Gewitsch-Moravia, 1835–1845
Photo
1 item
AR 7147

GE PM **KOHLBERG FAMILY**
Family tree and related documents (16th, 19th cent.); correspondence
16 items
AR 2256

PM SM **ABRAHAM KOHN**
Diary of experiences as immigrant in America (1842–1846)
1 item
AR 262

GE **CARL ISAAC KOHN FAMILY**
Family tree (19th–20th cent.)
1 item
AR 4783

FO = Photos · GE = Genealogical Material · PM = Primary Material · SM = Secondary Material

GE PM **KOHN FAMILY BAJA, HUNGARY**
Family history and related documents
(18th–20th cent.)
3 items
AR 4358

PM **FELIX KOHN**
Attorney, Vienna
Address by Jos. Schell, "Memories of
Felix Kohn" (1959)
1 item
AR 4975

FO **HAENLEIN SALOMON KOHN**
1803–1880
Portrait of Kohn and wife (mid–19th
cent.) and other photos
3 items
AR 4363

FO PM **HANS KOHN**
SM Historian, 1891–1971
Photo; clippings; manuscript;
correspondence
32 items
AR 259

GE PM **ISAAK KOHN FAMILY, BOHEMIA**
Family tree by John Henry Richter
(18th–20th cent.); correspondence
2 items
AR 4822

GE PM **PAUL KOHN**
SM Family documents and
correspondence (1791–1884);
clippings of the Karpeles, Kohn,
Tedesco family of Prague and New
Jersey
26 items
AR 7086

GE **KOHN-STEIN FAMILY**
Genealogical material
4 items
AR 4092

GE **KOHNSTAMM FAMILY**
Family tree (17th–19th cent.)
2 items
AR 1431

PM **ADOLPH KOHUT**
Historian, 1848–1917
Page proofs for a book by Kohut
1 item
AR 4160

PM **ANNETTE KOLB**
1875–
Autograph
1 item
AR 1756

PM **KOLBERG; JEWISH HOSPITAL**
Jewish convalescent hospital
Card for fees
1 item
AR 4746

PM **CARL KOLLER**
Opthalmolgist, 1857–1944
Letters; curriculum vitae
6 items
AR 4826

FO PM **GERTRUD KOLMAR**
SM Poet, 1894–1943
Clippings; photo; correspondence
(1938–1943)
10 items
AR 1346

FO **LEOPOLD KOMPERT**
Author, 1822–1886
Photo
1 item
AR 2721

SM **KONITZ (NOW CHOJNICE,
POLAND); JEWISH COMMUNITY**
Clippings about Moritz Lewy for
ritual murder trial
16 items
AR 3476

FO PM **KONSTANZ; JEWISH
COMMUNITY**
Photos of synagogue; list of Jews
deported from Konstanz (1940)
9 items
AR 2166

GE **KOPLIK FAMILY**
Family tree since 1744
1 item
AR 5051

PM **JACOB KOPPEL**
Rabbi
Personal documents (1816–1829)
10 items
AR 3465

FO = Photos · GE = Genealogical Material · PM = Primary Material · SM = Secondary Material

GE **NATHAN KOPPEL**
Family trees (18th–20th cent.)
2 items
AR 4423

PM **SCHEYER KOPPEL**
Passport (1808)
1 item
AR 1400

FO PM **PROFESSOR S. KORACH**
Photos; doctoral diploma
3 items
AR 961

PM **DAVID FERDINAND KOREFF**
1783–1851
Autographs (ca. 1830)
1 item
AR 1954

FO PM **KORITSCHAN FAMILY, AUSTERLITZ**
Documents; photos
39 items
AR 2444

SM **ARTHUR KORN**
Physicist
Obituary (1945)
1 item
AR 261

FO **KORNEUBURG/AUSTRIA; JEWISH COMMUNITY**
Drawings of former synagogue
3 items
AR 4973

FO SM **PAUL KORNFELD**
Photo; press clipping
2 items
AR 2502

FO PM **ERICH KORNGOLD**
Artist, composer, 1897–1957
Photo; note (1915, 1929)
7 items
AR 546

PM **JULIUS KORNGOLD**
Music critic (1860–1945), father of Erich Korngold
Autographs
19 items
AR 2946

PM **HEDI KORNGOLD-KATZ**
Violinist
Curriculum vitae
1 item
AR 1273

FO PM **FRITZ KORTNER**
SM Actor and director, 1892–1970
Photo; clippings; autograph
17 items
AR 1549, AR 1835

PM **G.I. KOSMOL**
Correspondence (1956–1957) concerning Gesellschaft für die Christlich-Jüdische Zusammenarbeit e.V.
18 items
AR 972

FO SM **HENRY M. KOSTERLITZ**
Photos: Oppeln synagogue; physiological chemistry article
2 items
AR 5234

SM **KOTSUJI, SETCHAN**
Japanese professor who saved Jews in Japan during World War II
Newspaper article on him
1 item
AR 5168

PM **OSKAR KOWALSKI**
Letter (1937)
1 item
AR 3436

PM **SIEGFRIED KRACAUER**
1889–1966
Autograph (1932)
1 item
AR 2175

PM **CLEMENTINE KRAEMER**
List of collection of articles and manuscripts by Kraemer
1 item
AR 2402

PM **LEOPOLD KRAEMER**
Teacher, cantor,1884–1963
Jewish teaching certificates; World War I military service book; cantor's material

33 items
AR 2994

PM **MAX KRAEMER**
World War I medals
1 item
AR 3211

GE **KRAFT FAMILY, GALICIA**
Genealogy written by Susan Kraft (76 pp.)
1 item
AR 5098

FO SM **WERNER KRAFT**
Photo; clipping
2 items
AR 973

SM **LOLA KRAMARSKY**
Leader of Hadassah
Newspaper clippings (1960)
2 items
AR 1432

PM SM **HELENE KRAMER**
Correspondence; certificates; clippings; biography; material on her work in Bertha Pappenheim's childrens' home
11 items
AR 2046

PM **FRIEDA KRAUS**
1886–1962
Poems originating in Theresienstadt
2 items
AR 5263

PM **HERTHA KRAUS**
Social worker, 1898–1968
Obituary (1968)
1 item
AR 3400

FO PM **KARL KRAUS**
SM Writer, 1874–1936
Photos; clippings; autographs
39 items
AR 1660, AR 1110

FO **KRAUTHEIM; JEWISH COMMUNITY**
Photos of former synagogue
6 items
AR 4072

FO **HANS ADOLF KREBS**
1900–
Photo (1900)
3 items
AR 3120

PM **RICHARD KREBS**
1884–
Family register
1 item
AR 4859

PM **KREFELD; JEWISH COMMUNITY**
Stamp; brochure
2 items
AR 2613

FO PM **FRITZ KREISLER**
Violinist, 1875–1962
Photo; concert program
2 items
AR 2090

SM **GEORG KREISLER**
Musician
Article (1964)
1 item
AR 2315

FO **KREMS-DONAU, AUSTRIA; JEWISH COMMUNITY**
Photos of synagogue articles
3 items
AR 4665

PM **SIMON KREMSER**
1775–1851
Biographical notices (19th cent.)
1 item
AR 4300

SM **KREMSIER; JEWISH COMMUNITY**
Article
1 item
AR 3221

PM **KREUZNACH; CHILDREN'S HOME**
Jewish children's convalescent home
Brochure
1 item
AR 3548

FO = Photos · GE = Genealogical Material · PM = Primary Material · SM = Secondary Material

PM **KREUZNACH; JEWISH COMMUNITY**
List of Jews with covering letter (1728–1788)
2 items
AR 4621

PM **KRIEG FAMILY**
Business documents (1794–1879); Jewish community lists from Goldberg, Silesia
1 item
AR 3108

FO SM **KRIEGSHABER; JEWISH COMMUNITY**
Clippings; photos of cemetery
5 items
AR 399

PM **ADA KRISTELLER**
Letters of Vassalage Lauenburg (17th cent.)
1 item
AR 2436

GE **KRONACHER FAMILY**
Family tree (18th–20th cent.)
2 items
AR 3288

PM **FRITZ KRONENBERGER**
Lawyer, 1902–1969
Correspondence (1934–1935)
4 items
AR 4045

FO **THEODOR KRONER**
Rabbi, 1845–1923
Photo (ca. 1920)
1 item
AR 1199

FO **ROBERT KRONFELD**
Glider pilot, 1903–
Photo
1 item
AR 2722

FO PM **EMIL KRONHEIM**
Photos; Red Cross certificates from World War I
6 items
AR 55

GE **KRONHEIM FAMILY**
Family tree (18th–20th cent.)
1 item
AR 959

GE **KRONHEIM FAMILY, SAMOTSCHIN**
Family history since 1820
1 item
AR 4852

GE **KRONTHAL FAMILY**
Family tree (16th–20th cent.)
1 item
AR 3511

PM **KROTOSCHIN (NOW KROTOSZYN, POLAND); JEWISH COMMUNITY**
List of graves
1 item
AR 760

FO PM SM **KRUMBACH-HUERBEN; JEWISH COMMUNITY**
Photos of synagogue; various religious objects; clipping
8 items
AR 4116

PM **JAN KUBELIK**
1880–1940
Autograph (1903)
1 item
AR 1842

SM **ARNOLD KUCZINSKI**
Book collector
Newspaper clipping (1959)
1 item
AR 805

FO **KUELSHEIM; JEWISH COMMUNITY**
Photos
10 items
AR 2928

PM **BERNHARD KUGELMANN**
Memoir; documents concerning Kugelmann's work in the development of telephonic electronics (1919–1957)
19 items
AR 1433

FO = Photos · GE = Genealogical Material · PM = Primary Material · SM = Secondary Material

PM **KUGELMANN FAMILY**
Marriage contract (1864)
2 items
AR 974

PM **SIMON KUHN FAMILY**
Birth certificates (1817–1827)
6 items
AR 4516

PM **OTTO D. KULKA**
Historian
Treatise on National Socialism and
Jewish Question in Germany
1 item
AR 5224

PM **EDUARD KULKE**
1831–1897
Autograph (1895)
1 item
AR 1701

PM **KULP FAMILY**
Biography; family documents (19th cent.)
3 items
AR 975

PM **KUNATH & MECKLENBURG**
Advertising brochure (1938)
1 item
AR 1434

PM **KARL F. KUNREUTHER**
School papers
5 items
AR 1274

GE **KUNSTADT FAMILY**
Family tree (18th–20th cent.)
1 item
AR 2662

FO **IGNAZ KURANDA**
Member of Austrian Reichsrat, 1812–1884
Photo
1 item
AR 2723

PM **HERBERT KURREIN**
Delegate's pass for 9th Zionist Congress (Hamburg, 1909)
1 item
AR 4311

PM **BARUCH KURZWEIL**
Professor
Manuscript "Die Fragwürdigkeit Jüdischer Existenz" (1964)
2 items
AR 2518

PM **MOYSES KUSSEL**
Contract for rental of estate property (1787)
1 item
AR 2845

PM **BERNARD KUSZNITZKI**
Letter (1937); biographical notices of his father
2 items
AR 264

PM **MAX KUZNITZKI**
Lawyer, 1852–1904
Career documents; death certificate (1876–1904)
8 items
AR 2869

PM **FRED LACHMANN**
Collection of Jewish sheet music; manuscripts relating to German-Jewish music
3 items
AR 5256

PM **LACHOTZKI FAMILY**
Family documents (1881–1940)
38 items
AR 4149

PM **LADENBURG; JEWISH COMMUNITY**
Letter; list of community members with their fate (1938)
2 items
AR 452

SM **PAUL DE LAGARDE**
Newspaper article, "The Latin Translations of Ignatius" (1883)
1 item
AR 1876

PM **LAHNER**
Yiddish poems entitled "Olluempf Lied" by Lahner (1847), partial transcription in German
1 item
AR 3910

SM **LAHR; JEWISH COMMUNITY**
Clippings
3 items
AR 4332

PM **HARRY W. LAIDLER**
Booklet about Social Security Plan (1943)
1 item
AR 5244

SM **HANS LAMM**
Newspaper article 1956 regarding number of Jewish Nobel Prize winners
1 item
AR 170

SM **ANNELIESE LANDAU**
Music teacher
Newspaper articles
2 items
AR 3600

PM **EZECHIEL LANDAU FAMILY**
Chief Rabbi of Prague, 1713–1793
Postcards of Ezechiel Landau
3 items
AR 3579

FO PM **LANDAU; JEWISH COMMUNITY**
SM Speech; photo of synagogue; articles
4 items
AR 3017

GE SM **LOLA LANDAU**
Biographical article; genealogical notes from family chronicle of Siegfried Porta in Bielefeld
2 items
AR 1435

PM **CHARLOTTE LANDAU-MUEHSAM**
1881–1972
Minutes of Citizens' Council at Lübeck for 1919–1921
1 item
AR 7256

PM **PAUL LANDAU**
Cultural historian, author 1880–
Curriculum vitae
1 item
AR 2951

PM SM **SOL LANDAU**
Rabbi
Biographical notes; clippings; articles
5 items
AR 727

GE PM **LANDAUER FAMILY**
Family trees; business papers
26 items
AR 207

SM **RICHARD LANDAUER**
Publisher, 1882–1960
Obituary
1 item
AR 2221

FO PM **JULIUS LANDEK**
Photos of three paintings; correspondence
3 items
AR 5257

PM **LANDMAN FAMILY**
Bound family history by Martha Wertheimer Landman (Washington, D.C. 1984, 174 pp.)
1 item
AR 5312

GE **LANDMANN FAMILY; SCHIFFERSTADT**
Family tree
1 item
AR 1289

SM **JULIUS LANDMANN**
Dictionary of the Social Sciences
1 item
AR 1436

PM **ROSE LANDMANN**
Correspondence; notes from N. Israel inscribed 1938; reports on Winfrid Israel (1962); silver plate, knife
7 items
AR 2204

PM **MAX LANDSBERG**
Rabbi, 1845–1928
Material about Jewish family in Berlin by Mark Brandenburg (manuscript)
1 item
AR 3219

PM **LANDSBERG/WARTHE; JEWISH COMMUNITY**
List of gravestone inscriptions
1 item
AR 4046

FO **ARTHUR LANDSBERGER**
Author, 1876–1933
Photo
1 item
AR 2724

FO PM **KARL LANDSTEINER**
Biologist, Nobel Prize winner, 1868–1943
Photo; stamp
2 items
AR 2979

SM **LANDSTUHL; JEWISH COMMUNITY**
Article
1 item
AR 5044

GE PM **ARTHUR LANG FAMILY**
Manuscript about Jews of Michelfeld (1550–1870); family tree (1749)
2 items
AR 1275

PM **LANGEN/HESSIA; JEWISH COMMUNITY**
History
2 items
AR 4925

SM **ALFRED LANGENBACH**
Newspaper clipping, *Wormser Zeitung* (1959)
1 item
AR 2186

FO PM **FRIEDA LANGENDORFF**
SM Singer, 1868–1947
Curriculum vitae; obituary; photos
6 items
AR 3323

PM SM **JIRI LANGER**
Writer, died 1943
Correspondence; article
2 items
AR 4401

PM **MAX LANGER**
Poet, 1914–1963
Curriculum vitae; poems
3 items
AR 5056

SM **ELIZABETH LANGGAESSER**
Writer
Article (1960)
1 item
AR 1364

FO PM **ERIKA LANGSTEIN**
Letter about situation of Jews (Vienna, 1938); photo
1 item
AR 3757

PM **ERAN LAOR**
Writer, 1900–
Letter with biographical data (1966)
1 item
AR 3745

FO SM **WALTER LAQUEUR**
Jewish Institute for National Security Affairs: articles and photo
5 items
AR 4583

PM **OSKAR LASKE**
Painter, 1874–1951
Brochure describing gallery exhibit (1965)
1 item
AR 2841

PM **EMANUEL LASKER**
Philosopher, chess master, 1868–1941
Autographs
3 items
AR 2649

GE PM **LASKER FAMILY**
Genealogies from 1680; correspondence; family papers
18 items
AR 5136

FO PM **ELSE LASKER-SCHUELER**
SM Writer, 1868–1945
Articles; clippings; correspondence; photos; poems; autographs
115 items
AR 983, AR 265

FO = Photos · GE = Genealogical Material · PM = Primary Material · SM = Secondary Material

FO GE **FERDINAND LASSALLE**
PM SM Socialist, 1825–1864
Family tree; articles; photo; Yiddish article about Lassalle (1923); flyer "Die französischen Nationalwerkstätten von 1848" by Lassale (Berlin, April 24, 1863); autographs
12 items
AR 984, AR 831

SM **J. LAUB**
Articles
2 items
AR 1282

PM **FERDINAND LAUCHHEIMER**
Letters about Jewish communities of Schopfloch (1960–1961)
2 items
AR 1283

FO PM **LAUPHEIM; JEWISH COMMUNITY**
SM Article; photos of synagogue and Judengasse; manuscripts; list of Lauphheim Jews killed 1933–1945; miscellaneous lists; decrees
34 items
AR 3560

SM **FRITZ ELIAS LAUPHEIMER**
Rabbi
Newspaper clipping
1 item
AR 2510

SM **ALFRED EDWARD LAURENCE**
Lawyer, industrial chemist, 1910–
Newspaper clippings
2 items
AR 4902

FO **LAUTERBACH; JEWISH COMMUNITY**
Photo of synagogue
1 item
AR 999

PM **LAVELSLOH-DIEPENAU-SULINGEN; JEWISH COMMUNITY**
Answer to questionnaire
1 item
AR 816

FO PM **ARNOLD LAZARUS**
SM Rabbi, 1877–1932
Curriculum vitae; funeral speech for his father; photo of German military chaplains 1917; articles about this photo in 1917 newspaper
5 items
AR 4497

GE **JULIUS LAZARUS FAMILY**
Family history (1938)
1 item
AR 3746

SM **LUDWIG LAZARUS**
Librarian, 1900–1970
Articles; obituary
4 items
AR 3670

GE PM **MORITZ LAZARUS**
SM Philosopher, 1824–1903
Family tree; letters to Ignaz Goldziher, Dr. Harrwitz, B. Felsenthal; photo; inventory of Lazarus archive in Jerusalem; report on Lazarus-Steinthal correspondence in East Berlin; autographs
53 items
AR 2051, AR 272

PM **MORITZ LAZARUS FAMILY**
Autographs
6 items
AR 3770

PM **NAHIDA RUTH LAZARUS**
1849–1927
Autographs
2 items
AR 3754

PM **PAUL LAZARUS**
Rabbi in Wiesbaden
Letter to Siegfried Guggenheim (1949)
1 item
AR 271

FO PM **ERNST LEBACH**
SM 1879–1941
Curriculum vitae; article; photo
3 items
AR 1688

FO = Photos · GE = Genealogical Material · PM = Primary Material · SM = Secondary Material

PM **JULES LEBELL**
Bill for cost of protected arrest
(October 1933)
1 item
AR 976

FO GE **LEBRECHT FAMILY**
Family tree (1700); pictures
2 items
AR 1293

PM **FRANK LEBRECHT**
Correspondence with the State
Department and F.B.I. about *Stürmer*
propaganda; postcards of Nazi
antisemitic street signs 1933–1936;
manuscript of English translations of
children's book published by *Stürmer*,
Trau keinem Fuchs und keinem Jud by
Elvira Bauer (1936)
7 items
AR 7140

PM **LEO LEBRECHT**
Identification cards, documents about
Leo Lebrecht (also known as Max
Fischer) and Gisela Fischer (alias of
Jenny Lebrecht), who lived
underground in Berlin, 1944–1945
6 items
AR 1308

FO **LEO LEDERMANN**
Sport enthusiast
Photo of World Championship
Record Swim across English Channel
(1895)
1 item
AR 3073

PM **LOUIS LEDERMANN**
Manuscript on Ledermann family
from 1714 (Breslau, 1934)
1 item
AR 275

GE PM **LEDERMANN-PRINGSHEIM**
Family trees of Ida Ledermann born
Pringsheim, manuscript by Bernhard
Pringsheim about the Pringsheim
family (Breslau, 1937)
3 items
AR 277

PM SM **ALFRED LEESTON**
Economist, 1897–
Curriculum vitae; list of publications
2 items
AR 3841

FO PM **MELANIE LEFFMANN**
1877–1969
Photos; ten certificates of refugee
status and emigration processing
cards; living underground in Cologne
(1943–1945); three letters of Jews
deported from Laupheim
24 items
AR 4264

PM **CARL LEHFELDT**
Certificates as a physician
(1831–1836)
5 items
AR 977

PM SM **BERENT LEHMAN**
Letter of protection in Warsaw
(1724); clipping
2 items
AR 2077

PM SM **ANTON & ALFRED LEHMANN AG**
Velvet and wool factory
advertisements; 75th anniversary
publication of Lehmann Inc.
2 items
AR 391

SM **ASCHER LAEMLE LEHMANN**
Newspaper article about his diary
(1976)
1 item
AR 4341

PM **DORA LEHMANN**
Manuscript memoir of life in Altona
1 item
AR 4632

FO PM **LEHMANN FAMILY**
Notes; family tree; photo of Isador
Lehmann (1776–1856), Reb Leime
(died 1791); letter of protection for
the court actor Michael Levy (Vienna,
1796)
5 items
AR 729

FO = Photos · GE = Genealogical Material · PM = Primary Material · SM = Secondary Material

GE PM **LEHMANN FAMILY, NOERDLINGEN**
Deportation list; genealogy; family papers; list of former members of Jewish community of Noerdlingen
13 items
AR 4881

SM **JOSEPH LEHMANN**
Rabbi
Obituaries by Jewish Reform Congregation in Berlin (1933)
1 item
AR 1596

FO **MARCUS LEHMANN**
Rabbi, 1831–1890
Photo
1 item
AR 2775

PM **MAX LEHMANN**
Relationship between Jews and Christians in Hanau (18th cent.); decrees; passport (1815)
11 items
AR 3168

PM **MAYER LEHMANN**
Schutzbrief for Lehmann
1 item
AR 5211

SM **ROBERT LEHMANN**
Obituary (1969)
1 item
AR 6009

FO SM **SIEGFRIED LEHMANN**
Physician, 1892–1958
Obituaries; photo
8 items
AR 4685

PM **WILHELM LEHMANN**
Writer, 1882–
Poem "Rosen" (1967)
1 item
AR 3289

GE **ABRAHAM SIMON LEHR**
Family tree (1774)
1 item
AR 278

PM SM **CUNO LEHRMANN**
Rabbi, 1905–1975
List of publications by Cuno Lehrmann; articles about Leo Baeck; manuscript "Heinrich Heine Kämpfer & Dichter"
5 items
AR 4731

PM SM **STEPHAN LEIBFRIED**
Professor
Articles about Leibfried's research on *Berufsrechte* and *Sozialpolitik* (1933–1945); biography of Dr. Friedrich A. Friedlaender
7 items
AR 4750

PM SM **BRUNO LEICHTENTRITT**
Physician, 1888–1965, director of the children's division of State Insurance Corporation in Breslau
Doctoral diploma; expulsion from teaching (1933); correspondence about restitution; obituary
13 items
AR 3335

FO PM **HUGO LEICHTENTRITT**
SM Music critic, 1874–1951
Obituaries; photo; curriculum vitae
9 items
AR 211

PM **EMANUEL LEIDERSDORFER**
Banker
Certificate as free mason from the Lodge "L'aurore naissante" (Frankfurt a/M, 1805)
1 item
AR 2804

PM SM **DAVID LEIMDOERFER**
Rabbi, 1851–1922
Writings; clippings; correspondence
33 items
AR 3369

FO PM **LEIPZIG; JEWISH COMMUNITY**
SM Historical articles; clippings; photos; estimate of properties and values (1945)
50 items
AR 2167

FO = Photos · GE = Genealogical Material · PM = Primary Material · SM = Secondary Material

PM **MARIA LEITNER**
Hungarian-born, German-speaking
Jewish writer
General information
1 item
AR 5319

FO GE **LEITZER PURWIN-SCHAAP**
PM Genealogies; photos; letters of Purwin
and Weil families; large photo of
Liederkranz Society, New York
3 items
AR 5268

PM **H. LEMLE**
Rabbi
Letter from Stefan Zweig (ca. 1940);
bill for celebration of Sukkoth in
Hechingen (1849)
2 items
AR 1928

PM **LEMOS FAMILY**
Report about Portuguese Jews of
Hamburg (1963)
1 item
AR 3330

GE **LENEL FAMILY**
Family trees of Richard Lenel
(Mannheim, 1938); genealogies since
1500
4 items
AR 3164

PM **ARTHUR LENKE**
Swedish passport for Mrs. Arthur
Lenke, issued in Budapest, 1944
1 item
AR 499

PM **ERNST LENS**
4 volumes of manuscripts:
"Physicians Talk about Life and
Death"; German and English
biographical notes on Popper;
Lynkens Papers
1 foot
AR 5133

PM **LEO LEOPOLD**
Travelling papers for apprentice
bookbinder Leo Leopold (1822)
1 item
AR 3619

PM **SABINE LEPSIUS**
1864–1942
Autograph
1 item
AR 731

PM SM **MAYER LERNER**
Rabbi, 1857–1930
Sermons (1913, 1916); obituaries;
article
6 items
AR 4271

PM SM **ADOLF LESCHNITZER**
Educator, 1898–1980
Various articles; background of
modern antisemitism, history of
German-Jewish immigration;
obituary
10 items
AR 249

PM **LOTTE LESSER FAMILY**
Tax certificates (1940); birth
certificates and military papers for
Carl Lesser (1847, 1869); certificate of
residence for Margarethe Sophie
Wolff (1940)
8 items
AR 2997

FO GE **LESSING FAMILY**
PM Certificates for Baruch Leiser Lessing
(1814, 1816, 1824, 1841); letters of
Berlin Jewish community (1939)
about Lessing family; Jewish identity
card (1939); photos (1864, 1918);
notes about family tree
23 items
AR 2019

FO SM **FRED W. LESSING**
Photo; clipping
3 items
AR 2235

SM **GOTTHOLD EPHRAIM LESSING**
1729–1781
Newspaper clipping (1963)
1 item
AR 1995

PM SM **THEODOR LESSING**
Philosopher, 1872–1933
Letters; articles; unpublished essays
24 items
AR 980

FO = Photos · GE = Genealogical Material · PM = Primary Material · SM = Secondary Material

PM **MAX (MEIR) LETTERIS**
1804–1831
Autograph (1858)
1 item
AR 1514

PM **ERNST LEUBUSCHER**
Speech at Bar Mitzvah (1880)
1 item
AR 3652

PM **ARON HEINEMANN LEVI**
1675–1736
Essay on Levi's descendants
1 item
AR 4130

GE **LEVI-BERLINGER-ELLINGER**
Family trees (1300–1934)
2 items
AR 1284

PM **ERNST LEVI FAMILY**
Travel papers for Salomon Levi
(Neustadt/Bavaria, 1838)
1 item
AR 1996

GE PM **LEVI FAMILY, GRIESHEIM**
Master's certificate as butcher (1858);
certificates; family trees of the family
of Herz Levi (18th–20th cent.)
4 items
AR 48

PM **HENRIETTE LEVI**
Album containing letters
1 item
AR 3669

PM SM **HERMANN LEVI**
Conductor, 1839–1900
Newspaper clipping (1963);
autographs
3 items
AR 2119, AR 2468

FO PM **JOSEPH LEVI**
Rabbi
Documents of Jewish communities of
Krefeld and Cleve; stories of various
other rabbis; photos
45 items
AR 3251

SM **JULIUS WALTER LEVI**
Physician
Articles
2 items
AR 7255

GE **SAMUEL ALEXANDER LEVI**
Family tree for Levi, Dann, Schiff,
and Mayer families since 1627
1 item
AR 3913

PM **JULIUS LEVIN**
Author, maker of stringed
instruments, 1862–1935
Manuscript about life of Julius Levin
1 item
AR 3298

PM **JULO LEVIN**
Painter, 1901–1943
Exhibition catalogues (1967, 1979)
1 item
AR 3383

FO **MEYER LEVIN**
American author, 1905–
Photo
1 item
AR 2725

PM **MORITZ LEVIN**
Rabbi, 1843–1914
Honorary certificates; notes by Levin
7 items
AR 2632

SM **BILL LEVINGER**
Article about geological trip to
Guatemala
1 item
AR 4320

FO **CHARLOTTE LEVINGER**
Photo album
3 items
AR 1270

PM **LEVINSOHN FAMILY**
Marriage contract Loevinsohn-
Samter (1853); related marriage
documents; certificate for master
exam for tailoring (1861); school
certificate (1866)

FO = Photos · GE = Genealogical Material · PM = Primary Material · SM = Secondary Material

6 items
AR 1632

PM ERMANNO LEVINSON
Certificate of voting register in Italy
1 item
AR 5186

FO GE FRIEDLAND LEVINSTEIN FAMILY
SM Family tree since 1772; photo of portrait for Levin Jacob Levinstein; article on Patents Act (1908)
4 items
AR 2193

SM HERBERT LEVINSTEIN
1878–1956
Obituary
1 item
AR 2280

GE AARON MOSES LEVY
Family tree for Levy family of Zachau
1 item
AR 5209

FO EMIL NATAN LEVY
Rabbi, 1879–1953
Photo
1 item
AR 792

PM SM GERARDO LEVY
Theater director, 1928–
Theater programs; reviews; letter
9 items
AR 3706

PM HANS LEVY
Lawyer
Permission to practice law before supreme court in Hamm and Essen (1932–1933); exclusion under Nazi legislation
15 items
AR 3467

FO PM MATTHIAS LEVY
Correspondence (1862); photo; notes; memoranda
6 items
AR 1261

FO PM NATHAN LEVY
1850–1912
105 letters as soldier (1870–1871); photo
106 items
AR 4535

PM RENE LEVY
Report about Levy's activities as artist in Swiss internment camps (1942); pencil drawing showing Rene Levy
2 items
AR 2103

FO PM RUDOLF LEVY
Painter, 1875–1943
Photo; clipping; memoir; exhibition catalogue; autograph
5 items
AR 2726, AR 3036

PM SALOMON WOLF LEVY
Letters (1860, 1871)
2 items
AR 4407

PM ZWI H. LEVY
Eulogy
1 item
AR 5

PM FANNY LEWALD
1811–1889
Correspondence; autographs
17 items
AR 849

PM SM LOUIS LEWANDOWSKI
Composer, 1821–1894
Program; clipping
2 items
AR 283

GE PM MANFRED LEWANDOWSKI
SM Cantor, 1895–
Family tree; family history; clippings; program notes
17 items
AR 1923

SM SI LEWEN
Book announcement (1957)
1 item
AR 281

FO = Photos · GE = Genealogical Material · PM = Primary Material · SM = Secondary Material

GE PM **LEWENZ FAMILY**
Family tree; family history and
related documents (19th–20th cent.)
22 items
AR 4842

PM **LEWEY FAMILY**
Military service documents (1850's)
2 items
AR 875

PM **ARTHUR LEWIN**
False identity papers from Nazi era
6 items
AR 3574

PM **RABBI LOUIS LEWIN**
Rabbi
Biography
1 item
AR 5205

SM **LUDWIG LEWIN**
Director of Lessing School,
1887–1967
Articles; obituary (1967)
3 items
AR 1803

PM **CARL LEWINSKY FAMILY**
Family papers; documents relating to
award of an Iron Cross (1813)
11 items
AR 3923

PM **JOSEPH LEWINSKY**
1835–1907
Autograph
1 item
AR 1843

SM **RICHARD LEWINSOHN (PSEUD. MORUS)**
1894–1968
Obituaries (1968)
2 items
AR 3370

SM **RICHARD LEWINSOHN**
Physician, 1875–1961
Obituary with photo
1 item
AR 1597

PM **ALBERT LEWKOWITZ**
Author, 1883–1954
Curriculum vitae
1 item
AR 280

PM **ELKAN LEWY**
1831–1912
Circumcision register for
Schildberg/Posen (1866–1906)
2 items
AR 3126

FO **ISRAEL LEWY**
Talmudist, 1841–1917
Photo
1 item
AR 3205

PM SM **KURT LEWY**
Artist, 1898–1963
Clippings; exhibition catalogues
9 items
AR 2320

PM **TONI LEWY**
Manuscript of play entitled *Moses Mendelssohn*
1 item
AR 282

SM **LEXIKON DES JUDENTUMS**
Dictionary of Judaism used for
advertising material (1967)
1 item
AR 3484

PM **ERICH LEYENS**
Documents protesting treatment of
Jewish veterans in Nazi Germany;
autographs
17 items
AR 4868, AR 7020

FO **LIBIN/BOHEMIA; JEWISH COMMUNITY**
Photo of synagogue
1 item
AR 7035

PM SM **ERWIN LICHTENSTEIN**
Lawyer, editor, 1901–
Correspondence; book reviews;
memoirs
5 items
AR 7193

FO = Photos · GE = Genealogical Material · PM = Primary Material · SM = Secondary Material

PM **H. LICHTENSTEIN**
Testimonial
1 item
AR 1691

PM **HEINRICH LICHTHEIM**
Doctoral diploma (Berlin, 1842)
1 item
AR 4140

SM **LEOPOLD LICHTIG**
Rabbi, 1872–1937
Obituary (1931)
1 item
AR 2293

PM **LICHTWITZ FAMILY**
Personal and official documents; correspondence of Jacob Lichtwitz, physician, and Leopold Lichtwitz (late 19th and early 20th cent.); memorabilia, ritual objects
55 items
AR 1704

GE **LIEBENTHAL FAMILY**
Family tree (19th–20th cent.)
1 item
AR 4765

SM **SAUL LIEBERMAN**
Address by Eli Wiesel (1977)
1 item
AR 4426

FO PM **BENJAMIN LIEBERMANN FAMILY**
SM Photo; eulogies; biographies
8 items
AR 3569

FO PM **ARTHUR LIEBERT**
SM Philosopher, 1878–1946
Photo; plaque; obituary
4 items
AR 4313

SM **HANS LIEBESCHUETZ**
Historian, 1893–1978
Articles; obituary
4 items
AR 2139

PM **WILHELM LIEBKNECHT**
1826–1900
Autograph
1 item
AR 778

GE **LIEBMANN FAMILY**
Family history (19th–20th cent.)
1 item
AR 4512

PM **JULIUS ISAAK LIEBMANN**
1863–
Military service documents (1880's)
4 items
AR 4373

FO **OTTO LIEBMANN**
Publisher
Photo (1930)
1 item
AR 2727

PM **GEORGE F. LIEBRECHT**
Family papers (1776–1814)
4 items
AR 284

PM **HEINRICH F. LIEBRECHT**
Play about Theresienstadt
1 item
AR 5215

FO SM **LIEGNITZ; JEWISH COMMUNITY**
Article on history with photo of synagogue
1 item
AR 5049

PM SM **HEINZ LIEPMANN**
Dust jacket from a book by Liepmann; autographs
3 items
AR 1287, AR 2493

GE PM **RENATE LIESSEM-BREINLINGER**
Family trees listing; autobiography of Jules Wertheimer
5 items
AR 5344

GE **H. D. LIFFMAN**
Family tree and history
1 item
AR 5166

SM **DR. LIFSCHITZ**
Bibliography of Hebrew literature published in Central Europe (17th–20th cent.)
1 item
AR 7115

FO = Photos · GE = Genealogical Material · PM = Primary Material · SM = Secondary Material

FO PM **E.M. LILIEN**
Artist, 1874–1925
Portrait photo of Lilien; postcards with reproductions of his sketches; autographs
24 items
AR 1944, AR 3054

GE **SIDNEY LILIENFELD FAMILY**
Family history (19th–20th cent.)
1 item
AR 2870

FO PM **ARTHUR LILIENTHAL**
Lawyer, 1899–1942, general secretary of Reichsverband Deutscher Juden
Doctoral diploma; portrait
2 items
AR 2871

GE **LILIENTHAL FAMILY**
Family tree and history (18th–20th cent.)
1 item
AR 2099

GE **LILIENTHAL FAMILY, KÜSTRIN**
Genealogy from 1786
4 items
AR 4952

FO SM **LEO LILIENTHAL**
Lawyer, 1867–1927
Photo; obituaries
4 items
AR 2069

SM **HIJMAN LIMBURG**
Chemist
Obituary (1955)
1 item
AR 286

GE PM **PAUL LINDAU**
Writer, dramatist, 1839–1919
Family history; family tree (18th–20th cent.); autographs
13 items
AR 6015, AR 547

PM **RUDOLPH LINDAU**
1829–1910
Autograph (1888)
1 item
AR 1970

FO **ANNA LINDE**
Artist
Photo
1 item
AR 537

PM **LINDHEIMER FAMILY**
Family papers (19th cent.)
1 item
AR 1376

PM **LINDHEIMER FAMILY, BAVARIA**
Death certificates (mid 19th cent.); passport (1861)
7 items
AR 4200

GE **LION FAMILY**
Family history and tree (18th–20th cent.)
1 item
AR 4602

FO PM **MAX LION**
Photo; letters (1920's) including two from Bernhard von Buelow
4 items
AR 3236

FO **FRITZ ALBERT LIPMAN**
Biochemist, 1899–
Photo
1 item
AR 3602

PM **PETER LIPMAN-WULF**
Sculptor, 1905–
Curriculum vitae; catalogues and reviews of exhibitions (1960's); clippings; articles
16 items
AR 3270

PM **LIPPE; JEWISH COMMUNITY**
List of Jewish communities
1 item
AR 3452

PM **LIPPERODE; JEWISH COMMUNITY**
Community record book 1846–1939; documents; business contracts; papers of individuals
72 items
AR 3666

FO = Photos · GE = Genealogical Material · PM = Primary Material · SM = Secondary Material

SM **JULIUS LIPPMAN**
Lawyer, 1864–1934
Press clippings
4 items
AR 2786

FO PM **ISRAEL LIPSCHUETZ**
Rabbi in Danzig, 1782–1960
Photo; letter by Sam Echt concerning the photo (1968)
2 items
AR 3384

PM **LIPSTADT FAMILY, ALTONA**
Wedding of Helene Munk: cables and poems, printed 1887
1 item
AR 1499

PM **LISSA; JEWISH COMMUNITY**
Petition to court
1 item
AR 2962

SM **FRITZ LISSAUER**
Composer
Opera score for *Adrian Brouwer*; clipping
4 items
AR 2517

PM **MENO LISSAUER**
Industrialist
Biography
1 item
AR 721

FO **EMANUEL LIST**
Singer
Photo
1 item
AR 3072

SM **LITERARY HISTORY**
Newspaper clipping, "Jewish Influence in German Literature"
1 item
AR 1927

SM **LITERATURE, EMIGRATION 1933–1945**
Newspaper clippings; articles; items from 1979 Heilbronn Exhibition
17 items
AR 981

SM **LITERATURE, GENERAL**
"Golah Index" (April, 1958)
1 item
AR 4763

PM **LITHUANIA-KONIACHOWSKY**
Data on work camp around Silute (in Yiddish)
1 item
AR 5273

SM **HANS LITTEN**
Announcement of lecture by Barbara Distel (1983)
1 item
AR 5112

SM **BERTHOLD LOEB**
1906–1976
Hiding from Gestapo, articles
2 items
AR 7250

GE **LOEB FAMILY, SOBERNHEIM**
Manuscript and family tree (1984, 52 pp.)
1 item
AR 5303

PM **FELIX LOEB**
Letters to papal nuncio in Madrid about transit visas through Spain (1940)
2 items
AR 1930

SM **HERMANN LOEB**
Publisher, 1897–1963
Obituaries
2 items
AR 2100

FO GE PM SM **JAMES LOEB**
Banker, 1867–1933
Curriculum vitae; correspondence; items from exhibition, Munich 1983
5 items
AR 4766

FO **BERT AND GERDA LOEBELL**
Reproduction of three costume photos
1 item
AR 4915

FO = Photos · GE = Genealogical Material · PM = Primary Material · SM = Secondary Material

FO PM **GUSTAV LOEFFLER**
1879–
Photo (1959); letter (1919); correspondence; report on *Verband der Jüdischen Jugendvereine Deutschlands*
3 items
AR 1622

FO PM **MARTIN LOEVINSON**
Lawyer, 1859–1930
Birth certificates; military service certificates; documents on legal career; photo
14 items
AR 3331

SM **MORITZ LOEVINSON**
Physician, 1820–1887
Article by Leonore Meyer (1981) on Loevinson's endowment established in 1887
1 item
AR 5041

GE **ELEASAR LOEW**
Rabbi, 1738–1837
Genealogy
1 item
AR 4845

FO SM **ERNST LOEW**
Clippings on Jewish communities of Ingelheim; photo album of German soldier in World War II (1939–40); photos of Jewish recipients of Iron Cross
5 items
AR 7200

PM **LOEW FAMILY**
Mortgazen Indenture (1659)
1 item
AR 5101

SM **IMMANUEL LOEW**
Book review of *Die Flora der Juden* (1925)
1 item
AR 1873

FO **ISAAK LOEW, EDLER VON HOFMANNSTHAL**
Industrialist; president of Vienna Jewish Community, 1759–1849
Photo
1 item
AR 2771

GE PM **KLAUS G. LOEWALD FAMILY**
Family history and history of Klaus G. and Rosel Loewald; varia
59 items
AR 4960

PM **EGON LOEWE**
1896–
Two volumes of scrapbook containing letters, telegrams, postcards from front (1915–1918)
2 items
AR 3738

FO **HEINRICH LOEWE**
Professor, librarian, 1869–1951
Photo
1 item
AR 791

SM **LUDWIG LOEWE**
Article on Loewe in *American Machinist* magazine (1901)
1 item
AR 5113

PM SM **LOEWENBERG FAMILY**
Correspondence about educational matters (1892–1928); correspondence and articles by Dr. Richard L. Loewenberg; autographs
52 items
AR 867, AR 868

GE **LEVI LOEWENBERG**
Family tree since 1806
1 item
AR 4521

FO **PETER LOEWENBERG**
Historian
Photo
1 item
AR 4947

FO PM **THEODOR LOEWENFELD**
Professor of Roman Law, 1848–1919
Photo, medal (1912)
2 items
AR 1201

PM **LOEWENHAAR FAMILY**
Family documents (1827–1880)
6 items
AR 289

FO = Photos · GE = Genealogical Material · PM = Primary Material · SM = Secondary Material

GE PM **LOEWENSOHN FAMILY**
Personal and official documents
relating mostly to Isidor Loewensohn,
lieutenant and major (1888–1933);
family tree and history since 1794
44 items
AR 2909

PM **ERNA LOEWENSON**
Correspondence with family
members (Tel Aviv and Jerusalem,
1946–1948)
14 items
AR 4874

PM **ARTHUR LOEWENSTAMM**
Rabbi, 1882–
Personal documents; manuscripts
40 items
AR 3132

SM **ARTHUR J. LOEWENSTEIN**
Industrialist
Obituary (1962)
1 item
AR 1804

PM **EGON LOEWENSTEIN**
French contract (1585)
1 item
AR 2125

PM **GRETE LOEWENSTEIN**
Memoirs about German Jews in
Egypt
1 item
AR 5011

PM **HEINZ WERNER LOEWENSTEIN**
Rabbi
Relationship to Karl Fischer expulsion
in 1933; letters about his work with
the *Jüdischer Pfadfinderbund*
3 items
AR 4659

PM **HUGO LOEWENSTEIN**
Rabbi
Permission for trading rights for R.
Salomon Frenckel (Rostock, 1813);
letter to Montefiore; Hebrew prayer
for the deceased
3 items
AR 1245

PM **JULIUS LOEWENSTEIN**
Innkeeper
Transfer of citizenship from Bavaria
to Baden (1895)
1 item
AR 3870

FO GE **KARL LOEWENSTEIN**
PM Photo of synagogue in Aachen;
emigration of Aachen Jews after 1933;
family tree of the Kohlberg family
from 1545; family tree of Bassevi of
Treuenberg including their code of
arms
9 items
AR 2529

FO PM **LEO LOEWENSTEIN**
SM Photos; obituaries; election placard
for Leo Loewenstein (1925); article
9 items
AR 31

SM **STEVEN LOEWENSTEIN**
Article, Jerusalem Post, 1983
"Information about Jewish
Immigration to Washington Heights,
New York"
1 item
AR 5184

GE **LOEWENTHAL FAMILY**
Family history and tree (Ladenburg,
since 1700)
2 items
AR 163

GE **LOEWENTHAL FAMILY,
BUETZOW**
Family history, also of Epstein Family
Lwow (Lemberg) in Hebrew
1 item
AR 7104

GE PM **LOEWENTHAL FAMILY, STETTIN**
Family papers (18th–19th cent.)
36 items
AR 3463

GE PM **LOEWI FAMILY**
Family business; religious documents
(1821–1886); family tree from 1740
21 items
AR 3218

FO = Photos · GE = Genealogical Material · PM = Primary Material · SM = Secondary Material

PM **ALFRED LOEWENGARD**
Architect, 1856–1929
Memorial pamphlet on Loewengard
1 item
AR 2872

FO GE **OTTO LOEWI**
Chemist, Nobel Prize winner,
1873–1961
Photo; notes on family tree
3 items
AR 2975

SM **FRITZ LONDON**
Physicist, 1900–1954
Obituaries
3 items
AR 986

GE **LONNERSTAEDTER FAMILY**
Family tree, Hassfurt a/M, Bavaria,
since 1790
1 item
AR 1629

PM **ALEXANDER LORCH FAMILY**
Lawyer, died 1951
Military service certificate,
replacement for Alexander Lorch of
Bingen and son Salomon Lorch
(1834); curriculum vitae for
Alexander Lorch
2 items
AR 288

GE PM **LORIE FAMILY, FRANKFURT**
Family history
3 items
AR 4869

PM **HIERONYMUS LORM**
Autograph
1 item
AR 1516

GE **LORRAINE; JEWISH COMMUNITY**
Notes on family genealogies (18th
and 19th cent.)
1 item
AR 7096

FO SM **ERNST G. LOWENTHAL**
1904–
Photo of family grave stone,
Luettringhausen, Rhineland (1947);
reviews of Lowenthal's book

Bewährung im Untergang (1965);
articles celebrating 60th, 70th, and
75th birthdays
10 items
AR 982

FO PM **ERNST LUBITSCH**
SM Film director, 1892–1947
Photo (1932); clipping; autographs
4 items
AR 2194, AR 1732

PM **HERMANN LUBLIN FAMILY**
Letter of citizenship; birth certificate
of Hirsch Lublin (born 1837)
2 items
AR 3485

PM **HUGO LUBLINER**
Autographs (1888, 1896)
2 items
AR 1702

FO PM **LEOPOLD LUCAS**
Rabbi, 1872–1943
Photos of Loeb Aron Lucas and
Leopold Lucas; letter from Leo Baeck
to Leopold Lucas 1924;
commemorative document of Glogau
Jewish community
5 items
AR 3673

PM **EMIL LUCKA**
Autograph
1 item
AR 1103

SM **GERTRUD LUCKNER**
Catholic Nazi foe who aided Jews
Newspaper articles (1977)
2 items
AR 4425

PM SM **EMIL LUDWIG**
Author, 1881–1948
Documents of Gestapo, Berlin, about
seizure of Emil Ludwig's property
(1933–1934); obituary; autographs;
general correspondence between
author Ludwig and attorney Tulin
11 items
AR 3441, AR 842, AR 7195

FO PM **LUDWIGSBURG; JEWISH COMMUNITY**
Photo of burning synagogue; list of documents
2 items
AR 3321

FO PM **LUDWIGSHAFEN; JEWISH**
SM **COMMUNITY**
Photo of synagogue; article; list of Jewish inhabitants
4 items
AR 2168

FO **LUEBECK; JEWISH COMMUNITY**
Photo of synagogue
1 item
AR 1226

GE **WALTER LUFT**
Luft family tree since 1775
2 items
AR 1388

SM **GEORGY (GEORG) LUKACS**
Communist Author
Newspaper articles (1961, 1964)
2 items
AR 1661

PM **LUNAU-MARUM FAMILY**
Memories of Nazi Germany; family histories
3 items
AR 5368

PM SM **ERNST LUSTIG**
Records (some confidential); excerpts from books on Jewish community of Gleiwitz early 20th cent.; memoir of Wilhelm Lustig
7 items
AR 7113

PM SM **LUSTIG FAMILY**
Honorary citizenship; membership certificate; clipping
3 items
AR 293

FO PM **FRITZ LUSTIG**
Letters from individuals; photo; letters about emigration to Australia (1939)
6 items
AR 987

FO **LEO LUSTIG**
Kommerzienrat
Photo
1 item
AR 1630

PM **MARTIN LUTHER**
Praise of Luther by rabbis; copy of letter to Count of Mansfeld
2 items
AR 5249

FO PM **ROSA LUXEMBURG**
SM Revolutionary, 1870–1919
Articles; photos (one dated 1914); police reports about Rosa Luxemburg 1914–1918
12 items
AR 1708

PM SM **HERMANN MAAS**
Protestant clergyman, 1877–1970
Letters; clippings concerning pro Jewish activities in the Third Reich
10 items
AR 297

FO PM **ERNEST MAASS**
Photos of buildings; documents of art work dealing with Jews of medieval Spain
19 items
AR 4017

PM **HEINRICH MACHOL**
Lawyer, 1871–1930
Correspondence on legislative draft concerning affairs of German-Jewish communities, 1900–1903
6 items
AR 4201

FO **HANS ROGER MADOL**
Photos
3 items
AR 2296

FO PM **MAERKISCH-FRIEDLAND (NOW**
SM **MIROSLAWIEC, POLAND);**
JEWISH COMMUNITY
Article; photos; documents (18th cent.)
5 items
AR 4260

FO PM **MAGDEBURG; JEWISH**
SM **COMMUNITY**
Photo of synagogue; deed; articles
6 items
AR 1626

SM **JUDAH MAGNES**
Rabbi, 1877–1948
Newspaper article
1 item
AR 4450

GE **BERNHARD MAGNUS**
Family tree (1880–1950)
1 item
AR 1006

FO PM **EDUARD MAGNUS**
Painter, 1799–1872
Photos (including album of works of family members); list of artistic works; personal and official documents; family history
17 items
AR 3948

FO **GOTTLIEB MAGNUS**
Marine engineer, 1883–1942
Photo
2 items
AR 3929

PM SM **ADOLF MAGNUS-LEVY**
Physician, professor of physiology (1865–1955)
Curriculum vitae; obituary
2 items
AR 46

FO PM **GUSTAV MAHLER**
SM Composer, conductor, 1860–1911
Photos; clippings; autograph
7 items
AR 1662, AR 1716

SM **HANS MAIER**
Bibliography
1 item
AR 2952

GE **JOSEPH VON MAIER**
Rabbi, 1797–1873
Genealogy
2 items
AR 5086

FO SM **PAULINE MAIER**
Social worker, 1887–1942
Photos; articles
9 items
AR 3803

FO GE **ROSALIE MAIER**
PM 1888–
Personal and official documents of family members; family history; genealogical tables since 1650; photos; cemetery photos
36 items
AR 786

PM **MAILERT FAMILY**
Correspondence between Carl Lucius Mailert and his brother, August Mailert, in Philadelphia (1835–1838)
16 items
AR 298

FO PM **SALOMON MAIMON**
Philosopher, 1754–1800
Photo of a portrait; biography
2 items
AR 3206

SM **MAIMONIDES**
Medical aphorisms, magazine article (1964)
1 item
AR 2611

GE SM **ISAAC M. MAINZ**
Obituary; family history (19th–20th cent.)
2 items
AR 1817

PM SM **MAINZ; JEWISH COMMUNITY**
Correspondence; flyer protesting religious reforms 1851; clippings, articles
14 items
AR 258

GE PM **MARTIN MAINZER**
Genealogy of Marx-Cohn family; documents of Jewish community in Halle/Saale (microfilm); memoirs of Adolf Bernhard Marx (1965)
3 items
AR 5265

FO = Photos · GE = Genealogical Material · PM = Primary Material · SM = Secondary Material

FO PM **MAX MAINZER**
SM Physician, 1872–1952
Correspondence; photo; press
clippings; obituaries
8 items
AR 173

PM **CARL MAISON**
Representative in State Diet,
1840–1898
Letter of Bavarian Ministry of State
to F. S. Perles in Israel (1981)
1 item
AR 5010

GE **HANS LEONHARD MAJER**
Family history and tree since 1796
2 items
AR 101

FO PM **HERMANN MAKOWER**
Photo; letter; pamphlet (1870's)
4 items
AR 3065

SM **JOSEF MAKOWSKI**
Polish authors tell of experiences in
Third Reich at end of war
(newspaper clipping)
1 item
AR 1805

PM **ABRAHAM MALACHOWSKI**
Director of Jewish Orphanage,
Berlin, 1811–1895
Family correspondence and other
documents
35 items
AR 4937

FO GE **MAMROTH FAMILY**
Family tree (1873–1930); portrait
2 items
AR 112

PM **MANASSE DAILY RECORD**
Business record
1 item
AR 5137

GE PM **DAVID MANDELBAUM**
Family history (19th and 20th cent.)
4 items
AR 4172

SM **ERIC MANDELL**
Essay; rare book catalogue
2 items
AR 4408

PM **MAX MANDERS**
Poems
1 item
AR 2053

SM **ALFRED MANES**
Insurance specialist, 1878–1963
Obituary (1963)
1 item
AR 2321

SM **URSULA VON MANGOLDT**
Book review (1963)
1 item
AR 2322

FO PM **JOHANNA MANHEIMER**
1874–1941
Memoirs; family dates; photocopies
of photos
10 items
AR 5008

GE PM **MANKIEWITZ FAMILY**
Official documents; family tree (19th
cent.)
24 items
AR 722

PM **FRANZISCA MANN**
Writer, 1859–
Family festivities
2 items
AR 2980

SM **GOLO MANN**
Newspaper clipping and articles
about antisemitisim in *Argentinisches
Tageblatt*
3 items
AR 1601

FO PM **JULIUS MANN**
SM Lawyer, 1853–1931
Eulogies; photo; bound handwritten
manuscripts on legal matters
4 items
AR 1290, AR 7028

FO = Photos · GE = Genealogical Material · PM = Primary Material · SM = Secondary Material

SM **KARL FRITZ MANN**
Economist, 1894–1979
Obituary (1979)
1 item
AR 4811

PM **LUDWIG MANN**
Memoirs of Gurs concentration camp
2 items
AR 1359

PM SM **THOMAS MANN**
Author, 1875–1955
Essays; letters; clippings related to Mann's 1921 essay "Zur Jüdischen Frage"
40 items
AR 536

PM **MANNABERG-MEITNER FAMILY, MORAVIA**
Documents; business papers; correspondence
12 items
AR 5062

PM SM **HANS MANNHEIM**
Physician, 1901–1972
Clippings; letters; obituary
5 items
AR 3943

FO PM **MANNHEIM; JEWISH COMMUNITY**
Photos; histories of the community; clippings; memorial book (1711–1938); marriage contracts (1776, 1804); list of protected Jews and widows (18th cent.)
82 items
AR 270

PM **MANNHEIM (JEWISH TEACHING INSTITUTE)**
Plans
2 items
AR 4223

PM **KARL MANNHEIM**
Sociologist, 1893–1947
Autograph
1 item
AR 1148

FO **ISAAK NOAH MANNHEIMER**
Rabbi, 1793–1865
Photo with notes
1 item
AR 2983

PM **MORITZ MANNHEIMER**
Letters (1861)
3 items
AR 294

PM **V. MANNHEIMER**
Brochure
1 item
AR 2494

SM **ROSYLN MANOWITZ**
Born 1942, New York
Newspaper article, review, "Unsere Zweite Generation; Mehr als Gewehre & Galgen" (*Aufbau*, 1978)
1 item
AR 4660

PM **HERBERT JOSEPH MANSBACH**
Dentist, 1912–
Correspondence dealing with Mansbach's residence in Switzerland (1938–1942), including correspondence with German and American consulates and Jewish organizations in America
50 items
AR 7073

FO **RAPHAEL MANTEL**
Cantor, Ingenheim/Pal.
Photos of cantor and of wife
2 items
AR 2780

FO PM **MARBURG; JEWISH COMMUNITY**
SM Photo of synagogue; antisemitic postcard 1897; clippings; articles
6 items
AR 2628

GE SM **MARC FAMILY, AROLSEN**
Genealogical tables and family history since 1967; article on family
7 items
AR 3014

PM **PAUL MARC**
Biography
1 item
AR 3170

FO = Photos · GE = Genealogical Material · PM = Primary Material · SM = Secondary Material

FO PM **MARCK FAMILY**
Letter; photos; family history
(18th–20th cent.)
6 items
AR 1786

FO **AHRON MARCUS**
Philosopher, 1843–1916
Photo
1 item
AR 3207

PM **ERNESTINE AND HERMANN MARCUS**
Photocopy of engagement correspondence (1867)
1 item
AR 5308

FO PM **MARCUS FAMILY, GILGENBURG**
Correspondence; photos; short memoirs
5 items
AR 3807

SM **LOUIS MARCUS**
Historian, 1798–1843
Obituary; bibliography
2 items
AR 800

FO PM **MAX MARCUS FAMILY**
Family documents (19th cent.);
Haggadah from Fuerth (18th cent.);
photos
13 items
AR 1251

PM **THEODOR MARCUS**
Memoirs
3 items
AR 2357

FO PM **WILHELM MARCUS**
SM Social worker, 1883–1954
Articles on Marcus and his role on executive committee of Jewish community in Berlin; photos; correspondence including letters to and from the German-Jewish Club, New York (1938–1940)
27 items
AR 20

PM **WOLFF MARCUS**
Membership certificate
1 item
AR 3497

PM **ERICH MARCUSE**
Photo certificate (1960)
1 item
AR 2101

FO **HERBERT MARCUSE**
Philosopher, 1898–1979
Photos
3 items
AR 3063

SM **LUDWIG MARCUSE**
Writer
Newspaper articles
7 items
AR 1664

GE PM **MARGOLIS-ARONOFF FAMILY**
Jeremy U. Newman family tree; other family histories
3 items
AR 4945

GE **MARGOLIUS FAMILY**
Family tree and additions
2 items
AR 5081

FO PM **HANS MARGOLIUS**
SM Librarian, philosopher, 1902–
Essays; clippings; short memoirs; articles on Albert Schweitzer
13 items
AR 716

SM **PETER MARK**
Physicist, 1931–1979
Obituary
1 item
AR 4813

PM **ISAAC MARKOWITSCH**
Hebrew and Yiddish letter
1 item
AR 7118

PM **MARKS-HAINDORFSCHE STIFTUNG**
Foundation letter to Leo Baeck Institute
1 item
AR 3848

SM **SIMON MARKS**
Politician, Zionist, 1888–1964
Obituaries
2 items
AR 2487

FO = Photos · GE = Genealogical Material · PM = Primary Material · SM = Secondary Material

PM **SCHILLER MARMOREK**
Manuscript
1 item
AR 2827

PM **MAROLDSWEISACH; JEWISH COMMUNITY**
Typescript
1 item
AR 398

FO **ALFRED MARUM**
Photo history of Marum textile factory (1860)
2 items
AR 1303

PM **ABRAHAM MARX**
Letter (1797)
1 item
AR 4689

FO PM **ALBERT MARX FAMILY**
Family documents; photos; prayer book; field Haggadah; parchment roll containing prayer on accession of new moon (18th cent.)
77 items
AR 2554

PM **HUGO MARX**
Letter
1 item
AR 3747

PM **JULIUS MARX**
Correspondence concerning Marx's book *Kriegstagebuch eines Juden*
2 items
AR 2519

SM **KARL MARX**
Editor, 1897–1966
Obituary
1 item
AR 3708

SM **KARL MARX**
Revolutionary, 1818–1883
Portraits; clippings; bibliography of items in the Tamiment Institute Library, New York
10 items
AR 202

FO **LEOPOLD MARX**
Writer, 1889–
Photo
1 item
AR 4727

SM **WERNER MARX**
Philosopher, 1910–
Newspaper clippings and articles, mostly about receiving Ruhr Prize in 1966
7 items
AR 2857

PM SM **AUGUST MASCHEL & CO.**
Correspondence; clippings
7 items
AR 4018

PM SM **FRITZI MASSARY**
Actress, 1882–1969
Clippings; photos; copy of a television film about her life; autograph
6 items
AR 1564, AR 3113

PM **MASSBACH; JEWISH COMMUNITY**
Official record of debt (1721–1777)
1 item
AR 2659

PM **PERCY MATENKO**
Material concerning research on Rahel Varnhagen
5 items
AR 7047

PM SM **ADOLF MATZNER**
Leather expert
Article on making parchment from animal skins; correspondence
2 items
AR 3615

PM **CHERI MAURICE**
1805–1896
Autograph
1 item
AR 1959

PM **HELENE MAUTNER**
Correspondence; clippings; testament (19th and 20th cent.)
20 items
AR 1246

FO = Photos · GE = Genealogical Material · PM = Primary Material · SM = Secondary Material

GE **HERBERT MAUTNER**
1923–
Gallinger, Schwab, Mautner, and
Wolff family trees (1800–1976)
1 item
AR 4715

GE **MAY FAMILY**
Family tree (18th–20th cent.)
1 item
AR 1389

SM **HENRIETTE MAY**
Eulogy
1 item
AR 295

SM **JAMES MAY**
Press releases; exhibition catalogue
Vienna: Workshop 1982
2 items
AR 5110

PM SM **MAX MAY**
Lawyer
Curriculum vitae; personal
documents; articles; correspondence
25 items
AR 4903

PM **OSCAR MAY**
Diploma
1 item
AR 323

PM SM **RICHARD MAY**
Journalist, 1886–1966
Clippings; personal papers
14 items
AR 1997

FO PM **SIMON MAY FAMILY, HAMBURG**
Personal and official documents (early
and mid–19th cent.); photos (19th
cent.); correspondence (mid–19th
cent.); report on May family
22 items
AR 159, AR 161

PM **WILL MAY**
1885–
Personal documents of Will May
including master's certificate (1912);
military service anmd veteran papers
from World War I (1905–1944)
11 items
AR 49

SM **IGNAZ MAYBAUM**
Rabbi
Articles; book review
3 items
AR 1880

GE PM **MAYER FAMILY, BRATISLAVA
AND VIENNA**
Family tree (18th–20th cent.); letter
2 items
AR 370

PM **MAYER FAMILY, FREIBURG**
Vital statistics and registration;
property; military service documents;
letters; clippings
32 items
AR 2007

PM SM **MAYER FAMILY,
WUERTTEMBERG**
Letters (1792, 1812); copies of
newspapers (1816–1824)
11 items
AR 1998

GE **FRED L. MAYER FAMILY**
Family tree (16th–20th cent.)
1 item
AR 3927

PM SM **FRITZ MAYER**
1907–1977
Biography; essay by Fritz Mayer
2 items
AR 4607

PM **JESSY MAYER**
1894–1934
Correspondence
2 items
AR 2998

GE **JONAS MAYER**
Family history (17th–20th cent.)
1 item
AR 1294

PM SM **JULIUS MAYER**
Clippings; program; letter; articles
(Nazi period)
10 items
AR 3152

FO = Photos · GE = Genealogical Material · PM = Primary Material · SM = Secondary Material

PM SM **PAUL MAYER**
Author
Clipping; bibliography; curriculum vitae; letters
11 items
AR 3989

SM **PETER MAYER**
Publisher
Article, *Aufbau* (1970)
1 item
AR 3718

PM SM **SAMUEL WOLF MAYER**
Doctoral diploma; articles
3 items
AR 4202

GE **MECKAUER FAMILY**
Family tree (19th–20th cent.)
2 items
AR 1939

PM **WALTER MECKAUER**
Autographs (1952, 1983)
2 items
AR 1844

PM SM **GEORG MECKLENBURG**
Reports; clippings; correspondence on Zionist activities in Saxony
14 items
AR 1007

PM **JACOB ZWI MECKLENBURG**
Essay on Rabbi Mecklenburg by Isidor Werczberger
1 item
AR 7057

PM **MECKLENBURG; JEWISH COMMUNITY**
List of Jewish communities
1 item
AR 3453

PM **MEHLINGEN; JEWISH COMMUNITY**
Typescript; registration of names of Jews of Mehlingen (1808)
2 items
AR 4639

FO PM **WALTER MEHRING**
SM Writer, 1896–
Photo; clipping; program
3 items
AR 2195

SM **ELSE MEIDNER**
Clipping; exhibition programs
5 items
AR 2511

FO PM **LUDWIG MEIDNER**
SM Painter, 1884–1966
Letter; clipping; photos, self-portrait; autographs
9 items
AR 2323, AR 1863

PM **JOSEF MEINDL**
Family documents (1857–1935)
8 items
AR 1230

SM **MEINERSHAGEN; JEWISH COMMUNITY**
Article and deportation list
1 item
AR 5208

PM **CARL MEINHARD**
1875–
Letter
1 item
AR 1971

FO PM **LISE MEITNER**
SM Physicist, 1878–1968
Photos; obituaries; family documents (18th–19th cent.); articles
14 items
AR 2729, AR 2729a

PM **MICHAEL MELAMID**
Biography; essay on petroleum concern
2 items
AR 220

FO PM **MARCUS L. MELCHIOR**
Rabbi, 1897–
Photo; biographical notice
2 items
AR 2781

FO **MELLRICHSTADT; JEWISH COMMUNITY**
Photo of synagogue
1 item
AR 5072

PM **MEMEL; JEWISH COMMUNITY**
Fliers; community reports
4 items
AR 3167

FO = Photos · GE = Genealogical Material · PM = Primary Material · SM = Secondary Material

FO **MEMMINGEN; JEWISH COMMUNITY**
Photo of synagogue
2 items
AR 2157

PM SM **MEMORIAL FOUNDATION FOR JEWISH CULTURE**
Articles on Foundation (1960's and 1970's); confidential reports involving allocations of funds (1973–1974); studies of various programs and functions (1960's and 1970's)
10 items
AR 2421

PM **KAETHE MENDE**
Social worker
Reminiscences of Mende written by her professor, Walter Friedlander (1964)
2 items
AR 2720

SM **EMANUEL MENDEL**
Physician, 1839–1907
Obituary (1907)
1 item
AR 2603

PM **FRITZ MENDEL**
Scrapbook
1 item
AR 1649

FO SM **ERICH MENDELSOHN**
Architect, 1887–1953
Photos; clippings
2 items
AR 1008

PM **SALOMON MENDELSOHN**
Instructor in gymnastics, 1813–1892
Biographical notice
1 item
AR 3893

PM **ERNST VON MENDELSSOHN-BARTHOLDY**
Orders from various crowned heads in Europe
3 items
AR 43

PM **ELEONORE MENDELSSOHN**
Actress
Letter (1928)
1 item
AR 2953

FO SM **MENDEN; JEWISH COMMUNITY**
Clipping; photo
4 items
AR 4176

FO PM **ANTON RAPHAEL MENGS**
Painter, 1728–1779
Photos; self-portrait
3 items
AR 1988

PM **JUERGEN MENNINGEN**
List of private collection about "Konservative Revolution" in Germany, 1918–1932
2 items
AR 4628

SM **YEHUDI MENUHIN**
Violinist, 1916–
Clippings; concert program
2 items
AR 3503

FO **MERCHINGEN; JEWISH COMMUNITY**
Photos of synagogue and memorial stone
8 items
AR 4073

PM **MERGENTHEIM; JEWISH COMMUNITY**
Excerpts from community minute book (19th cent.)
1 item
AR 4251

FO **WILHELM MERTON**
Active in Metal Industry, 1848–1916
Photo
1 item
AR 1202

GE **MERZBACHER FAMILY**
Family tree (18th–19th cent.)
2 items
AR 889

FO = Photos · GE = Genealogical Material · PM = Primary Material · SM = Secondary Material

SM **LEO MERZBACHER**
Rabbi
Newspaper article (1958)
1 item
AR 236

PM SM **METZ; JEWISH COMMUNITY**
Decree (19th cent.); broadside of *Wandering Jew* with poem; "La Dette Brancas" (ca. 1791); receipts in Hebrew (18th cent.)
4 items
AR 3220, AR 2064

PM **JACOB METZGER**
Business license (1813)
1 item
AR 1442

PM **LUISE METZGER**
Letters re Hedwig Strauss Eppstein; Mia Neter report card from Städtische Frauenschule, Mannheim
4 items
AR 5352

PM **IGNATZ MEUMANN**
Receipt; notice of aryanization of Ignatz Meumann's business (1938)
2 items
AR 1631

FO PM **ALEX MEYER**
SM Professor of law, aviator, born 1879
Photo; bibliography; list of awards; bibliographical notices
5 items
AR 3772

PM **ALFRED RICHARD MEYER**
1882–1956
List of letters to him
1 item
AR 1866

GE **EMIL LOUIS MEYER FAMILY, HANOVER**
Genealogy of this and related families
2 items
AR 5052

GE **EPHRAIM MEYER FAMILY**
Family tree, related documents (18th, 19th cent.)
9 items
AR 3117

FO PM **MEYER FAMILY; BARDEWISCH, OLDENBURG**
Photos; portraits; family estate
8 items
AR 5073

GE **MEYER FAMILY; BEROLSHEIN**
Family history (20th cent.)
1 item
AR 3765

PM **FELIX MEYER**
Letter concerning Theresienstadt
1 item
AR 1437

PM **FRIEDRICH MEYER**
Letter
1 item
AR 3719

PM **GEORG MEYER**
Biographical notices; letters from his wife
3 items
AR 506

FO **GERALD MEYER**
Lawyer
Photo
1 item
AR 3147

FO **HANS H. MEYER**
Pharmacologist
Photo
1 item
AR 2571

PM **HEINRICH MEYER**
Proclamations (18th cent.); letter of protection from Elector of Palatinate (1745); stock cerificates (1837)
9 items
AR 3634

FO **J. MEYER**
Rabbi
Portrait (ca. 1800)
1 item
AR 3223

PM SM **JOEL WOLF MEYER**
Clippings; biographical notices
2 items
AR 3523

FO = Photos · GE = Genealogical Material · PM = Primary Material · SM = Secondary Material

PM SM **KARL MEYER**
List of publications; memorandum; family documents; letters
15 items
AR 1009

SM **MICHAEL A. MEYER**
Book review of Meyer's *The Origin of the Modern Jew*
1 item
AR 3601

FO PM **SIGMUND MEYER**
Photos of portraits (late 18th–19th cent.); biography
6 items
AR 204

PM **SUSANNE MEYER FAMILY**
Family papers; army papers; Hebrew marriage contract; Yiddish poetry (19th cent.)
7 items
AR 1338

GE **MEYER-SUST FAMILY**
Family history (1657–1882)
1 item
AR 3165

SM **WOLFGANG MEYER-UDEWALD**
1893–1964
Eulogy
1 item
AR 3817

FO PM **GIACOMO MEYERBEER**
SM Composer, 1791–1864
Family trees and histories since 1677; photos (19th cent.); articles on Meyerbeer (1960's); autographs
42 items
AR 371, AR 851

FO PM **MAX MEYERFELD**
Family correspondence; business records; photos and reports of Jewish community Bielefeld
83 items
AR 4920

PM **PAUL MEYERHEIM**
1842–1915
Autographs
3 items
AR 1733

GE **MEYERHOF FAMILY**
Extensive family trees since 1742
2 items
AR 801

PM **ISRAEL MEYERHOF**
Family letters (1839–1840)
5 items
AR 162

FO PM **OTTO MEYERHOF**
Physiologist, 1884–1951
Photos; essay; letter
6 items
AR 1449

FO PM **EMILE MEYERSON**
Philosopher, 1859–1933
Photo; biography
2 items
AR 4050

PM **GUSTAV MEYRINK**
Autographs
3 items
AR 735

GE PM **JACOB MICHAEL**
SM Family history and documents; clippings
13 items
AR 2467

PM **DOLF MICHAELIS**
Banker, author, economist, artist, 1906–1983
Transcript of memorial meeting
1 item
AR 5266

PM **EVA MICHAELIS**
Social worker
Eva Michaelis' life story by Dolf Michaelis
1 item
AR 4870

GE PM **MICHAELIS FAMILY**
Family tree (17th–19th cent.); letter of citizenship (1844)
2 items
AR 2120

FO = Photos · GE = Genealogical Material · PM = Primary Material · SM = Secondary Material

PM **LEONOR MICHAELIS**
Physician, 1875–1949
Biography; invitation to Biochemical Society symposium (Weimar, 1980)
3 items
AR 4899

FO **ALBERT ABRAHAM MICHELSON**
Physicist, 1852–1931
Photo
1 item
AR 2982

GE PM **ERIC MIDAS FAMILY**
Family history (19th cent.); related documents
4 items
AR 3385

FO **MIDDLEMANN FAMILY**
Photos of 19th cent. portraits
1 item
AR 4777

PM **WALTER MIDENER**
Sculptor, 1912–
Exhibition catalogue (1976)
1 item
AR 4699

SM **MARTHA MIERENDORFF**
Sociologist
Articles on German theater in exile, "Gleichschaltung of German theater"
4 items
AR 1333

PM SM **FRIEDRICH MILCH**
Banker, 1870–1966
Biography; eulogy
2 items
AR 3085

FO **MILTENBERG; JEWISH COMMUNITY**
Photo of synagogue
1 item
AR 3900

SM **SYBIL MILTON**
Archivist
Articles on German-Jewish genealogical research, "Art of the Holocaust," the Stroop Report re: Warsaw Ghetto Destruction (in English), "Germany: Forty Years After"
4 items
AR 4767

SM **GEORG MINDEN**
Civil servant, 1850–1928
Obituary (1928)
1 item
AR 1881

FO **MINSK; JEWISH COMMUNITY**
Photo of Choral Synagogue
1 item
AR 7035

PM SM **CARL MISCH**
Journalist, historian, 1896–1965
Clippings; biographical material
9 items
AR 7214

FO PM **ADELE VON MISES**
Photo; notices concerning family
2 items
AR 4661

SM **MITTEILUNGSBLATT**
German-Jewish Refugee Journal, Tel Aviv; listings of data like birthdays, obituaries, etc. (1933–1980, 100 pp.)
1 item
AR 5082

SM **DIE MITTWOCHSGESELLSCHAFT**
Newspaper article, "The Sixteen Upright Germans" (*Welt am Sonntag*, 1982)
1 item
AR 5154

GE SM **MODEL FAMILY**
Family tree (18th–20th cent.); clippings
8 items
AR 93

FO **ALEXANDER MOISSI**
Actor, 1880–1935
Photo (1928)
1 item
AR 4343

FO = Photos · GE = Genealogical Material · PM = Primary Material · SM = Secondary Material

GE **MOLL FAMILY**
Family tree since 1516, additional
family tree since 1570
2 items
AR 3114

PM **WALTER VON MOLO**
Autographs
2 items
AR 2641

FO PM **ALFRED MOMBERT**
SM Poet, 1872–1942
Photo; clippings; autographs
5 items
AR 2968, AR 1142

PM **THEODOR MOMMSEN**
1817–1903
Autograph
1 item
AR 802

PM **CLAUDE G. MONTEFIORE**
1859–1939
Autographs
5 items
AR 1699

PM **MOSES MONTEFIORE**
Banker, 1784–1885
Leather briefcase; autograph
2 items
AR 4673, AR 2995

PM **RENATO MONTI (FORMERLY LEO BALAGUR)**
Actor, cantor, 1898–1979
Correspondence (1936); attestation
for employment; theater
announcements
4 items
AR 5084

GE PM **MOOS-MOORE FAMILY**
Personal documents since 19th cent.;
manuscripts including a two-volume
unpublished book on Jewish
community of Konstanz (1863–1940);
correspondence; clippings in reference
to Konstanz Jewish community
(1970's); family genealogy
12 items
AR 3127

FO PM **SALOMON MOOS**
Physician, professor of medicine,
1831–1924
Photo; biographical notices
4 items
AR 2514

PM **KONRAD MORGAN**
1909–
Proceedings of Military Government
Court (1946–1948), testimony by
Morgan against Koch
1 item
AR 5317

PM **PAUL MORGAN**
1886–1944
Autograph
1 item
AR 1972

FO SM **JULIUS MORGENROTH**
Bacteriologist, 1871–1924
Photo; obituaries
20 items
AR 2499

SM **DAVID MORGENSTERN**
Politician
Article on his parliamentary activities
with photocopy of photo (1851)
1 item
AR 2102

SM **LINA MORGENSTERN**
Clippings
4 items
AR 718

FO GE **MORGENTHAU FAMILY**
PM Diary of Lazarus Morgenthau (1842);
genealogy of Moses Morgenthau and
Brunhilda Lebrecht (1773–1968);
photos; family documents
40 items
AR 4980

SM **HANS MORGENTHAU**
Historian
Article, *Aufbau* (1975)
1 item
AR 4198

FO **SIGMUND MORGENTHAU**
Merchant, 1853–1948
Photos
5 items
AR 4288

FO = Photos · GE = Genealogical Material · PM = Primary Material · SM = Secondary Material

PM **SALOMON MORITZ**
Marriage license (1907)
2 items
AR 4131

GE **MORPURGO FAMILY**
Family tree (18th–20th cent.)
2 items
AR 1778

FO PM **MOSBACH; JEWISH COMMUNITY**
SM Photos; typescript; map
9 items
AR 2481

SM **BERNHARD MOSBERG**
Physician, 1871–1944
Newspaper articles
3 items
AR 4279

PM **IGNAZ MOSCHELES**
Pianist, 1794–1870
Lithograph; autographs
7 items
AR 396, AR 843

PM **JULIUS MOSEN**
Author, 1803–1867
Autograph
1 item
AR 2516

FO PM **SALOMON HERMANN VON MOSENTHAL**
Author, 1821–1877
Photo; autograph
2 items
AR 2731, AR 1517

PM **ALICE MOSER**
Letters (1940–1941)
14 items
AR 4033

FO SM **MOSES MOSER**
Banker, 1796–1838
Photo; clipping on Moser's friendship with Heinrich Heine
2 items
AR 1010

PM **ABRAHAM MOSES**
Letter of protection (Hanover, 1806)
1 item
AR 4366

FO PM **BERTHOLD MOSES**
Essays on family history; documents concerning Jewish youth movement in Germany (1919–1934); photo of synagogue in Braunschweig
10 items
AR 1342

PM SM **JULIUS MOSES**
Physician, Social Democratic politician, head of Mannheim Synagogue Council, 1868–1942
Bibliography; biographical notices; introduction to Julius Moses' memoirs (written 1940); article, "Politics of Social Hygiene in Germany, 1868–1942"; autographs
8 items
AR 3386, AR 1011

PM **LIEBMANN MOSES**
Testament (1899)
1 item
AR 3433

GE **SALOMON ISAAC MOSES**
1768–1837
Family tree (18th–20th cent.); notes
3 items
AR 4101

FO SM **SIEGFRIED MOSES**
Zionist, President of Leo Baeck Institute 1956–1974; 1887–1974
Clippings; obituaries; photo
25 items
AR 305

SM **ERNST MOSEVIUS**
Social worker
Articles; essay entitled "25 Jahre B'nai Brith in Deutschland 1882–1937"
3 items
AR 300

FO PM **ALBERT MOSSE**
SM Letters; essays by Professor Sakai concening Albert Mosse's role in drafting the Meiji Constitution, Japan; photo
32 items
AR 7124, AR 5367

FO = Photos · GE = Genealogical Material · PM = Primary Material · SM = Secondary Material

PM **ERICH MOSSE**
1891–
Autograph
1 item
AR 2647

FO SM **GEORGE L. MOSSE**
Historian, 20th cent.
Photo; bibliography
2 items
AR 2130

PM **ALEXANDER MOSZKOWSKI**
1851–1934
Postcard
1 item
AR 2601

PM **MORITZ MOSZKOWSKI**
Pianist, 1854–1925
Concert program (1892); autograph
2 items
AR 2091, AR 2067

PM **MUEHLHAUSEN-BAMBERG; JEWISH COMMUNITY**
Payment agreement
1 item
AR 4084

FO PM **MUEHLHEIM; JEWISH COMMUNITY**
Birth, marriage, death registers (1823–1847); photos
9 items
AR 822

FO PM **PAUL MUEHSAM**
SM Author, 1876–1960
Autobiographical notices; bibliography; publications; catalogue; photo
6 items
AR 719

FO SM **RICHARD MUEHSAM**
Surgeon, 1871–1938
Obituary; photo
2 items
AR 1013

PM **ABRAHAM MUELLER**
Document of naturalization (Ostrowo, 1834)
1 item
AR 4933

PM **MUELLER FAMILY, BARTERODE**
Official documents (19th cent.)
23 items
AR 3701

PM **HANS MUELLER**
1882–
Autograph
1 item
AR 1760

SM **R. MUELLER**
Mail carrier
Clipping about Jewish mail carrier in Frankfurt
1 item
AR 76

SM **SAMUEL MUELLER**
Teacher
Clipping with article on Mueller
1 item
AR 5159

PM **STEPHAN MUELLER**
Letter, marriage certificate, both signed by Leo Baeck (1925)
3 items
AR 1339

PM **MUENSTER; JEWISH COMMUNITY**
Historical material
2 items
AR 5090

FO **FRAU MUENSTERBERG**
Photo of portrait of Frau Muensterberg, painted by Curt Herrmann (1916)
1 item
AR 2178

SM **MUENSTEREIFEL; JEWISH COMMUNITY**
Clippings
6 items
AR 451

PM **CHAIM MUENTZ**
Philologist, 1884–
Letter by Karl Helfenstein to Baeck
1 item
AR 4048

FO = Photos · GE = Genealogical Material · PM = Primary Material · SM = Secondary Material

PM **ISAK MUENZ**
Rabbi, 1857–
Letters, one from Leo Baeck, one from chief rabbinate of Egypt (1930, 1935)
2 items
AR 4716

PM **DAVID MUENZER**
Letter from Muenzer in London to his parents in Breslau (1849)
1 item
AR 4609

SM **HANS MUENZER**
Lawyer
Newspaper clipping (1964)
1 item
AR 2222

FO GE **MUGDAN FAMILY**
PM SM Clippings; photo; family trees; poem (19th and 20th cent.)
21 items
AR 1012

FO **OTTO MUGDAN**
Photo
1 item
AR 788

PM **REGINA MUNDLAK**
Artist
Autographs
2 items
AR 3437

SM **PAUL MUNI**
Actor, 1895–1967
Obituary
1 item
AR 3720

PM **MUNICH; JEWISH COMMUNITY**
Jewish oath (15th cent.); clippings; circulars; copy of circumcision register (1913–1938); sermons; Rabbi Josef Perles Collection, community papers (1835–1894)
67 items
AR 143, AR 2945

SM **ELIE MUNK**
Rabbi
Book review of Munk's book (1935)
1 item
AR 4367

FO SM **GEORG MUNK (PSEUDONYM OF PAULA BUBER-WINKLER)**
Writer
Clippings; book reviews with photo
1 item
AR 1541

PM SM **MUSIC**
Manuscripts of music for synagogue services; articles on Jewish sacred and Israeli music
8 items
AR 3842

FO SM **ROBERT MUSIL**
Author, 1880–1942
Photo; clippings
4 items
AR 1203

FO **DAVID NACHMANSOHN**
Biochemist
Photo
1 item
AR 4398

PM **PERETZ FRITZ NAPHTALI**
Zionist, journalist, Israeli politician, 1888–1961
Correspondence; interview transcripts concerning Naphtali's life
9 items
AR 4670

FO **NAROWL (POLESIE, RUSSIA); JEWISH COMMUNITY**
Photo: drawing of wooden synagogue
1 item
AR 7035

FO PM **MAX NASSAUER**
Physician
Scrap book containing clippings, shorthand material, correspondence from the front (First World War), photos (1914)
1 item
AR 4873

FO PM **ALFRED NATHAN**
SM Lawyer, philanthropist, 1870–1922
Biography; clippings; photo concerning Nathan Foundation in Fuerth (1913–1968)

FO = Photos · GE = Genealogical Material · PM = Primary Material · SM = Secondary Material

9 items
AR 3460

PM SM FRITZ NATHAN
Architect, 1891–1960
Description of works; clippings;
photos of work; correspondence;
articles; licenses; obituaries
12 items
AR 1443, AR 7197

PM SM HELMUTH NATHAN
Doctor, artist, 1901–1979
Clippings; obituaries; sketches
7 items
AR 3911

PM KARL NATHAN
Banker, 1885–1964
Letter with biographical information
1 item
AR 2223

FO SM LEOPOLD NATHAN
Brewery chemist, 1864–1939
Obituary; autobiographical article;
advertising and brochure on his
brewery equipment; group photo
4 items
AR 1326

FO SM PAUL NATHAN
Politician
Newspaper clippings; photo
2 items
AR 52

FO PM GERDA NATHORFF
Permit for residency (1813); *ketubah*;
photo of Laupheim synagogue; photo
and material on Rabbi Leopold
Treitel and wife; material on
Laupheim community; poetry
10 items
AR 5207

PM NATIONAL CENTER FOR JEWISH FILM
Letter on film in Yiddish
1 item
AR 5264

PM NATIONAL-SOCIALISM; AUSTRIA
Postwar trials, Austria: a
documentation by Dr. Karl Marschall
(Vienna, 1977)
1 item
AR 5100

PM HANS NATONEK
1892–
Autographs
2 items
AR 2495

FO SM MAX NAUMANN
Lawyer, leader of the Reichsverband
Nationaldeutscher Juden (1875–1939)
Photo/essay; clippings
8 items
AR 226

FO GE ROBERT A. NAUMANN
PM Essay on Liegnitz Jewish community;
essay; photo; family tree of Fritz
Engel
4 items
AR 1229

PM BARUCH NAUMBURG
Marriage contract (German and
Hebrew, 1810)
1 item
AR 1392

FO GE NAUMBURG FAMILY
PM Family history; family tree; photo
(19th and 20th cent.)
6 items
AR 1783

FO NECKARZIMMERN/BADEN; JEWISH COMMUNITY
Photos
3 items
AR 4074

PM CAROLA NEHER
Autograph
1 item
AR 1761

FO GE NEISSER FAMILY
Family history since 1766; photo
2 items
AR 826

PM SM DAGOBERT NELLHAUS
Rabbi, 1891–
Correspondence; clippings; sermon
(19th cent.); Hebrew marriage
contract (1810)
12 items
AR 3237

SM **NEO-NAZISM**
Material on Social Nationalist Aryan People's Party and *National Zeitung*
2 items
AR 5111

FO PM **EMIL NETER**
SM 1875–
Correspondence; photos; press clippings of Neter and his family (19th and 20th cent.)
30 items
AR 1204

FO PM **MIA NETER**
SM Social worker, 1894–1975
Correspondence (1970's); photo; obituary
16 items
AR 4210

GE PM **RAPHAEL NETER**
Genealogy of Neter family; death list of people in Gurs camp
3 items
AR 5218

FO PM **KARL NETTER**
Photo of street sign in Israel; letter
2 items
AR 4964

FO PM **WOLF NETTER**
1895–1954
Corporate material (1895–1935); family papers; documents; industrial photographs
4 items
AR 7215

PM SM **PAUL NETTL**
Musicologist, 1889–
Essay; clippings on Jewish music; musical score
8 items
AR 3075

PM **NEU BREISACH NEAR COLMAR; JEWISH COMMUNITY**
List of 207 houses (1685); head tax list
2 items
AR 4904

SM **CARL NEUBERG**
Physician, biochemist, 1877–1956
Obituary
1 item
AR 56

PM **NEUBERG FAMILY**
Family documents (19th cent.)
4 items
AR 952

FO PM **NEUBURGER FAMILY**
SM Personal and official documents for individual family members since 18th cent.; family memorabilia (20th cent.); articles; clippings on family members (20th cent.); photos
19 items
AR 4462

FO **NEUDENAU/BADEN; JEWISH COMMUNITY**
Photos
4 items
AR 2482

FO PM **NEUENKIRCHEN; JEWISH**
SM **COMMUNITY**
Photos of synagogue; memorial book; article
5 items
AR 7083

SM **EDWARD NEUFELD**
Bibliography on material concerning halachic issues in *Monatsschrift für Geschichte & Wissensschaft des Judentums*
1 item
AR 7102

PM **SIGBERT NEUFELD**
Rabbi
Documents (1925, 1953)
2 items
AR 4120

FO **ERIC NEUGARTEN**
Photos of Neugarten, of synagogue in Zeven before and after Kristallnacht
4 items
AR 1058

PM **KARL NEUHAUSER**
1834–
Certificate stating that Karl Neuhauser graduated from vocational school in Munich (1847)
1 item
AR 4605

FO = Photos · GE = Genealogical Material · PM = Primary Material · SM = Secondary Material

FO PM **ALFRED NEUMANN**
SM Novelist, 1895–1972
Correspondence; clippings; photo; manuscripts; bibliography; poems; autographs
67 items
AR 1955, AR 4983, AR 1961, AR 2531

SM **NEUMANN FAMILY, BERLIN**
Article concerning history of cigar-producing firm of Neumann, Berlin
1 item
AR 1920

FO PM **NEUMANN FAMILY, ESSEN**
Family pictures; photos of synagogue in Essen (20th cent.); 40th anniversary catalogue of Neumann & Mendel garment factory
38 items
AR 4576

GE **NEUMANN FAMILY, PYRITZ**
Family tree (19th–20th cent.); genealogical table (1600–1980)
9 items
AR 4606

SM **HUGO NEUMANN**
Lawyer
Obituary (1915)
1 item
AR 2366

FO SM **HUGO NEUMANN**
Physician, 1858–1912
Clippings; photo
6 items
AR 1057

SM **J. B. NEUMANN**
Art dealer
Obituary (1961)
1 item
AR 2788

FO PM **ROBERT NEUMANN**
SM Author, 1897–
Clippings; photo; autographs
22 items
AR 1581, AR 1825

PM **RUDOLF NEUMANN**
Physician, Berlin
Plate specifying he can only treat Jews; letter from Erich A. Grunebaum regarding the former item
2 items
AR 5009

PM **SALOMON NEUMANN**
Physician, 1819–1908
Material concerning the Salomon Neumann Stiftung für die Wissenschaft des Judentums (1906–1940)
4 items
AR 3667

PM **SIEGFRIED NEUMANN**
Certificate announcing awards of honor (1888, 1908)
2 items
AR 1692

FO **SIGMUND NEUMANN**
Historian, 1904–1962
Photo
1 item
AR 3039

PM **LILLY NEUMARK**
Letter; reminiscences about living underground in Germany during 1940's
2 items
AR 504

FO PM **ALFRED NEUMEYER**
Judge, chairman of Jewish community of Munich
Correspondence (1914); photo
10 items
AR 3155

PM **NEUSS; JEWISH COMMUNITY**
Budgets of Jewish community; lists
4 items
AR 5297

PM **NEUSTADT B. PINNE; JEWISH COMMUNITY**
Memorial
1 item
AR 1604

FO = Photos · GE = Genealogical Material · PM = Primary Material · SM = Secondary Material

PM **NEUSTADT/SAALE; JEWISH COMMUNITY**
History of community
1 item
AR 3642

PM SM **NEUSTADT/WEINSTRASSE; JEWISH COMMUNITY**
Clipping; statutes of congregation
2 items
AR 2914

PM **NEUSTETTIN; JEWISH COMMUNITY**
Report of trial concerning burning of Neustettin synagogue (1884)
1 item
AR 3495

PM **NEUTITSCHEIN (NOW NOVY JICIN, CZECHOSLOVAKIA); JEWISH COMMUNITY**
Answer to questionnaire
1 item
AR 811

SM **NEUWIED; JEWISH COMMUNITY**
Press list for dedication of community stone for Neuwied community
1 item
AR 7233

SM **ALBERT EINSTEIN – BETTY NEWMAN COLLECTION**
Newspaper clippings; Einstein stamps; posters
37 items
AR 4988

GE PM **HILDE NEWMAN FAMILY**
Vital documents; notes on family history
4 items
AR 4780

GE **JEREMY U. NEWMAN**
1925–
Family trees of the Newman and related families (18th–20th cent.)
4 items
AR 4697

PM **FRITZ NEY**
Lawyer, 1897–
Autobiographical brochure
1 item
AR 4255

SM **NIEDERBUSCH; JEWISH COMMUNITY**
Clippings
4 items
AR 3828

PM **JUERGEN NIEDERMEIER**
Manuscript "Life in the Landkreis Kitzingen" (1982)
1 item
AR 5306

FO PM **NIEDERWERRN; JEWISH COMMUNITY**
Photos of synagogue; list of Jewish taxpayers (1812)
5 items
AR 2169

FO **NIKOLSBURG-MORAVIA (NOW MICOLAV, CZECHOSLOVAKIA); JEWISH COMMUNITY**
Photos
6 items
AR 3396

PM **ABRAAM NIMCOWITZ**
Letters from Bialystok
2 items
AR 3290

SM **MAX NIVELLI**
Film director, producer
Clippings; posters; related material
5 items
AR 4258

FO PM **N. A. NOBEL**
SM Rabbi, 1871–1922
Photo; obituaries; speeches; reminiscences by Erich Ahrens; clippings
8 items
AR 1576

SM **NOBEL PRIZE RECIPIENTS**
Clipping (1976)
1 item
AR 4603

PM **NOERDLINGEN; JEWISH COMMUNITY**
Report about fate of community during World War II; cemetery list
2 items
AR 3496

FO = Photos · GE = Genealogical Material · PM = Primary Material · SM = Secondary Material

PM SM **H. NOERDLINGER FAMILY**
Testament; press clipping (mid–19th cent.)
2 items
AR 1924

SM **EMMY NOETHER**
Mathematician, 1882–1935
Obituary
1 item
AR 2897

SM **NONNENWEIER; JEWISH COMMUNITY**
Article
1 item
AR 4972

PM SM **MAX NORDAU**
Author, 1849–1923
Letter; clippings; autographs
10 items
AR 441, AR 1145

SM **EDUARD NORDEN**
Literary historian, 1868–1941
Newspaper clippings
2 items
AR 2324

SM **NORDEN; JEWISH COMMUNITY**
Clipping
1 item
Ar 2265

FO **JOSEPH NORDEN**
Rabbi, 1870–1943
Photo
1 item
AR 2570

FO **NORDERNEY; CHILDREN'S HOME**
Children's convalescent home of Zion Lodge, Hannover
Photo album
1 item
AR 4986

FO PM **NORDSTETTEN/WUERTTEM-**
SM **BERG; JEWISH COMMUNITY**
Photos of synagogue; Torah binders; sermon; photo; history booklet
6 items
AR 2438, AR 5277

GE PM **CATHERINE NOREN**
Photographer, 1938–
Family histories
7 items
AR 4102

GE **NOTHMANN FAMILY**
Family trees (18th–20th cent.)
3 items
AR 4629, AR 5384

FO PM **NUREMBERG; JEWISH**
SM **COMMUNITY**
Photos of synagogue; clippings; list of surviving Jews in Nuremberg (1945); addresses of former residents
23 items
AR 1706

PM SM **ARTHUR NUSSBAUM**
Professor of law, 1877–1964
Clippings; obituaries; manuscript entitled "Die Juden in der Rechtsprechung des dritten Reichs"
9 items
AR 2404

PM **NUSSBAUM FAMILY; FRIEDBERG/HESSEN**
Vital business and family documents of Nussbaum family from Friedberg in Hessen, material on Groedel family in Budapest, including their patent of nobility and correspondence with the Nussbaums (1849–1922)
83 items
AR 2400

FO SM **FELIX NUSSBAUM**
Photos of works and synagogues; clippings on Nussbaum (20th cent.); exhibition information
29 items
AR 3922

PM **HANS NUSSBAUM**
1909–
Material on Jews of Suhl in Nazi era; biography of Nussbaum; text of Jewish melodies from Germany; correspondence
13 items
AR 4784

FO = Photos · GE = Genealogical Material · PM = Primary Material · SM = Secondary Material

FO PM **JAKOB NUSSBAUM**
Painter, 1873–1943
Photo; autograph
2 items
AR 2874–2875

FO PM **MAX NUSSBAUM**
SM Rabbi, Zionist, 1910–1974
Photo; obituary; reminiscences
5 items
AR 1693

SM **MEINHOLD NUSSBAUM**
Lawyer, 1888–1953
Newspaper clipping
1 item
AR 2325

PM **WILLIAM NUSSBAUM**
Correspondence; related documents on anthropological work; manuscript of Friedrich Sieburg entitled "France d'hier et de demain" (1941)
22 items
AR 725

PM **OBBACH/LOWER FRANCONIA; JEWISH COMMUNITY**
History of Obbach Jews with list of names (1938)
1 item
AR 4797

PM **OBERAULA; JEWISH COMMUNITY**
List of victims of Holocaust
1 item
AR 4570

SM **OBERDORF AM IPT; JEWISH COMMUNTIY**
Clipping
1 item
AR 1589

PM **OBERGLOGAU (NOW GLOGOWEK, POLAND); JEWISH COMMUNITY**
History
3 items
AR 3714

GE PM **LEOPOLD OBERLAENDER**
SM **FAMILY**
Family tree; vital documents; obituaries (19th and 20th cent.)
20 items
AR 4028

PM **OBERLAURINGEN; JEWISH COMMUNITY**
Birth, marriage, death registers (1812–1875)
1 item
AR 7091

GE **OBERNDOERFFER FAMILY**
Family tree (18th–20th cent.)
1 item
AR 726

PM **J. N. OBERNDOERFFER**
Letter of owners of Oberndoerffer bank (1872)
1 item
AR 1059

FO PM **SIEGFRIED OCHS**
Choirmaster, 1858–1929
Photo; autographs
4 items
AR 1932, AR 2422

PM **ODENBACH; JEWISH COMMUNITY**
Answer to questionnaire
1 item
AR 812

PM SM **LUDWIG OELSNER**
Historian and student of Leopold von Ranke, 1831–1910
Album containing degrees; articles; correspondence; book of poetry
4 items
AR 5267

PM SM **TONI OELSNER**
Historian, 20th cent.
Correspondence; clippings; articles; bibliography of Toni Oelsner
28 items
AR 3970

PM **OETTINGEN; JEWISH COMMUNITY**
List of Jews born (1822)
2 items
AR 3209

PM **OETTINGER FAMILY**
Testament, marriage contract and dowry (19th cent.); photo of family members (20th cent.); other family papers

7 items
AR 888

FO **JACOB JOSEPH OETTINGER**
Rabbi, 1780–1860
Photo
1 item
AR 3249

PM **RECHA OETTINGER**
1872–1957
Personal documents; official papers concerning Recha Oettinger's emigration to Holland; imprisonments in Westerbork and Theresienstadt (ca. 1940–1946)
30 items
AR 1698

FO PM **JACQUES OFFENBACH**
Composer, 1819–1880
Photo; autographs
3 items
AR 2924, AR 852

FO PM **OFFENBACH; JEWISH COMMUNITY**
Histories; photos; community burial statutes
15 items
AR 144

PM **OFFENBURG; JEWISH COMMUNITY**
"Blaue Beitragskarte" (1930's)
1 item
AR 4525

SM **MANFRED OHRENSTEIN**
New York State Senator
Newspaper article, 1960 (*Aufbau*)
1 item
AR 1448

PM **S. ADOLPH OKO**
Correspondence of Oko with Ernst Altkirch and Richard Beer-Hoffman (1940–1944)
32 items
AR 311, AR 312

FO PM **ARSONE OKUN COLLECTION**
Handwritten manuscript to poet Arno Nadel by Adolf Kestenburg (1914, 79 pp.); typescript of opera *Die Asferiden* by I. Jacobsen (72 pp.);

photo of cantors' meeting in Berlin (ca. 1906–1910)
3 items
AR 5116

PM **RUDOLF OLDEN**
1885–1940
Autographs
2 items
AR 1845

FO SM **OLDENBURG; JEWISH COMMUNITY**
Clipping; photos of arrest of community members (1938)
5 items
AR 2802

FO PM **GERALD OLIVEN**
Photo; correspondence concerning proposed history of Ludwig Loewe manufacturing companies, note on actions of G. Oliven's father to bring about cessation of reparation payments (1931)
3 items
AR 3148

GE **JACOB OLIVEN FAMILY**
Family history (18th–19th cent.)
1 item
AR 327

FO PM **FRIEDRICH OLLENDORF**
SM Social worker, 1889–1951
Photo; correspondence; clippings; obituaries
11 items
AR 2910

FO PM **PAULA OLLENDORF**
SM Teacher, social worker, 1860–1938
Lecture notes; clippings; photo, honorary medallion
21 items
AR 3060

SM **ALDO OLSCHKI**
Publisher, 1893–1963
Obituary (1963)
1 item
AR 2121

GE PM **OLSCHWANGER FAMILY**
Journal with genealogies, history, and family documents
1 item
AR 7242

FO **OPPELN; JEWISH COMMUNITY**
Photos of synagogue and its destruction (1938)
7 items
AR 810

SM **ABRAHAM FREIHERR VON OPPENHEIM FAMILY**
Clippings
2 items
AR 240

PM **BRUNETTE OPPENHEIM**
Poetry album (ca. 1800)
1 item
AR 1952

GE **OPPENHEIM FAMILY**
Family tree (18th–20th cent.)
1 item
AR 241

FO PM **OPPENHEIM FAMILY, ELMSHORN**
SM Family correspondence; clippings and photos (19th and 20th cent.)
7 items
AR 2060

PM **GERTRUD OPPENHEIM**
Letter from Theodor Fontane (1895)
2 items
AR 1356

PM **HEINRICH BERNHARD OPPENHEIM**
Lawyer, 1819–1880
Biography (1874)
1 item
AR 2378

PM **HERMANN OPPENHEIM**
Neurologist, professor of medicine, 1857–1919
Biographical lecture by Helmut Selbach (1978)
1 item
AR 4671

GE **JEFFREY OPPENHEIM**
1962–
Genealogy of family since 1397
1 item
AR 4954

FO SM **OPPENHEIM; JEWISH COMMUNITY**
Photo of medieval Hebrew inscription; clipping
3 items
AR 2803

PM **MAX VON OPPENHEIM**
Assyriologist, 1860–1946
Manuscript with notes by Alfred Vagts concerning Max von Oppenheim
1 item
AR 3419

PM SM **MICHEL OPPENHEIM**
1885–1963
Diary (Mainz, 1941–1943); clippings concerning Michel Oppenheim
4 items
AR 3408

FO SM **MORITZ DANIEL OPPENHEIM**
Artist, 1800–1882
Photos of works; pamphlets on exhibitions (20th cent.)
51 items
AR 2798

PM **NATHAN OPPENHEIM**
Attestation of military service (1851)
1 item
AR 2033

FO PM **PAUL OPPENHEIM FAMILY**
SM Photo; clippings; medallion of family members (19th and 20th cent.)
15 items
AR 2833

FO SM **RICHARD OPPENHEIM**
Architect
Articles; photo album of Jewish gravestones
9 items
Ar 3166

GE **SANWIL OPPENHEIM**
1598–1670
Family tree
1 item
AR 5286

PM **OPPENHEIMER**
Lawyer
Documents concerning the award of the Iron Halfmoon to Oppenheimer by the sultan of Turkey (1917)

FO = Photos · GE = Genealogical Material · PM = Primary Material · SM = Secondary Material

OPPENHEIMER FAMILY

5 items
AR 4105

PM **OPPENHEIMER FAMILY**
Family material (1799–1977)
1 item
AR 7106

SM **OPPENHEIMER FAMILY, BURGKUNSTADT**
Newspaper clippings about bank founded 1858 in San Antonio, Texas
1 item
AR 3295

GE PM **OPPENHEIMER FAMILY, FUERTH**
Family trees, family history (19th and 20th cent.)
4 items
AR 1060

GE PM **OPPENHEIMER FAMILY, HAMBURG**
Family tree; citizenship papers; marriage contract; constitution of the Oppenheimer Stiftung (19th and 20th cent.); letters
5 items
AR 4178

GE **OPPENHEIMER FAMILY, HIMSBACH-KANSAS CITY**
Genealogy
1 item
AR 5203

PM **OPPENHEIMER FAMILY, MARSBERG**
Personal and official documents including those in reference to mortgages (19th cent.); correspondence (20th cent.)
31 items
AR 2041

GE PM **OPPENHEIMER FAMILY, VREDEN**
SM Family history; family tree; obituary
4 items
AR 90

FO PM **FRANZ OPPENHEIMER**
SM Economist, 1864–1943
Photo; clippings; autographs
8 items
AR 2196, AR 2448

FO **FRITZ OPPENHEIMER**
Photo of soldiers on Eastern front (1916)
1 item
AR 1707

SM **FRITZ E. OPPENHEIMER**
Lawyer, 1898–1968
Obituaries (1968)
2 items
AR 3281

GE PM **ISRAEL OPPENHEIMER FAMILY**
Family history; family trees (18th–20th cent.); will
6 items
AR 4681

GE SM **J. ROBERT OPPENHEIMER**
Physicist, 1904–1967
Obituaries; family tree
4 items
AR 3730

PM **JOSEF OPPENHEIMER**
Painter
Reproduction of sketch
1 item
AR 7140

FO PM **JOSEPH OPPENHEIMER**
Banker, 1692–1739
Photos; engravings of Oppenheimer; contemporary fliers on his execution; documents
9 items
AR 554

PM **JOSEPH SUESS OPPENHEIMER**
Correspondence with the Duke of Wuerttemberg (photocopies)
17 items
AR 7114

PM **JULIUS OPPENHEIMER**
Diary: "Memories of Naples, 1831–1833" (306 pp.)
1 item
AR 4000

FO **MAX OPPENHEIMER**
Artist, 1885–
Photos
2 items
AR 2734

PM **MOSES LOEB OPPENHEIMER**
Documents concerning military
service (1868)
1 item
AR 4221

GE **OPPENHEIMER OF RIMBACH**
Family tree
1 item
AR 5139

FO **SAMUEL OPPENHEIMER**
Banker, 1635–1703
Photos of paintings
1 item
AR 2986

GE **ZACHARIAS OPPENHEIMER**
Letter giving family tree
1 item
AR 5248

FO PM **ERNST OPPLER**
Artist, 1867–1929
Photo; autographs
3 items
AR 1986, AR 2735

SM **ORAL HISTORY; COLUMBIA UNIVERSITY**
Columbia Library Journal (1960)
photocopy; proposal to inagurate oral
history project for study of German
Jews
2 items
AR 3748

PM **ORANIENBURG; JEWISH COMMUNITY**
Material about community election
(1929)
5 items
AR 3160

PM **ABRAHAM ORLEWICZ FAMILY**
Distiller, 1799–1892
Family album containing
memorabilia including personal and
official documents
1 item
AR 3138

FO PM **EMIL ORLIK**
SM Artist, 1870–1932
Photo; clippings; autographs
14 items
AR 1673, AR 949

PM **SALOMON ORNSTEIN**
Marriage contract (1851)
1 item
AR 3639

PM **MARIA ORSKA**
1893–1930
Autograph
1 item
AR 2417

PM **MAX OSBORN**
Art historian, 1870–1946
Autograph
1 item
AR 1064

FO **OSNABRUECK; JEWISH COMMUNITY**
Photos of synagogue
1 item
AR 5206

FO PM **MAX OSTERBERG**
SM 1865–1938
Biography; photos; obituaries
2 items
AR 329

PM **OSTHEIMER FAMILY, LIPPERODE**
Passports; commercial licences;
marriage certificate (19th cent.)
6 items
AR 3387

FO SM **KARL OTTEN**
Author, 1889–1963
Photo; obituaries; clipping
5 items
AR 1065

PM **OTTENSOSER FAMILY**
Passport; school documents
(mid–19th cent.)
6 items
AR 4042

SM **PADERBORN; JEWISH COMMUNITY**
Clippings
3 items
AR 1414

SM **HEINZ PAECHTER**
Author, 1907–1980
Obituary
1 item
AR 4936

PM **HANS PAGAY**
1845–1915
Autograph
1 item
AR 1846

PM **PALATINATE; JEWISH COMMUNITY**
Decrees (18th cent.); memorial book; correspondence with Munich government concerning the status of the community as public corporation; deportation lists (early 1940's)
15 items
AR 3041, AR 2039

FO PM **MAX PALLENBERG**
Actor, 1877–1934
Photo; autographs
5 items
AR 2736, AR 548

PM **ERWIN WALTER PALM**
Correspondence with Erich von Kahler (1945–1946)
3 items
AR 4347

PM **PAMPHLETS 17TH/18TH CENTURY**
Conception of new and "false" prophet Mahomet
1 item
AR 4820

PM **PAMPHLETS 19TH CENTURY**
Conversation between Ranke and Brennceke
1 item
AR 3597

PM **PAMPHLETS 20TH CENTURY**
Pro and con antisemitism
16 items
AR 3320

FO **ERWIN PANOFSKY**
Art historian, 1892– ?
Photos
3 items
AR 3647

FO PM **BERTHA PAPPENHEIM**
SM 1859–1936
Articles; newspaper clippings; letters; postage stamps; correspondence; photos
111 items
AR 331, AR 332, AR 54

PM **PAPPENHEIMISCHES HAUSARCHIV**
Decrees; tax lists concerning Jews in southern Germany (18th cent.)
5 items
AR 1504

PM **PARADIES FAMILY**
Letters of protection (Detmold, 1781, 1823)
3 items
AR 194

FO PM **PARCHIM/MECKLENBURG; JEWISH COMMUNITY**
Notes; Hebrew marriage contract (1824); photos of synagogues
22 items
AR 195

FO PM **ERNST PARISER**
Literary historian, 1883–1915
Curriculum vitae; photo; letters; title to synagogue seats and mortgage document (1808, 1817)
8 items
AR 3506

FO **PASSAU; JEWISH COMMUNITY**
Photos of old synagogue
2 items
AR 2580

PM **BORIS PASTERNAK**
Writer, 1890–1960
Correspondence concerning portrait of Pasternak's father in possession of the Leo Baeck Institute
2 items
AR 2737

SM **ARNOLD PAUCKER**
Writer, 1921–
Book review (1968)
1 item
AR 3985

PM SM **KURT PAUCKER**
Biologist, 1924–1980
Curriculum vitae; obituaries
3 items
AR 4900

FO = Photos · GE = Genealogical Material · PM = Primary Material · SM = Secondary Material

GE PM **PAULY FAMILY**
Family tree (17th–19th cent.);
correspondence; documents;
genealogies of Milch, Pauly, and
Kantorowicz families
14 items
AR 535

FO PM **SIEGFRIED PELTESOHN**
1876–
Identity card; photo; letter
4 items
AR 2043

FO SM **SIEGFRIED PELZ**
Physician, 1848–1936
Clippings; photo
9 items
AR 3332

FO SM **ARNO PENZIAS**
Physicist, 1933–
Clipping (1978); photo, Nobel Prize
(1978)
2 items
AR 4652, AR 7142

PM SM **FELIX PERLES**
Rabbi, 1874–1933
Correspondence; clippings; programs,
and appeals from Jewish community
(Berlin, 1908)
47 items
AR 1351

PM **HEDWIG PERLES**
Social worker, wife of Rabbi Felix
Perles, 1876–1954
Curriculum vitae; documents
3 items
AR 4993

PM **BERNARD PERLOW**
Doctoral dissertation on rabbinical
education in Germany with notes and
photocopies of documents (1954)
1 item
AR 7068

SM **FREDERICK S. PERLS**
Physician-psychiatrist, 1894–1970
Obituary
1 item
AR 3663

PM SM **PERLSTEIN/FREIMARK COLLECTION**
Theresienstadt materials: watercolors,
drawings, poetry, publication;
Maccabi Hazair, 3 issues (1939, 1940);
circular letter (1938) with Dr. Chaim
Weizmann's speech (1938)
4 items
AR 7246

FO PM **HANS PETERSDORFF**
Photo of Petersdorff's department
store in Breslau (1929); letter from
Field Marshall von Hindenburg
(1915)
2 items
AR 1360

PM **EDWARD PETRIKOVITSCH**
1896–
Biographical notices
1 item
AR 4377

SM **PETUCHOWSKI FAMILY**
Obituaries for Rabbi Dr. Marcus
Petuchowski and Rabbi Dr. Salomon
Petuchowski; magazine and
newspaper articles; book review
6 items
AR 1066

FO **JAKOB PETUCHOWSKI**
Photo
1 item
AR 5174

FO PM **MORITZ PFAELZER**
Lawyer
Correspondence with socialist leader
Ludwig Frank (1896–1912); other
correspondence; picture of the
Oberrat der Israeliten Badens
35 items
AR 4021

PM **PFEIFER FAMILY, FRANKFURT A/M**
Personal and official documents (19th
cent.); correspondence (mid–19th
cent.)
8 items
AR 3061

FO = Photos · GE = Genealogical Material · PM = Primary Material · SM = Secondary Material

SM **WILHELM PFEIFER**
Article about Jews in Prague (1958)
1 item
AR 355

SM **EDWARD PFEIFFER**
Liberal politician, 1835–1921
Obituary
2 items
AR 2433

FO **PFORZHEIM; JEWISH COMMUNITY**
Photos of synagogue
2 items
AR 2035

PM **PFUNGSTADT; JEWISH EDUCATIONAL INSTITUTIONS**
Lists of students and teachers (1860's and 1870's)
4 items
AR 4351

FO SM **ALBERT PHIEBIG**
Photos of family members; clipping
50 items
AR 352

FO PM **PHILANTHROPIN SCHOOL**
SM Modern religious school founded in 1804
Articles on history of school and its records since 1804; school bulletins (20th cent.); correspondence in reference to school (20th cent.); photos; medallion
53 items
AR 385

FO **MARTIN PHILIPPSOHN**
Historian, 1846–1916
Photo
3 items
AR 1945

PM **PHILLIP BROTHERS**
Metal dealers
Dissertation by Helmut Waszkis; letter by Dr. Grubel about history of Phillip Brothers
2 items
AR 5229

SM **JOHANNA PHILIPPSON**
1887–
Clipping (1977)
1 item
AR 4498

SM **PHILO VERLAG**
Catalogue (1927)
1 item
AR 2938

SM **FRITZ PICARD**
Book dealer, 1888–
Newspaper clipping (1963)
1 item
AR 2326

FO PM **JACOB PICARD**
SM Author, 1883–1967
Clippings; manuscripts; photo; medals of Picard
34 items
AR 351

PM **JULIUS PICARD FAMILY**
War medals of First World War; birth certificate; correspondence; family documents
14 items
AR 3586

FO PM **MAX PICARD**
SM Philosopher, 1888–
Article with photo (1958); autographs
3 items
AR 1067, AR 1762

GE SM **SALOMON PICARD**
Genealogical essays containing list of Jews from Alsace; Jewish marriages in Alsace during 18th cent.
1 item
AR 7075

PM SM **DAVID PICK**
Rabbi, 19th cent.
Articles; documents; report cards
21 items
AR 1951

PM **FRIEDRICH KARL PICK**
1875–1943
Biographical notice by his daughter; poems written by Pick during his imprisonment in Theresienstadt

FO = Photos · GE = Genealogical Material · PM = Primary Material · SM = Secondary Material

4 items
AR 1247

FO **GUSTAV PICK**
Composer of Viennese songs,
1832–1921
Photo
1 item
AR 2776

SM **FELIX DAVID PINCZOWER**
1901–
Bibliography on Jewish sports
(1930–1971)
1 item
AR 4578

PM SM **HENRY F. PINDAR**
Lawyer, 1885–1964
Curriculum vitae; obituary
2 items
AR 2999

PM **HERMANN PINEAS**
Documents (19th–20th cent.);
correspondence of Hitler period;
documents concerning World War II medals; letters from Reichsbund Jüdischer Frontsoldaten
52 items
AR 94

PM **PINNE; JEWISH COMMUNITY**
Journal
2 items
AR 3549

PM **ALBERT PINNER**
1857–1933
Letter
1 item
AR 3786

PM **LUDWIG PINNER**
Zionist, 1890–
Letters from Kurt Blumenfeld (1932, 1933)
6 items
AR 4708

GE **PINTHUS FAMILY**
Family tree (18th–20th cent.)
1 item
AR 57

FO **PIRMASENS; JEWISH COMMUNITY**
Photo of synagogue
2 items
AR 1995a

PM **ERWIN PISCATOR**
Artist, 1893–
Autograph
1 item
AR 1847

SM **EPHRAIM PISTINER**
Writer
Play by Pistiner, *Ein Mensch fliegt zu seinem Stern*
1 item
AR 4771

PM **EUGEN PLATKY**
Poetry album (1870)
1 item
AR 5254

PM **PLATZHEIM; JEWISH COMMUNITY**
Circumcision register (1826–1857)
1 item
AR 2640

PM **PLAUEN; JEWISH COMMUNITY**
Answer to questionaire about Jewish communal property (1944)
1 item
AR 3454

FO GE **PLAUT FAMILY, SCHMALKALDEN, ROTENBURG/FULDA**
Family tree, related information (18th–20th cent.); portraits of family members (18th–20th cent.); pictures of Rotenburg/Fulda (ca. 1900)
15 items
AR 4778

PM **PLAUT-FRENKEL-BESCHUETZ FAMILIES**
Documents; correspondence; family documents (19th-early 20th cent.)
20 items
AR 4880

PM SM **GUENTHER W. PLAUT**
Rabbi, 1912–
Biography; book review
2 items
AR 3899

GE **JACOB PLAUT FAMILY**
Family tree (17th–20th cent.)
22 items
AR 2394

PM **JOSEPH PLAUT**
1879–
Autograph
1 item
AR 2418

PM SM **THEODOR PLAUT**
Economist, 1888–
Curriculum vitae; publications; reviews; correspondence
35 items
AR 5019

SM **HELMUTH PLESSNER**
1892–
Clipping
1 item
AR 4499

PM **JACOB PLESSNER**
Sculptor, 1871–
Print from lithograph
1 item
AR 5027

SM **MARTIN PLESSNER**
Historian
Newspaper article (1962)
1 item
AR 1807

FO PM **ROBERT POHLY**
Photo; appointment as official consultant on scrap metal for state court in Dresden (1921)
2 items
AR 63

FO PM **ALFRED POLGAR**
Writer, 1875–1955
Photo; autographs
9 items
AR 2738, AR 1100

GE PM **HUBERT POLLACK**
Economist, 1903–1967
Family histories and trees since 18th cent.
5 items
AR 3858

FO PM **ADOLF POLLAK**
Zionist leader, 1879–1951
Correspondence; photo; autobiographical notices
7 items
AR 3498

SM **OSKAR POLLAK**
Publisher, 1894–1963
Obituaries (1963)
2 items
AR 2327

PM SM **STEFAN POLLATSCHECK**
Writer, 1890–1942
Three volume manuscript and synopsis of manuscript; bibliography of Pollatscheck's works
3 items
AR 4449

PM **DAVID POPPER**
Cellist, 1843–1913
Autograph
1 item
AR 2822

PM **GEORGE POPPER**
Family papers and documents on Austrian Jewish families: A. Zwillinger, Leopold Oskar Strauss, Adolf Jellineck, Hugo Kallberg
5 items
AR 4898

FO SM **JOSEF POPPER-LYNKEUS**
Philosopher, 1838–1921
Photos; list of works published by L. Loewit publishers (1931)
7 items
AR 1609

PM **MOSES PORGES**
German and Yiddish language versions of Moses Porges' memoirs; correspondence
6 items
AR 1450

PM SM **NATHAN PORGES**
Rabbi, 1847–1924
Letter; obituary
2 items
AR 1396

FO = Photos · GE = Genealogical Material · PM = Primary Material · SM = Secondary Material

PM SM **POSEN (NOW POZNAN, POLAND); JEWISH COMMUNITY**
Government decrees; clippings; community regulations
15 items
AR 1598

SM **ERNST POSNER**
Archivist, 1892–
Article in periodical (1967)
1 item
AR 3388

FO **POTSDAM; JEWISH COMMUNITY**
Photo of synagogue
1 item
AR 4392

PM **PRAEGER**
Assistant rabbi
Sermon for confirmation ceremonies in Oestringen (1843)
1 item
AR 3709

FO SM **BERNHARD PRAGER**
Editor and chemist, 1867–1934
Photo; obituary; eulogy
5 items
AR 4839

PM **EDWARD PRAGER**
Manuscript by Prager as eight-year-old child (1935)
1 item
AR 3135

FO PM **PRAGUE; JEWISH COMMUNITY**
Photos of synagogue in old quarter; documents
81 items
AR 377

PM **ROBERT PRECHTL**
Author, 1874–1950
Autograph
1 item
AR 1848

GE **PRERAUER FAMILY**
Family tree (18th–20th cent.)
1 item
AR 3340

PM SM **PRESS, JEWISH**
Typescript; clippings; list of publications of Jewish press in general as well as in Germany prior to World War II
7 items
AR 1750

SM **PRESS; NAZI GERMANY**
Photocopies of descriptive charts depicting organization and function of press and mass communications before and during Nazi regime
11 items
AR 3364

PM **PRESSBURG; JEWISH COMMUNITY**
Antisemitic fliers (1846)
2 items
AR 3307

PM **PRESSBURGER FAMILY**
Letter from Michael Pressburger about family history
1 item
AR 2385

PM **KENNETH A. PRESTON**
Sabbath lamp (brass)
1 item
AR 2576

FO **ERNST G. PREUSS**
Photo
1 item
AR 5212

FO **HUGO PREUSS**
Politician
Photo with text
1 item
AR 2805

PM SM **JOSEPH PREUSS**
Clipping; identification papers from Shanghai (1942)
2 items
AR 357

FO **JULIUS PREUS**
Physician, 1861–1913
Photo
1 item
AR 2670

FO = Photos · GE = Genealogical Material · PM = Primary Material · SM = Secondary Material

GE PM **PRINGSHEIM FAMILY**
SM Family tree and history; clippings;
curricula vitae (18th–20th cent.)
8 items
AR 887

SM **KLAUS PRINGSHEIM**
Article (1963)
1 item
AR 2328

FO PM **HERMANN PRINZ**
Photo (1935); correspondence
2 items
AR 4612

PM SM **JOACHIM PRINZ**
Rabbi, 1902–1988
Clippings; curricula vitae
14 items
AR 740

SM **GERTRUDE PROCHOWNIK**
Social worker
Article (1964)
1 item
AR 2427

SM **WILHELM PROKESCH**
Copy of release paper from
Sachsenhausen (1938); paperback:
Kommandant in Auschwitz
2 items
AR 5124

PM **PROSKAU, UPPER SILESIA;
JEWISH COMMUNITY**
Typescript
1 item
AR 3715

FO PM **BERNHARD PROSKAUER**
SM **FAMILY**
Chemist, 1851–1915
Personal and official documents for
family members; obituaries; photos
25 items
AR 3710, AR 3711, AR 3712

SM **CURT PROSKAUER**
Dentist and dental scholar, 1887–1972
Articles; obituary
6 items
AR 4004

SM **ERIC S. PROSKAUER**
Chemist, scientific editor, 1903–
Article on Proskauer
1 item
AR 4043

GE **MORITZ PROSKAUER FAMILY**
Family tree (18th–20th cent.)
2 items
AR 4158

PM **PROSTEJOV; JEWISH
COMMUNITY**
Letters to Otto Kaufler in Ecuador
1 item
AR 5151

PM **PRUSSIA; JEWISH COMMUNITY**
Letter concerning archival list of Jews;
proposed curriculum; miscellaneous
papers; 1981 exhibition material
20 items
AR 2177

SM **PRUSSIAN CULTURAL
POSSESSION**
Pictorial Archives (Preussischer
Kulturbesitz); pre-announcement of
exhibition: "Juden in Preussen"
(1981); NY article
3 items
AR 5014

FO **PRZEMSYL; JEWISH
COMMUNITY**
Photos of synagogue
13 items
AR 2876

PM **PSST; PARIS**
Weekly anti-Dreyfus, antisemitic
caricature journal
1 item
AR 7100

PM **PUDEWITZ (NOW POBIEDZISKA,
POLAND); JEWISH COMMUNITY**
Minute book (1835–1871)
1 item
AR 2873

PM **PYRITZ (NOW PYRZYCA,
POLAND); JEWISH COMMUNITY**
List of Jewish inhabitants (1813)
1 item
AR 2076

SM **QUERIDO-VERLAG**
Publisher
Newly published material (1933); list of books (1934, 1935); article by Hermann Kesten (1961)
3 items
AR 1610

SM **RABBIS; DECLARATION**
Declaration of German rabbis in opposition to antisemitic slander (1893)
1 item
AR 3244

PM **FREDERICK RABE**
Report of his death by British pay-office (Hanover, 1838)
1 item
AR 4406

FO **ISIDOR I. RABI**
Physicist
Photo, Nobel Prize (1944)
1 item
AR 3587

SM **SIMON RABINOWITZ**
Clipping (1957)
1 item
AR 476

PM SM **CURT RADLAUER**
Government official, 1884–
Information on Radlauer's wife, material on his activities helping Jews during Third Reich
6 items
AR 3621

SM **CHARLOTTE RADT**
Ethnobotanist, 1923–1978
Obituaries; articles
4 items
AR 4720

SM **RAESFELD/WESTPHALIA; JEWISH COMMUNITY**
Article on community
1 item
AR 7226

PM **JOSEF RAFF**
Letter (1845)
6 items
AR 1621

FO PM **RANDEGG; JEWISH COMMUNITY**
Photo of synagogue; circumcision register (1828–1881); tape of Jewish dialect
9 items
AR 2483

PM **RAPHAEL FAMILY, WESTPHALIA**
Family history
1 item
AR 5281

PM SM **GRETA RAPP**
Honorary documents (1973, 1974) for Marie Luise Hensel, recipient of Medal of Honor from Yad Vashem; letters from Yad Vashem (1970's) in reference to Marie Luise Hensel; letter from Marie Luise Kaschnitz; clippings (1973–1974) in reference to Hensel
31 items
AR 4375

FO **SALOMON JEHUDA LOEB RAPPAPORT**
Rabbi
Photo
1 item
AR 3578

GE **RASHI (R. SALOMON BEN ISAAK OF TROYES, FRANCE)**
Rabbi, 1040–1105
Family tree (11th–20th cent.)
2 items
AR 3607

FO PM **RASTENBURG (NOW KETRZYN, POLAND); JEWISH COMMUNITY**
Program; photo of synagogue; letters
4 items
AR 4184

GE PM SM **RATHENAU-AEG**
Family genealogies; material on Emil, Erich, and Walter Rathenau (1710–1938); article on AEG executives; photos; articles; clippings (60th anniversary of Walther Rathenau's assassination, 1982); information on 100th anniversary of AEG
5 items
AR 1451a

FO = Photos · GE = Genealogical Material · PM = Primary Material · SM = Secondary Material

FO SM **EMIL RATHENAU**
Industrialist, 1838–1915
Photos; clipping
13 items
AR 2626

FO PM **WALTER RATHENAU**
SM Industrialist, politician, 1867–1922
Photo; clippings, primarily on the
30th, 40th and 50th anniversaries of
his death; various articles and letters;
autographs
40 items
AR 1451, AR 276

PM **RATIBOR; JEWISH COMMUNITY**
Answer to questionnaire; typescript;
letter
3 items
AR 820

FO PM **MAX RAU**
Photo, grandmother; itinerary of
"First trip of American businessman
to Palestine" (1946)
2 items
AR 5358

SM **ERWIN RAWICZ**
Journalist, 20th cent.
Clippings from Central Verein
Zeitung in reference to resettlement
of Jews throughout world (1936)
61 items
AR 4841

SM **RAWITSCH (NOW RAWICZ, POLAND); JEWISH COMMUNITY**
Clipping
1 item
AR 3766

PM **RECHNITZ FAMILY**
Tombstone inscription; letters of
citizenship; award of medals
13 items
AR 419

FO **RECKLINGHAUSEN; JEWISH COMMUNITY**
Photo
1 item
AR 2158

GE PM **REE FAMILY**
Testament of Helene Ree (1918);
family history and tree since 1722
2 items
AR 4556

FO PM **REGENSBURG; JEWISH**
SM **COMMUNITY**
Circulars by Zionist organization;
photo of medieval synagogue; list of
Jews deported to Theresienstadt
(1942)
6 items
AR 1425

PM **DAVID REGENSBURGER**
Died 1879
Document on disposition of
Regensburger estate
1 item
AR 4368

FO PM **FABIAN REHFELD**
Conductor, 1842–1920
Photo; musical score
4 items
AR 1931

FO SM **HANS I. REHFISCH**
Writer, 1891–1960
Photo; clipping
2 items
AR 2329

PM **BERNHARD REICH**
Physician, 1841–
Dissertation in medicine (1864)
1 item
AR 4804

PM **EMIL REICH**
Autograph
1 item
AR 1763

PM **KOPPEL REICH**
Rabbi
Postcard (1905)
1 item
AR 2294

SM **WILHELM REICH**
Psychoanalyst, 1897–1957
Advertisement for book (1934)
1 item
AR 1611

FO = Photos · GE = Genealogical Material · PM = Primary Material · SM = Secondary Material

PM SM **FRITZ REICHE**
Physicist, 1883–1969
Curriculum vitae; obituary
2 items
AR 2573

GE **HANS REICHENBACH FAMILY**
Family tree (18th–20th cent.)
1 item
AR 3121

PM **REICHENBACH (NOW DZIERZONION, POLAND); JEWISH COMMUNITY**
"Synagogen Ordnung" (1863)
2 items
AR 450

PM **EMANUEL REICHER**
Autograph
1 item
AR 1925

FO PM **EVA REICHMANN**
SM Photo; clippings; speech by Eva Reichmann concerning antisemitism (1952–1977)
8 items
AR 904

FO PM **HANS REICHMANN**
SM Lawyer, representative of German Jewish refugees, 1900–1964
Photo; clippings; biographical notices
6 items
AR 2236

PM **REICHSVEREINIGUNG DER JUDEN IN DEUTSCHLAND; BADEN**
Circulars concerning regulations for Jews (1941–1943)
16 items
AR 2038

SM **ALBERT REIMANN**
Artist, 1874–
Clipping
1 item
AR 2428

SM **HEINZ REIMANN**
Physician, died 1977
Clipping
1 item
AR 4488

PM **HERTHA REINEMANN FAMILY**
Birth certificates; employment testimony (1843–1905)
3 items
AR 4723

FO PM **MAX REINHART**
SM Director, producer, 1873–1943
Clippings; catalogues of Reinhart's work; stamps; photos (1947–1948); autographs
26 items
AR 484, AR 1107

GE PM **VICTOR REIS**
1880–
Family tree (17th–20th cent.); list of Jews living in Steinau and Schluechtern; testament (1908)
6 items
AR 869

PM **ERICH REISS**
Author, 1887–1951
Catalogue of memorial exhibition
1 item
AR 3626

FO GE **REISS FAMILY, STARGARDT**
PM Family history and genealogy, including Perez and Driesen family; correspondence; photos; poetry journal
22 items
AR 5017

PM SM **H. G. REISSNER**
Historian, 1902–1977
Correspondence concerning manuscript; obituaries
2 items
AR 4147

PM **EDUARD REMENYI**
Hungarian violinist, 1830–1898
Autograph
1 item
AR 2823

PM **JOSEPH RENARD**
Testament (1837)
1 item
AR 4815

FO = Photos · GE = Genealogical Material · PM = Primary Material · SM = Secondary Material

PM **RENDSBURG; JEWISH COMMUNITY**
Program (1845)
1 item
AR 6003

GE **RENNER-RUBEN FAMILY**
Family tree (1650–1913)
1 item
AR 313

FO PM **REPZIN; JEWISH COMMUNITY**
Photo; card
2 items
AR 1946

SM **RESTITUTION**
Laws concerning restitution from Germany; articles
12 items
AR 4939

FO **JACOB RETWITZER**
Pictures of Retwitzer cigar factory and of Retwitzer house in Lampertheim (ca. 1900)
4 items
AR 3066

FO PM **REXINGEN; JEWISH COMMUNITY**
SM History; clipping; photo of synagogue
14 items
AR 1000

FO SM **RHEDA/WESTPHALIA; JEWISH COMMUNITY**
Article; photos
3 items
AR 4695

FO **RHEINBISCHOFSHEIM; JEWISH COMMUNITY**
Photo of synagogue
3 items
AR 2484

FO **RHEINBROHL; JEWISH COMMUNITY**
Photos
2 items
AR 4691

SM **RHEINPFALZ & SAARLAND; JEWISH COMMUNITY**
Review of book on area
1 item
AR 5169

PM **HEINRICH RHEINSTROM**
Lawyer, 1884–
Curriculum vitae
2 items
AR 1070

SM **MONIKA RICHARZ**
Historian, 1939–
Notice for lecture, "Jüdische Autobiographien als Quellen der Sozialgeschichte"
1 item
AR 4291

FO GE **JOHN H. RICHTER**
PM Correspondence with Lucius Clay; family tree since 1720; photos; photocopies of pictures of synagogues in Dessau, Essen; orphanage Berlin-Pankow
14 items
AR 1683

SM **HERTHA ROSA IRMA PATAKY RIESE**
1892–1981
Obituary in *Richmond New Leader*
1 item
AR 5074

PM **JACOB RIESE**
Court dwarf, Kingdom of Poland (18th cent.)
Item on Riese
1 item
AR 5318

PM SM **ADOLF RIESENFELD**
Freight mover, 1884–1977
Diary; related items and clippings
10 items
AR 7186

GE PM **ALFRED RIESER FAMILY**
Family tree (18th–20th cent.); copies of documents; correspondence
8 items
AR 4871

FO PM **ELLIDA RIESER**
Opera singer, 1889–1970
Pamphlet; photos; burial instructions; correspondence
44 items
AR 3924

FO = Photos · GE = Genealogical Material · PM = Primary Material · SM = Secondary Material

PM **MAX RIESER**
Philosopher, journalist
Personal papers; literary, philosophical, scholarly correspondence; literary manuscript
12 items
AR 7207

SM **HERMANN RIESS**
Clippings; eulogy
4 items
AR 507

FO PM **GABRIEL RIESSER**
Politician, 1806–1863
Photo of portrait; album with dedication to Riesser on occasion of his move to Frankfurt a.M (1840); correspondence; autographs
7 items
AR 2027, AR 853

SM **RIGA; JEWISH COMMUNITY**
Poster and program of theater performance
2 items
AR 3348

SM **RAINER MARIA RILKE**
Author, 1875–1926
Newspaper articles
2 items
AR 4211

PM **RING FAMILY**
Family poetry (Prague, 1883); diaries; school notebooks
3 items
AR 5080

PM SM **EDITH RINGWALD**
Lawyer
Newspaper article (1960); letters, Walter Rathenau (1920–21), Mathilde Rathenau (1888–1926)
30 items
AR 1269

PM **BENJAMIN RIPPNER**
Rabbi
Correspondence (1898); poetry; personal papers
23 items
AR 908

FO PM **LUCIE RITTER MARCUS**
Painter, 1895–1967
Curriculum vitae of Lucie; photos; reproductions of paintings
12 items
AR 4393

SM **RITUAL SLAUGHTER**
Articles and rabbinical decrees in reference to ritual slaughter (1866–1932)
27 items
AR 2112

FO **ELLIS RIVKIN**
Historian
Photo
1 item
AR 2253

SM **BETTY ROBBINS**
Cantor
Clipping (1955)
1 item
AR 4557

SM **ROBINSON BROTHERS**
Magazine article about Jewish store in Hamburg in Third Reich (1958)
1 item
AR 534

FO PM **ALEXANDER RODA-RODA**
Actor, 1872–1945
Pictures; film stills; autographs
9 items
AR 2960, AR 857

PM **MAX F. RODEN**
Author, 1881–1968
Autograph
1 item
AR 6013

PM SM **JULIUS RODENBERG**
Editor, 19th cent.
Clipping (1964); autographs
3 items
AR 2330, AR 438

PM SM **EDOUARD RODITI**
Art, literary critic
Article; letters from Paul Celan, Else Lasker-Schueler, Karl Wolfskehl
19 items
AR 4216

FO = Photos · GE = Genealogical Material · PM = Primary Material · SM = Secondary Material

FO **ROEDELSHEIMER BROTHERS, BACHINGEN**
Photos of seven brothers in uniform (1914–1918)
1 item
AR 4968

SM **LUDWIG ROERSCHEID VERLAG**
Declaration (1956), concerning Aryanization of firm in 1938
1 item
AR 2451

FO PM **KARL ROESSLER**
SM Actor, 1864–1948
Photo; obituary; letter
4 items
AR 1361

FO PM **ROGASEN; JEWISH COMMUNITY**
Photos of ritual objects; list of community members
4 items
AR 342

GE PM **ERNST VOM ROMBERG FAMILY**
Family tree; letters
3 items
AR 4229

GE **ROMBURG FAMILY**
Family tree since 1545
1 item
AR 4946

SM **FRANKLIN D. ROOSEVELT**
Memorandum of conversation between Franklin D. Roosevelt and King Ibn Saud concerning Zionism (1945)
1 item
AR 3944

PM SM **ELISE ROSEN**
Artist, 1895–
Letters; exhibition catalogues
6 items
AR 3767

PM **MICHAEL ROSEN**
Collection of material on German-Jewish industrialists
1 item
AR 5148

PM SM **WILLY ROSEN**
Cabaret artist
Newspaper clipping (1920); autographs
4 items
AR 2496, AR 884

PM SM **LEOPOLD AND BELLA ROSENAK**
Rabbi, 1869–1923
Letters, including one from Paul von Hindenburg; photo; biographical accounts; articles
20 items
AR 1071

PM **WILHELM ROSENAU**
Certificate of military service (1852)
1 item
AR 3980

PM **ABRAHAM ROSENBACHER**
Marriage contract (1843)
1 item
AR 3277

GE **SIMON ROSENBACHER, SULZBACH**
Genealogy of the Rosenbacher family (ca. 1750)
1 item
AR 5250

PM **EDUARD ROSENBAUM**
Letter concerning Rosenbaum's resignation from Deutsche Gesellschaft für Voelkerrecht (1933); commentary by Rosenbaum
2 items
AR 2882

GE **ROSENBAUM FAMILY**
Family history (19th cent.)
1 item
AR 4724

GE **ROSENBAUM-HALBERSTADT FAMILY**
Family genealogies
3 items
AR 883

PM **HEINEMANN ROSENBAUM**
Letters to his wife (1864)
3 items
AR 3341

FO = Photos · GE = Genealogical Material · PM = Primary Material · SM = Secondary Material

PM **HEINRICH ROSENBAUM**
Letters from the field (1914)
3 items
AR 2054

PM **MAX ROSENBAUM FAMILY**
Petition to King of Bavaria by
Mendel Rosenbaum (1854)
1 item
AR 2614

GE **SAMUEL ROSENBAUM**
Rosenbaum family tree (19th cent.)
2 items
AR 1617

PM **SIEGFRIED ROSENBAUM**
Birth certificate (1879)
1 item
AR 4069

PM **VALENTIN ROSENBAUM**
Letter
1 item
AR 1072

PM **ROSENBERG-BUCHENWALD**
Copy of first interrogation report
after liberation of Buchenwald
concentration camp
1 item
AR 5126a

PM **ERICH ROSENBERG**
Letter from Edmund Husserl (1921),
explanatory note
2 items
AR 3365

PM **ERNST ROSENBERG**
Certificate of commendation for
valor in the field (1916)
1 item
AR 2055

GE **ROSENBERG FAMILY**
Family tree, related documents
(18th–20th cent.)
4 items
AR 508

PM **GERTRUD ROSENBERG**
Reminiscences of experiences in
Theresienstadt
1 item
AR 2733

PM **HERBERT ROSENBERG**
Physician
Licenses, permision to treat Jewish
patients (1939); Shanghai certificate
4 items
AR 5121

PM **ROSENBERG (NOW OLESNO, POLAND); JEWISH COMMUNITY**
Typescript
1 item
AR 3716

PM **JULIUS ROSENBERG**
Athlete
Sports certificates (1913–1929)
13 items
AR 3545

GE **LEWIN ROSENBERG FAMILY**
Family tree, related documents
(19th–20th cent.)
3 items
AR 4630

PM SM **RENA ROSENBERGER**
Articles about Theresienstadt;
newspaper clippings about encounter
with a Falasha as a child; obituaries of
famous Jews
12 items
AR 4932

PM **SARA ROSENBERGER**
Letter of recommendation for a
former servant (1877)
1 item
AR 4321

SM **MARTIN ROSENBLUETH**
1886–1963
Clippings (1960's)
4 items
AR 1452

PM SM **PINCHAS ROSENBLUETH**
Israeli Minister of Justice, 1887–1978
Manuscript; obituary
2 items
AR 7114

FO **LOUIS ROSENDAHL**
Photo
1 item
AR 1206

FO = Photos · GE = Genealogical Material · PM = Primary Material · SM = Secondary Material

GE PM **ROSENFELD FAMILY, UHLFELD, BAVARIA**
Documents on family history (18th–20th cent.)
3 items
AR 4667

PM **MAX ROSENFELD**
Denial of application for name change (1915)
1 item
AR 1073

PM **MORITZ ROSENFELD**
Rabbi, 1876–1951
Family memorabilia (1882–1961); manuscripts
24 items
AR 1165

FO SM **SAMSON WOLF ROSENFELD**
Rabbi, 1782–1862
Photo of portrait; clipping
2 items
AR 2795

GE PM **THEODOR ROSENFELD**
Family tree (18th–19th cent.); correspondence; reminiscences of conditions in the Saar before plebiscite (1935)
23 items
AR 882

PM **FRITZ ROSENFELDER**
Letters
2 items
AR 3869

PM **ROSENGARDT FAMILY**
Birth records (19th cent.)
1 item
AR 1694

PM **JOSEF ROSENGART**
Letter on the subject of emigration to United States (1846)
1 item
AR 3901

FO PM **ALBERT ROSENHAIN**
SM Merchant, 1836–1916
Photos; advertising brochures, account of founding of foreign branches after 1933
20 items
AR 3272

FO PM **JACOB ROSENHEIM**
President of Agudas Israel and editor of *Israelit* (Frankfurt), 1870–1965
Correspondence with Rabbi Justus Tal, Amsterdam; photo
4 items
AR 5252, AR 4860

PM SM **MAX ROSENSCHEIN FAMILY**
Doctor's license (1890); Brazilian visa (1938)
2 items
AR 3486

FO PM **PAUL ROSENSTEIN**
SM Physician, 1875–1964
Clippings; photos; curriculum vitae; list and copies of scientific articles
16 items
AR 212

PM **WILLY ROSENSTEIN**
Account of experiences as World War I flyer (1924)
1 item
AR 3617

PM **JOSEPH ROSENSTOCK**
Conductor, 1895–
Autographs
2 items
AR 3018

PM **ADOLF ROSENTHAL FAMILY**
Engagement contract (1797); letter of protection and other business papers (1774–1797); family documents; business papers
35 items
AR 1260

FO PM **ARTHUR ROSENTHAL**
Rabbi, 1885–1951
Photo; original sketch of Torah scroll by daughter
2 items
AR 1205

PM SM **ARTHUR ROSENTHAL**
Professor, 1887–1959
Curriculum vitae; letter; eulogy
2 items
AR 1917

FO PM **FERDINAND ROSENTHAL**
SM Rabbi, 1835–1921
Photo; pamphlets; sermon
manuscripts; brochures on festivities
9 items
AR 2595

PM **GABRIELLA ROSENTHAL**
Writer
Six letters to Dr. Elizabeth
Petuchowski in Cincinnati (Israel,
1964–1970)
6 items
AR 4977

PM **JACQUES ROSENTHAL**
Correspondence; material on Verein
zur Abwehr des Antisemitismus
(1931–1933) and on the Israelitische
Union (1934–1935)
12 items
AR 3808

SM **JULIUS ROSENTHAL**
Poem, "Kapuziner Predigt"
1 item
AR 3867

PM **KARL ROSENTHAL**
Account of emigration of Jews from
Germany after 1933
1 item
AR 390

PM SM **KARL ROSENTHAL**
Rabbi, 1880–1952
Clippings from Reform newspapers;
bound sermons; two cassette tapes of
interviews with his widow (1976)
34 items
AR 909

PM SM **LOUIS ROSENTHAL**
Engineer, 19th cent.
Biography; clippings; documents
10 items
AR 1936

PM **LUDWIG ROSENTHAL**
Rabbi of Cologne
Poem (1934)
1 item
AR 2331

SM **LUDWIG ROSENTHAL**
Antique book dealer
Clippings
3 items
AR 1074

PM **LUDWIG ROSENTHAL**
Rabbi, 1855–1928
Curricula vitae
2 items
AR 509

PM **LUDWIG ROSENTHAL, HANAU**
Decrees; letters of protection
(1738–1796)
12 items
AR 2367

PM SM **MORITZ ROSENTHAL**
Pianist, 1862–1946
Concert programs; press clippings;
autographs
18 items
AR 2092, AR 2246

GE **STUUK ROSENTHAL, MUNCHHOLZHAUSEN**
Family tree
1 item
AR 5332

PM SM **WALTER ROSENTHAL**
Lawyer
Documents of various lawyers'
appointments; termination of
permission to practice law (1936)
6 items
AR 4934

FO PM **LEOPOLD ROSENTHALER**
SM Pharmacologist, 1875–1962
Biographical account; letter; photo in
the field with Crown Prince; obituary
of his brother
4 items
AR 2828

FO PM **CARL ROSENWALD**
SM Lawyer, 1873–1938
Documents; medals;
recommendations concerning service
in World War I; legal career; photo;
biography
10 items
AR 4551

FO = Photos · GE = Genealogical Material · PM = Primary Material · SM = Secondary Material

SM **LESSING J. ROSENWALD**
Philanthropist, 1891–1979
Clipping
1 item
AR 1808

FO PM **ADELE ROSENZWEIG**
Mother of Franz Rosenzweig, 1867–1933
Photo; correspondence concerning her memoirs
3 items
AR 4634

PM **CECILIA ROSENZWEIG**
Letters describing deportation of Polish Jews from Germany (1938)
2 items
AR 7128

FO PM **LOUIS ROSENZWEIG**
Merchant, Jewish community official, 1885–1960
Photo; letter; documents on business career and army service (1918–1919); imprisonment in Dachau (1938); emigration to the United States
15 items
AR 1207

SM **JOSEL VON ROSHEIM**
Printed version of diary (15th–16th cent.)
1 item
AR 1300

PM **MOSES ROSNER**
Naturalization documents (1833–1836)
3 items
AR 4166

PM **STELLA ROTENBERG**
Poet, 20th cent.
Poem, related correspondence (1976)
2 items
AR 4325

PM **B. M. ROTH**
Letter to son Solomon on America (1854); notes on Solomon Roth's activities in Civil War
2 items
AR 511

SM **CECIL ROTH**
Historian, 1899–1970
Obituary
1 item
AR 3707

PM SM **ROTH (INCLUDING NIEDERWALGERN); JEWISH COMMUNITY**
Clippings; history
4 items
AR 7230

PM **STEPHEN ROTH**
Anti-Nazi cartoons (1942); explanatory letter (1978)
2 items
AR 4558

FO **THERESE ROTHAUER**
Singer, (ca. 1870–ca. 1944)
Picture with biographical notices
1 item
AR 2409

SM **ROTHENBURG; JEWISH COMMUNITY**
Clipping
1 item
AR 2183

PM **JOSEPH ROTHENSTEIN**
Attestation of selection of family name (Danzig, 1816)
1 item
AR 3809

SM **HANS ROTHFELS**
Historian, 1891–1976
Obituaries
1 item
AR 5262

PM **HANS ROTHMANN**
Documents on the efforts of Hans Rothmann's father to enroll him in cadet corps (1914)
14 items
AR 2122

PM **FRANZ ROTHMUELLER**
Documents on Franz Rothmueller's imprisonment in Dachau (1938)
4 items
AR 4779

FO = Photos · GE = Genealogical Material · PM = Primary Material · SM = Secondary Material

GE **DAVID ROTHSCHILD**
1790–1853
Table of descendants of David Rothschild of Heldenbergen since 1790
1 item
AR 5026

GE **ROTHSCHILD FAMILY, STADTOLDENDORF**
Family tree (19th–20th cent.)
2 items
AR 713

PM **FELIX ROTHSCHILD**
Judge, 1868–1962
Biography
1 item
AR 3000

PM **FRANK ROTHSCHILD**
Liturgical music
2 items
AR 2545

PM SM **ROTHSCHILD, HOUSE OF**
Various articles about Rothschild family and museum; photocopies of letters
89 items
AR 512

PM **HUGO ROTHSCHILD FAMILY**
Documents
5 items
AR 3889

PM **KARL ROTHSCHILD**
1788–1855
Autograph
1 item
AR 830

PM **MORITZ ROTHSCHILD**
Hebrew marriage contract (1820); death notice (1874)
2 items
AR 1362

PM **SALOMON MEYER VON ROTHSCHILD**
1774–1855
Autograph
1 item
AR 1651

SM **SAMSON ROTHSCHILD**
Teacher, 1848–1939
Article, Wormser Zeitung (1964)
1 item
AR 2552

FO GE **ROTHSCHILD SIBLINGS**
PM Family trees; letters of protection (1741–1971); photos of paintings
7 items
AR 341

FO PM **ANNA ROTHSTEIN**
SM Artist, 20th cent.
Photos of her work; clippings; letter
5 items
AR 771

FO SM **IRMA ROTHSTEIN**
Sculptor, died 1971
Obituary; exhibition catalogues; photo of her work
4 items
AR 3752

PM **HERBERT RUBEN FAMILY**
Official documents (Hamburg, 1822–1855)
8 items
AR 1363

PM **LEVY RUBEN**
Foreign language teacher, tutor for Duke of Anhalt, 1772–1858
Letter of protection; correspondence; documents on Levy Ruben's career; biographical notices
7 items
AR 4833

PM **PAUL RUBEN**
Letter to Alfred Vagts (1934), with elaboration
2 items
AR 4663

PM **HANS J. RUBIN**
Nazi antisemitic posters
2 items
AR 1365

PM **KURT RUBIN**
Documents on military career and emigration from Germany
13 items
AR 1279

FO = Photos · GE = Genealogical Material · PM = Primary Material · SM = Secondary Material

PM **S. RUBIN**
Liturgical music
3 items
AR 1366

FO PM **ANTON RUBINSTEIN**
Russian pianist and composer,
1829–1894
Photo; autographs
4 items
AR 2814, AR 549

SM **ARTHUR RUBINSTEIN**
Artist, 1889–
Clipping
1 item
AR 1665

FO PM **EDUARD RUDNICKI
(PSEUDONYM OF ELI ROTTNER)**
born 1898
Documents; manuscript; diaries of
Lotte Brunner; drawings of
Constantine Brunner; photographs of
various people
2.5 feet
AR 7046

SM **MAX RUDOLF**
Clipping
1 item
AR 514

SM **REINHOLD RUEDENBERG**
Obituary (1962)
1 item
AR 1542

FO PM **ISAAC RUELF**
Editor, 1831–1902
Reports; manuscripts; photos; letters;
Russian silver cigarette box
20 items
AR 3179

SM **RUELZHEIM; JEWISH
COMMUNITY**
Clipping
1 item
AR 3693

SM **RUESSELHEIM; JEWISH
COMMUNITY**
Catalogue for 1980 exhibition
1 item
AR 4923

PM SM **ARTHUR RUPPIN**
Sociologist, 1876–1943
Clipping; autograph
2 items
AR 126, AR 829

SM **RUST; JEWISH COMMUNITY**
Clipping
1 item
AR 2507

PM **ERNST RYCHWALSKI**
Bound correspondence with Jewish
communities of Stettin, Stolp, Berlin
(1934–1942)
1 item
AR 2842

SM **MARTHA SAALFELD**
Author, 1898–
Book review (1966)
1 item
AR 3594

PM SM **MANFRED SAALHEIMER**
Lawyer, 1907–1967
Obituary; letters to Leo Baeck and
others; material on Jews of Saxony in
Nazi era; lists of Jewish emigrants
from Chemnitz
36 items
AR 3616

SM **SAARBRUECKEN; JEWISH
COMMUNITY**
List of Judaica in archives
1 item
AR 4319

SM **DAGOBERT SABATZKY**
Antique dealer
Catalogues of Jewish book dealers
and publishers; clippings on Jewish
subjects from 1930's
5 inches
AR 7222

FO SM **SABBATAI ZVI**
"False Messiah", 1626–1676
Review of biography of Sabbatai Zvi;
photo of contemporary woodcuts of
him
6 items
AR 2806

FO = Photos · GE = Genealogical Material · PM = Primary Material · SM = Secondary Material

SM **CURT SACHS**
Writer
Obituary (1959)
1 item
AR 772

FO PM **EDUARD SACHS**
Jewish communal official, died ca. 1930
Biography; photo negative
2 items
AR 3389

GE SM **ELLY SACHS**
Family trees (18th–20th cent.); clippings on genealogy (1920's)
7 items
AR 3068

FO PM **FRANZ SACHS**
Photo; doctoral diploma; dissertation; employment contract with Bayer chemical company; letters to Sachs' uncle, Paul Ehrlich
13 items
AR 456

GE **HANNELORE SACHS**
Family tree since 1759
1 item
AR 1390

PM SM **HANS F. SACHS**
Book dealer
Article; art catalogues for exhibitions (1940's); family letters (1860's)
14 items
AR 4327

SM **LESSIE SACHS**
Poet, 1898–1942
Poem; clippings; short stories
15 items
AR 4031, AR 4031a

FO PM **MICHAEL SACHS**
SM Rabbi, 1808–1864
Photo; clippings; memorial services
6 items
AR 384

FO PM **OSCAR SACHS**
German consular agent, Kansas City, Missouri, 1853–
Personal documents; family photos; scrapbook (1909–1917)
9 items
AR 4459

FO PM **RUDOLF AND YOLLA SACHS**
SM Photographers
Personal papers; obituaries; photos
5 items
AR 5163

PM **DOV SADAN**
Refers to memoirs of Adele von Mises
1 item
AR 5155

PM **AUGUST SAENGER**
Professor of law, 1884–
Curriculum vitae
1 item
AR 4241

SM **EDUARD SAENGER**
Writer, 1880–1948
Article on his poems (1963)
1 item
AR 2332

SM **KURT SAFRANSKI**
Publisher
Newspaper clipping (1964)
1 item
AR 2333

FO **HANS SAHL**
Author, 1902–
Photo
1 item
AR 2739

SM **MAXIM SAKASCHANSKY**
Actor
Theater, cabaret programs (1929–1933)
5 items
AR 4020

FO PM **ARTHUR SAKHEIM**
SM Author, 1884–1931
Obituary; photo; autographs
3 items
AR 325, AR 1973

GE **SAKHEIM FAMILY**
Family tree
2 items
AR 338

FO = Photos · GE = Genealogical Material · PM = Primary Material · SM = Secondary Material

PM **SALFELD POSTCARD COLLECTION**
Series of 57 postcards depicting painted scenes of Jewish holidays by Hermann Junker and Hugo Elkun
57 items
AR 5123

PM **SALIN FAMILY, THÜRINGEN**
"The Jewish Community in Thüringen 1811–1875"; Salin family history
2 items
AR 5060

PM **SALINGER FAMILY**
Marriage, burial documents (1860)
3 items
AR 2006

SM **ERNA SALM FAMILY**
Magazine clipping (1963)
1 item
AR 2530

SM **WILHELM SALOMON-CALVI**
Geologist, 1868–1941
Article
1 item
AR 4445

PM **CAROLA F. SALOMON**
Poem
1 item
AR 2447

SM **CHARLOTTE SALOMON**
Painter, 1917–1943
Exhibition catalogue
1 item
AR 1367

FO **GOTTFRIED SALOMON-DELATOUR**
Sociologist, 1892–1964
Photo
1 item
AR 3074

PM **SALOMON FAMILY, FRIESACK**
Author, graphic artist, 1920–1981
Resource notes; miscellaneous material
6 items
AR 5020

SM **MAX SALOMON**
Artist
Newspaper article (1961)
1 item
AR 1215

PM **SELIGMANN SALOMON**
Deed of sale (1770)
1 item
AR 1695

FO PM **FELIX SALTEN**
Author, 1869–1945
Photo; prospectus for collected works; autograph
3 items
AR 1543, AR 1426

SM **GEORG SALTER**
Graphic artist
Newspaper clipping (1957)
1 item
AR 216

FO PM **HUGO SALUS**
Writer, 1866–1929
Photo; autographs
5 items
AR 2740, AR 1703

PM **GEORG SALZBERGER**
Rabbi
Three sermons (1956)
3 items
AR 102

PM **MARCELL SALZER**
Artist, 1873–1930
Autographs
2 items
AR 1974

PM **FANNY SAMOSCH FAMILY**
Letters from Berlin and Theresienstadt (1941–1944)
13 items
AR 3084

GE **SAMSON FAMILY**
Various family trees (18th–20th cent.)
15 items
AR 4439

GE PM **SAMSON FAMILY, HAMBURG**
Family tree (18th–20th cent.)
1 item
AR 4721

FO = Photos · GE = Genealogical Material · PM = Primary Material · SM = Secondary Material

PM **GRETE SAMSON**
Nurse, 1922–
Nurses' training certificates (1940–1942); D.P. identification papers (1946)
5 items
AR 4038

SM **JOSEPH W. SAMSON**
Physician
Obituary (1961)
1 item
AR 1819

PM SM **OSKAR SAMTER FAMILY**
Newspapers (1800, 1840); letter of municipal citizenship (Posen, 1846); documents from Nazi era (1942–1945)
6 items
AR 1368

PM **ISRAEL SAMULON**
Letters (1825–1845, in Judeo-German)
3 items
AR 3350

FO **SANDBERG**
Physician, 19th cent.
Photo negative
1 item
AR 3845

FO PM **KLARA SANDER**
SM Published and unpublished essays on fashion and other topics; music scores; photos (1908–1920)
34 items
AR 4806

FO PM **WILLY SANDER**
Chemist, industrialist, 1875–
Autobiographical letters; photo
10 items
AR 1075

PM **SANGERHAUSEN/BEZ.HALLE; JEWISH COMMUNITY**
Local history
1 item
AR 4458

PM **MORITZ G. SAPHIR**
Journalist, 1795–1858
Autographs
2 items
AR 550

PM **SAXONY-ANHALT; JEWISH COMMUNITY**
History of Jews in region
1 item
AR 5146

PM **SAXONY; JEWISH COMMUNITY**
List of Jewish communities
1 item
AR 3455

SM **HJALMAR SCHACHT**
Letter to Hitler (Newspaper clipping, 1932)
1 item
AR 773

FO **SCHADOW FAMILY**
Photo of pictures of family members and of family residence
5 items
AR 2741

GE **SCHAEFFER FAMILY**
Family tree (19th–20th cent.)
1 item
AR 1792

PM SM **MORITZ FRIEDRICH SCHAEFFER**
1889–1917
Certificate; clippings on economics and politics
5 items
AR 3293

PM SM **RUDOLF SCHAEFFER**
Classicist, 1894–1970
Obituary; speeches; emigration documents
9 items
AR 3292

FO PM **ALBERT SCHAMES**
Banker, 1859–1905
Biographical notice; photo; condolence letters from Rothschilds on death of his mother
7 items
AR 1334

SM **SAMSON SCHAMES**
Obituaries; photocopy of monotype: "Cemetery in Frankfurt/M."; review of his British and New York shows
2 items
AR 3310, AR 7198

FO = Photos · GE = Genealogical Material · PM = Primary Material · SM = Secondary Material

SM **MORRIS U. SCHAPPES**
Editor, 20th cent.
Articles
5 items
AR 4875

PM SM **GEORG SCHAPS**
Judge, 1867–1918
Documents on legal career; obituary of his mother
12 items
AR 4789

PM **SCHARLACH FAMILY**
Lottery collectors, manufacturers
Personal and business documents (1833–1895)
42 items
AR 4010

SM **WALTER SCHATZKI**
Book dealer, 1899–
Clippings
5 items
AR 4382

PM **SCHATZLAR (CONCENTRATION CAMP)**
Inmate's birthday poem
1 item
AR 7131

GE PM **SCHECHTER FAMILY**
Meta Johanna Schechter memoirs; Jacob Bernstein and Schechter family trees
3 items
AR 5015

FO **MAX SCHELER**
Philosopher, 1874–1928
Photo
1 item
AR 2742

FO PM **MAX SCHERK**
1875–1942
Biography; photo
2 items
AR 4435

FO PM **SCHERMBECK; JEWISH COMMUNITY**
Photos; history
21 items
AR 4962, AR 5108

FO PM **HUGO SCHEUER**
Grain dealer, born 1878–
Biographical note; photo
2 items
AR 4538

PM **HERZ SCHEYER**
Rabbi of Mainz
Notebook on the Talmud (ca. 1820–1821, 176 pp.)
1 item
AR 7054

PM **ADELHEID SCHIFF**
Dissertation: "Names of Frankfurt Jews" (1917)
1 item
AR 5296

GE **SCHIFF FAMILY**
Trees of Schiff and related families (18th to 20th cent.)
4 items
AR 774

PM **SCHIFF FAMILY, HEIDENOLDENDORF**
Letters of protection (1810, 1843)
2 items
AR 4150

FO **JACOB HENRY SCHIFF**
American banker
Photo
1 item
AR 4387

SM **MORITZ SCHIFF**
Chemist
Newspaper article (1976)
1 item
AR 4597

PM **JOHN SCHIKOWSKI**
Editor
Autographs
5 items
AR 2954

PM **GERDA SCHILD**
1922–
Documents on imprisonment in Theresienstadt and release to Switzerland in 1945

5 items
AR 4285

SM **RICHARD SCHINDLER**
Physician
Article on new therapy with electrons
1 item
AR 5221

FO **SCHLAINING/BURGENLAND; JEWISH COMMUNITY**
Photo of synagogue
1 item
AR 4895

FO PM **DOROTHEA SCHLEGEL**
SM Romanticist, 1763–1839
Photo of portrait; clipping; autographs
8 items
AR 2187, AR 1823

SM **ABRAHAM SCHLESINGER**
Rabbi
Newspaper article by F. E. Bloch (1962)
1 item
AR 1647

PM **ABRAHAM SCHLESINGER**
Marriage certificate (1903), signed by Leo Baeck
1 item
AR 197

SM **ADOLF MARTIN SCHLESINGER**
Publisher
Newspaper clipping: "150 Years Music Publishing House Lienau in Berlin" (1960)
1 item
AR 2224

PM **DAVID SCHLESINGER**
Marriage certificate (Oppeln, 1903)
1 item
AR 1301

PM SM **FRITZ SCHLESINGER FAMILY**
Essay on the Bible (1929); Red Cross letters (1941–1942)
5 items
AR 2295

FO **JACOB SCHLESINGER**
Photo of portrait painted by Jacob Schlesinger
1 item
AR 2644

PM **JOSEF SCHLESINGER**
Physician
New Year's greeting (1829)
1 item
AR 3518

PM **M. O. SCHLESINGER**
Yahrzeit table
1 item
AR 4889

FO **SIEGFRIED SCHLESINGER**
Photo in uniform as consul of Persia (Dresden, ca. 1910–1918)
1 item
AR 3057

PM **SCHLESWIG-HOLSTEIN; JEWISH COMMUNITY**
Statistics about community budget
1 item
AR 1001

PM **GABRIEL SCHLEWINSKY**
Six manuscripts on religious issues (1958–1960)
6 items
AR 1424

FO PM **GEORG SCHLOCHAUER**
Businessman, 1870–1942
Photo; biography; documents on attempted emigration and heirs' restitution claims
7 items
AR 4272

PM **BENNI SCHLOTTMANN**
Physician
Lithograph; medical diploma (1848)
2 items
AR 1500

FO PM **LOUIS SCHLOTTMANN**
Pianist, 1826–1904
Photos; poems; conductor's baton
7 items
AR 1501

FO = Photos · GE = Genealogical Material · PM = Primary Material · SM = Secondary Material

PM **SCHLUECHTERN; JEWISH COMMUNITY**
History; letter
2 items
AR 5021

PM **SCHMALKALDEN; JEWISH COMMUNITY**
Answer to questionnaire
1 item
AR 814

PM **M. SCHMALZ (PSEUDONYM MARTINS)**
Letter: Dismissal from Kaiser Wilhelm Institute, Berlin-Dahlem (1933)
1 item
AR 5031

PM **JOSEPH SCHMIDT**
Singer, 1904–1942
Correspondence; personal documents
31 items
AR 2604

FO **SCHMIEHEIM; JEWISH COMMUNITY**
Photos
3 items
AR 4385

SM **MARIA SCHMOLKA**
Newspaper clipping (London, 1940)
1 item
AR 1620

FO SM **ARTHUR SCHNABEL**
Pianist, 1882–1951
Concert programs; photos
7 items
AR 2093

GE **SCHNAITTACH FAMILY**
Family history (17th–19th cent.)
1 item
AR 4513

PM **SCHNAITTACH; JEWISH COMMUNITY**
Letter
1 item
AR 85

GE **SCHNAPPER FAMILY**
Family tree (18th–20th cent.)
1 item
AR 1779

FO PM **MICHAEL SCHNEBEL**
Grain dealer
Business and family documents; photos (1828–1900)
17 items
AR 3013

PM SM **HEINRICH SCHNEE**
1895–
Biographical notices; bibliography of works
3 items
AR 2379

PM SM **SCHNEIDEMUEHL (NOW PILKA, POLAND); JEWISH COMMUNITY**
Clipping; documents concerning rights of Jews; purchase of land by Jewish community (1687, 1727)
4 items
AR 2600

PM SM **LENE SCHNEIDER-KAINER**
Artist
Correspondence; memo; album with newspaper clippings
3 items
AR 3180

PM **FRITZ SCHNIEWIND**
Manuscript of lecture, "Die Tragik der Deutsch-Jüdischen Symbiose"
1 item
AR 525

FO PM **ARTHUR SCHNITZLER**
SM Writer, dramatist, 1862–1931
Photo; clippings; autographs
73 items
AR 1527, AR 531

SM **HARRY G. SCHNUR**
Copies of newspaper clippings
2 items
AR 1552

PM SM **SALMAN SCHOCKEN**
Publisher, 1877–1959
Clippings; letter
22 items
AR 256

GE **EUGENE SCHOEMAN**
Genealogy
3 items
AR 5342

FO = Photos · GE = Genealogical Material · PM = Primary Material · SM = Secondary Material

FO PM **ARNOLD SCHOENBERG**
SM Composer, 1874–1951
Photos; clippings; obituary notice
(newspaper clipping, 1960);
autographs
11 items
AR 2334, AR 1149

PM SM **JAKOB SCHOENBERG**
Composer, 1900–
Typescripts by Schoenberg;
scrapbook; programs; reviews
(1921–1948)
14 items
AR 3390

PM SM **EUGEN SCHOENBERGER**
Champagne manufacturer, 1871–
Business letters, related papers;
clippings
17 items
AR 2829

PM **SCHOENENBERG FAMILY**
Military pass for Paul Schoenenberg,
Thuringian Infantry Regiment (1905)
1 item
AR 376

PM **ERNA SCHOENFELD**
1902–
Identity card bearing the letter "J"
(Berlin, 1939)
1 item
AR 4489

GE **SCHOENFLIES FAMILY**
Family trees and history since 1667
3 items
AR 1582

PM SM **SCHOENLANK FAMILY**
Correspondence; clippings
(1862–1963)
10 items
AR 2014

PM SM **SCHOENMANN FAMILY**
Album containing postcards and
letters (1914–1918); clippings
2 items
AR 4472

PM **FRANZ SCHOENTHAN**
1849–1913
Autograph
1 item
AR 1926

PM SM **HANS JOACHIM SCHOEPS**
Historian, 1909–1980
Letters; clippings
5 items
AR 2859

GE PM **ERNST SCHOLEM FAMILY**
Family trees and histories; official and
family documents (1776–1960)
8 items
AR 1340

FO SM **GERSCHOM SCHOLEM**
Historian, philosopher, 1897–1982
Typescripts; book reviews; speech on
acceptance of Bialik Prize (1977);
photos (1962–1980)
22 items
AR 1791, AR 5190

PM **DOROTHY AND MARVIN SCHOR**
Copies of documents while in
Shanghai
1 item
AR 5189

PM SM **EMIL SCHORSCH**
Rabbi, 1899–
Curriculum vitae; correspondence
with Leo Baeck and Max
Gruenewald; sermons by Schorsch;
programs; clippings; typescripts by
Schorsch and others on Hannover
Jewish community (1929–1963)
27 items
AR 4007

PM **SCHORSCH FAMILY**
Letter concerning Schorsch family
1 item
AR 2512

FO SM **ISMAR SCHORSCH**
Rabbi, historian, born 1935,
chancellor Jewish Theological
Seminary
Book review; photo
2 items
AR 4070

PM **JOSEPH SCHOTT**
Receipt for municipal citizenship fee
(1863)
1 item
AR 1922

FO = Photos · GE = Genealogical Material · PM = Primary Material · SM = Secondary Material

PM SM **SCHOTTLAENDER FAMILY**
Typescripts; clippings of family
histories (18th and 19th cent.)
3 items
AR 526

PM **SCHOTTLAENDER PUBLISHERS**
Typescript (1965) on history of
publishing house (1886–1933)
1 item
AR 2791

PM **RECHA SCHRAGENHEIM**
Government, finance documents for
Recha Schragenheim; family
documents (1901–1962)
11 items
AR 1937

SM **EDWARD L. SCHREIBER**
Obituary (1895); book announcement
2 items
AR 1553

GE **SCHREIBER FAMILY**
Family tree (1914)
1 item
AR 5298

GE SM **HEDWIG SCHREIBER**
Family tree from 1735; clipping
(1916)
2 items
AR 1375

PM **MEYER SCHREIBER**
Document granting permission to
settle in Eslohe (1829)
1 item
AR 4676

PM SM **HERMANN SCHUELEIN**
Brewery director, 1884–
Clippings; correspondence; awards;
documents on his career
34 items
AR 776

PM SM **SCHUELER FAMILY**
Inheritance settlement; clippings;
eulogy; engagement announcement
(1841–1880)
6 items
AR 900

SM **J. W. SCHULEIN**
Artist, 1881–1970
Catalogues of exhibitions; articles;
copies of paintings
27 items
AR 777

SM **BRUNO SCHULTZ**
Poet
Newspaper clipping (1962)
1 item
AR 1567

SM **KARL SCHUSTER**
Publisher
Newspaper article (1963)
1 item
AR 2335

PM **SCHUTZBRIEFE (LETTERS OF PROTECTION)**
Miscellaneous *Schutzbriefe*
18 items
AR 285

PM **SCHUTZJUDEN**
Documents concerning *Schutzjuden*
(1827)
2 items
AR 1153

GE PM **ALFRED SCHWAB FAMILY**
SM Correspondence; clippings; family
trees since 1495
9 items
AR 2623

PM **HERMANN SCHWAB**
1879–1962
Manuscript on Kristallnacht
(December, 1938)
1 item
AR 780

PM **JOSEF SCHWAB**
Merchant, 1801–1900
Memoirs
4 items
AR 4626

GE PM **SAMUEL SCHWAB FAMILY**
Family tree; postcard showing
Memphis department store
3 items
AR 4984

FO = Photos · GE = Genealogical Material · PM = Primary Material · SM = Secondary Material

FO **JULIUS SCHWABACH**
Banker, 19th cent.
Photo negative of Schwabach's family
(ca. 1880)
1 item
AR 4709

PM **ALBERT SCHWABACHER**
1896–
Letter (1823); notes on Schiller (ca. 1890)
3 items
AR 4127

FO SM **SCHWAEBISCH-GMUEND; JEWISH COMMUNITY**
Photos; clippings
8 items
AR 2660

SM **SCHWAEBISCH HALL; JEWISH COMMUNITY**
Article
1 item
AR 2572

PM **SCHWANFELD; JEWISH COMMUNITY**
Estimate value of community property
1 item
AR 3456

FO **ANDRE SCHWARZ-BART**
Writer, 1928–
Photo
1 item
AR 2743

PM **CLARA SCHWARZ**
Certificates for Red Cross Medal (1916)
1 item
AR 3960

GE **SCHWARZ FAMILY**
Family tree (17th–20th cent.)
1 item
AR 4672

PM **ISRAEL SCHWARZ**
Rabbi, 1830–1875
Silhouette (undated)
1 item
AR 2683

FO PM **JOSEF SCHWARZ**
SM Singer, 1880–1926
Photo; clippings; autographs
6 items
AR 2410; AR 2787

SM **KARL SCHWARZ**
Art historian and dealer
Articles about collecting of art
10 items
AR 1904

PM **LEON SCHWARZ**
1912–
Documents concerning Leon Schwarz's nationality (1924, 1938–1939); personal papers
10 items
AR 7135

PM **I. SCHWARZHAUPT**
Documents on history of Jewish community of Regensburg (1826–1933)
12 items
AR 1276

GE **SCHWARZSCHILD FAMILY**
Family tree (16th–19th cent.)
3 items
AR 3342

FO PM **FRITZ SCHWARZSCHILD**
Social worker, 1896–1967
Correspondence; reminiscences on emigration of Jews from Nazi Germany and emigration of D.P.'s after Second World War; photo
8 items
AR 885

SM **STEVEN SCHWARZSCHILD**
Review essay (1960)
1 item
AR 1093

PM **SCHWEINFURT; JEWISH COMMUNITY**
Prayers in German and Hebrew
2 items
AR 7024

PM SM **ALBERT SCHWEITZER**
Physician, 1875–1965
Clippings on Schweitzer's relations with Jews; autograph
3 items
AR 4058, AR 2832

FO = Photos · GE = Genealogical Material · PM = Primary Material · SM = Secondary Material

GE **SCHWEITZER FAMILY**
Family tree with elaborations
1 item
AR 3512

PM **ALFRED SCHWEIZER**
Lawyer
Letter to Schweizer by his wife (1958)
1 item
AR 3351

FO PM **ERNST SCHWERIN**
Photo; account of family textile factory in Breslau
2 items
AR 340

PM SM **KURT SCHWERIN**
Lawyer, librarian, born 1902
Curriculum vitae; manuscripts; clippings
9 items
AR 121

PM **SAMUEL SCHWERIN**
Apprenticeship certificate (1850)
1 item
AR 3409

SM **ARTHUR SCHWERINER**
Article: "In Defense of German-Jewish Resistors"
1 item
AR 5225

SM **SCHWETZINGEN; JEWISH COMMUNITY**
Clipping
1 item
AR 110

FO **ISRAEL SCHWIERZ**
Photos of cemeteries of Jewish communities in Unterfranken, Bavaria
129 items
AR 5042

FO PM **SCHWIRZ-STAEDTEL/SILESIA; JEWISH COMMUNITY**
Answer to questionnaire; photos of synagogue
5 items
AR 818

PM **HERMAN SECKELSOHN**
Receipt (1864)
1 item
AR 3474

PM **NORBERT SECUNDA**
Rabbi, born 1895
Correspondence; birth certificate; documents on rabbinical education and career
16 items
AR 3078

GE **SEELIG-DREIDEL-MOSS FAMILY**
Family tree
5 items
AR 4539

PM **SALOMON SEELIGMAN**
Deed of sale (1770)
1 item
AR 2056

PM **SEELOW; JEWISH COMMUNITY**
By-laws of commmunity (1841)
1 item
AR 72

PM SM **SEESEN, JACOBSON SCHOOL**
Articles; history; speeches; obituaries
20 items
AR 3502

SM **SEESEN; JEWISH COMMUNITY**
Clippings
2 items
AR 3662

FO PM **ARTHUR SEGAL**
SM Painter, 1875–1944
Photo; exhibition catalogues; clippings; manuscripts; correspondence
11 items
AR 4194, AR 7105

PM **HANS SEGAL**
Dissertation abstract (1968)
1 item
AR 3410

GE **BENJAMIN SEGALL FAMILY**
Genealogies, of descendents of John Henry "Josef Segall," Ann Arbor, Mich., since 1730
4 items
AR 2898

FO = Photos · GE = Genealogical Material · PM = Primary Material · SM = Secondary Material

PM **ANNA SEGHERS (PSEUDONYM OF NETTY RADVANY, BORN REILING)**
Letters about relationship with author Anna Seghers
1 item
AR 5179

PM **KARL SEIFART**
Manuscript
1 item
AR 459

GE **SELBIGER FAMILY**
Family tree (18th–20th cent.)
1 item
AR 4876

FO PM **SIEGFRIED SELBIGER**
SM Photo; essays; poetry
16 items
AR 528

PM **BENEDIX SELIG**
Letter of protection (1803)
1 item
AR 4356

GE **SELIGMAN-LIEBSCHUETZ FAMILY**
Genealogies of above, Bach-Gundelfinger, and Lindskold-Pederson families
1 item
AR 5202

FO PM **CAESAR SELIGMANN**
SM Rabbi, 1860–1950
Photo; clippings; essays; speech and sermon manuscripts
9 items
AR 1076

FO PM **ERICH SELIGMANN**
SM Bacteriologist, physician, 1880–1954
Biography; photos; documents; emigration (1939); obituaries; articles; curriculum vitae; publications list; correspondence diary; family history
12 items
AR 4104, AR 4104a

PM **MEYER JACOB SELIGMANN**
Copy of birth certificate (1938)
1 item
AR 1332

PM **F. SELIGSOHN**
Reminiscences on antisemitism in Germany (1961)
1 item
AR 3083

FO **JULIUS SELIGSOHN**
Lawyer, 1890–1942, member of Reichsvertretung
Photo
1 item
AR 2678

PM **ROBERT SELIGSON**
Letter from Leo Baeck (1948)
1 item
AR 1357

PM **JULIUS SELLING**
Correspondence on restitution claims
2 items
AR 3445

GE PM **LEO SELLO**
Report card on one-year voluntary military service (1906); apprenticeship contract as mason (1906); certificate of building committee of Berlin Jewish community (1909); certificate for military service (1912–1913 and 1914–1918) as sergeant; family tree; German passport with letter "J"
11 items
AR 1938

SM **HENRY SELVER**
Social worker
Obituaries (1957)
2 items
AR 109

PM SM **SELZ FAMILY**
Mohel book of Abraham Selz (1853–1881); newspaper article about Nanette Selz (1874); various letters about Adler family, Kitzingen and about Selz family; photocopy of *Congressional Record* (1981) about Edward M. Adler, descendant of Abraham Selz
8 items
AR 5018

FO = Photos · GE = Genealogical Material · PM = Primary Material · SM = Secondary Material

SM **TONY SENDER**
Social Democrat, 1888–1964
Photocopy of magazine article
1 item
AR 4800

PM SM **IMMANUEL SENFT**
Correspondence (1934, 1942–1944);
clippings on Austro-Indian Society
(1934)
7 items
AR 502

PM **SENNFELD; JEWISH COMMUNITY**
Letter
1 item
AR 2881

PM SM **MELANIE SERBU**
Mathematician, poet
Poems; certificate; exemption from
forced labor; testimony of University
of Brasov, Rumania
10 items
AR 4357

SM **ROBERT SEREBRENIK**
Rabbi, 1902–1965
Newspaper article; obituaries (1965)
2 items
AR 2579

PM **SERMONS**
Sermons (1847–1938), some given by
Rabbi Salomon Holdheim, Berlin
4 items
AR 3644

SM **SHALOM OF SAFED**
Artist
Clippings (1966, 1970)
2 items
AR 3721

PM **GEORGE BERNARD SHAW**
1856–1950
Autographs
2 items
AR 947

SM **WILLIAM L. SHIRER**
Newspaper clipping (1962)
1 item
AR 1809

PM **SICHEL FAMILY**
Family documents (1837–1870)
27 items
AR 621

PM **FRIEDRICH SIEBURG**
Documents concerning Sieburg's
Nazi past, his attitudes in the 1950's
4 items
AR 2015

FO PM **SIEGBURG; JEWISH COMMUNITY**
List of Jewish residents (1933–1942);
immigration and deportation lists;
photo of synagogue
7 items
AR 3077

PM **SIEGEL FAMILY**
Letter from Gesamtarchiv der Juden
in Deutschland (1938)
1 item
AR 1077

GE **PAUL SIEGEL FAMILY**
Family tree, related documents
3 items
AR 4394

PM **SILBER FAMILY**
Letter of municipal citizenship
(Berlin, 1831)
1 item
AR 948

FO PM **ARTHUR SILBERGLEIT**
SM Author, 1881–1943
Photos; clippings; poetry;
correspondence concerning attempted
emigration (1939–41); autographs
34 items
AR 301, AR 1518

PM **DOCTOR SILBERGLEIT**
Letter (1871)
1 item
AR 4369

PM **EDUARD SILBERMAN**
Lawyer, died 1917
Letter (1883)
1 item
AR 2009

FO = Photos · GE = Genealogical Material · PM = Primary Material · SM = Secondary Material

PM **FRIEDRICH SILBERSTEIN**
Physician
Correspondence on dissemination of antisemitic fliers among German troops in Finland (1918); Finnish Freedom Medal awarded to Silberstein
5 items
AR 3979

FO PM **SILESIA; JEWISH COMMUNITY**
Letter of protection (1786); histories of Silesia and of Jewish communities; photos
18 items
AR 292

PM SM **JACOB SILVEY**
Clippings; correspondence
10 items
AR 4801

PM SM **GEORG SIMMEL**
Sociologist, 1858–1918
Clippings; correspondence with Husserl, Rilke, Dietrich Schaefer; autographs
27 items
AR 388, AR 1108

FO SM **PAUL SIMMEL**
Cartoonist, 1887–1933
Photo; clippings
2 items
AR 2815

PM **BETTINA SIMON**
Medal; certificate; testimonial war work (1916, 1933)
3 items
AR 3978

PM **ELSE SIMON FAMILY**
Ritual objects (19th cent.)
8 items
AR 2844

FO PM **ERICH SIMON**
Musician, 1882–1943
Photo; biographic notes
2 items
AR 346

PM SM **ERNST SIMON**
Educator, born 1899
Curriculum vitae; clippings on Simon and on Jewish communities in Latin America
38 items
AR 108

GE PM **SIMON FAMILY**
Family tree; letter from Moses Mendelssohn to Friedrich Nicolai (1799)
2 items
AR 1355

PM **FRITZ SIMON**
Permission to continue employing an Aryan maid (1936)
1 item
AR 1078

PM **HERMANN E. SIMON**
Letter written during service in U.S. Army (1942–1945)
1 item
AR 5239

FO PM **JAMES SIMON**
Art collector, 1851–1932
Commemorative plaque (photo) on gift of excavations in Tel El Amarna to German Orient Society (1911–1914); miscellaneous letters, articles, photos; letters telegraphed by former emperor Wilhelm II
19 items
AR 2629

PM **KARL SIMON**
Correspondence of Karl Simon, Rumanian consul general in Germany (1900, 1916); explanatory note of his son (1958)
3 items
AR 321

GE **MAX SIMON**
Lehmann and Badmann family trees (18th–20th cent.)
4 items
AR 4446

PM **OTTO SIMON FAMILY**
Synagogue seat certificates (1857–1935); trees for Israel certificates (1961)
13 items
AR 1135

GE **SIMON SIMON FAMILY**
Family tree (19th–20th cent.)
1 item
AR 3631

FO = Photos · GE = Genealogical Material · PM = Primary Material · SM = Secondary Material

PM **THEODOR SIMON**
Chalizah levirate document (1881)
2 items
AR 1956

SM **WALTER SIMON**
Treatise: "The Position of a Jewish Agnostic"; bibliography of scientific publications
2 items
AR 5251, AR 2541

SM **WALTER B. SIMON**
Sociologist
Clippings; proposal for a scholarly study
5 items
AR 4261

FO PM **DAVID JACOB SIMONSEN**
Rabbi, 1853–1932
Photo; letters
3 items
AR 1208

PM **BERTHOLD SIMONSOHN**
1912–1978
Funeral notice
1 item
AR 4540

FO **JUSTIZRAT SIMONSON**
Photo
1 item
AR 3530

PM **M. H. SIMONSON**
Rabbi Manchester, mid–19th cent.
Notebooks of biblical commentary by Simonson
3 items
AR 7190

FO PM **EDUARD SIMSON**
SM Politician, 1810–1899
Photo; clippings; autographs
11 items
AR 1304, AR 1109

GE **SIMSON FAMILY, BAVARIA**
Genealogy (1716–1965)
1 item
AR 5104

PM **O. K. SIMSON FAMILY**
Diary (1864); school admission papers (1877); letter of municipal citizenship (1898)
3 items
AR 1377

FO **SINDOLSHEIM; JEWISH COMMUNITY**
Photos of ruins of synagogue
3 items
AR 3881

PM **J. SINGER**
Letter (1884)
1 item
AR 268

FO PM **PAUL SINGER**
Politician, 1844–1911
Photo (1903); autographs
3 items
AR 2744, AR 337

PM **SINN COLLECTION**
19th cent. documents; correspondence of Horwitz, Lambert, and Rautenberg families
67 items
AR 1160

PM **CLAIRE SINNREICH**
Writer
Poetry; diaries; correspondence
2 items
AR 5102

PM **JACOB SINNREICH**
Diary; miscellaneous papers;, documents
3 items
AR 5061

PM **SKLAREK AFFAIR**
Letter to *Berliner Tageblatt* on Sklarek affair (1927)
1 item
AR 1713

PM **FEDOR SKUTSCH**
Physician, 1821–1896
Correspondence (1847); personal, family documents (1771–1846)
11 items
AR 3116

FO = Photos · GE = Genealogical Material · PM = Primary Material · SM = Secondary Material

SM **MARTIN SOBOTKER**
1900–1977
Obituary
1 item
AR 4436

SM **SOCIALISM AND THE JEWISH QUESTION**
Clipping concerning scholarly conference on socialism and the Jewish Question (1977)
1 item
AR 4635

FO **WALTER H. SOKEL**
Literary historian
Photo
1 item
AR 2254

SM **SOLINGEN; JEWISH COMMUNITY**
Clippings
2 items
AR 3694

SM **BERNHARD SOLOMON**
"Ancestry of Bernhard Solomon" (Chart, 1977)
1 item
AR 5289

PM **EZECHIEL SOLOMON**
History of descendants of Ezechiel Solomon
2 items
AR 4577

SM **FREDERICK SOLOMON**
Painter, 20th cent.
Clippings; exhibition catalogues (1958–1970)
8 items
AR 3854

PM **FRANZ SOLON**
Membership certificate for Gesellschaft der Freunde (1886)
1 item
AR 4840

PM **FRITZ SOLON**
Poetry (1947–1951)
4 items
AR 2083

PM **WERNER SOMBART**
1863–1941
Autograph
1 item
AR 1849

PM **ARTHUR SOMMERFELD FAMILY**
Personal papers; correspondence; Dutch poetry; short manuscripts
27 items
AR 1983

PM **MARTIN SOMMERFELD**
Literary historian
Photo; curricula vitae; correspondence with Alfred Vagts (1920–1943)
65 items
AR 3217

PM **SONCINO-GESELLSCHAFT**
Membership list; printed material from organization (1924–1930)
5 items
AR 2358

PM **JACOB SONDHEIMER**
Photocopies of family documents; stories of persecution, emigration, restitution; Sosua refugee settlement in Dominican Republic; Miriam Sondheimer diary (1934–1942)
10 items
AR 4981

SM **ABRAHAM SONNE**
Author, 1883–1950
Four library cards of his writings
1 item
AR 3371

SM **RUDOLF G. SONNEBORN**
"Henriette and Steward Hirschman Foundation gives $100,000 for Dormitory Building" (*American Judaism*, newspaper clipping, 1958)
1 item
AR 238

PM SM **LEOPOLD SONNEMANN**
Journalist
Newspaper clipping commemorating 100th birthday (1931); autograph
2 items
AR 462, AR 756

FO = Photos · GE = Genealogical Material · PM = Primary Material · SM = Secondary Material

GE **SONNENBORN FAMILY**
Family history (18th–20th cent.)
1 item
AR 4802

PM SM **JOSEPH VON SONNENFELS**
Statesman, 1733–1817
Photo of painting; article on
Sonnenfels; autograph
3 items
AR 2745, AR 444

FO PM **ADOLF VON SONNENTHAL**
Actor, 1834–1909
Photo; autographs
7 items
AR 1492, AR 1491

PM SM **HEINRICH SONTHEIM**
Singer, 1820–1912
Official documents; correspondence
of various sorts; clippings (19th cent.)
200 items
AR 520

SM **SOSHANA**
Painter, 20th cent.
Exhibition catalogue (1973)
3 items
AR 4190

PM **JURA SOYFER**
Poet, 1912–1939
Biographical notices
2 items
AR 4395

SM **SOZIALDEMOKRATISCHE
PARTEI DEUTSCHLANDS**
Newspaper clipping (1981): Prague
Exile – Reports 1934–1940
1 item
AR 5196

SM **SPANDAU; JEWISH COMMUNITY**
History of Jews (clipping)
1 item
AR 5194

SM **ADOLF SPANIER**
Book of memorial prayers (1918)
1 item
AR 3513

SM **JULIUS SPANIER**
1880–1959
Obituary (1959)
1 item
AR 1079

GE SM **MEIER SPANIER FAMILY**
Bibliography of Meier Spanier's
works; family tree
2 items
AR 3566

PM **NATHAN SPATZ**
Documents on Nathan Spatz's
military service and family affairs
(1833–39)
3 items
AR 442

FO SM **HENRY SPETT**
Publisher, born 1898
Clipping; photo of Spett and of
Mannheim Jewish burial society
(1925)
3 items
AR 2162

GE **SPEYER FAMILY**
Family tree (19th–20th cent.)
1 item
AR 3843

PM SM **SPEYER; JEWISH COMMUNITY**
Clippings; speech
3 items
AR 3361

PM **MARIA SPEYER**
Autograph
1 item
AR 1850

PM **WILHELM SPEYER**
1887–1952
Autograph
1 item
AR 1379

SM **ALEXANDER S. SPIEGEL**
Writer
Newspaper clippings (1956, 1957,
1958)
3 items
AR 192

PM **JULIUS SPIEGEL FAMILY**
1884–1961
Files on restitution claims; family documents; correspondence
11 items
AR 7235

GE PM **SPIEGELBERG FAMILY**
Original documents relating to veterinary doctor Jos. Spiegelberg (1822–1844); family papers; genealogy
8 items
AR 5292

FO PM **HILDE SPIEL**
Writer, 20th cent.
Photo of Hilde Spiel; reviews of her biography of Fanny Austen (1962)
5 items
AR 1810

PM **MORITZ SPIER**
Poetry for wedding (1913)
1 item
AR 3247

PM SM **SELMAR SPIER**
Newspaper article about memoirs (1961); letter from Selmar Spier, Frankfurt
2 items
AR 2336

PM **SIMON SPIER**
Cantor, teacher; 1864–1931
Wesel/Rhein and Haifa memoirs; sermons; poems
4 items
AR 4990

PM SM **HEINRICH SPIERO**
Literary historian
Document giving exemption from escort and protection money (1810); baptism certificate for Moritz Simon and wife; correspondence; articles of influence of Jews and non-Aryan Christians on German life; autograph
20 items
AR 1235, AR 1851, AR 5341

PM **ELSE SPIES**
Membership card for Jüdischer Kulturbund; letter on emigration (1938)
3 items
AR 1081

FO SM **BARUCH DE SPINOZA**
Philosopher, 1632–1677
Clippings on 300th anniversary of Spinoza's death; photo of Spinoza's house
5 items
AR 4344

FO PM **GEORGE SIMON SPIR**
1851–1896
Postcards; letters as soldier in war of 1870/71 to his family; photo; miscellaneous letters
7 items
AR 3576

PM **SPIRO COLLECTION**
Hebrew record books of Jewish community of Neustadt (19th cent.); sermons in Hebrew (17th cent.); notes in Hebrew
3 items
AR 7055

PM SM **EUGEN SPIRO**
Painter
Newspaper clippings; curriculum vitae; clippings: "Dialogue with Professor Eugen Spiro;" autographs
9 items
AR 503, AR 1080

PM **IRMA SPITZ**
Red-Cross letters from Irma Spitz in Berlin to her children in Argentina (1942)
2 items
AR 4490

PM **ELIAS SPITZER**
Austrian passport (1868)
1 item
AR 2288

FO **SAMUEL SPITZER**
Rabbi, Hamburg
Photo
1 item
AR 2290

FO = Photos · GE = Genealogical Material · PM = Primary Material · SM = Secondary Material

PM **AXEL SPRINGER**
Publisher, philanthropist, 1912–1985
Manuscript; interviews; speeches
(1967–1984); honors given by Leo
Baeck Institute
85 items
AR 2338

PM **PETER STADELMAYER**
Correspondence of Stadelmayer
concerning Jewish publishers (1968)
3 items
AR 3501

PM **STADTHAGEN; JEWISH COMMUNITY**
Typescripts; letters
5 items
AR 128

SM **FRANK L. STAHL**
Engineer, born 1920
Article (*Aufbau*, 1980)
1 item
AR 4877

FO PM **FRIEDRICH JULIUS STAHL**
Politician, 1802–1861
Photo; autographs
4 items
AR 2746, AR 2082

FO SM **HEINRICH STAHL**
Jewish community official,
1868–1942
Photo; obituaries; press clippings
15 items
AR 463

SM **LEO STAHL**
Journalist, 1888–1960
Obituary (1960)
1 item
AR 1092

PM **RUDOLF STAHL**
Essay, "Vocational Retraining of Jews
in Nazi Germany 1933–1938"
1 item
AR 3722

SM **HANS STAMM**
Review by Stamm of the book *Von
der Novemberrevolution zur Räterepublik
in München* (1958)
1 item
AR 1082

SM **RUDOLF L. STAMM**
Literary historian
Clipping (1974)
1 item
AR 4559

SM **FRIEDRICH STAMPFER**
Journalist, Social Democrat,
1874–1957
Clippings including biography
(1968–1969)
3 items
AR 4636

GE **CHARLES P. STANTON**
Genealogies of Steinheim and
Kaufmann families from Franconia
(200 pp.)
1 item
AR 5096

FO PM **STARGARD (NOW STARGARD SZCZECINSKI, POLAND); JEWISH COMMUNITY**
Photo of synagogue; history
3 items
AR 4139

PM **ELSE STAUDINGER**
Social worker, 1889–1966
Testimonials to and memorials for
Else Staudinger
8 items
AR 2359

GE PM **STEEGMAN FAMILY**
Family tree; official documents on
Steegman Family in Mannheim (ca.
1800)
6 items
AR 4883

FO **STEIN A. KOCHER; JEWISH COMMUNITY**
Photos
3 items
AR 4075

PM **ARNOLD AND ERNA STEIN**
1927–1942
Photocopies of diary (1927–1939);
correspondence to Gerda Stein from
relatives; notes and commentary by
Gerda Meyer (born Stein)

FO = Photos · GE = Genealogical Material · PM = Primary Material · SM = Secondary Material

3 items
AR 5085

SM **EDITH STEIN**
Nun, 1891–1942
Clippings
4 items
AR 2624

GE **STEIN FAMILY**
Family tree (18th–20th cent.)
1 item
AR 4103

PM SM **FRED STEIN**
Photographer, 1909–1967
Clippings; biography
8 items
AR 808

FO PM **LEOPOLD STEIN**
Rabbi, 1810–1882
Photos of Stein and the girls' school he directed; biographical notices; memorial booklet; letters; sermon manuscripts
17 items
AR 45

FO PM **LUDWIG STEIN**
Philosopher, 1859–1930
Photo; reminiscences of Stein by Arthur Kallmann
4 items
AR 1084

FO PM **NATHAN STEIN**
SM Economist, 1881–1966, Jewish communal official
Photo; obituaries, correspondence with his father; letters from Leo Baeck and Zacharias Fraenkel; history of Jewish Council of Baden
29 items
AR 1209

SM **SIGMUND STEIN**
Lawyer
Newspaper clipping (1968)
1 item
AR 3420

PM **STEINACH A.D. SAALE; JEWISH COMMUNITY**
History; family reminiscences
2 items
AR 4526

SM **STEINBACH/GLAN;JEWISH COMMUNITY**
Newspaper article on burning synagogues
1 item
AR 5045

FO PM **HANS WILHELM (WILLIAM)**
SM **STEINBERG**
Conductor, 1899–1978
Photo; letter; autographs
5 items
AR 5023, AR 3019

PM SM **STEINBERGER FAMILY**
Personal documents; clippings (1917–1935)
7 items
AR 1705

PM **EDUARD STEINER**
Austrian passport (1865)
1 item
AR 1784

SM **GEORGE STEINER**
Author of play about Adolf Hitler
Photocopy of a critique of play
1 item
AR 5157

SM **ELEANOR STEINER-PRAG**
Newspaper clipping concerning address book of German book trade (1961)
1 item
AR 1674

SM **HUGO STEINER-PRAG**
Painter, 1880–1945
Clippings; exhibition catalogues
14 items
AR 2969

PM **SIMON STEINER FAMILY**
Photocopies of correspondence (1879–1891); report card (1879); birth certificate (1822)
3 items
AR 5362

FO PM **ADOLF STEINHARTER**
Antiques dealer, 1853–1918
Photo; eulogy; bound volume containing pictures of the Steinharter mansion

FO = Photos · GE = Genealogical Material · PM = Primary Material · SM = Secondary Material

4 items
AR 2883

**FO ADOLF AND ROSA
STEINHARTER**
Photo album (ca. 1910)
1 item
AR 7170

FO SOLOMON LUDWIG STEINHEIM
Philosopher, physician, 1789–1866
Photo
1 item
AR 4246

FO PM HANS STEINITZ
Journalist, born 1912
Biographical notice; photo
2 items
AR 3444

GE MORITZ STEINITZ FAMILY
Family tree (18th–20th cent.)
1 item
AR 4203

GE SALOMON STEINITZ FAMILY
Family tree (18th–20th cent.)
2 items
AR 4257

FO SM MORITZ STEINSCHNEIDER
Historian, 1816–1907
Photo; clippings; list of Hebrew manuscripts
7 items
AR 1696

PM F. L. STEINTHAL FAMILY
Rabbi
Court documents; case against administration of synagogue (1826); autographs
27 items
AR 954–955

GE STEINTHAL FAMILY
Family tree (18th–20th cent.)
2 items
AR 1393

PM STEINTHAL FAMILY
Family documents; poesie albums (Dessau and Coethen, 19th cent.)
23 items
AR 627

FO PM HEYMANN STEINTHAL
SM Psychologist, 1823–1899
Photo; letters; autograph
3 items
AR 2922, AR 1519

SM ELEANORE STERLING
Sociologist, 1923–1968
Obituary (1969)
1 item
AR 4268

FO STERN MAGAZINE
Photos: six snapshots of rabbis (1934–1935)
6 items
AR 5315

**GE ABRAHAM STERN FAMILY;
SILESIA**
Family tree (18th–20th cent.)
1 item
AR 4144

PM ADOLF STERN FAMILY
Family papers of Stern and Friedlaender families (mostly Berlin 19th and early 20th cent.); document on Adolf Stern, Minister of Public Works (Berlin, 1904)
34 items
AR 1277

PM SM ALFRED STERN FAMILY
Official, commercial, family documents (Neustadt/Saale, 1828–1941); clipping on Alfred Stern (1970)
26 items
AR 2631

PM SM ARTHUR STERN
Clippings; correspondence (1925–1937)
30 items
AR 3759

FO PM STERN FAMILY
SM Family papers (1806–1936), including passport (1806); letter of appointment for Moritz Stern at Göttingen (1859); photo; obituary of historian Alfred Stern
7 items
AR 752

FO = Photos · GE = Genealogical Material · PM = Primary Material · SM = Secondary Material

PM **STERN FAMILY, SCHMALLENBERG**
Excerpt on Stern family in Schmallenberg, their textile factory
1 item
AR 4383

FO GE **STERN FAMILY, STEINACH**
PM SM Family tree; annotations; letters; clippings; photos of family members (1838–1942); photos of socialist politician Adolf Braun
19 items
AR 2070

PM SM **FRED STERN**
Businessman, 1895–
Curricula vitae; clippings on Stern's literary activity
7 items
AR 1948

SM **FRITZ STERN**
Clippings and articles on Bleichroeder
8 items
AR 4370

SM **GERSON STERN**
Writer, 1874–1956
Typed copy (245 pp.) of novel *Die Waage der Welt*; copies of other writings
4 items
AR 172

FO PM **GUY STERN**
SM Professor of German literature, born 1922
Photo; curriculum vitae; clippings; essays
11 items
AR 1085

SM **ISIDOR STERN**
Liquor wholesaler, 1857–1943
Obituary; biography
2 items
AR 44

SM **JULIUS STERN**
Educator
Programs for graduation, Gymnasium in Hohenbaden (1963); article
2 items
AR 2244

GE SM **MALCOLM STERN**
Rabbi
Book reviews of Stern's genealogical studies (1977–1979)
2 items
AR 4710

FO PM **MAX STERN**
SM Engineer, 20th cent.
Business contracts; photos; clippings (1926–1966)
24 items
AR 3161

SM **MAX STERN**
Born 1904 (Duesseldorf); Art dealer (Montreal)
Exhibit catalogues; booklet on art market
5 items
AR 7070

SM **MAX M. STERN**
Psychoanalyst, 1895–1982
Clippings; bibliography; obituaries; articles
6 items
AR 4786

FO PM **OTTO STERN**
Physicist, 1888–1967
Photos; biographical notes
3 items
AR 1405

PM **PAUL STERN**
Flour-milling industrialist, born 1878
Correspondence on business; account of imprisonment in Buchenwald (1938)
13 items
AR 1086

SM **RUDOLF STERN**
Physician, father of Fritz Stern
Recommendation (1938)
1 item
AR 4641

SM **SIEGFRIED STERN**
Banker, 1884–1961
Obituaries
4 items
AR 1949

FO = Photos · GE = Genealogical Material · PM = Primary Material · SM = Secondary Material

SM **SIGISMUND STERN**
Bibliography
1 item
AR 3939

FO **SUESSKIND STERN**
1610–1687
Color photo of painting
1 item
AR 4135

PM **WILLIAM STERN**
Psychologist, 1871–1938
Biographical notices
3 items
AR 3787

PM **FRITZ STERNBERG**
Socialist, 1875–1963
Manuscript, "Die Welt von Morgen" (1943), on prospects for socialism after Second World War
1 item
AR 7174

PM **HILDE STERNBERG**
Letter from Stefan Zweig (1927)
1 item
AR 1935

PM **STERNBERG; JEWISH COMMUNITY**
Letter; Jewish birth and death register (1813–1933); community minute book
3 items
AR 3507

FO **WILHELM STERNBERG**
Physician, 1865–
Pictures of Sternberg with medical invention
2 items
AR 3581

PM SM **FANNY STERNFELD**
Letters from Johann Nepomuk Ritter von Nussbaum; eulogy for Fanny Sternfeld; clipping (history of Neustaetter family)
26 items
AR 622

FO SM **CARL STERNHEIM**
Author, 1878–1942
Clippings; photo
3 items
AR 1667

GE PM **STERNHEIMER FAMILY**
Family tree (18th–20th cent.); chronicle of Jewish life on the Rhine
10 items
AR 3294

FO **NATHAN STETTHEIM**
Photos of portraits of Nathan Stettheim and wife (early 19th cent.)
2 items
AR 4244

PM SM **STETTIN (NOW SZCZECIN, POLAND); JEWISH COMMUNITY**
Typescript about deportees (1940); clippings
3 items
AR 3790

PM SM **ANITA STEVENS**
Psychiatrist, born 1911
Curriculum vitae; professional opinions; articles
9 items
AR 4309

FO **WILHELM STIASSNY**
Architect, 1842–1920
Photo
2 items
AR 2748

SM **STIEBEL**
Physician
Newspaper clipping (1959)
1 item
AR 1088

PM SM **ERNST C. STIEFEL**
Lawyer
Booklet *Crime, Law and the Scholars*, by Gerhard O. W. Mueller; correspondence
6 items
AR 5230

GE PM **ERNST STIEFEL FAMILY**
SM Family documents; clippings (19th and 20th cent.); family trees since 1735
51 items
AR 3591

GE **NATHAN STIEFEL FAMILY**
Family tree (19th–20th cent.)
1 item
AR 4491

FO = Photos · GE = Genealogical Material · PM = Primary Material · SM = Secondary Material

GE **STIEGLITZ FAMILY**
Family history (18th–20th cent.)
1 item
AR 3430

PM **HEINRICH STIEGLITZ**
1801–1849
Autograph
1 item
AR 1852

FO **KURT STILLSCHWEIG**
1905–1955
Photo
1 item
AR 1395

PM **STOLZENAU/WESER; JEWISH COMMUNITY**
History (14 pp.)
1 item
AR 4809

FO **STRALSUND; JEWISH COMMUNITY**
Photo of synagogue
1 item
AR 3322

PM **STRASSBOURG; JEWISH COMMUNITY**
Letter
1 item
AR 4917

SM **STRAUBING; JEWISH COMMUNITY**
Clippings
2 items
AR 2464

GE **ELIAS STRAUS**
Genealogy since 1470
1 item
AR 1397

GE **EMANUEL STRAUS**
Family tree since 1815
1 item
AR 3962

FO GE **STRAUS FAMILY, OTTERBERG**
PM Founders of Macy's
Family histories; family trees since 1725; records from Worms (1826); personal documents (mid–19th cent.); correspondence; photos
8 items
AR 4492

PM **OSCAR STRAUS**
1870–1954
Autographs
3 items
AR 1653

FO SM **RAHEL STRAUS**
Physician, 1880–1963
Photo of family; obituaries
16 items
AR 1454

PM **STRAUS-SONTHEIMER FAMILY**
Vital document (1938); correspondence (1939, 1945)
5 items
AR 4286

PM SM **BRUNO STRAUSS**
Historian, philologist, 1889–1969
Correspondence; clippings; obituaries; memorabilia of Herman Cohen; letter (1964) concerning Rabbi Nobel
45 items
AR 3753, AR 3876

PM **STRAUSS-EPPSTEIN, HEDWIG**
Social Worker, wife of Dr. Paul Eppstein (1903–1944)
Part of letter to Mia Neter (1939); photo
2 items
AR 5369; AR 5235

GE **STRAUSS FAMILY**
Family history (17th–19th cent.)
1 item
AR 4922

GE PM **STRAUSS FAMILY, DITTIGHEIM-TAUBERBISCHOFSCHEIM, BADEN**
Family tree from 1658; family notes;, documents; copies of manuscripts; data on World War I participation; withdrawal of admission to practice law (1938); letters
15 items
AR 77

SM **HANS STRAUSS**
Clipping; URO circular on restitution (1952, 1956)
2 items
AR 4879

FO = Photos · GE = Genealogical Material · PM = Primary Material · SM = Secondary Material

SM **HEINRICH STRAUSS**
Art historian, 1899–
Reviews; clippings on Strauss
3 items
AR 4610

PM SM **HERBERT STRAUSS**
Historian, born 1918
Personal documents; articles; clippings
(1938–1976)
21 items
AR 3372

FO PM **ILSE STRAUSS**
SM 1920–
Family histories trees, and documents since 1768; correspondence with reference to immigration to Australia (1939–1947); clippings from Australia; general clippings on family members (1940–1979)
43 items
AR 3273

FO PM **LEO STRAUSS**
SM Philosopher, 1899–1973
Bibliographies; photo; clipping; biographical notes
6 items
AR 2205

PM **LEOPOLD STRAUSS FAMILY**
Letter (1915); pass (1942); notices on deaths of family members in concentration camps
4 items
AR 3407

PM **LUDWIG STRAUSS**
1892–
Autographs
4 items
AR 1150

GE **STRAUSS-NEUGASS FAMILIES, BAD HOMBERG VON DER HOEHE**
Family notes and trees Strauss family (1776–1961), Neugass family (1818–1914)
3 items
AR 5275

PM **RICHARD STRAUSS**
1864–1949
Autographs
3 items
AR 2397

SM **HUGO STREISAND**
1878–1955
Obituary
1 item
AR 2226

FO GE **KATE STREIT (BORN LIPPMANN)**
PM 1895–1977
Family histories and trees since 1580; personal documents (19th cent.); photos
20 items
AR 4507

FO **FRITZ STRICH**
Literary historian, 1882–1963
Photo
1 item
AR 2749

FO PM **BETHEL HENRY STROUSBERG**
SM Financier, 1823–1884
Family documents (18th and 19th cent.); clippings; correspondence (19th cent.); photos
36 items
AR 1406

FO PM **HERMANN STRUCK**
SM Artist, 1876–1944
Photos; clippings; exhibition catalogue; autographs
28 items
AR 1548, AR 1455

PM **STRUEMPFELBRUNN; JEWISH COMMUNITY**
Notes
1 item
AR 3362

PM **MAX STRUPP FAMILY**
Official documents (1812–1938)
6 items
AR 3981

FO PM **MANFRED STURMANN**
SM Author, (1903–
Photo; clipping; autograph
3 items
AR 2176

FO = Photos · GE = Genealogical Material · PM = Primary Material · SM = Secondary Material

FO PM **STUTTGART; JEWISH**
SM **COMMUNITY**
Clippings; photo of synagogue; articles; circular letters; programs
45 items
AR 2391, AR 2045

PM **EDUARD SUESS**
1831–1914
Autographs
1 item
AR 2620

GE **SUESSKIND FAMILY, GUESTEN**
Genealogies, family tree
2 items
AR 4959

PM **SUGENHEIM; JEWISH COMMUNITY**
Typescript, Kahlsbuch
2 items
AR 453

GE **ARTHUR HAYS SULZBERGER FAMILY**
Family tree (17th–20th cent.)
1 item
AR 3042

SM **SULZBURG; JEWISH COMMUNITY**
Clipping
1 item
AR 558fi

FO PM **SALOMON SULZER**
Cantor, 1804–1890
Photo; musical score
2 items
AR 3304

PM **CURT SUSSMANN**
Promissory note (1808)
1 item
AR 806

GE PM **SUSSMANN FAMILY, HAMBURG**
Family tree; marriage contracts; vital, commercial, registration documents (1852–1913)
15 items
AR 2049

GE **SUSSMANN FAMILY, STORKOW**
Family tree and history since 1774
2 items
AR 2227

PM **ABRAHAM SUTRO**
Rabbi, 1784–1869
Autograph
1 item
AR 1726

SM **ITALO SVEVO (PSEUDONYM FOR ETTORE SCHMITZ)**
Writer, 1861–1926
Newspaper and magazine articles
2 items
AR 2339

PM **SWARENSKY FAMILY**
Family documents (1917, 1955)
3 items
AR 3758

SM **GERSHON SWET**
Journalist
Newspaper clipping (1968)
1 item
AR 3411

FO **SYNAGOGUES; PHOTOS**
Photo of synagogues in Germany
4 items
AR 4878

SM **ZOSA SZAJKOWSKI**
1911–1978
Book review of his *Analytical Franco-Jewish Gazetteer 1939–1945* (1967)
1 item
AR 3214

FO **OTTO SZASZ**
Mathematician, 1884–1952
Photo
1 item
AR 3228

FO **EUGEN SZENKAR**
Conductor, 1891–
Autographed photo
1 item
AR 2419

FO **MORITZ SZEPS**
Journalist, 1833–1902
Photo
1 item
AR 2750

FO = Photos · GE = Genealogical Material · PM = Primary Material · SM = Secondary Material

PM **BENJAMIN SZOLD**
1829–1902
Testimonial letter (1858)
1 item
AR 2663

SM **HENRIETTE SZOLD**
1860–1945
Articles
2 items
AR 2081

FO **JACOB JOSEPH TACHAU**
Railroad freight expert, 1828–1900
Photo with wife
1 item
AR 4372

PM SM **LUDWIG TACHAU**
Philologist, 1858–1919
Bound volume containing offprints, clippings, manuscript, correspondence (1890's)
15 items
AR 3851

SM **PAUL TACHAU**
Esther Megillah
1 item
AR 3401

FO GE **DAVID TACHAUER FAMILY**
PM SM Professor of mathematics, 1885–1976
Personal documents (1885–1914); correspondence (1930–1969); articles; family trees and histories since 1590; photo album
44 items
AR 4396

FO PM **EUGEN TAEUBLER**
Historian, 1879–1953
Photos; obituaries; poetry; correspondence with Nazi authorities (1933); papers from estate
16 items
AR 174

FO SM **URIEL TAL**
Historian, 20th cent.
Photos; essays; reviews of books
14 items
AR 3773

FO SM **TANN RHOEN; JEWISH COMMUNITY**
Photos; article
3 items
AR 5075

SM **MARC H. TANNENBAUM**
Rabbi; director of American Jewish Committee
Address to World Council of Churches
1 item
AR 5233

FO SM **TARNOWITZ (NOW TARNOWSKIE GORY, POLAND); JEWISH COMMUNITY**
Photo; cliipings
3 items
AR 2963

SM **ARYEH TARTAKOWER**
Lecture at conference in Vienna (1976), "Die soziologischen Grundlagen der modernen hebräischen Sprachforschung und der hebräischen Renaissance"
1 item
AR 7087

PM SM **MAX TAU**
Author, 1897–1976
Newspaper clippings; autographs
8 items
AR 1568, AR 1765

FO **ALFRED TAUBER**
Mathematician, 1866–1942
Photo
1 item
AR 4142

FO PM **RICHARD TAUBER**
Singer, 1892–1948
Photos; autograph
3 items
AR 2751, AR 1102

FO PM **TAUBERBISCHOFSHEIM; JEWISH COMMUNITY**
Correspondence; photos of synagogue; list of Jewish residents (1933) and their fate
14 items
AR 3028

FO = Photos · GE = Genealogical Material · PM = Primary Material · SM = Secondary Material

FO **KARL TAUSIG**
Pianist, 1841–1871
Photo
1 item
AR 2782

PM **WALTER TAUSK**
1890–
Introduction to memoirs of life in Theresienstadt
1 item
AR 4215

FO **THEODOR RITTER VON TAUSSIG**
1848–1909
Photo
1 item
AR 2752

SM **MIKE TAYLOR**
Copies of reminiscence of Klaus Barbie (newspaper articles)
2 items
AR 5135

FO **JOSEPH TENENBAUM**
Physician, 1887–1961
Photo
1 item
AR 2789

GE **TENZER FAMILY, GALICIA**
Family tree (18th–20th cent.)
2 items
AR 7116

GE **TEUTSCH FAMILY**
Family history and tree (18th–19th cent.)
2 items
AR 382, AR 5118

PM **GUMBEL THALMANN**
Teacher
Correspondence; documents on education, career (1878–1911)
7 items
AR 4027

GE PM **THALMESSINGER FAMILY**
Family tree (19th–20th cent.); essay on Jewish community of Wallerstein; correspondence
5 items
AR 333

SM **SIEGFRIED JOSEPH THANNHAUSER**
Physician, 1885–1962
Obituary
1 item
AR 2029

SM **THEATER; VIENNA**
Newspaper clipping (1963)
1 item
AR 2340

PM **PAUL THEILHEIMER FAMILY**
Family and official documents (19th cent.)
6 items
AR 1399

GE **THELMA FAMILY**
Family tree (18th–20th cent.)
1 item
AR 3956

FO SM **FRIEDRICH THIEBERGER**
Philosopher, 1888–1956
Photo; bibliography
2 items
AR 2360

GE PM **THORSCH FAMILY**
Family and official documents (19th cent.); family histories and trees since 18th cent.; sheet music with words
34 items
AR 1878

PM **JOSEF TICHAUER**
Letter (1966); essays
3 items
AR 3608

FO PM **TIEFENTHAL FAMILY**
Marriage contract (1831); photo (ca. 1860); excerpt from speech by Graf Zeppelin (1916)
3 items
AR 2884

FO **ALBERT U. TIETZ**
Assistant treasurer of Associated, Metals & Minerals Corporation
Photo
1 item
AR 3149

FO = Photos · GE = Genealogical Material · PM = Primary Material · SM = Secondary Material

FO PM **GEORG AND EDITH TIETZ**
Department store owner, 1889–1953
Personal documents; photos; family
histories (19th cent.); correspondence
1930–1960
15 items
AR 2276

FO PM **HERMANN TIETZ**
SM Department store owner, 1837–1907
Clippings; photos; correspondence
(1930)
38 items
AR 1943

FO SM **LEONHARD TIETZ**
Clippings; photo of Tietz
Department Stores; excerpts from
their catalogues
19 items
AR 2434, AR 5357

FO SM **LUDWIG TIETZ**
Social worker, 1897–1933
Photos; obituary
3 items
AR 1882

PM **OSCAR AND BETTY TIETZ**
Documents from the Landesarchiv
Berlin on Oscar-und-Betty Tietz
Stiftung (1912–1939)
71 items
AR 4123

FO **ABRAHAM TIKTIN**
Rabbi, 1764–1820
Photo
1 item
AR 4164

PM SM **BERTHOLD TIMENDORFER**
Lawyer, 1853–1931
Clippings; official letters (1913–1947)
5 items
AR 1933

PM **ERNEST TOCH**
Composer, 1887–1967
Autograph
1 item
AR 4548

SM **MARVIN TOKAYER**
Rabbi
American rabbi in Japan: newspaper
clippings (1982)
1 item
AR 5195

FO **NELLY TOLL**
Painter, 20th cent.
Photos of her work
44 items
AR 4664

FO PM **ERNST TOLLER**
SM Writer, revolutionary, 1893–1939
Photo; wanted poster; police records
on Toller; abstract of thesis by
Elsasser; autographs
12 items
AR 1641, AR 1734

PM SM **FRIEDRICH TORBERG**
died 1979
Essay; letter; obituary
4 items
AR 1942

PM **TOST, UPPER SILESIA; JEWISH
COMMUNITY**
Manuscripts
2 items
AR 3724

SM **JAKOB TOURY**
Historian
Book reviews of Toury's *Social and
Political History of the Jews in Germany
1847–1871*, newspaper clipping
(Bonn, 1980), same clipping contains
review of Monica Richarz's history
covering 1780–1971
1 item
AR 5064

FO **TOVACOV/MORAVIA; JEWISH
COMMUNITY**
Photo of synagogue
1 item
AR 7035

SM **HANS TRAMER**
1905–1979, Social worker, vice-
president Leo Baeck Institute,
Jerusalem Obituaries
7 items
AR 4696

FO = Photos · GE = Genealogical Material · PM = Primary Material · SM = Secondary Material

SM **SALO TRANSLATEUR**
Essay (ca. 1963), "Theodor Herzl's 'Judenstaat' und der 'Staat Israel': Traum und Wirklichkeit"
1 item
AR 2380

PM **ALFRED TRAUBE FAMILY**
Family history (1968); family documents, including vital registration papers (1813–1920); papers on a schoolteacher's career
17 items
AR 3137

PM **TREITEL FAMILY**
Naturalization document (1837); diploma from Breslau Rabbinical Seminary (1876)
2 items
AR 4063

PM **HERMANN TREITEL**
Documents on Hermann Treitel's army service (1904–1917, 1936)
7 items
AR 3928

GE PM **TREPP FAMILY**
Family tree (17th–20th cent.); letter
3 items
AR 4828

PM **TREUCHTLINGEN; JEWISH COMMUNITY**
Estimate of value of community property; letter
2 items
AR 3457

GE **TREUENFELS FAMILY**
Family history (16th–20th cent.)
1 item
AR 4242

SM **CAROLA TRIER**
Magazine articles: "Beauty Bulletins" (1963)
3 items
AR 2108

GE SM **TRIER FAMILY**
Family history (17th–20th cent.); family obituaries
2 items
AR 3622

PM SM **TRIER; JEWISH COMMUNITY**
Clipping; list of Judaica in local archives; signatures on behalf of equality of Jews (1843)
3 items
AR 3106

SM **WALTER TRIER**
Artist, 1890–1951
Copy of newspaper article (1977)
1 item
AR 4460

PM **IRENE TRIESCH**
Actress, 1877–1964
Photographic postcards of Irene Triesch on stage; autographs
4 items
AR 1550, AR 3797

SM **ERNST TUCH**
Essays; clippings on Galician Jews, on white slave trade and related topics (1897–1899)
10 items
AR 7025

GE PM **TUCHMANN FAMILY**
Grain dealers
Official document (19th cent.); family history, and tree since 1774; correspondence; restitution; architectural drawings
8 items
AR 1401, AR 1401a

FO PM **KURT TUCHOLSKY**
SM Author, 1890–1935
Photo; clippings on his life and work; autograph
16 items
AR 1210, AR 2126

FO SM **TUEBINGEN; JEWISH COMMUNITY**
Clippings; photos of synagogues; reviews
8 items
AR 1484

PM SM **GUSTAV TUGENDREICH**
Physician, born 1876
Curriculum vitae; clippings; essays; correspondence on pediatrics, public hygiene, and attempts to reduce infant mortality (1905–1936)

FO = Photos · GE = Genealogical Material · PM = Primary Material · SM = Secondary Material

34 items
AR 3080

PM **HERMANN TURBIN**
Documents concerning Jewish survivors in Germany (1945–1947); list of restrictions on Jews (1943); GDR visa (1957)
11 items
AR 3366

PM **EDGAR TUTEUR FAMILY**
Marriage license (1862)
1 item
AR 3129

SM **WERNER TUTEUR**
Psychiatrist, 20th cent.
Articles on psychiatry
22 items
AR 1407

SM **SINAI UCKO**
Rabbi, 1905–1976
Obituaries
3 items
AR 4345

PM **JOSEPH UFFNER**
List of items taken along on move from Koenigsberg, Germany, to United States (1938)
1 item
AR 5028

GE **UHLFELDER FAMILY**
Family tree (18th–20th cent.)
1 item
AR 316

PM **ARNOLD ULITZ**
Autograph
1 item
AR 1853

PM **BER BERNHARD ULLMAN**
1751–1837
Chronicle of his false imprisonment for counterfeiting (1803)
1 item
AR 7090

PM **DAVID ULLMAN**
Letter of protection (1747)
1 item
AR 4274

PM **ULLMANN FAMILY**
Orders and awards from King of Bavaria and Emperor of Austria to family members (1866–1906)
9 items
AR 3343

SM **MARTIN ULLMANN**
Booklet containing prayer for new moon (18th cent.)
1 item
AR 3049

FO GE **ULLSTEIN FAMILY**
PM SM Publishers
Correspondence including letters from Carl Zuckmayer, Maximilian Harden (19th and 20th cent.); clippings on family (1940's–1950's); family histories and trees (18th cent.); photos (19th–20th cent.)
68 items
AR 1133

FO PM **ULM; JEWISH COMMUNITY**
SM Clippings; photo; circular; lists
11 items
AR 3169

PM **AGNES ULMAN (BORN SPEYER)**
Correspondence by Hugo von Hofmannsthal family and Karl Wolfskehl; poetry by Hofmannsthal and Wolfskehl (1890's–1930's)
45 items
AR 1867

PM **GABRIEL ULMANN**
Copies of letters from Ulmann to Goethe (1797, 1807, 1819)
3 items
AR 3299

PM **UNGER FAMILY**
Family documents Erfurt, including correspondence with authorities; testimonial letters; letters of municipal citizenship (1807–1834)
25 items
AR 4807

SM **HEINZ UNGER**
Conductor, 1895–1965
Obituary
1 item
AR 2542

PM **BRUNO UNGERLEIDER**
Lawyer, 1891–1941
Biography
1 item
AR 3894

SM **UNIVERSITIES IN GERMANY, 1933–1945**
Clipping on University of Bonn during Nazi era (1964)
1 item
AR 2435

SM **UNIVERSITY OF BONN**
Clippings; exhibition catalogue (1967), on Jews at the University of Bonn
4 items
AR 3352

FO **UNIVERSITY OF HEIDELBERG**
Photos of 72 Jewish professors who taught at the University of Heidelberg
75 items
AR 3008

SM **UNIVERSITY OF TUEBINGEN**
Clippings on Institutum Judaicum at the University of Tuebingen (1967)
1 item
AR 3590

SM **UNNA FAMILY, MANNHEIM**
Article, "Reminiscence of the Youth" (1981) by Victor Unna
1 item
AR 4992

SM **FRITZ VON UNRUH**
Author, 1885–1970
Clippings; prospect for collected works
5 items
AR 4541

PM SM **UNSLEBEN; JEWISH COMMUNITY**
Articles; lists
4 items
AR 4725

FO **UNTERBALLBACH; JEWISH COMMUNITY**
Photo
1 item
AR 4233

PM **GEORG URDANG**
Pharmacist
Documents on Urdang's career (1906–1939)
4 items
AR 4090

FO **URSPRINGEN; JEWISH COMMUNITY**
Photos of synagogue
1 item
AR 4504

SM **ELSE URY**
Writer, 1877–1943
Clipping
1 item
AR 4500

FO SM **LESSER URY**
Painter, 1861–1931
Photos; clippings
12 items
AR 1094

PM **PAULA VALK FAMILY**
Marriage, birth records (1845–1867)
5 items
AR 2454

PM **HERMANN VAMBUERY (PSEUDONYM FOR BAMBERGER)**
Historian, 1823–1913
Autograph
1 item
AR 2621

PM **KARL AUGUST VARNHAGEN**
Husband of Rahel Varnhagen (1785–1858)
Autographs
2 items
AR 1824

FO **CONRAD VEIDT**
Actor, 1893–1943
Photo
3 items
AR 2411

PM **VEIT & CO.**
Firm history (1924)
1 item
AR 2188

FO = Photos · GE = Genealogical Material · PM = Primary Material · SM = Secondary Material

PM **JOHANNES VEIT**
Painter, 1790–1854
Autograph
1 item
AR 3225

FO PM **PHILIP VEIT**
Painter, 1793–1877
Photo of painting (1838); autograph
2 items
AR 2972, AR 850

SM **GEORG OTTO VENEDIGER**
Antique collector, 1871–1937
Newspaper clipping (1959)
1 item
AR 1456

SM **GEORGE VIDA**
Clippings (1955) on Dachau from the series "Dachau 10 years after"
2 items
AR 7084

FO SM **VIENNA; JEWISH COMMUNITY**
Articles; photos
84 items
AR 2432, AR 7035

PM **VIERNHEIM; JEWISH COMMUNITY**
Typescript
1 item
AR 4571

SM **VIERSEN; JEWISH COMMUNITY**
Book review
1 item
AR 3829

PM **VILNA; JEWISH COMMUNITY**
Program
1 item
AR 3349

SM **STEVEN VINAVER**
Composer, son of Mascha Koleko, 1937–1968
Obituary (1968)
1 item
AR 3541

GE **VOGEL-WAGNER FAMILY, HALBERSTADT**
Family tree (1653–1957)
1 item
AR 5120

FO GE **VOGELSTEIN FAMILY**
PM SM Family and official documents (19th cent.); excerpts from Jewish registers from city of Lage (19th cent.); articles; family histories and trees since 1729; photos
19 items
AR 3141

PM **WACHENHEIM FAMILY**
Marriage contracts; greeting cards; poems on festive occasions (1821–1887)
11 items
AR 1570

SM **HEDWIG WACHENHEIM**
Social worker, 1891–1969
Eulogy pronounced by Ernst Fraenkel
1 item
AR 4133

FO **BERNHARD WACHSTEIN**
Historian, 1868–1935
Reproduction of portrait
1 item
AR 2992

PM **WAECHTERSBACH; JEWISH COMMUNITY**
Documents (1838)
2 items
AR 3733

PM SM **JOSEF WAGNER**
Musician
Sheet music; correspondence; clippings
4 items
AR 5125

PM **FERDINAND WAGSCHAL**
Naturalization papers; doctor's licenses; war award (1886–1916)
5 items
AR 3632

FO PM **WAHL FAMILY**
Poetry album, photos, marriage documents (1823–1870); letter from Theresienstadt (1943); letter on family history (1966)
7 items
AR 3373

FO = Photos · GE = Genealogical Material · PM = Primary Material · SM = Secondary Material

SM **HANS WAHL**
Chemist
Newspaper clipping
1 item
AR 2341

SM **SAMUEL WAHRMANN**
Antique dealer
Newspaper clipping (1939)
1 item
AR 1457

SM **WAIBSTADT; JEWISH COMMUNITY**
Clipping
1 item
AR 2950

PM **WALDBAUM FAMILY**
Memorial album
1 item
AR 5959

FO PM **HERWARTH WALDEN (BORN GEORG LEVIN)**
Writer, husband of Else Lasker-Schueler, editor of *Der Sturm* (1878–1939)
Letter; photo; autograph
3 items
AR 2753, AR 2021

PM **FELIX WALDHEIM**
Report card; birth certificates (1853–1898)
2 items
AR 3633

PM **ERNST WALDINGER**
Poet, 1896–1970
Poems; letter; notes; obituary; autographs
12 items
AR 2830, AR 3528

SM **ERNST WALLACH**
Newspaper clipping (1937, Centralverein newspaper)
1 item
AR 1408

FO PM **MORITZ WALLACH**
SM Textile printer, born ca. 1890
Photo; memoirs; clippings; exhibition catalogues; correspondence on Wallach's work
19 items
AR 1259

SM **MOSHE WALLACH**
Physician
Newspaper clipping (1962)
1 item
AR 1602

FO **OTTO WALLACH**
Chemist, 1847–1931
Photo
1 item
AR 2978

FO PM **OTTO WALLBURG**
Actor, died ca. 1943
Photos; autographs
4 items
AR 1976, AR 1975

PM **WALLDUERN; JEWISH COMMUNITY**
Typescript
8 items
AR 3029

SM **HANS WALLENBERG**
Journalist, 1907–1977
Obituaries, eulogy by Axel Springer
6 items
AR 4417

GE PM **WALLERSTEIN-WECHSLER FAMILIES**
Family trees from 1695; correspondence; notes
3 items
AR 5271

SM **ROBERT WALSER**
Writer, 1878–1956
Clippings (1978)
3 items
AR 4614

FO PM **BRUNO WALTER**
SM Conductor, 1876–1962
Photos; concert program; obituaries; autographs
17 items
AR 1458, AR 1717

SM **FRITZ WALTER**
Obituaries
2 items
AR 4456

FO = Photos · GE = Genealogical Material · PM = Primary Material · SM = Secondary Material

SM **HILDE WALTER**
Essays; publicity concerning her
books (1952–1963)
9 items
AR 482

PM **HANS WALZ**
Letters to Walz from Leo Baeck
(1945, 1948)
3 items
AR 3142

FO PM **WANGEN; JEWISH COMMUNITY**
Photos of synagogue; circumcision
register (1861–1893)
3 items
AR 2170

SM **WANKHEIM; JEWISH COMMUNITY**
Clipping
1 item
AR 4254

SM **ABY WARBURG**
Art historian, 1866–1929
Newspaper clippings
2 items
AR 1883

PM SM **WARBURG FAMILY**
Banking documents (1872); clippings;
notes on Warburg banking house
(20th cent.); partnership contract
(1810); autographs
13 items
AR 1154, AR 1155, AR 7013

SM **FELIX M. WARBURG**
Banker, 1871–1937
Newspaper clipping (1955);
photocopies of two books about Felix
Warburg and of 250 archive cards
3 items
AR 274

PM **FREDERICK WARBURG**
Memorial service (1973)
1 item
AR 4890

SM **FRITZ M. WARBURG**
Banker, 1879–1964
Obituary
1 item
AR 2361

PM **WARBURG; JEWISH COMMUNITY**
Letter
1 item
AR 4527

FO PM **MAX M. WARBURG**
SM Banker, 1867–1946
Photo; correspondence (1933–1938);
essay by Warburg (1913); essay about
Warburg (1937, 1977)
16 items
AR 1211

SM **OTTO WARBURG**
Biologist, Nobel Prize winner 1931,
1883–1970
Newspaper clippings concerning
award and on occasion of 80th
birthday; obituaries
14 items
AR 1569

PM **ARREST WARRANTS (STECKBRIEFE)**
Warrants of 1802 and 1842
2 items
AR 158

PM **ERNST WARSCHAUER**
Note on his experiences during Nazi
era
1 item
AR 1415

FO PM **MALVIN WARSCHAUER**
Rabbi, 1871–1955
Correspondence (1941–1948);
biographical notes for eulogies
(1930–1931); photo
10 items
AR 794

GE **ISIDOR WARTENBERG FAMILY**
Family tree (18th–20th cent.)
1 item
AR 4493

SM **WARTENBURG (NOW BARCZEWO, POLAND); JEWISH COMMUNITY**
Clipping
1 item
AR 4536

FO = Photos · GE = Genealogical Material · PM = Primary Material · SM = Secondary Material

PM **MOSES WASSERMAN**
Chief rabbi of Wuerttemberg,
1834–1884
Collected census of all Jews in Europe
1 item
AR 5161

SM **AUGUST PAUL VON WASSERMANN**
Physician and bacteriologist,
1866–1925
Article by Dr. Erich Cohn (3 pp.),
with photo
1 item
AR 4998

PM **GUSTAV WASSERMANN**
Letter (1933) with explanation (1978)
2 items
AR 4579

FO PM **JACOB WASSERMANN**
SM Author, 1873–1934
Photos; letter; clippings;
reminiscences of Wassermann written
by Rudolf Kaiser; autographs
60 items
AR 2189, AR 253

PM **OSCAR WASSERMANN**
Banker
Autograph (1932)
1 item
AR 1143

FO **SIGMUND WATERMAN**
Photo
1 item
AR 7133

SM **FRANZ WAXMAN**
Composer, 1906–1967
Philharmonic Hall program (1968)
1 item
AR 3311

PM **HILLEL WECHSLER**
Rabbi, 1843–1894
Autograph
1 item
AR 3416

PM **MARGA WEGLEIN**
Antisemitic business note (1938)
1 item
AR 5372

PM **SIGMUND WEGLEIN**
Circular on Reichsvereinigung der
Juden in Deutschland concerning
deportations (1942)
1 item
AR 1255

PM SM **ARNIM WEGNER**
Author, 1886–
Letter to Hitler on negative
consequences of persecution of Jews
(1933); clippings; reviews; honorary
documents (1930–1967)
16 items
AR 3173

FO GE **WEHLE FAMILY**
PM SM Official documents (19th cent.);
clippings; offprints (20th cent.);
family histories and trees since 1700;
photos; autographs
21 items
AR 350, AR 863

PM SM **HERBERT WEICHMANN**
Politician, civil servant, born 1896
Speech-transcript (1974); clipping
(1976)
2 items
AR 4110

SM **JULIUS WEIGERT**
Lawyer
Obituary (1961)
1 item
AR 1820

GE SM **KARL WEIGERT FAMILY**
Family trees (18th–20th cent.);
clippings on life of biochemist Karl
Weigert
23 items
AR 83

PM **MAX WEIGERT**
Factory owner, 1842–1922
Honorary plaques
2 items
AR 2834

GE **WEIL FAMILY, AUFHAUSEN**
Branch of Gutmann family
(genealogy)
1 item
AR 5178

PM **FRANK L. WEIL INSTITUTE FOR STUDIES IN RELIGION AND THE HUMANITIES**
Cincinnati, Ohio
Minutes; papers
2 items
AR 4125

FO **FREDERICK DAVID WEIL**
1877–1953
Photo
1 item
AR 1461

SM **HERMAN WEIL**
Professor of psychology
Clippings concerning "Statistics on Jewish Teachers and Students in Germany under the Hitler Regime 1933–1938"
1 item
AR 4132

PM SM **HERMANN MAX WEIL**
Law professor, 1894–1942
Letter; obituary; eulogy
3 items
AR 1462

PM **HERMINE WEIL**
Remembrance of confirmation celebration (1889)
1 item
AR 1603

SM **JAKOB BEN JEHUDA WEIL**
Rabbi, 1381–1456
Articles by Peter Puhlmann (1981)
3 items
AR 5016

SM **JULIUS AND HELEN WEIL**
Clipping (1978)
1 item
AR 4560

GE **LEHMANN WEIL**
Family tree with elaboration (18th–20th cent.)
3 items
AR 1618

PM **MICHAEL WEIL**
Letter of protection (Parchim, 1790)
1 item
AR 3282

SM **NATANAEL WEIL**
Rabbi, 1687–1769
Newspaper article (1957)
1 item
AR 87

PM **SALOMON WEIL**
Birth certificate (1857)
1 item
AR 3355

GE PM **SIGMUND WEIL**
Family tree (18th–20th cent.); official documents concerning Weil family (1887–1939)
12 items
AR 1416

PM SM **WEILBURG; JEWISH COMMUNITY**
Letter; articles
6 items
AR 4195, AR 5278

PM **ALEXANDRE WEILL**
Writer, 1811–1888
Letter (1843)
1 item
AR 2831

FO SM **ERNA WEILL**
Sculptor, 20th cent.
Clippings; exhibition programs; photos of her work
28 items
AR 1417

GE PM **ERNEST WEILL**
Correspondence on genealogy (1957)
17 items
AR 1306

GE **WEILL FAMILY, KIPPENHEIM**
Family tree (18th–20th cent.)
1 item
AR 3926

FO SM **KURT WEILL**
Composer, 1900–1950
Photo; article (1984)
2 items
AR 2754

PM **HERMANN WEILLER FAMILY**
Notes on the family
1 item
AR 3849

FO = Photos · GE = Genealogical Material · PM = Primary Material · SM = Secondary Material

PM **ARTHUR VON WEINBERG**
Chemist, 1860–1943
Short biography
1 item
AR 3699

PM **BERNHARD WEINBERG**
Naturalization certificate; letter of municipal citizenship; lease with attached floor-plan (1843–1861)
7 items
AR 3775

FO PM **WEINBERG FAMILY**
Maps and photos of gravestones of Rheda; diary of Heinrich Meyer (1824–1890)
2 items
AR 5307

PM SM **GUSTAV WEINBERG**
Writer, 1856–1909
Personal documents; curriculum vitae; correspondence; reviews; poetry
24 items
AR 4752

PM **HUGO WEINBERG**
Born 1896 in Rhoda
Military pass; photocopies of other documents and medals; letters
6 items
AR 4999

GE **RICHARD WEINBERG**
Genealogy of Weinberg family, Westphalia
1 item
AR 5201

FO SM **WEINHEIM/BADEN; JEWISH COMMUNITY**
Photo; article
2 items
AR 2485

PM **OTTO WEININGER**
Philosopher, 1880–1903
Autographs
4 items
AR 2755, AR 1151

GE PM **ROBERT WEINLAUB FAMILY**
SM Family histories (19th–20th cent.); clippings on theater in Breslau (1932–1933); inventory of the Walter Wicclair productions (1962)
5 items
AR 3640

PM **MAX WEINMANN FAMILY**
Memorabilia (20th cent.)
15 items
AR 2352

SM **URIEL WEINREICH**
Newspaper clipping about Guggenheim Fund (1959)
1 item
AR 741

SM **B. WEINRYB**
Two articles on modern Jewish history (1959)
2 items
AR 1307

GE **WEINSCHENK FAMILY**
Family tree and history (17th–20th cent.)
1 item
AR 4457

SM **WILLI WEISBECKER**
Lawyer
Newspaper clippings (1917–1938)
4 items
AR 483

FO **GUSTAV WEISHUT**
Photo
1 item
AR 1646

PM **MAYER WEISKOPF**
Rabbi, 1832–1915
Biography
1 item
AR 4388

PM SM **BERNHARD WEISS**
Police official, 1880–1952
Clippings; letter
4 items
AR 4926

FO PM **ERNST WEISS**
SM Author, 1882–1940
Photo; clipping; essays on Weiss; autograph
9 items
AR 2342, AR 1652

FO = Photos · GE = Genealogical Material · PM = Primary Material · SM = Secondary Material

SM **GUIDO WEISS**
Editor, 1822–1899
Obituary (1899)
1 item
AR 2513

SM **PETER WEISS**
Writer
Newspaper clipping (1964)
1 item
AR 2343

PM **WALTHER WEISS COLLECTION**
Items on members of board of Jewish Community in Munich; items about Reichsvertretung of Jews in Germany and about Munich Jewish Community
3 items
AR 4830

SM **A. WEISSBARTH**
Newspaper clipping "Underground in Berlin"
1 item
AR 1089

PM **JOSEF WEISSE**
Rabbi, 1812–1897
Correspondence; Hebrew writings; documents
15 items
AR 4032

PM SM **SAMSON WEISSE**
Rabbi, son of Rabbi Josef Weisse, 1857–1946
Documents; report cards; letters; articles; notes
21 items
AR 4096

PM **RAIMUND WEISSENSTEINER**
Composer
Sheet music with text
1 item
AR 4243

FO PM **MAX WEISSMAN**
Psychiatrist, 1895–
Photo; recommendations; documents on his medical career
8 items
AR 3796

SM **S. WEISSMANN**
Newspaper clipping about Jewish population in Baden (1938)
1 item
AR 1460

SM **FREDERICK WEITZEN**
Articles about UNWRA, including Children's Center
2 items
AR 4951

PM SM **CHAIM WEIZMANN**
Zionist leader, 1874–1952
Correspondence with Leo Baeck (1939); stamps; clippings; autograph
6 items
AR 472, AR 4528

SM **JULIUS WELLHAUSEN**
Newspaper clipping in Hebrew (1982) by Brinowski about Wellhausen
1 item
AR 5160

SM **SIEGMUND WELTINGER**
Opera manager, 1854–1941
Photocopy of newspaper clipping (1969)
1 item
AR 3565

PM **LUTZ WELTMANN**
Publisher, born 1901
Curriculum vitae (1965); lists of correspondence; autographs
5 items
AR 1766, AR 2970, AR 2971

PM **GUSTAV WENDEL FAMILY**
Correspondence with Lion Feuchtwanger (1954); appointment of Michel Wendel as chairman of Jewish community of Flamersheim (1833)
3 items
AR 544

FO PM **WENKHEIM/BADEN; JEWISH COMMUNITY**
Typescript; photos
12 items
AR 3045

FO = Photos · GE = Genealogical Material · PM = Primary Material · SM = Secondary Material

PM SM **HILDE WENZEL**
Writer, 1905–1972
Clippings of short works by Wenzel (1950–1962); poetry; manuscripts (1913–1923); correspondence (1915–1969)
82 items
AR 1418, AR 3861

PM SM **ALMA WERFEL**
Artist, 1879–1965
Newspaper article; obituary; autographs
4 items
AR 1663, AR 2605

FO PM **FRANZ WERFEL**
SM Author, 1890–1945
Photos; essay on Werfel; questionnaire filled out by him; autographs
15 items
AR 2756, AR 836

SM **DR. WERNER**
German versions of stories about famous rabbis
6 items
AR 1324

FO GE **ELLA WERNER**
PM SM Social worker, 1880–1964
Curriculum vitae; articles; photos; official family documents (18th and 19th cent.); family histories and trees
38 items
AR 3079

PM SM **ERIC WERNER**
Author
Book reviews; clippings; curriculum vitae
6 items
AR 2179

PM **IGNATZ WERNER**
Religious teacher
Speeches given by Werner at confirmation ceremonies of his pupils (19th cent.)
6 items
AR 3620

FO PM **MORITZ WERNER**
SM Educator, 1873–1939
Clippings; lectures; curriculum of Jewish school in Frankfurt a/M (1933–1936); correspondence; photos
84 items
AR 304

PM **SIDONIE WERNER**
Letters concerning her life (1957)
4 items
AR 1463

FO PM **WERTHEIM, BADEN; JEWISH**
SM **COMMUNITY**
Lists of Jews in Wertheim before and during Nazi period; clippings; photos; local calendar
34 items
AR 2929

FO PM **WERTHEIM DEPARTMENT STORES, BERLIN**
Photos; letters; family papers; documents
21 items
AR 2630

PM SM **FERDINAND WERTHEIM**
Civil servant, 1841–1891
Obituary; birth certificate; document naming him tax inspector
5 items
AR 3514

FO GE **ERNST WERTHEIMER FAMILY**
PM Family tree since 1738; memorabilia; family documents; photos
45 items
AR 3356

FO GE **WERTHEIMER FAMILY**
Family tree (16th–20th cent.); photos of portraits of family members (18th–19th cent.)
4 items
AR 1347

FO GE **WERTHEIMER FAMILY, BODERSWEIER AND EMMERDINGEN**
Album containing family tree, histories, and photos since 1754
1 item
AR 4549

FO = Photos · GE = Genealogical Material · PM = Primary Material · SM = Secondary Material

GE **WERTHEIMER FAMILY, EICHSTATTEN/BADEN**
Family history (56 pp.)
1 item
AR 2919

PM SM **MAX WERTHEIMER**
Psychologist, 1880–1943
Articles; correspondence
8 items
AR 4030

PM **DR. RICHARD WERTHEIMER**
Letters (1941)
4 items
AR 5407

SM **WESEL; JEWISH COMMUNITY**
Clippings
2 items
AR 2940

PM SM **WESSELING; JEWISH COMMUNITY**
Letter; articles
3 items
AR 4918

SM **WEST PRUSSIA; JEWISH COMMUNITY**
Issue of *Briesener Kurier* (1884); circular
2 items
AR 3525

GE **BETTY WESTERFELD**
Family tree of her ancestors (19th–20th cent.)
1 item
AR 4173

FO PM **PAUL WESTHEIM**
SM Art historian, 1886–1963
Obituary; clippings; photos of caricatures; invitation to circumcision of grandfather of Westheim's widow's first husband (1864)
6 items
AR 2163

PM **WESTPHALIA; JEWISH COMMUNITY**
Documents and reports (1805–1830); synagogue melodies
3 items
AR 2075

SM **WETZLAR/LAHN; JEWISH COMMUNITY**
Articles
2 items
AR 4950

PM **ALBERTO WEYL**
Documents on history of Weyl & Nassau textile firm, Reichenbach
4 items
AR 91

FO PM **HERMANN WEYL**
Mathematician, 1885–1955
Letters to Alfred Vagts (1948–1950); corespondence concerning Weyl and his wife, Helene; pictures of Helene Weyl
12 items
AR 3344

SM **HERMANN WEYL**
Physician, 1894–1961
Obituary (1961)
1 item
AR 1821

PM **M. WEYL**
Speech given by Weyl at his Bar Mitzvah (1854)
1 item
AR 3852

PM **SAMUEL WEYL**
Transcript of document, granting Samuel Weyl permission to serve as rabbi of Upper Alsace (1711)
1 item
AR 4437

GE **WICKERT FAMILY**
Genealogy
1 item
AR 5223

SM **WILLY WIEGAND**
Publisher, 1884–1961
Obituary (1961)
1 item
AR 2225

PM SM **ALFRED WIENER**
Librarian, 1885–1964
Obituaries; autographs
15 items
AR 1464, AR 2585

FO = Photos · GE = Genealogical Material · PM = Primary Material · SM = Secondary Material

PM **EVA WIENER**
Memoirs of her childhood, written 1951
1 item
AR 4633

PM **GEORG WIENER**
Correspondence containing his reminiscences of Leo Baeck (1957)
5 items
AR 4275

FO **KARL WIENER**
Composer
Photo (1937)
1 item
AR 5272

GE PM **LEOPOLD WIENER**
Medalist
Various medals; family history
2 items
AR 5087

FO PM **MAX WIENER**
SM Rabbi, 1882–1950
Lectures; sermons; clippings; photos; correspondence
61 items
AR 1822, AR 3760

FO PM **WIESBADEN; JEWISH**
SM **COMMUNITY**
Photos of synagogue; German prayers; articles
6 items
AR 761

FO GE **WIESENTHAL FAMILY**
PM SM Photos; vital and official documents; clippings (1847–1924); correspondence from the Jacob family (1844–1878); family tree of the Jacob-Wiesenthal family (18th–20th cent.)
50 items
AR 375

PM **WIESENTHAL FAMILY, HOMBURG**
Promissory note (1813)
1 item
AR 7119

SM **SIMON WIESENTHAL**
"Hunter of Nazi War Criminals"
Holocaust studies: newspaper clippings
4 items
AR 2132

FO **LUDWIG WIHL**
Author, 1807–1882
Portrait (etching); photo
2 items
AR 1419

PM **FIELD CHAPLAIN WILDE**
Pamphlet from First World War, entitled *Sabbathgedanken für jüdische Soldaten*
1 item
AR 4751

FO SM **KURT WILHELM**
Rabbi, 1900–1965
Photo; obituary; clippings
14 items
AR 111

PM **CURT WILK**
Autographs (1940's and 1950's)
38 items
AR 1152

FO PM **RICHARD WILLSTAETTER**
SM Chemist, 1872–1942
Essay; photos; list of honors he received; autographs
10 items
AR 2612, AR 1718

GE PM **WILMERSDORFER FAMILY**
Family tree (18th–20th cent.); ex libris (1897)
3 items
AR 3016

PM **BENJAMIN WILSTAETTER**
Speech on the Torah (1826)
1 item
AR 3762

GE **WINDMUEHL-COHN FAMILY**
Family history (18th–20th cent.)
1 item
AR 267

FO = Photos · GE = Genealogical Material · PM = Primary Material · SM = Secondary Material

FO GE **WINDMUELLER FAMILY**
PM Family trees and histories since 1690;
photos; George Washington's letter to
Hebrew congregations (photocopy)
20 items
AR 4012

SM **JACOB WINDMUELLER**
Newspaper clipping concerning 90th
anniversary of Central Savings Bank,
New York
1 item
AR 1466

PM SM **FRANZ WINKLER**
Banker
Clipping (1966); document about
Military Rescue Service Jos. Winkler
(1864)
2 items
AR 2959

PM **HEINRICH WINKLER**
Material on his lumber corporation
(1975)
2 items
AR 4174

SM **LUCY WINTERFELDT**
Jewish calendar for 1872–1873
1 item
AR 125

PM **MARK WISCHNITZER**
Report on visit to South Africa,
Rhodesia, and Kenya (1936), to
explore possibilities for Jewish
emigration from Germany
1 item
AR 3134

PM **PHILLIP WITKOP**
1880–1942
Autographs
4 items
AR 1854

GE PM **WITKOWSKI FAMILY**
Memorabilia (19th cent.); family
histories and trees since 18th cent.;
photos
19 items
AR 470

SM **FRITZ WITTELSHOEFER**
Obituary notice (1958)
1 item
AR 334

SM **LUDWIG WITTGENSTEIN**
Engineer
Newspaper clipping (1961)
1 item
AR 1420

SM **DR. ERIE D. WITTKOWER**
Physician, Professor
Editorial article McGill University
1 item
AR 5099

PM SM **RUDOLF WITTKOWER**
Art historian, 1901–1971
Catalogue of auction for the benefit
of Rudolf Wittkower Fellowship
(1977); testament of Nina Cohen
(1797)
2 items
AR 1642

SM **WITTLICH; JEWISH COMMUNITY**
Clipping
1 item
AR 4305

SM **FRITZ WOEHRN**
Trial and verdict for being accomplice
to a murder as Gestapo officer
1 item
AR 5147

FO PM **ADOLF WOHLBRUECK**
Actor, 1900–
Photo; autographs
2 items
AR 2412, AR 1855

SM **PAUL WOHLFAHRT**
Newspaper clipping about his
ancestors (1957)
1 item
AR 1467

FO GE **IMMANUEL WOHLWILL FAMILY**
PM Educator, 1799–1847
Writings; family tree; photo;
photocopies of letters (1822–1834);
personal and official documents;
memorabilia; manuscripts; autographs
19 items
AR 2671, AR 517, AR 758, AR 2675

FO = Photos · GE = Genealogical Material · PM = Primary Material · SM = Secondary Material

SM **ALICE WOLF (BORN FRISCH)**
Art historian, 1905–1983
Book review; lists of publications
2 items
AR 7252

PM **CLAIRE WOLF**
Report on her experiences in Gurs (1940); letter
2 items
AR 4935

GE PM **WOLF FAMILY, EISENSTADT**
Letter (1940); family history (17th–20th cent.)
2 items
AR 1439

GE **WOLF FAMILY, STUTTGART**
Family tree and histories (18th–19th cent.)
4 items
AR 4386

FO **GERSON WOLF**
Historian, 1823–1892
Photo
1 item
AR 2757

FO PM **GUSTAV WOLF**
Graphic artists, 1887–1947
Photo; samples of work
7 items
AR 3676

PM **HUGO WOLF**
Author
Autographs
14 items
AR 1438

FO **IRMA WOLF FAMILY**
Photos of portraits of family members (18th–19th cent.)
7 items
AR 7060

GE **SIMON WOLF FAMILY**
Family tree (18th–20th cent.)
1 item
AR 4637

FO **ZELEV WOLF**
Photo of tombstone
1 item
AR 4787

SM **WOLFENBUETTEL; JEWISH COMMUNITY**
Clippings
8 items
AR 1999

PM **WOLFENBUETTEL; SAMSON SCHOOL**
Letter
1 item
AR 1302

FO PM **ALFRED WOLFENSTEIN**
Poet, 1888–1945
Photo (1932); autographs
3 items
AR 2817, AR 1715

PM **WOLFENSTEIN FAMILY**
Vaccination and military registration certificates (1851, 1870)
2 items
AR 3653

PM **LAURA WOLFENSTEIN**
Album with poetry and illustrations (1880–1883)
1 item
AR 3668

PM **ADOLF WOLFERMANN**
Personal documents (1930's); correspondence including communications from concentration camps (1940's)
21 items
AR 1957

PM **BELLA WOLFERMANN**
German passport (1939)
1 item
AR 1934

GE **WOLFERMANN FAMILY**
Family tree (18th–20th cent.)
1 item
AR 4514

GE **WOLFES FAMILY**
Family tree and history (18th–20th cent.)
2 items
AR 1468

FO = Photos · GE = Genealogical Material · PM = Primary Material · SM = Secondary Material

PM **ALBERT WOLFF**
Journalist, 1838–1891
Autographs
2 items
AR 1531

PM SM **EMIL WOLFF**
Music promoter, 1846–1926
Obituary; letters from musicians
3 items
AR 1537

PM **ERNST WOLFF**
Miltary cap (ca. 1806) with explanatory letter
1 item
AR 1623

PM **ERNST WOLFF**
1899 doctoral dissertation, "Die Haftung des Ratgebers"
1 item
AR 4379

GE **WOLFF FAMILY, ZERBST**
Genealogy
4 items
AR 4953

SM **FRITZ F. WOLFF**
Newspaper clipping (1960)
1 item
AR 1469

PM SM **KAETE WOLFF**
Artist, 1881–1968
Prints of her work; poetry; correspondence; clippings on and eulogies of Julius Bab
32 items
AR 1538

SM **KURT WOLFF**
Lawyer
Obituary
1 item
AR 4005

SM **KURT WOLFF**
Publisher, 1887–1963
Newspaper articles; obituaries
11 items
AR 1310

FO PM **LEO WOLFF**
Lawyer, 1870–1958
Typescripts; lectures; correspondence (1913–1938); photos; minutes of meetings of Anti-Zionist Committee (1912–1914)
121 items
AR 4059

GE **LEOPOLD WOLFF FAMILY**
Family history and tree (18th–20th cent.)
1 item
AR 4517

PM SM **MARGO WOLFF**
Letter; clippings (1956–1977)
3 items
AR 1470

PM **MARTIN WOLFF**
Professor of law, 1872–1953
Medals; certificates on his legal career and relations to Prussian court; visiting card of Hugo Preuss
13 items
AR 2369

FO PM **ROSEMARIE WOLFF**
Documents on her education in Germany (1931–1933), on her life in and migration from Shanghai (1942–1947); photos of Arnswalde (1929–1930), of Jewish children's home in Wyk (1935); poetry albums (1929–1930)
25 items
AR 4888

SM **URSULA WOLFF-SCHNEIDER**
Photographer, 1906–1977
Photocopy of newspaper article (1981)
1 item
AR 5070

PM SM **THEODOR WOLFF**
Journalist, 1868–1943
Clippings; copies of Theodor Wolff's correspondence (1923, 1928); autographs
11 items
AR 1090, AR 1712

FO = Photos · GE = Genealogical Material · PM = Primary Material · SM = Secondary Material

PM **URI WOLFF**
Testament (1843)
1 item
AR 3882

PM **WOLFFBERG FAMILY**
Manuscript: "Lauenburg –
Pommerania and Wolfberg Family"
(photocopy)
1 item
AR 5389

FO PM **DAVID WOLFFSOHN**
Zionist, 1856–1914
Photo; autographs
3 items
AR 3208, AR 1144

PM SM **WOLFRATSHAUSEN; WOMEN'S SCHOOL FOR ECONOMICS**
Article; letter
1 item
AR 4640

PM SM **KARL WOLFSKEHL**
Author, 1869–1948
Correspondence; clippings; obituaries; documents concerning Wolfkehl's grandfather Otto; autographs
68 items
AR 471, AR 757

PM **JULIUS WOLFSOHN**
Sermons (1906–1908)
1 item
AR 2835

PM **JULIE WOLFTHORN**
Painter, 1868–ca.1944
Examples of her work
5 items
AR 1495

FO GE **WOLLENBURG-EICHELBAUM**
PM SM **FAMILY**
Eichelbaum family tree (19th–20th cent.); official documents (1865–1937), including documents on Adolf Eichelbaum's military career; photos; Wollenberg family tree (17th–20th cent.); clippings on and obituaries of family members; vital documents of Landsberg family (1845–1871, 1936)
36 items
AR 4550

PM SM **EDUARD WOLLHEIM**
Painter, 1896–1963
Obituary; biographical letters
2 items
AR 6010

PM **WOLLMANN FAMILY**
Family documents; report by Lili Wollmann on her activities in child care for the Jüdischer Frauenbund in Breslau (1930's)
4 items
AR 717

PM **MOSHE WOOLF**
Biographical note (1978)
1 item
AR 4615

FO PM **WORMS; JEWISH COMMUNITY**
SM Articles; copies of documents; photos of synagogues and cemetery; reports
176 items
AR 145, AR 7111

FO **SAMUEL WORMSER FAMILY**
Photos (19th cent.)
3 items
AR 4065

FO SM **BRUNO WOYDA**
Engineer; publisher of Jewish liberal newspaper, 1900–1968
Newspaper article (1969); photo
2 items
AR 4956

FO **WRONKE/POSEN; JEWISH COMMUNITY**
Photos
3 items
AR 7035

PM SM **WUERTTEMBERG; JEWISH COMMUNITY**
Circular (1938) for resettlement of Rexingen Jews in Palestine; typescripts; clippings; statistical material on fate of Baden-Wuerttemberg Jews; decrees of Israelitische Oberkirchenbehoerde (1914–1933); circumcision register; government documents about Jewish vagabonds; court decision; correspondence

FO = Photos · GE = Genealogical Material · PM = Primary Material · SM = Secondary Material

38 items
AR 147

PM SM **WUERZBURG; JEWISH COMMUNITY**
Deportation and survivors lists; list of Würzburg Jews in United States; letter; article (1977)
15 items
AR 3788

GE PM **WUERZBURGER FAMILY**
SM Family tree (16th–18th cent.); clippings; notes; short essays on the family
9 items
AR 1633

PM **JOSEPH WULF**
Historian, 1912–
Curriculum vitae (1973)
1 item
AR 4052

GE PM **WUNDERLICH FAMILY**
Notes on family history (1957, 1968)
2 items
AR 1311

PM **GUSTAV WURZWEILER**
Philanthropist, 1896–
Biographical notes (1970)
1 item
AR 4374

SM **WILLIAM WYLER**
Movie director
Article in Swiss-Jewish paper
1 item
AR 5158

SM **YESHIVA UNIVERSITY**
Exhibition catalogue, related items (1977)
4 items
AR 4505

SM **YIDDISH LANGUAGE**
Newspaper clipping, "Das Jiddische im Bayrischen" (1964)
1 item
AR 2527

SM **YIVO**
Articles on YIVO (1956–1975)
11 items
AR 473

FO **HEINRICH YORK-STEINER**
Author, 1859–1934
Photo
1 item
AR 2790

PM **EUGEN ZADEK**
Autographs
6 items
AR 1637

PM **WALTER AND LILLI ZADEK**
Letters from Walter Zadek in Amsterdam to to his sister, Lilli in Israel; letters from Lilli Popper, born Zadek, from Israel to various places
2 items
AR 5000

PM **KURT ZADIG**
Draftee, 1895–1916
Scrapbooks of letters and postcards from the front (1914–1916)
2 items
AR 3791

PM **LUDWIG LAZARUS ZAMENHOF**
Autograph
1 item
AR 1669

PM **KURT ZANDER**
Lawyer, 1860–1926
Personal and official documents for family members since 1838; family tree; manuscripts by Zander on construction of Baghdad railroad (1909–1918); manuscripts; correspondence of Marthe Brunnemann, governess to Zander children (1904–1905)
42 items
AR 4371

SM **WALTER ZANDER**
Article from *New Outlook* (1976)
1 item
AR 5387

PM **OTTO ZAREK**
Letter (1952)
1 item
AR 1856

FO = Photos · GE = Genealogical Material · PM = Primary Material · SM = Secondary Material

PM **EGMONT ZECHLIN**
Historian, 1896–
Correspondence with Ernst
Hamburger on Zechlin's book, *Die deutsche Politik und die Juden im Ersten Weltkrieg* (1969–1970)
16 items
AR 4113

PM **EGON ZEITLIN**
Sociologist
Curriculum vitae; correspondence (1961–1968)
4 items
AR 3391

PM **HARTMUT ZELINSKI**
Essay (1878), on Richard Wagner
1 item
AR 4580

FO PM **FRIEDRICH ZELNIK**
Actor
Photos (ca. 1916); autograph
3 items
AR 1978, AR 1977

PM **MARTIN ZELT**
Letter (1863)
1 item
AR 1625

SM **JOHN PETER ZENGER**
Article in *Staatszeitung* (1956)
1 item
AR 169

SM **BOGUMIL ZEPLER**
Artist
Newspaper clipping (1938)
1 item
AR 1473

PM **ZERBST/ANHALT; JEWISH COMMUNITY**
Papers of Jewish community; correspondence; photocopies of documents
119 items
AR 4965

PM **ZERKOW; JEWISH COMMUNITY**
Record book of Chevre Kadishe, with statutes
1 item
AR 5165

SM **CHARLOTTE E. ZERNICK**
Photocopies of clipping showing experiences in Ingolstadt (1918–1938)
1 item
AR 5283

SM **KONRAD ZIEGLER**
Educator, born 1884
Newspaper clipping (1964)
1 item
AR 2344

PM **LEOPOLD ZIEGLER**
born 1881
Autograph; biography; notes
2 items
AR 1857

PM **SIEGFRIED ZIEGLER**
Painter, born 1894
Biographical notes
1 item
AR 3278

PM SM **KURT ZIELENZIGER**
Journalist, 1890–1945
Article by Zielenziger; biographical notes on his son
2 items
AR 2913

PM SM **RUDOLF ZIELENZIGER**
Lawyer, 1905–1963
Typescripts; invitations; programs of Freie Wissenschaftliche Vereinigung and Juedischer Kulturbund, Berlin; lectures and articles by Zielenziger
55 items
AR 4044

SM **HIMRICH ZILLE**
Draftsman, 1858–1959
Newspaper article (1979)
1 item
AR 5038

SM **LUDWIG ZIND**
Educator
Newspaper clippings (1958) on new antisemitism
3 items
AR 191

FO PM **ZIONISM**
SM Clippings; fliers; photos; exhibition catalogue on German Zionism (1898–1965); bond issued by the Jewish Colonial Trust (1901)

10 items
AR 1410

SM **RUDOLF ZIPKES**
Articles (1945, 1949)
2 items
AR 1474

PM **ZITTAU; JEWISH COMMUNITY**
List of community property
1 item
AR 3459

PM **THEODOR ZLOCISTI**
1874–1943
Autographs
2 items
AR 2072

PM SM **MAX ZODYKOW**
Author, 20th cent.
Clippings; poetic manuscripts (1920's)
7 items
AR 3434

PM **OTTO ZOFF**
1890–
Autograph
1 item
AR 1858

SM **HARRY ZOHN**
Articles on Jewish thought and authors, including J. C. Wagenseil, "Christian master of Jewish studies."
18 items
AR 1797

FO **ZOLKIEW; JEWISH COMMUNITY**
Photo of synagogue
1 item
AR 7035

SM **JOSEPH ZOLLMANN**
Photocopy of *Stamp Review* showing Judaic stamp
1 item
AR 5261

FO **BERNHARD ZONDEK**
Physician
Photo
1 item
AR 2818

FO SM **HERMANN ZONDEK**
Physician, 1887–
Photo; clipping
2 items
AR 2860

SM **PAUL VON ZSOLNAY**
Publisher
Newspaper clippings (1933); obituaries (1961)
3 items
AR 1613

SM **ZSOLNAY VERLAG**
Catalogues (1937–1938, 1951–1959)
24 items
AR 3336

GE SM **DAVID S. ZUBATASKY**
"Sources of Jewish genealogies," bibliography
1 item
AR 5238

PM **M. ZUCKER FAMILY**
Marriage contract; letter (1825)
2 items
AR 2020

SM **HUGO ZUCKERMANN**
Poet, 1881–1914
Newspaper article on occasion of "100th birthday" (1981)
1 item
AR 5001

PM **ZUCKMAYER-LIPMANN**
Three letters from Carl Zuckmayer (1945–1946, typed)
3 items
AR 5399

FO = Photos · GE = Genealogical Material · PM = Primary Material · SM = Secondary Material

SM **ZUELZ; JEWISH COMMUNITY**
Clipping
1 item
AR 3990

PM **ZUELZER FAMILY**
Letter (1934)
1 item
AR 2071

FO PM **ARNOLD ZWEIG**
SM Author, 1887–1968
Photos; clippings; obituary; autographs
10 items
AR 2164, AR 1635

PM **MAX ZWEIG**
Letter concerning Zweig (1968)
1 item
AR 3412

FO PM **STEFAN ZWEIG**
SM Author, 1881–1942
Obituaries; clippings; photos of Zweig and his relatives; letters, essay by Zweig, reminiscences of him; autographs
38 items
AR 1476, AR 834

PM **ZWICKAU; JEWISH COMMUNITY**
Questionnaire on Jewish community property
1 item
AR 3458

PM **ZWINGENBERG/BERGSTRASSE; JEWISH COMMUNITY**
Chronicle
1 item
AR 5287

FO = Photos · GE = Genealogical Material · PM = Primary Material · SM = Secondary Material

Schriftenreihe wissenschaftlicher Abhandlungen des Leo Baeck Instituts

Alphabetical Listing

ADLER-RUDEL, Scholem: Ostjuden in Deutschland 1880–1940. 1959. *Vol. 1.* – Jüdische Selbsthilfe unter dem Naziregime 1933–1939 im Spiegel der Berichte der Reichsvertretung der Juden in Deutschland. 1974. *Vol. 29.*
BACH, Hans I.: Jakob Bernays. 1974. *Vol. 30.*
BELKE, Ingrid – *see:* Lazarus, M.
BERNAYS, Jakob – *see:* Bach, H. I.
BARKAI, Avraham: Jüdische Minderheit und Industrialisierung. 1988. *Vol. 46.*
FEILCHENFELDT, Werner, Wolf Michaelis, and Ludwig Pinner: Haavara-Transfer nach Palästina und Einwanderung deutscher Juden 1933–1939. 1972. *Vol. 26.*
FISCHER, Horst: Judentum, Staat und Heer in Preußen im frühen 19. Jahrhundert. 1968. *Vol. 20.*
FREEDEN, Herbert: Jüdisches Theater in Nazideutschland. 1964. *Vol. 12.*
GANS, Eduard – *see:* Reissner, H. G.
GILBERT, Felix (ed.): Bankiers, Künstler und Gelehrte. Briefe der Familie Mendelssohn. 1974. *Vol. 30.*
GILCHRIST, Silvia – *see:* Paucker, A.
GLATZER, N. N. – *see:* Zunz, L.
GRAETZ, Heinrich: Tagebuch und Briefe. Hrsg. von R. Michael. 1977. *Vol. 34.*
HAMBURGER, Ernest: Juden im öffentlichen Leben Deutschlands. 1968. *Vol. 19.*
HEGEL, G. W. F. – *see:* Liebeschütz, H.
HOMEYER, Fritz: Deutsche Juden als Bibliophilen und Antiquare. ²1966. *Vol. 10.*
KESTENBERG-GLADSTEIN, Ruth: Neuere Geschichte der Juden in den böhmischen Ländern. Teil 1: Das Zeitalter der Aufklärung 1780–1930. 1969. *Vol. 18-1.*
KISCH, Guido, and Kurt Roepke: Schriften zur Geschichte der Juden. 1959. *Vol. 4.*
KREUTZBERGER, Max: (ed.): Leo Baeck Institute New York, Bibliothek und Archiv. Katalog, Band 1. 1970. *Vol. 22.*
LAZARUS, Moritz, and Heymann Steinthal: Briefe, Band I. 1971. *Vol. 21.* – Band II/1. 1983. *Vol. 40.* – Band II/2. 1986. *Vol. 44.* (All ed. by Ingrid Belke.)
LICHTENSTEIN, Erwin: Die Juden der Freien Stadt Danzig unter der Herrschaft des Nationalsozialismus. 1973. *Vol. 27.*
LIEBESCHÜTZ, Hans: Das Judentum im deutschen Geschichtsbild von Hegel bis Max Weber. 1967. *Vol. 17.* – Von Georg Simmel zu Franz Rosenzweig. 1970. *Vol. 23.* – Liebeschütz, Hans, and Arnold Paucker (eds.): Das Judentum in der deutschen Umwelt 1800–1850. 1977. *Vol. 35.*
MENDELSSOHN, family letters – *see:* Gilbert, F.
MICHAEL, Reuven – *see:* Graetz, H.
MICHAELIS, Wolf – *see:* Feilchenfeldt, W.

Mosse, Werner W. (ed.): Juden im Wilhelminischen Deutschland 1890–1914. 1976. *Vol. 33.* – Mosse, Werner E., and Arnold Paucker (eds.): Deutsches Judentum in Krieg und Revolution 1916–1923. 1971. *Vol. 25.* – Entscheidungsjahr 1932. ²1966. *Vol. 13.* – Mosse, W. E., A. Paucker, and R. Rürup (eds.): Revolution and Evolution 1848 in German-Jewish History. 1981. *Vol. 39.*

Paucker, Arnold, mit S. Gilchrist und B. Suchy (eds.): Die Juden im Nationalsozialistischen Deutschland. The Jews in Nazi Germany 1933–1943. 1986. *Vol. 45* – *see* also: Liebeschütz, H.; Mosse, W. E.

Pinner, Ludwig – *see:* Feilchenfeldt, W.

Prinz, Arthur: Juden im deutschen Wirtschaftsleben. 1984. *Vol. 43.*

Reinharz, J. (ed.): Dokumente zur Geschichte des deutschen Zionismus. 1981. *Vol. 37.*

Reissner, Hanns G.: Eduard Gans. 1965. *Vol. 14.*

Richarz, Monika: Der Eintritt der Juden in die akademischen Berufe. 1974. *Vol. 28.*

Roepke, Kurt – *see:* Kisch, G.

Rosenzweig, Franz – *see:* Liebeschütz, H.

Rürup, R. – *see:* Mosse, W. E.

Simmel, Georg – *see:* Liebeschütz, H.; Susman, M.

Simon, Ernst: Aufbau im Untergang. 1959. *Vol. 2.*

Steinthal, Heymann – *see:* Lazarus, M.

Stern, Selma: Der Preußische Staat und die Juden. Band 1/1–2: Die Zeit des Großen Kurfürsten Friedrich I. 1962. – *Vol. 7.* – Band 2/1–2: Die Zeit Friedrich Wilhelms I. 1962. *Vol. 8.* – Band 3/1–2: Die Zeit Friedrichs des Großen. 1971. *Vol. 24.* – Band 4: Gesamtregister. 1975. *Vol. 32.*

Suchy, B. – *see:* Paucker, A.

Susman, Margarete: Die geistige Gestalt Georg Simmels. 1959. *Vol. 3.*

Taeubler, Eugen: Aufsätze zur Problematik jüdischer Geschichtsschreibung. 1908–1950. 1977. *Vol. 36.*

Toury, Jacob: Die politischen Orientierungen der Juden in Deutschland. 1966. *Vol. 15.* – Die Jüdische Presse im Österreichischen Kaiserreich. 1983. *Vol. 41.* – Jüdische Textilunternehmer in Baden-Württemberg 1683–1938. 1984. *Vol. 42.*

Turnowski-Pinner, Margarete: Die zweite Generation mitteleuropäischer Siedler in Israel. 1962. *Vol. 5.*

Weber, Max – *see:* Liebeschütz, H.

Wilhelm, K. (ed.): Wissenschaft des Judentums im deutschen Sprachbereich I/II. 1967. *Vol. 16.*

Zunz, Leopold: Jude – Deutscher – Europäer. Gesammelte Schriften. Ed. by N. N. Glatzer. 1964. *Vol. 11.*

Please ask for our complete catalogs
J. C. B. Mohr (Paul Siebeck), P. O. Box 2040, D-7400 Tübingen